HISTORY

OF THE

ROMAN-DUTCH LAW.

BY

THE HON. J. W. WESSELS.

ONE OF HIS MAJESTY'S JUDGES OF THE SUPREME COURT OF THE TRANSVAAL.

New Introduction

by

Michael H. Hoeflich

John H. & John M. Kane Professor of Law,
University of Kansas School of Law

THE LAWBOOK EXCHANGE, LTD.
Clark, New Jersey

ISBN 978-1-58477-657-4

Lawbook Exchange edition 2005, 2013

The quality of this reprint is equivalent to the quality of the original work.

THE LAWBOOK EXCHANGE, LTD.
33 Terminal Avenue
Clark, New Jersey 07066-1321

Please see our website for a selection of our other publications and fine facsimile reprints of classic works of legal history:
www.lawbookexchange.com

Library of Congress Cataloging-in-Publication Data

Wessels, J. W. (Johannes Wilhelmus), Sir, 1862-1936.
History of the Roman-Dutch law / Johannes Wilhelmus Wessels ; with a new introduction by Michael Hoeflich.
p. cm.
Originally published: Grahamstown, Cape Colony : African Book Co., 1908.
Includes index.
ISBN 1-58477-657-9 (alk. paper)
1. Roman-Dutch law--Netherlands--History. 2. Roman-Dutch law --History. I. Title.
KKM120.W47 2005
340.5'4--dc22 2005000819

Printed in the United States of America on acid-free paper

INTRODUCTION

Roman-Dutch law is the hybrid legal system created from the merger of Roman law, primarily as set out in the *Corpus Iuris Civilis,* and Germanic law and custom as adopted and developed in the Netherlands. This unique mélange continues to play a major role in the modern legal systems of the Netherlands and South Africa, and is of importance as well in the jurisprudence of Scotland.

Roman-Dutch law, as a legal system, first developed in Holland during the sixteenth and seventeenth centuries. Most important to its development was the publication of Hugo Grotius' *Inleidinge tot de Hollandische Rechtsgeleerheide* in 1631, a work that organized the whole of its jurisprudence in a systematic fashion. This pioneering work was greatly supplemented in the eighteenth century by the Dutch "Elegant School" of Roman jurists, which included such men as Cornelius van Bynkershoek and Johannes Voet. Immediately popular throughout Europe and America, the treatises produced by this school became the standard texts on modern Roman law. Colonial settlement by Afrikaaners brought Roman-Dutch law to South Africa. Although its influence was diminished after the subsequent triumph of the British, it remained influential in such areas as the law of property.

The work of J.W. Wessels reprinted here is of great importance. For the practicing lawyer it provides an easy introduction to the difficult substantive areas of Roman-Dutch law. For the legal historian and comparative lawyer, it offers a number of important features. While the account of ancient and medieval law is now outdated, the general history of Dutch legal development continues to be useful and is one of the few short histories of the subject in English. More important is his chapter on the Dutch jurists of the sixteenth, seventeenth, and eighteenth centuries. Many of these men, such as Joost de Damhouder, an expert on criminal law, wrote treatises that are still significant to the history of European law and the development of modern substantive law. Despite their importance, they are little known to Anglophone scholars. Wessels' chapters on these jurists provide an accurate and brief summary of their lives and work.

Wessels was a judge of the Supreme Court of the Transvaal, one of British South Africa's major provinces. When he wrote his book materials in English on Roman-Dutch law were scarce, a situation that continues today. Though almost a century old, it is still cited today by lawyers and scholars. In short, no one with an interest in South Africa, the Netherlands, or Scotland, nor any scholar of comparative law or European legal history can fail to benefit from this classic text.

Michael H. Hoeflich
May 2005

HISTORY

OF THE

ROMAN-DUTCH LAW.

BY

THE HON. J. W. WESSELS.
ONE OF HIS MAJESTY'S JUDGES OF THE SUPREME COURT OF THE TRANSVAAL.

GRAHAMSTOWN, CAPE COLONY.
AFRICAN BOOK COMPANY, LIMITED

1908.

AFRICAN BOOK COMPANY, LTD.,
GRAHAMSTOWN,
CAPE OF GOOD HOPE,
PRINTERS.

DEDICATED TO

SIR JAMES ROSE-INNES, K.C.M.G.

(CHIEF JUSTICE OF THE TRANSVAAL),

AND

THE HONOURABLE J. G. KOTZÉ

(JUDGE-PRESIDENT OF THE EASTERN DISTRICTS' COURT AND CHIEF JUSTICE OF THE LATE SOUTH AFRICAN REPUBLIC).

THIS WORK OWES ITS EXISTENCE TO THE ENCOURAGEMENT OF THE FORMER AND TO THE TEACHING OF THE LATTER.

CONTENTS.

PART II.

Law of Persons, Things and Obligations.

LIST OF AUTHORITIES.

Aanteekeningen op Lybrecht.
Arntzenius, *De Conditione Hominum.*
Baluzius, *Capitularia Regum Francorum.*
Beijnen, *Overzicht van de Staatsregeling van ons Vaderland.*
Blok, *Eene Hollandsche stad onder de Bourgondisch-Oostenrijksche heerschappij.*
Bluntschli, *Staatswörterbuch.*
Boey, *Woorden-tolk.*
Bort, *Tractaat van het Hollandsch Leenrecht* (in his *Verzamelde Werken*).
Brandt, *Leven van Hugo de Groot.*
Brissaud, *Histoire du Droit Français public et privé.*
Brouwer, *De Jure Connubium.*
Burge, *Colonial Law.*
Burton (Judge), *Insolvency Law of the Cape*, 1829.
Bynkershoek, *Opera Omnia.*
Caesar, *De bello Gallico.*
Cape Statute Law, 1714–1863.
Cattenburgh, *Leven van Hugo de Groot.*
Cicero, *Pro Caec.*
Consultatiën and *Advysen* of Van den Berg, Schrassert, Schomaker, Kop and others.
Consultatiën Hollandsche (the six original volumes and the Amsterdam volume).
Cuq. *Institutions Juridiques des Romains.*
De Villiers, *De Injuriis.*
Droysen, *Historicher Atlas.*
Ducange, *Glossarium mediae et infimae latinitatis.*
Esmein, *Droit Canonique.*
Fockema Andreae, *Bijdragen tot de Nederlandsche Rechtsgeschiedenis.*
—— *Oud-Nederlandsch Burgerlyk Recht.**
Glück, *Ausführliche Erlaüterung der Pandekten.*
Grimm, *Deutsche Rechtsalterthümer.*
Groenewegen, *De Legibus Abrogatis.*
Groen van Prinsterer, *Handboek der Geschiedenis van het Vaderland.*

* This valuable work only reached the author after the greater portion of this book was through the press.

Groot Charter Boek.
Groot Placaat Boek.
Grotius, *De jure Belli ac Pacis.*
—— *Inleiding tot de Hollandsche Rechtsgeleerdheid.*
Gudelinus, *De jure Novissimo.*
Guetât, *Histoire Elementaire du Droit Français.*
Heineccius, *Elementa Juris Germanici.*
—— *Historia Juris Romani ac Germanici.*
Heusler, *Institutionen des Deutschen Privaatrechts.*
Hofdijk, *Ons Voorgeslacht.*
Hollandsche Consultaties.
Holzendorf, *Encyclopaedie der Rechtswissenschaft.*
Huber, *Hedendaagsche Rechtsgeleerdheid.*
Jutphaas, *Sachsenspiegel in Nederland.*
Kersteman, *Woordenboek* and *Aanhangsel.*
Kluit, *Geschiedenis van het Vaderland.*
Kotzé, Translation of Van Leeuwen.
Locale Wetten der Z.A.R.
Maasdorp, *Institutes of Cape Law.*
—— Translation of Grotius' *Introduction.*
Mathyssen, *Rechtboek van den Briel*, by Pols and Fruin.
Matthaeus, *De Auctionibus.*
—— *De Nobilitate.*
—— *Paroemiae.*
Meyer, *Institutions Judiciaires des Pays-Bas* (vol. 5).
Morice, *English and Roman-Dutch Law.*
Muller, *Rechtsbronnen der stad Utrecht.*
Munniks, *Handleiding tot de Hedendaagsche Rechtsgeleerdheid.*
Nathan, *Common Law of South Africa.*
Nederlandsche Placaatkundig Woordenboek.
Neostadius, *Decisiones.*
Noordewier, *Nederdeutsche Rechtsoudheden.*
Orange River Colony Proclamations and Ordinances.
Ortwyn, *Standhoudend Roomsch Recht.*
Peckius, *De jure Sistendi* and *De regulis juris canonici* in his *Opera Omnia.*
Pollock and Maitland, *History of English Law.*
Poullet, *Origines, developpements et transformations des institutions dans les Anciens Pays-Bas.*
Proclamations of the Government of the Cape of Good Hope, 1805–1825.
Raepsaet, *Analyse historique et critique de l'origine et des progrès des droits des Belges et Gaulois*, vols. 3–5 of his *Œuvres Complètes.*
Rechtsgeleerde Observatiën.
Reports—Cape, Transvaal, O.R.C. and Natal.

Ritterhuisius, *Differentiae juris civilis et canonici.*
Roby, *Roman Private Law.*
Rogers, Thorold, *Holland.*
Sande's *Decisiones.*
Savigny, *Geschichte des Römischen Rechts in Mittelalter*
—— *System des heutigen Römischen Recht.*
Scheltinga, *Commentary on Grotius.*
Schomaker, *Consultatiën.*
Schorer, *Notes to Grotius.*
Schrassert, *Consultatiën.*
Schröder, *Lehrbuch der Deutschen Rechtsgeschichte.*
South African Law Journal.
Stallaert, *Glossarium van verouderde Rechtstermen.*
Star Numan, *Leven van Bynkershoek.*
Statutes of the Cape of Good Hope, 1652 up to date.
Tacitus, *Germania, Annals* and *History.*
Tennant, *Notary's Manual.*
Transvaal Proclamations and Ordinances.
Troplong, *Droit Civil.*
Van den Berg, *Nederlandsche advysboek.*
Van der Aa, *Biographisch Woordenboek der Nederlanden.*
Van der Bergh, *Verhandeling over de oude wijze van straf vordering*
Van der Keessel, *Theses Selectae.*
Van der Linden, *Judicieel Praktijk.*
—— *Koopmans Handboek.*
Van der Schelling, *Histori van het Notarisschap.*
Van der Spiegel, *Oorsprong der vaderlandsche rechten.*
Van Leeuwen, *Censura Forensis.*
—— *Crimineel en Judicieel Praktijk.*
—— *Roomsch Hollandsch Recht.*
Van Loon, *Aloude regeeringswyze van Holland.*
Van Mieris, *Charterboek.*
Varro, *de re Rustica.*
Verhandelingen ter nasporinge van de wetten en gesteldheid onzes vaderlands. Door een genootschap "pro jure excolendo patrio."
Vinnius, *ad Institutiones.*
Viollet, *Histoire du droit Français.*
Voet, *Commentary.*
Wagenaar, *Nederlandsche Historie.*
Wassenaar, *Judicieel Praktijk.*
—— *Notarieel Praktijk.*
Wet Boek van de O.V.S.
Zypaeus, *Notitia Juris Belgici.*

THE HISTORY OF THE ROMAN-DUTCH LAW.

INTRODUCTION.

As far as I am aware there is no work on the history of the Roman-Dutch law which deals with the whole subject in a compact form. There certainly is none in the English language. There are quite a number of Dutch works which set out the history of Dutch institutions or which devote themselves to the history of the laws and customs of particular towns. The nearest approach to a history of the Roman-Dutch law are the contributions to the history of law in the Netherlands (*Bijdragen tot de Nederlandsche Rechtsgeschiedenis*) of Professor Fockema Andreae. This work treats of the family law, the constitution of the courts and the condition of persons. Owing to the fact that the history of the above subjects is traced in detail with reference to every province and many towns the work is very diffuse. Besides the *Bijdragen* of Fockema Andreae there are several monographs on the laws of different towns, such as *Het Rechtsboek van den Briel,* by Fruin and Pols; *Rechtsbronnen der Stad Zutphen,* by Hordijk; *De Friesche Stadrechten en Stadboek van Groningen,* by Telting; *De Saksenspiegel in Nederland,* by Van Jutphaas, and several others. These works are extremely useful to the student of Dutch history, but they are too antiquarian and too bulky to interest the South African student of the Roman-Dutch law.

The general history of the Roman-Dutch law can only be gathered from a number of writers, each of whom contributes his share upon some particular subject. The influence of the Roman law upon the development of Dutch law was very fully set out by Van der Spiegel in his little book on the *Oorsprong der Nederlandsche Rechten*, and by the Belgian writer Raepsaet in his *Analyse Historique et Critique de l'origine et des progrès des Droits des Belges et Gaulois*, forming the third, fourth and fifth volumes of his *Œuvres Complètes*. There are a few other works of the eighteenth century, such as Arntzenius' *De Conditione Hominum*, which concern themselves with special branches of law, and from which a great deal of historical information can be gathered. Besides these less known works there are of course the text-books of Grotius and Van Leeuwen, the *Commentary* of Voet, Groenewegen's *De Legibus Abrogatis* and other well-known authorities.

From all these I have endeavoured to gather sufficient material to give a sketch of the gradual development of the Roman-Dutch law in the Netherlands and in South Africa. No ambitious attempt has been made to write a complete history, partly because here at Pretoria, where this work was written, the material at my disposal has been very scanty, and partly because I have tried to keep the book within a moderate compass so as to endeavour to stimulate an interest in the subject rather than to terrify students with its bulk. I have endeavoured to follow as much as possible the main stream of the legal development of our law, and to disregard the various tributaries, each of which, if traced to its sources, would in itself yield a small volume.

The history of the Roman-Dutch law has been sadly neglected in South Africa, so that the ideas which prevail in the profession as to the origin and development of the Roman-Dutch law are extremely crude. Ancient law books are often quoted in the courts with little or no conception of who the authors were or what place they occupy in the development of the law. Practitioners know that Neostadius preceded Voet if perchance they have noticed that he is quoted by the latter. Bynkershoek is often a mystery, and the old Dutch Consultations are regarded with respect more on account of their black-letter print than on account of any knowledge of their authors. It is surely high time that the legal profession as a body should become acquainted with the whole course of the history of the system of law they are called upon to practise. Something of the fountain-head students know, for a meagre acquaintance with the history of the Roman law is picked up from the text-books for the legal examinations; and the mouth of the stream they are familiar with, because they must read the recent decisions of the courts and the Acts of the legislature, but the course of the vast stream from its fountain-head to its mouth is a *flumen incognitum*. If a person's knowledge of butterflies were confined to the egg and the full-grown *imago*, no one would dream of calling him a naturalist; yet numbers of men teach and practise the Roman-Dutch law who only know the egg and the *imago*, but to whom the larva and the pupa are either wholly unknown or wrapt in a profound mist.

I must warn the reader that he will find little if anything in this work to enable him to pass any of our university examinations. We in South Africa do not require law to be studied as a science. The University of the Cape of Good Hope grants a degree in law without requiring a knowledge of the history of the Roman law, much less of the Roman-Dutch law. Instead of making its requirements such that the student is compelled to study law as a science, and not as a mere tool, it is quite satisfied if he can digest enough law to be able to plead some elementary cause.

This used to be thought enough to enable a student to be called to the English Bar, but it is no longer regarded as sufficient in the universities of England or of the Continent. No doubt when the scales have fallen from our eyes we shall require law to be studied as a science, and then a knowledge of the history of Roman law, before and after the days of Justinian, will be considered as necessary as the *Institutes* of Justinian or the *Introduction* of Grotius. Meanwhile the student who is not satisfied with a mere empyrical knowledge of law will do well to study the history of the Roman law as well as the history of our own law.

In every law school of Europe the history of the particular system which is taught is at present regarded as a natural concomitant to the study of that system. The history of the Roman law has long been a compulsory subject wherever law is taught as a science, and where mere empyricism is discouraged. In Germany Schröder's *Manual of the History of German Law* and Heusler's *Institutes of German Private Law* are well-known text-books. In France the history of law has made great progress, whilst in England the work of Sir

Frederick Pollock and Professor Maitland has supplied a long-felt need.

In South Africa it has been quite impossible for the ordinary student to find out much about the history of the Roman-Dutch law. The only English book where a sketch of this history is to be found is Chief Justice Maasdorp's introduction to his translation of Grotius, and, good as it is, it had necessarily to be very brief. It was this absence of any English work which led me to contribute a few articles to the *South African Law Journal.* The editor, Mr. W. H. S. Bell, who became interested in the subject, asked me to publish the articles in book form. It soon became apparent that most of them, written as the occasion demanded, had to be entirely recast and considerably amplified. I hope this little book may serve as a finger-post to the study of the subject it professes to deal with. In many cases conclusions are stated as if no controversy existed about them. Let me warn the reader at the outset that there are few statements in this little work which have not been the subject of long and furious controversy. I have, however, thought it preferable to give the conclusions of what I thought the better authorities, than to trouble the unfortunate student with the views of every writer and pamphleteer. By referring to the authorities cited he can at his pleasure soon be plunged into the mass of divergent views. If I have succeeded in giving a bird's-eye view of the development of our law, and in stimulating a desire to know more, I shall be supremely satisfied. No critic can be better aware of the shortcomings of this work than I am myself. If I wait for publication until the work satisfies myself I am afraid it will be a very long time before it sees the light.

A great deal of the early history of the Roman-Dutch law is hidden in deep darkness. Our information is extremely scanty, and conjecture often has to take the place of accurate information. From records scattered over a wide area, and from customs which crop up here and there, we have to build up and reconstruct the past as best we can. That our laws have been formed in the main from German customs, modified by the principles of the Roman law, will admit of no doubt. But when we are asked to give the exact value of any particular custom we must fail, because our records are too fragmentary, and often too indefinite.

In the development of law generally there must necessarily be a great deal of resemblance in various systems, if for no other reason than that law is the product of the human brain, and that a great number of human acts are common to the cultured classes of Europe and the savages of Central Africa and Patagonia. A custom therefore common to the Dutch of Holland and the early Egyptians does not imply that the Dutch borrowed the custom from an Egyptian source. In order, therefore, to trace the history of laws we must have some acquaintance with the political history of the country whose laws we are studying. If one knows that Holland formed part of the Frankish monarchy, and that the early inhabitants of Holland were Franks, one would expect to find Frankish customs in Holland, and the fact that similar customs existed in Lombardy would be a coincidence and no more. If, however, the Lombards were known to be of the same race, and to have spoken a similar language, it would be a fair inference that these customs were common to the ancestors of the two races. So in tracing the history of

Dutch customs we often have to consider the customs of other nations of the same stock, such as the Alemanni, the Burgundians, the Lombards, and even the Visigoths. Just as it is the business of the comparative philologist to build up the *ursprache* of the race, so is it the function of the comparative jurist to ascertain the original laws and customs of the race. Much of his work is conjecture, but it is based on a process of reasoning from the known to the unknown.

In the following pages I have had to make use of several of such conjectures, though I have endeavoured to build upon well-ascertained facts. In the conflict of influences it is often difficult to attribute to each its due effect. Where, therefore, I speak of the influence of the German laws, or of the Roman, Canon, or English law, I mean the preponderating force which gave the law a certain direction. This direction is usually the resultant of many forces, but it always lies nearest to the direction of the greatest. If, for instance, we take our Marriage Ordinances in South Africa we see at once, when we compare them with the Roman-Dutch law, that the direction they have taken is mainly due to the law of Holland; but there is a considerable deflection, and that deflection is due to the influence of English law. So again, if we look at our law of Contract we at once conclude that the Roman law forms the greatest factor in that branch of law; but we soon recognise that German customs and English practice have altered its direction very materially.

I have frequently had to refer to the local customs of various towns in the Netherlands. It may be said, what have we to do with the customs of Amsterdam or the keuren of Leyden; these customs do not form part of our common law?

If customs grew up quite independently, and wholly unconnected with the general law, this would be true, but such is not the case. The customs of a town are often but a variation of what they accepted as the customs of their ancestors, or when we find these customs appearing in many towns at the same time we may legitimately infer that this was the trend of public opinion as to what the law should be. I have endeavoured to be as sparing as possible in my references to local customs, though they are often interesting as pointing out dangers which we in our hurried and feverish factory of new laws often forget.

In explaining a subject I have often taken into consideration the whole of the Netherlands. It may be said, why discuss what took place in Groningen when our law is derived from Holland? The answer is obvious. Holland was not cut off from the rest of the Netherlands, but formed part of it; and in the development of its law the adjoining provinces played a very important part. If we want to solve a particular legal problem we must go to the law of Holland and see how that system would solve it; but if we want to know why and how that particular rule of law prevailed in Holland we must see what the law was which prevailed in the neighbouring provinces, and so trace its common origin.

I have confined myself as much as possible to the law of Holland, though it has been necessary in many cases to go outside the law of that particular province in order to understand how our present law has assumed its present form. The Roman-Dutch law was not created at any particular date; it is linked to the past, and therefore I have endeavoured to go back as far as possible, though it must be confessed that when we go further back than the fifteenth century the light is not always clear. There is, however, enough light to trace the outlines of large and important objects. I have been obliged to touch briefly upon the political and constitutional history of the Netherlands and upon the development of some of its institutions, for without a knowledge of the outlines of these subjects it is impossible to grasp the history of the development of the Roman-Dutch law.

The work has been divided into two parts. In the first part I trace the general development of the Dutch system of law. In this part I have included a sketch of the principal Dutch jurists. In the second part I deal with the development of special branches of law in greater detail. For the chapters which deal with the administration of law in South Africa I am indebted to the Rev. Mr. Leibrandt and to Mr. C. H. van Zijl for much valuable information. The work is merely an attempt, and I hope it will be received as such.

PART I.

GENERAL DEVELOPMENT OF THE DUTCH SYSTEM OF LAW.

CHAPTER I.

THE PERIODS OF DUTCH HISTORY.

IN considering the history of the Roman-Dutch law it is absolutely necessary to have some idea of the history of the people who inaugurated and developed that system. A detailed account would carry us too far afield, but a general review is indispensable. The Netherlands have since the Christian era been so often overrun by various nations that, without analysing the influence of each invasion, we may form an incorrect idea of the effect of these invasions upon the later laws, customs and institutions. Antiquarian research has shown us that most of the European nations have clung tenaciously to their ancient customs, and that modern laws and modern customs have their roots fixed in a distant past. The nations and tribes which have from time to time occupied the territory now known as Holland and Belgium have formed no exception to this rule. Before proceeding to deal with the laws, customs and institutions of the Netherlands I shall first sketch out the periods into which I propose to group my survey. These periods may be regarded as landmarks in the history of the Netherlands to which reference will have to be frequently made.

The history of the Netherlands can be conveniently considered under the following periods:—

(1) The Early German period. This period refers to the time prior to the Roman conquest of the Low

Countries, when the German tribes in their westward march occupied the country along the banks of the Rhine, Maas and Schelde.

(2) The Roman period. This includes the four centuries during which the Netherlands formed part of the Roman Empire.

(3) The Early Frankish invasion. When the troubles in eastern Europe compelled the Roman emperors to withdraw their legions from Gaul, the Salic Franks attacked the weakened Roman forces and eventually succeeded in driving them out of the country now known as Holland and Belgium.

(4) The Saxon invasion. The Saxons during the fifth century spread along the coast of the North Sea and gradually drove the Franks out of Holland and Zeeland. These provinces they occupied for some time until they in their turn were driven out by the Frisians. This invasion of the Frisians will constitute our fifth period.

(5) Invasion of the Frisians.

(6) The Frankish monarchy. The Salic and Ripuarian Franks joined their forces and, fighting under one king, occupied northern Gaul, and then turning back to Holland drove the Frisians out of that province.

(7) The weakening and gradual disruption of the Carolingian monarchy gave rise to the rule of the hereditary counts. This period, which may be called the rule of the House of Holland, lasted from 922–1299.

(8) This and the following periods are determined by the various houses that held sway in the Netherlands.

The House of Holland was followed by the House of Henegouwen (Hainault) (1299–1345).

(9) The House of Bavaria (1345–1425).

(10) The House of Burgundy (1428–1482).

(11) The House of Austria (1482–1572).

(12) The Dutch Republic (1572–1795).

(13) Holland under Napoleon (1795–1814).

The later history of Holland does not concern us in this history of the Roman-Dutch law.

CHAPTER II.

EARLY GERMAN PERIOD.

THE Netherlands was inhabited at the beginning of the Christian era by various tribes of Germanic origin. At that period the German people were wandering over central and western Europe. This wandering (*völkerwanderung*) went on for several centuries, so that it is difficult to say with certainty what particular lands in western and central Europe these nations occupied. At the time of Caesar the Frisians and Caninefates held the coast-line from the Elbe to the Rhine. Between the Rhine and the Schelde dwelt the Batavians. South of them were the Menapii and the Toxandrii. Round the Zuyder Zee (*Lacus Flevo*) lived the Catti (probably a Frankish tribe), and the Chamavi.

Later on, as the westward movement of the Germans continued, we find certain well-known branches of that people occupying fairly well-defined tracts of country. Thus after the *Völkerwanderung* in the fourth century the Frisians occupied the coast-line from the Ems to the Rhine. West of them were the Saxons stretching to the Elbe. On the right bank of the Rhine were the Ripuarian Franks, while the Salic Franks occupied the countries now known as Belgium and Luxembourg. The Alemanni occupied central Europe, with the Burgundians to their west and the Bavarians to their east. Spain and Italy formed part of the West Gothic kingdom, whilst a large portion of western Europe was under the sway of the East Goths. About the middle of the sixth century the Long Beards or the Lombards occupied Italy, and part of Austria and Hungary, (Droysen's Atlas; Schröder's Map).

The Netherlands, therefore, was occupied by Frisians on the north, Ripuarian Franks on the east, and by Gauls and Salic Franks on the south. Of the various tribes that occupied Holland in the early days the Batavians were the most renowned. Tacitus tells us that the Batavians who dwelt west of the Rhine were a part of the Catti, and that, driven from their native country, they settled on a waste tract of land on the extreme confines of Gaul, and on an island with the ocean on its north, and on both sides the Rhine (Tacit. *Hist.* iv, 12). These Batavians belonged to the Great Frankish nation which was destined to play so important a part in the history of western Europe.

Roughly speaking, we may say that the provinces of Zeeland and South Holland were inhabited by the Batavians; North Holland by the Caninefaten; Friesland and Groningen by the Frisians; and Overijssel by the Catti.

We shall now inquire what manner of men these Germans were, and what were their institutions, their customs and their laws. When first we become acquainted with the Germans they had already acquired a certain amount of civilisation. Though they were nomadic and warlike, they had emerged from the state of the huntsman pure and simple. They were essentially a pastoral people, but at the commencement of the Christian era we find them occupied in agricultural pursuits; of trade they knew little or nothing. Before their contact with the Romans they were unacquainted with money, and barter was their only means of exchange. Their standard of exchange was cattle Their years were reckoned by winters; their time not by days, but by nights. Life in towns was unknown to them. They lived either on isolated farms or in small, straggling villages (Schröder, pp. 1–15).

The social unit was not the individual, but the family. The family consisted of the husband, wife and young children, for the grown-up sons left the household to form their own homes, whilst the grown-up daughters married into other families. When the husband died the eldest son took his place, if old and strong enough; if not, the family was absorbed in that of one of the husband's brothers. As in all uncivilised communities, the head of the family was a warrior and the defender of his family. The wife and children helped to tend the flocks and to till the soil (Tacit. *Germ.* 25). The Germans were greatly addicted to divination by omens and lots, and it was always the head of the family who in private did the interpretation. The husband had the right to punish his family, and if the wife committed adultery he cut off her hair, stripped her, and in the presence of her relatives expelled her from his house, pursuing her with stripes through the village (Tacit. *Germ.* 10, 19).

The collection of families formed the tribe, but the voice of the tribe was the voice of the majority of the men capable of bearing arms. There was no distinction between the army and the tribe, and the administration which applied to the former also applied to the latter (Schröder, p. 16). The army was divided into bodies of a thousand, and these again into bodies of a hundred men. The commander of the former was called by the Romans a *millenarius* and of the latter a *cente-*

narius. The bond between commander and men was at first a purely personal bond; in time, however, it came to be not only personal, but territorial. Hence the tribe was divided into Hundreds (*centena*) and into Thousands (*canton* or *gau*). The Thousand (*tausendschaft*) was composed of ten Hundreds. It was known in Latin as the *pagus*, in German as the *gau* (Dutch, *gouw*). A collection of *gauen* formed the tribe, nation or *civitas* (Fock. And. vol. 4, p. 14).

The great distinction between the east and west Germans is, that when we first become acquainted with them we find the former under kings, whilst the latter, at any rate in times of peace, knew neither hereditary nor elective rulers. In time, however, the west Germans, like the east Germans, came to adopt the kingship. The kingship, however, was elective, and the choice lay with the assembled people.

The king was at first chosen out of the noblest families, but in time the election came to be limited to one particular noble family (Schröder, p. 25). The king was the head of the nation, he led its army, presided at its councils and was also the chief priest. In war his power was great, but limited in peace. Prior to the establishment of the kingship the sovereign ruling power was the great meeting of all the shield and spear bearing men of the tribe. Tacitus calls this meeting a *concilium.* He tells us that on affairs of minor importance the chiefs (*principes*) consulted one another. By princeps he means the headman of the *gau* or *pagus.* For matters of greater importance the whole tribe assembled. Before they assembled, however, the headmen came together and deliberated about the matters to be submitted to the council or *fylkisthing.* The new or the full moon was the most auspicious time for meeting. The assembly sat down armed, the priests proclaimed silence and then the chief or other headman (*rex aut princeps*) addressed the people. If a proposal displeased it was rejected by a murmur of disapproval, but if they approved they clashed their arms (*honoratissimum assensus genus est armis laudare*) (Tacit. *Germ.* c. 11).

Before this council accusations were heard and capital offences were prosecuted. Punishments varied with the nature of the crime. Traitors and deserters were hanged upon trees, cowards were suffocated in the mud. For most crimes a penalty was imposed upon the accused, part of which went to the king or state, and part to the injured person or his relatives. In this assembly also the various district and hundred chiefs were elected (Tacit. *Germ.* c. 12). This assembly no doubt also determined with regard to war or peace. The principes or canton chiefs (*gouwvorsten*) were the administrative heads of the gau or canton, and also the judges in minor cases (*jura per pagos vicosque reddunt.*—Tacit. *Germ.* c. 12); the more serious crimes were tried by the assembly. Most authorities seem to think that just as the head of the canton possessed judicial functions so the head of the Hundred also presided in a Hundred Court (Fock. And. vol. 4, p. 17). The headman was accompanied by a number of youths (*comitatus*) in times of peace as well as on the field of battle (Tacit. *Germ.* c. 13, 14).

This comitatus or companionship was a great factor in the German national life, and has led in the course of time to important developments. It existed in the Frankish monarchy as late as the eighth century, and was probably the model upon which the Byzantine bodyguard was formed. There is little doubt that it was the origin of feudal chivalry. It rested upon a voluntary bond between the chief and his followers. The chief protected and maintained his followers, whilst they, on the other hand, promised him service and assistance. The service was such as one freeman might tender to another, and as they mostly belonged to one family they could rely on one another's loyalty (Schröder, p. 32).

The Kelts possessed an ecclesiastical hierarchy—the Druids—but according to Caesar no such institution was known to the Germans (Caesar, *Bel. Gal.* 6, c. 21). That the Germans possessed priests there can be no doubt, for Tacitus tells us that in the assemblies *silentium per sacerdotes quibus tum et coercendi jus est, imperatur* (*Germ.* c. 11). What their functions were we do not know, but it is very probable that the influence of the priest was not so great amongst the Germans as amongst the Gauls and Romans.

The people were divided into three classes—nobles, freemen and slaves. In the course of time the west Germans (especially the Franks) came to recognise a fourth class, called *lites, liti,* or half-free (German, *hörigen;* Dutch, *hoorigen*). The slaves were either captives or persons who had fallen into that state through debt. They were not as a rule domestic servants, but each had allotted to him a hut and land where he raised crops and bred cattle, of which a certain percentage belonged to him and the rest to his master (Tacit. *Germ.* c. 25). Originally the Germans did not recognise individual ownership in the soil. The land belonged to the tribe and was parcelled out by lot from time to time to the various families (Caesar, *Bel. Gal.* 6, c. 22). The nobles in all probability did not take part in this division. At a very early period the nobles seem to have had tracts of land allotted to them on which they built their strongholds with dwellings for their followers and slaves (*hof*) (Schröder, p. 59).

Of the private law of the early Germans we know very little. There are no written laws or customs. Of the procedure of their courts we are also ignorant, though by comparing the various customs prevalent in later times we gather that they were fond of using alliterative formulae, such as *morth motma mit morthe kela* (murder we must cool with murder), and symbols such as straws, staves, rods, &c. The father was the guardian of his young children, but directly they left the house the father's legal power ceased. They acknowledged no *patria potestas*. The marriage laws were very strict, and the wife brought no dos to her husband; on the contrary, she received a dowry from him (Tacit. *Germ.* c. 18). We know nothing of their contracts, though they seem to have attached great importance to a promise (Tacit. *Germ.* c. 24).

It may be asked of what value can the customs of the early Germans be to a student of the Roman-Dutch law? With a view to a practice of the law, none whatever. But for a person who takes an intelligent interest in the development not only of the Roman-Dutch, but of the English law, these customs are of the greatest interest. As we proceed in our investigation it will be found that a great many of the rules of both Dutch and English law have their beginnings in some of the simple customs of our Teutonic forefathers.

CHAPTER III.

ROMAN PERIOD.

WHEN the Romans had conquered Gaul they made the Rhine their natural frontier. It has been a matter of dispute whether the Batavians were ever conquered by the Romans. It is, however, clear that Batavia was incorporated in the Roman Empire, and that the province furnished the Roman armies with excellent troops. The country was considered by the Romans difficult to colonise on account of its low-lying fens and woods. The Batavians were skilled horsemen, and their valour made them welcome auxiliaries to the Roman forces. Under a chieftain, called Claudius Civilis by the Romans, they raised a revolt during the reign of Vitellius. This revolt spread all along the Rhine, and Rome was in danger of losing the fairest province of her Empire. Civilis was, however, defeated at Votera, and the Romans occupied Batavia. So strong was the power of Civilis and so insecure was the victory, that the Romans treated with him and accepted his excuse that he did not intend to subvert the Empire, but to support Vespasian against Vitellius. What became of Civilis we do not know (Tacit. *Hist.* bk. iv, c. 13 *et seq.*; bk. v, c. 14–18).

The history of Civilis shows us that, even prior to the revolt, the Roman influence was strong in all that part of the Netherlands which lay on the left bank of the Rhine. After this revolt the Batavians remained faithful to the Roman Empire, until at the downfall of the Western Empire in the early part of the fifth century they were merged in the Salic Franks. The country inhabited by the Batavians, Menapii, Toxandrians and others formed the Roman province of Germania Inferior, whilst the Nervii and other Gallic tribes that lived in the present south Belgium and north-eastern France formed the province of Belgica. According to Droysen north Holland and Friesland never formed part of the Roman Empire.

For four centuries south Holland and Belgium remained part of the Roman Empire and aided Rome in her wars. It is therefore inconceivable that Roman influence did not make itself felt in the country between the Rhine and the Schelde. To what extent, however, this influence permanently affected the customs of the people it is difficult to say. The effect of Roman influence upon Gaul we can gauge, for Gaul was civilised under Roman rule; but the dense woods and extensive morasses of the Netherlands made communication difficult, and hindered the progress of civilisation. What the influence of the Roman conquest was upon the laws and customs of the peoples around the mouths of the Rhine, Maas and Schelde we do not know.

Though the fundamental principles of the laws of the Netherlands remained German, there is no doubt that the great body of the laws which prevailed in the Netherlands, as elsewhere in western Europe, must have been modified by its contact with Roman law.

It is difficult to determine to what extent the Roman conquest over the Batavians, Salic Franks and Saxons was effective. That the Romans at various times held sway over the greater part of the Netherlands admits of little doubt, and that they imposed upon these peoples a Roman administration is extremely probable; but whether the people who lived in Germania Inferior were brought under Roman influence to the same extent as were the inhabitants of Gaul is a question by no means easy to solve.

In Gaul Roman customs had been everywhere introduced, and Latin was as well known to the people as their own dialects. The Roman religion had completely taken the place of the Celtic cults, and Roman priests had largely usurped the functions of the Druids. If this was the case in Gaul the probability is that the same influences produced similar effects in the Netherlands, though no doubt to a less extent. Although it was the practice of the Romans to allow conquered nations to retain their laws and customs, yet a period of Roman rule for several centuries must have had the effect of considerably modifying the barbarous customs of the German tribes. We have no proof whatever of the influence of Roman law upon the early inhabitants of the Netherlands, yet it seems improbable to suppose that with the removal of the Roman legions all traces of Roman customs and Roman law entirely disappeared. At any rate, though we may think it probable that the early Roman occupation left some mark upon the later development of the law of Holland, we must remember that there is absolutely no proof of such effect.

CHAPTER IV.

EARLY FRANKS, SAXONS AND FRISIANS.

SOME writers are of opinion that the Batavians and Toxandrians formed part of those German tribes who were known later as Franks, whilst others, admitting them to have been Germans, deny that they were Franks (Fock. And. vol. 4, p. 18). Whichever view we accept, it is quite clear that at the time the Romans left Gaul the Franks were in possession of a large portion of the Netherlands. In the time of Maximinian and Constantine the Franks were undoubtedly moving in the direction of Holland, and occupying the country around the mouths of the Rhine. Eumenius, writing about Constantine (*paneg. Constantino*, c. 5), says, *Qui terram Bataviam sub ipso quondam alumno suo a diversis Francorum gentibus occupatam omni hoste purgavit.* Who the *alumnus* was we do not know. An anonymous writer of that period speaks of the thousands of Franks who invaded Batavia. These Franks were in all probability Salic Franks. Van der Spiegel thinks that the Salic Franks or Salii were the Sea Franks, as distinguished from the Ripuarii or River Franks. He also thinks that the Zeelanders derived their name from these Sea Franks (Van der Spiegel, p. 13).

Besides Batavia the Salic Franks occupied Toxandria, which corresponds to the modern province of Brabant. Julianus, one of the generals of Constantius, and later the Emperor Julian, seem to have fought against them about the middle of the fourth century, though apparently after their defeat he left them in occupation of the land.

It is about this time that the Saxons first appear upon the scene. As we have seen in a former chapter, the Saxons had in their western movement occupied the country between the Weser and the Ems. On their western frontiers during the fourth century they came in contact with the Salic Franks and sought to drive them out of the country between the Rhine and the Schelde. Melis Stoke (p. 3) and Klaas Kolyn (p. 136), two old Dutch chroniclers, tell us that the land from Nijmwegen to the western Schelde and thence to the sea was called Nether Saxony (*Neder Saxen*). From this we may conclude that the Saxons occupied a large portion of Holland and Zeeland. The Venerable Bede tells us that the Britons employed Saxon troops against the Picts and Scots (*Ecc. Hist.* bk. 1, c. 15). These Netherland Saxons certainly joined the other Saxons and Angles in their invasion of England, and those who remained were so weakened by this exodus of warriors that they fell a prey to the Frisians (Van der Spiegel, p. 26). During the fifth century the hold of the Romans upon the Germanic and Gallic tribes began to slacken, for the Roman troops had to be withdrawn from western Europe to defend Rome and the Eastern Empire against the onslaught of Goths and Huns. At that time the southern Netherlands was occupied by the Franks, and the north by the Frisians. So strong was the Frisian occupation of Holland that the whole country along the coast from the Weser to the Schelde was called Friesland; south and east of the Frisians dwelt the Franks. We saw that the Franks who dwelt in the Netherlands were called Salic Franks, but near them along the right bank of the Rhine dwelt another tribe of Franks known as the Ripuarian Franks. These Ripuarian or River Franks formed an independent nation, and occupied the country immediately adjoining that of the Salic or Sea Franks.

About the middle of the fifth century the Salic and Ripuarian Franks formed a bond for purposes of offence and defence. The first king of the Salic Franks was Clodion. He was succeeded by Childeric, who died in 481 at Doornik. Clovis, the son of Childeric, was the most important of the early Frankish kings. He conquered the Roman general Lygarius, and extended the dominion of the Franks as far south and west as the Loire. He became the recognised king of both Salic and Ripuarian Franks.

In 496 A.D. Clovis was converted to Christianity, and this was an important factor in the development of the great empire of the Franks. By supporting the Church he gained the support of the Gallo-Roman Christians, and was thus enabled to spread in western Europe the Roman civilisation of which the Church had become the heir. Clovis perceived the influence which the bishops had over the Christians of Gaul, and by joining the Church he utilised that influence for his own purposes. The bishops, on the other hand, welcomed to the Church a strong monarch like Clovis, for the Roman Empire was crumbling away, and, unsupported by temporal power, the Church could make no headway against the encroaching German barbarism. Clovis required the bishops as they required him, and both together strove to build up a new empire on the ruins of the one which had begun to totter. Clovis married Clotilda, the Christian daughter of the Christian king of the Burgundians, and his victory at Tolbiac over the heathen Alemanni was attributed by the Christian bishops to the God of the Christians. Clovis extended his empire southward as in turn he defeated Burgundians and Visigoths. The influence of the Church was established. Between the temporal and ecclesiastical powers a strong alliance was formed. The kings approved of the election of the bishops, whilst they in their turn became important councillors of State. The Church of Rome carried on in the west the institutions and laws of Imperial Rome. Clovis was not a territorial king; he was merely the leader of a people in arms, and the Gallo-Romans saw in him only the successor of the Roman proconsuls. Later on the kings of the Franks styled themselves *Reges Francorum et Romanorum.*

This early empire of the Franks is known as the Merovigian dynasty, from Merowig or Merovech, an ancestor of Clovis. This dynasty ruled until 752 A.D., when it was succeeded by Pepin the Short, the first of the Carolingian monarchs. Upon the death of Pepin, Charlemagne or Charles the Great consolidated the Frankish Empire (768 A.D.).

I shall now return to the Frisians. We saw that the Frisians had settled themselves in Holland and Zeeland, and had driven out the early Salic Franks from those provinces. From the time of the bond between the Salic and Ripuarian Franks the Frisians and Franks constantly fought in the Netherlands for the mastery of that country. In time, however, the Franks were victorious, and Holland and west Friesland fell under Frankish sway. The other provinces of the northern Netherlands remained under Frisian rule until Charlemagne completely conquered the Frisians, and the whole of Holland, Zeeland and Friesland became part of the Frankish Empire. It was during the eighth century that Willibord, Bonifacius and other missionaries converted Holland to the Christian faith. It rapidly spread through the northern provinces, and Utrecht became the seat of Bishop Boniface. The bishopric of Utrecht was destined to play a great part in the later history of the Netherlands, and the bishops of Utrecht became next to the counts of Holland the most important persons in the State.

Before discussing the influence of these various invasions on the legal history of Holland, I shall briefly resume its earlier history. We saw that the Low Countries were inhabited at the beginning of the Christian era by German tribes in the north and Gauls in the south. The Romans conquered or made allies of the Batavians, Catti, Toxandrians, Menapii and others, and established along the lower Rhine the province of Germania Inferior. When the Romans retired from western Europe the Salic Franks occupied the Netherlands. They were driven from Holland and Zeeland and some of the other northen provinces by the Saxons, who in turn gave place to the Frisians. The Frisians remained in occupation of the northern Netherlands until they were conquered by the united Salic and Ripuarian Franks, and then the Netherlands became a portion of the great empire of the Franks.

We have seen that the Netherlands were inhabited by Saxon and Frisian tribes as well as Franks. The Saxons we learnt were conquered by the Frisians and the latter by the Franks. Now it was not the habit of the Franks to abrogate entirely the laws and customs of those whom they conquered, but on the contrary to allow the conquered nations to retain to a certain extent their own laws. Hence it is not surprising to learn that in Holland and other parts of the Netherlands Saxon customs and Frisian usages lived side by side with the laws of the

Franks, and so in the course of time came to be incorporated in the common law of the Netherlands. The sources of the Saxon law are to be found in the *Lex Saxonum,* which dates from the eighth century. The old Frisian law is embodied in the *Vetus jus Frisicum* or the *Lex Frisionum,* which also probably dates from the eighth century.

CHAPTER V.

CHARLEMAGNE.

IN 768 Carloman and Charles the Great began their joint reign. In 772 A.D. Carloman was dead and Charles the sole inheritor of the kingdom of the Franks. He was a devout Catholic and fond of the rites of the Roman Church. He was first and foremost a conqueror. He annexed to the kingdom of the older Franks the Lombard kingdom, Saxony, Spain and the Slavonic lands of the Elbe. The Papacy had been alienated for some time from the Eastern Empire, and Pope Leo III conceived the idea of placing the Church under the protection of the great and growing empire of the west. In 800 A.D. the Pope placed the imperial crown upon the head of Charlemagne. Charles was now not only the military head of a great empire, the elected king of the Franks, but the protector of Christendom and the emperor crowned by God. In placing the crown upon the head of the victorious Frank, Leo III said, "God grant life and victory to Charles the Augustus crowned by God, great and pacific emperor of the Romans."

This union of Church and State had a great influence not only upon the temporal power of the emperor, but upon the development of the system of law which was spread if not inaugurated by him. This union of Church and State was not entirely the work of Charlemagne and Leo. It had been brought about under the Merowigs, but the bond was then a loose one, whilst under Charles the Great it became a publicly acknowledged fact. Charles was now the legitimate emperor of the Romans, and the Pope was recognised as the highest power that could confer imperial title. From the point of view of legal development this union of Church and State was most important. It gave a new force to the Church as the interpreter and later on as the maker of laws. It aided the spread of the Canon law and added to its prestige, and through the Canon law it indirectly helped the spread of the Roman civil law throughout western Europe. Charles encouraged learning and aided the clergy in their civilising influence. He inaugurated a strong system of imperial government, and above all established a code of imperial law. He sent out representatives to all lands under his sway. His lieutenants, the Missi Dominici and Missi Decurrentes, kept him in touch with the farthest ends of his empire. He divided the empire into territories ruled over by dukes and counts, and where he thought it advisable he gave the Church territorial rights and substituted bishop for duke. This was regularly done where it was considered necessary to check hereditary power. Hence sprung the dukedom of Brabant, the countships of Flanders, Holland and Guelderland, and the bishoprics of Utrecht and Münster.

The foundation upon which the legislation of Charlemagne was built consisted of the early bodies of German law, known as the *Lex Salica* and the *Lex Ripuaria*. From time to time these laws had been modified by the Frankish kings, so that when Charlemagne succeeded the confusion was very great. Now the Franks, when they invaded northern France, and spread their conquests, came in contact with a civilisation far greater than their own. They found the Gallo-Roman living under a system of law far superior to the crude codes of the barbaric Germans. They learnt that the Roman respected the laws of the conquered, and they followed his example. The influence of the Church in smoothing over the effect of the Frankish conquest upon the inhabitants of the Roman provinces must not be forgotten. The Merovigian kings were Christian monarchs, and the power wielded by the bishops and other ecclesiastics in the kingdom of the Franks was very considerable. The *Lex Ecclesiastica* ruled side by side with the *Lex Mundana*, and tended to soften and modify the latter. Of these factors Charles the Great was well aware, and as he was a conqueror it was in his interest to keep the Church and the people satisfied. Hence he made no innovation on the practice of his predecessors; but whilst leaving the people to live under their own law, he strove by means of his statute law (*capitularia*) to introduce as much unity as possible into the administration of law. In the Netherlands it was the policy of Charles to invest the bishops with great political power, and for a long time the power of the Bishop of Utrecht was as great, and often greater, than that of the counts.

The institutions of the Franks may be briefly summarised as follows:—

(1) The King, or Emperor, as he was called after the coronation of Charlemagne by the Pope. He was the executive head of the nation, but his laws were made with the consent of the Assembly of the Freemen *Lex fit constitutione Regis consensu autem populi.*

(2) The Court of the King. This consisted of the principal officers attached to his household. The Court was composed of the chancellor, the comes palatii or grand

justicier, usually an ecclesiastic, the chamberlain, the seneschal, the constable and others.

(3) Missi Dominici or Royal Commissioners. Each Commission consisted as a rule of two members, one a high dignitary of State, the other a bishop or abbot. They acted both as high administrative and judicial functionaries.

(4) The National Assembly, composed of bishops, abbots, counts, dukes, and other magnates as well as of freemen.

(5) Counts, hundredmen (*centenarii*) and vicars.

(6) Placita Communia or Generalia or General Assemblies of Freemen, for transacting legal and other business.

(7) Placita Indicta or Special Assemblies of Freemen, for judicial and other purposes.

(8) Rachimburgii and Scabini (Schepenen, Echevins) or Members of Local Courts.

(9) The country was divided into Great Pagi, and these into *pagi medii* and *pagi minores*. Holland, Oostergoo, Westergoo, Kennemerland, de Veluwe and Betau formed a Great Pagus. The pagi were ruled over by dukes and counts, and the subdivisions of the pagi by the *centenarii* and *vicarii*.

(10) The tenure of land was either *dominium directum* (allodial land, *alleu*) or *dominium utile* (*benefices*, feudal property). These again were parcelled out into plots held under servile tenure.

(11) The various divisions of land were known as manses or small farms, *casae* or dwelling plots, *hospitia* or small rural holdings, and *villae* or villages.

(12) The people were divided into clerics and laymen. The latter were either freemen, divided into optimates, land-owners (*boni viri*) and others, or half-free (*lites*), or, lastly, serfs (Poullet, *Origines*, vol. 1, pp. 66–110).

CHAPTER VI.

THE LAWS OF THE FRANKS.

I SHALL now proceed to give a brief account of the laws of the Franks, for these have played an important part in the development of the law of the Netherlands. I shall first discuss the early laws of the Franks, known as the *Lex Salica* and *Lex Ripuaria*, and then pass on to the body of laws, which consist of statutes passed by the Carolingian monarchs and known as Capitularia. From a brief account of these laws I shall pass over to a discussion of a cardinal factor in the development of law in western Europe—the personality of Law. This will enable us to deal with an important part of our investigation, viz., the introduction of Roman Law into the Common Law of the Netherlands.

Lex Salica.—Our knowledge of the early laws of the Franks is derived from two bodies of law, one of which dates back to the sixth century. These laws are known as the *Lex Salica* or the Laws of the Salii or Sea Franks, and the *Lex Ripuaria* or Laws of the Ripuarii or River Franks.

It was before the death of Clovis (511 A.D.) that the *Lex Salica* was drawn up. It was no doubt a compilation of the customs and laws of the Salic Franks, but it is clear from the text that the ecclesiastics played a great part in its production. It was written in Latin, and much of it was borrowed from the Roman law. To what extent the Roman law was drawn upon we do not know, though, judging from the chapter on contracts, the influence of that system was probably considerable. It is possible that the first compilation of the *Lex Salica* was written in the language of the Franks. During the reign of Clovis it was in all probability translated and edited by Roman priests, and the language of the Roman law-books was used to express the ideas of the Franks. We find in the *Lex Salica* many of the laws and customs which Tacitus mentions as belonging to the other German tribes. Like the earlier Germans the Salic Franks reposed in the Great Council of the Freemen, the *Concilium Generale,* full jurisdiction over all persons in the State. Besides this general assembly there were other courts presided over by the chief of the district (*thunginus* or *tunginus*) or by the chief of the hundred (*centenarius*). The exact jurisdiction of the thunginus is not clear, for we find him also presiding over the *mallum legitimum.* Next to these two officials the *Lex Salica* recognised two others called the *grafio* and the *sacebaro.*

The grafio (later graaf or count), as the representative of the princeps, had charge of the administration. He was, as it were, the executive officer of the princeps. Originally he had no judicial functions, but as the power of the thunginus decreased the grafio came to possess judicial as well as administrative functions. The sacebaro was also an executive officer, and his functions appear to have been limited to the collection of taxes. At the time of Clovis it would appear that the right of pronouncing judgment over a freeman was not confined to the *mallum legitimum,* but that some selected persons termed *rachimburgii* had the power of pronouncing a doom or judgment. Of these I shall treat more fully when I come to deal with the development of the law courts. These rachimburgii do not belong exclusively to the Salic Franks, for they are mentioned in the *Lex Ripuaria* (Schröder, p. 223; Fock. And. pp. 17 *et seq.*).

The greater part of the *Lex Salica* deals with criminal law and with the penalties attached to various transgressions. Some titles deal with the administration of justice, others with succession and with the various formulae for contracts. Some of the chapters treat of the possession of land, sale, lease, exchange and payment.

Lex Ripuaria.—The *Lex Ripuaria*, or the Laws of the River Franks, is considerably younger than the *Lex Salica*. It was probably compiled some time during the sixth century, probably before 596 A.D. The compilation with which we are acquainted dates from the reign of Charlemagne. In character it was very similar to the *Lex Salica*, and a great deal of it is devoted to the penalties due for injury to person or property. The Franks had in all probability no public officer charged with the prosecution of crime. Each freeborn citizen took into his own hands the pursuit of the criminal, and called upon his relatives to assist him. The injured party undertook the prosecution before the Hundred Court or the Gau Court or even the Great Council, and claimed the penalty which the law accorded to him—*Judicis non est quemlibet judicare vel condemnare absque legitimo accusatore.* Neither the Salic nor Ripuarian laws mentioned the death penalty or corporal punishment. These were apparently in the hands of the injured party who had not received the *wergeld* due to him. Thus the *Lex Ripuaria* provided that for the theft or injury of an ox the penalty was three soldi. A horse was valued at six soldi; a cow at one; a cuirass at twelve; and a trained hawk at six. Not only was the delinquent liable, but his family as well, unless they renounced their family connection (*se de parentela tollere*). In the latter case the accused was brought before the princeps, where his prosecutor again claimed the penalty. If he still refused he was declared an outlaw, *extra sermonem regis,* and could be put to death by the injured party (Raepsaet, vol. 3, pp. 382 *et seq.*).

Both the Salic and Ripuarian Codes were recognised as law in various parts of the Netherlands. Van der Spiegel says (p. 60): "There can be no doubt that the laws of the Salic and Ripuarian Franks were of force in the Netherlands from the time that the Frankish monarchs conquered that territory. As regards the Netherlands, there is a donation mentioned by Fokkens in the *Nova Collectio Diplomatum Belgicorum* (pt. 1, c. 4) by which certain lands situated in Holland were granted *according to the laws of the Salic and Ripuarian Franks.* Besides this there is more than one instance of manumission of slaves according to the provisions of these laws, of which we see one in Mieris' *Groot Charter Boek,* vol. 1, p. 29. This was not only according to the *Lex Salica,* but also in accordance with one of the formulae of Marculfus, a jurist who flourished in the seventh century. This shows us that the work of Marculfus was used in the Netherlands, and that the formulae gathered from the Frankish and from the Roman law were used by our ancestors as precedents of judicial procedure."

The sources of law, therefore, in the Netherlands at the time of the Carolingian monarchy were:—

(1) The ancient customs of the Germans, which regulated

the relations of the ruling classes to the rest of the freemen and established many of the principles of the family law.

(2) The *Leges Barbarorum,* such as the Salic, Ripuarian, Burgundian, Saxon and Frisian laws.

(3) The *Lex Ecclesiastica,* which consisted of the canons of General Councils, and such legislations of the Popes as applied to that territory.

(4) The *Lex Romana,* and

(5) The *Capitularia.*

I shall now proceed to deal more fully with the last of these sources.

CHAPTER VII.

CAPITULARIA.

THE Capitularia were the ordinances or statutes of the Carolingian monarchs. They were called capitularia either because they were divided into chapters or because they were made by the emperor in council; for *capitulum* means either the chapter of a book or a body of persons, just as we speak of the chapter of a book or the chapter of a cathedral (Van der Spiegel, p. 63). They constituted the body of laws passed by the Great Council under the presidency of the king. As this legislation was regarded as imperial, it applied to all the subjects of the king wheresoever they might live. The capitularia applied, therefore, not only to the Frankish subjects of the Carolingian monarchs, but also to Austrians or Italians. Not only did the capitularia form a part of the *Lex Mundana*, but they also formed an important part of the *Lex Ecclesiastica*. They were called at the Council of Troffi (909 A.D.) the Companions of the Canons. At the same time the emperors did not allow them to be superseded by the canons of the Church. Thus we find in a *capitulare* of Charles the Bald (844 A.D.) "that the bishops may not, under the pretext that provision is made by the canons, refuse to receive and to carry out the constitutions of the emperor" (*Cap. Carol. Calvi*, tit. 5, c. 8; Raepsaet, vol. 4, c. 9).

Church and State mutually assisted one another. The temporal power was supported by the spiritual power. Without a due appreciation of this important fact it becomes almost impossible to understand how the rough, uncultured Teutons could, in so short a period, have established a monarchy which absorbed all that was most virile in Roman civilisation. The Church preached to her sons and daughters respect for established authority, and respect for the law, whilst to the rulers she preached moderation and the brotherhood of man. The emperors in their capitularia enjoined respect for the Church and for her teaching. The Church was the heir of Roman culture, and of Roman culture in those days the greatest factor was the civil law. Hence the marriage of Church and State meant the softening of manners and the spread of the civilising influence of the Roman law.

There are several extant collections of the *Capitularia*, the chief ones being those of Angésisse and Benôit. The first printed collection is that of Vitus Amerpachius, dated 1545. The edition used by me is that of Baluzius, 1772. How long the capitularia were regarded as the law of the empire we do not know. Heineccius thinks that they were still recognised as the law of Germany as late as 952 A.D. Raepsaet is of opinion that the capitularia were considered to have had the force of law in Flanders and in the Netherlands as late as the end of the tenth century. He says, "They have never been formally abolished either in France, in the empire or in the Netherlands; and it is therefore still in the capitularia that we should search for the sources of our civil and public laws" (Raepsaet, vol. 4, c. 65). Van der Spiegel expresses a similar opinion, and points out that a great many of the later customs and usages are almost identical with the laws of the capitularia. Unless therefore, we assume that the capitularia were always looked upon as a legal force, we should be driven to assume that from the ninth to the thirteenth centuries there was a period of anarchy, after which we meet with the same customs and usages stated in almost the same words as we find them in the capitularia (Van der Spiegel, chap. 3).

He goes on to say (p. 64), "There can be no doubt that the capitularia had the force of law in our country, for they applied to all countries over which the Frankish kings held sway. This appears clearly from the capitularia themselves; and, inasmuch as many of them dealt with the privileges of the ecclesiastics, the Popes themselves admitted their authority. In one of the great Church councils at Ravenna (904 A.D.) all persons were threatened with excommunication who did not acknowledge the capitularia of Charlemagne and his successors (Labaeus in *Concil.* tit. ix, p. 508). As clear proof of the authority of the capitularia in the Netherlands we have the *Capitulatio de partibus Saxoniae* (ed. Georg. p. 578), where the words occur, *De perjuriis secundum legem Saxonicum fit,* and also the *capitulare* in bk. 6, sec. 366, where a command is laid upon all the subject tribes who are specially mentioned, as the Romans, Franks, Alemanni, Bavarians, Saxons and Frisians. Again, inasmuch as the counts of Holland obtained their rule and territory from the Frankish monarchs whilst the capitularia were still in force, it will bear no contradiction that the laws and prohibitions of these monarchs were, at any rate at that time, recognised in Holland."

CHAPTER VIII.

PERSONAL LAWS.

We have seen above that it was the practice of the Romans to interfere as little as possible with the laws and customs of the people they conquered. By the force of their superior civilisation they hoped gradually to induce the conquered nations to accept their institutions and laws. This policy worked very well, and we know that Gaul was almost completely romanised. When, therefore, the Franks overran Gaul, they found there a civilised people living under the Roman law. The Franks adopted the same principle as the Romans, and allowed the conquered peoples to live under their own law (*jure suo uti; sua lege vivere*).

This right of choosing your own law had a considerable effect upon the later development of our law, and therefore it will be advisable to explain fully what was meant by living under your own law, the choice of law, or, to express it more in conformity with modern terminology, the personality as opposed to the territoriality of law.

According to our modern system of legislation our laws are territorial, *i.e.* they bind all the individuals within a certain territory. This is a development of later times, and certainly did not prevail during the Merovigian dynasty. Each inhabitant of the Frankish kingdom was subject to the law of his own nationality. Thus in France the Frank was subject to the *Lex Salica;* the Burgundian to the *Lex Burgundionum;*

the Visigoth to the *Lex Antiqua Visigothorum;* whilst the Roman lived under the *Lex Romana.* According to this system the laws were personal and not territorial. Their applicability was determined not by the place where the person lived, but by the nationality to which he belonged. That this system, which appears so strange and unreasonable to us, did really exist is borne out by a large mass of reliable authority.

In an edict of Lothair we find the following: *Volumus ut omnis senatus et populus Romanus interrogetur quali vult lege vivere ut sub eâ vivat* (capit. Lotharii, I, sec. 37). In another edict we find, "We decree that in suits between Romans the judgment shall be according to the *Lex Romana*" (*capit.* add. iv, sec. 45, ed. Georgius). In the formulae of Marculfus (660 *circa*) we find the following: "You will govern, according to the law and custom of each one, all the peoples who live under your jurisdiction, the Franks, Romans, Burgundians and others" (bk. 1, f. 8). In the *Lex Ripuaria* we find the following: "We have decided that he who lives in the land of the Ripuarians, be he Frank, Burgundian, Alleman or of any other nationality, must answer when summoned before a court of law according to the law of the country in which he was born." "If a person is condemned he must pay his penalty according to his own law, not according to that of the Ripuarian Franks" (*Lex Rip.* tit. 33, art. 3; tit. 31, art. 4).

Agobardus, a favourite of Charlemagne, wrote: *Cupio per pietatem vestram nosse si non huic tantae divinae operationis unitati obsistat tanta diversitas legum quanta non solum in singulis regionibus et civitatibus sed etiam in multis domibus habetur. Nam plerumque contingil, ut simul eant aut sedeant quinque homines et nullus eorum communem legem cum altero habeat externis in rebus transitoriis cum internis in rebus perennibus unâ Christi lege teneantur* (Legem. Gund. c. 4, pt. 3, art. 2, ed. Balurus; Van der Spiegel, p. 82).

Matthaeus gives us a number of instances where father and son, husband and wife lived under different personal laws (*De Nob.* 1, c. 27); and, as we see above from Agobardus, you might sometimes find five persons congregated in one place each of whom lived under a different system. Here are a few more examples; "*Nos supradicti jugales qui professi sumus lege vivere Salica;*" "*Ego Maria quae professa sum lege vivere Romana*" (Matthaeus, *De Nob.* 1, c. 27). *Qui professus sum ex natione meâ lege vivere Salica et Leah legalis filia quondam Adelberti de praedicto loco Agrano quae professa sum ex natione meâ lege vivere Longobardorum* (Van Loon's *Aloude Regeeringswyze*, vol. 1, p. 201).

Savigny, in his history of Roman law in the middle ages, discusses the *raison d'être* of this personal law. He finds it inconceivable to imagine that the primitive laws of the Germans could have dealt satisfactorily with the advanced civilisation which the conquerors encountered throughout France. At the same time the Franks were too proud and too stubborn to submit to the civilisation and the laws of the conquered. Extermination of the conquered was out of the question, and, therefore, the only method out of the difficulty was to allow the conquered to retain their own laws, whilst the Germans who lived amongst them should retain theirs. From this fact that the two peoples did not live apart, but occupied one territory, it followed that if each citizen was to retain his own law it could be only a personal law, depending on the nationality to which he was born (Savigny, *Gesch. des R. R. in M. A.* vol. 1, ch. 3, sec. 31). Although it was a general principle that each one lived under his own law, we must not imagine there was no territorial law whatever.

As the Franks were the conquerors, they imposed upon the conquered their system of punishments by means of fines. The Salic law compelled the Roman to submit to compurgation in case of arson, and, as the Frank was the conqueror, in some cases the penalty for injuring a Roman was less than that for an injury to a Frank.

It is in the domain of civil law that the personality of Law applied more particularly. Suits between Romans were judged by Roman law: *Inter Romanos negocia causarum Romanis legibus praecipimus terminari* (Capito Lothair. I, 560). If the suit, however, were between Franks or Burgundians their respective laws were appealed to. By the *Lex Gondobada* if a question arose between a Burgundian and a Roman, then the Roman law was to be consulted in order to decide the dispute (*Lex Gond.* tit. 55, art. 2). The son followed the law of his father, the wife that of her husband, and the freed man the person under whose *mundeburdium* or tutelage he stood.

The judges were bound to find out what the personal law of the parties was, and to judge accordingly, and if they refused they were subjected to a money penalty (*Lex Sal.* tit. 60, arts. 1 and 2).

Whether it was possible at will to change from one system of law to another has been much discussed. The probability, however, is that a man was obliged to submit to the law of the nationality to which he was born, and that he could only effect a change by express consent of the king or of some other authority (*Lex Sal.* tit. 60, art. 4).

Gradually, however, during the Merovingian dynasty, laws were enacted which applied to all the inhabitants of the king's territory. These laws were territorial, and existed side by side with the personal laws. In course of time their scope was extended until they came to form a very important body of law. At first they were called the Edicts of the Frankish kings, but in the Carolingian period they came to be known by the name of Capitularia. I have dealt with these in the former chapter.

CHAPTER IX.

FEUDALISM AND FEUDAL LAW.

CHARLEMAGNE was succeeded by Lewis the Pious. The end of this unfortunate reign was the commencement of the breaking up of the empire, which had been built up with such care by Charles the Great. The wretched custom of partitioning the empire amongst the sons of the reigning monarch brought the Carolingian dynasty to the same woeful end to which it had brought the Merowigs. The important factor of this period in the development of law was the usurpation of the secular by the clerical authority. In consequence of this the influence of the Canon, and, therefore, also of the Roman law was spread throughout the empire. Lewis the Pious died in 840, and the next century saw the darkest hour of European history. The Vikings descended on Europe in the north and the Moors extended their victories to Italy.

Up to the time of Charlemagne the Northmen had confined their attacks upon western Europe to the Saxons and Frisians. During the latter half of the eighth century they commenced their raids upon the east coast of England, and early in the ninth century began to fall upon the undefended portions of the Frankish Empire. During the reign of Charles the Great their raids were frequent, but not so serious as to be a real danger. During the latter half of the ninth century, however, the descents of the Northmen upon the coasts of the Frankish Empire became frequent and serious. The Danes ravaged the coast of Friesland year after year, and the Emperor Lothair was obliged to cede the island of Walcheren to Rorik the Viking. In France the Vikings went up the Seine and sacked Paris, and early in the tenth century (911 A.D.) Charles the Simple ceded Normandy to Rollo the Dane.

Holland formed no exception to the inroads of the Northmen. The coast was constantly ravaged, and year after year the Danes sailed up the Maas. The influence of the Danes upon the development of the Roman-Dutch law was quite inappreciable. Their frequent invasions no doubt tended to throw the country back to barbarism and so to check the growing influence of the Roman law, but they exercised no positive influence in modifying the laws of the Franks.

The attacks of the Danes in their ships on the north and of the rapid moving Saracens on the south could not be repelled by the heavy, slow foot-soldiery of the Franks. It became necessary to raise horsemen wherever possible, and these bands of cavalry, raised and maintained by the dukes and counts in the territories over which they were appointed governors, formed one of the principal factors in the establishment of the feudal system. It has often been asserted that the incursions of the Northmen and Saracens compelled the emperors to place strong military leaders on the northern coasts and on the frontiers of the empire, and that fiefs were granted to them as a reward for their services. They in turn parcelled out these fiefs to their followers upon condition of service, and so arose the feudal system. This no doubt is true to some extent, but the best authorities tell us that this is not the whole truth. The origin of the feudal system is far more complicated than the grant of benefices for services against Dane and Saracen.

Feudalism in Holland, like the whole feudal system of western Europe, was not created by a legislative Act. It was the slow growth of centuries. The rise of feudalism on the Continent differed very materially from the establishment of that system in England. Feudalism did not exist in England as a system until its introduction in 1066 by William the Conqueror. William divided the country into a number of baronies, and placed over each either one of his followers or an Anglo-Saxon noble favourable to his cause. He compelled each baron, great or small, to swear fealty to him direct. Feudalism in England was, therefore, an act of conquest. In Holland, as in the rest of Charlemagne's dominions, feudalism grew up from small beginnings until at last it became a vast system of government.

The germ of feudalism is to be sought in the land laws of the Germans and Romans, and in the relationship which existed between the German chief and his followers. It is, therefore, impossible to say here ended the system of government of the Franks and there began the feudal system (Schröder, pp. 158 *et seq.*).

Feudalism was based upon two elements; the one was personal service and the other was beneficial ownership. The vassal (*homo, fidelis, vassus*) swore that he would faithfully serve his overlord (*senior, dominus*), and the overlord gave to his vassal a fief or territory for the use of himself and his descendants. The services of the vassal were such only as could be demanded from a free man—knight's service and attendance at court.

The Germans had from olden times been accustomed to such services, and the freemen expected in their turn services from their various classes of serfs. In the service which the *litus* (or half-free) owed to his master we see all the elements of vassaldom. This relationship of *litus* to master was similar to the relation of vassal to overlord, though by no means the same. In both cases we have service, and in both cases the use of land in return for service. During the Merovingian monarchy many of the king's followers had become large land-owners and on their land lived freemen, half-freemen (*liti*), and enfranchised slaves of all descriptions. The large land-owner thought it in his interest to fight for his sovereign, and his tenants made his interest their own.

Brunner has pointed out that the need for horse-soldiers to defend the Church against the Turk, and the empire against the Dane, was also a cause which operated in the establishment of vassaldom. Modern German historians doubt very much whether the old view is correct that the Merovigian monarchs gave benefices to their followers in order to defend their frontiers against the Northmen and the Arabs. That such may have been one of the reasons is highly probable. Roth thinks that the benefices were given in usufruct to the vassals like the leases of Church lands to its tenants.

It is a matter of dispute whether this combination of vassaldom and benefice—service and land—had its origin in Gaul or in Lombardy. Van Leeuwen gives the following account of the introduction of the *jus feudi* in Holland: "The origin of the feudal law, and by whom and when it was introduced among us, is uncertain. The common opinion is that it was first introduced by the further Saxons and ancient German tribes in Italy, particularly in the duchy of Milan, where they made their first inroad and for a long time had the upper hand under the name Long Beards (whence the term Lombard is still in use), in order to make the fealty of their subjects more certain; and having become an institution of the emperors Henry, Lothair, Conrad and Frederick Barbarossa it was transmitted, about 1100, to us as well as to other nations" (Van Leeuwen's *Commentaries*, Kotzé's trans. 2, 14, 1). Most of the modern German writers reject this view, that feudalism was introduced by the Lombards, and regard France as the place of its birth. Kindred systems were, however, in all probability introduced about the same time in various parts of German territory, though no doubt the feudal system, as it prevailed in Holland, owed its origin to Charles Martel and his successors. Bluntschli's view is that feudalism originated in a mixture of the Germanic custom of making the chief and his lieutenants mutually dependent, and the Roman custom of settling soldiers on the frontiers (*Staatswörterbuch, sub voce Lehnrecht*).

The feudal system as such was born just about the time when the Germans had made themselves masters of northern Italy, and when they became subject to attacks on all their frontiers. It seems reasonable to suppose that it was the result of a fusion of Roman institutions, the practice of the Church, which was again based on Roman law, and the native customs of the Germans. The system, however, as introduced into Holland was the feudalism as perfected by the Merovingian and Carolingian monarchs. It is difficult to say exactly at what period the introduction into Holland took place, but it was probably considerably earlier than the date suggested by Van Leeuwen. In course of time the feudal system became so crystallised that the relation of lord to vassal, and their mutual rights and duties towards each other as regards the land tenure, could be accurately formulated and defined.

The *feudum* or *beneficium* (*leen*) was an estate which was granted by the lord to his vassal, subject to the condition that the *dominium civile* remained with the lord, whilst the *dominium utile* went over to the vassal, provided that the vassal swore fealty to his lord and performed the required services. Originally personal and real rights were indissolubly mixed, but in time fealty came to be regarded as attached, not so much to a particular person as to the person by virtue of his ownership (*fidelitas realis*). The Roman law was invoked to systematise and codify both the personal and the real rights.

Although, as we have seen, it is very doubtful whether the feudal system as such had its origin in Lombardy, there is but little doubt that the feudal law as a system of jurisprudence came originally from Milan. In 1158 and 1168 two judicial officers of Milan collected and systematised the law regarding feudal property as it had been recognised by the Milanese courts. These two officers, Obertus ab Orto and Gérardus Niger, published the law regarding feudal property in a book called the *Libri Feudorum*. It soon became universally recognised as the text-book for feudal law. Hugolinus and Columbinus wrote commentaries and glosses on the *Libri Feudorum*. These glosses were afterwards placed as a *decima collatio* at the end of the *Corpus Juris*, where they are still to be found under the designation of *Jus Feudorum et Consuetudines Feudorum*.

As the feudal system had been extended to Holland, the *Jus Feudorum* applied to that province as it did to the other countries of Europe. It is, however, a noteworthy fact that the

Frisians never accepted the feudal law as part of their legal system, for, as Huber tells us, they could not endure that the word "service" should apply to their customs Huber, *Hed. Recht.* 2, c. 36). This *Jus Feudorum* was another channel through which the principles of the Roman law flowed into Holland. Its influence upon the general law of Holland was not very great, though it must be remembered that for a long time there was a well-recognised court which dealt with feudal relations and feudal property (*leenhof*). In time, however, the feudal law in Holland only applied to a particular kind of tenure. In an indirect way it influenced Roman-Dutch law, for it kept alive such principles of the Roman law in the middle ages as had been introduced into the *Consuetudines Feudorum*, more especially with regard to *erfpacht* or emphyteusis (Schröder, pp. 158 *et seq.*; Holzendorf's *Encyclopædie*, vol. 1, pp. 160–62; vol. 3, p. 545; Bluntschli's *Staats Wörterbuch, sub voce Lehnrecht; Guetât Histoire*, p. 274; Bort, *Leenrecht*).

CHAPTER X.

SKETCH OF THE HISTORY OF THE NETHERLANDS.

In this and the following chapter it is my intention to set out, as briefly as possible, the main features of the history of the Netherlands from the rule of the counts to the establishment of the Batavian Republic in 1795. My chief object is to give the student some idea of the constitutional history of the Netherlands, for that history is so bound up with the development of its laws and institutions that it is somewhat difficult to appreciate the latter without having some knowledge of the former. The main facts to which I would wish to draw the student's attention are: (1) That the counts of Holland and other sovereign princes who held sway in the Low Countries were not monarchs, but overlords of separate provinces; (2) that the influential forces in the State, until the reign of the House of Burgundy, were the count, the nobles and the clergy; (3) that the fourth estate, the towns, grew from small beginnings to great power, and that they formed a powerful burgher aristocracy; (4) that, stirred up by the Reformation and the hatred of the Spanish Inquisition, the towns brought about the Dutch Republic; and (5) that this form of government lasted practically until the French rule. In order to grasp the constitutional history I shall first give a brief sketch of the early political history of the Netherlands.

The Netherlands, as we have seen, formed part of the empire

of the Franks. They were not ruled by a single governor or representative of the emperor, but were divided into a number of provinces and cantons or *gouwen*, and these were presided over by dukes and counts (*graven*). In the north the most powerful provinces were Gelderland, Utrecht, Friesland and Holland; in the south Flanders and Brabant. Gelderland and Brabant were dukedoms; Flanders and Holland were countships (*graafschappen*); whilst Utrecht was a bishopric. Overijssel, Drenthe, Groningen and the Ommelanden were considered part of the bishopric of Utrecht. Holland included North Holland, South Holland and West Friesland.

In 922 A.D. Charles the Simple conferred upon Count Dirk I the fief of Holland together with the Church of Egmond. Dirk I was the first hereditary count of Holland and the founder of the House of Holland. The counts of Holland through their connections became extremely powerful. In order to give the student an idea of the influence of the counts of Holland I can do no better than quote the words of Kluit and Groen van Prinsterer (sec. 38): "Many have too slight an opinion of our earliest counts. They were related to the crowns of the principal houses of Germany and France. Kings married their daughters. They were the possessors of princely incomes and of property either inherited from the emperors or won by the sword or purchased with their gold. Floris II was called the very rich count. Dirk II married a daughter of the king of France. Philip I of France was the son-in-law of Floris I. The sister of the Emperor Lothair was married to Floris II; the sister of the king of Scotland was the wife of Floris III; whilst John I married a daughter of a king of England." Their wealth was great and their courts were equal to, if not better than, those of most European princes. The Church was powerful and well endowed. Holland possessed many abbeys of considerable influence, such as those of Egmond and Rijnsburg. The noble houses were many and influential. The houses of Egmond, Brederode and Voorne are names well known to the later history of Holland. The counts were staunch adherents of the Church, took part in the Crusades, helped the Pope against the emperor, and aided the Church in the suppression of heresy. It was during the rule of the counts that the towns of Holland began to grow in importance, and to aid the counts against the encroaching power of the nobles.

The House of Holland was succeeded by the House of Henegouwen or Hainault (1299). William III added Zeeland to the fief of Holland, and the counts of Holland became counts of Holland, Henegouwen and Zeeland. Under the House of Henegouwen the trade of Holland increased, and with that the wealth of the province. In 1345 the House of Henegouwen died out, and Holland, Zeeland and West Friesland passed by succession to the House of Bavaria. It was during this period that the feud, known as the feud of the Hoeken (Hooks) and Kabeljauwen, broke out. Civil war disturbed the country and injured its trade.

In 1428, after the death of John of Bavaria, the provinces of Holland, West Friesland and Zeeland passed to Philip the Good, and thus was founded the House of Burgundy. Philip was Duke of Burgundy, Flanders, Mechlin, Franche Comté, Artois, Salins, Namur, Brabant, Limburg, Hainault, Holland, Zeeland and West Friesland. Philip was the first ruler of the Netherlands who conceived the definite policy of gradually amalgamating the heterogeneous countships, dukedoms and bishoprics into one homogeneous state. His rule, however, over the Netherlands was not a happy one. He constantly broke his promises and disregarded the privileges of the towns. In 1448 he imposed a tax on salt without the consent of the Estates (*Staten*). Ghent resisted, and was reduced only after a four years' struggle. The cruel punishment of Ghent caused great misery amongst the industrial population and incensed the Flemish towns.

Philip the Good was succeeded in 1467 by Charles the Bold (*le téméraire*). This ruler was even more untrustworthy than his father. No oath was sacred to him. His ambition was to extend his dominions from the North Sea to the Mediterranean. For this purpose he engaged in numerous wars, and in order to pay for these he oppressed and taxed the Netherlands. He continued the work of his father in forcing tribute from the towns. In Holland Charles established a military despotism, while in the southern Netherlands, after the revolt of Liége, he deprived all the important towns of the liberties they were so jealous and proud of. In 1477 he marched against the Swiss Confederation, and was killed at the siege of Nancy. He continued the policy of his father to form a monarchy out of his numerous possessions. As he was not entirely dependent on the Netherlands he had but little scruple in exacting from the towns of Holland, Utrecht, Brabant and Flanders as much as he could manage to squeeze out of them. It was during his reign that the idea of a protective union of various provinces and towns became more than a mere political speculation.

The heir of Charles the Bold was his young daughter Maria—the Lady Mary of Burgundy. Louis XI immediately strove to lay his hands on the possessions of the House of Burgundy. He sought to marry her to the Dauphin, a lad of eight years, or else to a French noble. When these projects failed Louis seized the duchy of Burgundy and occupied Artois. This roused the Flemish towns, and they sided with the Lady Mary against the French king. She had, however, to pay for their support and to promise to maintain their liberties. In March 1477 she granted to the Netherlands their great Charter—*De Groote Privilegie*—in return for their assistance. "It was this constitution which Mary's grandson violated, which the Netherlands took up arms to recover and maintain, and which Holland fought for during more than fifty years, and finally secured. It provided that offices should be filled by natives only; that the Great Council and Supreme Court of Holland should be re-established and should be a court of appeal, having no jurisdiction over the other tribunals; that the cities and Estates should hold diets when they chose; that no new taxes should be imposed without the consent of the Estates; that no war should be undertaken without the consent of the Estates; that the language of the people should be used in all public and legal documents; that the seat of Government should be the Hague; that the Estates alone should regulate the currency; and that the sovereign should come in person before the Estates when supply was required" (Thorold Rogers' *Holland*, p. 41). It also provided that the sovereign could not marry without the consent of the Estates. The provinces then suggested that the Lady Mary should marry Maximilian of Hapsburg, the son of the Emperor Frederick III. This proposal was entertained, and in August, 1477, she became the wife of Maximilian, and their son Philip the Fair was the first of the Austrian line (1482–1506).

Philip the Fair married Johanna, the daughter of Ferdinand

and Isabella, and their son, the great Emperor Charles V, was born at Ghent, a Dutch sovereign, King of Germany, King of the two Sicilies, Archduke of Austria, Count of Burgundy, Holland and numerous other places. From the death of Philip to 1517 the Netherlands were governed by a regent.

In 1494 Philip the Fair assembled the States at Gertruidenberg, and informed them that he did not intend to abide by the provisions of the Great Privilege. The provinces objected, but eventually a compromise was arrived at. After that the towns strove hard to gain back what they had lost, but neither Philip nor Charles V were inclined to budge. After the end of the fifteenth century the period of Privileges was closed. During the following century the provinces and towns had to win their liberties by the sword.

In 1555 Charles abdicated the sovereignty of the Netherlands in favour of his son Philip, who during the following year became Philip II of Spain.

Charles V was very favourably disposed towards the Netherlands. He never forgot that he was born a Netherlander. On the whole he may be said to have respected the liberties and the privileges of the provinces except where they were used to further heresy, and they in turn were loyal to the emperor. A great deal of important legislation, as we shall see later, was the work of Charles. Philip II, on the other hand, was at heart a Spaniard, and showed but little sympathy with the people of the Netherlands. It was during his reign that the great struggle for freedom took place which has been so eloquently depicted by Motley in his *Rise of the Dutch Republic.* Spain was forced to relinquish her hold on the northern provinces of the Netherlands, soon after destined to become a strong republic.

The House of Austria continued the policy of the House of Burgundy to unite the Netherlands into one great State. The main object of Charles was to create a powerful bulwark against French aggression. The States themselves desired a defensive union, and Charles thought that it was easier to get contributions from the representatives of the provinces collected in one council than from seventeen different councils. In 1548, by the treaty of Augsburg, the seventeen provinces of the Netherlands were declared independent of the empire though under its protection. The effect of this attempt at union was not quite what Charles contemplated, for instead of increasing the power of the House of Austria in the Low Countries it soon taught the provinces that if they banded together they were far better able to defend their liberties and privileges than if they stood apart. It was this policy of union which eventually brought about the loss of the United Netherlands to Philip of Spain.

In dealing with the history of the law during the reign of the counts, we are apt to be confused by the fact that the same person is Count of Holland, Count of Brabant, Count of Friesland and Duke of Burgundy. The beginner often thinks that as we change from the House of Bavaria to that of Burgundy the laws of Holland must naturally be affected thereby, so that at one time Bavarian and at another time Burgundian customs would be introduced. The reader will be spared a great deal of this confusion if he remembers that whether a Bavarian or a Burgundian, Austrian or Spaniard ruled over Holland he always ruled over the province as Count of Holland, Zeeland and West

Friesland. The laws that were administered in Holland were the laws promulgated by the Bavarian or Austrian prince solely in his capacity as Count of Holland. These laws were usually framed by the Estates of the provinces, and were promulgated after receiving the sanction of the Count of Holland. No doubt the foreign and home policy varied in accordance with the views of the different princes, but the great bulk of the common law of the various provinces of the Netherlands was unaffected by the change of House. The laws promulgated by Charles V, as Count of Holland, were valid in Holland, Zeeland and West Friesland, and had no effect beyond those provinces, while the laws which he promulgated in Germany or Spain had no recognition in the province of Holland. When, therefore, we speak of the laws that were promulgated in Holland or the privileges, keuren, charters or handvesten that were granted to the various cities in Holland we must always remember that these were granted by the various princes as counts of Holland, Zeeland and West Friesland.

CHAPTER XI.

EARLY CONSTITUTIONAL HISTORY OF THE NETHERLANDS.

WE saw that in the early German period the king was the head of the State, and that the land was parcelled out into cantons or gouwen. The greater part of the government was carried on by the king and his followers, though at stated times all the freemen assembled, and their voice determined how graver questions should be solved. Every gouw was governed by a chief, whilst under them stood the leaders of the hundred. This system was continued by the Franks, but owing to the introduction of Christianity and the gradual growth of towns, to which the early Germans were unaccustomed, it was found necessary to modify the old form of government. Under the Frankish monarchs it became impossible to summon all the people to a general council, and so the Frankish sovereign and his entourage obtained a power far more extensive than that of the early German princeps. As large provinces fell under the sway of the Merovigian and Carolingian monarchs it was found necessary to send deputies (*missi*) from the central government to control the provinces and to keep the emperor in touch with them. The influence of the Church on the Crown had also a far-reaching effect. The ecclesiastical power was mingled with the temporal in a manner wholly unknown to the early Franks. As trade increased the necessity for towns began to be felt, and the primitive village

E

gradually grew into the fortified town. Again, as the tribe settled down upon the soil, and territorial interests sprang up, the larger land-owners began to assert rights unknown to the early freemen. The freeman who had distinguished himself by his valour in the field became a territorial noble, and on his estates were freemen who paid him tribute for the privilege of living on his land, slaves whom he had emancipated and who now belonged to the land (*lites, hoorigen*), and slaves still in a state of thraldom. The king and his followers, the Church, the territorial nobles, the freemen and the burghers of the towns began to act and react upon one another, and so to compose that complicated system known as the State.

We have traced the growth of the feudal system, and shall now trace the rise of a new element in the government—the voice of the burghers of the chartered towns. The idea that the sovereign power should consult the four Estates (*Standen* or *Stenden*) was one of slow growth, though the germs of it go back to a remote past. In the early German times, as we have seen, the king consulted his nobles and other freemen, but after the introduction of Christianity and the growth of the Church's power she insinuated herself into the councils of State. Though in theory the freemen were still to be consulted, in practice it only occurred when special money grants were sought. As the towns grew in importance they took the place of the freemen, until they forced themselves to be recognised as a fourth Estate. In many respects the constitutional history of the Netherlands is very similar to that of other European states, but the insignificance of its territory, the wealth and rapid growth of its towns, and the independent spirit of its people, caused it to emerge from feudal oppression and from autocratic rule earlier than its neighbours. Its chartered towns at first modified the feudal system and then caused it to disappear almost entirely.

I shall now briefly describe the four Estates, and then show how they were united in the great councils of the State.

The Estates (Staten).—The term "Estates" was first used by Philip the Good in 1428 in the treaty made by him with the Countess Jacoba. Mention was then made of the Estates of Hainault, Holland, Zeeland and Friesland. The term *Staten* was not used in Holland until 1558, though the four Estates existed in that province long before.

Sovereign Power.—The sovereign power in the Netherlands was originally vested in the emperors of the Franks; after the disappearance of the Carolingian monarchs it passed to the emperors of the Holy Roman Empire. This sovereignty, however, became entirely nominal, for after the days of the hereditary counts the bond of allegiance between count and emperor was by no means strong. The Netherlands were in the early days a collection of provinces which had a common interest, but were not united by any common bond. Nor was the whole of the country nominally under one overlord, for Flanders was a fief of France. During the thirteenth and fourteenth centuries the overlord of a particular province (*landsheer*), whether he bore the title of duke, count, bishop or lord, except for the shadowy feudal bond to the German Empire, was the sovereign of that province. He made peace or war, he granted privileges and charters, he levied tolls and collected taxes, and disposed of these as he thought fit. During the reign of the House of Burgundy the sovereign power of the various counts became even greater than before. It extended over all the Netherlands, and was in its nature monarchical. The constant aim of the counts was at unification and centralisation. They strove to make of the Netherlands a kingdom like that of France or England. Though they consulted the towns and convoked general councils they retained in their own hands the sovereign power. The House of Austria continued the work of centralisation, and though Charles V extended the powers of the States-General, he never allowed the sovereign power to slip from his hands.

The Nobles (de Edelen).—Next to the overlord stood the nobles. Their authority and prestige dated back to the early German period. At first they were bound to the chief by a purely personal bond, but in the course of time they became the hereditary possessors of large territories, and their influence grew from a personal to a territorial one. Under them stood freemen of various grades as well as slaves. The nobles were bound to the sovereign by fealty, just as their vassals were in turn bound to them. They possessed great privileges, amongst which the chief were to lead their own vassals in the field and to attend the council of their sovereign. Their relation to their sovereign was ruled entirely by feudal law. Their combined power was very great, sometimes so great as to threaten the rights and privileges of the overlord; and it was, therefore, not unnatural that the House of Burgundy should have sought to place as a counterpoise to the nobles the freemen of the towns.

The nobles were divided into three classes: (1) those descended from houses which had been regarded as noble from time immemorial; (2) persons ennobled by the sovereign; and (3) the *patricii* or persons who held high offices of State and their descendants (*Ridderschap*). In the province of Holland the nobles who formed one of the Estates were persons enrolled in the Ridderschap and citable by special summons (*Resolutie van Holland*, 19th March, 1678). In the early days they had their own courts, to which their vassals were subject, but this right disappeared with the disintegration of feudalism. They retained, however, even after the Revolution, a certain number of privileges.

Clergy (Geestelijken).—From the time of the Frankish Empire to the fifteenth century the influence of the clergy was very great, both directly and indirectly. The influence of the Church was exerted directly through her wealth and her large territorial holdings, such as the bishopric of Utrecht, and indirectly because, amidst a people lacking in civilisation and knowledge, she was the proud possessor of learned and educated men. Moreover, the Church represented the might of ancient Rome, which, though traditional, was during and even after the middle ages a strong moral force. In the course of time, however, the influence of the Church began to decline. In the State the Church was represented by the large abbeys, and as these became corrupt they lost their moral force. In Gelderland the Church ceased to have any influence in matters of State. In Holland even the Abbot of Egmond had no voice in the administration. In Zeeland and Friesland the power of the Church was greater than in Gelderland or Holland. As a general rule, however, it may be said that the Church exercised a greater temporal control in the south than in the north, and the wealthy abbeys of Hainault exerted during the reign of the House of Austria considerable influence in matters of State.

After the Reformation and after the establishment of the

Dutch Republic the clergy ceased to have any direct influence in the State. In Holland the monasteries were suppressed and their goods confiscated for the benefit of the State, and their revenues devoted to the maintenance of churches, schools and charities. All legacies to Roman Catholic institutions were prohibited, and the only ecclesiastical body recognised by the State was the Protestant clergy. Their jurisdiction, however, was limited to church discipline in accordance with the XXXIV Articles of May, 1591. After the Revolution, therefore, the Church ceased to be recognised as an Estate. At the same time we must not forget that the indirect influence of the clergy in matters of policy was exceedingly great during the seventeenth and eighteenth centuries both in Holland and in the other provinces of the Union.

The Towns.—The rise of the towns is an important factor in the constitutional history of Holland. Starting as insignificant villages under the entire control of the nobles, they rose in power during the rule of the House of Burgundy, and became during the Republic the ruling force in the State. In order to understand the development of the history of the Roman-Dutch law and the institutions by which that law was administered, the student must become acquainted with the history of the rise in power of the towns of Holland.

The chief event during the rule of the counts which tended to increase the influence of the towns was the Crusades (1096–1291). The towns of the Netherlands were not, like the towns of France and Italy, the successors of the Roman *municipia*. The Romans never colonised the Netherlands to the same extent that they colonised Gaul. There were, no doubt, Roman towns in the Low Countries, but they never attained the wealth and position of such places as Paris, Rheims or Cologne. It was during the Crusades that the southern towns of the Netherlands began to grow in importance, but it was not until the thirteenth century that the towns of the northern provinces exerted any real influence. The Crusades gave an impulse to trade, not only along the coast of the Mediterranean, but even on the shores of the German Ocean. The Crusaders brought to the West a knowledge of the commercial instincts and the civilisation of the East. The road followed by the Crusaders became the trade route, and along this route sprang up prosperous towns. In order to pay for the Crusades the counts wanted money, and as the traders in the towns were the only people from whom this commodity could be got the counts granted them liberties, and they in turn gave money. The preparations for a Crusade were left to the burghers of the towns, and in this way a great deal of money was earned. The nobles found it easier to get money from the towns than from the cultivators of the soil, and so in time they came to recognise that their own prosperity depended directly on the opulence of the towns in their possession.

The count stipulated with the town that he was to receive yearly a certain sum, and in consideration of this grant he conceded certain privileges to its citizens. These privileges took various forms. Sometimes it was the right to elect magistrates, at other times the exemption from military service or the right to levy toll by road or river. The rapid increase of the trade of the Low Countries with England, France, the Hanseatic towns and other localities brought in its train contracts and treaties. Regulations had to be made as to payments, and as to the consequences of failure to meet obligations. The laws of a pastoral and agricultural community were not adequate to solve the difficult questions which arose, and therefore men had to resort to the only legal system which dealt with such questions—the *Lex Romana*, and later on the law of the *Corpus Juris*. The rise of the towns, therefore, was one of the factors which facilitated the introduction of the Roman law, as we shall see in a later chapter. The Church also exerted its influence in favour of the towns, partly because it required contributions and partly because the bulk of its priests were the sons of citizens.

From the beginning of the thirteenth century representatives of the towns were called as witnesses to treaties or to take part in the settlement of internal disputes. In 1296 Floris V requested the towns to assist in the negotiations with the king of England regarding the marriage of the young prince. On that occasion the count spoke of *Nobiles homines et communitates bonarum villarum*. The principal privileges and charters were granted between the reigns of William II (1256) and John of Bavaria (1425). The Great Privilege of 1477 was not so much a charter granted to the towns as a compact between the sovereign and her people.

The privileges of the towns consisted mainly in freedom from tolls and tribute; in the right to hold yearly fairs or markets and to tax the citizens; in the possession of courts of law and the power of coining their own money as well as keeping their own accounts. On the other hand, they were obliged to pay to the count or noble (*landsheer*) under whose jurisdiction they fell a fixed tribute under the name of *beden*, and to contribute, in case the income of the overlord's domains was not sufficient, towards the cost of his military expeditions.

One of the oldest keuren was that granted by Count William I and the Countess Joanna of Flanders to the town of Middelburg. It was signed in 1217, and was the model upon which many privileges were granted in later years to the various cities. The epitome of this charter as given by Motley (*Rise of Dutch Republic*, vol. 1, p. 31) is as follows: "The inhabitants are taken into protection by both the counts. Upon fighting, maiming, wounding, striking, scolding; upon peace-breaking, upon resistance to peacemakers and to the judgment of schepenen; upon contemning the Ban; upon selling spoiled wine, . . . fines are imposed for the benefit of the count, the city and sometimes the schepenen. To all Middelburgers one kind of law is guaranteed. Every man must go to law before the schepenen. If any man being summoned and present in Walcheren does not appear or refuses submission to sentence he shall be banished, with confiscation of property. Schout and schepenen denying justice shall, until reparation, hold no tribunal again. A burgher having a dispute with an outsider (*buiten man*) must summon him before the schepenen. An appeal lies from the schepenen to the count. No one but a householder can be a witness. All alienation of real estate must take place before the schepenen. If an outsider has a complaint against a burgher the schepenen and schout must arrange it. If either party refuses submission they must ring the town bell and summon an assembly of all the burghers to compel him. Any one ringing the town bell except by general approval and any one not appearing when it tolls are liable to a fine. No Middelburger can be arrested or imprisoned in Holland or Flanders except for crime."

One of the most important institutions of the towns of the Netherlands was the guild, *collegium opificium*, or trading corporation. When this institution was first adopted by the towns of the Netherlands is not clear. In all probability it was introduced during the rule of the early counts. The main object of the guild was to form a number of trade unions for particular trades. It tended also to keep together the respectable citizens, and to separate them from the rougher classes which were constantly flowing into the towns. Each guild (*gild* or *burger collegie*) was a corporation ruled over by a president and council (*hoofdman en dekens*) elected by the members. The guilds came in course of time to be recognised by the counts, and to be protected by various privileges. In the province of Gelderland the guilds had the power of electing the representatives of the towns. The name of the elected member was submitted to the magistrate, who had no right to reject the elected member except for good cause (*Ned. Jaar boek*, 1765).

As the guilds grew in wealth and importance it became an inestimable privilege to belong to a guild. In time the right of membership in many of the guilds was made hereditary. So great was esteemed the privilege of becoming a member that many nobles were enrolled in the guilds, and many wealthy men increased the coffers of these institutions by purchasing membership at high prices. They became in the course of time not only important political, but also charitable institutions supporting the widows and educating the children of deceased members.

In 1443 Philip the Good conceded to the town of Delft the right to elect a council called a *vroedschap* (*vroed* = wise). The vroedschap was a corporation composed of the wisest and richest burghers of the town for the purpose of representing the town and maintaining its rights and privileges. Vroedschappen probably existed long before the concession of Philip, though Delft appears to have been the first vroedschap which obtained sovereign recognition. It was not a town council, such as we know, to manage the affairs of the town, but a political body to watch over and protect its liberties and privileges.

In course of time the vroedschappen of the other towns obtained state recognition, and during the rule of the Bavarian and Burgundian Houses the vroedschappen played important political rôles. When the towns obtained recognition as one of the Estates the vroedschappen elected some of their members to represent the town in the councils of the State. In this respect the towns of the southern provinces were far more energetic than those of Holland. The former were always anxious to be represented, whilst the latter, at any rate before the sixteenth century, sought to avoid the expense and trouble. In Holland the representatives of the towns were usually persons who had held some office such as schout, baljuw or schepen, and were known as the *leden van de Gerechte*. The towns of Holland had the privilege of electing certain men to a *collegie* or *kies collegie* from the noblest and wealthiest of the citizens (*uit den buik der stede*), and from these alone could the count appoint his magistrates and high officials. In this way gradually grew up a powerful and wealthy burgher aristocracy which in time acted as a strong check on the absolutism of Philip of Spain.

The government of the towns was entrusted to a baljuw, hoofdschout or schout with a certain number of advisers called schepenen, or sometimes raden. As the towns increased poortmeesters, burgermeesters or schatmeesters (burgomasters) were appointed out of the raden or councillors.

The schout and schepenen formed both an administrative and a judicial body. Of its judicial functions I shall treat later. The baljuw was as a rule the count's representative in the district, the schout in the town. On the whole the baljuw was superior to the schout, and the baljuw and schepenen dealt with the more serious matters, whilst matters of less importance were entrusted to schout and schepenen. In the larger cities, such as the Hague, Leyden, Amsterdam, &c., the administration of the town was entrusted to two or three burgermeesters, as they were called in Flanders, or poortmeesters or schatmeesters, as they were called in Holland.

During the Burgundian rule a functionary grew up who was destined in later times to play an important part. This was the pensionaris or, as he was called later, the Raadpensionaris (i.e. *raad en pensionaris*). He was paid by the town, and was usually a lawyer of high attainments (*e.g.* Grotius and Oldenbarneveld). His duties were to act as the spokesman of the town's representatives. He also advised the municipal body in difficult matters and conducted their lawsuits.

From what has been said above it will be manifest that the towns of Holland were very different from the European towns of to-day. They were virtually small republics governed by a burgher aristocracy. Though they formed part of the domain of a powerful noble they usually treated him as an equal, not as a governor. In the course of time so many contracts had been made between the overlord and the town, in the shape of keuren, privileges, charters and handvesten, that the town regarded itself as an independent contracting party. All the rights granted to the town were carefully registered from time immemorial, and these registers or archivès were regarded as a precious possession. Between the thirteenth and fourteenth centuries the towns of Holland followed the example of the larger towns of Germany, such as Cologne and Strasburg, and collected all that was important in these registers into a kind of law-book for the town, called in Holland a *stadboek*, in Germany a *stadtbuch*. These stadboeken are of the greatest interest to both the legal historian and the antiquarian. I do not think it will be out of place at this stage to give some account of one of these stadboeken. It will enable us to form some idea of the state of the laws and the administration of justice in those far-off days.

Each town had its own body of municipal law, but this was so different from what we understand by municipal law that it would be very misleading to use that term. I prefer, therefore, to adopt the term "local law," though I know that this is also open to great objection. As a matter of fact we find that each town had a body of laws and regulations which applied to matters of great weight and importance as well as to things of a most trivial nature. In many respects they remind one of the Transvaal Grondwet, which regulated the gravest affairs of State in one part, and in another the duties and charges of the market-master. The scientific study of law was unknown, and men made their laws as the necessities called for them, without any regard to order and sequence. After the revival of learning and the assiduous study of the *Corpus Juris*, a great change came over the scene, and these undigested local laws gave place to the scientific treatises of a Grotius or a Voet, though even then the different districts and towns retained their own peculiar privileges and customs. In order to illustrate the local legislation of the fourteenth and fifteenth centuries, I shall take the town of Groningen,* because its stadboek is perhaps somewhat fuller than the others I have come across, and because it has been fully explained by the society, *Pro excolendo jure patriae,* in one of the volumes of the *Verhandelingen ter nasporinge van de wetten en gesteldheid onzes vaderlands.*

The Stadboek of Groningen is divided into nine books or parts, and is dated 1425, though it contains provisions made all through the fourteenth century. It was drawn up by the burgomasters because, as they themselves say, they were desirous of maintaining their ancient rights and privileges. It begins with an account of how the town council and the burgomasters are to be chosen, and how their discussions and proceedings are to be regulated. The second book deals with the law of intestate succession, and the subject is treated of in a series of articles very much in the same way as a modern code divides up the subject-matter, though of course not so logically or clearly. In this book we find the peculiarity of the Frisian law as to community of property. Article 8 reads as follows: "In the year of our Lord, 1324, on Saint Peter's day, the council and burghers of the town decreed that if a man takes to wife a woman or a young maid, and the marriage is consummated, then the property of the spouses shall be in community immediately after the consummation." In dealing

* As the law of South Africa is principally the law of Holland, in attempting to give an idea of the local laws of the towns I should perhaps choose some principal town of Holland. After careful consideration, however, I prefer to take the stadboek of the town of Groningen. It is true that the common law of Groningen was not quite the same as that of Holland, but for the purposes of giving a sketch of how the law was administered in the towns of the Netherlands we may with equal propriety take the stadboek of a town of Friesland or of Holland.

with succession the stadboek incidentally treats of legitimacy, the children of monks and nuns, secret marriages and the sale of an inheritance. This shows that logical sequence was not a matter of great importance in those days.

The third book or chapter begins by telling us what fines and penalties a person incurs by breaking the law. It then goes on to treat of the penalties or damages a person incurs for slandering another. For the first offence the slanderer had to pay half a mark to the town and another half to the party slandered. Similar provisions are found in the laws of Amsterdam and many other cities of the Netherlands. After this follows a series of special libels or slanders, such as calling a person a knave, a whoreson, a murderer, &c., with the appropriate special penalty for each. This book then proceeds to deal with various kinds of assaults and maiming and the penalties attached to each limb that is cut off or injured. The fourth book deals with homicide, riot and serious breaches of the peace. It begins with the words *De wergeldo dats mangeld*, and then goes on to deal with the various penalties for manslaughter. The 30th article of this book treats of a curious old custom which seems to have prevailed throughout the greater part of the Netherlands. If a person was killed, and it was not a deliberate murder, the guilty party was bound to pay wergeld both to the town and to the relatives of the deceased; if, however, it was not known who had committed the homicide it was the custom for one of the relatives of the dead man to go to the grave and to call upon the unknown perpetrator or his relatives to pay the wergeld. This book provides that if he does not come forward to pay, after being called upon to do so over the grave, then the homicide will be considered murder (*so sal men dat voer ene mœrtdaet holden*). This custom existed in the seventeenth century, and was specially abolished at Drenthe in 1614: *Den dooden te gelde te bieden, hier bevorens in gebruik geweest zynde, zal niet meer geobserveert worden en de naaste vrienden van den dooden zullen geenen moort over den dooden by het graf roepen laten.*

The fifth book still continues with breaches of the peace, and then proceeds to deal with injuries to property, setting out in detail the damages to be paid for injuring cattle, pigs, corn, grass, &c. Amongst other provisions we have one that if a dumb animal (*onweten dier*) of one person kills the dumb animal of another then no penalty is due. The sixth book deals with who are burghers, what their duties are and their privileges, and ends up with the rules as to sea-fishing. The seventh book opens with the various building regulations that obtained in Groningen; it deals with churches and schools, and concludes with the penalties for being out after dark without a permit. The eighth book begins by imposing a penalty of five marks on the owner of a house who allows any gambling therein. The passion of gambling seems to have been inveterate with the Germans. Tacitus in his *Germania* (c. 24) tells us that the Germans when quite sober play at dice as a serious business, and that so desperately that they will stake their liberty on a throw; if they lose they voluntarily go into slavery. The customs of the various towns of Holland teach us that this passion was by no means extinct in the fourteenth century. In some towns it was the policy of the council to profit by this passion by setting up public gambling places (*dobbel scholen*). In others, again, there was an attempt to check gambling by imposing severe penalties on the keeping of gaming houses. Article 2 provides that "He who by gambling wins the clothes off another's back shall, if the clothes are of any value, forfeit five marks to the town." In Amsterdam a person was allowed to lose the money he had with him and his clothes, but no more. In the next article, however, a certain form of dice play called *worp tafel* was permitted, provided it was not indulged in at night. If a person played with loaded dice he was punished, and the money he won was forfeited to the town, and not returned to the loser. The next and following articles deal with robbery, theft and their punishments, and, after discussing witchcraft, coining offences and poisoning, it suddenly proceeds to consider the punishment for living with another man's wife. The book ends up with a few articles regarding pleading, which are rather important. "Neither man, widow, minor nor guardian may bring an action on worldly matters before an ecclesiastical court." If he did he forfeited one mark to the town. Such cases, however, as were customarily brought before the ecclesiastical courts he might bring without fear of penalty, but the onus of proving the custom lay on the plaintiff. When once a matter had been disposed of in the civil courts it might not be again ventilated before the Church courts, and if it were, the penalty was one mark. In Utrecht, where the sovereign lord was a bishop, the ecclesiastical court had great influence. This was a source of friction between Utrecht and Groningen. We find, therefore, that the stadboek provides that no priest in Groningen may act on any instructions of the Bishop of Utrecht if such are in conflict with the privileges of the town. The priest is told that he must disobey the orders of the bishop and report the matter to the town council, who will see him through the difficulty and pay all the costs and expenses incurred by him.

The next and last book opens with provisions regarding betrothal and marriage. As has been pointed out above, community followed consummation of the marriage, but if the parties chose they could marry with antenuptial contract. This contract had to be made before some members of the council, but the terms could afterwards be varied by consent of parties and of two of the next of kin. Then follow the most minute provisions as to the expenses, dishes, pipers and other preparations that are allowed at bridal feasts. If the entertainers exceeded the limits laid down in the stadboek they forfeited various sums for the various breaches. It seems strange to us to find sumptuary laws with regard to bridal feasts, but as these are not confined to any particular part of the Netherlands, we can only conclude that our forefathers were extremely lavish whenever a marriage took place, and that the good men of the council thought this lavishness undesirable. The law compelled the entertainers to appear before the council and give an account of the expenses incurred, and if they refused to do so they were mulcted in a fine. The rest of the book contains nothing but laws which would correspond to our town regulations.

The country around Groningen was called the Ommeland. It possessed a code of laws of its own called the *Landrecht van Ommeland.* The origin of both these systems is to be found in the ancient customs of the Germans, but the more recent source from which most of these laws sprung was the *vetus jus Frisicum,* a privilege granted to the Frisians by Charlemagne. It is quite manifest, when we consider the provisions of the stadboek, that it could hardly have been a sufficient code of laws to regulate all the relations of the citizens towards each other. Where the stadboek was not sufficient to decide a question recourse was had to the *Jus Frisicum* or the *Capitularia* of the emperors, or to the Roman law. This occurred more especially towards the end of the fifteenth century.

Groningen has been merely taken as an example. Every town of any importance had its local laws, and as these were usually insufficient to meet the numerous cases that fell outside of their provisions it was everywhere necessary to fall back upon some wider system of law. We have seen that in Groningen the *Lex Frisica* was appealed to, but in the provinces of Holland and Zeeland the *Lex Salica*, and sometimes the *Lex Ripuaria*, were resorted to in the first instance, together with the modifications introduced by the *Capitularia*. If these, however, were insufficient, the Roman law was appealed to. In Utrecht the Canon law had great influence, for there the administration of justice was very largely in the hands of the ecclesiastics.

CHAPTER XII.

THE COUNCILS OF STATE.

We are now in a position to understand how the Councils of State came into existence and developed. The ordinary Council of State (*Curia Comitis*) prior to the reign of Philip the Good consisted of the count or overlord (*landsheer*), his relatives, friends and favourites. The number of councillors was not fixed, nor was the place of meeting. It served not only as a parliament, but also as a supreme court for the nobles, and as a court of appeal for the provinces. Besides the ordinary council there was the traditional Great Council consisting of the count, nobles and freemen. This, however, was only assembled in times of great trouble.

Towards the end of the thirteenth century it first became customary to summon representatives of the great cities, such as Dordrecht, Delft, Haarlem, and Leyden, to the council of the count.

During the fourteenth century there are many occasions upon which the towns were called upon to send representatives to the Council of State. In 1465 Philip the Good called together a Council of State at Brussels, to which he summoned the nobles, the clergy and the representatives of the larger towns. This meeting was convoked for the purpose of obtaining supplies for the war with France, and to proclaim Philip's son Charles as his successor. From that time onwards it became the custom to summon representatives from the towns to the General Council together with the nobles and clergy. No particular rule was followed in summoning the towns, though apparently the large towns were always appealed to, and the smaller only when the count thought fit to do so. Dordrecht, Haarlem, Leyden, Delft, Gouda and Amsterdam were always summoned, and in 1553 a petition was presented to Charles V by Rotterdam, Schoonhoven, Gornichem, Schiedam, Heusden, Vlaardigen, the Hague and other towns with a request that representatives from them also might be summoned. In 1583, after the War of Independence, twenty-three towns were summoned to the Great Council of the States-General.

The representatives of the towns were not elected by the burghers, but by the vroedschappen, or in some cases by the kies collegies, and in a few others by the guilds. As the various counts were not kings of a definite territory, but overlords of separate provinces before the rule of the House of Burgundy, the count seldom summoned a General Council of the various provinces. If he wished the advice of his Estates he convoked an assembly in each province, so that the Estates of Holland might be summoned independently of the Estates of Friesland, Zeeland and the other provinces.

An important Council of State created in 1455 was the Great Council of Mechlin. The object of Philip in creating this council was mainly to establish a supreme court of appeal for all his provinces. Its influence in the unification of the Roman-Dutch law was very great, though it was always looked upon with distrust by the provinces as an infringement on their liberties. What especially vexed them was to be deprived of the right of refusing to appear before a judge who was not a judge of the province (*jus de non evocando*). Besides acting as a judicial body, this Great Council developed into a privy council clothed with great power.

Philip the Good initiated the practice of summoning the Estates of all his provinces to meet in one general council. It was mostly for the purpose of obtaining supplies (*beden*), and no legal right of being convened was acknowledged thereby. The Lady Mary was compelled, on account of the attitude of Louis XI, to appeal frequently to the assembled provinces. When, however, Margaret of Savoy was regent of the young Emperor Charles the General Assembly of the Estates of all the provinces was so frequently assembled that its power became very real, and it succeeded in making itself felt as an important element in the government of the State. It was during this period that the General Assembly was convened almost every year and sometimes two or three times in the same year. The Assembly dared to refuse supplies, and even went so far as to request Maximilian to put an end to the regency of Margaret of Savoy when Charles was only fifteen years of age.

Charles V completed what was initiated by the House of Burgundy. The General Council became, not only in name, but in fact, a legislative body with supervision over the administration. During the reign of Charles the Council General of the provinces was called together more than fifty times. The convocation of the General Council in which the towns were so largely represented had the inevitable consequence of aggrandising their power, for their wealth and influence constituted the backbone of the Netherlands. In this General Council, therefore, we see the precursor of the States-General of the seven provinces which formed the supreme governing body of the Dutch Republic. An account of the States-General and the States of Holland will be given in the next chapter.

CHAPTER XIII.

FROM THE TIME OF THE REPUBLIC TO 1795.

IT is not my intention to give a lengthy account of the history of this period. I shall confine myself to such important facts as are necessary for a due comprehension of the development of the legal history of the Netherlands. The Reformation may with justice be regarded as the origin of the Dutch Republic. The direction the Reformation took in Holland was not the ecclesiastical system of Luther, but that of Calvin. Luther did not seek to divorce the Church from the Crown and so to destroy the doctrine of the divine right of kings. Calvin's doctrine, on the contrary, had that effect. Hence the form of government which was most acceptable to the religious revolutionaries of the northern provinces was a republic. To this cause, however, must be added the revival of learning, which inclined the minds of the learned, and they were many in the Netherlands of the sixteenth century, towards the glorious days of the Greek and Roman republics. Besides these there were other reasons which induced the northern provinces to establish a republican form of government. They could find no foreign sovereign to protect them: Elizabeth of England had refused the trust. As the people had just emerged from a struggle with kings, it was but natural for the Dutch to adopt a form of government which resembled their own municipal institutions and which had made Rome mistress of the world.

The great influence which the Reformation had in moulding the later history of Holland must not be overlooked. It was not a sudden outburst of religious enthusiasm. For a long time past the people of the Netherlands had been dissatisfied with the dissolute lives and selfishness of the monastic orders. Gerard Groote (1340–84), Wessel Gansfort (1419–89), and Erasmus (1467–1536) were all reformers. The glowing embers were ready for a Luther to cause them to burst into flame. The persecutions of Charles V and of Philip of Spain only tended to harden the hearts of an obstinate and courageous people, and to drive them to extreme Calvinism. Hatred of foreign tyranny and the love of freedom, especially the freedom of religious worship, caused the Dutch to draw the sword; an indomitable courage and a firm trust in Providence kept that sword in their hands until the tyrant was conquered and the Protestant religion safe. The revolutionary States cried out for tolerance of the Protestant religion; the victorious Republic was as intolerant of Roman Catholicism as Philip had been of Protestantism. The Calvinistic Church became a pillar of the State, and demanded that all officials of the Republic should be Protestants. As we shall see later on, the laws which had grown up under the ægis of the Church were altered. Marriage was no longer regarded as a sacrament, and the authority of the Canon law was completely undermined.

The story of William of Orange is familiar to every one. On the 9th August, 1559, William received his commission from Philip II as Stadhouder of Holland, Zeeland, and West Friesland. The title of stadhouder has nothing to do with the word *stad*, meaning a town. It is derived from the word *steede*, and means the *steede* or *plaats houder*, *i.e.* the person who holds the place of another, a representative.* Hence in the commission, which was written in French, William is called *Lieutenant.* The counts of Holland had from early days been accustomed during their absence to appoint *stedehouders* in the provinces to act as their representatives. The stadhouder had no legislative functions. He was an executive and administrative officer.

After William of Orange took up arms against Philip, his commission as stadhouder was naturally revoked, but he nevertheless retained the title. In the early days of the struggle the provinces pretended that they were not fighting the sovereign of the Netherlands, but his foreign emissary, Alva the Spaniard. At the convocation of the Estates of Holland on the 18th July, 1572, William was recognised as the Stadhouder of Holland and Zeeland. In 1576 came the pacification of Ghent, when Holland and Zeeland and thirteen provinces swore to uphold the liberties of the Netherlands. In 1578 followed the union of Brussels, and in 1579 was concluded the union of Utrecht, which was virtually the constitution of the Dutch Republic. In 1580 Philip declared the Prince of Orange an outlaw, and promised a purse of gold and a patent of nobility to his assassin. The next year (1581) saw the Declaration of Dutch Independence.

The Declaration of Independence was issued on the 26th July, 1581, in the form of a placaat. It was called the Act of Abjuration, and was signed by the deputies of Holland, Zeeland, Utrecht, Friesland, Brabant, Flanders, Gelderland, Zutphen, Overijssel, and Mechlin. It deposed Philip from his sove-

* *In steede van* = instead of.

reignty, but it placed no hereditary sovereign in his place. An attempt was made to place Francis, Duke of Alençon and Anjou, at the head of the confederacy, but this failed because Holland and Zeeland would have no other sovereign than William of Orange. There were, therefore, two confederacies—Holland and Zeeland under the stadhoudership of William, and the rest of the provinces under the leadership of the Duke of Anjou. The Prince of Orange refused to accept the title of Count of Holland. He preferred to retain the title of Stadhouder until the end of the war.

By the Act of Abjuration the provinces declared that the King of Spain had no authority over the Netherlands, and the use of his name and seal was forbidden under severe penalties. In 1582 the Prince of Orange accepted the hereditary sovereignty of Holland and Zeeland under the title of "Graaf van Holland," but before the preliminaries had been completed he was assassinated by the hand of Balthazar Gérard. Upon his death the Catholic provinces of the south made their peace with the King of Spain. After the Act of Abjuration the sovereignty of the United Provinces resided in the people as represented by the Estates of the nobles and the towns. The Estates had wished to confer the sovereignty upon William, but after his death they retained it in their own hands.

The States-General established a State Council to exercise the executive power in the provinces of Holland, Zeeland, Utrecht, Friesland and such parts of Flanders and Brabant as formed part of the Union. At the head of this council was placed the young Maurice, son of William the Silent, with the title of Stadhouder of Holland, Zeeland and West Friesland.

The constitution as established in 1584 remained the constitution of the seven northern provinces, though modified in detail from time to time. In 1593 it took the shape which it practically retained as long as the United Netherlands existed. The Union consisted of the provinces of Holland, Zeeland Friesland, Overijssel, Gelderland, Utrecht, and North Brabant. The sovereign power was the States-General, consisting of the representatives of these seven provinces. Each province was independent as far as local government was concerned, and possessed its own council or raad, but the seven provinces formed a Bond State of which, as I have said, the States-General was in reality the sovereign power, though its permanent executive head was Prince Maurice. Each province was a member of the Bond State, and possessed a single vote. The number of deputies, however, varied. Holland and Gelderland usually sent six, the spokesman of the representatives of Holland being the Raadpensionaris. The president of the Council changed from week to week. The senior deputy of each State presided in turn. The stadhouder only appeared in the Council when he had some proposal to make. Up to 1656 the title of the States of Holland was *De Edele Mogende Heeren;* after that it was changed into *De Edele Groot Mogende Heeren.* The title of the States-General from 1653 was *De Hoog Mogende Heeren, myn Heeren de Staten Generaal.*

The functions of the States-General were:—

(1) To determine peace or war; to provide for the army and navy;

(2) To levy taxes for the purposes of the Union;

(3) To exercise supreme control over the Dutch possessions oversea;

(4) To promulgate Placaats and Ordinances affecting the seven provinces;

(5) To appoint officials, control the mint and do such things as affected the welfare of the Union.

The nobles were represented in the Council, but they had only one vote, and this was recorded by the Raadpensionaris. After 1608 eighteen towns were represented in the Council, each with one vote, recorded by the pensionary of the town. The provincial councils (*Staten van Holland, Gelderland*, &c.) made laws affecting the provinces, levied taxes each for its own province, and appointed both superior and inferior magistrates. Gradually, however, Holland sought to obtain the first political place amongst the provinces. She began to assert that the States of Holland were independent, and that in them resided the sovereign power of Holland. She did not wish to withdraw from the Union, but she desired to act independently where she thought fit, and so by virtue of her wealth and power to obtain the hegemony of the provinces. The death of William II (1650) gave her the opportunity. From 1650 to 1672 there was no stadhouder. During this time Holland usurped the lead of the other provinces, and the latter were obliged to acquiesce. Hollanders were appointed as officials in nearly all the provinces, and Hollander influence was exerted in every quarter of the Union. In 1658 de Wit, at the age of twenty-eight, was, as Raadpensionaris, at the head of the Republic, and the main objects of his policy were the aggrandisement of Holland and the downfall of the House of Orange. The former object was attained, but the murder of de Wit and the war against Louis XIV brought back the stadhoudership under William III (1672). After the death of

William III once more a period intervened during which there was no stadhouder. In 1747 the House of Orange again took the reins of government in hand under William IV. After his death followed a regency, and then William V became stadhouder. As a sovereign he was incompetent, as a man he was contemptible. The States-General once again asserted their right of sovereignty, substituted the arms of the States for those of the House of Orange in public documents, on the regimental colours, and even on the State furniture. In 1789 broke out the French Revolution, and the stadhouder joined the alliance of European monarchs. The revolutionary party in Holland gained the upper hand, and during the winter of 1794–95, when the stadhouder fled to England, the Dutch welcomed the French. The Dutch Revolution was complete and the Batavian Republic established. Holland then fell completely under the French, at first as a kingdom under Louis Napoleon, and later as an integral portion of Napoleon's empire.

CHAPTER XIV.

INTRODUCTION OF THE ROMAN LAW INTO HOLLAND.

I SHALL now proceed to consider how the Roman Law came to be introduced into Holland. In dealing with this subject I shall first treat of the *Lex Romana* as it existed during the Frankish monarchy, and shall endeavour to show that the influence of the *Lex Romana* was constant and never died away completely. I shall then pass over to the revival of the study of the Roman law in Italy and western Europe, and show how the consequence of this revival was the disappearance of the old law books, such as the *Breviarium Alaricum*, and the introduction of the law books of Justinian. This will bring me to a consideration of the gradual development of the study of Roman law from the twelfth to the sixteenth century. I shall then briefly summarise the manner in which the Roman law came to be regarded as almost equivalent to the common law of Holland. This part of our subject will, therefore, naturally divide itself into, (*a*) the *Lex Romana* during the Frankish period; (*b*) the Roman law during the rule of the early counts; (*c*) the Roman law during the twelfth and later centuries; and (*d*) the position of the Roman law in Holland during the fourteenth and fifteenth centuries.

(a) Lex Romana during the Frankish Period.—In addition to the laws embodying the German customs, our forefathers in the Netherlands were acquainted with and frequently employed the Roman law or the *Lex Romana*, as it was called in contradistinction to the bodies of Germanic or Frankish law. It has been a favourite subject of controversy at what exact time the *Lex Romana* was introduced into the Netherlands. Some authors deny that Roman law had any influence in Holland. Fockema Andreae (*Bijdragen*, vol. iv, p. 434, says: "The force of the Roman law in Holland and Zeeland has often formed a subject for discussion. As far as this refers to the question when and by what statute or resolution it has been incorporated the investigation must be fruitless: such a legal acceptance of the Roman law has never occurred. . . . We see, therefore, there has never been any recognition of the Roman law even as a subsidiary law."

In 1782 the Brussels Academy proposed the following question: *Depuis quand le Droit Romain est il connu dans les provinces des Pays-Bas autrichiens et depuis quand y a-t-il de force de loi?* De Bergh, whose essay was crowned by the academy, answered that there was no trace of the Roman law having been in use in the Netherlands prior to the twelfth century, and that it was not recognised as *raison écrite* until the end of the fourteenth century. This called forth a very virulent article by Raepsaet in support of the view that Roman law had been constantly invoked in the courts of the Netherlands from the days of the Frankish monarchs.

Although it is clear that there was no special Ordinance by which the authority of the Roman law was established, it does seem more reasonable to accept the view that the Roman law was always appealed to since the days of the Frankish monarchy, than to believe that what was undoubtedly the common law of Friesland in the fourteenth century and of Holland in the fifteenth century was introduced *en bloc* as a foreign law some time after the rule of the counts. The tenacity with which all people, and the German nations in particular, cling to their laws and customs seems to militate against the view of a sudden introduction of the Roman law. If we accept the view that the *Lex Romana* prevailed and was appealed to throughout the Frankish dominions and, therefore, in the Netherlands, at the time when the monarchy of the Merowigs was founded, then the gradual extension of its authority in Friesland, Holland and the other provinces of the Netherlands is easily understood. But if we accept the conclusion that the Roman law was not in any way appealed to until the fourteenth century, then it becomes difficult to understand its complete and universal reception a few centuries later. This reasoning is purely *à priori* and therefore, by no means conclusive; but I think that the conclusion arrived at can be supported by sufficient facts to justify the acceptance which it has received from such writers as Merula, Huber, Raepsaet, Van der Spiegel and De Haas.

We have seen that for four centuries the Romans ruled in the Netherlands. During that time no doubt Roman laws and customs exercised some influence on the people; but as this period was followed by the invasions of the Saxons and Frisians almost all, if not all, traces of Roman law must have disappeared. We cannot, therefore, regard the Roman occupation as the period from which dated the adoption of the Roman law. It was not until after the introduction of Christianity into the Netherlands that the Roman law once more began to influence the settlement of disputes. The ecclesiastics did not refer directly to the Roman law, for their law was to be found in the canons of the Church; but these very canons, as I shall endeavour to show later, embodied many of the principles of the Roman law, and were founded upon Roman jurisprudence. Indirectly, therefore, a reference to the Canon law meant a reference to the Roman law. The use of the *Lex Ecclesiastica* familiarised the inhabitants of the Netherlands with many of the principles of the *Lex Romana*. In order to understand the influence of the *Lex Romana* in the Netherlands after they became a portion of the Frankish monarchy, and after the establishment of the rule of the counts in Holland, we must first form some idea of the position of the Roman law in the courts of the Carolingian monarchs.

Besides the *Lex Salica* and the *Lex Ripuaria* there were two other bodies of law which applied to a considerable portion of the Frankish monarchy—the *Lex Burgundionum* and the *Lex Visigothorum*. Although the Burgundian kingdom did not long survive Gondebaud, for it fell into the hands of the Franks in 534 A.D., the national law of the Burgundians survived for some time, until it was almost completely replaced by the *Lex Visigothorum*. The latter was probably first started in the reign of Eurick, though its first important compilation was made by Alaric II in 506 A.D. It was then known as the *Lex Romana Visigothorum*, and was the law applicable to the Gallo-Roman subjects of Alaric. The collection of laws was made by Anianus, Alaric's chancellor, from whom it came to be known as the *Breviarium Aniani*. After the tenth century it was usually called the *Breviarium Alaricum*. Its preface begins thus: *Incipit Lex Romana; in hoc corpore continentur leges sive species juris de Theodosiano et ex diversis libris selectae et sicut preceptum est explanatae anno XXII regnante domino Alarico rege ordinante viro illustri Goiarico comite, exemplar auctoritatis.* Alaric enjoined that this *Breviarium* should be regarded as an authoritative code, for he says: *Providere ergo te convenit ut in foro tuo nulla alia lex neque juris formula proferri vel recipi praesumatur.* This *Breviarium* contained not only a summary of the *Codex Theodosianus,* but also extracts from the *Institutes* of Gaius, and the *Sentences* of Paul.

Heineccius (*Hist. Jur. Germ.* 1, 1, 15), Van der Spiegel (*Oorsprong,* p. 74) and Savigny (*History of Roman Law in Middle Ages,* chaps. 8 and 9) are of opinion that this *Breviarium* was, during the earlier part of the middle ages, the favourite text-book from which the principles of the Roman law were gathered. It was frequently called the *Codex Theodosianus, Leges Theodosianae* or even simply the *Lex Romana.* Although the law-books of Justinian were promulgated soon after the compilation of the *Breviarium,* it was not until a much later date that they became familiar to the jurists of western Europe. As we have already seen, the Franks were not in the habit of suppressing the laws of those whom they conquered. There existed, therefore, in France, on both sides of the Loire, recognised bodies of law which were known by the generic term of *Lex Romana,* and of these the *Breviarium Alaricum* came in time to be considered as the most convenient text-book.

In addition to the *Breviarium* there existed another compilation, also mainly based on the Theodosian *Code* and chiefly used by the Burgundians, called the *Librum Responsorum Papiani* (Hein. *Hist. Jur. Germ.* 2, 1, 15, 17). Both these text-books were used throughout the Frankish monarchy, and therefore, also in the Netherlands when reference had to be made to the *Lex Romana.* Though botn the *Lex Salica* and the

Lex Ripuaria contain references to the Roman law, yet upon examination of these Codes we find that they are mainly concerned with the *Jus Personarum*. Of the *Jus Rerum* and the *Jus Obligationum* very little is found in the early laws of the Franks. It is, therefore, easily understood that as soon as the legal relations of men became more complicated, recourse was had to some body of law more advanced than that of the conquering Germans.

As commerce, which was practically unknown to the early Germans, began to grow, the disputes engendered thereby had to be settled by reference to some stable and scientific principles. What more reasonable than that the judges should have recourse to those Roman laws which had for centuries regulated the legal relations of a highly civilised and energetic people. It was not as though these laws were only to be found in learned books; they were daily referred to in the decisions of disputes which arose amongst the Gallo-Romans, for the conquered inhabitants of Gaul continued even after the establishment of the Frankish monarchy to live under their own laws. This will also account for the fact that most of the cases that have come down to us, where the Roman law was applied, were disputes between persons of considerable means. These were the persons in a position to make wills and donations, to endow their wives and to manumit their slaves, and to enter into commercial transactions. Examples of such transactions may be found in Matthaeus, *De Nobilitate*, bk. 1, c. 27. We learn that Agathias, who wrote in the sixth century, speaking of the Franks and Germans, says: *Romanae eos politiae non omnino exsortes esse Romanasque inter se leges et eosdem in contractibus connubiisque mores servare.*

The learned men of those days were the ecclesiastics, and they were also the lawyers of that time. In the Roman laws they found the Church supported as a State institution, and respect inculcated for her functionaries and her possessions. What therefore was more reasonable than that they should teach a reverence for the Roman law and reliance on its authority. Gregory of Tours thus praises a certain Andarcius (bk. 4, c. 41): *Quod operibus Vergilis, legis Theodosianae libris, arteque calculi adplene eruditus fuerit* (Van der Spiegel, pp. 74–77).

In his *History of the Roman Law in the Middle Ages* Savigny devotes several chapters to the influence of the Roman law in the Frankish monarchy. He points out that in the *Capitularia* there are many references to the Roman law. The books from which these are taken are principally the *Breviarium*, the *Code* of Theodosius, the *Epitome* of Julian, the *Sentences* of Paul, and in the later laws even the *Code* of Justinian. Van der Spiegel (p. 81) quotes a *capitulare* of Charles the Bald in which these words occur: *Super illam legem (Romanam) vel contra ipsam legem nec antecessores nostri quodcumque capitulum statuerunt nec aliquid constituimus.*

Savigny, dealing with the extant documents, says (ch. 9, sec. 37), "There exists a number of documents which bear testimony to the use of the Roman law in the Frankish Empire." He then proceeds to enumerate a large number of these, but as they refer exclusively to France it is unnecessary to quote them here. In dealing with the teaching of Roman law in the Frankish monarchy he tells us that there were in those days no schools of law properly so called. The study of law both for the Gallo-Romans and for the Germans was practical. The notaries and the scabini had a practical knowledge of law, but the sources of the Roman law formed part of the subjects read in the schools; and Roman law was studied side by side with dialectics. Besides those Frankish writers who wrote glossaries on the *Breviarium* there were compilations of formulae in which we find a good deal of the principles of the Roman law, such as (*a*) the formulae of Angers; (*b*) those of Marculfus; (*c*) those of Sirmond; (*d*) the formulae Bignonenses; (*e*) the formulae Baluzianae minores; and (*f*) the formulae Mabillonis. In addition to these Savigny mentions the *Petri Exceptiones* (*i.e. excerptiones*) *Legum Romanorum*, which was a text-book containing a systematic exposition of law, and to a very large extent of the Roman law (Savigny's *History*, vol. 2, c. 9, secs. 44–56).

We have seen in a former chapter that laws were to a great extent personal, and that in the Frankish Empire people lived under their own law. This applied to the Netherlands as well as to the possessions of the Franks in Gaul. The judges were, therefore, obliged to have some knowledge of the various laws which prevailed in the Frankish Empire, and more especially of the *Lex Romana*, as this not only occurred more frequently, but as it was the only jurisprudence on which systematic treatises were to be found, and the one most useful for settling disputes arising out of commercial transactions. No doubt there was a considerable confusion in the application of all these laws, but as the *Lex Romana* was the most widespread, and as it was more in agreement with the *Jus Canonicum*, it was the one system least likely to increase the confusion. Bishop Hincmarus writes in the ninth century: *Quando sperant ob id lucrari ad legem Romanam se convertunt quando vero per legem non aestimant acquirere ad Capitula confugiunt.* A contemporary of Hincmarus says, "Let them know that on the

Day of Judgment they will be judged neither by the laws of the Romans, nor of the Salic Franks, nor yet of the Burgundians, but by the laws of God" (Van der Spiegel, p. 83).

As the *Capitularia* gradually became more and more complete they took the place of the various German and Frankish laws. The *Lex Romana* also lost a great deal of its force, though part of it was no doubt incorporated in the *Capitularia*. There is frequent reference in the *Capitularia* to the *Lex Romana*: "*Ut justa Romanam legem hoc corrigantur;*" "*Inter Romanos negotia causarum Romanis legibus praecipiumus terminari*" (Hein. *Jur. Germ.* 2, 1, 44; *Capit.* 4, sec. 45). In a constitution of Chilperic reference is made to the *Lex Tricenaria*, which is taken directly from the *Codex Theodosianus*. Wherever business was carried on to any extent the native laws and customs of the Germans were quite inadequate to deal with the new order of things, and the principles of the *Lex Romana* were resorted to in order to supplement the lacunae of the Frankish laws.

The *Lex Romana* was never recognised in the Netherlands, either during the period of the Frankish monarchy or during the rule of the counts, as the common law of that territory. It was only admitted in a modified form to supplement the deficiency in the local laws and customs. All that I have tried to show is that during the Frankish period the Roman law was not dead and forgotten, and that when later on it played so vigorous a part in the legal system of the Netherlands it was not appealed to as a newly discovered system of jurisprudence, but as a system which, for several centuries before the birth of the Bologna school of law, had been referred to in the courts of the Netherlands.

CHAPTER XV.

(b) ROMAN LAW DURING THE RULE OF THE EARLY COUNTS.

It has often been asserted that during the anarchy which followed upon the splitting up of the Carolingian dynasty law-books were destroyed and the Latin language lost. No doubt during the inroads of the Northmen on the coasts of Holland and France a great number of books, legal as well as ecclesiastical, were destroyed; yet it seems somewhat far-fetched to hold that the destruction of law-books was so great that all knowledge of the *Lex Romana* was lost. The lists of several of the libraries of that time contradict this assertion most emphatically. A more important factor in the decline of the Roman law was the ignorance of the Latin tongue during the tenth and eleventh centuries. The inroads of the Northmen coincide with the period of private wars and of the anarchy of the middle ages.

Gerlache, speaking of this period (*Essai sur les Grandes Epoques*, p. 97), says: "Eighty years of plunder and murder had made a wilderness of the fields; the towns were like oases in the desert; the wealth of the monasteries was destroyed; the people were either slain or else they joined the raiders; all the essentials of political life were confused; kingship, nobility and clergy were confounded; and every tie of civil society broken." This state of anarchy and confusion continued all through the tenth, eleventh and twelfth centuries.

Mabillon called the tenth century a century of slaughter and misery (*saeculum ferreum et infaustum*). No wonder that during these dark ages Latin had lost ground as a language, and Roman law was in a period of decadence. The Council of Mayence (847 A.D.) complained that the priests were ignorant of Latin, and enjoined them if they could not compose sermons to read the homilies in the vulgar tongue. It seems quite clear that during these dark centuries the Roman law could not have been readily referred to except in the highest courts. By this time, however, a great deal of the Roman law had been so accepted in the territory of the Carolings that it formed part of the customary law of the land.

It is extremely difficult to lay one's hands on the writings of any author who recognised the Roman law as authoritative or as supplementary. Hence some writers have gone so far as to say that with the loss of the Latin language Roman law completely disappeared in the Netherlands between the tenth and fourteenth centuries. If the priests could not understand Latin, the probability is that the judges were also ignorant of the language; and if the judges knew no Latin how could they refer to the Roman law? Both Raepsaet and Van der Spiegel deal with this question, and the conclusion they come to is that the Roman law was neither forgotten nor allowed to fall into disuse. *Ce prétendu oubli et cette désuétude dans lesquels serait tombé, le droit romain du Xe au XIIIe siècle en France et dans les Pays-Bas est donc une chimère inventée par les écrivains légers et superficiels et accreditée par ceux qui trouvent plus commode de réduire toute la jurisprudence à l'aequum et bonum cerebrinum que de se livrer à de longues études.*

Van der Spiegel points out that if we compare the language

of the charters with the Frankish and the Roman laws we find that there is a great similarity. Moreover, he thinks it highly improbable that the counts of Holland would have suddenly abandoned the laws of the monarchy under which they lived, and to which they looked for support. To what laws did they refer their disputes? It is hardly credible that at a time when the towns began to assert their importance, and when the growth of trade and commerce became marked, the people of the Netherlands should have resorted to the ancient Germanic laws rather than to the later laws so much better adapted to the needs of a civilised people. "I think from all these facts I may safely conclude that the state of the laws in this country remained the same after the commencement of the rule of the counts as it had been in the Frankish period. It is for him who alleges the contrary to show that a change took place" (Van der Spiegel, p. 93).

Professor Poullet, who has recently written a history of the institutions of the Netherlands, points out that towards the latter end of the Carolingian monarchy the distinction between the law administered in the various provinces of the Netherlands was not very great. Naturally the nearer to France the greater the influence of the Roman law. In dealing with the sources of the law of the Netherlands he says: "In the Netherlands, as in the north of France, the *Droit Coutumier* prevailed. The Roman law was never regarded as the principal law. The only question is within what limits was the Roman law considered as having any force in this territory during the middle ages. This matter has given rise to considerable disputes, and during the reign of Joseph [of Belgium] in the former century (eighteenth) it was obscured by political views. This is not a place to go too deeply into the question. It is enough to say concerning this matter that there are two essential points to be remembered. Numerous facts prove that the Roman law has never been completely forgotten in the Netherlands, and that certain rules established by this law have never fallen into desuetude. Other facts no less numerous and no less convincing show that the rules of the Roman law, accepted as the basis for legal decisions, were observed less on account of their legislative origin than because they had passed into a tradition which regarded them as necessary, and which constantly invoked them [*que pour être passées dans une tradition constante et nécessaire*], and that if the judges and the national practitioners had recourse to the Roman law it depended on the extent of their knowledge merely as a reference, and not because it was obligatory" (*Histoire des Institutions des Pays-Bas*, vol. 1, p. 340).

Naturally the influence of Roman law in the northern provinces was less than in the south; it would, however, have been extremely difficult in the tenth century to say on this side of a line the influence of Roman law was felt, but not on that. The more reasonable view seems to be that the influence of Roman law infiltrated the whole of the Netherlands, and its principles became mixed up with those of the customary law, which formed so large a part of the jurisprudence of the Frankish monarchy. In other words, it helped to mould and shape the customary law which was so jealously guarded. The counts were obliged to swear to the people that they would maintain the laws and charters that obtained at their accession. "*Ego Florentinus, &c., omnibus nobilibus ut hanc legem sive Chartam eligerent sibi, concessi, quam ego, et dominus Henricus de Voorne confirmamus.*" "*Die grave van Zeeland is schuldich de keure van Zeeland te zweren met zijne burggrave*" (*Keure van Zeeland*, 1290, sec. 80).

It is clear that besides the keuren* and handvesten† there existed a kind of common law or *landrecht* composed of what was called the *oude costumen*. What these old customs were our authorities do not state, but from numerous charters and extracts Van der Spiegel concludes "that it is certain that these old customs were nothing but the old laws and customs which had grown up with our forefathers; they were the *mores Germanorum*, the laws of the Franks and the neighbouring nations, and the then known *Lex Romana*" (Van der Spiegel, p. 95).

That the Roman law was often referred to before and during the tenth and later centuries as *Consuetudo Romana* is capable of proof. We find in the *Lex Burgundionum: Si quis post haec barbarus testari voluerit vel donare aut Romanam Consuetudinem aut barbaricam esse servandam sciat* (tit. 60, c. 1).

In the catalogue of the library of St. Bertin, in the town of St. Omar, the Roman law is indicated by the words *Consuetudinum legum Romanarum.* This shows, moreover, that in 1104 A.D. Roman law-books were to be found in the towns of the Netherlands (Raepsaet, vol. 4, p. 95).

It may be that a great deal of this *Consuetudo Romana* was traditional between the ninth and thirteenth centuries, unless we are mistaken in our supposition that the Latin language had fallen so into disuse as not to have been understood. But even if the Latin language was not universally

* Local enactments. † Charters.

understood at the court and in the larger towns, at any rate there were always ecclesiastics and lawyers who could read and understand it. Raepsaet points out that where the schepenen were ignorant of the law they used to refer their difficulties to persons skilled in the law, called *assessores*. This idea of reference to a jurisconsult was no new one. It had existed in the Roman law. The reference was known to the Franks when a suit had to be determined between two persons of different nationalities and the judge was ignorant of their laws. Although we find no mention of *assessores* in the writers of this period, we find them later in the towns of the Netherlands. The *pensionaries* are probably a relic of this custom. In Flanders there was an old law that the judges in the seignorial courts had to send the records of cases heard by them to three advocates (called *advocati pro judice*) of an adjoining town for their advice. This law was probably the legislative enactment of a custom which had existed ever since the days of the Franks (Raepsaet, vol. 4, p. 94). The practice of Hofvaart (*i.e.* for the schepenen of smaller towns to consult the courts of the larger towns), Van der Spiegel thinks, was not on matters of fact, but on questions of law. In the larger towns there were always either laymen or ecclesiastics skilled in the Roman law, and when questions were referred to them which the local statutes could not solve they resorted to the system they knew most about, viz., the Roman law.

As against the view that the Roman law was used to supplement the defects in the Codes of the Franks, it has been pointed out that there are a number of charters which show that the judges were required to give their judgments according to their innate feelings of what was right, if they could find no definitely accepted custom (Fock. And. *Bijdr.* vol. 4, p. 435). They were required to pronounce judgment "*na recht en na oordeel;*" "*na oude Costumen en na beste oordeel;*" "*na den gemeenen landrecht en na hunne fijf zinnen;*" "*na de beste redelijkheid en na den ouden hercomen.*" Now what was meant by the terms in accordance with the *landrecht, i.e.* law of the country, and "*na hunne fijf zinnen,*" i.e. according to their common-sense.

We find that the *Capitularia* as early as 802 A.D. required the judges to give their opinion according to the *Lex Scripta,* "*ut judices secundum scriptam legem non secundum arbitrium suum, judicant.*" They were expressly enjoined not to judge according to their sweet will, but to follow the *Lex Scripta.* What was the *Lex Scripta?* Van der Spiegel is of opinion that the *Lex Scripta* meant the various compilations of laws then in existence, such as the *Lex Salica, Lex Ripuaria,* the *Leges Burgundionum* and *Visigothorum,* the privileges of the towns and the *Capitularia.* To these must be added the Roman law as found in the *Breviarium Alaricum* and a great deal of the Canon law. We find similar language used in the charters of the fifteenth and sixteenth centuries, and there the words *beschreven wetten;*" "*gemeene beschrevene wetten;*" and "*beschrevene rechten,*" always mean the Roman law (Scheltinga, *ad Grot.* 1, 22).

Raepsaet points out that the seignorial courts were required to pronounce their judgment *secundum Rectum,* and that *Rectum* meant the Roman law (Raepsaet, vol. 4, p. 92; Du Cange, *Glossarium, sub voce Rectum*). A further proof adduced by Van der Spiegel is that in many cases the judges of the small towns were required to consult the judges of larger towns, such as Leyden (Van Mieris, *G.C.B.* vol. 1, p. 63). If, therefore, by the words *na hunne fijf zinnen* were meant their peculiar notions of what was right, then it seems objectless to have required them to refer to the practice of other towns. Van der Spiegel thinks that the reason the judges of the smaller towns were required to follow the practice of the larger towns was that the lawyers of the larger towns were supposed to have a greater knowledge than they of the *landrecht* and the *Lex Scripta*. The expression, therefore, "according to their five senses," meant little more than according to their conscience and according to such legal principles and precedents as the judges knew of, or could become acquainted with by reference to those who knew more than they.

CHAPTER XVI.

(c) THE STUDY OF ROMAN LAW DURING THE TWELFTH AND LATER CENTURIES.

I HAVE shown that the Roman law to which reference was made during the Frankish monarchy was not the law as found in the law-books of Justinian, but that which had been compiled by Anianus from the *Codex Theodosianus.* About the twelfth century a purer and better form of the Roman law came to be introduced. The law-books of Justinian, though not known to western Europe, had never been quite forgotten in Italy. In the eleventh century the law school of Bologna took up the neglected study of the Roman law. In the twelfth century it had become a seat of learning of great importance. A tale is told that in 1135 A.D., after the siege of Amalfi, a valuable manuscript containing the whole of the *Corpus Juris* of Justinian fell into the hands of the Pisans. Some have attributed the revival of the study of Justinian to this fact, though according to the best authorities this view is fanciful. The *Corpus Juris* of Justinian was studied before the siege of Amalfi, though the date of this siege synchronises with the great activity in the study of the pure Roman law. A crowd of students flocked from all parts of Europe to Bologna to study Roman jurisprudence, and returning to their own countries taught the Roman law of the *Corpus Juris* of Justinian.

Bernardus, Abbot of Clairvaux, complained that at the palace of Pope Eugenius he heard more about the laws of

Justinian than about the laws of God. The Church dignitaries in Germany were well acquainted with the *Code* of Justinian, and there is no reason to believe that the high Church dignitaries of so important a see as that of Utrecht were not as well informed as those of Münster. We know that scholars went from Friesland and Flanders to study law in Italy (Savigny, *History*, p. 19), and we may, therefore, fairly assume that the law-books of Justinian were not unknown to the higher Church and State officials of the Netherlands. Its superiority to the law of the Theodosian *Code* came to be recognised, and in time it completely supplanted the latter.

In Germany the *Corpus Juris* of Justinian was well known in the time of Henry II (1002–1024), for he passed a law with regard to the oaths of ecclesiastics in which, *inter alia*, we find, *Cum divus Justinianus jure decreverit ut canones patrum vim legum habere* (Van der Spiegel, p. 105). This very law was in all probability known to the ecclesiastics of Utrecht, for this emperor was a great supporter of the bishops of that city. Frederick Barbarossa in 1158 summoned to the Council of Roncalie four of the pupils of Irnerius, the great Bologna professor of Roman law. Now at these Councils were present many of the counts and bishops of the Netherlands, and they must have become acquainted with the influence and prestige of the teachers of the civil law of Justinian. Moreover, many of the counts of Brabant, Luxembourg and Limburg had studied law in Italy, where at that time only the *Corpus Juris* of Justinian was recognised as authoritative. In this way, then, the law of Justinian took the place of the law of Theodosius, and helped to build up the common law of the Netherlands.

In order to understand fully the impulse which the study of Roman law received in the eleventh and twelfth centuries, we must have some comprehension of the great influence exerted by the Italian universities. Bologna, Pisa, Padua, Perugia and Venice were practically small, though extremely energetic republics. They vied with each other not only in commerce, but also in learning. Their universities differed from ours inasmuch as they were the sole seats of learning. No gymnasia, colleges and high schools competed with them. Hence they attracted not only all the young men of their respective towns, but the youth of the empire. Learning did not then consist of the numerous subjects taught to-day; it was practically confined to dialectics, law, theology and medicine, and of these law and theology were the favourite subjects. Again, the study of law was practically confined to the *Corpus Juris* of Justinian, and the *Epitome* of Julian. From Italy the study of the Roman law spread to the universities of France (Paris, Montpellier, Orleans) and to those of Spain, Portugal and England.

A short account of the men who spread the knowledge of the Roman law of the *Corpus Juris* throughout Europe may not be amiss here. All historians seem to agree that the founder of the Bologna school of law was Irnerius. He was born at Bologna, and was during the years 1113–18 in the service of the Countess Mathilda and of Henry V. Besides teaching law at the University of Bologna he edited the *Corpus Juris*, and wrote glosses upon the text. The compilation of the *Novels* as printed in the *Corpus Juris* is believed to be due to Irnerius. He is also credited with having collected or composed a volume of formulae for the use of notaries. Certain writers of the thirteenth century refer to some *Quaestiones* as those of Irnerius. Few of the above works have come down to us except in so far as they have been incorporated in the works of later authors (Savigny, *History*, vol. 4, c. 27).

Towards the middle of the twelfth century there lived at Bologna four jurists who had acquired so great a reputation that they are always cited as the *Quatuor Doctores*, or the four doctors. Their names are Bulgarus, Marthinus Gosia, Jacobus and Hugo. They are said to have been pupils of Irnerius. Of these four doctors Bulgarus seems to have held the first place in public esteem. Besides being a professor of law, he held very high political and judicial offices. He wrote glosses, a commentary on the *De Regulis juris*, and a treatise on the law of procedure. Marthinus Gosia was a Ghibelline, and as such was banished from Bologna. He is chiefly known by his glosses. Of Jacobus we know very little except that he composed glosses. The same may be said of Hugo, or Ugo, as he is often called.

The four doctors acquired considerable reputation during the twelfth century. They were great favourites at the court of the Emperor Frederick, and were consequently violently attacked by writers belonging to the anti-imperial party. Their glosses, however, enjoyed much reputation during the twelfth and thirteenth centuries. Other lawyers of the twelfth century were Rogerius, Placentius, Bassianus, Cyprianus, Otto, Burgundio and Vacarius. The last of these taught law at Oxford.

The first great law teacher of the thirteenth century was Azo. A story is told that he had as many as 10,000 students, so that he was obliged to lecture under the open sky. He occupies an important place amongst the glossators, and a knowledge of his works was apparently regarded as essential to the success of a lawyer, for there existed an Italian saying—*Chi non ha Azo non vada a Palazzo* ("He who did not know the summary of Azo had poor chance of success at court"). Another great lawyer of the thirteenth century, and a contemporary of Azo, was Hugolinus. He was ambassador of Bologna at Rome, Florence and Reggio. His chief works are glosses, *Quaestiones,* and controversies on disputed points of law.

Jacobus Balduinus, Carolus de Tocco and Accursius were the last great names of the old school of glossators. Accursius was the pupil of Azo. He was a lecturer on law for a period of forty years, and became assessor to the Podesta of Bologna in 1252. He died an exceedingly wealthy man in 1260. His gloss is unquestionably the most important of those composed by the old glossators. Savigny, in dealing with the gloss of Accursius, says (*History,* vol. 4, p. 149): "The gloss [of Accursius] is of great historic value to us, because the greater part of the works referred to by Accursius have been lost or are unpublished. It has rendered to the science of law the same service as did the compilations of Justinian. Indeed, it has preserved the memory of the glossators and of their works better perhaps than would have done those works themselves. . . ." The success of this gloss was extremely great. Before the tribunals it almost obtained the force of law, and Accursius was looked upon as the most eminent lawyer, not only of his own, but of all preceding centuries. Some towns decreed that Accursius' interpretation of the Roman law was to be accepted as final. When once the authority of the gloss of Accursius was established the ancient glosses were completely neglected, and neither read nor copied. Often the ancient glosses were actually destroyed and erased in order to enable the copyist to use the parchment for the gloss of Accursius.

Accursius was the last of the old glossators. Their influence upon the study of Roman law had been very great. We may smile at their useless disquisitions and refinements, yet we must acknowledge that they did a great deal towards the scientific study of the Roman law. They helped to establish the text of the *Corpus Juris*, and by their exegetical as well as dogmatic treatises they assisted the jurists of the fifteenth and sixteenth centuries to understand the true meaning of the Roman law. No doubt a great deal of their work was useless, for they often had to grope in the dark. Of the history of the development of the Roman law they knew little or nothing, for the works of Gaius, Ulpian and other pre-Justinian writers were very imperfectly known to them. Though our knowledge to-day is far greater and our method superior to theirs, we owe to them a debt of gratitude for the activity they displayed in resuscitating the study of the Roman law.

From the middle of the thirteenth century the schools of law changed the character of their teaching. Instead of a scientific exposition of the civil law we come upon an era of great prolixity, with very little originality. The first of the new school, or perhaps the last of the old school, was Odofredus, the pupil of Balduinus and for some time the contemporary of Accursius. To the latter half of the thirteenth century belonged Guido de Suzaria, Andreas de Barulo, Vicentius and others whose names may be passed by.

The fourteenth century saw a revival in the scientific

method of teaching and expounding law. The jurists of this century largely introduced dialectics in the study of law. The number of writers on the theory and practice of law during this century was very large, and I shall, therefore, content myself with some of the most eminent names. In France Johannes Faber had acquired a great reputation. He criticised the prolixity of his contemporaries, taught in the French language and became a great authority on the practice of the courts. In Italy the principal jurists were Cinus, Bartolus de Saxoferato, Baldus, and Lucas de Penna. Of these Bartolus was the most celebrated. In Spain the opinions of Bartolus were long considered as conclusive upon the questions discussed by him. His commentary on the *Code* was translated into Portuguese, and regarded of equal value to the text and the glosses. At Padua lecturers explained the text of the *Corpus Juris,* the gloss and Bartolus. Many consider him (though according to Savigny erroneously) the founder of the Commentary so largely used by the writers of the fifteenth and sixteenth centuries. It was during this century that the *Consultation* came to be adopted as a method of expounding law. The ancient glossators very seldom had recourse to this method, but during the fourteenth and fifteenth centuries jurists wrote consultations upon disputed points of law and published their collections. There are numerous *Consultations* of Bartolus, Baldus, Jason and others.

There was very little difference between the jurists of the fourteenth century and those of the first half of the fifteenth. Towards the end of the fifteenth century came the earnest revival of learning in general, and with that a great development in the study of Roman jurisprudence. It was during this century that the Eastern Empire was completely overthrown by the Turks, and the learned men of Constantinople and the other eastern towns were compelled to migrate from the east to western Europe. Every science and every form of learning was improved, and in consequence of this activity the teachers of Roman law came to regard their science in a new light. The frivolous disputations of the teachers of the last two centuries made way for the solid learning and great acumen of the new school. Moreover, the art of printing facilitated reference to the original texts of the *Corpus Juris*, and the study of the civil law became less laborious than it had been in the previous centuries. During the fifteenth century a very large number of jurists continued the work of Accursius, Bartolus and Baldus. The principal names of those who followed the methods of the fourteenth century are Jason and Paulus de Castro. Of the jurists of the end of the fifteenth century who saw the necessity for reform the names of Ambrosius, Camaldulensis, Nicolaus Everard, Rebuffus and Voerda must suffice.

With Udalricus Zazius and Andreas Alciatus we enter upon a new period in the study of the Roman law—a period during which flourished Cujacius and Donellus, the greatest and most scientific expounders of the Roman civil law. Zazius was born in 1461, studied at Tubingen, became registrar of the court of Constance, and afterwards professor of law. He wrote a number of *Responsa* and *Consilia* as well as commentaries on several titles of the *Pandects*. Alciatus was born at Milan, taught at Avignon, Bourges, Bologna and Ferrara. He died in 1550. His chief works were annotations on the *Code*, disputations and consultations.

These two authors may be regarded as the founders of the New School of Commentators. The former introduced the modern method of teaching the civil law into Germany, whilst the latter did the same for France and Italy. Men began to study law in the same way as they studied the other monuments of antiquity. The *Institutes*, the *Digest*, and the *Code* were no longer regarded as though they embraced a system of law which stood separate and apart from all other branches of learning. The history of Roman institutions, the texts of the works of ante-Justinian authors and the literature of Rome were all examined with a view to arriving at the true meaning and spirit of the legislation of Justinian. This was the method adopted by Alciatus and Zazius, and followed by those illustrious commentators Cujacius and Donellus, whose works are still regarded as the greatest commentaries on the civil law. Cujacius (Cujas) was born at Toulouse in 1522, and died in 1590. He lectured on law at Valence and Bourges, where he taught a number of men who became illustrious jurists. He was a man of great learning, and brought to bear upon the interpretation of the text his immense knowledge of Roman literature and Roman institutions. He possessed a critical faculty of a high order and a remarkable method of exposition. His emendations, corrections, restitutions and conjectures were stamped with the mark of genius, and soon came to be recognised as authoritative. His principal work is a commentary on the *Digest, Code, Novels* and the *Decretales.* Besides his commentaries he wrote a number of treatises on special branches of the civil law, and edited the *Codex Theodosianus*, the *Institutes* and a number of other law-books. Next in rank to Cujacius stands Donellus (Hugo Doneau).

He was born in 1527 at Chalon sur Saône. He taught law at Bourges, at Heidelberg and at Leyden.

From both these illustrious jurists the lawyers of the Netherlands borrowed a great deal, and we find them freely quoted by all the Dutch lawyers of the seventeenth century. The influence which Donellus had upon the study of the Roman law in Holland was exceedingly great, both through his personal influence and through his wonderful commentary on the civil law—a work which is to-day still one of the best and most methodical expositions of the Roman law. Of all the writers on the Roman law, this man seems to be the most lucid and most interesting. But for the fact that the commentary is written in Latin, it reads like a legal treatise of our own time. He was one of the first professors of the University of Leyden, and there he lectured for nearly ten years. If his oral lectures were as clear and interesting as his books, he must have contributed in no small degree to the spread of the Roman law in Holland. The extent of his influence upon the later lawyers of the Netherlands is manifest from the frequency and respect with which he is quoted by all the great Dutch writers on law, and especially by Johannes Voet.

The influence of Cujacius and Donellus upon the common law of Holland, nay, indeed, upon the common law of the Continent generally, cannot easily be exaggerated; and without constant reference to their works it is by no means easy to understand the great *Commentary* of Voet, and for that reason alone the works of Cujacius and Donellus should be constantly referred to by the student of Roman-Dutch law.

Besides Cujas and Doneau, the sixteenth century produced

a number of eminent jurists of whom the following were the most celebrated. To the French School belonged Duarenus (François Le Douaren), who was born at Moncontour in 1509, and died at Bruges in 1559. He was a pupil of Alciatus and the teacher of Donellus. Balduinus (François Badouin) 1520–1573. The brothers Pithou (*Pithoei fratres*), Barnabas Brisson (1531–1591), the author of the *De Significatione Verborum*, and the compiler of a collection of formulae, Petrus Faber (Pierre Du Faur), 1540–1600, and Godofredus (Denis Godefroy), the celebrated editor and annotator of the *Corpus Juris*. To the German School belonged Haloander (Gregorius Meltzer), 1501–1531, celebrated for his edition of the *Corpus Juris*; Franciscus Hotomanus (1525–1590), professor of law at Strasburg, Valence, Lausanne, Ghent and Bourges. To the Spanish School belonged Antonius Augustinus (1517–1586); and to the Dutch School, Viglius Zuichemus (Van Zwickem) 1507–1577.

This review of the great European jurists brings us to the beginning of the seventeenth century. During that century the Netherlands, as we shall see later on, produced a large number of eminent lawyers and commentators, so that the influence of foreign writers ceased to be as great as it had been during the previous centuries.

CHAPTER XVII.

(d) THE POSITION OF THE ROMAN LAW IN HOLLAND DURING THE FOURTEENTH AND FIFTEENTH CENTURIES.

WE are now in a position to understand the reception of the civil law into Holland; and how, towards the end of the fifteenth century, it came to be regarded, at any rate by the superior courts, as almost equivalent to the common law of the Netherlands. As we have seen, there was no ordinance or law by which either the sovereign imposed the Roman law upon the people, or by which the people deliberately accepted that system as their common law. There are some who would deny to the Roman law even the force of subsidiary law until late in the sixteenth century. They base their arguments upon the want of documentary evidence to that effect, and upon the assumption that the people were ignorant of both the Latin language and the law-books of Justinian. They admit that it was not only referred to freely during the sixteenth century, but that it formed the basis of the decisions of the courts of appeal during that century. The argument of those who hold the view that the reception of the Roman law was comparatively late is based on the fact that the judges in the towns were not skilled lawyers, and that, therefore, a reference to the Roman law was improbable. The records do not disclose that there were many persons skilled in Roman law during the first years of the fifteenth century. The *keurboeken* show few traces of Roman law, and their unsystematic arrangement suggests that they were not drawn up by skilled lawyers, at any rate before the latter half of the fifteenth century.

It is very difficult to come to a definite conclusion from the documentary evidence in our possession. If proof is adduced of some document full of references to the Roman law, its force is minimised by saying that it is an exception and was the production of some specially learned person. Those who maintain that the influence of the Roman law was unbroken, and that it was already in the fifteenth century regarded as the most important body of law for settling disputes, rely not only on documentary proof, but on the assumption that it is highly improbable that the Roman law, which was of such pre-eminent importance during the latter half of the sixteenth century, had acquired this importance almost within the recollection of Damhouder or of Paul Merula, the teacher of Grotius.

That a people should so suddenly have had recourse to a system of law which was *ex hypothesi* foreign to them, and that within a period of a little more than fifty years this foreign law should become the common law of that people, is so contrary to experience and to the history of legal development that it is very difficult to accept the proposition, unless the proof of it were overwhelming.

There is no doubt whatever that during the fifteenth century the civil law was scientifically studied in Holland, and the *keurboeken* show the effect of this study in their better and more methodical arrangement. If we compare the *keurboeken* of Leyden of the fourteenth century with those of 1406 and 1450 we find a great alteration. From a crude collection of administrative regulations and legal provisions mixed up in hopeless confusion, the *keurboeken* gradually assume a methodical arrangement and a legal language which shows the influence of the Roman law.

Not only in the Netherlands, but throughout a great part of the continent of Europe, the monarchs of the fifteenth century saw in the introduction of the Roman law their only hope of reducing into one system the divergent customs that prevailed in their provinces. It was the only means at their disposal to obtain some general law for all their subjects. The German rulers looked with great distrust upon the Canon law, and as the study of the Roman law of Justinian had engrossed so many lawyers from all quarters of Europe, it was resorted to as the universal common law.

The House of Burgundy encouraged the spread of the Roman law as a solvent of the various almost contradictory customs which had grown up throughout the provinces (Blok, *Ned. Stad.* p. 195). This same idea had, however, occurred sporadically to earlier rulers when Holland formed part of the Holy Roman Empire. That Empire was looked upon as a continuation of the Roman Empire, and it was therefore urged that the laws of the latter ought to prevail in the former. This was not only the case in the Netherlands, but also in the German provinces. Brunner tells us that there was no special introduction of the Roman law into any portion of the German Empire. "The introduction of foreign laws, and especially of the Roman law, did not take place by some sudden or special Act; it was the result of a long process. . . . It dates back to the twelfth century, and was rooted in the idea that the Holy Roman Empire was a continuation of the ancient Roman Empire, and that, therefore, the laws of the Roman emperors were the laws of the predecessors of the German monarchs, and, therefore, of force as a subsidiary law (Holzendorf's *Rechts Encyclopaedie*, vol. 1, p. 185).

The Holland of the twelfth century formed part of the Holy Roman Empire, but above all it had formed part of the Frankish monarchy. The *Lex Romana* had been recognised as part of the system of law which prevailed among the Franks, and there is no evidence that any break occurred during the rule of the counts. Gradually the people had come to look upon the *Lex Romana* as part of their ancient customs (*oude costumen en hercomen*), and we find it referred to as such in many of the charters, privileges and handvesten. Hence the rulers of the House of Burgundy found no difficulty in encouraging the adoption of a system of law already known by name, and of which a number of principles had become familiar to men in their daily intercourse. If it had lain dormant during the earlier centuries it certainly began to bud after the establishment of the Supreme Court of Mechlin and the court of Holland and West Friesland during the fifteenth century, and to burst into leaf during the sixteenth century.

With the establishment of the Supreme Court of Mechlin the reception of the Roman law as the basis of the common law was assured. In the Supreme Court of Mechlin the number of civil lawyers was larger than the number of canonists. These judges, and the advocates who practised in the Supreme Court, were educated in the universities where the Roman law of Justinian formed, as we have seen, one of the most important branches of study. It is, therefore, not to be wondered at that the Court of Mechlin exercised a great influence in the spread of the Roman law, especially as its judgments formed precedents for the lower courts. The influence of the other high courts was also directed towards this same end during the fifteenth and sixteenth centuries (Blok, *loc. cit.* p. 196; Star Numan Bynkershoek, p. 241). In 1531 the Court of Holland was composed almost entirely of jurists who had been educated in the Roman law. The town courts of schout and schepenen, and the district courts of baljuw and mannen followed suit, for to almost all the important lower courts officials were attached skilled in the practice of the Roman law. The pensionaries of the towns during the fifteenth and sixteenth centuries were nearly all skilled lawyers, whilst advocates educated in the Roman law began to practise not only in the superior courts, but also in the town courts of schout and schepenen, (Blok, *loc. cit.* p. 197).

It would therefore be more correct to speak of the gradual infiltration of Roman law into the law of Holland prior to the fifteenth century, and to regard that century as the century during which the reception of the Roman law began. It was then used as a subsidiary law where the old laws and customs were inadequate. During the fifteenth century the whole aspect of the life of Holland changed. From a pastoral and agricultural province it rapidly developed into a commercial country. Trade began to grow by leaps and bounds. Commerce brought with it increasing disputes, almost impossible to solve by the old customs, and the Roman law was more freely invoked as the only known scientific system by which these disputes could be satisfactorily settled. Bynkershoek has therefore rightly said, *Ubi silent leges Patriae, cedo mihi, quid succedat nisi Romana?*

When we turn to the text-writers of the Roman-Dutch law we see that some of them favour a special introduction. Thus Van Leeuwen says, "This agrees with the opinion of those who hold that the Roman law was introduced into this country by King William II (1256), who, being crowned and confirmed as king of the Romans by the princes of the empire when he was about twenty years of age, resolved that the Dutch should use the Roman law in future" (Van Leeuwen's *Commentaries*, Kotzé's Tr. vol. 1, p. 7). Neither Grotius, Bynkershoek, nor Huber pretend to fix any definite period for the introduction of the Roman law, though they all agree that in olden times the Roman law had the force of subsidiary law.

I have pointed out in an earlier chapter that the *Lex Romana* was founded on the Theodosian *Code*, but the law which was accepted during the fifteenth century was the law of the *Corpus Juris* of Justinian as explained by the glossators. In the time of Philip II the authority of the *Corpus Juris* was so great that it became the custom to abrogate such parts of it as were no longer to be regarded as law. In 1564 chapter 2 of the fourth book of the *Novels* and the *Authentica hoc si debitor* (*C.* 8, 14) were specially abrogated (Scheltinga, *ad Grot.* 1, sec. 22). By a special Constitution passed about the same time the title *De Juris dictione* in the *Digest* was declared to be no longer in force. Hence Grotius was able to say in 1631 A.D.: "In the absence of any written law, charter, privilege or custom on any particular subject the judges have from times of old been enjoined on oath to follow reason to the best of their knowledge and discretion, and as the Roman laws, particularly in the form in which they were codified by Justinian, were regarded by the learned as replete with wisdom and equity, they were first adopted as examples of wisdom and equity, and in course of time through custom as laws." In a later chapter I shall show that the writers of the sixteenth century regarded the Roman law as the common law of Holland. This no doubt was not quite correct, but it shows the great respect in which that law was held by the leading jurists of Holland.

CHAPTER XVIII.

THE CANON LAW.

As mention has frequently been made of the Canon law and of its influence upon Roman-Dutch law, it seems necessary to give a sketch of the origin and nature of that law, and to state what effect its introduction into the Netherlands has had upon the development of the law of those provinces. Inasmuch as the Canon law was the law of the Roman Church, it has not had a very fair treatment at the hands of the Protestant writers who were near to the intense struggle between the adherents of the old Church and those of the reformed religion. As a system of law which ruled the intimate relations of men for several centuries, it cannot be passed by with a few derogatory remarks, as is so often done by Protestant writers, nor, on the other hand, need it be extolled as being of almost divine origin, as is done by Zypaeus.

As the Church grew in power, both temporal and spiritual, it sought to impose its will upon Europe, step by step, through channels which during the preceding centuries had met with general approval. The canonists sought to do for the Canon law what the development of the Roman Empire had done for the Roman law. The whole of the Roman Empire had been ruled by one system of law, of which the emperor in the last resort was the supreme expounder. The Church strove to establish one system of law, whenever her influence was undisputed, in which the Roman pontiff occupied the same position as the Byzantine emperor. The Roman Curia was to be the chief court of appeal, and the fountain-head from which would flow such new laws as were required to meet new circumstances. The *decretales* of the Popes were to have the same effect as the rescripts and constitutions of the emperors. This was the principle the Curia strove to establish, and though Protestant writers have tried to minimise the power and influence of the Canon law, there can be little doubt in the mind of an unbiased inquirer that during the twelfth, thirteenth and fourteenth centuries the Popes had succeeded remarkably well in placing Europe under this system.

The Canon law was admitted as the only valid law in the courts of ecclesiastics; and even in the secular courts its authority rose from century to century, until the corruption of the Church and the advent of the Reformation completely wrecked the whole system. The Canon law had borrowed very largely from the Roman law. It used the same legal terms, it approved of the same forms, and the maxims of the Roman law were used as the foundation upon which the structure of the Canon law was raised. If the student wishes to get an insight into the principles and practice of the Canon law, I should not advise him to begin with the *Corpus Juris Canonici*, for there is much in it that does not appeal to a student of law. A far better work to form an idea of the principles upon which the canonists proceeded is Peckius' *De Regulis Juris Pontifici*. He shows clearly how closely the canonists adhered to the maxims of the civil law, and how they combined the *Regulae Juris* with biblical texts.

As, however, Christianity had introduced new ideas into the policy of, and as it drew its chief support from, the new Germanic nations of western Europe, it was but natural that the Canon law should contain much that the civil law had not required. The laws of divorce, the ceremonies for marriages, the executors to wills, the testimony of witnesses, the punishment of heretics, the sanctity of oaths, the pledge of faith, and many other matters both in procedure and in substantive law, were dealt with by the canonists somewhat differently from the civilians. In time, however, as the Church became corrupt, and as the study of the Roman law became a passion in Italy, France, and Germany, the Canon law began to decline as well in intrinsic value as in the estimation in which it was held. It was not only the Continent which was influenced by the Canon law, for even England, the home of the common law, owes a great deal to the *decretales* of Gratian. It was a fashion to deny its influence in England, but Pollock and Maitland, the learned authors of the *History of English Law*, have at last given to the Canon law due recognition (vol. 1, pp. 111 *et seq.*).

In the same way, if we read the Protestant writers on the law of Holland we are led to believe that the Canon law was some unholy system of law from which nothing but evil could be learnt. On the contrary, the civilising effect of the Canon law upon the customs of our forefathers was very great, and it went hand in hand with the Roman law to help to build up the system we call the Roman-Dutch law. One of the great services rendered by the canonists was the simplification of the law and the abolition of unnecessary formalism. This left its mark on our law of contract and law of procedure.

Although we ought to recognise the influence of the Canon law in the development of our modern Roman-Dutch law, we must not forget the great difference which existed between canonists and the civil jurists. The former always appealed to the Bible as the ultimate authority, whilst the latter relied on the *Corpus Juris*. The canonist went to the Roman law for the general tenor of his law, but he relied on scriptural texts for guidance when the precepts of the Church conflicted with the rules of the civil courts. If, for instance, we take the law of marriage as an example, we see that the Canon law followed the Roman law very closely, but where the rule of the Church or special texts are incompatible with the Roman law the precepts of the Church and not the rules of the civil law were adopted by the canonists. Thus a widow was free to marry a second time, but if she took a vow of chastity then Timothy, 1, 5, 11, was relied upon to pronounce her second marriage void (*Decret*, pars. 2, cons. 27, Q. 1). Again, the Church was strongly opposed to divorce, whereas the Roman law freely allowed it. The canonist, therefore, relied on Genesis, 2, 21, 22, 24, and Matthew, 19, 9, and adopted a rule diametrically opposed to the policy of the Roman law (*Decret.* Greg. 4, 19, 8).

The oldest trustworthy sources of the Canon law are to be found in the resolutions of the various Church Councils held in the fourth century. In the East the Councils of Nicaea (325 A.D.), Ancyra (314), and Neocaesarea furnished the first collection of Church laws. The Councils of Antioch, Constantinople and Chalcedon furnished a second collection. They had but little influence in western Europe until they were translated into Latin some time in the sixth century. The first collection of Church laws arranged upon some definite plan was that of Dionysius. It was translated into Latin, and in western Europe it received the sanction of Charlemagne. Besides the *Collectio Dionysiana* there were other collections, portions of which were later incorporated into the *Corpus Juris Canonici*, but none of these were recognised as being of supreme authority. In consequence of these various collections there was no Church law which was binding on all members of the Romish Church. During the twelfth century Gratianus, a monk of St. Felix in Bologna, conceived the idea of making a collection of all the resolutions, constitutions, and *litterae decretales* of the Popes that were of such a character as to be recognised all through western Europe. He not only collected, but brought the mass of laws into some sort of system and published them in the form of a law-book. This work came to be known as the *Decretum Gratianum*, and formed the foundation upon which the *Corpus Juris Canonici* was built. The next century saw a great deal of papal legislation, and this, together with the *Decretum Gratianum*, was published by Gregory IX, and known as the *Decretum Gregorianum* or *Epistolae Decretales* of Gregory. About 1303 Boniface VIII made another collection, known as the *Liber Sanctus*, in which he incorporated all that had gone before, together with recent decrees. Clement V made another collection in 1334, and in the following century Pope John XXII added the last collection, which may be compared to the *Novellae* of the *Corpus Juris*. In 1582 all these collections received the sanction of Gregory XIII, and were thereafter known as the *Corpus Juris Canonici*.

Having dealt with the origin and composition of the Canon law, we shall proceed to consider how it came to influence the administration of law in western Europe generally, and then its particular influence on the Roman-Dutch law; and we shall find that its effect was twofold. In the first place, it modified the system of Justinian in a great many respects, and secondly, its connection with the Justinian legislation and its acceptance by the Churches of the Netherlands, caused the study of the *Corpus Juris* to be more widely spread, for the Canon law was to a great extent founded on the *Corpus Juris.*

In the earlier centuries the Church did not have sufficient power to attempt to exercise over her members a jurisdiction which was not derived from the temporal power. The emperor protected the Church, and the Church ruled her functionaries and her members through the emperor. In the sixth *Novel* Justinian deals with the ordination of bishops, and there he tells us that the two great gifts of God are priesthood and empire. Inasmuch as the priest prays for the prosperity of the empire, it is to the interest of the emperor that the prayers of the priest should be heard; and, unless the life of the priest is pure and holy, there is but little chance of his prayers being acceptable. It is, therefore, incumbent upon the emperor to see that the lives of priests are pure and well regulated, and consequently Justinian proceeds to legislate with regard to bishops and higher priests in the same strain as he had already legislated for monasteries and monks.

In Justinian's time, therefore, it was still the civil power which by civil legislation regulated the affairs of the Church and the conduct of its priests. In western Europe also the Church got her authority not from the decree of the Pope, but from the sanction of the Emperor. Just as Justinian dealt with Church law in his *Novels*, so Charlemagne dealt with it in his *Capitularia.* Charlemagne accepted the collection of Church laws made by Dionysius, and gave to them, by his formal sanction, the force of law. Charlemagne conceded to the Church the right of the Pope to regulate the affairs of the Church, and to have jurisdiction over its priests, but he never acknowledged the right of the Pope to legislate without the sanction of the temporal power. During the ninth and tenth centuries the Popes strove hard, but did not succeed, in getting from the emperors an acknowledgment of their right to legislate for, and to exercise jurisdiction over, the laity in their disputes with Church officials. In the eleventh century the Popes boldly claimed that they obtained their authority from God, whilst all temporal kings owed their power to the devil.

Quis nesciat reges et duces ab iis habuisse principium qui Deum ignorantes, superbiâ, rapinis, perfidiâ, homicidiis, prostremo universis pene sceleribus, mundi principe diabolo videlicet agitante super pares, scilicet homines, dominari caecâ cupidine et intolerabili praesumptione affectaverunt (*Regist.* Greg. vii, bk. 8, ep. 21). (Who does not know that kings and counts have their origin in those who, ignorant of God, with blind lust and unbearable presumption, strive to rule their equals, human beings, by means of pride, rapine, perfidy, murder, and almost every form of crime at the instigation of the ruler of the world, namely, the devil.)

The legislation of the Popes was directly inspired by God, and, therefore, superior to that of temporal emperors and kings. This view came to be accepted in many parts of Europe, and as the Western Empire declined, the power of the Popes increased. In the first place, all matters concerning priests were withdrawn from the temporal and handed over to the ecclesiastical courts; in the next place, certain persons were allowed to appeal for redress to the Church courts, such as widows, orphans, slaves, &c., called *personae miserabiles;* and lastly, all matters which were considered to be more of a spiritual than of a temporal nature were entrusted to ecclesiastical courts. In this way the latter came to deal with the *causae spirituales*, such as matrimonial causes, disputes arising out of wills, cases concerning Church property, usury and *bonae fidei* contracts. In criminal matters the Church courts took cognisance of heresy, simony, blasphemy, bigamy, witchcraft, perjury, fraud, and other matters affecting the conscience of its members.

The twelfth and thirteenth centuries saw the aggrandisement of the Church, and the consequent extension of the Canon law over the whole of western Europe. Though the Dutch writers, after the Reformation, tried to minimise the influence of the Canon law, we cannot shut our eyes to the fact that the Canon law played a great part in the development of the Roman-Dutch law. Its direct influence upon the law of Holland may not have been very great, but its indirect influence, through the law of Utrecht and Middelburg, must have been considerable. If we consider the great influence that the Romish Church had in the Netherlands during the twelfth and thirteenth centuries, more especially in Utrecht, Middelburg and the southern provinces, together with the numerous references to the Canon law which are to be found scattered through the various law-books, we cannot come to any other conclusion than that the Canon law has left a great mark on the Roman-Dutch law of the seventeenth century. If we take the charters of the counts we see they admitted that the ecclesiastics did not fall under temporal courts, but that the ecclesiastical courts alone had jurisdiction over them (Van Mieris, *Groot Chart. Boek*, p. 153). The courts were called Consistory Courts, and the judges Provisory Judges. They dealt not only with all matters affecting the conscience, but also with such as were called *res mixti fori*, without any regard as to whether the cases brought before them affected ecclesiastics or others. From these provisory judges an appeal lay to the bishop. All these officers judged according to the dictates of the Canon law; and in this way it came to be regarded as an important part of the law of the land. Lawyers who were admitted to practise in the courts of Holland were required to be *doctores Utriusque Juris*, *i.e.* persons skilled in the Canon as well as in the civil law, and Hollanders, such as Phillipus à Leidis, taught the Canon law not only in their own universities, but even in Paris. Grotius, Bynkershoek, Huber, Van der Keessel, Van der Linden and Van der Spiegel, all acknowledge the fact that the Roman-Dutch law is largely indebted to the Canon law, and if we consult the various *Consultatiën* and *Adviesen*, we shall find that the Canon law is very frequently quoted and relied upon. Inasmuch as most of these opinions were given after the Reformation, we can conjecture how much greater the authority of the Canon law must have been before the time of Luther.

In order to show how intimately the Canon law was connected with the civil law of Justinian, and how wide its scope was, some principal maxims accepted during the twelfth century may be quoted (Ritterhusius, *de Diff. Jur. Can. et Civil*, p. 9).

(1) *Quoties res obscura aut dubia est jure civili, jure autem Canonico clare definita standum esse canonibus et quidem in utroque foro.* (Whenever a matter is obscure or doubtful in the civil law, but is clearly defined in the Canon law, then the latter must prevail as well in temporal as in ecclesiastical courts.)

(2) *Quando aliquid est jure Civili definitum et non jure Canonico standum est jure Civili etiam in foro Canonico.* (Whenever a matter is defined by the civil law, but not by the Canon law, then the civil law must prevail even in ecclesiastical courts.)

(3) *Cum jus Civile et jus Canonicum inter se pugnant jus Civile debet servari in foro imperii sed jus Canonicum in terris Ecclesiae.* (If the civil and Canon laws are opposed to one another, then the civil law must prevail in courts where the lands are not held by the Church, but in lands held by the Church the Canon law prevails.)

(4) *Quoties tractatur de materiâ peccati et conscientiae si pugnet jus Civile cum Canonico potius sequenda est dispositio juris Canonici quam Civilis etiam in foro Civili.* (If the Canon and civil laws differ and the question regards some matter of conscience and sin, then even in civil courts the Canon law must be accepted.)

In time certain classes of cases came to be ruled in Holland rather by the Canon law than by the civil law. "Illegitimate children born *ex prohibito concubitu* may not take under the will of their parents either directly or indirectly, except that by the Canon law, which is followed in this particular, they may be left sufficient to provide for their necessary sustenance" (Grot. 2, 16, 6).

"Although according to Roman law children may not claim

the Trebellian fourth over and above their legitimate fourth, it is nevertheless the practice with us in accordance with the Canon law for children to draw their legitime from the whole inheritance and their Trebellian from the residue, if charged to give this over to another" (Grot. 2, 20, 10).

"It is a rule of the Canon law that oaths, not contrary to the will of God or against morals, are to be respected, and this principle is so far taken over by us that no one can refuse to fulfil a promise made by him under oath, even though he would not ordinarily be bound" (Huber, *Hed. Reg.* 3, 22, 49).

"We cannot deny that the Canon law has had some influence on our practice with regard to matrimonial matters, but we must endeavour to see that this influence does not become any greater than it need be" (Bynkershoek, *Quaest. Jur. Priv.* bk. 2, c. 10 *in inst.*).

Voet tells us (1, 1, 2) that we must first resort to the local laws and customs of the country, then to the Roman, and lastly to the Canon law. *Quod si nec ex his expediri res possit tum demum Romani juris decisiones et Canonici illustrationes admittendae sunt.* This is sufficient to show that the Canon law was admitted even as late as the seventeenth century as having authority in the Dutch courts. How much greater, therefore, must not its influence have been before the Reformation in the time of the counts, when the Church of Rome held sway over the whole of the Netherlands. The Canon law was also a very important factor in keeping alive, and in spreading, the principles of the civil law. Not only did this take place through the Church courts, but also through the temporal courts. In the Church courts the civil law came to be quoted and relied upon, because the Canon law borrowed from the *Corpus Juris* of Justinian in its arrangement, principles and procedure. It may be considered as the Roman civil law adapted to meet the requirements of the Church of Rome. In the temporal courts, on the other hand, the Canon law went hand in hand with the Civil law; for inasmuch as the churchmen were to a great extent educated in both Canon and Civil law, and inasmuch as a great many ecclesiastics were notaries, they relied first on the Canon and then on the Civil law in giving their advice when consulted by their parishioners. When these matters, upon which they had advised, were carried into the temporal courts it was but natural that the Canon law should have been referred to and quoted as an authority. In many places, indeed, such as Utrecht and Middelburg, extremely important towns in those days, the judges of the higher courts were ecclesiastics, and as they naturally preferred the Canon to the Civil law, their decisions were based on the former rather than on the latter system. As these decisions helped to mould the future practice we see how the Canon law principles helped to form a part of the judge-made law of Holland.

Cujacius tells us that most of the *decretales* were taken either out of the *Corpus Juris*, or out of the glosses, and in this way the glosses themselves came to have the force of law. It follows that the spread of the Canon law meant the spread not only of the Civil law as found in the *Corpus Juris*, but also as developed and extended by the glossators. In many ways, therefore, the Canon law represented the Civil law as brought up to date. We also know that many treaties were made between the different counts of the Netherlands in which the Canon law was taken as the basis of reference in disputes relating to matrimonial causes, legacies *ad pias causas*, and matters regarding ecclesiastics, and thus it acquired an authority from the temporal prince in addition to that of the Church (Arntzenius, specimen 21). Even the legislation of the counts of Holland prior to the seventeenth century bore numerous traces of the Canon law, and thus again introduced its principles into the temporal courts. Its influence may be seen in the *Instructiën Van den Hove,* where it helped to mould the procedure of the courts in the manner of hearing witnesses, and in the rules regarding evidence (Arntzenius, *ibid.*). The procedure of the Canon law, from which so much was taken over by the temporal courts, had according to Paul Voet its origin principally in the writings of the glossators and interpreters of the Roman law.

Already in 1531 the provinces of Holland began to fear the increasing influence of the Canon law and the rescripts of the Popes, for in that year an ordinance was passed prohibiting judges from paying any attention to papal rescripts unless first accepted by the temporal authority (*Instructiën Van den Hove*, art. 221). From that time on its influence was on the wane, and the policy of the later legislation was to reduce rather than to extend its authority. It was, therefore, not quoted as an authority for the living law during the seventeenth century, but merely as the source of such customs as had been derived from it and had been incorporated in the common law, not *ex jure Divino*, but *ex inveteratâ consuetudine.*

The influence of the Canon law may, therefore, be thus summed up:—

(1) It influenced largely the courts of the southern provinces, and of Utrecht and Middelburg, and so, indirectly, the law of Holland.

(2) It helped to spread the civil law and the interpretation of the glossators.

(3) It profoundly affected certain branches of law, such as matrimonial law, the law of wills, legacies, the law of evidence and matters affecting conscience.

(4) It had a great effect on the law of procedure, and helped to do away with the antiquated procedure of Justinian and to introduce the procedure of modern times.

CHAPTER XIX.

ADMINISTRATION OF JUSTICE.

History of early courts.—In this chapter we shall consider how the various courts of Holland were built up in the course of time from the primitive courts of the early Germans. In discussing this subject I shall first deal with the place where and the time when the courts were held, next with the nature of the early courts, and then I shall endeavour to show how the ordinary courts of Holland, the courts of baljuw and mannen, and of schout and schepenen were established. After which I shall treat of the courts of appeal, and explain how the great courts of Holland, the Provinciale Raad and the Hoogen Raad had their origin. I shall then pass over to a consideration of the development of the procedure, and show how our present rules of court are directly descended from the procedure that prevailed in Holland during the sixteenth century.

The place where justice was administered.—Before the conversion of the Saxons to Christianity the priests played an important part in the administration of law (Tacitus, c. 10, 11). The courts were opened with due sacrifice to the gods, and a great deal of the procedure was regulated by religious rites. On the other hand, a free burgher could only be judged by the free burghers of his district, or perhaps of his ward, so that the court was bound to be assembled at some definite place convenient for the meeting of free burghers.

Hence the place where a Saxon court met in heathen times had to be both a holy place and a place open to the public.

The only public meeting-places known to the early German races were under the open sky. Their sacred places were generally groves on rising ground in the neighbourhood of some stream. Hence we find that the courts of the early Saxons were usually conducted on some hillock under the shade of spreading trees, and in the neighbourhood of a stream (Tacitus, *Germania*, c. 9, c. 39; Noordewier, p. 365; Van den Berg, pp. 3 *et seq*). The old high German name for the place where the court was held was *mahal;* the Gothic term was *mathal;* in Anglo-Saxon it was termed *mael;* and in old Frankish *mallum*. The term *mallum* (sometimes *mallus*) was the one adopted by Latin writers on the ancient laws and customs of the Germans. In the Netherlands there are still a number of relics of this ancient word *mallum*. In Gelderland we have a village called Malbergen, which clearly points to this as one of the places where the *mallum* or court was held. In the Netherlands the terms *mael, maelstede, malburg,* and *malberg* were in use as late as the fourteenth century (Van Mieris, 2, 418; Van den Berg, p. 4).

Another feature of the ancient Saxon court was the large block of blue or black stone on the *mallum*. The exact use of this stone is somewhat obscure, but Grimm and others lean to the view that it was used as a sacrificial altar. There are numerous places in the Netherlands where such *blauwe of zwarte stenen* are still found. The stone is usually on some hillock, and there is no doubt that in later times courts were held at these blue or black stones. It is difficult to say whether courts were held in the neighbourhood of these stones as the result of tradition or not. In Reinaert de Vos (vs. 2756) the king sat upon a stone when he held his court. Orlers, writing in the sixteenth century, says: *De gerechtigheyt van den blauwen steen van outs als yet sonderlings en heylichs gehouden.* He tells us that at Leyden as late as 1614 no civil imprisonment could be decreed against a free citizen until he had been deprived of his citizenship (*ontporteerd*) and until the schout had placed his rod on the blue stone. The debtor was then led three times round the stone, and the bystanders were asked if they would become sureties for him. Similar practices in which the old stones played an important part existed elsewhere in the Netherlands (Noordewier, 369; Van den Berg, p. 7).

After the introduction of Christianity the courts were frequently held in the churches or churchyards. Already in the days of Charlemagne this practice was considered objectionable. In one of the *Capitularia* we find, *Mallus neque in ecclesiâ neque in atrio ejus habeatur* (*Cap.* 1, 819 A.D. sec. 14). Notwithstanding these prohibitions the practice continued even to the fourteenth century, for in 1310 A.D. we find Bishop Guido of Utrecht issuing a proclamation that no worldly trials (*placita*) should be conducted either in the church, in the portico or in the churchyard (Van Mieris, 2, 98; Noordewier, p. 370).

The next step was to hold the court either in front of the palace of the prince or else in a building specially set aside for this purpose. The *Capitularia* are the earliest documents which mention a definite building for conducting trials. They require the counts to see that such buildings are properly roofed in, so that the public be not inconvenienced by sun or rain (*Cap.* 2, 809 A.D. sec. 13; *Cap.* 1, 819 A.D. sec. 14; Noordewier, p. 37). In the thirteenth century such buildings were known as *praetoria* (Van Mieris, 1, 221), and later they were called *scepenhuus* (Van Mieris, 2, 865) and *dingehuus* (Maerlant, *Spieg. Hist.* 2, 236). In Germany they were known as *sprakhus*, *dinchus*, and *spelhus* (Grimm, *R.A.* 746, 747, 806).

We see, therefore, that in the early days of heathendom the Saxons and other German tribes in the Netherlands held their courts in the open on some hill under the shade of sacred trees. After the introduction of Christianity for the hill with its sacred stones were substituted the churchyard and church, and these in turn were abandoned for some building called the praetorium or council chamber. But though the building was there, to be used in case of inclement weather, the ordinary place for holding the court, as late as the fourteenth century, was in front of the praetorium under the blue sky (Van den Berg, p. 10).

We still speak of a "bench" of judges, or sitting on the bench; in Dutch we have *rechtbank* and *op de rechtbank zitten*. This brings us back to the old *mallum*, and the bench upon which the judge and jurors sat who spoke the doom or judgment. In the Market Book of Luttle in Overijssel we find, *Die richter zal sitten gaan op die Bencke mytt twee buren toe cornooten en heghen een gerichte als gewoontlyck.* What the exact shape of the bench was in Holland in the early days we do not know, but in Germany, Grimm tells us, the benches upon which the judges sat were arranged to form three sides of a square, whilst the fourth side was closed with iron rods (Grimm, *R.A.* 812). Van den Berg suggests that the word *vierschaar*, meaning a court, may be derived from this ancient practice. From the expression *de bank spannen* it is possible that the arrangement of benches was the same in Holland, and that instead of rods a cord was drawn across the opening. Noordewier, on the other hand, thinks that the old arrangement was mostly circular, and to support this view he refers to the term *ring* for an assembly and the expression *ring en ding*. The circle was not entirely closed with benches. Where the public stood there was probably a break, and in front of this either a rope was stretched or a hedge was placed made of hazel twigs (Noordewier, p. 372). In later times when the schepenbanken were instituted, there is no doubt that the form of the court was a square; the judge occupied the one bench, the schepenen the two benches to his right and left, whilst the fourth bench was occupied by the other officials of the court. Behind stood the public. This arrangement we find in the miniatures and early prints.

Time for holding the court.—By the early Roman law according to the Twelve Tables (Bouchaud, vol. 1, p. 295) law-suits began at sunrise and ended with sunset. The same rule seems to have applied to the Dutch courts during the earliest period. The judge opened the proceedings by asking the assembly of freemen whether it was a proper time to begin. If they replied that it was, the trial began. The commencement of the trial was *by klimmender zon*, *i.e.* before the middle of the day. A similar practice prevailed in early Rome—*ante meridiem causam conscito.* It is difficult to determine whether this practice was derived from Roman procedure or whether it was connected with the religious rites of the early Germans. We know that the sun was regarded as holy, that the judge sat facing the east, and that when he took his oath of office he turned his face to the sun. Moreover, it would have been very inconvenient to keep an assembly of freemen so late that they could not easily return home. The probability is, therefore, that the practice of the middle ages to try causes between sunrise and sunset dates back to a very remote antiquity. All punishments were to be inflicted between sunrise and sunset, and in case of capital punishment the execution had to be carried out before midday (Noordewier, pp. 373 *et seq.*).

Whether the heathen Saxons had *dies fasti* and *dies nefasti*, like the Romans, is a matter which antiquaries have not yet settled. Some think that Tuesday was the favourite court day of the ancient Germans (Noordewier, p. 375), though others believe this to be fanciful (Van den Berg, p. 17). After the introduction of Christianity it would appear that the court could be assembled upon any day of the week except Sundays and feast days. In one of the *Capitularia* (813 A.D.) we find: *Ne dominicis diebus mercatum fiat neque placitum et ut his diebus nemo ad poenam vel ad mortem judicetur* (Van den Berg, p. 17), though as a matter of fact this prohibition was not always strictly observed. It seems that the August vacation of the modern European courts dates back to a remote antiquity, for the Franks held no court during that month. The probable explanation is that during this month the agricultural population was too busy to attend the *mallum*. In one of the keuren of Zeeland of 1256 (Van Mieris, 1, 307) there is an express provision that the count should not hold a court in August on any account, and this practice has continued down to the present day in the superior courts of several European countries. There was no special time of the year except August that courts could not be held, though the period between the waxing and waning moon was not regarded as favourable.

Nature of the court.—In heathen times the chief of the tribe usually presided at the *mallum*; but as the tribe gave way to the nation, the king became the nominal president of the court. Inasmuch, however, as his time was fully occupied with other matters, he generally appointed some nobleman or, after the introduction of Christianity, some ecclesiastic to act in his stead. The older monarchs, however, made a point of presiding over a *mallum* at certain times of the year. These general assemblies became in the course of time more of the nature of parliaments than of courts, though they never entirely abandoned their judicial functions. The fact that the House of Lords is the Supreme Court of Appeal in England is a relic of this, for prior to 1399 the judicial power resided in the whole Parliament.

Such assemblies were held by the Carolingian monarchs once and by other princes two, three or even four times a year. Civil and criminal complaints were laid before these assemblies and were dealt with as by an ordinary court. Inasmuch as these assemblies met at definite times during the year, they were called the general or principal courts (*conventus generales*; *malla principalia*; *placita generalia*, or *communia*). It is from this last term that the English court of Common Pleas derived its name. The court of the Placita Generalia was, prior to the twelfth century, the chief court of appeal (Van den Berg, pp. 19 *et seq.*; Noordewier, pp. 379, *et seq.*)

Besides the Placita Generalia or Communia there were other sittings of the courts specially convened by the sovereign or his substitute. These were called *Placita Indicta*. To the courts appointed to sit on fixed days of the year all freemen were bound to come or to tender a valid excuse for non-attendance, but no one was bound to attend special courts except those directly interested.

There is little doubt that criminal cases were brought before the Placita Generalia, and that trials of a serious nature were conducted before those courts. The special courts were convened primarily for the transaction of civil business, and it was not originally a general practice to try prisoners at the special courts, though from the thirteenth century onward the special courts appear to have tried all kinds of complaints, criminal as well as civil (Van den Berg, p. 22).

In addition to the Placita Generalia and the Placita Indicta a number of inferior courts grew up throughout the Frankish Empire. In the Netherlands these courts gradually shaped themselves into district courts and town courts. As many of the courts grew up under the feudal system the lord of the territory or manor (*ambacht*) was the recognised judge within his own domain. His jurisdiction was, therefore, strictly limited to the territory over which he was lord, and to the persons who were his vassals. The lord of a district had the right to appoint inferior judges to act in his stead, and in this way there grew up a complicated system of manorial courts. Many of the old German courts, however, existed side by side with the feudal courts; the former exercised jurisdiction over free men, whilst the latter were chiefly engaged in settling disputes between the lords of manors (*ambachts-heeren*) and their *hofhoorigen* or between the *hofhoorigen* themselves. To the old German courts belonged the land courts, the gouw courts (canton courts), the mark courts and the town or village courts. The judges of these courts were appointed by the count, and their jurisdiction extended over all freemen within the limits of their districts.

During feudal times a great confusion existed between personal and territorial jurisdiction. Thus in 1361 the Emperor Charles IV gave to Bishop Jan van Arkel the right to act as judge over all Salland and Twente. His jurisdiction did not exclude, but existed concurrently with, that of the territorial courts. Certain courts were established from time to time to deal with some special subject. Thus the *Cynsgericht* was established for the purpose of dealing with disputes about taxes and contributions, the *Dykgericht*, presided over by a dykgraaf, dealt with matters affecting the boundaries of farms and their protection from floods. Besides these there was a number of similar special courts. The dykgraaf and watergraaf presided over courts in which *heemraden* sat as judges and jurors very much in the same way as the schepenen sat with the schout.

The word *heemraad* has an interest for us, for our early South African courts were courts of Landdrost and Heemraden. The word *heem,* from which this word is derived, means a homestead, and is connected with a German word meaning a hedge; *raad* means councillor. The heemraden were members of the dyk court and other courts whose principal functions were to determine boundaries. They were defined as *septem viros diffinitores terminorum et limitum discretos et idoneos vulgariter heemrade appellatos* (Stallaert, *Glossarium, sub voce Heemraad*). From the nature of their court they often settled disputes in the open, and in this way arose the erroneous idea that the word *heemraden* was derived from *hemel* (open sky), as though heemraden only sat under the open sky. When the early Dutch settlers came to the Cape they called the president of their court landdrost, and the members heemraden. Why they selected the term heemraden in preference to schepenen or mannen I have not been able to find out. It may be because the original courts were engaged in delimitations of boundaries, or because some of the early settlers were seafaring folk from the districts where heemraden was the usual term for the members of the court.

In criminal matters the Placita Generalia took cognisance of all cases which fell under what was called the *bloedban* (blood ban). This included murder, arson with intent to murder (*moordbrand*), wounding with intent, rape, kidnapping of women, robbery, and serious cases of theft. The trial was before the king or special officer appointed by him (*e.g.* the count) and the judges of fact were the freemen. There is a *capitularium* of Charlemagne which specially prohibits the local judges, such as the gaugraven or markgraven, from trying such cases: *Nullus homo in placito centenarii neque ad mortem neque ad libertatem suam ammittendam aut ad res reddendas vel mancipia judicetur sed ista in praesentia comitis judicetur* (*Cap.* Car. M. iii, 812 A.D. c. 4). Gradually, however, as the territorial power of the various courts and landsheeren increased they either obtained the right of *bloedban* from the emperor or else they assumed it without special leave being granted. The smaller feudal lords, however, had no right of *bloedban*. Hence it became the practice for the overlord either to go from place to place in person or to send some official to hold circuit courts in his province. In these courts the more serious crimes were tried.

Some towns possessed courts (*schepenbanken*) with full powers; these had both civil and criminal jurisdiction. Others, again, had *schepenbanken* for trying civil cases only. Here the criminal jurisdiction was exercised by some special circuit judge. In the country (*platte land*) we must distinguish between those district courts which were composed of freemen and those of which the members were persons with a qualified freedom (*hofhoorigen*). In the former case from very ancient times the courts had criminal jurisdiction to a certain limited extent. In the case of the *hofhoorigen*, however, the courts had no criminal jurisdiction, though in the course of time they obtained this by virtue of special handvesten (Van den Berg, 20–24; Noordewier, pp. 380 *et seq.*).

CHAPTER XX.

ADMINISTRATION OF JUSTICE.

Constitution of the ordinary courts during the thirteenth, fourteenth and fifteenth centuries.—As we have seen above, the old German procedure started with the fundamental principle that the free burgher could only be tried and condemned by those members of the tribe or nation who possessed the same status as himself. When the tribe was small no doubt all the freeborn members of the tribe took part in the trial, but, as the tribe gave place to the State or nation, only trials of extraordinary gravity were heard before the whole of the assembled people. Trials of less importance were relegated to the district council, and probably trifling offences tried before the hundred court. In any case, however, the accused was condemned by his equals and sentenced by the president of the court. In the case of the Great Council the king, as the representative of the executive power, announced the verdict of the people, and saw that the punishment was carried out. In the district and hundred courts presidents took the place of the king. We see, therefore, that the court was composed of a president corresponding to our judge, and of persons corresponding to our jurors who voted for the condemnation or acquittal of the prisoner.

In various cities of the Netherlands, however, especially in Holland and Zeeland, courts were also held once a year by a judge appointed by the count. Inasmuch as these courts were not open to the public, and as the accused were charged not openly by the complainant, but by an officer of the court, they were called *stille waarheden*. In time they came to be so hated by the citizens of the free towns as partaking of the nature of a *veemgericht*, that many of the charters specially forbid the holding of *stille waarheden*, except in the cases of murder, and arson with intent to murder (*moord* and *moord brand*). During the fifteenth century these courts gradually disappeared, and all cases were tried in the open courts (*openbare vierscharen*).

In Holland the fountain of justice was the count. He derived his jurisdiction during the Frankish period from the Carolingian monarchs, and later from the emperors. During the thirteenth and fourteenth centuries the presidents of the various minor courts were appointed by the count. The principal courts were the court of baljuw and mannen and the court of schout and schepenen. The former was in the early days the most important, but later on, as the towns obtained their privileges, the court of schout and schepenen became as important as that of baljuw and mannen. In some parts of Holland (*e.g.* Kennemerland) certain persons skilled in law were appointed to assist the courts with their judgment. This advice might be given either verbally or in writing—*zijn tuijg doen onder zijn zegel* (Fock. And. vol. 4, p. 304).

In civil cases the courts of baljuw and schout were of equal jurisdiction. No one could be cited except before his usual judge (*dagelijksche rechter*) whether baljuw or schout. Nobles, however, had the privilege of refusing to appear before schout and schepenen, unless these were well born, and of insisting upon their cause being heard before a baljuw and welgeborene mannen.

The court of schout and schepenen always took cognisance of questions regarding immovable property, whoever the parties might be. In criminal matters the court of the baljuw had jurisdiction over all crimes, whilst the court of the schout had jurisdiction over smaller delicts only. In the large towns, however, the jurisdiction of the court of the schout was equivalent to that of the baljuw (Fock. And. pp. 304 *et seq.*).

The above remarks are general, but it would be wrong to suppose that they applied to every district and town of Holland. In Amstelland, Gooiland and Waterland the courts of schout and schepenen had a very extended jurisdiction in civil and criminal matters, whereas in Kennemerland and South Holland the court of the baljuw was the more important.

We shall now pass over to consider the constitution of the ordinary courts during the fourteenth, fifteenth and sixteenth centuries. The courts were not like ours, composed of expert lawyers. The president or judge was the representative of the count, and the other members were appointed either by the count or, where some special privilege existed, by the people. The president had no voice in the judgment; this was the function of the rest of the court. These courts differed, therefore, from an English judge and jury court, where the judge supplies the law and the jury simply find the facts.

(1) *The judges of fact.*—Originally the only persons who could act as judges of fact were freemen of the tribe. The trial was *coram populi multitudine* or *coram maxima parte populi istius provinciae,* as it is expressed in documents of the tenth and eleventh centuries. It was impossible, however, for this

practice to continue, and during the Frankish monarchy, instead of the whole body of freemen acting as judges of fact, a certain number was chosen. These were called by the Franks *rachimburgii* or *rachineburgii*, which probably meant counsellors. On what principle they were selected we do not know. When a cause was tried according to the Salic law seven or more of these rachimburgii took their seats on the bench (*rachineburgii sedentes*), whilst the rest of the panel apparently stood around (*rachineburgii circumstantes*) (Noordewier, p. 94; Fock. And. *Bijd.* vol. 4, p. 26). Grimm (*R.A.* p. 775) quotes an old formula regarding these rachineburgii: *Praesentibus quam pluribus viris venerabilibus rachimburgis qui ibidem ad universorum causas audiendum vel recta judicia terminandum residebant vel adstabant.*

The duties of those who sat are fairly clear—they were the judges of fact; but the duties of those who stood around are obscure. Some (Schroeder, p. 168; Fock. And. p. 27) think they merely agreed or disagreed, though the practical difficulties of this view are great. Suppose the sitting rachimburgii found the prisoner guilty, and those standing around thought him innocent, what was to happen? It seems to me more likely that there was a body of men called rachimburgii who were appointed to act as judges; from these a panel was chosen (*rachimburgii sedentes*) to try the particular case; and the rest stood around (*rachimburgii circumstantes*) so as to be available for some other case.

It is doubtful whether rachineburgii existed in the Netherlands. Their place was probably taken by the scabini; Dutch, *schepenen;* French, *échevins;* German, *schöffe.* The schepenen date back to the reign of Charlemagne (Grimm, *R.A.*

p. 775). They differed from the rachineburgii in so far that they were permanently appointed to act as such, whilst the latter were only appointed as rachineburgii sedentes for a certain case, or number of cases. The word scabinus is derived from *scapan-ordinare decernere, cf.* Dutch, *scheppen* (Noordewier, p. 356). Originally they were chosen by the king's representatives (*missi*) with the approval of the people—*ut missi nostri ubicumque malos scabinos inveniunt, ejiciant et totius populi consensu in loco eorum bonos eligant.* Gradually, however, different methods of election prevailed in the various districts and towns. Sometimes they were elected by the people, sometimes by the count and the people, whilst at other times by the count alone. Thus in Staveren in the Veluwe the count elected the schepenen, in Nijmegen the election was by the people, whilst in Zalt Bommel the count elected one-half and the people the other half. The *Capitularia* enacted that for the smaller courts there should be seven schepenen and for the larger twelve. Gradually, however, the numbers varied; thus at Zutphen, Arnhem, Nijmegen and other towns there were twelve schepenen, Venlo had nine, Zalt Bommel had eight, whilst Delft had seven. On the whole, however, seven and twelve were the usual numbers (Van den Berg, pp. 27 *et seq.*).

The schepenen were appointed for a certain fixed period, generally a year, and could be dismissed if they did not do their duties properly. No one could be appointed to the office unless he was a free and well-born citizen of certain means. He had to belong to a class known as *schepenbare mannen. Nec scultetus nec scabinus debet esse nisi nobilis et bene natus nisi scabini de aggere* (*i.e.* proprietors of land). In

Zeeland schepenen were required to own at least fourteen morgen of land (Van Mieris, *G.C.B.* 1, 518). In time, however, persons came to be appointed as schepenen who did not possess the above qualifications. After their appointment they took an oath of office and could then be punished if they refused to act (Van den Berg, p. 29). In Friesland the schepenen were called *azigen.* Grimm tells us that *azig* meant lawgiver. It is from these two words that we get the well-known Schependoms recht and Aasdoms recht (Van den Berg, p. 31). Though schepenen were appointed by Charlemagne, we must not conclude that the people were completely deprived of their right to try their fellow citizens. Up to the thirteenth century we find this right asserted in various landrechten and keuren. The free burghers who took part in the trial had to take an oath that they would give an impartial verdict, and were consequently called *gezworenen* or *witachtige mannen.* Thus Van Mieris (*G.C.B.* 1, 535) quotes a landrecht of Kennemerland: *Waer dat een man ghewondt worde of ghequetset daer sal die Rechter ende die gezworen toe komen ende die wonde oft die quetsinge bezien ende bij heuren rade dat te beschuldigen alst redelijk is.* The verdict of the *gezworenen* was known as *stille waarheid.* In Zeeland the number was limited to forty-four in the west Schelde, and twenty-four in the east Schelde (Van den Berg, p. 33). The schepenen gave their verdict upon the whole case, law as well as fact, and differed therefore in this respect from an English jury.

(2) *The president or judge.*—There were two classes of courts in the early days, the court where the freeman and the court where the half-free or the serf (*hofhoorigen*) was tried.

In the former case the judge was the president of the court, and was obliged to speak the doom which the people, the rachineburgii or the schepenen decreed. In the latter case the judge was competent to find the facts and pronounce the doom himself. It is to the latter class that our inferior magistrates owe their origin.

In earliest times the chief or king presided at the *mallum*. During the Frankish monarchy the king usually presided at least once a year at the great council. In time this became impossible, and he deputed various high-placed officials to preside at the various courts held in his dominions. In the Netherlands the great courts were presided over by the hereditary counts. The lesser courts of freemen were presided over by vice-counts, markgraven, baljuws, drossaats, or schouten. In Holland the president of the court of schepenen was usually the schout. Hence these courts came to be known as the courts of the schout and schepenen. This word schout (Latin, *scultetus*) is connected with the word *schuld*, meaning a debt or obligation. In Germany these officers were known as *dorffs schulzen* or *gerichts schulzen*. A schout is therefore equivalent to a *schuld invorderaar*, or person who saw that debtors paid their debts (Noordewier, p. 338). He was the representative of the count, and presided over the court in the name of the count. When dealing with the procedure of these courts we must dismiss from our minds the idea of a single judge hearing evidence and then giving a judgment. The schout never sat alone; he simply directed the schepenen to hear the charge against the accused or the plaint against the defendant. The court, therefore, of the *scultetus cum scabinis* was the original form of the delegated jurisdiction

L

of the counts. In time, as we shall see, the court of schout and schepenen came to be regarded as the special court for town and village.

In the country district, or, as it is called in Dutch books, *het platte land*, the administration of justice was entrusted to the baljuw en mannen, baljuw en goede or welgeboren mannen or in feudal language to the baljuw and leenmannen (Hofdijk, *Voor Ouders*, vol. 4, p. 45; Van Leeuwen, *Manier van Procedeeren*). Besides these courts there were special courts, such as the courts of waldgraven, dijkgraven, watergraven, heigraven and markenrigters. The jurisdiction of these courts was confined to subjects relating to forests, dykes, sluices, waterways, &c. In some places the baljuw was called marschalk, in others drossaat or drost, from which we in South Africa took our word land-drost.

In Gelderland, Brabant, Drenthe and Overijssel the drost or drossaat was the equivalent of the schout. In Overijssel the schout was at first called *schulte*, afterwards *drost*. In Zutphen he was sometimes called drossaat or drost and at other times landdrost (Fock. And. *Bijd.* vol. 4, pp. 233, 278). The drossaat was originally a seneschal or marshal, and he was called in mediæval Latin a *senescallus, oeconomus* or *drossartus*. His duties were partly administrative and partly judicial, though in time his judicial functions became the more important. In Brabant he was called a chief judge, *opper gerechtsheer* or *haut justicier*. His office was called the *drossaerdij* or *drossaartschap* (Stallaert, *Glossarium, sub voce Drossaat*). In the Cape Colony the drosdy originally meant the district over which the landdrost had jurisdiction, but afterwards it came to be applied to his residence, *i.e.* his office was confused with his dwelling. When the courts of justice were established at the Cape the president of the court of the Cape district was called landdrost. Why this name was selected for the president of the court instead of the more usual schout or baljuw I have not been able to discover. In the Indies the more common term schout was apparently adopted.

The schout was appointed by the count, and his duties appear to have been both judicial and administrative. In this respect he resembled our resident magistrate, though, unlike our magistrate, he could not act judicially without the assistance of the schepenen. In the towns the schout and schepenen looked after the well-being of the citizens, saw that the city was properly policed and made such regulations as are usually made with us by municipal councillors.

The court of schout and schepenen came in time to be the ordinary court of first instance in civil matters (Merula, p. 95; Hofdijk, vol. 4, p. 171). Before this court all questions between poorters, burghers and domiciled inhabitants were brought, unless by some privilege as to the person or cause of action the matter could be brought in the first instance before some superior court without going to the schout and schepenen.

As the towns grew in importance and bought or earned their distinctive privileges, the right to appoint schout and schepenen was surrendered by the counts to them, and in this way a great number of towns came to appoint their own magistrates. In 1587 the duties of schout and schepenen were set out in the following terms: "The duty of the burgomaster is to deal with all political matters as well in the administration of the property and finances of the town, as in such things as appertain to the general welfare and peace of the town; the schepenen as a rule see to the administration of justice in criminal as well as civil cases, and they exercise a jurisdiction in great matters as well as in small" (*G.P.B.* vol. 1, p. 44). After the secession from the Spanish rule it was in Holland a *sine quâ non* that schepenen should be of the Protestant religion (Van Leeuwen, *Manier van Procedeeren*; Kersteman, *sub voce Collegie van schout en schepenen*).

(3) *Other officers of the court.*—The orders of the judge were carried out by the *bode*, who usually carried a rod before the judge (Van Mieris, 4, 217). He was not a messenger in the ordinary meaning of the word. He often combined the functions of the registrar and of the clerk of the court. In the larger courts the principal officials were the *griffier* or registrar, the *bode* or messenger, and the *deurwaarder* or process-server. In many respects the latter resembled our sheriff (Van Mieris, 2, 419; 4, 217).

In the middle ages, and even as late as the thirteenth century, the execution of the judge's sentence or order was carried out either by the complainant or, strange as it may appear to us, by the judge himself. Thus in one of the keuren of Zeeland (Van Mieris, 1, 303, 517) dated 1256 we find the following: *Qui cumque furtum vel rapinam fecerit si cum recenti furto captus fuerit statim ille qui cepit eum si adeo potens fuerit quod eum suspendere possit presente sculteto et judicio scabinorum infra ortum solis et occasum solis suspendet eum, sed si hoc fecere non possit tradet eum sculteto qui eum cum hominibus officii suspendet.* I have little doubt that what the old writers meant by saying that the judge must execute the culprit unless the complainant chose to do so, was nothing more than that the judge was responsible for the carrying out of the execution in the same way as the sheriff is with us.

About this time, however, it became customary to appoint a special hangman to conduct the execution of condemned persons. He was called a *hangdief*, and later a *scherprechter*. In Nijmegen his assistants were called *klick steenen;* these were entitled to the underclothing of the person executed (Van den Berg, p. 41).

CHAPTER XXI.

ADMINISTRATION OF JUSTICE (*continued*).

Courts of appeal.—The counts of Holland recognised at a very early date the danger of allowing the judgment of a lower court to become *res judicata* immediately after its pronouncement. The judges were often not skilled in the law; family and other interests produced bias and prejudice, and therefore an opportunity was given to bring the decisions of the lower courts in review. The one method adopted to arrive at a sound judgment we have already mentioned. I allude to the Hofvaart. It was not an appeal at the instance of one of the parties, but a reference on the part of the court itself to men considered more skilled in legal matters.

The *Capitularia* of the Carolingian monarchs are the first authorities which mention the right of appeal. No doubt the older Franks had some similar institution, but we find no trace of it in the *Lex Salica* or the *Lex Ripuaria*. The *Capitularia* provide that the court of the count is to hear all appeals from the local courts, whilst the *missi imperatoris*, or royal representatives, are entitled to review the decisions of the counts. The ultimate court of appeal was the king or king and council (*Capit.* v, Lud. Pii. A.D. 819; *Capit.* ii, Lud. Pii, A.D. 819, c. 15).

When the counts of Holland became hereditary the *missi* disappeared, and the court of the count became the national court of appeal for the Netherlands. From the count, however, an appeal still lay to the king or emperor. The count, therefore, reviewed all such decisions of the baljuw and mannen, and of the schout and schepenen, as were brought before him on appeal. It was naturally impossible for the count to attend personally to all this business, and he got over the difficulty by delegating these matters to some high nobles of his court, with the assistance of men skilled in the law. Some of these assessors were laymen, but a great number of them were ecclesiastics, and as these representatives, at any rate during the thirteenth and fourteenth centuries, were acquainted with the laws of Justinian and the Canon law, it was but natural that they should have resorted to the principles of the Roman law in deciding appeals.

The count and his court in the old days travelled about from place to place, and litigants never knew where an appeal would be heard. This became a grievance in the fourteenth century, and several requests were made to the counts to fix the court of appeal at some definite place. Several towns acquired the privilege of a fixed court of appeal, but as the count was usually in person in the province of Holland, no fixed court of appeal was established there, though in practice most appeals were heard at the Hague. The Court of the Hague came, therefore, to be recognised as the court of appeal for Holland, but it was apparently not until the fifteenth century that the Court of Holland, Zeeland and West Friesland was first established. The exact date at which this occurred is a matter of considerable dispute (Merula, bk. 4, tit. 1, ch. 1, p. 161, *in notis*).

De Haas contends that the Court of Holland, or the Provincial Court, as it was sometimes called to distinguish it from the Supreme Court shortly afterwards established at Mechlin was founded long before 1429. Grotius, Bynkershoek, Lulius and Van der Linden, on the other hand, are of opinion that the Court of Holland was first established by Philip the Good in 1429. Philip himself in a letter written in 1445 says that some time previous to that date he had established a court at the Hague for Holland, Zeeland and West Friesland. *Comme pour le gouvernement en justice de nos pays, contes et seigneuries de Hollande, Zeelande et Frise nous avons puis aucun temps ença ordinné un président et certain nombres de conseillers en nôtre ville de la Haye en Hollande* (Van der Linden's *Jud. Prakt.* vol. 1, p. 43). Dr. Blok is of opinion that the Court of Holland (*De Raad* or *Het Hof van Holland* or *De Provinciale Raad*) dates back to the days of the hereditary counts, but that prior to 1429 the court was not necessarily assisted by jurists (Blok, *Eene Holl. Stad,* p. 387).

The court of 1429 consisted of five noblemen, with power to add certain jurists to their number if they required legal assistance. That they did so appears from a certain Middelburg case referred to by Van Mieris (*G.C.B.* vol. 4, p. 1023). It must not be supposed that the nobles who were appointed as judges of the court were necessarily ignorant of law, for legal studies formed part of a liberal education in those days. In 1436 two jurists sat as permanent members of the court. In 1440 the jurists had increased to four. Shortly before 1462 the Court of Holland was composed of ten or twelve members. Of these four or five were jurists, others high officials, and the rest nobles.

In 1462, however, all the members of the court were dismissed and a new court constituted. This court consisted of a president and eight members; of these seven were jurists and one a nobleman. The eight were said to be *notable mannen wel bezocht ende geexperimenteert in saecken van justitie.* The *Instructie* of 1462 not only reformed the old court, but laid down a set of rules for its guidance; these we shall see in a later chapter became the *Instructies van den Hove* upon which our present practice is partly moulded. From 1462 onwards lawyers predominated in the Court of Holland, until eventually in 1510 the nobles were completely excluded. From that date the Court of Holland was composed entirely of jurists taken from the college of advocates or from the professors of the universities. The *Instructies* of 1531 show that it was at that date a court of justice and a court of appeal composed entirely of lawyers and conducted upon the same principles as our modern courts. In fact if we adopted to-morrow the rules of court of 1531 our procedure would be more cumbersome, but our cases would still be carried on in all essentials as they are conducted under our present rules of court.

To this court was attached a number of minor officials called secretaries or clerks of the registers. One of these secretaries was the *griffier* or registrar. He was always a jurist of repute, and was often promoted to a seat on the bench. The financial administration was entrusted to a board called the *Rekenkamer*, consisting of two *Meesters der Reekeningen.* The Attorney-General (*Procureur-generaal*) and the Advocaat-Fiscaal were since 1462 subordinate officers of the court. The messengers and process-servers (*boden* and *deurwaarders*) completed the list of functionaries attached to the court (Blok, *Hol. Stad*, pp. 387 *et seq.*).

Since 1429 the Court of Holland sat at the Hague as a

fixed court of appeal. It was not a court of appeal for all the Netherlands, but only for the provinces of Holland, Zeeland and West Friesland. At a later date the court was composed of a president and eleven members called *Raadsheeren;* of these eight had to be Hollanders and three Zeelanders (Van der Linden's *Jud. Prakt.* vol. 1, p. 44).

The jurisdiction of the Court of Holland was both civil and criminal, and the court was a court of appeal as well as a court of first instance. It took cognisance of all cases in which the rights and privileges of the States were involved, as well as those of the nobles and other privileged persons born in these States. The Court of Holland was the court of first instance for all the officers of the court, such as the registrar, secretaries, advocates, attorneys and clerks. Cases brought by widows, orphans, paupers and other privileged persons could be heard before the Provincial Court in the first instance. All unmarried women, and women in needy circumstances, could pass by their ordinary magistrate and come direct to the Provincial Court. The Provincial Court was also a court of appeal and revision for all judgments, civil or criminal, which had been pronounced by any judge in the three provinces. This Court of Holland became one of the most renowned courts of Europe, as will appear from the fact that several European potentates, who had nothing to do with the Netherlands, on various occasions requested this court to decide their private disputes (Kersteman, *sub voce Hof van Holland*).

Besides establishing the Court of Holland on a sound basis, Philip the Good, in furtherance of his policy of unification and centralisation, established the Supreme Court at Mechlin. It was founded in 1446, but it first obtained its jurisdiction as a court of appeal in 1455. This court was established in order to have one central court of appeal and revision for all the different provinces, over which the House of Burgundy ruled. It was known as De Groote Raad, De Hooge Raad van Mechelen, or Le Grand Conseil de Malines. It was the supreme court of appeal for the whole of the Netherlands. It was not exclusively a judicial body, but, like the Parliament of Paris, was endowed with administrative powers and a control of the State finances. The towns were strongly opposed to Philip's policy because the court encroached upon their liberties and privileges, especially upon their treasured right that a burgher could not be compelled to appear before any but his daily judge—the celebrated *jus de non evocando.*

Charles the Bold carried out the policy of his father, and was determined, notwithstanding the opposition of the towns, to create a strong central court. He separated in 1473 its financial administration from its judicial functions, and established the supreme court of appeal of Mechlin with a jurisdiction over all the provinces of the Netherlands. It consisted of thirty-six members, and was presided over by the chancellor or by one of his two deputies. Of the thirty-six members several were ecclesiastics and a large number jurists. It exercised the functions of a supreme court of all the Netherlands until 1582 (Van Beijnen, *Staats regeling,* p. 27; Poullet, *Origines,* vol. 2, pp. 250 *et seq.*). Its decisions as collected by Christinaeus have always been regarded as of high authority.

After the establishment of the Republic the Court of Mechlin ceased to exercise any jurisdiction or influence over the northern provinces. In its stead was established

Supreme Court of Holland, Zeeland and West Friesland. It was known as the Hoogen Raade or Hoogen Raade van Holland, Zeeland en West Friesland. It was composed of a president and nine members, of whom six were always Hollanders and three Zeelanders. It became very soon a court of great importance, and its president, whose election was a weighty matter full of great and solemn ceremony, was regarded as one of the highest officers of state.

All judgments of the Provincial Court could be brought before the Supreme Court by way of appeal or review. The usual practice with regard to appeals was to bring a case heard by the local magistrate, first before the Provincial Court and then before the Supreme Court, but certain towns were privileged to bring their appeals direct from the local magistrate to the Supreme Court, without first going to the Court of Holland. The Supreme Court was, however, not only a court of appeal, it was also a court of first instance in the following matters: (1) disputes arising between foreign merchants who had no domicile in Holland, Zeeland or West Friesland; (2) in all matters where by law or custom no appeal was allowed; (3) in all admiralty and maritime cases. The Supreme Court also took the place of the sovereign power in giving relief against unlawful and immoral contracts, in granting the benefits of inventory and of *cessio bonorum*. If litigants agreed to submit their disputes to the Supreme Court, then the court could consent to hear the matter in the first instance and so pass by the ordinary judge, though this permission was only granted in very weighty matters (Kersteman, *sub voce Hoogen Raad;* Merula, bk. 1, tit. 6, c. 1, n. 13, *in notis*).

Besides the Supreme Court of the Union, and the Court of Holland, the provinces of Utrecht, Gelderland, Friesland, Overijssel, and later Groningen and Drenthe, each had a superior court of its own to which appeals were brought from the lower courts. In addition to these were the Council of Brabant, the Council of Flanders, and the Raad van Staaten. The latter was a body with both administrative and judicial duties. It was a court of first instance regarding public property and revenue, and a court of appeal from the colonies and from the Council of Flanders. As a rule it referred the appeals to the Hooge Raad and the Council of Brabant respectively, and then pronounced the judgment of these courts (Maasdorp's *Introduction to Grotius*, p. xxvi).

The establishment of permanent courts sitting at the Hague had a great effect in fixing the Roman law as the common law of Holland. It was a source of constant complaint that the Provincial and Supreme Courts did not sufficiently respect the local laws and customs of the towns from which the appeals were brought (Hofdijk, v, 7). These courts tended to centralise the administration of justice and to introduce uniformity not only in the procedure, but also in the law. The judges looked more to the Roman law, with its well-developed system of jurisprudence, than to the numerous local laws and customs of the various places from which the suits were brought. The decisions of the superior courts were binding on the inferior courts, and in this way the Dutch jurists were enabled to build up on the foundations of the Roman law their own magnificent system of jurisprudence.

CHAPTER XXII.

DEVELOPMENT OF PROCEDURE.

THE procedure of the courts during the Frankish Empire is but very imperfectly known to us. It was entirely different from the procedure of our modern courts. With us there is a great deal of formality in the preparation of the trial, and the hearing of a cause forms but a small part of its actual course. In the middle ages, on the contrary, outside of the actual hearing in the court there was very little formal procedure. The matter to be tried by the judge or judges, whether civil or criminal, was regarded in the light of a duel. The plaintiff or complainant was the attacking, and the defendant or accused the defending party. The judge determined who was the winner.

The self-help procedure of early times was gradually disappearing, though here and there traces of it still remained. The judge was called in to arbitrate instead of allowing the injured person and his relatives to take the matter in their own hands. At first the judge only exercised his jurisdiction when the parties both appeared before him. Where the defendant refused to appear the procedure of self-help was still often resorted to. In time, however, on a refusal to appear the principle of self-help received legal sanction from the judge.

The principle that the court sees to the execution of its sentence belongs to modern ideas of jurisprudence. The principle of the middle ages was to deprive the obstinate defendant of the protection of the law. Every opportunity was to be given to the defendant to appear before the judge, and mere absence, unless it was wilful, was not regarded as a confession of guilt or of being in the wrong. There were two reasons for this. The first was that self-help had given place to the judge, and the idea that he was merely an arbitrator had not yet disappeared; and the second was that freedom was sacred to the German people, and a freeman was not to be lightly placed under a ban. Three times at least, and then at considerable intervals, he had to be called to appear before he could be condemned as a defaulter. This tenderness towards the defendant always formed a marked feature in the procedure of the Dutch courts. It prevailed in the Cape Colony before our modern rules of court were promulgated. If the defendant persisted in his default the sovereign could declare him first a provisional outlaw (*vor ban*), and later on a complete outlaw (*ban*).

Gradually, however, the procedure of the Roman law and of the Canon law modified the simple practice of the Franks. Formalism became an important feature in the conduct of a suit. The slightest departure from the due order brought with it the danger of losing a case. The very procedure was known as legal danger (*Rechtsgefahr*, *vare*, *insidia verborum*) (Schröder, pp. 359 *et seq.*, 765 *et seq.*). The strictness of the procedure was, however, not so great in the Netherlands as in Germany, and in time the latitude allowed to the Flemish merchants seems to have helped to break down the formalism of pleading (Schröder, p. 765).

There is very little doubt that the procedure of choosing a

particular kind of action by formula existed in Holland as it did in Germany. Actions were not scientifically classified, though on the whole we may say that they were divided into actions for payment of debt and actions for recovery of property. For this purpose there were a number of actions available to the plaintiff. These were called *formulae,* though they had nothing in common with the formulary system of the Romans. They derived their origin from Frankish procedure, and were in many respects similar to the writs of the old English courts. Here are a few of their names: "*Malo ordine possides,*" e.g. *Petre, te appellat Martinus, quod terra quae in tali loco est sua est et tu eam possides malo ordine;* "*Dare mihi debes;*" "*Quod tu conventasti mihi solvere,*" &c. The defendant's answer was also couched in the form of a formula thus to the claim, *Tenes malo ordine terram meam,* &c.; the plea was, *Ipsa terra mea est propria per successionem de parte patris mei or per usumfructum,* &c. (Heusler, *Institutionen Klagensystem,* vol. 1, p. 384).

The Church courts disregarded these formulae, and strove to settle disputes with as little technicality as possible. The views of the canonists gradually gained ground in this respect, and as commerce increased the extremely technical form of pleading gradually gave place to our modern system.

During the Frankish period there was very little difference between civil and criminal procedure, but during the twelfth and thirteenth centuries a distinction came to be drawn between these classes of cases. Civil actions came to be divided into those by which debts were claimed, those which were brought for the recovery of property, and those in which an inheritance formed the subject of a suit. No proper distinction was drawn between criminal matters and delicts. Hence an action for the recovery of stolen property was partly a civil *vindicatio*, partly a claim for damages, and partly an inquiry into crime. It was only during the latter portion of the middle ages that our modern conception of the State prosecuting the criminal began to dawn. I shall now pass over to the procedure in the lower courts during the thirteenth and fourteenth centuries.

Procedure in court.—The judge, baljuw, schout or drost, and the schepenen or goedemannen sat on the bench. Behind the judge was hung a shield; he held a rod in his hand whilst before him lay a naked sword. In many courts besides a sword were added as symbols of his office iron gloves, a rope and an axe. A cord or rod was drawn so as to separate the bench from the public. The proceedings began by the judge asking the schepenen, "Is it the right time to open the court?" The schepenen answered, "It is." The judge then said, "Is there a quorum?" To which the schepenen replied, "There is" (*i.e.* there is a majority of them present). This formula was in actual use in Amsterdam during the eighteenth century. The judge then enjoined silence, and the breach of that order was followed by severe punishment. After that no one might enter or leave the court without leave of the judge. The plaintiff and defendant or complainant and accused stood. In the Landrecht of Nieuwbroek, 1328, they are ordered *tho recht staen,* and so they are represented in the miniatures of that period (Noordewier, p. 397; Van den Berg, p. 43).

If there was a criminal charge against an accused then the complainant, who must be a freeman, was bound to appear with a naked sword and clad in armour. If the accused repelled the charge he also appeared fully armed, though if he admitted the charge, but pleaded some excuse, he appeared bare headed and barefoot, in his shirt, without armour and without weapons—*ende hem onschuldigen wil, die sal komen ant gericht in eenen hemde, bloots hoovds, bairvoets . . . sunder ijser of staal* (*Pro excol.* vol. 1, p. 389; Van den Berg, p. 43). The complainant (*clamans*) called the defendant before the court and made his claim or laid his charge. The defendant or accused denied the claim or repelled the charge. If the charge was one of murder the complainant brought the corpse into court, and addressing the judge said, "I have brought you here my dead brother (or other relative), do you believe the corpse is here?" The judge then answered, "I do." Some official then shouted, "Vengeance, vengeance, vengeance" (*wraeck*). Thereupon the usual formula for such a charge was read and the matter proceeded with. The claimant thereupon took an oath and gave security that he would not involve in this charge any but the accused or his accomplices (Matthaeus, *De Crim.* pp. 514 *et seq.*), and asked the judge to name a day for the trial (Van Mieris, 2, 29). If the complainant or accused was a priest, woman or child the judge appointed a representative to conduct the prosecution or defence. The reason for this was that neither priest, woman nor child could be challenged to single combat.

In course of time pleading by representative became the rule, so that from the fifteenth century onwards the defence was nearly always conducted by a special class of representatives called *procuratores, procureurs* or *taalmannen.* As a general rule if there was no plaintiff or claimant the case was dismissed, *geen Klager, geen rechter.* In some cases, however, the State took up the prosecution through the baljuw, or in the ecclesiastical courts through the bishop (Noordewier, p. 398). The complainant then took an oath, told his tale, and called upon his relatives and friends to substantiate the value of his oath. These were called *eedhelpers* (oath helpers), *mede-zwerenden, volgers* or *conjuratores.* They no doubt owe their origin to the old German custom of the family undertaking to avenge the death of one of its members. The family received part of the wergeld, and from this it followed they were bound to assist in the recovery of it. The conjuratores were, so to speak, the sureties for the complainant; they swore that they accepted the oath of their relative or friend as true (Van den Berg, 1, p. 45). The conjuratores were not witnesses in our sense of the word. They might or might not have known anything of the charge. All they practically did was to say, "We are convinced that the claimant's charge is well founded, for he is a man worthy of belief." Towards the end of the fifteenth century their presence lost its weight, and they gradually disappeared in the towns, though in the country we sometimes find them as late as the sixteenth century (Van den Berg, p. 48).

To substantiate his oath the complainant called the witnesses to the act or crime. These were freemen mostly from the neighbourhood or from the same mark. Not only did they testify to having been present at the occurrence, but to the worth of the complainant and to such matters as formed common knowledge. Rigid proofs such as we require in our courts were unknown in the fourteenth and fifteenth centuries. A witness to the fact (*oog of oorgetuige*) could be punished for perjury if he swore falsely, but a conjurator was not subjected to any penalty (Noordewier, p. 400). The usual number of witnesses to convict a freeman were three. Thus in the Keuren of Zierikzee and Middelburg (Van Mieris, 1, 242) we find the following provision in the thirteenth century: *Ubicunque tres legales homines aliquid viderint et juramento ammoniti fuerint hoc scabini testabuntur* (*cf.* Van Mieris, 1, 518, n. 88). Though this was the general rule there were of course many exceptions, and the gravity of the charge often determined the number of witnesses required for a conviction.

Besides proof by witnesses there existed the proof by ordeal (*Bewijs bij God's oordeel*). If a crime had been committed, but the proof was obscure, then our German ancestors believed that the gods as the highest judges could be appealed to in order to determine guilt or innocence. The English word "ordeal" is derived from the Anglo-Saxon *ordal,* old Frisian *ordel,* old German *urteil,* Dutch *oordeel.* It means, therefore, the god's *oordeel,* or the judgment of the gods. This procedure was based upon heathen practice; but after the introduction of Christianity it was taken over by the priests, and for the gods of the heathen was substituted the God of the Christians.

The principle was that there was some higher power which would protect the innocent and punish the guilty. In practice it was the person upon whom the onus lay of proving his innocence who could appeal to trial by ordeal. It has always been a principle of the German criminal law that the accused should be in a more favourable position than he complainant. This arose from the fact that freedom was regarded as inviolable (Noordewier, p. 400). Hence every difficulty was put in the way of the complainant. He was constantly hindered by formalities and technical requirements, so that the proof of guilt was made difficult and the proof of innocence rendered easy. The appeal to the ordeal, therefore, gave the accused an extra chance of escape. The means used were such as to impress the public with the innocence of the accused who successfully went through the ordeal. How often it took place and what its general effect was is obscure to us, for the chroniclers dwell mostly on the few cases of extraordinary success on the part of the accused (Noordewier, pp. 434 *et seq.*).

The principal forms of ordeal were: (1) Ordeal by fire. The accused had to hold his bare hand in the flames. If he was burnt he was guilty, if not he was innocent. (2) Ordeal by hot water. The accused had to plunge his bare arm and hand into boiling water and to extract some object like a ring or stone. (3) Ordeal by cold water. The accused was thrown in the water. If he floated he was guilty, if he sank he was innocent. (4) Cross ordeal. In this case both parties, complainant and accused, took part in the ordeal. They stood against a cross with uplifted hands; the one who let his hand fall first was the losing party. This form of ordeal was used in civil suits. It is said that Charlemagne and Radboud used this ordeal to determine to whom Friesland should belong. Charlemagne dropped his glove, Radboud picked it up, and so lost his cause. Whilst the contest went on the priests prayed and read the mass. (5) Ordeal by duel or trial by combat. This was the noblest form of ordeal, and was the origin of our modern duel. It was resorted to long after the other forms of ordeal had fallen into disuse or been applied to slaves and other persons of low degree. Its origin dates back to a very remote antiquity (Tacit. *Germ.* 7 and 10), and we sometimes find it employed to end the quarrels of nations, where the opposing chiefs fought instead of, and in the presence of, their followers. The towns, the great civilising centres, were the first to prohibit trial by combat. The Keur of Middelburg forbade it in 1217, and the Keur of Haarlem in 1245. Later on the maxim was adopted, *Kamprecht kwaadrecht,* and it became a general rule that *poorter mag poorter niet ten campe roepen* (burgher could not challenge burgher to combat). (6) *Baargericht.* If a murder had been committed, and one or more persons were strongly suspected, they could be compelled to approach the corpse and touch it. If it began to bleed afresh at the touch of the suspected person he was declared guilty. This ordeal was used in the middle ages, and survived until the fifteenth century. In one of the landrechten it is thus expressed: *Wie betegen of berucht word voer moert, die sal den dooden aantasten die vermoert is; onsculdiget voer God soe is hy onsculdich.* (7) Ordeal by the holy bite. The suspected person was bound, and a slice of bread placed in his mouth. If he managed to eat it he was innocent, but if it stuck in his throat he was considered guilty. In Anglo-Saxon it was called *corsnæd.* After the introduction of Christianity consecrated bread was used (Noordewier, pp. 437–443).

The law of evidence which prevailed in the courts of Holland before the sixteenth century was naturally crude. Gradually the courts began to adopt the rules of evidence which we find scattered through the *Corpus Juris.* In the seventeenth century, however, the law of evidence had attained a high degree of perfection, as will be found on reference to Matthaeus, *De Criminibus*, and Matthaeus, *De Probationibus*.

When the evidence had been heard by the court the schepenen had to declare to the schout how they found the case (*Hoe zij de zaak vonden*). It was their *vondenesse* or *vonnis* that they uttered. This *vonnis* or judgment not only found whether the accused was guilty, but also what penalty should be imposed upon him. In this respect the finding of the schepenen differed from the exclusive finding on fact of our jury. In another respect the schepenen differed materially from our jury. A jury is called upon to find the facts as they appear to them, and if they wish to know the law they must consult the judge; but the schepenen had the right in case of doubt to leave the court and make inquiries as to the law and the form of their judgment. They had the right to consult about the case or, as it was expressed, *raad halen; toeloop hebben; aan een kennige of hofvaart gaan; ordel ten hofvaart halen*. This right to seek counsel applied to civil as well as criminal cases. The schepenen would naturally not seek counsel on the facts, for of these they could judge as well as any other person; but as neither they nor the schout were learned in the law they were obliged to get their legal knowledge from some other quarter. In the days of Charlemagne the schepenen referred to the sacebarones or sapientes (Grimm's *R.A.* 783), but later on to the judicial officers at the court of the count, or even of the emperor. During the thirteenth and fourteenth centuries the laws of the towns or districts determined where the schepenen should go. Middelburg and Leyden required them to go direct to the count (Van Mieris, 1, 171). The smaller towns were required to consult the courts of the larger and older towns. Thus the schepenen of the smaller towns of Zeeland went to Middelburg, of Holland to Leyden or Haarlem, of Gelderland to Zutphen or Roermond. This practice did not mean that the courts of Leyden, Middelburg, &c., were courts of appeal for the smaller towns. It merely meant that the lawyers of the larger towns had greater experience, and were therefore capable of advising the courts of the smaller towns. The schepenen took the advice, and then gave their own judgment (Noordewier, p. 408; Van den Berg, pp. 121 *et seq.*).

During the fifteenth century permanent courts of appeal had been established in the Netherlands as well as in the provinces of Holland and West Friesland. The result of this was to systematise the practice of the courts and to build up a legal procedure on the lines of the Roman procedure, but adapted to the circumstances and customs of the people.

The procedure of the fifteenth century could not have differed very materially from that of the sixteenth century. The *Instructies van den Hove* (rules of court) of 1531 are founded upon the earlier Instructions of 1462 (*Rechts. Obs.* vol. 2, obs. 100). Hence the practice of the sixteenth century is based upon a practice which prevailed in the fifteenth century. It is difficult to conceive that after definite rules of practice were established in 1462 they would have been so entirely swept away in a hundred years as to have left no permanent mark on the later procedure. It is most unlikely that a practice similar to that of the *Instructies* of 1531 could have been invented in the space of a century. The probability is that during the fifteenth century the superior courts adopted a great deal of what was then the practice of the lower courts, and amended and amplified that practice by reference to the procedure of the Roman and Canon law.

As we have seen in a former chapter, the Canon law did a great deal towards simplifying the procedure of the courts. It elaborated a system of rules with regard to testimony which forms the basis of our modern law of evidence. It also helped to break down the formalism in pleading. The full effect of its influence was felt during the fourteenth and fifteenth centuries, so that the latter may be regarded as the transition period from the procedure of the middle ages to the modern practice. By the end of the fifteenth century, therefore, the practice of the courts was more or less similar to the procedure promulgated by the *Instructies* of 1531. The *Instructies* took over and improved what was good, and abandoned what was obsolete and cumbersome, and so laid what we may call the foundations of our modern practice.

CHAPTER XXIII.

PRACTICE OF THE COURTS AND WRITERS ON PRACTICE FROM THE SIXTEENTH CENTURY ONWARDS.

WE have detailed and accurate information of the procedure, both civil and criminal, of the various courts of Holland during the sixteenth century. The procedure of the lower courts in the towns as well as in the country was fixed towards the end of the sixteenth century by two Ordinances. In 1570 an Ordinance was passed known as the *Ordonantie over de Procedeeren van de Crimineele Saaken in de Nederlanden.* This regulated the criminal procedure throughout the Netherlands.

In 1580 an Ordinance was passed to regulate the civil procedure throughout the Netherlands. It was known as the *Ordonantie op 't stuk van de Justitie binnen de Steden en ten platte landen van Holland en West Friesland.* This Ordinance recited that great confusion had been caused throughout Holland by the different modes of procedure adopted by the various towns and districts, and, therefore, the States of Holland enacted that in future the procedure as laid down in this Ordinance should be followed in all the courts of Holland. *Dat van nu voortaen over geheel Holland voor alle vierscharen ofte geregten zoo wel van de steden, baljuwen en mannen, als schouten ende schepenen ofte gezworens van de dorpen geprocedeert zal worden navolgende d' Instructie hierna verklaard.* This procedure followed to a large extent the procedure that had been adopted by the superior courts. The first Instructions of the

Court of Holland that I know of are the *Instructies van den Hove van Holland, van 4 Sept.* 1462 (*Rechts. Obs.* vol. 2, obs. 100). I regret that I can give no account of these, as I have been unable to procure a copy. In 1531, however, Rules and Regulations were published by Charles V, known as the *Instructiën van den Hove van Holland, Zeeland en West Friesland.* These Instructions are very similar to a charter of justice and rules of court combined. The stadhouder is enjoined, together with the president and judges of the court, to see that law and justice are administered to all such as choose to seek the aid of the courts. The court is to see that all its judgments are carried out and that its orders are put into execution. In the absence of the stadhouder it was the duty of the president of the court to introduce the matter to be discussed, and then, after discussion, to take the vote of the judges and to pronounce the judgment of the court in accordance with the majority of votes. The president called the judges together, kept the seal, and had the general control of the court. In addition to their purely judicial duties the judges were also required to see that the baljuws, schouten, schepenen and other magistrates behaved themselves, and could, if need be, suspend them, especially in cases where magistrates allowed the nobles to oppress ecclesiastics, women or children. The Instructions also deal with the duties of the Attorney-General or Advocaat-Fiscaal, the registrar, the secretaries of the court, the advocates, attorneys, and other officers. The Instructions contain rules regulating the practice of the court. If an unsuccessful litigant wished to appeal from a lower court he must give notice of appeal within twenty days. The judge of the lower court was required to send up the record to the court of appeal, and execution was stayed provided sufficient security was given.

Another form of appeal was called *Provisie in cas van reformatie.* In this case the losing party could, within a year after judgment was given, come to the superior court and ask that court to review the decision of the lower court. If the court thought fit to grant *Provisie,* the respondent had to give security that he would restore what he had obtained by virtue of the judgment of the lower court. In order to avoid frivolous appeals the appellant could be mulcted not only in the costs of the suit and of the appeal, but also in a penalty of 30 guldens. As we have seen, it was a general rule that parties had, in the first instance, to go before the magistrate of their district or town (*voor hunnen dagelijkschen rechter*), and this was specially laid down in a rule of court. In certain cases, already referred to, they could come direct to the Provincial Court. In order to do this the plaintiff took out a summons returnable after fourteen days if the defendant lived in Holland, and three weeks if he lived in Zeeland. Then elaborate rules follow with reference to the various defaults allowed to a plaintiff or a defendant, and in this respect the rules of the Provincial Court differed greatly from our own. With us one default is enough to bar the other party from proceeding unless that default has been purged, but in the Court of Holland it was usual to require a series of defaults before the other party could take advantage of his opponent's non-appearance. The reason why so many defaults were allowed is no doubt historical, as has been explained in a former chapter. Courts are very slow to alter their procedure, and one century takes its procedure from a former century often in ignorance of the original reason. The *Instructiën* then dealt with the plea, the replication, their various defaults, and the particular way in which each had to be served. Special rules deal with the kinds of exceptions that may be made, and the manner in which documents are to be produced and proved.

Judgments are divided into interlocutory and final, and the effect of each kind is set out at length. After dealing with judgments, the rules proceed to state how these are to be put into execution, and in what cases execution can be stayed. The Instructions end up with a short account of criminal procedure. The language of these Instructions is very antiquated, and by no means easy to understand, but one is struck with the great similarity that exists between these Instructions of the sixteenth century and our modern rules of court. In some cases the very words of the old Instructions might stand for one of our rules of court. "If a party wishes to avoid the trial before the court or wishes to allege *lis pendens,* or that a suit is pending before another court, he must plead this by way of an exception, because if he neglects this he will not be allowed to do so afterwards unless the court determines otherwise" (No. 117). From time to time these Instructions were amended and revised, as, for instance, by the *Instructiën in Kleine zaken,* dated 21st December, 1579, those of 1580, and numerous others called *Ampliatiën.*

The first *Instructiën* of the Supreme Court, or Hoogen Raad, is dated 31st May, 1582. After dealing with the duties of the judges, the registrar, the secretaries, advocates and attorneys, we come to the procedure of the court. The first of the rules of procedure is as follows: "In the first place the judges shall cause the messengers (*deurwaarders*) to cry silence, and the advocates and attorneys shall take their seats according to rank, and shall not be permitted to walk or wander about, or to come up to the registrar's desk, unless their cases have been called, and if they do they shall be liable to the arbitrary penalty to be fixed by the court." We then get a set of rules dealing in detail with the procedure before the Supreme Court very similar in their general character to those of the Court of Holland.

We shall deal with the early procedure of the Cape courts in a later chapter.

CHAPTER XXIV.

THE PRACTITIONERS IN THE OLD DUTCH COURTS.

In a former chapter we have dealt with the judges and the lay members of the court. The other salaried officers of the court were the registrar or *griffier*, or, as he was sometimes called, the secretary, and the deurwaarders or process-servers. These were very much the same in the seventeenth century as we found them in the older courts. Besides these salaried officers were the legal practitioners, who were also regarded as officers of the court, but whose emoluments were not paid by the State, but by the litigants.

The classes of persons who practised before the old Dutch courts were very much the same as those who practise to-day before the South African courts. The pleader who addressed the court was not the same as the representative of the litigant, who saw that all the necessary steps in the lawsuit were properly taken. In other words, the functions of the advocate were distinct from those of the attorney. Besides these there was the notary, who took part in legal work of a non-litigious nature. These three—the advocate, the attorney and the notary—were officers of the court, and subject to its direct control. In case of improper conduct they could be deprived of the privilege of appearing before the court or preparing legal documents.

Advocates.—The word advocate is derived from the Latin *advocatus*, and means the person called to the side of another to render him some assistance. Thus Varro (*De re Rustica*, 2, 5) calls a person who is asked to witness the receipt of some money his *advocatus*. The persons who accompanied Caecina to take possession of his estate were called *advocati*. *Eodem tempore se in fugam conferunt una amici advocatique ejus* (Cicero, *Pro Caec.* ch. 8). Gradually, however, the meaning was specialised, and the term *advocatus* came to be applied to the person who undertook to assist litigants in court by speaking on their behalf. As the *patronus* usually pleaded the cause of his client, advocates were sometimes called *patroni*. Another term for an advocate was *orator*. The word *advocatus* is frequently met with in the *Digest*. Ulpian says, *Advocatos accipere debemus omnes omnino qui causis agendis quoquo studio operantur* (*D.* 50, 13, 11). We ought to regard as advocates those who apply themselves to pleading causes. Such persons are said *advocationem praebere* or *praestare*, to offer their advocacy to those who required their services.

In early times they acted gratuitously, and their only reward was fame or the good opinion of their fellow-citizens. Gradually the practice of gratuitously pleading causes disappeared, and in imperial times the advocates received fees, though these were often disguised as loans (*C.* 2, 6, 3), showing that it was still regarded dishonourable to receive an emolument. The *Lex Cincia* had specially forbidden advocates or senators to accept fees *ne quis ob causam orandam pecuniam donumve accipiat*. Though during the period of the early emperors gratuitous practice was more honoured in the breach than in the observance, yet so as not to shock public opinion there was a constant pretence that advocates rendered their services gratuitously. The charges of advocates had become so excessive that during the reign of Claudius the consul Silius proposed to the Senate to renew the provisions of the *Lex Cincia*, and to compel advocates to render their services free of charge. The arguments for and against the practice of paying fees to advocates are set out by Tacitus in his *Annals* (bk. 2, c. 6 and 7). The Senate limited the charge of an advocate to *dena sestertia*.

In the days of Charlemagne the *advocatus* was no longer a pleader of causes, but a defender and protector of the Church: the pleader took the name of *causidicus* (Du Cange, *sub voce Advocatus*). The question as to what fees should be paid to advocates was a constant source of legislative attention. Beaumanoir says of the old French advocates: *Ils doivent estre paiés par journées selon ce que il sevent (savent) et selonc leur estat et selonc che que lequerelle est grant ou petite . . . car il n'est pas raison que chel que peu set (sait) ait autant que chel qui set assez* (ch. 5). This sensible practice was the one adopted by the courts of the Netherlands.

Advocates were responsible for what they said in court unless instructed by their clients to use the language employed by them. Hence arose the phrase so often seen in the *Dutch Consultations*, "*onder correctie.*" According to Beaumanoir (ch. 5), if an advocate found himself in a position to advance some fact or proposition which his client might repudiate he could safeguard himself against personal responsibility by using the formula, *Sous la correction de la cour.*

During the thirteenth century certain advocates in the Netherlands were called *taelmannen.* These persons were apparently attached to the court in some way, for they were appointed by the judge at the request of a defendant. In

Latin they are called *antiloqui* or *praelocutores*. The advocate was distinguished from the counsel. The former was a pleader who addressed the court (*narrator* or *conteur*); the latter were persons skilled in legal matters who gave their advice, but who did not address the court. The *taelman* alone addressed the court, and the other counsel (called *raed*) were only required to advise their client. The advocate who addressed the court and the other advisers who sat by him were called *taelman* and *raed* (*conteurs et conseil*). A similar practice prevailed in France, and to this is probably due the fact that with us, as in England, only one counsel can address the court on fact (Raepsaet, vol. 5, p. 264). The origin of the court assigning an advocate to a pauper defendant in criminal cases is probably due to the fact that the *taelman* was appointed by the judge at the request of the client (Raepsaet, vol. 5, p. 266).

When, however, the supreme courts were established in the different provinces and the Great Court sat at Mechlin, the advocates were organised into an order and their dignity and importance increased, so that they were brought back to the same plane they occupied in the days of the Roman Empire. Advocates were attached to the towns to defend their interests, and these came to be known as *pensionarisen* or *raad pensionarisen*.

By the Roman-Dutch law any person who obtained a diploma of *doctor utriusque juris* in any Dutch university was entitled to practise as an advocate, provided he professed the Christian religion. In 1658 the court refused to admit a Jew who had obtained his doctor's degree. At present all English and Irish barristers and Scotch advocates as well as those persons who have obtained the LL.B. of the Cape of Good Hope University can practise as advocates in the Cape Colony irrespective of what religion they belong to. In the Transvaal it is sufficient for admission to the Supreme Court to have practised exclusively as a barrister in any English colony. The duties and privileges of a Dutch advocate were almost identical with those of an English barrister (Raepsaet, vol. 5; Kersteman, *Woordenboek, sub voce Advocaat*).

Attorneys.—In early Roman times the office of an attorney was only performed by men of low degree. It was said to be an *onus odiosum infamissimae vilitatis.* During the reign of Diocletian and Maximilian, however, it began to lose its servile character (Merula, 4, tit. 18, c. 1, 1 and 2). What the exact functions were of the attorney during the Roman Empire it is difficult to say. During the middle ages the *Lex Romana* recognised two classes of attorney—the *atturnatus judicialis* and the *atturnatus extra-judicialis* The former was a person employed by a litigant to assist him in the conduct of his lawsuit (*procurator ad causas*), and the latter a mere agent to assist in the transaction of business (*procurator ad negotia*). The latter might be a man of servile condition; the former could only be a man of honourable conduct. The attorney of the present day is the *atturnatus judicialis,* whereas in the words "power of attorney" we see the *atturnatus extra-judicialis* (Raepsaet, vol. 5, p. 273). The *atturnatus judicialis* differed from the *advocatus* or the *taelman* in that he merely represented his client *in judicio,* whilst the latter spoke for him.

Attorneys were credited with encouraging useless litigation, and to prevent this Charlemagne by a *Capitulare* of 802 prohibited litigants from pleading through the agency of an attorney except in such cases as the judge thought fit. This prohibition lasted for a considerable time, for in the Landrecht of Flanders (39) we find that attorneys could only represent unmarried women, priests, clerks, children and persons so old that they have no sense left to them. Gradually, however, the prejudice against attorneys wore away, and they were allowed to act for clients charged with minor offences. Thus we find in a keur of Zeeland of 1496 that persons may be represented by attorney where life and limb were not at stake: *Dat een yeghelijch sal voortaen moghen maecken ende stellen eenen procureur oft meer wie hij wil voor drie manden om alle synen saken te hanteren die hij tot deze hoogher vierschare te doen sal moghen hebben uit genomen van saken daar men lijf of lit mede winnen of verliesen mach* (*Rechts. Obs.* vol. 2, obs. 72).

During the fourteenth century attorneys first began to organise themselves into corporations, and since then their power and prestige increased. They had so far advanced in public esteem during the sixteenth century that no one might appear before the Court of Holland to conduct his own case. Pleadings had become so technical that the court required litigants to be assisted by attorneys and advocates.

From the sixteenth century onward the function of the attorney was not to advise his client as to the law applicable to his case, but to see that every necessary step in the law-suit was duly taken, and to prepare the case so that it could be properly conducted and argued by the advocate. He was an officer of the court, and subject to its discipline. His fees were fixed by tariff, and neither he nor the advocate could make any contract to share in the proceeds of the lawsuit (*Pactum de quota litis*). Our law to-day in South Africa with regard to attorneys, except in so far as it has been modified by statute, is the same as prevailed in the Dutch courts during the eighteenth century (Raepsaet, vol. 5; Kersteman, *sub voce Procureur*).

Notaries.—The word "notary" comes from the Latin word *notarius*, and this again is derived from the word *nota*, a mark. The Romans called those persons *notarii* who took down in shorthand the speeches of orators. They were, therefore, equivalent in the early days to what we call stenographers or shorthand writers. As their characters were different to the ordinary writing of the day it became customary to employ these persons to put on record in this abbreviated character contracts, wills, &c., which parties intended to keep secret. The notary was entrusted with the secret, and as he alone knew the meaning of his abbreviated characters it could with safety be put on record. Such memoranda were known as *notae hieroglyphicae*.

Not only was the notary employed because of his secret characters, but also because he could write down rapidly at the dictation of parties what they desired. Thus Nicolaus in his work *De siglis veteribus* says: *Romani hujus rei gratia notarios adhibebant, auctore Suida, quos scribas, a secretis vocant, qui notarent res seu notis, seu zifris scriberent quas non liceret propulare. Ita etiam jurisperiti ad tegendos actus suos, inquit Cicero pro Muraena, notas invenerunt ne plebs sciret quibus diebus fas nefasre esset lege agere* (c. 3).

During the middle ages, and especially in the kingdom of the Franks, notaries were employed to write secret letters.

The chief letter writer to the king was called a *protonotarius* or chancellor (Mabillon, bk. 2, c. 11, p. 114). During this period *notarii* are sometimes called *cancellarii*, *secretarii*, and even *lectores*. Gradually we find two kinds of notaries mentioned in the old documents, the notaries belonging to the Church and the notaries who help to record worldly transactions. The Church notaries were again divided into those appointed by the Pope, and those appointed by bishops. The papal notaries could exercise their profession wherever the Church of Rome was recognised, whilst the episcopal notaries could only practise within the jurisdiction of the bishop who appointed them. The secular notaries were those attached to the king or to some high official, and those who exercised their profession independently.

The notaries of the Frankish Empire resembled the *tabelliones*, the *exceptores* and the *actuarii* of the Roman Empire, and gradually came to exercise the functions of all three. The first drew up extra-judicial documents, whilst the two last wrote out contracts, wills and other matters which were registered in the public registry of the judge. These deeds were called *gesta*, *publica monumenta*, *instrumenta forensia*, *publicae chartae* or *tabulae*.

The word "notary," therefore, had originally a very wide meaning, but in the course of time its signification became more specialised and restricted, so that the work of the notary resembled that of the *tabellio* of the later Roman Empire, who received imperial authority to reduce to writing contracts, testaments and other instruments, and to preserve copies for future use. These notaries appointed by the secular or ecclesiastical powers came to be known as *Notarii*

Publici (notaries public), and their deeds as *instrumenta publica* (Van der Schelling, *Histori der Not.* 1–36).

Public notaries were probably known in the Netherlands before the eleventh century, and during the beginning of the thirteenth century they were already in possession of protocols (*loc. cit.* 39). *Chartae indentatae*, or indentures, drawn by notaries existed during the thirteenth century in the Netherlands as well as in France. As the art of reading and writing became less common after the eleventh century, and was mostly confined to ecclesiastics, the ecclesiastical notary gradually supplanted his secular brother, so that the public notary of a town or village was nearly always a priest or clerk.

From the earliest times the public notary was required to pass some sort of examination, and owing to the trust reposed in him he was usually a man of character. He wore a signet ring, with which he sealed the instruments executed by him. As learning improved the ecclesiastical notary lost his monopoly, and public notaries were appointed not only by the counts, but by the towns. The result of this was that the notaries greatly increased in number and decreased in efficiency. Charles V was therefore constrained to issue a Placaat in 1524 by which the number of notaries was limited and the nature of their examinations fixed. Since then the number of notaries practising in the towns of Holland has always been limited. After 1592 notaries were forbidden to exercise their functions outside the town in which they were admitted to practice. Various Placaten have made provisions for the kind of protocol the notary must keep and for the manner in which he must carry on his profession.

During the seventeenth century a notary had first to pass an examination before the Provincial Court and then to be admitted by the States of Holland and placed upon the list of notaries of some town. He was required to be a trustworthy person of good character, and as the authorities were careful in their choice the profession of a notary was always regarded in Holland as a most honourable one.

In the Cape Colony the notary has always held a high place in the legal profession, and the influence of English law has not yet brought him down to the level of an English notary. His chief functions are to protest negotiable paper, to make antenuptial contracts, wills, and generally to attest deeds. Our present conveyancer executes many of the instruments which were drawn up by the Dutch notary before the annexation of the Cape Colony.

In all the South African colonies the notary must pass an examination, and when admitted by the court is regarded as one of its officers. His protocol is subject to inspection. The rules which notaries have to follow in the Cape Colony were drawn up in 1793 by the commissioners Nederburg and Frykenius. Many of these have fallen into disuse, though a great number are still in force (Van der Schelling, *Histori van 't Notarischap;* Kersteman, *sub voce Notaris;* Tennant's *Notary's Manual*).

CHAPTER XXV.

THE LAW OF THE SIXTEENTH AND SEVENTEENTH CENTURIES.

What was the law administered by the courts of justice throughout the Netherlands during the sixteenth and seventeenth centuries?—I know of no text-book on the Roman-Dutch law written before the latter half of the sixteenth century. Damhouder wrote his *Praxis* in 1562, and Paul Merula his *Manier van Procedeeren* in 1592. Although those writers do not deal with substantive law, but with procedure, we can gather fairly well from their works what the substantive law must have been. It is inconceivable that the two works above mentioned were the first of their kind. From a perusal of them it is also quite clear that the practice of the latter half of the sixteenth century was not then newly inaugurated, and from our knowledge of the nature of the development of law in other countries it is safe to assert that in its general form the practice of the middle of the sixteenth century could not have very materially differed from that of the middle of the fifteenth century. Again the whole practice is founded upon the laws and customs which then prevailed, and a very casual reference to the above-mentioned works will show that the Roman law forms the most important part of the law administered by the superior courts of the Netherlands.

In one sense the civil law may be said to have been the common law of the Netherlands, for whenever neither statute, custom nor privilege applied to a particular case the judge sought in the Roman law a solution of the problem presented to him. On the other hand, it is erroneous to suppose that the Roman law was the sole law of the Netherlands during the sixteenth century. In the law of Persons the customs and privileges of former days, some traditional and others embodied in charters, keuren and handvesten, had so qualified the Roman law that this modified law had come to be regarded as a distinct system of law. Not only in the law of Persons, but also in the law of Things and in the law of Obligations, the Roman law had been so altered that its modified form may be regarded as the fundamental law of the land.

Looking at the matter from this point of view, we may say that the common law of the Netherlands was not the Roman civil law, but this new system compounded of the ancient customs of the people, the ordinances, charters and privileges of the towns, and the principles of the *Corpus Juris*. In the provinces of Holland and Zeeland this composite law was called the Roman-Dutch law (*Roomsch Hollandsch Recht*).

The manner in which this Roman law was applied in the different provinces of the Netherlands varied considerably. Friesland after the time of Duke Alfrecht adopted the Roman law almost in its entirety, and this we must always bear in mind when we consult such authorities as Sande and Huber. In Utrecht the Roman law was considerably modified by the Canon law. Thus although Community of Property was the common law both in Holland and Utrecht, in the former province it applied directly the marriage was celebrated, whilst in the latter, following the Canon law, only after its consummation. In the superior courts, whose judges were skilled in the theory and practice of both the Civil and Canon law, the Roman-Dutch law took shape and became a definite system of jurisprudence. In the inferior courts the president was often a lawyer, though the members were seldom other than burghers of good social standing, and therefore the ordinances and customs of the country or the decisions of the superior courts were the authorities which guided them. Though the *Corpus Juris* was the principal text-book in the superior courts, its principles were not quoted at first hand in the lower courts. Nor is this at all surprising when we consider the practice of our own magistrate courts.

Besides the Roman law there were few general laws that applied to the whole of the Netherlands. As each province before the establishment of the Republic was entirely independent of the others, though one sovereign ruled over them all, it followed that the laws of one province had no effect outside its own frontiers. In many cases, no doubt, the legislation ran on the same lines, but very often the laws of one province differed from—nay, were diametrically opposed to—those of other provinces. Hence the law which prevailed in Holland, Friesland, Gelderland, Utrecht, Overijssel, Brabant and the southern provinces was by no means the same.

In dealing with the development of the towns, I pointed out that at any rate the larger towns came to have many of the attributes of small republics. Privileges were granted to them by handvesten and charters, and these privileges in many cases modified the civil law which was administered in the town. Hence in the course of time each town acquired a body of special laws which applied to its own burghers, but which had no application in other towns. It was this fact which made it so important that the *jus de non evocando* should be strictly observed. The burgher knew the rights and duties which the law of his own town granted to or imposed upon him, and he was therefore exceedingly jealous of the right of being sued before his own judge, by whom he knew his rights would be protected. On the other hand, if he found himself in a dispute with a stranger within the walls of his city it was but natural that he should strive to bring the stranger before the courts of his own town. In this way arose the law of arrest so peculiar to the cities of the Netherlands. To make confusion still worse, there were certain privileged classes of citizens who were not bound even by the general laws of their own town, but could appeal to the special privileges accorded to their order. To these privileged classes belonged amongst others the nobles, the knights (*ridderschap*), and the professors and students of the universities.

The importance of the civil law is seen in Damhouder's division of law into *jus scriptum* (*beschreven recht*) and *jus non scriptum* (*onbeschreven recht*). The *jus scriptum*, he tells us, "is really that law which the Romans of old committed to writing for the purpose of governing the Republic, . . . so that when we speak of the written law we mean nothing but the Roman law." It was the law adopted by the nations of Europe, and was therefore called the *jus commune* or *jus universale scriptum*. By the *jus non scriptum* Damhouder means the particular privileges, statutes, ordinances, customs and manners which exist in each town or province according to the needs of the place (*Praxis Civil*, c. xii). The division of Damhouder is very important, for it shows the great authority which the author, as a practical jurist, attributed to the Roman law.

Merula deals more logically with the subject, and though he also attributes a very great authority to the Roman law, he perceives that the enactments of the provinces are of greater force than the civil law. He divides the *jus civile* (*landrecht of burgerlijk recht*) into the *jus scriptum* and *jus non scriptum*. The *jus scriptum* he divides into (1) law introduced from elsewhere, and (2) native law. By the former he means the Roman law (*jus Romanum*), by the latter the ordinances, placaten, privilegen and keuren. Merula points out that inasmuch as the native written law is more recent than the Roman law, where these differ the native law is to be preferred to the *jus introductum*.

By unwritten law he means the ancient customs of the people. He tells us that recourse must be had to the customs of the people (*oude gewoonte*), when neither the native ordinances, &c., nor the Roman law applies. He looks upon a custom as a traditional law. *Oude gewoonte welke is eene ongeschreve wet en Burgerlijk recht bevestigt door langheid van tijd ingevoerd en aangenomen door lang plegen en een stilzwijgend consent en bewilligen van luiden niet strijdende met de wet der Natuure.* These customs he divides into general customs applicable to the whole country, and special customs applicable only to certain localities.

It is important to note that Merula, like Damhouder, is still so mastered by the dignity and force of the Roman law that he places its authority above the general customs of the country. In this he was wrong. The general customs of the country are superior to the rules of the Roman law where in the course of time the former have obtained the recognition of law. Thus the community of husband and wife in the province of Holland prevails over the rules of the Roman law. Again, the law of *Naasting* (*jus retractus*) was a special custom of great antiquity, which applied to certain places such as Delftland, Rynland, South Holland, Voorne and elsewhere.

Of recent years some Dutch writers have striven to throw doubts not only on the antiquity of the reception of the Roman law, but also on its effect. I think no better answer can be given to this desire to detract from the authority of the Roman law than the views of two such eminent and authoritative writers as Damhouder and Merula. Surely they are better judges than ourselves of the scope of the Roman law at the time they were writing and during the immediately preceding period. If then we find them treating the Roman law as the common law of Holland, we must conclude that they attributed to that law a very high authority. It may be wrong to say that the Roman law was the common law of Holland, for in many respects the ancient customs and native legislation had modified the civil law into the Roman-Dutch law. It certainly was a *jus subsidiarium* of such authority as to be almost equivalent to the common law, for there were so many cases in which the old customs and native laws were insufficient to deal with the rapidly growing trade and commerce of the Netherlands that the Roman law was the system most generally resorted to.

We see, therefore, that in the time of Merula (end of the sixteenth century) the law to be applied was :—

(1) The general Ordinances which referred to all the provinces of the union.

(2) The Ordinances which applied to the particular province in which the cause of action arose.

(3) The special privileges of the district, town, village or estate.

(4) The special privilege which applied to the individual plaintiff or defendant.

(5) The Roman-Dutch law, *i.e.* the ancient customs engrafted on the Roman law.

(6) The Roman law of the *Corpus Juris*, or in some cases the Canon law.

I shall now pass over to consider these in greater detail.

(1) Statute Law.—Merula defines the Statute Law as embracing all laws that have been passed by the sovereign power, whether such power resided in one person or in a council. After the union of the seven States there were two kinds of statute law: (1) statutes which applied to all the provinces of the union, and (2) those which applied only to a particular province. The statute law was divided into ordinances and privileges (*ordonantiën* and *privilegiën*). Ordinances are laws passed by the sovereign power, to be strictly observed by all to whom they apply. These ordinances bore different names, such as *edicten, missiven, approbatiën, confirmatiën, revocatiën, instructies, ampliatiën*, &c.

Some ordinances were general and applied to the subjects of the whole province, whilst others only applied to particular towns, districts, wards or persons. These were called special ordinances. The heading of the ordinance varied according to the period at which, and the province where, it was issued. Here are a few examples:—

Karl by der Gratie Gods Roomsche Keiser, &c., *Grave van Holland.*

Phillips by der Gratie Gods Koning van Castilien, &c., *Grave van Holland.*

De Ridderschap, Edelen, en de Steden van Holland, &c., *representeerende de Staten van de zelve landen. De Staten van Holland, Zeeland en West Friesland.*

Grotius says, "The general written law consists of enactments of the States, *i.e.* of the knights, nobles and representatives of the large towns; or placaats of the heads of provinces (*lands hoofden*) to whom such power has been lawfully granted by the States under the title of counts, lords, governors or chief magistrates" (*Introd.* 1, 2, 17). If we examine the *Groot Placaat Boek* we shall find many examples of general enactments, either by way of a placaat of the count, or by way of an ordinance passed by the States of Holland and West Friesland, or by the States of all the provinces.

An example of the former class is the Political Ordinance or Perpetual Edict of the Emperor Charles V of the 4th of October, 1540, regarding bankruptcy, marriages, usury, testaments, protocols of notaries, &c. (*G.P.B.* vol. 1, p. 311). The Intestate Succession Ordinance of the 18th December, 1599 (*G.P.B.* vol. 1, p. 343), is an example of a placaat of the knights, nobles and towns of Holland and West Friesland. It begins thus: "The Knights (*ridderschap*), Nobles and Towns of Holland and West Friesland representing the several Estates of those provinces proclaim," &c. Sometimes an ordinance was passed by the States-General of all the provinces, and then it affected the whole Republic. Such, for instance, is the Ordinance of the 26th July, 1581 (*G.P.B.* vol. 1, p. 25), by which the authority of the King of Spain was abrogated in the united provinces. This placaat begins: "The States-General of the United Netherlands to all who may see, hear or read these presents, greeting," &c. The ordinances relating to particular districts or towns that were passed by the States-General or by the States of Holland were in the same form as the ordinances of general application, but the local ordinances of the Supreme Court or of the Court of Holland began thus: "Inasmuch as it appears to the Supreme Court (*Hoogen Rade*) that," &c., or, "The President and Councillors of Holland, Zeeland and West Friesland, to all who may see, hear or read these presents, greeting," &c.

Besides these legislative bodies of greater power there were local assemblies who had the power of legislation in certain matters. Ordinances were passed "by the lawful assembly of the schout, burgomaster and schepenen with or without the councillors or vroedschappen in the towns, dyk, graaf and heemraden, baljuw and mannen and also schout and schepenen outside the towns in so far as they have received from the States-General or the heads of Provinces the right to make laws" (Grotius' *Introd.* 1, 2, 18).*

(2) Privileges were special benefits accorded to an individual or to a particular district or town. These privileges were extremely important during the sixteenth and seventeenth centuries, for special advantages in the way of tolls, jurisdiction, succession, &c., had been granted to nearly all the large towns and important villages. As they differed materially from one another, the laws within a very small radius might be in hopeless conflict with one another. Students in the universi-

* The statute law is to be found in the *Groot Placaat Boek* and *Jaarboeken*, whilst privileges, charters, &c., are collected in Van Mieris' *Groot Charter Boek*.

ties had numerous special rights accorded to them, *e.g.*, they were toll free, they could not be cited before the ordinary judge, their books could not be sold in execution, &c.

(3) Keuren.—Many of the towns had obtained from the thirteenth century onwards the privilege of making certain laws and regulations for their burghers. These had to be submitted to and approved of by the count or his representative, and were then known as keuren (*wille keuren*, i.e. *Geboden of Statuten van de Stad of plaatse*).

(4) Ancient Customs.—The ancient customs which were recognised during the sixteenth century as part of the common law of the land were such as had from time immemorial been recognised as law. They were derived from various sources, from the *Lex Ripuaria*, the *Lex Salica*, the *Jus Saxonicum*, the *Jus Frisicum*, the *Lex Romana*, the *Capitularia* and other ancient bodies of law. Besides the community of goods and naasting above referred to, the following may serve as examples: immovable property had to be transferred before schout and schepenen; hypothecations had to be registered before schout and schepenen; stolen property sold in market overt could not be reclaimed in many parts of Holland. Many other examples will occur during the course of this work.

(5) Roman Law and Canon Law.—This subject has already been dealt with. For the mode of its application I shall refer the reader to Van der Keessel's *Theses Selectae*, Nos. 10–23.

Let us now consider how the judges applied the law. If a case were tried before a lower court in the country (*platte land*) then the judge would apply such statute law as affected the whole of the province. If no such statute law applied to the case then he would consider whether there existed any privilege or special charter which would solve the difficulty. Failing these he would consider whether any general or special ancient custom (*oude gewoonte*) applied. If such a custom did apply he would interpret it according to the canons of interpretation of the Roman law. If no custom applied his decision would be governed by the principles of the Roman law. In the southern provinces he might apply the Canon law if that were in conflict with the Roman law. If the dispute came before a town court the judges would first refer to the charters, keuren or privileges of the town. If no such special law existed then the same procedure was adopted as in the district court, and where no general ordinances applied the case would be decided by the Roman-Dutch law.

The higher tribunals and courts of appeal would proceed in a similar manner to apply the ordinances, privileges and common law in turn. Inasmuch, however, as the judges of these courts were composed of lawyers skilled in the Roman law and trained to apply that system of law to settle disputes, the influence of the Roman law in the higher courts was far greater than in the courts of baljuw and mannen or of schout and schepenen. This, as we have seen in a former chapter, was often a matter of complaint.

As the modifications were very slight in this respect during the seventeenth and eighteenth centuries the above will serve as a statement of the general application of the statute and common law in Holland, the province with which we in South Africa are mostly concerned.

CHAPTER XXVI.

LEGISLATION OF THE SIXTEENTH AND BEGINNING OF THE SEVENTEENTH CENTURIES.

BEFORE I pass over to the writers on substantive law who flourished towards the end of the sixteenth and the beginning of the seventeenth centuries, it will be as well to give a short account of the legislative activity of that period. I have already pointed out how, in the fourteenth and fifteenth centuries, the various towns had modified and altered the *jus commune* by obtaining from the counts various privileges, charters, handvesten and keuren. The tendency during those centuries was to modify the *jus scriptum*, according to the needs of the particular place or district. People very soon perceived the advantage of bringing the law up to date, and of adapting the great principles of equity contained in the *Corpus Juris* to the exigencies of a more active commercial life. There were great general causes at work throughout the length and breadth of Europe, which necessitated a change in the laws that had prevailed during the middle ages. Amongst these causes we might enumerate the decay of rigid feudalism, the spread of commerce, the growing influence and importance of the towns, and the revolt against Papal authority which followed upon the general revival of learning. These causes affected the Netherlands in the same way as they affected the rest of western Europe, though in

Holland and the other northern provinces they produced their effects more rapidly, owing to the intensity of the struggle between the people and their hereditary sovereigns.

It was during the reign of the House of Burgundy that the first attempts were made, on a large scale, to secure some uniformity in the administration of law. This desire for uniformity was fostered by the House of Austria, and when the Revolution ended in the establishment of the Dutch Republic there was such a breaking away from the old crystallised system, that the great geniuses that Freedom had given birth to were enabled to impress upon the nation the necessity of accepting the new ideas, that had been struggling for more than a century to obtain general recognition.

Men saw that the country had greatly suffered in its development on account of a lack of uniformity, and they sought to remedy this defect in every branch of law. It was during the reign of Charles the Bold that the burghers of the Netherlands began to appreciate their power. When he fell Louis XI of France stretched out his arms towards the Netherlands, but the wary burghers of Antwerp, Ghent, Utrecht, and the other great towns saw that more was to be gained by supporting the Lady Mary of Burgundy than the crafty French fox. They called an assembly together at Ghent and swore to support the young princess. In return, however, for this support they made her promise to the provinces and cities of the Netherlands a Charter of Liberties. This charter, called *De Groot Privilegie*, the Great Privilege or Magna Charta of the Netherlands, was granted in 1476 (*G.P.B.* vol. 2, p. 658). Its provisions have been enumerated in a former chapter. This shows clearly the great power to which the towns had attained, and also points to the weakening of the arbitrary authority of the hereditary princes.

From this time onward the struggle between the people and the hereditary counts began in earnest, until at the end of the sixteenth century the seven northern provinces threw off the Spanish yoke and began a new and vigorous life as the Dutch Republic. One of the first steps that inaugurated the policy of attaining uniformity of law was the establishment of the Great Council or Supreme Court at Mechlin, already referred to in a former chapter. The next step was to ascertain what the various customs were throughout the Netherlands, for whenever an attempt was made to pass some general law one or other city would bring forward, in opposition to the law, some ancient privilege of which the advisers of the hereditary sovereign had never heard. The earlier princes had tried to cope with this difficulty, but as they were mostly aliens and their policy suspected, they did not achieve much of what they desired. Charles V, however, was regarded as a native prince, and it was chiefly during his reign that the great innovations began to be introduced, and that a strong attempt was made to carry out the policy of introducing uniformity into law and administration. This period has been called by Dutch writers the period of the *nieuwe reformatiën* or new reforms. These reforms were not issued, as in olden time, by the counts as privileges or keuren, but were promulgated as general laws.

In 1531 Charles V issued a placaat at Utrecht (*Groot Placaat Boek van Utrecht*, vol. 1, p. 414), in which he clearly expressed the tendency of the new legislation "that the customs of our lands on this side of the Rhine shall be reduced into writing within six months, and that these customs so reduced to writing shall be presented to us in order that we may examine them, and after due deliberation promulgate them, in the interest of reason and justice, and for the well-being, profit and advantage of all our vassals and subjects." He also gives us his reasons for this step—"because often these customs conflict with one another, and the burghers are thereby injured and suffer great loss, and all because of the fact that they are not reduced to writing and duly approved of." Litigants were caused great annoyance and expense, because whenever a custom was pleaded it had to be proved by witnesses, and as a *turbe van getuigen*, or a great number of witnesses, were required, the inconvenience of the practice will be readily appreciated. Two strong reasons, therefore, made for uniformity, (1) to reduce expense, and (2) to make the law certain (Zypaeus, *Not. Juris. Belg.* p. 38). In 1540 a similar proclamation was issued referring to the whole of the Netherlands. Some of these customs affected certain towns only, others affected districts, whilst others, again, obtained in several of the provinces. So suspicious, however, were the burghers, that it was no easy matter to obtain the desired information, and we consequently find Philip II, as late as 1570, complaining of the difficulty of ascertaining what the customs and privileges really were.

If, therefore, we consider the tendency of the legislation of the sixteenth century, we shall readily appreciate that its main object was to do away with these floating, inconvenient customs, and to legislate in such a way that the new laws would regulate the legal relations of the inhabitants, if not of the whole country, at any rate of the various provinces.

I shall now consider somewhat in detail the various enactments which dealt with private law, and which so profoundly modified the common and customary law of the country. I shall endeavour, as much as possible, to adhere to chronological order; but where it will be easier to appreciate the change by grouping together cognate legislation I shall not rigidly adhere to the sequence of time.

The Placaat of 1515, regarding lessees, exemplifies very clearly the difficulties that were caused by the prevalence of unwritten customs and the means that were adopted to overcome the difficulty. The preamble to this placaat states that complaints were daily growing more and more frequent, that whenever land was leased the lessees at the expiration of the term alleged some custom or other, by which they claimed the right to hold over. Not only did the lessees hold over themselves, but they sublet or sold their alleged *jus retentionis* to third parties, who naturally clung to the land they had paid for. This state of affairs led to constant breaches of the peace, and it was therefore considered advisable to put a stop to these unreasonable claims on the part of lessees and sub-lessees. Charles V therefore provided that no one could lay claim to any land as a lessee or sub-lessee, unless he could show that he held a written lease from the owner. This placaat, however, did not entirely remedy the evil, for it was apparently disregarded in many places; hence we find similar provisions made at various times both in Holland and Zeeland, *e.g.* in 1580, 1658 and 1664 (*G.P.B.* vol. 1, pp. 330, 363; vol. 2, p. 2515; vol. 4, p. 1035).

In 1521 an ordinance was passed which provided that justice must have its course, and that no plea of privilege could be set up against the process of a superior court (*Instructiën van den Hove*).

The Roman Church in Holland, as elsewhere, had acquired, principally by way of gift or legacy, vast feudal and other domains. For these no service was rendered and no taxes were paid to the Crown. Public opinion was very hostile to the Church all through the sixteenth century on account of the abuses which had crept in, and even good Catholics sought to check the growing tendency of the Church to acquire large possessions. In 1524, therefore, a great blow was dealt to the Church by the promulgation of a placaat that ecclesiastical bodies were forbidden from acquiring lands by testament, legacy or donation (*G.P.B.* vol. 1, p. 1588). In 1529 an important placaat was published with regard to the alienation and hypothecation of immovable property (*G.P.B.* vol. 1, p. 373).

It was an immemorial custom in Holland, differing therein from the Roman law, that no pledge of land held good unless it had been effected *coram judice loci rei sitae*. Gradually, however, a custom appears to have crept in to mortgage the land, not before the court of the place where the land was situated, but before any court in the province. The practice grew up to execute the mortgage *coram judice*, but not *coram judice rei sitae*. This naturally led to great abuse, and defeated the very object of the law requiring registration. Hence the Ordinance of 1529 was passed to stop this growing custom. It recited that it had become customary for persons to alienate and hypothecate their land before judges other than those within whose jurisdiction the property was situated, and that thereby purchasers of lands were defrauded and a multiplicity of lawsuits engendered. Moreover, in this way the payment of proper duties was evaded, inasmuch as the judge did not know the true value of the land. To obviate this the Ordinance enacted that in future no alienation or hypothecation of immovable property should take place, except before the judge within whose jurisdiction the land was situated, and all transfers and mortgages not complying with this provision of the law were declared null and void. This matter of registration was dealt with in several later placaats, notably in the Politique Ordonantie of 1580, arts. 35–38.

We now come to one of the great consolidation acts of Charles V. This is the Perpetual Edict of the 4th October, 1540 (*G.P.B.* vol. 1, p. 311). The preamble to this very important placaat states that it was promulgated in order to check the heresy that was creeping into the provinces, to remedy the expense connected with lawsuits, and to provide for a pure administration of justice which would deal equally with both rich and poor. The preamble goes on to point out the great impulse trade had received, and that, in order to guard and foster that trade, debtors must be compelled to pay their debts and must be prevented from evading their liabilities by flight. The Ordinance, therefore, provides that all persons who absent themselves from their ordinary residences with the object of defrauding their creditors are to be regarded as common thieves, and if caught may be summarily dealt with and publicly hanged. Persons who aid and abet such fugitives, as well as the wives of the latter, are to be held liable for the payment of the whole debt, and unless they pay in full they may be imprisoned or otherwise punished.

Article 3 declares that all contracts made with fugitive

bankrupts, and all sales or alienations made by them, are void if prejudicial to creditors. This article is the origin of our law with regard to fraudulent alienations and undue preference. It was considered so heinous an act to leave the country in order to avoid paying one's debts that the Ordinance insisted on their punishment, even if afterwards they paid their creditors in full.

Article 6 provides that the wives of bankrupts can make no claim upon the estates of their husbands until all the creditors are paid in full, though they retained their preference with regard to goods brought by them to their husbands, either by antenuptial contract or by succession. It was on this article that the well-known case of *S. A. Bank's Trustees* v. *Chiappini* (Buch. 1869, p. 143) was decided.

Article 7 provided against corners in any particular article. No merchant, tradesman, or other person may make contracts of the nature of a monopoly, or prejudicial to the public welfare, as, for instance, to buy up all goods of a certain kind in order to create a corner, and so obtain excessive prices. The penalty was the confiscation of the goods so cornered and "arbitrary punishment." The same article also forbade the granting of monopolies by any town or corporation.

Article 8 launches out against usurers, inasmuch "as they cause the loss of many souls and do great damage to the public welfare." The Ordinance, therefore, limits interest to 12 per cent., "for the preservation of souls, the conservation of the holy Christian belief, and the convenience of the public."

We have seen above that the Houses of Burgundy and

Austria strove as much as possible to make the law in the Netherlands uniform. In order to achieve this object, article 10 provides that all customs must be reduced to writing, and receive the approval of the court.

The next article aims another shaft at the Church. It provides that ecclesiastics may not censure the judgments of the secular courts, but if they have any objection to such judgments they must enter these objections by way of requisition.

Article 12 provides that all testaments, legacies, donations *inter vivos* or *mortis causâ* by persons under twenty-five years of age, whereby their tutors, curators, or administrators are benefited, are *ipso facto* void.

The Ordinance also makes provision for the keeping of protocols by notaries, and compels them to keep a proper register of all instruments passed by them. They are forbidden to make any will or contract unless they are acquainted with the parties, or unless the witnesses vouch for the identity of such persons. The notary is also obliged to fill in the proper address of any person who may appear before him.

Article 16 makes provision for the limitation of certain actions. The fees or emoluments of all advocates, attorneys, secretaries, doctors of medicine, surgeons, apothecaries, clerks, notaries, or other workmen, as well as the wages of servants, are prescribed within two years; so also the price of goods bought for consumption and moneys due by sureties. If, however, the obligation has been reduced to writing, then the period of prescription is ten years against the principal debtor. If the principal debtor dies the creditor has two years, from the time he knew of the death, within which he can claim the debt from the heir.

Article 17 provides that if a man marries a girl under twenty, without consent of parents or nearest relations, he can derive no benefit from any property she may leave. Similarly, a woman who marries a man under twenty-five, without the necessary consent, forfeits all claim on his estate. This applies even where, after marriage, the requisite consent has been obtained. The article also provides that all persons who knowingly assist at such marriages are subject to arbitrary correction.

From the provisions above set out it is clear that the edict was not a law dealing with some single subject, but an ordinance which strove to amend existing abuses and to introduce some uniformity into the practice of the courts. It dealt, therefore, with what may be described as the pressing needs of the day, with very little regard to logical order or method. This Ordinance of 1540 is important, not only because it contains some provisions which are still law, but because it is the precursor of the Politique Ordonantie of 1580, which had so great an effect upon the later Roman-Dutch law.

There are several ordinances between this and the Politique Ordonantie of 1580, which were of great importance in those days in helping to consolidate the Roman-Dutch law, but which, having been either superseded by later legislation or fallen into disuse, are of little importance at present. Amongst these I may mention the Placaat of the 22nd February, 1576, regarding the right of sureties to demand the excussion of immovable property specially pledged, and the Instructions with respect to the Administration of Justice of the 21st day of December,

1579, and of the 1st day of April, 1580. The next great ordinance with which every student of the Roman-Dutch law must be familiarly acquainted is the Politique Ordonantie of 1580, by which the States of Holland strove to do away with a great many difficulties and disputes which had arisen not only in the province of Holland, but also in the neighbouring provinces.

The Placaat of the 1st April, 1580, or *Ordonantie van de Policien binnen Hollandt,* is usually cited as the Politique Ordonantie or Political Ordinance. It is undoubtedly the most important law promulgated in Holland during the sixteenth century. As this law was passed a year after the Union of Utrecht (1579), it is published in the name of the knights, nobles and towns representing the States of Holland. It recites that inasmuch as there is great confusion in Holland with regard to the laws of marriage, succession, sales, leases, mortgages and registration, because the Roman law as to these matters had been modified by custom and legislation, and inasmuch as the various ordinances by which the common law had been altered were deliberately disobeyed or had fallen into disuse, therefore the Raad van Staten, by way of interpretation, amendment, or extension, determined to publish as a Perpetual Edict the laws that follow.

The enactments in the Politique Ordonantie or Ordinance for regulating the statute law may be divided into various chapters:—

Chapter I (articles 1–18) deals with the law of marriage and divorce.

Chapter II (articles 19–29), succession.

Chapter III (articles 30–34), leases.

Chapter IV (articles 35 and 36), mortgage of immovable property and preference.

Chapter V (article 37) provides machinery for registration of alienations and hypothecations.

Chapter VI (article 39) deals with fees that are payable to officers, &c.

Chapter VII (article 40) fixes the new style of reckoning time from the first of January.

Chapter VIII repeals all laws in conflict with the Ordinance.

The first two articles of the chapter on the law of marriage and divorce deal with persons whose marriages were irregular in some way or another, and allow them within three months after publication of the Ordinance to report the circumstances and to get the marriage duly legalised.

The third article makes provision for the manner in which marriages are to be celebrated in the future. The parties are to appear before the officials or Church authorities and request that their banns be published on three successive Sundays or market days in the church, or at the council chamber, or at other places where justice is administered, so as to give interested parties the opportunity of objecting to the celebration of the marriage. The publication of banns is, however, to be refused if the parties are under the legal age (*i.e.* twenty-five for men and twenty for women), and cannot prove to the satisfaction of the authorities that they have obtained the consent of their parents. Even if above the legal age, the consent of parents must be obtained or leave to marry granted by the court. By a later placaat the word "parents" was interpreted not to include grand-parents. If there are no objections, the parties may be married by the Church authorities or by the magistrate.

Article 4 sets out that as doubts exist as to what the degrees are within which parties may not marry, the forbidden degrees are definitely fixed by the States. Articles 5, 6, 7, 8, 9, 10 and 11 set out what these forbidden degrees are (*vide* Grotius, 1, 5, 6 *et seq.*). Article 12 provides that if the Church authorities have any doubt they must refer the matter to the civil authorities. Article 13 makes all marriages not complying with the provisions of the Ordinance void, and in case the parties marry within the forbidden degrees they are liable to be punished for incest.

Articles 14, 15, 16, 17 and 18 provide for divorce in case of adultery, and enumerate the various pains and penalties to which the adulterous man or woman may be subjected.

With article 19 we begin the chapter on the law of succession *ab intestato.* This chapter is of particular importance to us, for the law of intestate succession prevalent throughout South Africa is founded upon this chapter of the Politique Ordonantie. On the 19th June, 1714, the Governor of the Cape of Good Hope, in Council, passed a resolution that in cases of succession *ab intestato* this chapter of the Political Ordinance should be followed, together with the interpretation Ordinance of the 13th May, 1594 (*G.P.B.* vol. 1, p. 341), in so far as they had been adopted by the Placaat of the 10th January, 1661 (*G.P.B.* vol. 2, p. 2633). In *Raubenheimer* v. *Executors of Breda* (F. p. 114), Sir Henry de Villiers gave a short sketch of the history of our law of intestate succession, which I shall repeat here. "The charter granted by the States-General to the Dutch East India

Company on the 10th January, 1661, regulates the law of intestate succession in this colony. That charter adopted as the law of succession the provision of the Political Ordinance of 1580, as interpreted by an edict of the States bearing date 13th May, 1594." A resumé of articles 19 to 29 will be found in Tennant's *Notary's Manual*, and I shall refer the reader to that work for further information. It will be unnecessary to pursue this subject at present, as I hope to deal fully with the development of the law of intestate succession in some future chapter.

Article 30 begins a new chapter, in which the subject of the letting and sub-letting of lands is once more dealt with. It declares that the Placaat of February, 1515, is in future to be rigidly observed, and that no lessee can claim any *jus retentionis* unless this right is publicly registered, or unless the claimant has some document signed by the owner of the land. If a lessee should interfere with an owner, who rightly claims possession, he can be severely punished, and can be adjudged to pay half the value of the lease.

The next chapter begins at article 35, and deals with hypothecation of immovable property. It provides that a mortgage of immovable property will only be of force and effect if passed before the judge of the place where the mortgaged property is situated. It also provides that a later special mortgage of immovable property properly executed takes precedence of an earlier general mortgage, even though the latter has been executed before the same court. This provision of the Placaat differs from the Roman law, which provided that a general mortgagee was to be preferred to a person who had obtained a special mortgage over one of the things pledged under the general mortgage (*D.* 20, 4, 2). If there are several general mortgages and unsecured creditors, the earliest general mortgage is preferred to a later, and the person with a general mortgage is preferred to an unsecured creditor, nor does it make any difference before what judge the general mortgage is passed. Article 36 provides that a creditor may proceed against immovable property specially mortgaged to him without being bound first to excuss the debtor or his heirs.

The next articles (37 and 38) deal with the machinery for registering the alienations of immovable property, and the burdens imposed thereon. The rest of the Ordinance is of little importance at present, and may, therefore, be passed over.

I have dealt with this Ordinance at length because it is frequently quoted in the various Roman-Dutch law books, and in no text-books, that I am aware of, has a general idea of the Ordinance been given, for, as their readers all understood Dutch, it was merely necessary to refer to the *Placaat Boek*. It is, however, so important a landmark in the history of the development of the Roman-Dutch law, that a knowledge of its provisions is indispensable. It summed up all that was then peculiar in the law of Holland with regard to the celebration of marriage, the succession *ab intestato*, the requisites of leases of *praedia rustica*, the registration of alienations and mortgages, and the preferent rights of mortgagees. It also contributed largely towards the extinction of local customs in the matters that fell within its scope, and to the establishment of a uniform law throughout the province of Holland.

We have seen that articles 19 to 29 of the Political Ordinance dealt with the law of intestate succession. On the 13th May, 1594, an Ordinance was passed with the object of interpreting more clearly the above-mentioned articles of the Political Ordinance. Neither of these ordinances pleased the people of North Holland, and, in order to make the compromise in the matter of intestate succession more effectual, a further ordinance was passed regarding succession *ab intestato,* on the 18th December, 1599. This ordinance was more in accordance with the Aasdoms law, or the law of North Holland, and after 1599 it regulated the succession *ab intestato* in the northern districts. As I intend dealing later with intestate succession, I shall content myself with merely mentioning these ordinances here.

Several very important ordinances were passed towards the end of the sixteenth century with regard to public and constitutional law, such as the Union between Zeeland and Holland in April, 1576; the Pacification of Ghent, of November, 1576; the Placaat of the 29th January, 1579, called the Union of Utrecht, by which Holland, Zeeland, Zutphen and Friesland formed a political bond; and the Placaat of the 26th July, 1581, by which the *Staten Generaal der Geunieerde Nederlanden* solemnly declared that the King of Spain had ceased to have any control or authority in the Netherlands, and that his seal should no longer be used in that territory.

In 1602 the States-General of the United Netherlands granted a charter to the East India Company (*G.P.B.* vol. 1, p. 529). The preamble recites that commerce was flourishing on account of the zeal and industry of the coast ports of Holland and Zeeland, and that it is, therefore, advisable to consolidate the various industries. The Company possessed the monopoly of the trade east of the Cape of Good Hope. There were sixty-five directors, divided into six boards, which sat at Amsterdam, Middelburg, Delft, Rotterdam, Hoorn and Enckhuisen. To these the nobles of Holland (*ridderschap*) sent two representatives, one from North and one from South Holland. Three times a year representatives were sent from these six boards to a general meeting. This general meeting sat sometimes at Amsterdam and sometimes at Middelburg. Another committee of ten met at the Hague to answer letters from India. The Company appointed the Governor-General and other high officials. The Company swore allegiance to the States of Holland, but it had a free hand in the conduct of war, the making of peace and in receiving embassies from the Indian princes. The Company was also entitled to colonise such places as it thought fit, to found cities and to keep on foot an army. A great number of ordinances were subsequently passed amending this charter and enlarging the powers of the directors. The West India Company obtained its charter in 1621 (*G.P.B.* vol. 1, p. 566).

With the impulse given to Dutch trade during the latter half of the sixteenth century various laws were passed with regard to insurance and merchant shipping. Insurance had towards the beginning of the seventeenth century assumed large proportions, and disputes were growing more frequent and more difficult of solution. The Roman law afforded the judges but little help, inasmuch as the idea of marine insurance was first practically applied during the fifteenth century. There was no uniform law of insurance, and each maritime nation or town made its own regulations. Spain, Portugal and Holland and the Hanseatic towns were the first to elaborate a system of marine insurance, and it seems to be universally acknowledged that Holland contributed the most important share in the development of that branch of law throughout Europe.

The first Placaat that dealt with insurance was that of the 31st October, 1563 (*G.P.B.* vol. 1, p. 796), or the Great Placaat on Maritime Law. One article of this Placaat (art. 7) dealt with marine insurance, and it provided that no insurance could be effected unless the ship complied with all the requirements of the Ordinance. Incorporated in this Placaat is a form of policy, which is the first, as far as I know, that obtained legal recognition. The Ordinance was constantly amended and its compass extended. The next step was to establish boards with jurisdiction over matters concerning insurance.

In 1612 a *Kamer van Assurantie*, or an Insurance Chamber, was established at Amsterdam, with somewhat greater authority than the Chamber which had for some time been in existence, and which owed its origin to the burgomaster and councillors. This new chamber was founded by the States of Holland and West Friesland, and dealt with questions of insurance as a court of first instance, in very much the same way as a French *cours de commerce* deals, nowadays, with these questions. The members of this chamber or court were experts in maritime affairs. Similar provisions were made for the other seaport towns. These laws were constantly amended and amplified during the seventeenth and eighteenth centuries, and if we examine them we find that they contain all the fundamental principles of maritime insurance that are in vogue to-day in all the great commercial countries of Europe. The Roman-Dutch law of insurance is fully set out in Lybrechts' *Redeneerend Vertoog*, vol. 2, c. 17, and Van Leeuwen's *R.H.R.* bk. 4, c. 9.

This was the law that prevailed at the Cape until 1879, when an Act was passed which provided that "In every suit, action, and cause having reference to questions of fire, life, and marine insurance, stoppage *in transitu* and bills of lading . . . the law as administered by the High Court of Judicature in England for the time being . . . shall be the law to be administered by the Supreme Court or other competent court of this Colony" (Act No. 8 of 1879, sec. 2). This was found necessary because, although the fundamental principles of both the Dutch and English systems were almost identical, commerce and navigation had made such strides during the nineteenth century, that new legislation was required to deal with the new circumstances which had arisen.

Having briefly sketched the history of the law of insurance, I shall now give a short account of the legislation with regard to merchant shipping.

The great commercial activity in the Netherlands during the sixteenth and seventeenth centuries gave rise to a number of Merchant Shipping Acts. The first important Ordinance was passed in 1551 (*G.P.B.* vol. 1, p. 783). It set out fully the relation between the master and seamen, made provision for ocean and coasting voyages, regulated questions of freight, collision at sea, and such other matters as usually occur in navigation codes. This crude Act was considerably modified and enlarged by the *Placaat op Zee-rechten* of 1563 (*G.P.B.* vol. 1, 796). This latter Ordinance was promulgated by Philip II, and was based, to a great extent, upon the Spanish navigation laws, which were then the best in Europe. This

Placaat is a very full code, and deals minutely and methodically with the various incidents which relate to merchant shipping. In order to show how wide the scope of this code was, I shall merely mention the headings of its different chapters. In each chapter the matter with which it deals is worked out in considerable detail. Chapter 1 treats of the fitting out of ships, and what the requirements are of a seaworthy ship; chapter 2 deals with shipmasters and merchants; chapter 3 with officers and seamen; chapter 4 with accidents to ships, jettison and average; chapter 5 with collisions at sea; chapter 6 with jurisdiction in shipping cases; and chapter 7 with marine insurance.

This Placaat practically remained the general law of Holland with regard to merchant shipping, though individual articles and matters of detail were modified by later placaats. The exact way in which this Ordinance was altered, and the various placaats that amended this law, it is unnecessary for our purpose to set out, for by Act No. 8 of 1879, sec. 1, the merchant shipping law of the Cape Colony was assimilated to that of England, and the Roman-Dutch law in this respect ceased to be administered by the Cape courts.

There are several other placaats that I might mention, but as my intention is rather to show the way in which the Dutch legislature strove to weld the customs, privileges and different systems of law into one uniform mass, than to give a detailed account of all the laws, I consider that I have sufficiently illustrated this subject. It forms a very important preface to the due appreciation of the *Introduction* of Grotius, to which I intend to devote more than a mere passing reference. Now that I have given a bird's-eye view of the legislation of the sixteenth and earlier part of the seventeenth century, the student will be better able to grasp the state of the statute law of Holland when that great Dutch jurist planned and wrote what must always be regarded as the greatest Dutch legal work of the seventeenth century. I refer to the *Introduction to the Jurisprudence of Holland.*

CHAPTER XXVII.

WRITERS ON THE PRACTICE OF THE DUTCH COURTS, REPORTERS AND AUTHORS OF CONSULTATIONS.

THE oldest Dutch jurists did not write treatises on the substantive law of Holland, but confined their attention to the practice of the courts. Incidentally, of course, they dealt with the early law of Holland, though their main object was to expound the procedure of the courts. It will be convenient to deal in this chapter with the writers on the procedure of the Dutch courts, the reporters of cases and the authors of the *Consultations*.

PRACTICE.

Joost van Damhouder is one of the earliest writers on procedure. He was born in 1507 at Bruges in Flanders, and studied law at the universities of Louvain, Padua and Orleans. He became Pensionaris of Bruges, and great favour was shown to him by Charles V, who in 1551 raised him to the peerage and gave him the appointment of Commissioner of the Treasury. Philip II continued him in that office until 1581, when he was created a member of the Raad. During the same year he died at Antwerp. His principal works were treatises on the practice of the civil and criminal courts of Holland. These works were originally written in Latin, but in the middle of the seventeenth century they were translated into Dutch by Van Nispen, and accepted as the standard work on the practice of the courts throughout the Netherlands. The elaborate illustrations of the first editions formed an extraordinary feature of the work, and one can hardly understand now-a-days why a book on practice should have been adorned with copious, and not always very edifying, wood-cuts. Both the civil and the criminal practice are arranged in a scientific manner, and the exposition of the rules of practice is thorough and masterly. Although Damhouder professes to treat only of civil and criminal practice, he incidentally deals with the substantive law of Holland, and gives us a very good idea of the Roman-Dutch law of the sixteenth century.

Andreas Gail (1525–1587), a contemporary of Damhouder, though a German, had so great an influence on the law of procedure in Holland that his name should be included amongst the writers on practice. His *Practicae Observationes* were regarded by the Dutch jurists as a work of the highest authority, and we find them quoting his *Observationes* as if he were a writer upon the practice of their own courts.

Paul Merula, a professor of law and the teacher of Grotius, published in 1592 his treatise on the *Civil Procedure of the Courts of Holland, Zeeland and West Friesland.* This work may be considered the standard work on the practice of the Dutch superior courts. It has been edited and annotated by numerous lawyers, and is an important book in a Roman-Dutch law library. Merula refers to all the most celebrated writers on the Roman law between the twelfth and sixteenth centuries, and often quotes Gail as an authority on practice. The latest edition of Merula, considerably augmented and brought up to date, is the one by Lulius and Van der Linden. This is the edition usually referred to nowadays, and although the text is that of Merula, the commentary and the notes exceed the text not only in bulk, but in value.

Willem de Groot (1597–1662), the brother of Hugo de Groot, published an *Introduction to the Practice of the Court of Holland* in 1656. It was called *Inleyding tot de Praktyke van den Hove van Holland.*

Bernhard van Zutphen published at Leeuwarden in 1664 a work called *Praktycke der Nederlandsche Rechten.* It is a collection of opinions and decisions of eminent jurists on various questions of practice, methodically arranged in the form of a lexicon.

Gerard Wassenaar was born towards the end of the sixteenth or beginning of the seventeenth century. He studied at Utrecht, and after taking his degree practised as an advocate in that city. He afterwards became burgomaster of Utrecht, where he died in 1664. He published a work on procedure during the first half of the seventeenth century. Its title is *Praktyk Judicieel ofte Instructie op de forme en manier van procedeeren voor Hoven en Rechtbanken.* The last edition of this work was published at Utrecht in 1746. Wassenaar's *Praktyk* is a work of considerable merit, and is frequently referred to by Voet. It deals very exhaustively with the law of executors and administrators, of which we find very little in Grotius.

Simon van Leeuwen published in 1666 a running commentary on the Procedure Ordinances of 1570 and 1580. It bears the title *Manier van procedeeren in Civiele en Crimineele Saaken.* The work was afterwards considerably added to by Verduijn and Aller, and has always been regarded as a text-book of great value.

Pieter Vromans published about 1669 a treatise on the nature of the cases which can in the first instance be brought before the superior courts, together with the usual procedure of those courts. It is called *Tractaat de Foro Competenti.*

Willem van Alphen was born at Leyden in 1608. He was appointed to the high office of Secretary of the Court of Holland when only twenty-three years old. This appointment he held until 1684. He died in 1691. He is chiefly known as the author of the *Papegaai,* a collection of legal forms and precedents. It was first published prior to 1668, for in that year a second edition of the work was issued. Since then many editions have been published, the last and best having appeared in 1720.

Johannes van der Linden is the most recent author on the practice of the courts of Holland. He published in 1794 a work entitled *Verhandeling over de Judicieele Praktijk of Form van Procedeeren,* which may be regarded as the best text-book for the practice of the courts during the latter half of the eigtheenth century.

Decisions and Consultations.

I shall now pass over to a class of work which stands midway between the procedure and the substantive law, and which plays so important a part in the subsequent development of the law that it deserves more than a mere passing notice. I allude to the collections of cases decided in the superior courts of the Netherlands. These reports contain decisions upon the practice of the courts and upon the law as then prevalent in the country. During the sixteenth and early part of the seventeenth century there were several collections of decided cases, all of which have helped to form what we now know as the Roman-Dutch law. They show

how the customs of the country modified the Roman law of Justinian, and what was the living law as accepted by the superior courts of the Netherlands under Spanish rule as well as after the secession of the seven provinces. The oldest decisions of the Supreme Court and of the Court of Holland that I have been able to lay my hands on are to be found in a collection of decided cases published by **Næranus** at Rotterdam in 1662. Its title is *Sententiën en gewezen zaken van den Hoogen en Provincialen Raad.* The preface to this book might serve as a preface to a volume of English reported cases. The author tells us that the weight attached to the decisions of the superior courts is such, that though they are not actually regarded as law they are of such authority as to pass for law. He points out that although the *Advijsen and Consultatiën* of eminent lawyers have always been regarded in the Netherlands as of great authority, yet they have not the same weight, and are not considered so binding upon the lower courts as the decisions of the superior tribunals. These decisions, as coming from judges appointed by the sovereign power, are regarded as decisive interpretations of the law, and are binding on all until amended or altered by some legislative enactment.

The decisions, therefore, of the superior courts of the Netherlands were regarded by the lawyers of those days in exactly the same way as we regard the decisions of our own superior courts. They definitely established the Roman-Dutch practice, they decided in how far the customs of the Netherlands modified the Roman law, and they admitted in an unquestionable manner that the basis of law of the Netherlands was the civil law as contained in the law books of Justinian. The oldest decision is one dated 1501. The matters discussed in these reports are of the greatest importance to us, for they form the foundation upon which later decisions and legislation have been built. One example will suffice. In 1515 the case of *Thon* v. *Thon* was brought before the Court of Holland, in which the issue raised was whether in case of a divorce granted on account of adultery the husband forfeited the goods he had brought into the community. The court decided that the defendant, by having committed adultery, forfeited all the property he had brought into the marriage, and condemned him to allow the plaintiff to have, for her own use, the said property, together with all such fruits as he had obtained therefrom since the *litis contestatio*, and further adjudged to the plaintiff all property in the defendant's possession which she had brought into the marriage, together with the fruits, and ordered the defendant to pay the costs of the suit. In *Higgins* v. *Higgins* (5 E.D.C. 344) the Eastern Districts' Court of the Cape of Good Hope admitted the principle which underlies the decision of *Thon* v. *Thon*, and though it did not go quite as far as the old Dutch court, it decided that the guilty spouse forfeited her benefit in a life policy settled on her by her husband by antenuptial contract.

Another important collection of decisions is that of **Christinaeus**, an advocate of the Supreme Court of Mechlin. These date from the latter half of the sixteenth century. In the very first decision the author tells us that the decisions of the Supreme Court of Mechlin are binding on all inferior courts.

Whilst dealing with this subject, there are some other collections of decided cases whose influence upon the Roman-

Dutch law has been so great that they cannot be overlooked. The first is that of **Cornelis van Nieustad** (Neostadius). He was one of the judges of the Supreme Court of Holland, Zeeland and West Friesland in the beginning of the seventeenth century. He collected and reported a great number of most important decisions, both of the Supreme Court and of the Court of Holland. The earliest decision, so far as I know, was one of the Supreme Court at Mechlin, given on the 19th November, 1568. He also collected the judgments of the feudal courts of Holland and West Friesland, to which he appended a treatise on the feudal law of those provinces. In addition to these he made a special collection of all the important decisions that had been given in his time on antenuptial contracts. These decisions of Neostadius have always been regarded by later writers as being of the very highest importance and authority, more especially in determining the difference between the Roman and Roman-Dutch law.

The next important reporter is **Jacob Coren,** also a judge of the Supreme Court of Holland, Zeeland and West Friesland. He flourished about the first half of the seventeenth century. He continued the work of Neostadius, and published reports of cases with remarks of his own upon them. In addition to these he also published a volume of *Consultatiën* and *Advijsen*. He has always been admitted to be a great authority on the practice of the Roman-Dutch law.

The next is **Jan van Sande.** He was a member of the Council of Friesland, and flourished during the first half of the seventeenth century. He published a collection of decisions of the Supreme Court of Friesland. These were published more after the manner of a modern text-book than of a volume of reported cases. It is practically a commentary on the law of Friesland arranged under definite headings, and the decisions of the Supreme Court are quoted as illustrating the text. These *Decisiones Frisicae* have always been regarded as of extremely great authority where the law of Holland and the Frisian law are the same. It must be remembered in dealing with Sande that the Frisians adhered more closely to the Roman law than the Hollanders, though where both follow the Roman law the writings of Sande are admitted to be of high authority. In addition to the *Decisiones Frisicae* he wrote a treatise on the Prohibition of Alienations (which has been translated into English by Mr. Walter S. Webber), a commentary on the *De Regulis Juris*, and a treatise on the *Cession of Actions*, lately translated by Dr. P. C. Anders.

Another important collection of decided cases is that of **Lœnius,** who was also one of the judges of the Supreme Court of Holland, Zeeland and West Friesland. These cases cover the period from 1621 to 1641. In 1712 they were published with numerous annotations by Tobias Boel, advocate of the Court of Holland. This edition with the notes of Boel is the one always quoted by the lawyers of the eighteenth century. Like Nieustad, Coren, and Sande, Loenius was present at the trials reported by him, and was therefore acquainted with the reasons that moved the court to come to the reported decision. It is for this reason that the reports of these judges have always been considered of such great weight and authority.

Besides these collections of such great importance there are several other volumes of reported cases to which constant reference is made by the later text-writers, such as the *Casus enucleati* and the *Observationes rerum Judicarum* of

Zaccharias Huber, published about the beginning of the eighteenth century; **Beucker's** decisions of the Frisian courts; **Radelant's** decisions of the Court of Utrecht; **Stockman's** decisions of the Court of Brabant; and **Wynant's** decisions of the Supreme Court of Brabant. The influence of the decisions of the courts of Friesland, Utrecht and Brabant upon the development of the Roman-Dutch law cannot be compared with that of the older decisions of the Supreme Courts of Mechlin and of Holland and Zeeland as reported in Christinaeus, Coren, Nieustad and Loenius. I have not included the *Quaestiones Juris Privati* of Bynkershoek under the head of decisions, for they do not really belong to this class, and I intend later on to devote some considerable attention to the works of this gifted jurist. The latest collection of decisions of the Court of Holland is a volume of *Gewysden,* published by **Johannes van der Linden** in 1803. He intended to publish a second volume, but probably abandoned the idea when the *Code Napoléon* supplanted the old law of Holland.

Consultatien.—As I have been dealing with the various collections of decided cases which contributed so largely to the development of the Roman-Dutch law, I think it will be convenient, though not strictly in its place, to devote some attention to those numerous collections of opinions of eminent jurists which are to some extent akin to the decisions. These opinions (*Consultatiën* and *Advijsen,* as they are called in Dutch, or *Consilia* in Latin) must not be regarded as being equivalent to the *Responsa Jurisprudentium* of the later Roman law. It will be remembered that the Roman jurisconsults, in the early days of the Republic, exercised a great influence on the development of the Roman law. The most eminent lawyers of the day were resorted to by private persons, magistrates and judges for advice upon questions of law, and their opinions, or *responsa*, were quoted as the interpretations of skilled persons upon the questions submitted to them. Before the time of Augustus the judge was not bound to accept the view of any particular lawyer, but was free to choose which opinion he would adopt. The opinions of the great jurists were carefully collected, and their views were so often adopted by the law courts that in course of time they came to be regarded as authoritative interpreters of the law. Augustus recognised the weight and authority which usage had given to their opinions, and in order to make the interpretation of the law more certain, he gave to some jurists the right of giving opinions. If the opinions of these privileged persons agreed the judge was bound to accept their view, but if they differed he could follow any particular opinion he pleased. After the time of Augustus and until the days of Hadrian there was, therefore, a privileged class of authoritative jurists. Now the collections of the opinions of the Roman-Dutch lawyers were regarded in the light of the pre-Augustan *responsa*. and never had any authoritative value, such as those of the post-Augustan lawyers who had obtained the *jus respondendi*. It is therefore but natural that the older the collection of opinions the more familiar their conclusions were to the profession, and, therefore, the greater the weight of authority. For this reason, then, the *Hollandsche Consultatiën*, which consist of opinions given in the sixteenth and during the first half of the seventeenth century, have acquired by usage a foremost place in the legal literature of Holland. The opinions were given to private persons upon certain facts stated, and were quoted, if not before the higher courts, at least before the courts of schout and schepenen. Many of them are frequently alluded to by the great lawyers of the seventeenth century, and both Van Leeuwen and Voet refer to them in the same way as they quote the decisions of Neostadius and Coren. It may, therefore, be safely asserted that the *Consultatiën en Advijsen* have played a very important part in the development of the Roman-Dutch law. Not only did the writers of the seventeenth century refer to them, but they are quoted by the very latest Roman-Dutch lawyers with the greatest respect as holding an important place among the authoritative works on Roman-Dutch law.

When first collections were made of the opinions of eminent lawyers in the Netherlands is a matter of some doubt. That some collections existed in the early part of the seventeenth century is extremely likely, though, as far as I am aware, they were not published in printed form. There are no references to the *Consultatiën* in the works of the early part of the seventeenth century. Judging, however, from the printed collections of later date it seems most likely that some of these had been collected and published in manuscript for the use of lecturers and lawyers. At any rate the first printed collection was published in 1645 by Næranus, a well-known publisher of law-books at Rotterdam. In the preface of the first volume we are told that in no branch of science is a theoretical knowledge enough, and least of all in the study of law. Students should not only know the law of Justinian, but also the decisions of the various courts, the customs, and the alterations in the law brought about by legislation. The publisher was therefore requested to print a collection of opinions emanating from well-known advocates and eminent jurists. He mentions the names of Reynier van Amsterdam and Willem de Cocq as the writers of *Consultatiën* that were much prized in his day. Their opinions were apparently well known at the time, and must, therefore, have been available to many persons in manuscript. In forming this new collection the publisher did not confine himself to the opinions of these lawyers, but included those of many other famous advocates, such as Grotius and Groenewegen. The first series, known as *Hollandsche Consultatiën* or *Responsa Juris Consultorum Hollandorum*, was published in six volumes. In this collection there are a great number of Grotius' opinions. These have been collected and translated by the late Advocate De Bruyn. The others are as yet untranslated, and having been printed in black letter type and written in a peculiar antiquated style, they are by no means attractive reading to the ordinary student of Roman-Dutch law.

Naturally they are not all of the same authority, and often we find different views on the same question. They are all solutions of questions that have actually arisen in practice, and they give us, therefore, an excellent insight into the manner in which the older lawyers treated the questions submitted to them. The advocate who gave his opinion was not satisfied with a mere statement of the facts and his opinion thereon, but he invariably set out his reasons and based each statement of the law upon some well-known authority, or some judgment of a higher court. After the first two volumes had been published by Næranus there appeared at Amsterdam a volume which purported to be a continuation of the *Hollandsche Consultatiën*. This was published by Johannes Colom, and is known as the *Amster-*

damsche Derde Deel (or Amsterdam Third Volume). The publisher in his preface jeers at some of the advocates whose decisions formed part of the first and second volumes of Næranus' collection, and he proposes in his volume to give the opinions of only very eminent advocates. That the opinions in this volume are of exceedingly great value is undeniable, though his detraction of the former collections seems to have been animated solely by trade jealousy. Næranus continued his work, and at first recognised the volume of Colom as a third volume, and called his own third volume the second part of the third volume, the Amsterdam publication being considered as the first part of the third volume. In 1688, however, Næranus called the volume, which he originally published as the second part of the third volume, the third volume of his collection. This volume is known as the *Rotterdamsche Derde Deel* (or Rotterdam Third Volume). There are, therefore, two third volumes to the *Hollandsche Consultatiën*, the one called the Amsterdam Third Volume and the other the Rotterdam Third Volume. It may be useful to know that Voet quotes the Amsterdam volume as *Respons. Jurisc. Holl.* part 3, vol. 1; and the Rotterdam volume as part 3, vol. 2. The whole work was completed in 1685 by the publication of the sixth volume. Later on, in 1696, a *kort begrip* or index was published by Van Someren at Amsterdam.

In 1661 the same publisher printed a collection of opinions by **Jacob Coren** before he became judge of the Supreme Court. These were originally published in Latin, but in 1665 a Dutch translation was issued.

So popular and so useful did these *Consultatiën* of Næranus become, that **Isaac van den Berg,** in 1692, began a new series of opinions known as Van den Berg's *Advijs Boek.* This work was completed in four volumes. It passed through several editions, the last and best being that of 1781.

Van den Berg's work was continued by **De Haas** and **Van der Kop.** The former called his collection *Nieuwe Hollandsche Consultatiën,* and the latter gave to his the title of *Nieuw Nederlands Advijsboek.*

In 1671, Ketell, a bookseller at Utrecht, published three volumes of opinions by well-known advocates who had practised, or were then practising, before the Court of Utrecht. These are known as the *Utrechtsche Consultatiën.*

In 1738 **Schomaker** began to publish a collection of opinions given by himself and others. These referred generally to the Roman-Dutch law, but more especially to the law that obtained in the provinces of Gelderland and Zutphen. The work was completed in six volumes.

In 1740 another collection of opinions was compiled by **Johan Schrassert.** These were mostly by Schrassert himself, though there are several opinions given by other well-known advocates. Both of these collections have been accepted as containing opinions of great weight and authority.

In 1712 Van Poolsum published at Utrecht an interesting volume of opinions known as the *Bellum Juridicum* or *Oorlogh der Advocaten.* This work was one of considerable novelty. It not only contained the opinions of well-known advocates, but also the decisions of the courts upon the questions discussed. We first get the opinion of one advocate (*casus primus*), then the opposite opinion of another (*casus secundus* or *contrarium superiori*), and, lastly, the decision of the court.

Practical questions of the day were, therefore, treated in the same way as Cocceijus and others dealt with the disputed points of law in their works on the *jus controversum*.

In order to illustrate the method adopted by the compiler of these opinions and decisions I shall give a resumé of one case as an example:—

FIRST CASE.

Whether stolen cattle sold to a third person on a free market can be reclaimed by the owner.

The advocates Jonas Cabbeljauw and Jacob Deym gave an opinion in 1673 in which, relying on the Code, *de furtis*, 1, 2, they answered the question above stated in the affirmative.

CONTRARY OPINION.

In the same year the advocates Kerkhoeven and Swaenswijk gave it as their opinion that, by the custom of Holland, stolen cattle sold on a free market could not be reclaimed without restoring to the purchaser the price he paid for them.

DECISION.

In the following year this very case came before the Court of Holland, and judgment was given against the plaintiff, so that the court upheld the views of Kerkhoeven and Swaenswijk.

In 1745 another important collection of opinions was published under the title of *Bort's Advijsen*. These opinions were given by the famous jurist **Pieter Bort**, as well as by several other eminent lawyers. They were all collected by Bort during his lifetime, and published posthumously under the title mentioned above.

Barels collected and published two series of opinions. In 1778 he published a collection of opinions on criminal matters, and in 1780 another collection on commercial and maritime law. The latter are known as Barel's *Advijsen over den Koophandel and Zeevaart.*

In 1780 Gartman published a series of important opinions by some of the best-known advocates of Holland and Zeeland. To this work he gave the name of *Vervolg op de Hollandsche Consultatiën.* Besides the above there were other collections of opinions on special branches of law, as, for instance, Van Hasselt's opinions on military law and on feudal law, Schelling's *Advijsen* and Lamsweerde's *Guelderlandsche Consultatiën,* but they are not frequently quoted by the text-writers. Various indexes or digests have been published to these decisions, as, for instance, the *Kort begrip der Hollandsche Consultatiën* and the *Kort begrip van Van den Berg's Advijsboek;* but the best and most complete digest of the *Consultaties,* and of the various collections of decisions, is undoubtedly Nassau La Leck's *Algemeen Register op Rechtsgeleerde Advysen, Consultatiën en Sententiën,* published at Utrecht in 1778.

The value of these *Consultatiën* and *Advijsen* to any one who desires to acquire a thorough grasp of the Roman-Dutch law can hardly be exaggerated. De Bruyn's translation of the opinions of Grotius forms an excellent introduction to the study of the *Consultatiën.* Students are no doubt repelled by the black letter type of the *Hollandsche Consultatiën,* but all the other collections can be obtained in the ordinary Roman character, and a careful perusal of these will, to my mind, more than anything else, enable the student to grasp the great legal acumen, clear reasoning powers and common sense of the Dutch lawyers of the seventeenth and eighteenth centuries.

CHAPTER XXVIII.

THE IMMEDIATE PREDECESSORS OF GROTIUS.

WHEN the Union had cast off the yoke of Spain it soon developed into a powerful and respected Republic. It was recognised by the surrounding kingdoms as an important factor in Europe. Its trade increased, its mercantile marine was one of the largest in Europe, it formed ambitious schemes of colonising the East, and though its European territory was small it was gradually acquiring a large territory in the East and West Indies. Its alliance was sought by the great European States, and its ambassadors were treated abroad with great respect.

With all this rapid development it was necessary for the Republic to have men to fill the many responsible positions created by this sudden expansion. The builders of the Republic were educated men who saw the necessity of creating universities and schools for the education of the people. The nation became enthusiastic in every branch of art and science. Law was studied with vigour, and some of the ablest jurists of Europe lectured in the universities and law schools of Holland. It is, therefore, no wonder that the end of the sixteenth and the whole of the seventeenth century beheld the Netherlands as one of the great centres for the study of law. Who the men were that expounded the Roman and the Roman-Dutch law in the universities and in the courts of law I shall now explain.

In a former chapter I have already referred to Damhouder, Paul Merula, and other writers on Practice. Contemporaneous with these writers on Practice, and the reporters who strove to bring the decisions of the superior courts into some system, were the professors of law and practising advocates, who published works on the substantive law as then accepted in the Netherlands. Head and shoulders above his contemporaries stands Hugo de Groot, who by his *Jus Belli ac Pacis* established the basis upon which modern international law was built up; whilst by his *Introduction to the Jurisprudence of Holland* he systematised the confused mass of law which obtained in Holland, and laid the foundation of the Roman-Dutch law as a legal system.

We have seen how German customs, Roman and Canon law, and the legislation of the emperors were all welded into one confused mass of laws, so that it was no easy matter to know under which particular system any individual fell. Throughout the whole of the Netherlands there was the one conservative idea that the customs and privileges of the people should remain intact. Their customs, laws and privileges the people held sacred, but as commerce grew and intellectual life increased this conservatism had to give way to the more practical requirements of the times. Law, like everything else, came to be treated more methodically and more scientifically, and it was found that a series of disconnected enactments, independent of some general system of principles, no longer satisfied a people burning to take up a position in the forefront of progress. The legal system of Justinian was at hand, but it had in many respects become antiquated, and the prolific legislation of the sixteenth century stood entirely outside of it. Moreover, the Canon law had to a large extent modified the principles of the *Corpus Juris.* Several writers strove to weave the newer law into the old, so as to make the old and the new homogeneous, but until Grotius appeared their success was comparatively small.

In the Netherlands Grotius was the giant intellect that brought about the complete *débâcle* of the legal ideas that prevailed in the middle ages. His *Jus Belli ac Pacis* separates the new from the old in the field of General Jurisprudence, and his *Introduction* is the first modern work on Roman-Dutch law. At the same time we must not imagine that the work of Grotius appeared like Minerva, for his immediate predecessors made it possible for him to achieve what he did. Without Cujacius and Donellus, Damhouder and Merula, the *Introduction* of Grotius would not have been possible. We shall, therefore, continue with our account of the principal writers of the end of the sixteenth and the beginning of the seventeenth century.

Brederode (Pieter Cornelius van) lived in the latter half of the sixteenth century, and was a lawyer of great repute. He was chosen as ambassador of the Republic at the courts of several German princes. His chief work is the *Repertorium Sententiarum et Regularum juris civilis ex Universo juris corpore,* first published in 1585 and again in 1664.

Peckius was born in 1529 at Zierikzee. He studied at Louvain, and was in 1562 appointed regius professor of Civil and Canon law at that university. In 1586 he became one of the judges of the Supreme Court at Mechlin, where he died in 1589. He wrote a large number of legal treatises. His best-known work is the *De jure sistendi et mannum injiciendi quam arrestationem vocant.* This is his well-known treatise on arrest. This work was translated into Dutch and annotated by Simon van Leeuwen. Until the appearance of Borts' work on arrest this treatise of Peckius was the chief authority on that branch of our law. It is still quoted as an authoritative work, though its greatest value at the present day is historical. Besides this he wrote the *De testamentis conjugum* and the *Regulae juris canonici.*

Gudelinus.—One of the immediate predecessors of Grotius, who in all probability had some influence on the production of the *Introduction,* was Petrus Gudelinus (Pieter Goudelin). He was born in 1550 at Ath in Henegouwen, and carried on his legal studies at Louvain. In 1574 he started practising as an advocate before the Supreme Court of Mechlin, and soon made for himself a great name. In 1582, the year before Grotius was born, he became a professor at Louvain, where he filled numerous offices until his death in 1619. He was a staunch Catholic and belonged to the Order of Jesuits. His principal work was a manual of the law in vogue in the Netherlands in his time. The title of this work is *Commentarium de jure novissimo optimâ methodo accurate ac erudite conscriptum additis harum vicinarumque regionum moribus.* The work was not published until a year after Goudelin's death, though it was in all probability well known to lawyers before that date, for we must remember that the works of professors were often dictated to their students, and not printed until after their death. This custom existed in Holland even in the time of Van der Keessel, whose *Dictata ad jus hodiernum* have never been printed, but have come down to us only in manuscript. Though the commentary of Gudelinus was not published until 1620, and though Grotius had then already written, though not published, his *Introduction*, it is difficult to believe that Grotius was not acquainted with the work of so eminent a jurist as Goudelin. Moreover, there is considerable internal evidence in the *Introduction* to make this supposition more than a mere conjecture.

Goudelin took the *Novels* of Justinian as containing the most recent Roman legislation, and, starting from these, he dealt methodically and under various heads with the Roman law as well as with the later legislation of the Western Empire. He did not adhere to the order of the *Novels*, but divided his treatise into six books, and each book into various chapters. In the first he deals with the *Jus Personarum*, in the second with the *Jus Rerum*. The third book deals with the law of obligations, and the fourth embraces the law of procedure. In the fifth book he treats of public law, the rights and duties of magistrates, the execution of sentences, and ends up with a brief sketch of the criminal law. The sixth book is wholly devoted to ecclesiastical law. In giving a short resumé of what he intends to discuss in his Manual (Isagoge) he tells us: "I intend to embrace in this work not only the *Novels* of Justinian, but also whatever has been established by later legislation (*quidquid est juris novissimi*). In this, however, I do not include the *Novels* of Theodosius, of Valentinianus, and of other post-Justinian emperors, since all these lack the authority of Justinian. I intentionally omit the *Novels* of Leo, of Constantine, and of the later Greek emperors, which Godefroi has included in his edition of the *Corpus Juris Civilis*, for these *Novels* were never taken over by the Western

Empire, and were never recognised by the Emperor Lothair. In the place of these I have incorporated the Constitutions of Frederick and of the other emperors of every period, . . . for these have been accepted by us as law. I shall add, also, the more general customs of these and of the neighbouring provinces, in order that this Manual may be useful to persons engaged in the study of our native laws."

We have in this work of Goudelin an attempt to weave into one whole the Roman law as it was received in the Netherlands, together with the local customs that had survived from the German forefathers, and the customs that had been adopted in the course of time from various quarters. The Manual presents the law as a homogeneous whole. Inasmuch as Goudelin was a Jesuit and a staunch Catholic, his work embraces a great deal of the Canon law, which the Protestant Netherlands gradually rejected.

It would hardly be profitable to give a lengthy account of the whole work, though a more than cursory account of some typical chapter will be useful in showing how these early text-writers dealt with their subject. I shall take chapter 7 of the first book as an example. The chapter is called *De potestate maritali et societate conjugali*; and I may here mention that the whole work, unlike the *Introduction* of Grotius, is written in Latin. He tells us that the power that a Roman husband had over his wife was very different from that possessed by a Dutch husband. That the Roman had some power over his wife is a natural consequence of marriage, and approved of by divine law, natural reason, and the use of all nations; at the same time, that power was not great in the time of Justinian (*attamen certum est exiguam fuisse potestatem mariti*). The husband had the custody and administration of his wife's goods, but he could not meddle with her affairs if she objected, and, therefore, she often managed her own private business. Even where the husband managed his wife's affairs he was obliged to render her an account of his administration. Inasmuch as they were married, lived together, and brought up their children in common, the one spouse naturally made use of the goods of the other, but there existed no such community of property as we understand by the term.

He then treats historically of the marital power of the husband amongst the Gauls of Belgium, and shows how much more extensive than the Roman were the rights of the Belgian husband over his wife: *Vires ibi in uxores etiam vitae necisque potestatem habuisse qualis videlicet apud Romanos fuit dominorum in servos, nec non patrum in filios.* The spouses held their property in common, and if one died the other succeeded to his or her share. Though the modern law throughout Belgium and the rest of Gaul is not quite the same as that of the ancient Gauls, there is a striking similarity.

He then passes over from his historical sketch to the actual law of the Netherlands in his day. "The law which we follow to-day, and which prevails in almost every city, is that the husband has the wife completely in his power, and he is as it were her tutor and father, so that the wife cannot contract without the consent and authority of her husband. She cannot appear before a court, nor can she enter into any business transactions without the consent of her husband, unless she follows the calling of a public trader, and depends on her trade for a livelihood. In this case she binds her husband, for he is considered to have approved of her acting as a tradeswoman. On the other hand, the care of the whole estate devolves upon the husband, and he has the full and free administration of the common property, without the necessity of rendering any account. He may, in general, alienate her property, except where by the custom of a particular place immovable property belonging to a wife cannot be alienated."

Gudelinus then proceeds to deal with the law of divorce. He first explains the Roman law regarding divorce, then states the Canon law, and boldly adopts that law as the only law on divorce existing in the Netherlands. That Holland never adopted the Canon law on divorce to its full extent is not mentioned by him, and he lays it down as a general rule for the Netherlands that "death alone can dissolve the marriage, and that, therefore, neither captivity, servitude, long absence, nor adultery can break the bond of marriage. By the judgment of the Church the parties may be separated in case of adultery, heresy or of incompatibility of temper, but such a separation will not enable either party to marry." This is an enunciation of the Canon law pure and simple, and certainly not of the customs of the Netherlands.

It is true that Gudelinus was not writing the law of Holland; but as he professed to deal with the customs *harum vicinarumque regionum*, one would have expected that he would point out that Holland at any rate did not adopt the Canon law rules as to divorce. A book which omitted to mention so important a fact as that adultery was in Holland and in the other northern provinces a good ground for divorce can hardly be called a hand-book for practitioners, in which is set out the customs *harum vicinarumque regionum.* The book is, however, fairly methodical, and the new is interwoven with the old so as to give the reader a general idea of every branch of law he deals with.

If, however, we compare the manner in which Gudelinus treats the subject of marriage and its consequences with that of Grotius, we shall soon perceive how far more scientific and logical is the treatment of the subject by the latter author. Gudelinus begins this branch of his subject by discussing the marital power of the husband over the wife. He then proceeds to deal with another consequence of marriage, viz., community of property. This he follows up with a discussion of *dos* and donations *propter nuptias.* In the next chapter he considers the requisites of a valid marriage, and then deals with divorce, the rights of the surviving spouse, and second marriages. The arrangement is obviously faulty, for the cart is placed before the horse. The consequences of marriage are dealt with before the requisites of a valid marriage have been considered.

Now, see how Grotius handles the same subject. He defines marriage, considers who can and who cannot marry, and then gives the statutory requirements for the due and legal solemnisation of the marriage. He then proceeds to set out the consequences of the marriage, its effect upon both husband and wife with regard to their personal relationship towards each other, and with reference to their legal capacity. This part of the subject is concluded by a statement of how marriage is dissolved. In a later chapter he proceeds to discuss the confusion of the property of husband and wife by reason of the marriage. This portion of the subject he deals with when he is considering the acquisition of ownership generally by accession and confusion, and he treats community of property as one of the methods of acquiring ownership. Grotius then somewhat illogically goes over to antenuptial contracts and *boedelhouderschap*, though no doubt these subjects could be conveniently brought in whilst dealing with community.

Here, then, we perceive the difference between the orderly and logical arrangement of Grotius, as compared with the somewhat loose method of exposition adopted by his contemporary. If we look more narrowly into the way in which the subject is presented in detail and in style, we are still more struck with the difference. With Grotius the subject is expanded step by step, and our knowledge is gradually and systematically increased, whereas with Gudelinus we are incorrectly assumed to know what should have been, but was not, told to us. In style, too, there is a difference: Grotius is crisp and clear, and almost every paragraph contains a rule of law; Gudelinus, though not nearly so involved as some of his contemporaries, is apt to crowd too much into one sentence, thereby making it difficult to follow his meaning.

In dealing with the subject of divorce, Gudelinus allows his religious prejudices to interfere with his exposition of the law as accepted in several of the most important provinces of the Netherlands; for he would make it appear as if the Canon law had been universally adopted throughout the whole of the Netherlands, whereas in so important a province as Holland the law of the Franks, that adultery was a ground for divorce, was always the customary law. These few remarks will sufficiently show how greatly the work of Gudelinus differs from that of Grotius.

Before I proceed to give an outline of the work of Grotius, there are two other lawyers of note, who wrote before or at the same time as Grotius, of whom mention must be made—the one is Zypaeus and the other Zoezius. They are both writers of considerable authority, and are frequently referred to by the jurists of the seventeenth century.

Zypaeus or **Van den Zype.**—Zypaeus belonged to the class of notaries attached to some ecclesiastical dignitary. These notaries were known as apostolic notaries, and were usually appointed by the Pope or by a bishop to look after the affairs of the Church, and to draw up all documents in which the Church was concerned. Zypaeus afterwards became a protonotary, and was attached as such to the see of Antwerp. He was highly skilled both in the Canon law and in the Civil law, as it obtained in the Netherlands towards the end of the sixteenth and the beginning of the seventeenth century. He was a contemporary of Grotius, though the book by which he is known was apparently published after the *Introduction.* This work is called the *Notitia Juris Belgici.* It deals briefly with both the Civil and the Canon law as it obtained in his day.

The method of exposition adopted by Zypaeus in his *Notitia* is very much the same, though not so good, as that of Gudelinus, and entirely different from that followed by Zoezius. The work is divided into twelve books, and each book deals with a number of more or less cognate subjects, though their connection is often impossible to ascertain. Sometimes the same book deals with subjects in no way connected.

The sixth book, for instance, opens with a treatise on slaves, and immediately thereupon proceeds to deal with wills. There is no definite system and no proper arrangement, so that the work seems a bewildering mass of indiscriminately arranged legal tracts.

Zypaeus, however, is not a mere commentator on the law of the *Corpus Juris*, for he shows us how the Roman law had been modified by custom and legislation. He freely quotes the placaats prior to 1629, but as he belonged to the southern States, and remained a fervent Catholic, he deals chiefly with the changes brought about by the legislation of Charles V and Philip II. The placaats cited are those contained in the first two volumes of the *Placaat Boek*. As an ecclesiastical notary his book is redolent of the Canon law. He begins his *Notitia* by inveighing bitterly against the heretical spirit of the times, which had given birth to such arch heretics as Luther, Calvin and Menno. The *Notitia* of Zypaeus is quoted by later writers as an authority for the law that prevailed in the Netherlands prior to the secession of the northern provinces, as well as for the law as it existed in the southern provinces when he wrote the work; but it is manifestly of little authority for the law of Holland after the establishment of the Republic.

Henricus Zoezius (1571–1627).—Zoezius was a predecessor of Grotius. He was born at Amersfoort in 1571, and studied at the University of Louvain. After taking his degree he went to Spain and lectured on law at the University of Salamanca. He was descended from a family of lawyers and senators, who had occupied in the Netherlands high positions in both Church and State. He returned to Louvain and was elected, in 1606, professor of Greek in that university. In 1619 he was elected regius professor of law in the place of Peter Gudelinus. Later on he became rector of the university, where he died in 1627. His principal work is the *Commentary on the Pandects*, which was not published until 1651. This work was held in great repute in Holland, and is very frequently quoted by Voet. It was written on the same principle as the *Commentary* of Voet, though it dealt almost exclusively with the Roman law, and only very cursorily with the law that obtained in the Netherlands. His other works were *Commentarii ad Institutiones; Commentarii ad jus Canonicum; Commentarii paratitulares ad Codicem;* and *Commentarii ad decretales et epistolas Gregorii IX.*

CHAPTER XXIX.

HUGO DE GROOT (GROTIUS).

I SHALL now consider that great genius of the Netherlands who may be justly described as the founder of modern international law and of the system of jurisprudence known as the Roman-Dutch law. I allude to Hugo de Groot or Grotius. I do not wish to convey the idea that Grotius invented and propounded the Roman-Dutch law. Such an idea would of course be absurd. What I do wish to impress upon my readers is that Grotius was the first great Dutch lawyer who systematised the confused mass of law which obtained in his day, and who by his *Introduction to the Jurisprudence of Holland* enabled subsequent legislators and jurists to build upon a solid foundation.

The body of rules now known as the Roman-Dutch law was there. Attempts had been made to expound the law methodically, as we saw in the last chapter, but no one had come forward to reduce the existing law into a system. This task was completed by Grotius, and so well was it carried out by this marvellous and many-sided man, that from the date of the publication of the *Introduction* down to our own time it has been recognised as the most authoritative exposition of the law of Holland. Some have commented upon almost every paragraph, and others have written more extensive treatises on the Roman-Dutch law, but one and all have gone to Grotius' *Introduction* as an acknowledged authority of the greatest weight. The influence of the *Introduction* on the subsequent development of Roman-Dutch law may be compared with that of the *Institutes* of Justinian upon the spread of Roman law. As this great man played so important a part in the development of the Roman-Dutch law, I propose to devote some considerable space to an account of his life and work.

Grotius, as he is commonly called, or Hugo de Groot, as he was known to his countrymen, was born at Delft on the 10th April, 1583. His real name was De Cornets, but his great-grandfather had assumed the name of De Groot when he married Ermgard, daughter of Dirk Huigen de Groot, the burgomaster of Delft. Grotius at a very early age had given promise to become a great scholar. When eight years old he composed Latin verses. He appeared to have such natural gifts in acquiring a knowledge of Latin and Greek that the great Greek scholars of the day took a peculiar interest in his education. As a boy he was the constant companion of the learned Scaliger. Junius, Snellius, Clusius and Merula were some of the learned men of the day who helped to instruct the boy Grotius. Before he was thirteen he was interested in the great religious dispute between the Catholics and Protestants, and it is said that he helped at that early age to convert his mother, a Catholic, to the Protestant faith.

At the age of fourteen he held his first public disputation. At the age of fifteen he had completed his university course at Leyden, and was selected by Oldenbarneveld and Justinus van Nassau to accompany them on their mission to the King of France (Henry IV). Henry was astonished at the marvellous learning and judgment of this young diplomatist, and presented him with a gold chain and his miniature as a token of his regard, at the same time pointing to Grotius and saying to his courtiers, "Voilà le miracle d'Hollande." The University of Orleans conferred upon this young Hollander the degree of Doctor of Laws. In the following year Grotius returned to Holland and there joined the Bar of the Court of Holland.

About this time Grotius began to study the religious disputes with great earnestness. His instructor in these matters was Johann Uitenbogaard, Court Minister to Prince Maurice. Uitenbogaard was a follower of Arminius, and it was therefore no wonder that Grotius embraced so eagerly the views of the Arminians.

Although Grotius had a large and ever-increasing practice at the Bar before he was twenty-one years of age, he nevertheless found time to edit classical works and to write numerous literary compositions in the Latin language. In 1607 Grotius was appointed Advocaat-Fiscaal of the province of Holland, and shortly after he obtained this appointment he married Maria van Reigersbergen.

In 1609 he published his first work of European fame, the well-known *Mare Liberum*. It was written as a plea in favour of Holland's right to navigate the open seas without the leave or license of any Power. In this work Grotius for the first time laid down the general proposition, which now appears to us so commonplace, "that according to the law of nations every person is free to sail to such coasts as he may please, and that therefore the Portuguese, even though they are the lords of the places to which the Hollanders are sailing, have no right whatever to hinder them in their course thither."

In this treatise he urged his countrymen to see "that whether they were at war with Spain or not, their freedom to sail upon the sea which nature had given them should not be curtailed." In the same year the great Arminius died, and Grotius composed a panegyric upon the deceased preacher in Latin verse, entitled *In Mortem Arminii.* In the following year he published a dissertation on the *Antiquity of the Batavian Republic.* Inasmuch as this book was a strong appeal to his countrymen to maintain the freedom they had won amidst so many difficulties, it was placed upon the *Index Expurgatorius* at the instance of the Spanish ecclesiastics. Amidst all the troubles of his later life he steadfastly continued to write the history of his native land, but this work was not published until after his death, in 1657.

In 1609 began the civil troubles in Holland, which proved to be so disastrous to Grotius. Though the United Provinces had cast off the Spanish yoke and wrested from Spain their freedom, the war with Spain went on long after the independence of the provinces had been acknowledged by the neighbouring European States. It was, however, shortly after the accession of James I that the United Provinces were compelled to endeavour to obtain peace, for James, though profuse in his promises of assistance, was virtually helping the Spaniards in their prosecution of the war.

The Spaniards were prepared to make peace upon three conditions: (1) Freedom for the Catholic religion; (2) a Spanish protectorate over Holland; and (3) that the Hollanders should renounce their right to trade with India. It was this last clause which turned both James and Henry IV to the Court of Spain. They were both anxious to exclude Holland from the Indian trade, in order afterwards to wrest that trade from Spain. It was under these circumstances that the peace party grew up in Holland, and this party did not meet with the approval of Prince Maurice. To this party belonged Oldenbarneveld, the great Raad-Pensionaris, and as Grotius was a strong supporter of Oldenbarneveld he naturally joined that party.

In 1609, at the instigation of Oldenbarneveld, a truce was made with Spain which lasted until 1621. This was one of the first breaches between Grotius and the House of Orange. It was about this time also that the religious dissensions began to divide Holland into the Arminian and Gomarist groups—dissensions which became so bitter and violent that they bade fair at one time to subvert the whole State.

It is impossible to understand the life of Grotius without some account of these religious dissensions. There were two professors of the University of Leyden whose differences of opinion on religious matters caused the terrible civil strife to which Oldenbarneveld fell a victim. The name of the one was Arminius, that of the other Gomarus. The belief in Predestination was accepted in 1562 as an article of belief in Holland, and became one of the main pillars of the national faith. Gomarus was a strong supporter of this article of faith, and when Arminius, his fellow-professor, openly scoffed at the doctrine and preached that it reduced God to a tyrant and allowed men to commit all manner of iniquities, under the plea that whatever their conduct may be their salvation or damnation had been pre-ordained long before their birth, the adherents of the national faith were up in arms and ranged themselves round the other Leyden professor, Gomarus.

From Leyden the strife spread over the whole of the United Provinces. To the Gomarists belonged the great mass of the people, whilst among the adherents of Arminius were the leading lights of Holland. Uitenbogaard, Barneveld, Grotius and others ranged themselves on the side of Arminius, who, in the eyes of the people, was regarded as a heretic plotting for the subversion of the Protestant Church.

In 1610 the flame of religious dissension was spreading fast and dangerously throughout the whole land, and the wiser men saw that it could only end in the destruction of the Republic, especially as it was fed and fostered by the trade rivals of the Netherlands—England and France.

In order to allay the passion, Grotius drew up a "Resolution for the Peace of the Church," which was adopted by the States of Holland. The States of Holland called upon Maurice to use his influence in order to get this resolution adopted by the other States. It was here that religion and politics met. The Arminian party was the great obstacle to the unlimited sovereign power which Maurice coveted, for all its leaders were strongly opposed to an absolute hereditary sovereign. On the other hand, the large mass of the people were Gomarists, and Maurice thought that by supporting that party he would increase his chances of obtaining sovereign power. He therefore hesitated no longer, but declared himself a Gomarist.

For several years the strife went on with ever-increasing bitterness and fury. In 1613 Grotius was appointed Pensionaris of Rotterdam in the place of the brother of Oldenbarneveld, who died during that year. Soon after his appointment to this high office Grotius went to England with a view to induce the English statesmen and clergy to side with the Arminians or Remonstranten. In England, however, he met with little success. The province of Holland was openly accused of heresy, and though it was defended by De Groot in a tract on the "Religion of the State of Holland," the greater part of the United Provinces sided with the opponents of Oldenbarneveld and Grotius.

In 1618 the crisis came. The disturbances in Holland became so great that the States of Holland thought it necessary as a precautionary measure to call out the troops under the control of the municipal authorities. This gave Maurice his opportunity. He alleged that this act on the part of the States of Holland was a breach of his prerogative and a revolt against him as Commander-in-chief of the Dutch forces. He took the power into his own hands and, supported by the middle classes throughout the United Provinces, he disbanded the municipal troops and caused Oldenbarneveld, Hoogerbeets and Grotius to be arrested. Oldenbarneveld, at the age of seventy-two, was sentenced to death and executed. Hoogerbeets and Grotius were sentenced to lifelong imprisonment in the castle of Louvenstein.

If any one desires to be staggered with amazement at the violent passions engendered by religious disputes, I should advise him to read Brandt's "History of the pleadings held in 1618 and 1619 with regard to the three prisoners Johann van Oldenbarneveld, Rombout Hoogerbeets and Hugo de Groot." It was whilst a prisoner in the castle of Louvenstein that Grotius conceived the idea of writing a systematic treatise on the law of Holland, and it was during confinement, with all the difficulties necessarily attending prison life, that he wrote the *Introduction to the Jurisprudence of Holland.*

By the aid of his wife Grotius escaped from Louvenstein in the year 1621. The means of his escape were devised by his wife. Grotius was allowed from time to time to receive books from Professor Erpenius. These books were sent in a large box, and the books that were no longer required were returned in the same box. At first the box was rigidly examined by the warders, but in time they grew somewhat careless about the examination. The wife of De Groot conceived the plan of liberating her husband by means of this box. For several weeks she made her preparations, and at last by the aid of a servant, Elsje van Houwening, got her husband into the box and obtained permission to have it carried out by the soldiers. Elsje took charge of the box with its precious contents, and though suspicions were aroused at several stages of the journey, the faithful Elsje managed to get the box safely conveyed to Gorkum. From there in the guise of a mason Grotius escaped to Antwerp. Thence he fled to Paris, where he remained an exile for many years.

It was during his stay in Paris that he wrote his great work, *De jure Belli ac Pacis.* It was this work which raised Grotius to the first rank among European jurists and publicists. The work was dedicated to Louis XIII, who was so pleased with it that he granted Grotius a pension. This pension, however, was taken away from him in 1631 by Richelieu, who greatly disliked De Groot.

Shortly after these events Prince Maurice died, and his brother Prince Frederik Hendrik became Stadhouder. This change aroused in the friends of De Groot the hope that he would be allowed to return to his native land. He sought the aid of Richelieu, but he tells us that though Richelieu promised to help him he added at the same time, "In politics the weakest party is always the party in the wrong."

In 1630 Grotius thought that the time was ripe for his return to Holland. He left France and arrived at Rotterdam, where he reported his arrival to the burgomaster. Although Frederik Hendrik had shown himself well disposed towards Grotius, the enemies of the latter were too strong, and the prince was compelled to agree to a decree of perpetual banishment from the Republic. Grotius thereupon went to Hamburg, where he obtained offers from the Danish, Polish and Spanish Governments to enter their service. These, however, he refused. In 1634 the Swedish Government requested him to enter the Swedish diplomatic service. The offer was made at the original instigation of Gustavus Adolphus, who had a profound admiration for the author of the *De jure Belli ac Pacis.* The Swedish offer was accepted, and Grotius was appointed Swedish ambassador to the Court of France.

Richelieu now became his bitter enemy, and did his best to get Grotius removed; but for ten years he remained at Paris as the trusted representative of the Swedish Court. In 1645, however, Grotius asked for his recall on account of some annoyance which his failure to obtain certain rights for Sweden had caused. He went back to Sweden and remained there for some months, and then again took ship to Holland. It would appear that there was some tacit understanding that he would be allowed to return to his native land to take up an important position at Amsterdam. In the passage to Holland he was overtaken by a storm and driven to the coast of Pommern, where he caught a cold, fell ill, and died on the 28th August, 1645.

Grotius, as we have seen, was a very learned and many-sided man. He was a man of the greatest probity and a noble patriot. The fame, however, which Grotius has obtained is in no way due to his political career. Outside of Holland Grotius has never been regarded as a politician. It is as a jurist and publicist that he has gained the fame which all Europe has accorded him. For our purposes there are two works of Grotius to which we must devote some attention. The first is the *De jure Belli ac Pacis,* and the second is the *Introduction to the Jurisprudence of Holland.* It may be said that we should dismiss the *De jure Belli ac Pacis* with a passing notice, inasmuch as we are considering the development of the Roman-Dutch law. The answer to this is that it is in the *De jure Belli ac Pacis* that we find a full exposition of De Groot's philosophy of law, and that a due appreciation of this is necessary in order to grasp fully the work that he did for the Netherlands in composing the *Introduction.*

It was the *De jure Belli ac Pacis* which raised Grotius to the first rank among European jurists and publicists. It placed international law upon a new footing, and sought to base the relations of civilised nations towards one another upon law and morality. It created a new epoch and a complete breach with the views that prevailed during the middle ages. It breathed the spirit of the Reformation, and liberated mankind from the theocratic views then predominant. Whatever there had been of international law, prior to this work of Grotius, was based upon the unity of the Church and the authority of the Pope. Grotius sought to base the law of nations not upon religious belief and Church authority, but upon a general idea of law and order. The papal authority had been so undermined that some new compensating foundation had to be sought upon which to build a law of nations. Grotius sought that foundation in a new fundamental idea of Right which was to regulate the relation of the individual to other individuals, of the individual to the State, and of the State to other States.

The new philosophy required an *à priori* conception of what was right and proper, that the individual should conform to this idea, and that in his social intercourse with other individuals he should recognise that a community could only exist if the individual sacrificed some of his natural liberty for the benefit of all. The State then becomes a common existence, born of the will of all, and regulated by that will. In the same way as the common will of all forms the State, so the common will of the various States forms the law which ought to guide them collectively, and this Grotius called the Law of Nations.

The object of Grotius in writing this book was to endeavour to put an end to the light-hearted manner in which one Christian nation made war with another. The terrible struggle which Holland underwent had taught Grotius the cruelties and inhuman acts which attended war, and he strove in some way to regulate the necessary violence. In the same way as the individual owed a duty to God not to ill-treat his fellow-man, so each State owed a duty to that same God not to ill-treat the individuals of another State beyond the limits accorded to it by the declared will of God and the teachings of Christ. It was De Groot's strong feeling of right and justice, and his humanitarian sentiment, which led him to compose the *De jure Belli ac Pacis*. For a century after its appearance the work was regarded as a text-book, and its principles were universally accepted.

I shall conclude my remarks upon this work of Grotius by a quotation from Hallam's *Literary History* (vol. 3, p. 181): "It is acknowledged by every one that the publication of the *De jure Belli ac Pacis* made an epoch in the philosophical and almost, we might say, in the political history of Europe. Those who sought a guide to their own conscience or that of others, those who dispensed justice, those who appealed to the public sense of right in the intercourse of nations, had recourse to its copious pages for what might direct or justify their actions. Within thirty or forty years from its publication we find the work of Grotius generally received as an authority by professors of the continental universities, and deemed necessary for the student of civil law, at least in the Protestant countries of Europe. . . . The book may be considered as nearly original in its general platform as any work of man in an advanced stage of civilisation and learning can be. It is more so, perhaps, than those of Montesquieu and Adam Smith. No one had before gone to the foundations of international law so as to raise a complete and consistent superstructure."

Such, then, was the fame of the author of the Law of Nations, and we must bear this in mind when we come to regard the influence of Grotius in the development of the civil law of Holland. When, therefore, in 1631, Grotius published his *Introduction to the Jurisprudence of Holland*, the work was enhanced with all the prestige Grotius had gained as the author of the Law of Nations. The fact, therefore, that Grotius was the author of the *De jure Belli ac*

S

Pacis had a great deal to do with the reception accorded to the *Introduction.* Apart from the intrinsic value of the *Introduction,* the fame acquired by Grotius as a jurist helped to make the *Introduction* a work of great authority. The *Introduction* was called in Dutch *De Inleiding tot de Hollandsche Rechtsgeleerdheid,* and was written during De Groot's captivity in the castle of Louvenstein.

There is a popular notion that Grotius wrote the *Introduction* without the aid of books, but this of course is absurd. Grotius had full opportunity of obtaining books, and it is most unlikely that he would not have availed himself of this opportunity in writing so technical a work as the *Introduction.* Moreover, the work was not published until 1631, so that there was ample opportunity for revision and correction. As a matter of fact Grotius, in a letter to his children, laments that he had *so few* books wherewith to accomplish so important a work. As this letter was intended originally by Grotius as a preface to his *Introduction,* but as it was never actually printed as such for fear that it might injure the sale of the work, and as I have not yet seen it printed in English, I shall give the reader a translation. The original is to be found in *Rechtsgeleerde Observatiën* (vol. 1, p. 9):—

MY DEAR CHILDREN,

Some of you were with me in the prison at Louvenstein; others have no doubt heard about it. God knows how unjustly I was placed there, and some of my published writings show it. Whilst there I passed the wretched time with such matters as have always deeply interested me, viz., God's word and other honourable studies. My notes to the New Testament and my six books on the Christian religion testify to the first, and as to the rest my translation of Stobæus and this work bear testimony.

I leave you this work containing instructions in the law prevailing in Holland. In its composition I have been careful to deal with the whole subject in proper order, and I hope I have succeeded as well as Justinian in his *Institutes.* I have also taken great care to express the subject-matter in its proper terms, a matter often neglected by lawyers. I have also striven to fit the divisions of the subject in their proper order, as you will see from the accompanying five tables.

In this work, as in the six books on the Christian religion, I have used our mother-tongue, and sought to honour it and to show that this subject can be very well explained in that language. I have used many old Dutch terms which, though somewhat archaic, are still good Dutch words found in the handvesten and keuren. I have also coined some words by coupling others together, but in such a way that their meaning is easy to catch. So that those persons who have been accustomed to use Latin and bastard words may not be inconvenienced, I have appended these in the margin, marking the former with an L and the latter with a B.

With respect to the Roman law, I have inserted here what is in use with us, not only such as has been taken out of the *Institutes* of Justinian, but also what has been gathered from other law-books. To this I have added our own law so far as I was acquainted with it in the old handvesten, judgments and other precedents.

There is one matter, however, which I regret, and that is that when I wrote this work I had but few books and little assistance. I had no intercourse with other persons with whom I should have liked to consult about the customs and usages of Holland. Seek, therefore, to come to know experienced lawyers in order to add here and there where this work falls short.

Accept this work in the meantime as a legacy, inasmuch as, with great injustice, the other means which I should have left you have been taken from me. Hold God before your eyes and know that He loves justice.

Your affectionate father,

HUGO DE GROOT.

Unlike most of the law-books of his time, the *Introduction* was written by Grotius in Dutch, and the use of Latin terms was scrupulously avoided. The original work had no notes whatever, and no authorities were cited. This deficiency was supplied by Groenewegen van der Made, who, with the approval of De Groot, published in 1644 an annotated edition of the *Introduction.*

Grotius was fully aware of the value of this work, for in a letter to his brother-in-law dated December, 1631, he writes as follows: "I am astonished at the bitterness so many members of the Council exhibit towards me; . . . the trouble that I have taken to acquaint our countrymen with their national laws, for the honour and glory of Holland, seems to me sufficient to have caused a ship to be sent to fetch me home, just as Athens sent for Demosthenes for services far less than mine." Time and experience have shown that the value placed by Grotius upon his work was in no way exaggerated. This *Introduction* marked an epoch in the history of the law of Holland, just as the *De jure Belli ac Pacis* marked an epoch in the development of international law. From the date of its publication it came to be regarded as an authority, and its value has not diminished during the three centuries that have elapsed.

Grotius broke away entirely from the method of dealing with the law of Holland prevalent in his time. No jurist before Grotius regarded the law of the Netherlands as a system, but treated it either in an unmethodical and unsystematic way as a confused mass of laws and customs, or else it was dealt with incidentally in works on the Roman law. Gudelinus, we have seen, strove to treat the matter in a more systematic way than usual, but he did not incorporate the legislation of his own time, and he attached too much importance to the Canon law. It was an ingrained habit of Grotius to use as few words as possible, and to write succinctly and methodically. When asked what books he thought the most useful, he replied, "Those which contain the fewest superfluous words." This is the keynote to the composition of the *Introduction*. The subject-matter is conceived as a whole and then subdivided, so as to enable each part to be dealt with fully and completely; but in dealing with the separate sections of the work not a superfluous word is employed. The great principles of the Roman law are laid down accurately and succinctly, and where these have been modified the modification is clearly set out; but where the principles of our law differ from the Roman law they are enunciated as substantive principles. In this way Grotius has been able to treat of the community of goods between spouses, the law as to antenuptial contracts, and the law of intestate succession as bodies of law depending on principles which had been developed in the Netherlands independently of the Roman law.

Grotius clung to no authority and adopted a method of his own. He treated the jurisprudence of Holland as a living system of law, and proceeded to arrange and expound it scientifically and methodically. He followed the general plan of the *Institutes* of Justinian, and divided the whole subject into the *Jus Personarum*, the *Jus Rerum* and the *Jus Obligationum*; but directly he had to explain the various subdivisions of each great class he adopted a method of his own, a style of his own, and a language which had not been used before for expounding any learned subject. If we take his chapter on Marriage and examine it in detail, we shall be able to see more clearly how Grotius differed from his contemporaries in his treatment of the subject. He begins by giving us a definition which is to a certain extent based on the Roman law, but to a certain extent also original. He then proceeds to explain the nature of the contract, and weaves into one continuous and orderly exposition the German customs, the Roman law principles and the legislation that had modified the law. He deals with the question of who may marry, and after stating the general disabilities found in the Roman as well as in most other systems, he tells us what the prohibitions are as laid down by the States of Holland in 1580. Here and there we find a decision of the Court of Holland and West Friesland, or some custom of our German forefathers.

If we compare this method of treating the subject with that of Gudelinus or of even later writers, we are struck with the great originality of Grotius. He writes no commentary on the work of another; he digests the law of his time and reproduces it in a form both novel and methodical. The *Introduction* formed the basis upon which was built up the structure of the Roman-Dutch law. Some of the greatest jurists of the Netherlands were content to write commentaries to the *Inleiding*. Schorer annotated Grotius largely; Van der Keessel's elaborate and exhaustive treatise on the Roman-Dutch law, called *Dictata ad jus Hodiernum*, is nothing more nor less than a commentary on the text of Grotius. In fact, it became the practice in Holland, Friesland and Zeeland for professors to take Grotius as their text-book and to expound the Roman-Dutch law to their students by way of explanation to the text. There are several of these commentaries that have never been printed, such as the *Dictata* of Van der Keessel and the *Verklaringen* of Professor Scheltinga. The latter is a work of great merit, though almost unknown nowadays. Groenewegen, Van Leeuwen, Matthaeus, Voet and Bynkershoek all quote Grotius in the same way as Coke, Hale or Blackstone are quoted by writers on English law. If we had lost all the subsequent works on Roman-Dutch law, and had retained only the *Introduction* of Hugo de Groot, we could administer to-day the Roman-Dutch law very much in the same way as it is actually interpreted by our courts. Since the days of Grotius there have been a great many statutory alterations of the law, but the great principles of the Roman-Dutch jurisprudence are the same to-day as they were enunciated by that wonderful genius who changed mediæval law into modern law.

After the publication of the *Introduction* two methods of expounding the law of Holland were followed: the one school followed the method of Grotius, and the other still adhered to the old system of writing a commentary on the *Corpus Juris* and weaving the modern law into the Roman law. Of the latter method, the *Commentary* of Voet is the best known and most authoritative; but this system does not possess the clearness and the great advantages of the method of Grotius, and we therefore find that the works of Van Leeuwen, Huber, Van der Keessel and Van der Linden were more widely read and studied than the learned, though somewhat cumbersome, treatise of Voet.

The fact also that Grotius wrote in Dutch, and not in Latin, had a great deal to do with the popularity his *Introduction to Dutch Jurisprudence* always enjoyed. It came to be considered in Holland as the text-book of the student, the *fons hodierni juris* of the professor, and the authoritative exposition of the law for the magistrate in the lower, and the judge in the superior courts. Van Cattenberg in his life of Grotius, written about a century after the publication of the *Introduction*, speaks of his manual in these terms: "A work which in these days is still esteemed not only by all skilled in the study and practice of the law, but by the superior and inferior courts of Holland and of the adjoining provinces as a legal oracle (*wet-orakel*), and which is daily quoted in law-books and in the judgments of our civil courts."

It may be safely asserted that not a single law-book of any importance was written in the Netherlands after the publication of the *Introduction* that did not refer to this work of Grotius. Not only in the Netherlands, but in our own South African courts the manual of Grotius has been in constant use as an authoritative exposition of the jurisprudence of Holland. When in 1859 the Volksraad of the Transvaal determined the text-books from which the Roman-Dutch law was to be gathered they took the later work of Van der Linden, the *Roman-Dutch Law* of Van Leeuwen, and the *Introduction* of Grotius as authoritative works. They adopted the first modern exposition of the principles of the law of Holland, the first great commentary on the *Introduction* of Grotius and on the Roman-Dutch law, and the latest text-book for law students. These three books were in all probability chosen because they were all written in Dutch, and covered the whole field of Dutch law from the establishment of the Dutch Republic to the conquest by Napoleon.

The *Introduction* has been twice translated into English, but the only translation in use throughout South Africa is that by Sir Andries Maasdorp, the Chief Justice of the Orange River Colony (Maasdorp's translation), and this is the translation I shall employ when reference is made to the *Introduction* in these notes.

CHAPTER XXX.

GROTIUS' PHILOSOPHY OF LAW.

I SHALL now proceed to give a brief outline of what, for want of a better term, I shall call the Philosophy of Law as understood by Grotius.

Grotius adopts Aristotle's division of law into Natural Law and Voluntary or Positive Law (*De jure Belli ac Pacis,* bk. 1, ch. 1, 10, 2). Throughout both his *Introduction* and his *De jure Belli ac Pacis* Natural Law plays a very important part. It is, therefore, necessary to know exactly what he meant by Natural and Positive Law, for without an accurate knowledge of these terms we cannot rightly understand the *Rechtsphilosophie* of Grotius. Right (*regt, jus*) in its wider sense is defined by Grotius as the agreement of the act of a reasonable being with reason, in so far as another person has an interest in such act (1, 1, 5).

Right in its narrower sense is the relation that subsists between a reasonable being and something which belongs to such being, as when I speak of my right (1, 1, 6, *De Jure Belli ac Pacis,* 1, 1, 4).

That is unjust which is contrary to the nature of a society of rational beings.

Law (*lex, de wet*), which is sometimes also called *Jus* or Right (because it prescribes what is right), is the outcome of reason, settling something which is honourable for the good of the community. So far the definition might include

Natural Law, but Grotius goes on to say that it must be enacted and promulgated by some one who has the supreme rule over a State. The last part of the definition restricts law to Municipal Law.

He then defines Natural Law, or, as he calls it in the *Introduction, Aangeboren Recht,* as the dictate of Right Reason, indicating that any act from its agreement or disagreement with the rational and social nature of man has in it a moral turpitude or a moral necessity, and consequently that such an act is forbidden or commanded by God, the author of Nature. This is Whewell's translation of the original Latin, which I subjoin: *Jus naturale est dictatum rectae rationis, indicans actui alicui, ex ejus convenientiâ aut disconvenientiâ cum ipsa natura rationali ac sociali inesse moralem turpitudinem aut necessitatem moralem ac consequenter ab auctore naturae Deo actum aut vetari aut praecipi.* Grotius therefore starts with the assumption that there is an inborn Reason in man which tells him what is morally good and what is morally bad. This capacity of reasoning is part of the Nature of Man. Now Man's Reason teaches him that it is for his own good to spend a tranquil, social life (*Proleg.* 8), and to do everything in his power towards the conservation of Society. Those things, therefore, which it is necessary for him to do in order to preserve this tranquil, social life are virtually the sources of Natural Law or Law *par excellence.* In his *Introduction* Grotius defines Natural Law as the dictate of Reason pointing out what things are in their very nature honourable or dishonourable, with an obligation to observe the same imposed by God (*Intro.* 1, 2, 5).

He enumerates the main principles or axioms of Natural Law as follows: (1) To abstain from that which belongs to others; (2) to restore to others what belongs to them; (3) to restore any gain made by the property of another; (4) to fulfil promises; (5) to make good loss caused by negligence; (6) to recognise that certain crimes require punishment (*Proleg.* 8). Again, as this Natural Law is part of what we call Human Nature, it would exist even if there were no God. But as there is a God, and as the will of God is revealed in the Bible, we know that God has ordained that the breach of these principles of Natural Law shall be punished. Moreover, God has also promulgated certain other laws in the Bible. These laws are the Positive Laws of God or Divine Positive Law (*Proleg.* 13 and 14). In addition to these laws human experience has learnt that other laws are necessary in order to regulate the social life of man. These laws are framed by man and imposed by man upon man. They are therefore called Human Positive Laws. Before the multiplication of mankind there was only one kind of human positive law, viz., the law promulgated by some supreme law-giver; but as mankind increased, and the original family broke up into many communities or nations, there arose another kind of human positive law, known as the Law of Nations (*Intro.* 1, 2, 10). The Law of Nations is that which is universally adopted by all nations for upholding the great human society (*Intro.* 1, 2, 11). The law which obtains in each particular State is called Municipal Law or Civil Law, and it is a law which derives its origin from the will of the supreme power of the State (*Intro.* 1, 2, 13).

Grotius' Division of Law may be therefore expressed in the following table:—

- Law
  - Natural
  - Positive
    - Divine
    - Human
      - Law of Nations
      - Civil or Municipal Law

The development of the idea of law according to Grotius may therefore be expressed in the following steps: Human Nature endowed with Right Reason; Natural Law; Divine Positive Law; Human Positive Law; Civil or Municipal Law; and International Law.

The Law of Nature is, therefore, according to Grotius, the basis of all our ideas of law. It is the law without which human society cannot exist, whilst Positive Law depends on utility, and varies in different communities, or even in the same community, according as circumstances alter (*Proleg.* 16). However much Positive Laws may vary, Natural Law remains immutable, and regulates not only the relations of man to man, but also of nation to nation, or people to people. In this way, therefore, Grotius was able to give to the Law of Nations some stable basis upon which he could systematically and methodically build a definite and rational system of International Law. In dealing with Municipal Law he gave to it a greater authority by referring its ultimate principles to Natural Law.

We must not for a single moment imagine that Grotius

was the first jurist who attached this great importance to Natural Law. The spread of Greek literature had taught Europe the Hellenic ideas of ethics, justice and law, and Natural Law played a very important part in the Ethics of Aristotle (*Nicom. Ethics*, bk. 5, c. 10). Earlier jurists, like Cujacius and Donellus, had fully discussed Natural Law, but Grotius was the first Netherlander who gave to his countrymen a systematic treatise on their Municipal Law, based upon the general idea of Natural Law, instead of a haphazard collection of laws and rules of laws.

I shall now proceed to show, as briefly as possible, how Grotius built up on the foundations of Natural Law his system of Municipal Law.

When he comes to deal with the Law of Things he tells us that it is an axiom that by Natural Law all things are common to all men. If this be the case, he stands face to face with the difficulty that no one can be said to be the exclusive owner of any particular thing. This view would strike at the root of ownership. To get over this difficulty he divides all created things into two classes: (1) those which are in such abundance that they suffice for all mankind, as light, air and sea water; and (2) such as cannot be simultaneously used by all and do not suffice for all. Of the latter class some are consumed by use, either immediately or in the course of time. Inasmuch, therefore, as the amount to be consumed is not sufficient for all, some must go without, and therefore these things cannot be owned by all mankind in common. He then goes on to assume that Reason, in order to prevent strife and disputes, allowed men to retain for themselves and their family what they had themselves produced. Thus arose ownership. Mere possession also gave a right to the thing possessed by virtue of the principles of Natural Law (*Intro.* 2, 3, 2). When once things came to be divided amongst the various members of the community, Natural Law once more stepped in and taught men that each must be content with what he had acquired for himself, for if he acted otherwise the tranquillity of Society would be disturbed, and such a state of things was contrary to Right Reason; hence arose the maxims, *Nemo debet locupletari ex alterius incommodo* and *Sic utere tuo ut alienum non laedas.*

If, then, Natural Law allows the acquisition of ownership and the free control over the acquired object, it also allows the object when once acquired to be transferred to another. Since Natural Law recognises ownership, it follows as a corollary that the owner can regain the possession of the article from the person who deprived him of that possession. Here, however, Natural Law ceased to supply an effective remedy, for the only means of re-obtaining possession known to Natural Law is force, and as the use of force would lead not to tranquillity, but to disturbance, man himself had to make provision by means of Municipal Law to enable the owner to regain possession, or, in other words, to vindicate his property. For this purpose Municipal Law called into being Courts of Justice (2, 3, 3). Natural Law made no distinction between the strong and the weak, the adult and the minor, but man's sense of Right and Justice devised by means of Municipal Law a distinction between those who had sufficient sense to know what was for their own interest and those who had not. Municipal Law, therefore, determined who had the power to alienate their property and who had not, and in this way arose the various restraints on alienation (*Intro.* 2, 5, 3).

Passing over from the *Jus Rerum* to the *Jus Obligationum*, Grotius tells us that in this great division of law Natural Law recognised two sources of personal claims: (1) *Promissio;* and (2) *Inequality* (3, 1, 3).

Promissio is the voluntary act of a man whereby he promises something to another with the intention that that other shall accept the same and thereby acquire a right against the promissor (*Intro.* 2, 3, 10). The regulations with regard to the manner in which this personal claim is to be enforced are left by Natural Law to the Municipal Law of the community.

Inequality is the obligation to compensate another, either for some benefit received at the expense of another or for some loss caused by a direct injury (*Intro.* 3, 1, 14 *et seq.*). Grotius' system recognises the free will of man. His ethical and religious views as an Arminian would not admit man to be destitute of a free will. Man is a free agent, and has, according to Grotius, the power of determining his own conduct. This capacity of man to determine his own acts is one of the qualities of human nature. Natural Law, therefore, also recognises a free will, and only recognises obligations in connection with a free will, and therefore where there is no will (*e.g.* in the case of a lunatic) there can be no obligation. Municipal Law has, however, for the good of the community restricted obligations to such cases as are not *contra bonos mores* or *contra legem.*

Sometimes Natural Law operates through both *Promissio*

and Inequality simultaneously; *e.g.* if I purchase a horse which is delivered to me I must pay the price, (1) because I have promised to do so, and (2) because I should otherwise be enriched at the expense of another (*Intro.* 3, 1, 20). Grotius even calls in Natural Law to show that interest is more than a mere municipal provision. Natural Law prescribes that I should place the person who lends me a thing in the same position in which he would have been if he had not lent me the article. If, therefore, the lender is deprived of the use of the article for a year, he ought to get back not only the article, but what the possession of that article was worth to him. When the thing lent is money, the lender is entitled by Natural Law to get back the money he has lent together with a sum equivalent to what that money under ordinary circumstances would have enabled him to earn with it. Though Natural Law allows the stipulation of interest, Municipal Law determines what the amount shall be according to the circumstances of the community (*Intro.* 3, 10, 9). For very much the same reason Natural Law approves of rent and profit (*Intro.* 3, 52, 2), but Municipal Law determines the outside limit of this profit (*e.g. laesio enormis*) and when it is inequitable to charge rent (*remissio mercedis*).

Grotius divides Inequality into amicable and inimical inequality. The former we have considered; the latter gives rise to delict. Right Reason teaches us that it is contrary to Natural Law to do an injury to another, and if an injury is done it should be compensated (*Intro.* 3, 32, 1 *et seq.*). In this way, then, Natural Law prohibits one person from depriving another of his property (*furtum*). It also provides compensation for molestation, breaking one's word, defamation, &c.

The mere breach of a Municipal Law is contrary to Natural Law, for Right Reason teaches us that no society can exist without general laws, and those, therefore, who do not conform to them act unreasonably (*Intro.* 3, 32, 6). The obligation to remove the inequality depends on Natural Law, but the exact liability is more closely defined by Municipal Law (*Intro.* 3, 32, 7). Grotius then proceeds to show in detail that every delict is prohibited by the principles of Natural Law, but that the amount and quality of the compensation is regulated by Municipal Law. After dealing with delicts he proceeds to show that crimes also are contrary to the Law of Nature, and that the punishment for crime is also a provision of Natural Law.

Reason teaches us that some men are good and others wicked, and that wickedness can only be controlled by fear. Reason also teaches us that fear can only be induced by inflicting pain, hence the punishment for crime is a dictate of Right Reason, and therefore within the province of Natural Law. What, however, the punishment should be varies according to the degree of culture attained by the community, and thus belongs to Municipal Law (*Intro.* 3, 32, 7). Judicial procedure belongs wholly to Municipal Law, for Natural Law does not determine how the compensation is to be claimed or arrived at.

Such then is the Philosophy of Law which Grotius has taken over from the schoolmen and applied to the law of Holland. The theory of Natural Law had not reached with him the revolutionary character it attained in the following century. He merely used it to distinguish Positive Law from that sense of justice which some philosophers considered to be innate in man and to have existed ever since man came into the world. During the next century, however, it was boldly asserted that Positive Law which did not conform to the principles of Natural Law was no law at all, and could be disobeyed with impunity. This view during revolutionary times served as a pretext for overthrowing such portions of the Positive Law as had become so antiquated as to be no longer maintainable in the community. Natural Law was then advanced to destroy the old and to introduce a new Positive Law. We find, however, in Grotius the germs of this view, for he tells us, "What is forbidden by Natural Law cannot, circumstances remaining the same, be commanded, nor can that which is commanded by it be forbidden; and in this sense this species of law is called immutable" (*Intro.* 1, 2, 6).

We do not nowadays base our systems of jurisprudence upon Natural Law, and therefore students of law are apt to forget the immense importance which the Law of Nature had for the jurists of the sixteenth, seventeenth and even the eighteenth centuries. The whole theory of the Law of Nature is now so thoroughly exploded that it is difficult for the modern student to imagine how the jurists of former years ever came to attach such importance to the abstraction—Natural Law. Unless, however, he does make some effort to grasp the theory of Natural Law, he will never be able to understand the jurisprudence of the seventeenth and eighteenth centuries.

Almost every jurist of the seventeenth century firmly

believed that there once was a time when no organised communities existed, and when each man was a law unto himself. They also believed that God had implanted in the original man the gift of reason, and that by this reason he was able to discover the elemental rules of right and wrong conduct. These elemental rules constituted the Law of Nature. They were as obvious to the thoughtful jurist as the material objects around him (*De jure Belli ac Pacis,* Proleg. 39).

Although jurists and philosophers like Grotius, Puffendorff and Hobbes differed materially as to the origin of the Law of Nature, they never doubted its existence. As the development of law came to be studied historically, so the theory of a Law of Nature became more and more untenable. The investigation of the manners and customs of ancient nations has shown us that there never was a time when man reasoned out what was in conformity with, and what did not conform to, Nature. Customary rules of conduct are adopted unconsciously and without any deliberate plan, and are always the resultant of a great number of forces almost impossible to isolate. Man never was the free reasoning agent which the priests of Natural Law would have us believe. He has always been fettered by a thousand invisible forces which we call circumstances, and for his own preservation he has adopted such laws and customs as have seemed to him best for himself and his race. Moreover, propounders of the Law of Nature have really confounded what has virtually taken place with what they conceived should have taken place, and once convinced that there ought to have been an abstract Natural Law they accepted it as having existed through all time, and started building upon it their systems of jurisprudence. As, however, their Law of Nature usually represented a high moral code, the structure built upon this foundation, though perhaps scientifically inaccurate, was practically sound, and tended very largely to eradicate all that was barbarous and brutal in the customs of the people.

We owe to the theory of Natural Law far more than is usually imagined. We owe to it our modern international law and a great deal of the law reform of the seventeenth and eighteenth centuries. A correct appreciation, therefore, of the philosophy of law as accepted by Grotius and adopted by nearly all the great writers on the Roman-Dutch law is not unnecessary and not the waste of time which so many believe it to be. It was only after the Roman-Dutch law had been supplanted by the *Code Napoléon* that these hypotheses were seriously attacked, and that the system of jurisprudence based on Natural Law fell into discredit. In order, therefore, to understand the scientific development of the Roman-Dutch law the student should never lose sight of the fact that Natural Law or the Law of Nature was the corner-stone of the whole fabric.

CHAPTER XXXI.

WRITERS OF THE SEVENTEENTH AND EIGHTEENTH CENTURIES.

I SHALL now pass over to consider the other Dutch jurists who wrote on the Roman-Dutch law. Some of them were the contemporaries of Grotius, but all the more important works on Roman-Dutch law were published after 1631—nay, indeed, after the death of Grotius in 1645. By this time the Roman-Dutch law was a well-established system, and the common law of one of the greatest commercial nations of Europe. By the middle of the seventeenth century the Dutch had succeeded in adapting the principles of the civil law to the exigencies of modern trade. Just as the Italian universities had been the principal law schools during the twelfth, thirteenth and fourteenth centuries, so the Dutch universities became the chief European centre for spreading a knowledge of the Roman law as adapted to modern uses.

Vinnius (1588–1657).—Arnold Vinnius was born at the Hague in 1588. He was therefore a contemporary of Zoesius, Grotius, Groenewegen van der Made and Paul Voet. He became rector at the Hague in 1619, and professor of law at the University of Leyden in 1633, or two years after the publication of the *Introduction* of Grotius. His *Commentary on the Institutes of Justinian,* published in 1642, raised him to the first rank not only amongst the lawyers of Holland, but of the great jurists of Europe. This work was edited in 1726 by the famous jurist Heineccius, and remained for a long time the universal text-book of Justinian's *Institutes* in European universities.

The method adopted by Vinnius was to set out the text of a section of Justinian's *Institutes*, then to append short textual and explanatory notes, and to continue with an exhaustive commentary on the subject-matter of the particular section. At the end of the commentary he explained in what way the law had been altered in Holland. His work is therefore not only a commentary on the Roman law, but a valuable exposition of the Roman-Dutch law in relation to the law of the *Institutes* and the *Corpus Juris*. Most of the later German and French commentators on the *Institutes* have freely borrowed from Vinnius, and many indeed have translated whole passages, often without acknowledgment. He is one of the writers whom Voet is very fond of quoting, and Sir Henry de Villiers has often expressed his appreciation of the work of this great Dutch jurist.

Another work of great importance and European fame is his *Selectae juris Quaestiones*. In this work he deals with a number of disputed points of law, and his exposition of each problem is so lucid, exhaustive and full of common sense that his views with regard to the matters dealt with have greatly influenced subsequent writers on law. Though these *Quaestiones* deal chiefly with Roman law, they are not mere academic dissertations on the old law, but practical discussions on the law that obtained in his time. In other words, they deal with the *Jus Antiquum* in order to illustrate the *Jus Novissimum*.

In addition to these works he wrote some smaller treatises

on Pacts, Jurisdiction, Collation and Compromise. His works have always been very popular with French jurists. The best edition of the *Commentary on the Institutes* is that of Heineccius, published in 1755. Heineccius, himself a jurist of repute, devoted a great deal of attention to the *Institutes,* and speaks of Vinnius with the greatest respect and highest praise. *Rationibus enim solidis legumque auctoritate munivit omnia quae docuit: nec in ullius juravit verba magistri.*

Antonius Matthaeus II (1601–1654). — There were three Dutch lawyers of the name of Antonius Matthaeus, and they are usually distinguished as Matthaeus I, Matthaeus II, and Matthaeus III.

The elder Matthaeus was a professor at Marburg, and was the author of a *Commentary on the Institutes of Justinian.* As a Roman-Dutch lawyer he is of no importance. His son Antonius Matthaeus II is, however, one of the great authorities on the Roman-Dutch law. He was born at Herborn in 1601, and became professor of law first at Harderwyk, and later on (in 1634) at Utrecht. Here he lectured on law until his death in 1654. His chief works are: *Commentarius de Criminibus; De Auctionibus libri duo; De Judiciis disputationes; Paroemiae usitatissimae;* and *Illustriores juris controversi quaestiones.* Of these, the three works known as *De Criminibus,* the *Paroemiae,* and the *De Auctionibus* are standard works of a high order.

The *De Criminibus* is one of the earliest treatises we possess on the criminal law as administered in Holland, and is still frequently referred to in the South African courts. The *Paroemiae* or *Maxims* is a short sketch of the essential differences between the Roman law and the Roman-Dutch law. Matthaeus selects some of the best-known maxims of our law, such as "*Man en wyf hebben geen verscheiden goed;*" "*Erfenis is geen winste;*" "*Meubelen hebben geen gevolg,*" &c., and then explains the origin of the maxim and the manner in which it is applied. To the student of the history and development of the Roman-Dutch law these maxims are of the greatest value, for the work is full of historical and antiquarian research. To the student of the law as it actually obtained in the Netherlands the work is also important, for Matthaeus has always been regarded as an accurate exponent of the law as recognised by the courts in his day.

The *De Auctionibus* is primarily a treatise on sales by public auction and sales by judicial process. In dealing with this subject, however, Matthaeus has allowed himself considerable latitude, and the work may be regarded as a disquisition on the law of sale, letting and hiring, as well as emphyteusis. The work has always been regarded as one of great merit, and we find it constantly referred to by Voet in his great *Commentary* as an authority of the first rank. Though the treatise professes to deal only with one aspect of the law of sale, the author constantly digresses into other branches of law, and whatever subject he touches upon he illustrates with a great wealth of learning.

As a consummate Roman lawyer and a great student of the antiquity of his own country, he spares no trouble to explain the origin and development of the various customs that had grown up in the Netherlands. In this respect his *De Auctionibus* is not only useful to the practitioner, but also to the student of Roman-Dutch law who, not satisfied with knowing the mere rule of law, is desirous of tracing its history and understanding its connection with the past. In his preface he tells us what his views are with regard to persons who study law empirically. "The uneducated lawyer puts on an air of contempt when any passage is quoted out of the Roman law, however apposite the quotation may be, as if there is such an enormous gulf between the knowledge of the past and that of to-day, and as if what he considers extremely recent has not been taken over from the past." Approaching his subject, therefore, both as a lawyer and as an historian, he has rendered the Roman-Dutch law a great service in tracing the modern law to its various sources. From a practical aspect the work is also of great importance, for it contains a full and clear account of the Roman-Dutch law of sale, especially if such sale takes place by judicial decree or public auction.

Johannes Jacob Wissenbach (1607–1665).—Johannes Wissenbach was one of the immediate predecessors of Voet. He was born at Fronhausen in 1607, and studied both at Groningen and Marburg. He left Holland after he had taken his degree, and went to Paris. He was elected professor of law at the Franeker University, and held that position until his death in 1665.

His chief works are a *Commentary on the Digest* and a *Commentary on the first seven books of the Code.* In both these commentaries he dealt with the Roman-Dutch law as well as the Roman law, and the method he adopted was very much the same as that of Zoesius. He is one of the seventeenth century jurists whom Voet often quotes. His work is of little value nowadays, except to throw some light upon those passages of Voet in which he is appealed to as an authority.

Johannes Christenius (1608–1672) was born near Glückstadt in Holstein. He studied at Leyden in 1628–29, and after trying his fortune in France and Germany, eventually settled in Holland. He taught law at Amsterdam, Rotterdam, Deventer and Harderwijk, where he was elected university professor of law. He died in 1672. His chief works were *Exercitationes Juridicae; Tractatus de Obligationibus;* and the *Dissertationes de jure Matrimonii* (1615). The last of these is his best-known work.

Christiaan Rodenburg (1618–1688).—Rodenburg was born at Utrecht in 1618. He studied law, and became secretary of the Court in 1642: His reputation as a sound lawyer was so great that the States-General requested him in 1644, when only twenty-six years of age, to go to England for the purpose of settling the dispute between the English and Dutch East India Companies. Later on he became one of the deputies to the States-General, and apparently retained this honour until his death in 1688. He assisted Matthaeus in his work *De Auctionibus.*

His chief legal work is the *Tractatus de jure conjugum.* In this he discusses the marital power, community of goods, antenuptial contracts and other incidents of marriage. He deals with most of the controversial points which had arisen with reference to this subject. He also added a chapter on the conflict of laws as to marriage and its consequences. The work dealt primarily with the law of Utrecht, but was not confined to this system; it embraced the laws relating to the consequences of marriage that obtained in his day in the various provinces of the Netherlands. The book is quoted by Voet with the greatest respect, and is still one of the best Roman-Dutch law-books upon this subject.

Paul Voet (1619-1677).—The Voets were a family of lawyers. Gysbert Voet was the father of Paul Voet, and Paul Voet was the father of Jan Voet. Gysbert Voet wrote several books on law, which are referred to in the works of his son and grandson, though none of them are of any importance to modern lawyers. Paul Voet, who is so frequently quoted in the works of Jan Voet as the *pater piae memoriae*, was born at Heusden in 1619. He studied at the University of Utrecht, where he became professor *extraordinarius.* In 1644 he was elected as ordinary professor to the chair of Greek and metaphysics, and later on to that of law. Some give 1667 as the date of his death, whilst others place it in 1677. The latter appears to be the more correct date.

He wrote a number of works on law, of which the most important are his *Commentary on the Institutes*, the *De Statutis* and the *De Naturâ rerum mobilium et immobilium.* Besides these, he wrote several treatises on religion and metaphysics and a biographical work on the *Oorspronk Voortganck en daden van de doorluchtige Heeren van Brederode.* Paul Voet was therefore a contemporary of Van Leeuwen. His *De Statutis* was one of the first systematic works on the comity of nations or private international law, and it is often referred to by Story with great respect in his treatise on the *Conflict of Laws.* In his *Commentary on the Institutes* he frequently points out the difference between the

Roman and the Roman-Dutch law very much in the same way as Vinnius does.

Simon Groenewegen van der Made (1613–1652).—Simon Groenewegen was born at Delft in 1613. Grotius was therefore a man of thirty when his great annotator was born. He studied law at the University of Leyden, where he took his degree. He started practising as an advocate, but soon gave up the practice of law and became secretary of the town of Delft. He died in 1652, at the age of thirty-nine. He wrote three works in all—*Annotations on the Introduction of Grotius;* an *Index to Grotius;* and a work entitled *Tractatus de Legibus Abrogatis et inusitatis in Hollandiâ vicinisque regionibus.* He has always been regarded as one of the great exponents of the Roman-Dutch law, and has been repeatedly quoted by Sir Henry de Villiers with great respect.

Though quite a young man when he died, he achieved a great reputation with the jurists and judges of Holland. He is chiefly known by his *Tractatus de Legibus Abrogatis,* and by the fact that he annotated the *Introduction* of Grotius. Both his *Annotations to Grotius* and his *De Legibus Abrogatis* have had an enormous influence upon later jurists, and have always been regarded as works of high authority. It has been mentioned before that the *Introduction* of Grotius appeared without any annotations. Groenewegen supplied this want, and his labours were greatly appreciated by Grotius himself. Groenewegen tells us that he began to annotate Grotius' *Introduction* in 1638, and published the result of his labours some years afterwards. He was an extremely careful annotator, and personally verified all his references.

Whenever he referred to a decision of a court of law as a precedent he took the trouble to refer to the original records of the case, and therefore his notes have always been accepted as an accurate exposition of the law as recognised by the Provincial Court and the Court of Holland and West Friesland.

The greatest work of Groenewegen is the *Tractatus de Legibus Abrogatis*, published in 1648. In his preface to this stupendous work he tells us that after devoting a great deal of labour to the acquisition of a correct knowledge of the theory of the law (without which the practice is often elusive), he applied himself to the practice, and constantly compared the older practice with the more recent, the Roman law with the law that obtained in Holland, and the common with the statutory law so as to form an accurate idea of their differences. In this way he came to write his *De Legibus Abrogatis*. In speaking of the magnitude of the undertaking he in no way exaggerates when he says: *Arduum profecto neque unius hominis opus! Quis enim mortalium in tanta consuetudinum copia, morum obscuritate, experientia difficili, opinionum varietate certum quid de jure nostro praedicare posset?* Groenewegen starts with the *Institutes*, and deals specifically with each paragraph, pointing out how the law of Justinian has been modified or abrogated by later customs or later legislation. He does this in the briefest possible way, and refers to some well-known authority for each statement. He then takes the *Digest* and treats every *Lex* in the same way as he treated the various sections of the *Institutes*. The same method is adopted with the *Code*, the *Novels*, the *Constitutions of Leo* and the *Jus Feudorum*. In other words, Groenewegen takes the *Corpus Juris* as his basis, and then proceeds to show how every principle of law laid down in that *Corpus Juris* has been modified by the Roman-Dutch law, or how and when it has fallen into disuse.

The *De Legibus Abrogatis* is therefore an extensive commentary on the code of laws which had come to be accepted as the common law of the Netherlands. As the work was executed with great care, and as it embodied all that was important in judge-made law and in legislation, it came to be looked upon as a work of the highest importance and of the greatest authority. In such a mass of controversial law which the work was necessarily bound to contain, it is no wonder if we find that later writers on law and the judges of the principal courts have not always adopted the views advocated by Groenewegen. At the same time we cannot but wonder at the strong common sense, the practical tendency and the astuteness of many of the views expressed by Groenewegen. It is therefore not a matter of astonishment to find that such a jurist as Voet always quoted Groenewegen with the greatest respect as the expounder of the salient differences between the law of the *Corpus Juris* and the *Jus Novissimum* of the Netherlands.

I think one may safely say that the *De Legibus Abrogatis* is one of the books without which a student of the Roman-Dutch law will find it extremely difficult to understand the development of that system of law. It is not a work of genius like the *Introduction* of Grotius, but it is a work of great practical utility, and a reservoir from which every subsequent writer on the law has freely drawn. A few examples will suffice to illustrate to those who are not acquainted either with the book or with Latin the method pursued by the author. Justinian in his *Institutes* tells us, "The Law of Paternal Power which we have over our children is peculiar to the citizens of Rome, for there is no other people who have such a power over their children as we have over ours" (*Inst.* 1, 9, 2). Groenewegen refers to this passage in the *Institutes* and says, "This great and peculiar power of the parent which belongs exclusively to the Roman people, together with its peculiar effects, has fallen into disuse according to our customs and that of other nations (Grot. *Intro.* 1, pt. 6; *Consult. Juris. Bat.* pt. 1, con. 44; Gudelinus, *De jure Nov.* l. 1, c. 13, &c., &c.)."

In the example just given Groenewegen merely refers to the passage in the *Institutes*, and then comments upon it that it has fallen into disuse, and quotes his authorities. Sometimes, however, he adopts another method. In *Inst.* bk. 2, tit. 8, pr., Justinian lays down the rule that he who is owner of a thing cannot always alienate it, whilst he who is not the owner may do so under certain circumstances, and quotes as an example that the husband may not alienate the *praedium dotale*, even though it had been given to him *dotis causâ*. Groenewegen takes the example here as the most important statement, and gives us a short sketch of the Roman-Dutch law of community of property arising from marriage: "According to our customs and that of other nations the goods which belong to the spouses before marriage, whether movable or immovable, become the common property of both as soon as the marriage is celebrated, not only *quoad* possession, but also *quoad* ownership (Grot. *Intro.* bk. 2, pt. 11, n. 4; Sande, 2, 5, 5; Goris, *Advers. de Soc. conj.* c. 1 *et seq.*)." He then continues to discuss the law of Holland with regard to this subject in the cases where nobles marry and where the property owned by one spouse consists of feudal property. He proceeds to discuss the relationship between husband and wife, and tells us that she becomes a minor and that he has the full power of alienating the goods of the community, and ends up by dealing with antenuptial contracts.

For every statement he quotes his authority. In this case he not only deals with the principle contained in the section of Justinian, but goes far beyond the text, and uses the statement that the Roman husband could not alienate the *praedium dotale* as a text to furnish him with the opportunity of discussing briefly the whole relationship between husband and wife. Sometimes different writers on the Roman-Dutch law have held different views as to whether the Roman law had been modified or not. In these cases Groenewegen states the various views, adding the authorities, and ends up by expressing his own view. For this he usually relies on some decision of the courts.

Hendrik Brouwer (1625–1683).—Brouwer was born at Leyden in 1625, where he studied and took his degree. He then practised at the Bar and afterwards became a judge of the Court of Leyden. He represented Leyden in the Council at the Hague. His principal work is an extensive treatise on the law of marriage, called *De jure Connubiorum*.

This work was published in 1664, and is a monument of research. The number of authors referred to is astounding.

Though he deals with the marriage laws of the Hebrews, Romans, Germans and other European nations, his main object was to expound the marriage laws of the Netherlands, and this he does very fully and in a practical manner. For every statement he quotes his authority, and the various decisions of the courts of Holland and the other provinces are cited to illustrate the text. The Canon law regarding marriage is also fully dealt with and compared with the law of Holland. The work is extremely diffuse—it consists of some 800 closely printed pages—but contains a mass of information as to mediæval customs. He died in 1683.

Simon van Leeuwen (1625–1682).—Simon van Leeuwen was born at Leyden in 1625, and was therefore six years old when Grotius published his *Introduction.* He studied at Leyden. The first work published by him was called *Paratitula Juris Novissimi.* It was dedicated to the burgomasters, schepenen and raden of the city of Leyden. In the dedication, dated 1652, he tells us that scarcely three years had passed since he had obtained his *Meesterschap in de Regten,* and that he is presenting them with the first fruits of his *versch en noch ongezouten oordeel.*

In the preface to this work Van Leeuwen points out that the law of Holland is a substantive system of law, based indeed upon the Roman law, but by no means the antiquated system of Justinian that prevailed in the middle ages. The changes which had taken place since the time of Justinian were so great and important "that we really require a new Emperor Justinian in order to do away with what is old and abrogated, and to lay down anew and codify the laws that are in general use."

He is very careful to guard against a spirit of reform that would cast aside all that time and experience had taught the world, though he pleads that since the time of Justinian the world has altered its ideas and its practice, and that it was therefore necessary once more to delete what had fallen into disuse, and to set out the changes that had been introduced, and the new customs that had gradually grown up and been incorporated into the law of Holland. *Eodem modo quo Imperator in Institutionibus suis breviter exposuit et quod antea obtinebat et quod postea inumbratum* (*Inst. Proem.* 5).

His object is, therefore, to publish institutes of the law of Holland, showing the laws that have fallen into disuse and the laws that obtained in Holland during his time. He criticises severely the teachers of his day, who taught the Roman law as an abstract study, and who forgot to instruct their students in the manner in which the Roman law was applied to the matters that daily came before the courts. They forgot that law was not a science that reached its perfection in the time of Justinian, and that it was ever growing and adapting itself to the new needs and circumstances of mankind. At the same time he has no sympathy with people who do not treasure the vast experience of the ancient world stored up in the marvellous works of antiquity, or with those who would lightly throw aside the precedents established by courts of justice.

With those commentators, however, who write long commentaries upon simple texts, so that in the end we are more confused than edified, he has no sympathy whatever. "And therefore," in the words of Van Leeuwen, "I have compiled a work out of the materials embodied in the whole of the Roman jurisprudence which is applicable to our daily needs and in constant use, together with the law that obtains to-day in our midst and which is to be found in all sorts of placaats, handvesten, privileges, keuren, uses, customs and decisions of the courts of justice. I have also compared these latter with the Roman law, and shown where they agree and where they differ, and in this way I have made a sort of compendium of all that may be considered to belong to the jurisprudence of Holland, or rather to the Roman-Dutch law."

He then goes on to explain why he has used the Dutch rather than the Latin language. Though a great deal of the law of Holland is to be found in the *Corpus Juris*, yet there is outside of this collection a vast body of law of great importance promulgated in the Dutch language. He does not wish to use the Dutch language as a jurist, differing in that respect from Grotius; but he desires to write in the language which is daily heard in the courts of law with all the phrases borrowed from the French courts and from the Roman lawyers. In other words, he does not despise the *vulgo vocabula artis,* but uses them as they were actually used in the living language of a judge or a pleader.

To the student of the history of the Roman-Dutch law this work of Van Leeuwen's is of the greatest interest, for there can be no doubt that this book, and not the *Censura Forensis,* was the basis of his great work on the Roman-Dutch law. Pages and pages of the *Paratitula* are incorporated verbatim in the *Roomsch Hollandsche Regt,* published some sixteen years later. In classifying his subject he employed a method somewhat different from that usually adopted by legal writers. He begins by dealing with law in general, the constitutional law of Holland and the law of persons. In the next book he treats of the law of procedure, and then goes on to expound the substantive law to which the law of procedure applies. That this is an inconvenient and incorrect method he recognises in his *Roman-Dutch Law*, and therefore abandons it in his great work, where he deals first with the substantive and then with the adjective law.

His next work of importance, the *Censura Forensis theoretico-practica id est totius juris civilis Romani usuque recepti et practici methodica collatio*, was published in 1662. It is usually known as the *Censura Forensis*. Although Van Leeuwen had written a text-book in Dutch, he felt that there was a need for a treatise on the Roman-Dutch law in Latin, inasmuch as Latin was still the accepted medium for legal education. He therefore wrote his *Censura Forensis* in Latin. The object of the work was to give in a connected form the principles of the Roman law that constantly occurred in practice, and to show in what way they had been modified by custom, judicial decision and legislation. He divided the subject-matter into two parts. In the first he dealt with substantive law and in the second with the law of procedure.

Van Leeuwen tells us that his object in writing the *Censura Forensis* was to bring within a moderate compass so much of the Roman law as was necessary for the due comprehension of the common law of Holland, together with the important modifications which had grown up in Holland from the earliest times. He inveighs bitterly against those commentators who have written such lengthy disputations upon minor details that they have forgotten the fundamental principles of our law. He wishes to do away with long commentaries and controversies, and to produce a work which will deal with the whole field of living law. Into this, however, he incorporates so much of the ancient law that the student is able to trace the connection between the new and the old, and to perceive clearly the principles upon which rests the living law of the Netherlands. He discards the disputations of the scholiasts *quae ad rem ipsam usumque parum aut nihil conferunt.*

The work opens with an introductory chapter (*prolegomena*), in which he gives a summary of the more important jurists from the time of Q. Mucius Scaevola to his own day. In dealing with the commentators who preceded Cujacius, Donellus and Duarenus, he speaks of their works as *ingentes immanes et insanos juris scholastici commentarios;* of the three commentators mentioned he speaks with the greatest respect. In dealing with the writers on the law of the Netherlands he specially mentions Grotius, *vir incomparabilis,* Gudelinus, Christinaeus, Damhouder, Merula and Groenewegen.

In the *Censura Forensis* he deals at far greater length with the Roman civil law than we find either in the *Paratitula* on in the *Roomsch Hollandsche Regt;* at the same time he gives a very lengthy and accurate account of the modifications which the Roman law had undergone in the Netherlands and in the neighbouring States, more especially in France. On account of its methodical exposition the

Censura Forensis has always held a high place amongst the Roman-Dutch law-books.

In 1663 he published an edition of the *Corpus Juris* with the notes of Godofredus, which, on account of its accuracy and excellent workmanship, has always beeen considered an edition of great merit. In 1665 he published in Dutch a text-book for notaries called the *Nederlandse Praktyk ende Oeffening der Notarissen.* This small work dealt with so much of the law as a notary was expected to know. As it was intended to be a practical hand-book, it contained all such forms and precedents as were usually adopted by the notaries of his day. The matter is treated by way of question and answer, and the book was the precursor in form and substance of Wassenaars' and of Lybrecht's *Notarial Practice.*

About the same time he published a small work in Dutch on the civil and criminal practice of the courts, called the *Manier van Procedeeren in Civiele en Crimineele Saaken.* He also published a treatise on the origin of the nobles and well-born in Holland, and a work on the *Costuymen van Rhijnland.*

In 1664 he first published his greatest work, *Het Roomsch Hollandsche Regt,* in which the Roman law is briefly set out and the Netherlands law in full. In support of his statements he quotes the various ordinances, placaats, handvesten, keuren, customs and decisions of the courts of Holland and the surrounding territories. As I have said before, this was based upon the *Paratitula.* It was, however, a work of much larger scope and better method. Immediately after its publication it took a place in the legal literature of Holland second only to the *Introduction* of Grotius. It was written in Dutch, and this, no doubt, had a great deal to do with its popularity. The great difference between the *Introduction* of Grotius and the work of Van Leeuwen is that the former states succinctly the principles of the law of Holland with hardly any comment or references, whilst the latter deals at greater length with the historical development of the law, and with the various decisions that have helped to establish the customary law of the Netherlands. Grotius confines himself almost entirely to the law of Holland, whilst Van Leeuwen is constantly bringing in the law of the various provinces as well as the law which in his day obtained in France and other neighbouring territories.

In many respects Van Leeuwen's *Roman-Dutch Law* may be likened to the *Commentaries* of Blackstone. In his introduction or *korte inhoud* he gives a resumé of the whole work. This forms an excellent sketch *in parvo* of the whole field of Roman-Dutch law, and it is a pity that Mr. Justice Kotzé in his excellent translation has left out this introduction. Let us hope that it may be inserted when a new edition of this translation appears. Necessarily, of course, the *Roman-Dutch Law* and the *Censura Forensis* have a great deal in common, for both works treat of the same subject.

There is, however, a considerable difference between them, and it is a great mistake to imagine that they are similar in substance and differ only in language. The difference between the two works arises mainly from the fact that their scope is not the same. The *Roman-Dutch Law* was chiefly intended for the use of practitioners in the courts of Holland and

West Friesland. Van Leeuwen was Registrar of the Court of Holland when the *Roman-Dutch Law* was published. The *Censura Forensis* dealt with the development and modification of the Roman law not only in Holland, but also in the neighbouring provinces and States.

I will illustrate this difference by taking the law of succession *ab intestato* as an example. In the *Censura Forensis* Van Leeuwen begins by giving us an account of the Roman law of intestate succession; he then tells us that this forms the basis of the law of succession in a great number of States, but that each State has introduced its own statutory peculiarities. He next deals with the difference in the succession to movables and immovables introduced by private international law or comity. Next, he proceeds to discuss the order and degree of the succession of descendants and ascendants, and refers to the rules observed in Saxony, Holland, Germany and Savoy. When he comes to speak of the order of succession of collaterals his field of view becomes very large, and he discusses the laws of Holland, Flanders, Brabant, the southern provinces of the Netherlands, Spain, France and Germany. Not content with a general review, he deals with the specific statutes of the cities of Antwerp, Utrecht, Mechlin, Bergen op Zoom, Brussels and Liège. He then devotes a special chapter to the statutory succession *ab intestato* in Holland and Zeeland and the *Politique Ordonnantie* of 1580. Other chapters are devoted to the statutory succession of the diocese of Utrecht and the duchies of Gelderland, Zutphen and Overijssel, Brabant, Liège and Flanders. Having completed his review of the provinces and cities of the Netherlands, he proceeds to discuss *in extenso* the statutory law of succession in France, England, Scotland, Spain, Italy, Prussia, Poland and Hungary.

This part of the *Censura Forensis* may therefore be described as a treatise on the law of intestate succession as it obtained in the various countries of Europe. The method employed may be considered a commentary on the Roman intestate succession as adopted and modified by the various statutory and municipal laws of the countries and cities of Europe. The law of the intestate succession of Holland and Zeeland forms but a small part of the whole. If we turn to the *Roman-Dutch Law* the difference in the treatment of the subject becomes very apparent. In the latter work he deals almost exclusively with the laws of Holland and Zeeland, the Aasdoms recht and Schependoms recht, and only refers very briefly to the systems prevailing in other parts of the Netherlands. In fact he specifically states at the end of the 13th chapter: "In the district of Utrecht and Gelderland the written laws are mostly followed; but it is not our intention to treat specially of these laws."

I have taken the law of intestate succession because there the difference in treatment is most marked, but I might equally well have chosen marriage, guardianship, testaments or any other of the great branches of law. The best edition of the *Censura Forensis* is that of De Haas (1741), and of the *Roman-Dutch Law* there is no edition to be compared with that of Decker (1780). Decker has not only edited the *Roman-Dutch Law*, but added to it a body of most valuable notes, by which the book was brought up to date. There are two English translations, one executed in Ceylon about 1820, and the translation by Mr. Justice Kotzé. The former is seldom met with, as it is out of print, whilst the latter is so excellent a translation that there is no excuse for neglecting Van Leeuwen as an exponent of the Roman-Dutch law.

If we compare the work of Grotius with that of Van Leeuwen we cannot help recognising that the former writer is a greater genius, and that his style and method are superior. At the same time Van Leeuwen takes a high place in the history of Roman-Dutch law. Though his work is undoubtedly based on that of Grotius, he has treated his subject in a clear, full and methodical manner, and considerably added to the work of his predecessor. He has given us more of the history of the Roman-Dutch law than Grotius, and his treatment of case law and statute law is wider and fuller than that of the older writer. Moreover, he brought the law up to date and pointed out how it had been altered since the time of Grotius.

In Holland he was always regarded as a classic, and later writers like Voet and Bynkershoek always quote him with respect as an authority of great weight. In the Cape Colony and in the Privy Council his works have been held in high esteem, whilst the Transvaal Republic recognised his *Roman-Dutch Law* as one of the three authoritative sources of our law. Van Leeuwen died in 1682, when Jan Voet was thirty-five years old.

Someren (1634–1706).—Johan van Someren was born at Utrecht in 1634. He was a pupil of Antonius Matthaeus, and afterwards went to Paris to continue his legal studies. He returned to Utrecht, where he became a judge of the Utrecht Court. He died in 1706. His chief works are *Tractatus de Jure Novercarum* and *Tractatus de Repraesentatione.*

Abraham a Wesel (1635–1680).—Abraham à Wesel was born at Bommel in 1635. He was a pupil of Antonius Matthaeus at Utrecht, and took his degree at that university. In 1669 he became advocate-fiscal of the province of Utrecht, and died in 1680. He was a great authority not only on the law of Utrecht, but also on the law of Holland, and is constantly quoted by Voet.

His chief works are: (1) *Commentarius ad Novellas Constitutiones Ultrajectinas*, dealing almost entirely with the law of Utrecht; (2) *Tractatus de Connubiali Societate bonorum et Pactis dotalibus*, which is one of the recognised authorities on the law of community of goods and antenuptial contracts, and ranks with the works of Brouwer and Rodenburg; it deals with community of goods in the Netherlands generally, and is not confined to the law of Utrecht. (3) *Tractatus de Remissione Mercedis.* These works were all collected in one volume and published in Ghent in 1729.

Antonius Matthaeus III (1635–1710).—Antonius Matthaeus III was a son of the famous Matthaeus. He was also a lawyer of great repute, and became professor of law at Utrecht, Groningen and Leyden. He was born in 1635, and died in 1710. He is better known as an historian than as a jurist, though his work on Evidence (*De Probationibus*) was long the standard work on Evidence in the Dutch law courts. His chief works are the *Observationes Rerum Judicatarum* and the *De Nobilitate Principibus*, &c., *Hollandiae et Ultrajectinae.* He was a friend of Jan Voet, who delivered the funeral oration over his grave.

Ulrich Huber (1636–1694). — Ulrich Huber was descended from a Swiss family. His grandfather entered the military service of the Netherlands. Ulrich was born at Dokkum in 1636. He studied at the universities of Franeker and Utrecht. In 1657 he became professor of law at the University of Franeker. He was twice offered the chair of law at Leyden, but refused each time. He was afterwards appointed as a member of the Provincial Court at Leeuwaarden, but shortly before his death he returned to Franeker. He died in 1694, or four years before Voet pubished his *Commentary*.

Ulrich Huber was regarded as one of the first rank in the Dutch school of law. His principal works are *De Jure Civitatis; Praelectiones Juris Civilis; Digressiones Justinianiae; Eunomia Romana;* and the *Hedendaegse Rechtsgeleertheyt zoo elders als in Frieslandt gebruikelyk.* In addition to these works he wrote a considerable number of works on theological and philosophical subjects. Of his legal works the most important are the *Praelectiones ad Pandectas*, the *Praelectiones ad Institutiones*, or, as they are called collectively, the *Praelectiones Juris Civilis*, and the *Hedendaagsche Rechtsgeleerdheid.*

The *Praelectiones* form a commentary on the *Digest* and *Institutes*, in which Huber briefly points out the modifications of the Roman law introduced into the Netherlands. His most important work, however, for the student of Roman-Dutch law is the *Hedendaagsche Rechtsgeleerdheid*, or *Treatise on the Roman-Dutch Law.* As Huber was a judge of the Provincial Court of Friesland, his work was intended principally for Frisian lawyers and law students; but inasmuch as he did not confine himself to an exposition of the law of Friesland, but of the Roman-Dutch law as in vogue in the Netherlands, it has always been regarded as a work of great value and of high authority.

The best edition is the one edited by his son Zacharias Huber, who added considerably to the work of his father. The work is written in Dutch, and the language used is so simple and clear that it presents no difficulty to any one acquainted with modern Dutch. As the work was intended for Frieslanders, the decisions of the Frisian courts are freely quoted, more especially those contained in the *Decisiones* of Sande. Inasmuch as the Roman law was less modified in Friesland than in the other provinces of the Netherlands, it is not surprising to find in the *Hedendaagsche Rechtsgeleerdheid* a great deal of pure Roman law. Ulrich Huber, however, did not confine himself to the law that obtained in Friesland, and his work was therefore held in high esteem over the whole of the Netherlands. Originally published in 1686, it had reached a fourth edition in 1742, when it had become one of the acknowledged authorities on the modern Roman-Dutch law. The work is divided into six books or divisions. The first three books deal with the substantive law. The arrangement is orderly and methodical, and follows to a large extent the method of exposition adopted by Grotius. In the fourth book he deals with public law, and especially with the constitution and jurisdiction of the various courts. The fifth book is devoted to the practice and procedure of the courts, whilst the sixth book deals with the criminal law.

To the student acquainted with the Dutch language this book of Huber will be found extremely useful, as its language and style are more modern than the works of Grotius or Van

Leeuwen. It is a great pity that so lucid an exposition of the modern Roman-Dutch law, and so important a law-book, has not yet been translated into English.

The fact that Huber was a Frisian judge, and that a great deal of this work deals with Frisian law, has led many to assume that his work is not of great use as an authority in the courts of South Africa, but this view appears to me quite erroneous. Although Huber deals extensively with the Roman law, his exposition of that law is not purely academical, but pre-eminently practical, and consequently we learn from him how the Roman law was applied in the Netherlands to the questions that were daily brought before the courts. With Huber, therefore, the Roman law is not an antiquated system of law, but a system that was applied in his day to the solution of legal problems. Except, therefore, in those matters where the Frisian law differs from the law of Holland, Huber is an excellent guide, and his masterly way of dealing with his subject makes him a very attractive writer.

Pieter Bort.—Pieter Bort flourished during the middle of the seventeenth century. He was born at the Hague and practised there as an advocate. He was one of the leading legal practitioners of his day. His chief works are: *Tractaat van de Hollandsche Leenen; Tractaat van Crimineele Zaken; Tractaat van de Domeijnen van Holland; Tractaat van Complaincte;* and *Tractaat van Arresten.* The last is perhaps his best-known work. He died about the end of the seventeenth century.

CHAPTER XXXII.

WRITERS OF THE SEVENTEENTH AND EIGHTEENTH CENTURIES.

Johannes Voet (1647–1713). — Johannes Voet was the son of Paul Voet. He was born on the 3rd October, 1647, at Utrecht. He studied and took his degree in law at the university of his birthplace, and became law lecturer at Herborn in 1674. From Herborn he went to Utrecht in 1681 as professor of law. A few years later he was elected to the law professorship of Leyden University, and there he remained until his death in 1713. For thirty years he occupied the chair of law in that university. He was twice elected Rector Magnificus. His principal legal works are: *Commentarius ad Pandectas*, first published in 1698; *Compendium juris adjectis differentiis juris Civilis et Canonici*, 1682; *De Usufructu*, 1704; *Elementa juris secundum ordinem Inst. Just.; De familia erciscunda: De jure Militari;* and the *De Tutoribus*. The great work of John Voet is the *Commentary to the Digest*, or, as it is called in Latin, the *Commentarius ad Pandectas*. He tells us in the title page that he intends to treat not only of the principles of the Roman law and the well-known controversies on that subject, but also of the law that obtained in his day and that was practised in the law courts. His method of exposition is one that had been adopted by the Italian jurists of the twelfth and thirteenth centuries, and copied by all the great professors of law in the universities of western Europe. The commentators on the Roman law had adopted two principal methods of exposition. The one method was to examine critically *Institutes, Digest* or *Code,* and to expound *lex* by *lex.* The text of each paragraph was annotated and explained, and compared with similar passages in the rest of the *Corpus Juris.* Of this method of exposition the works of Brunnemann on the *Pandects* and on the *Code* afford an excellent example. Cujacius and Donellus have also done a great deal of work of this description. The other method, the more usual one in the seventeenth century, was to take a title of the *Digest,* and then to expound the law upon the subject-matter of the title in a systematic and methodical manner. The commentator who adopts this method does not confine himself to the *Digest,* but brings in the *Institutes, Code* and *Novels* in order to make his treatise as complete as possible. Where questions of law arise, upon which former jurists have held different views, these controversial matters are discussed, and usually one or other opinion is adopted. This is the method followed by Zoesius, Noodt, Voet and a great many others. Voet, however, differs from most of the other Dutch commentators on the *Pandects* in his thorough and masterly exposition of the Roman-Dutch law as it obtained in his day. He was not satisfied with a mere academic treatise on the civil law, but he showed how that law should be applied to the affairs of everyday life, and how it was actually practised in the courts of Holland and the adjoining provinces. Into his treatise on the Roman law he wove the legislation of the United Provinces which had altered or modified the civil law, the decisions of the courts which had interpreted the law, and the disputes on controverted points of law which had been ventilated in the courts or in the works of Dutch and other jurists. Voet's *Commentary on the Pandects* is therefore just as much a treatise on the law of Holland as the *Introduction* of Grotius or the *Roman-Dutch Law* of Van Leeuwen.

As Voet was a professor at the University of Leyden, and as his *Commentary* was used by him for teaching law at the university, he did not use the Dutch language as Grotius and Van Leeuwen had done, but wrote in Latin, then the language in which almost all university teaching was conducted. In explaining his subject Voet usually gives us the Roman law first and then passes over to the Roman-Dutch law. The words *sed nostris moribus* are generally used to mark the transition.

His conception of law is as a rule the same as that of Grotius, and he constructs his whole system upon the Law of Nature as a foundation. He tells us that if we look back to the remotest times of the history of our race we shall find that in no place and in no time did the race exist without laws regulating what is right and honourable. After the Fall of Man we lost our full knowledge of what was right, but we retained sparks of the principles of what was just and proper. "Thus there remained in the hearts of men some remnants of an imprinted, inborn divinity; some rules of justice and equity, divinely ingraven and inborn, dictating unto each one what was lawful and what unlawful, what to do and what to avoid" (1, 1, 1). He then discusses a number of more or less mythical law-givers in order to show how every nation had some conception of law, and passes over somewhat abruptly to the sources of the Roman law.

He next explains the plan of his own work. "I thought that it would be a useful labour if I should illustrate the fifty books (of the *Pandects*) by a commentary, and also weave into the definitions of the Roman law such amendments, additions or interpretations as have been adopted by us and by neighbouring nations owing to change of circumstances. Any one who considers that laws have their day and perish will agree that a great deal of the explanation of the civil law would lose its value if the exposition of the modern law were omitted, for much of what was formerly considered wrong is now considered right; what was formerly forbidden is now allowed; moreover, it must be borne in mind that in settling disputes amongst litigants the law of Justinian no longer holds the foremost place."

Voet is never tired of telling us how important it is to the jurisconsult to study carefully both the theory and the practice of the law. He quotes with approval a saying of Pinellus that theory without practice can give no solid knowledge of law, and that practice without theory makes but a sorry lawyer. It is this intimate acquaintance with both the theory of the civil law and the practice of the courts of Holland which has made the *Commentary* of Voet a work so useful both to the teacher and to the practitioner. His method is, however, not always all that is to be desired, and his manner of treating a subject not always so clear and methodical as that of Grotius. I shall take his first book as an example of what I mean. When we consider Grotius' explanation of natural law either in his *Introduction* or in his *Law of Nations* we grasp his meaning at once, for he proceeds step by step and gradually unfolds his subject. If we turn to

Voet's exposition of the same subject we find that he is diffuse, and that he does not unfold his subject with the same mathematical precision and method. He begins with our inborn sense of what is right and wrong. He then refers to the scope of his work. He then treats of the sources of the Roman law and its authority in Holland. After this he reverts to the philosophy of the law, discusses what is *aequum et bonum*, and when equity should be allowed to interpret the law. He then returns to a consideration of justice and the natural law (*jus naturale*) of Ulpian (what nature has imprinted in all animals), and then, without distinguishing his terms, he passes on to a consideration of the Law of Nature as defined by Aristotle and the schoolmen. He then proceeds to discuss the Law of Nations, and lastly the civil law. If we compare this with the treatment of Grotius we find that Voet does not advance step by step like the former. and that he does not work on the same methodical plan. It may be said that Grotius wrote a manual whilst Voet was writing a commentary, and that therefore the former could afford to be much more concise and methodical. This no doubt is true to a great extent, but it does not take us away from the fact that Grotius' manner of exposition is more methodical and more systematic. There is much more in Voet than there is in Grotius, but what there is in Grotius is much more concise and much more methodically arranged.

Voet shows us repeatedly in his *Commentary* that he was no narrow, hide-bound lawyer seeking refuge in forms and technicalities so dear to timid men of weak intellect. He recognised law as a science and an art, and not merely a bundle of unconnected rules which had to be applied to every case in a stereotyped and rigid manner. Every page of Voet's great *Commentary* shows us how he strove to get at the reason of every *lex* of the *Digest*, and how he analysed every case to get at the underlying principle. The verbal quibbles of the older commentators had no charm for him. Whenever he discusses a point of law that has been the subject of controversy he sifts the grain from the chaff, and allows his strong common sense and practical view of the affairs of men to guide him to his conclusion. We may not always agree with his view, but we must always acknowledge that his reasoning is keen, logical and practical. We may not accord to him the highest place as a methodical expounder of the law, but we cannot deny to him an inimitable power of interpreting the law on any particular point.

If we compare Voet as an interpreter of the law with the older commentators, we are struck with his practical sense as compared with their dialectical subtlety. The range of our knowledge on many subjects is far greater than that of Voet, and therefore no doubt there are many propositions in the *Commentary* which we cannot accept to-day; but when we consider how slowly and amidst what difficulties science has advanced, and how our horizon has gradually widened, we need not be surprised at these shortcomings. That Voet discusses whether a lessee can quit the house he has hired because he believes it to be haunted, is no reason for considering him antiquated and redolent of the middle ages. Haunted houses have not yet gone quite out of fashion, and ghosts are still familiar objects in many quarters. Though we do not cancel a lease on account of ghosts, we still believe many strange and improbable things. The basis of legal interpretation has been and always will be common sense and an intimate knowledge of human nature and of the affairs of men. In every title Voet shows us that he possessed a sane common sense, and that he was intimately acquainted with man and his affairs. His philosophy was not the philosophy of our century, and he often confused Morality and Law, because the foundation of his legal system was the Aristotelian Law of Nature; but his ethics were of a high order, and therefore when he strove to make the law conform to his idea of what was ethically right he appeals strongly to our sense of justice.

I have said before that Voet is always strong in the interpretation of the law. Let me illustrate that by a single example. Equity has been constantly resorted to by strong judges in order to alter the formal or antiquated element in the common law, and by weak judges in order to avoid what would appear to them a harsh rule of law. Voet has shown us with admirable sense what equity is and when it should be invoked. The *lex* of the *Code* (3, 1, 8) has it: *Placuit in omnibus rebus praecipuam esse justitiae aequitatisque quam stricti juris rationem,* and this is the *lex* which has been so often relied upon to show that equity is more important than strict law.

Voet compares this with an expression of Paulus in *D.* 39, 3, 2, 5, where the latter says: *Haec aequitas suggerit etsi jure deficiamur.* Paulus is dealing with a case where the *stricti juris actio* of *aquae pluviae arcendae* would not apply, but where an action based on analogy or a *utilis actio* should be granted. Here there is no conflict between equity and law, for the decree of the praetor was as effective as the decree of the magistrate. There were two ways in Rome of attaining the same end, but both ways ended in a decree according to the rules of law administered in the particular court. Equity did not therefore mean some varying idea of justice which if rightly understood would supplant the law, but it meant those rules of law which were followed in the court of the praetor. The judge, Voet points out, must judge according to the law where the case in question clearly falls within the terms of the law, and he must not allow his moral or ethical sense to interfere with his judgment; in other words, he may not say, "The words of the law are clear and the case undoubtedly falls within the terms of the law, but the law is monstrously severe, and therefore I shall not be doing equity if I apply the law to the case in point."

It will then be asked, Are we never to appeal to the judge's sense of justice and equity? This difficulty is solved by Voet's keen sense as a legal interpreter. Voet feels, like many of the German writers on jurisprudence, that law is a branch of Morals, and that the judge in administering the law must always bear in mind the fact that the ultimate end and object of all law is to regulate the relations of individuals according to that sense of right and wrong which prevails in any particular community. If we call this sense of right and wrong Equity, then the judge is bound to take Equity into account; and Voet points out that the judge is not to do this when the words of the law are clear or when the circumstances exactly fit the terms of the law, but when the law-giver has so expressed himself that his words may be capable of different meanings or when they do not exactly apply to the case in point.

The law-giver may have shown what cases it was his intention to cover by the law, and so expressed the *ratio legis*, then it would be contrary to our sense of Right and Wrong to apply the law to a case outside the scope of the *ratio legis*. Equity, then, is necessary in order to interpret the meaning of the law-giver, and to apply the law to the vast variety of cases which present themselves.

Throughout his whole *Commentary* Voet adheres to these principles, and to my mind it is this quality more than his learning that makes Voet so great a jurist and so admirable an authority on the law of Holland. It is a quality he possesses in common with Bynkershoek.

The *Commentary* of Voet has always held a very high place amongst the authorities of the Roman-Dutch law, both in the courts of Holland and in those of South Africa. No judge, however, either in Holland or in South Africa, has relied on Voet more firmly or shown his best qualities more clearly than Sir Henry de Villiers. The Chief Justice of the Cape Colony has taught us that in the *Commentary* of Voet we possess a legal work of a very high order both for the purpose of understanding the theory of the civil and of the Roman-Dutch law, and for the purpose of applying the principles of the Roman-Dutch law to the everyday affairs of life. After the long and brilliant career of the Chief Justice as an expounder of the Roman-Dutch law at its best, Voet can never fall into oblivion in South Africa.

A great number of the titles of Voet have been translated into English, but it is a great pity that there is not an English version of the whole of the *Commentary* of this great lawyer. It is astonishing to me that the legislatures of the various South African colonies have not yet combined to obtain an authoritative translation of a work which deals so fully and so admirably with our common law. It may be said that every South African lawyer should know enough Latin to be able to read Voet. Such a consummation is devoutly to be wished, but the older I have grown the more confirmed I am that its attainment is far off. On the contrary, Voet is read less and less in the original, and authorities written in Latin are consulted less and less every day. The money voted for a translation of Voet would be money better spent than that which is wasted on a thousand and one madcap projects and useless commissions. An adequate translation of Voet, like that of Berwick, would convince the better class of English lawyers that our system of law is not an antiquated and an obsolete system, but a jurisprudence founded on reason, scientific in its method, a model of legal thought and abounding in principles which have stood the test of ages.

Besides the *Commentary* there are two other works of Voet which deserve special mention here. The first is the *Elementa juris secundum ordinem Inst. Justiniani*, or, as it is called in the Dutch translation, *De Beginzelen des Rechts*. In this work Voet has followed the arrangement of Justinian's *Institutes*, and has written a short commentary on that manual. In writing this commentary he has borrowed very largely from Vinnius, and has given us a resumé of the Roman and Roman-Dutch law. This book of Voet was always used during the eighteenth century by

Dutch students as a companion to the *Institutes.* It enabled the student to grasp the Roman law and the Roman-Dutch modification of that law when he was still busy with his first text-book. The extent of its use during the eighteenth century we see from the works of Lybrecht, Kersteman and others who, writing for a public not conversant with Latin, constantly refer to this hand-book of Voet as an authority.

The next work is the *Compendium juris juxta seriem Pandectarum adjectis differentiis juris Civilis et Canonici.* This also was a student's book. Every title in the *Digest* is treated in the same way as in the *Commentary,* only very much more succinctly. At the end of each title we find the word *Moribus,* and then follows a short exposition of the Roman-Dutch law upon this subject. The work was written in Latin, and was in use not only in the universities of Holland, but also in those of Italy.

The other works, like the *De familia erciscunda* and *De Tutoribus,* are monographs, and their substance is to be found in the *Commentary.*

Joan Cos (17th–18th centuries).—Joan Cos was an advocate who practised his profession at the Hague. I have not been able to find out the date of his birth. It must have been, however, about the middle of the seventeenth century, for in 1733, when his *Rechtsgeleerde verhandelingen* appeared, he was already dead. He did not write much, but the little that he wrote is extremely good. His principal work is a systematic account of the law of marriage. Its title is *Verhandeling over het huwelyk.* In addition to this he wrote a work on community, antenuptial contracts, the *ex hâc Edictali,* and the conditions of future succession. These two works form a complete treatise on the law regarding marriage and its consequences. He also wrote a monograph on *Rei vindicatio* and another on the *Actio Publiciana.* The works on marriage are constantly referred to by the best authorities, especially by Voet.

Gerard Noodt (1647-1725).—Noodt was born in the same year as Jan Voet, and survived his great contemporary by twelve years. He was born at Nijmwegen in 1647. He studied at Leyden, Utrecht and Franeker; and after obtaining his degree as doctor of laws at the latter university he settled at Nijmwegen as an advocate. Here he lectured on law. From there he went to Utrecht in 1679 as professor of law. In 1686 he left Utrecht and took the chair of law at Leyden. He retired from Leyden in 1706, and died in 1725.

Noodt was a jurist of European fame, and has always been regarded as a great authority on Roman law, of which throughout his whole life he was an ardent student. Besides a commentary on the first twenty-seven books of the *Digest,* his works consist chiefly of commentaries on particular titles of the *Digest.* He never dealt with the Roman-Dutch law as a substantive system of law in the way that it was handled by Grotius and Van Leeuwen. Whenever Noodt deals with the Roman-Dutch law it is merely incidental, for his deep and learned inquiries are usually confined to the Roman law. On this subject he was acknowledged to be a master both by his friend Jan Voet and by Bynkershoek. Barbeyrac, who edited his works, speaks of Noodt with the greatest admiration. Mr. Justice Kotzé classes him with

Vinnius, Huber, Voet and Bynkershoek. His principal works are: *Probabilia Juris Civilis; De Jurisdictione et Imperio; Ad Legem Aquiliam; Observationes; De Usufructu; De pactis et transactionibus;* and the *Commentary* on the first twenty-seven books of the *Digest.* This *Commentary* has been much praised for the critical ability displayed in dealing with disputed texts.

Zacharias Huber (1669–1732).—Zacharias Huber was the son of Ulrich Huber. He was born in 1669 and studied at Franeker, Utrecht and Leyden. In 1690 he graduated in law and practised as an advocate at Leeuwarden. He became professor of law at Franeker in 1690. In 1716 he was appointed a judge of the Frisian High Court, and filled this office until his death in 1732. His two best-known works are the *De Casibus enucleatis quaestionum forensium ex jure Romano et Hodierno* (1712), and the *Observationes rerum forensium ac notabilium in Supremâ Frisiorum Curiâ judicatorum.*

Bynkershoek (1673–1743).—Cornelis van Bynkershoek was born at Middelburg in 1673. His father was a merchant who had considerable interest in ships and in oversea expeditions. The early years of Bynkershoek were spent in his native city, but in his sixteenth year he was sent to the Frisian University of Franeker. Here Bynkershoek studied Latin and Greek, and became very proficient in both these languages. He then devoted himself to the study of theology with a view to joining the ministry of the Hervormde Kerk. At the end of the seventeenth century, however, the disputes between the various theological professors seem to have been quite as lively as they were towards the beginning of that century. At Franeker there were two professors, Vitringa and Roëll, whose views about the Logos were diametrically opposed, and it was entirely owing to the fact that Bynkershoek chose the unpopular side that he became a famous jurist. He openly defended the views of Roëll, and that immediately cut off all chance of success as a minister of the Hervormde Kerk. He then bade farewell to theology and embraced the study of law. One of his teachers in this new branch of study was the well-known Ulrich Huber, for whom Bynkershoek always had great esteem and respect, though differing from him on many occasions. He obtained his degree at Franeker and started his practice as an advocate at the Hague in 1699.

Bynkershoek had no great admiration for the *societeit der advokaten* of his day, and he has often criticised them with considerable severity. These are some of his expressions: "The advocates were not much respected, because instead of selling law they sold their pleadings at a very high price." "Every [advocate] who has drunk a little of the *decoctum philosophicum* can easily dish up a dozen reasons tempered more or less with a little equity." He also accuses them, and particularly the attorneys, of protracting lawsuits unto eternity, not for the benefit of their clients, but for their own pockets. He was always of opinion that an advocate should be a man of a high order of intelligence, learning and honesty, and he constantly complained that this was not the case even with regard to those who pleaded before the Supreme Court. A great number of them, he tells us, were nothing more or less than *rabulae* or pettifoggers, who adhered rigidly to the formularies of the law and now and then indulged in some *regula juris* which they only half understood (Preface to the *Observationes Jur. Rom.*).

It is important to know the opinion he had of the practitioners of his day in order to understand his attitude towards the reform of the law and its practice. He had a profound hatred of sheltering ignorance and weakness behind platitudes, formalities and technicalities. He had a great contempt for practitioners who built their whole case upon the dictum of some obscure commentator without accurately investigating the original text of the law and its reasons. He must have gained considerable fame as an advocate, for it is said that Peter the Great was very anxious for Bynkershoek to accompany him to Russia in 1697, and that the reason he refused the offer was his ignorance of the Russian language. In 1704, however, when only thirty-one years of age, he was appointed by the province of Zeeland as one of the judges of the Supreme Court of Holland, Zeeland and West Friesland. He was elected President of the Supreme Court in 1724, and filled that office until his death in 1743. He was therefore a judge of the highest tribunal of Holland for nearly forty, and Chief Justice for nearly twenty years. It is manifest that he must have influenced very greatly the jurisprudence of Holland during the first half of the eighteenth century.

The history of Bynkershoek's election to the chief-justiceship is instructive as showing some of the weak points in the constitution of the highest court of Holland. As we have seen in a former chapter, the Supreme Court was composed of nine members, three of whom were chosen by the province of Zeeland and six by the province of Holland and West

Friesland. The Zeelanders had frequently complained that they never could get a Zeelander elected president because they were in a hopeless minority, and that Holland had on every occasion appointed a Hollander to this important post. When the vacancy occurred in 1703 Zeeland sent a strong appeal to the States-General to use their influence to get a Zeelander appointed. When the election took place a Hollander, Simon Admiraal, received the majority of the votes. This caused great ill-feeling between Holland and Zeeland, and covert threats were used that Zeeland would withdraw from the *accoord* by which the Supreme Court had been constituted. The Hollanders realised that the Zeelanders were in earnest, and they promised to use their best endeavours to put in a Zeelander when the next vacancy occurred, provided Zeeland was prepared to assist them in other matters. In the following year Admiraal died and a new election was to take place for the presidency of the council. On this occasion Bynkershoek was elected. Nothing was said officially that the protest of Zeeland had anything to do with the election. The official declaration stated that Bynkershoek was "chosen on account of his good knowledge of law, his love of justice and his loyalty." Bynkershoek's letters show that he was not passive in the matter, but that he actively canvassed for the appointment.

Though no doubt there was a great deal of intrigue to get Bynkershoek the Zeelander elected, once the election was over, the towns of Holland, as well as of Zeeland, were highly satisfied with the choice. The office of President of the Supreme Court of Holland and Zeeland was one of the highest and most honourable positions in the State. The Court was one of the great European courts, and Bynkershoek himself reminded his colleagues, *Et quid attinet dicere publice notum est! ad judicium vestrum quotidie provocant, etiam qui judicio vestro subjecti non sunt.*

Bynkershoek had the greatest respect for the judges of the Supreme Court and the Court of Holland, but for the *judices minores* he did not always show the same regard. The idea that a person should be appointed to any bench who did not possess the highest qualifications for that office was repugnant to him, and he expressed his views with his usual strength and energy.

Bynkershoek was held in the very highest esteem by his contemporaries. He was constantly appealed to as an arbiter by the various cities of the Netherlands in any grave dispute that arose between them. He was universally admired for his great learning, his acute reasoning powers, his keen sense of justice, as well as for his noble and independent character.

From his youth onwards Bynkershoek was a great student of the Roman law. All his spare moments were devoted to that study. He tells us in his preface to the *Observationes juris Romani* that this study was his favourite pastime: *Ab his (occupationibus curiae) reversus et mihi, ut ita dicam, reditus in his deliciis juris Romani versatus sum, utili et dulci otio.*

If we consider the works of Bynkershoek we are struck by the fact that they all have a fragmentary appearance. He has given us no system of Roman law or of the Roman-Dutch law. He has confined himself almost entirely to discussing isolated legal questions. He calls his works "*opuscula,*" "*opera minora,*" "*observationes*" or "*quaestiones.*"

The reason he himself gives for not having been able to write a complete treatise is that he was too much interrupted by the ordinary judicial work of the courts to enable him to devote his time to some systematic work. The fact that he was actively engaged in one of the greatest tribunals of Europe not only influenced the form of his work, but also its contents. As a judge he was daily called upon to decide practical questions which arose between man and man, and therefore his writings are not merely theoretical disquisitions on abstruse points of law, but observations on such matters as had actually occurred in practice, and therefore likely to occur again. Not only did he devote himself to questions of civil law, but he followed Grotius in his study of international law.

To the student of Roman-Dutch law Bynkershoek is a great authority on the Roman law and on the law of Holland, but to the student of international law Bynkershoek ranks amongst the great pioneers of that branch of study. The works of Bynkershoek may be divided into three classes: (1) works on Roman law; (2) works on Roman-Dutch law; (3) works on international law.

(1) *Roman law.*—Bynkershoek loved the Roman law. *Scias juris prudentiam Romanam cordi et curae esse,* he writes to one of his friends. He speaks of the Roman law as *jus optimum, deliciae, amoenitates, juris Romani.* He studied Roman law as a whole, and had the greatest respect for the ancient jurisconsults. When asked why students should be worried with a knowledge about *res mancipi et nec mancipi* he answered, "You ask what is the good of a knowledge of the ancient law? What is the use of studying

an ancient jurisprudence dead and buried? Why disturb its ashes and waste the precious hours? Forsooth, these are questions asked by those who are ignorant of the fragments of the ancient jurisconsults, and who know not how to draw from those fountains of clear water, but who resort to the turbid pools of the commentaries of the so-called doctors." The ancient jurisprudence was to him the key of the civil law. He was a critic both of the text and of the substance, and his master in both these departments was Cujacius. His principal works on Roman law are *Observationes juris Romani* (1710–1733); *Opuscula varii Argumenti* (1719); and *Opera Minora* (1730).

The *Observationes juris* consist of a series of dissertations upon texts and controversies, annotations and emendations, historical essays on the development of special branches of the law and on legal antiquities. Heineccius wrote the preface to these *Observationes*, and speaks of them in terms of the highest praise. The *Opuscula varii Argumenti* and the *Opera Minora* all consist of dissertations upon particular subjects or branches of law.

As these works did not constitute a systematic treatise on the Roman law they gradually lost ground, and as our knowledge of the Roman law is greater to-day, owing to new discoveries, than it was in the time of Bynkershoek, his works on the Roman law are not as popular as they were in the eighteenth century. In the opinion of all his contemporaries he was one of the greatest civil lawyers. *De Bynkershoekio id tantum, ut semel dicam, quid sentio, addo me illi nullum juris consultorum ne ipsum quidem Cujacium anteferre* (Hamberger). Modern German opinion is not quite so enthusiastic, though Mommsen and Bluhme had a high opinion of him.

(2) *Roman-Dutch law.*—Whatever the value of Bynkershoek's works on Roman law may be, there can be no doubt about the value of his contributions to the Roman-Dutch law. Here he ranks with the greatest authorities on our law. His chief work, the *Quaestiones Juris Privati*, has always been regarded as one of the most important works on the Roman-Dutch law as accepted in the courts of Holland. His *Absoluta legum Patriarum Cognitio* has been recognised by every judge and jurist who followed him. Van der Keessel, Van der Linden, the writers of the *Rechtsgeleerde Observatiën*, Kersteman, Schorer and others constantly quote the *Quaestiones Juris Privati* as a work of the highest order and authority. The *Quaestiones Juris Privati* consist of a number of dissertations on various branches of the law of Holland. The work is to a great extent controversial in its nature, but as the object was to present the law of Holland as it was actually practised in the courts, it is one of great value to the practitioner. Bynkershoek constantly refers to the cases which were heard in his own court, and, where he differed from the judgment of the majority, he sets out his arguments with considerable force. He was no great admirer of those lawyers who resorted to authorities merely to find some passage upon which to build their conclusions. He invariably went to the root of the matter and endeavoured to grasp the principle upon which a case was decided, and if that principle was not sound he never hesitated to say so, and refused to follow the decision however great the

prestige of the judge or jurist who decided the case contrary to sound principle. In this sense Bynkershoek, like Lord Mansfield in England, was a great reformer of the law of Holland. Sometimes, no doubt, he goes too far, and, carried away by the spirit of controversy, he seeks to upset what had become a settled practice, simply because in his opinion it was built up upon a wrong foundation. At other times he becomes so violent an advocate that his view and temper are not judicial. He shows repeatedly in his *Quaestiones Juris Privati* that he was no admirer of the shibboleths of the law, and where a practice had become obsolete and inconvenient and no longer suited to the new circumstances, he was quite prepared to throw it aside even though it had met with the approval of eminent predecessors. He regarded law not as an arrested growth, but as a living organism, and held that it should adapt itself to its surroundings, though its fundamental principles, which had stood the test of ages, should not be interfered with.

He was not only skilled in the Roman law and in the law of Holland, but he had a vast knowledge of most of the systems of law that were practised on the Continent. The views expressed by him in the *Quaestiones Juris Privati,* owing to the prestige he had gained both from his great learning and his long tenure of office as President of the Supreme Court, exercised considerable influence on the judges and practitioners of the courts of Holland. In this way, therefore, during the latter half of the eighteenth century Bynkershoek's works made a great impression on the development of the Roman-Dutch law. When we add to this that as an international lawyer and an authority on shipping and commercial law he had made for himself a name not only in the Netherlands, but also throughout the whole continent of Europe, we can well understand that his opinions as a judge and his writings as a jurist mark an epoch in the development of the Roman-Dutch law. What strikes one forcibly in reading his *Quaestiones* is how much more modern he is in his views than a great many of the lawyers who came after him. The *Quaestiones Juris Privati* were translated into Dutch as *Burgerlijke Rechtszaken,* and this no doubt greatly added to their popularity with the practitioners of the courts of Holland.

(3) *International law.*—As it is beyond the scope of this work to deal with international law, I shall merely mention his principal work on that subject—the *Quaestiones Juris Publici.* It is constantly referred to by all subsequent publicists.

Hobius van der Vorm.—Van der Vorm flourished during the first part of the eighteenth century. He started his legal career by founding a law school at Middelburg called Collegium Grotianum, and afterwards devoted himself to the practice of law as an advocate at Hoorn. In 1702 he published a work on succession, which came to be regarded as the leading authority on that subject. Its title was *Verhandeling over het Hollandsch, Zeelandsch en West Frieslandsch Versterfrecht.* A later edition was published in 1774, by which the work of Van der Vorm was brought up to date and considerably augmented by Blondeel. This edition by Blondeel is the best and latest work we have on the law of intestate succession as it obtained in Holland when the Cape Colony became British.

Gerloff Scheltinga (1708–1765).—Scheltinga studied law at Franeker and was a pupil of Heineccius and Voorda. He also studied at Leyden. He became a professor of law, first at Deventer and later at Leyden. Here he twice became Rector Magnificus. He was looked upon by his contemporaries as a very able lawyer and lecturer. He wrote several learned works, but his only work of importance for us is a *Commentary on the Introduction of Grotius.* Like the *Dictata* of his pupil Van der Keessel, the *Commentary* of Scheltinga has never been printed. He died in 1765.

Willem Schorer (18th century, latter half).—Schorer was President of the Court of Flanders. He flourished in the latter half of the eighteenth century. He is chiefly known as the editor and annotator of Grotius. In his *Notes to Grotius* he attempted to bring the *Introduction* up to date by incorporating the work of later writers. Most of his notes, however, are references to Voet. He was also a pamphleteer, and wrote several pamphlets on law reform. His *Notes to Grotius* have been translated from the Latin and incorporated in Maasdorp's *Introduction to Grotius.*

Franciscus Lievens Kersteman.—Kersteman flourished in the second half of the eighteenth century. He was professor of law at Heusden. In 1774 he was arrested for issuing a forged bill, and was condemned to thirty years' imprisonment at Rotterdam. In 1786, however, he was liberated, and continued to practise his profession until his death. Most of his works were of an elementary character, and written for the use of students, such as *De Academie der Jonge Practicyns; Nieuwe Oefenschool der Notarissen: Regtsgeleerd*

Kweekschool of Sleutel der Crimineele Practijk; Rechtsgeleerd Katechismus, &c.

His best work, however, is a sort of law lexicon called *Hollandsch Rechtsgeleerd Woordenboek* (1768). It is a dissertation on various legal subjects arranged alphabetically. In the production of the *Rechtsgeleerd Woordenboek* Kersteman was assisted by a society of jurists. The work was undertaken by subscription, and in the preface it is stated that, in order to supply the omission of certain important articles on various subjects, an *Aanhangsel* or supplement to the *Woordenboek* would be published. For some unexplained reason Kersteman, however, declined to complete the *Aanhangsel*, and ultimately that was done by an unknown jurist, who wrote under the motto *Nisi utile est, quod facimus, stulta est gloria* (completed in 1772). This same jurist is probably also the author of the *Aanteekeningen op Lybrechts' Notaris Ambt*, for that author likewise adopted the above motto, and frequently transcribes whole passages from Voet, a practice we also find adopted in the *Aanhangsel* to Kersteman's *Woordenboek*. In fact, many of the articles in the *Aanhangsel* are bodily taken from Voet's *Commentary*, such as, for instance, the articles on Payment, Sale, Feudal Tenure, *Injuria*, Hypothecations, *Fidei-commissum*, and many others. The work is of value as an encyclopædia of the law of Holland, although there are a great number of important subjects which are either not treated of at all or else very cursorily referred to. As a work of reference to put the practitioner in the way of finding where the subject may be further studied, the dictionary of Kersteman can be recommended

J. Munniks. — Of Munniks we know very little. He flourished towards the end of the eighteenth century, and was an advocate who practised before the Court of Holland. In 1776 he published a *Manual of Modern Law for the United Netherlands according to the order of the Digest.* This work is constantly quoted by Arntzenius, and is of considerable merit. It may be regarded as a series of notes on the *Pandects,* showing how the Roman law had been modified by custom and statute law. It is useful as a guide to the legal opinion of the latter half of the eighteenth century.

Hendrik Jan Arntzenius (1735–1797).—Arntzenius was born at Nijmegen in 1735. He studied law at the University of Franeker, where he took his doctor's degree. For some time he taught classics, but eventually took up law once more. He was appointed professor of Roman law at Groningen in 1774. Subsequently he became professor of both Roman and Roman-Dutch law. In 1788 he left Groningen for Utrecht, where he was elected professor of Roman law, Roman-Dutch law and of the history of law. Later on he was appointed professor of international law as well. He remained at Utrecht until his death in 1797.

Arntzenius was a great admirer of Noodt, and considered him one of the best models for a jurist. He was a man of great talent and versatility. His best-known legal work is the *Institutiones juris Belgici de conditione hominum.* This work was apparently never completed. It is a marvel of learning, but a very difficult book for the student to master. No Roman-Dutch law-book shows more clearly how utterly impossible it was to deal with the whole of the law of the Netherlands in one treatise. In the three volumes which constitute the work Arntzenius first gives us a sketch of the history of the Roman-Dutch law, then he deals with the division of law into *jus scriptum* and *jus non scriptum*, and lastly with his principal subject—*De conditione hominum.* In considering the different conditions of men, he discusses the various divisions of Justinian, and explains the law prevailing not only in every province, but also in almost every city of the Netherlands. The most important part of his work is that part in which he deals with the law of marriage and the law of guardianship.

He is not satisfied with stating the law which prevailed in his day in every city of the Netherlands, but he traces the various laws and customs to their origins. For each statement he quotes his authority, and as he is dealing with the laws and customs not only of every province and district, but of every town, the mass of laws, customs and authorities becomes overwhelming. Add to this that the language and the style are very terse, and the reader will easily understand how difficult it is to find one's way through this maze. At the same time the work is as systematic as a work of this description can be, and is very valuable to the student of the history of the Roman-Dutch law. It is greatly to be regretted that this learned author did not investigate the whole field of the Roman-Dutch law in the way he treated the *De Conditione Hominum.*

Arent Lybrecht.—Arent Lybrecht was a notary practising in the Hague. We know very little about him except that he lived in the eighteenth century, and was still alive in 1780. His first work was *Burgerlijke Rechtsgeleerdheid, Notarieel en Koopmans Handboek.* This book gave

Van der Linden the idea of writing his *Institutes*. Lybrecht's principal works, however, are the *Redeneerend Vertoog over 't Notaris Ambt* and the *Redeneerend Praktijk over 't oefenen van 't Notaris Ambt.* Of these the *Redeneerend Vertoog over 't Notaris Ambt* is his most important law-book. Notwithstanding that severe criticisms were levelled against this work, six editions were published between 1738 and 1780.

Lybrecht was not an advocate, but a notary, and had therefore not had the advantage of the theoretical training usual with members of the Dutch Bar. Though acquainted with the Latin language, he was not a very efficient Latin scholar, and therefore he could not refer with facility to the numerous Dutch writers who had written in that language. At the same time he had a very good knowledge of the Roman-Dutch law, particularly of those branches with which a notary should be acquainted. His *Notary's Manual* was intended as a practical work for notaries, and not as a scientific treatise on the Roman-Dutch law. That it was highly popular in Holland cannot be disputed, for otherwise the anonymous author of the *Aanteekeningen op Lybrecht's Notaris Ambt* would not have taken the trouble to write so extensive a commentary on Lybrecht's text. This anonymous writer, an able lawyer himself, gives Lybrecht no scant praise for the good work he had done.

The *Notaris Ambt* of Lybrecht, together with the *Aanteekeningen,* have done a great deal towards the better understanding of the practice of the Roman-Dutch law during the eighteenth century. The annotator supplied that theoretical part of the subject in which Lybrecht himself was somewhat deficient. The *Redeneerend Praktijk* gives us the ordinary forms in use during the latter part of the eighteenth century, and if we compare them with the forms used by notaries to-day we notice that the change has not been very great. These works, therefore, are of the greatest value to the practitioner and to the student of the history of our law. Tennant's *Notary's Manual*, a book very popular with the profession, is very largely founded on the work of Lybrecht.

These works of Lybrecht are all written in the Dutch of the eighteenth century, which is quite a different language from the Dutch in which modern law-books are written. French words with a Dutch form are constantly used, such as *participeeren, conquesten, compareeren, expresseeren,* and so on, though in this respect Lybrecht is not nearly so great a sinner as Kersteman. It was apparently the language of the forum in those days, and no one will dare to call it beautiful. At the same time Lybrecht expresses himself very clearly, and his style is well suited to his subject. Those students of the Roman-Dutch law who can read the lawyer's Dutch of the eighteenth century will find the works of Lybrecht and his annotator most useful towards understanding the practice of the Roman-Dutch law as it obtained in Holland during the eighteenth century.

Johan Jacob van Hasselt (1717–1783).—Johan Jacob van Hasselt was born at Zutphen in 1717. He studied at Harderwijk and practised as an advocate before the Supreme Court of Gelderland. He was a lawyer of considerable reputation in his day. His chief works are the *Aanteekening tot de Hollandsche Advysen* (Notes on the Dutch Consultations) and, in collaboration with Moorman, the *Verhandelingen over de Misdaden en derzelver Straffen.* Other works are the *Consilia Militaria, Rechtsgeleerde Brieven,* and antiquarian researches.

Gerard de Haas.—Gerard de Haas lived during the eighteenth century. He is known chiefly for his notes to Merula's *Manier van Procedeeren,* and a volume of consultations known as the *Nieuwe Hollandsche Consultaties.*

Cornelis Willem Decker.—Cornelis Willem Decker lived towards the end of the eighteenth century, and practised as an advocate at Amsterdam. His chief works are the *Notes to Van Leeuwen's Commentaries* and a treatise on divorce. The *Notes to Van Leeuwen* show him to have been a jurist of no mean order. They form an excellent commentary on Van Leeuwen's great work, and help materially to elucidate the text.

Didericus Lulius.—Didericus Lulius lived during the latter half of the eighteenth century. He practised as an advocate in the Court of Holland. He was a friend of Van der Linden, and published several works in collaboration with Van der Linden and Van Spaan. Of these the chief were: *Notes to Merula's Manier van Procedeeren;* an edition of the *Placaat Books* subsequent to Cau's collection, and the *Rechtsgeleerde Observaties* and *Dertig Vragen.* The last works are of great importance from an antiquarian point of view, and very necessary to a correct understanding of Grotius' *Introduction.*

Renier van Spaan.—Renier van Spaan was one of the judges of the Court of Holland during the latter half of the eighteenth century. He was a poet and a strong supporter of the democratic party. He published works in collaboration with Van der Linden and Lulius (*vide* Lulius).

Timon Boey.—Boey was secretary of the Court of Holland, and a lawyer learned in the history of law and the antiquities of his native land. He died towards the end of the eighteenth century. His chief works are a history of the Court of Holland and a law lexicon called *Woorden tolk of Verklaring der voornaamste woorden in de hedendaagsche en aloude rechtspleging voorkomende* (1773).

Dionysius Godefried van der Keessel (1738–1816).—Van der Keessel was born at Deventer in 1738. He studied at Leyden, where he was a pupil of Professor Scheltinga, the author of a commentary on Grotius. After obtaining his degree he settled at the Hague and practised as an advocate. His learning and knowledge of law were so great that he was appointed professor of law at Groningen at the early age of twenty-four. He remained at Groningen from 1762 until 1770, when he accepted the professorship of law at the University of Leyden. Here he remained as professor of law for thirty-eight years. Three times he was elected Rector Magnificus of the university. He retired from the professorship at Leyden in 1808, and died in 1816. His chief legal works were: *Dictata ad Jus Hodiernum; Dictata ad Jus Criminale; Dictata ad Institutiones Justinianeas* and the *Theses Selectae Juris Hollandiae et Zeelandici ad Supplendam H. Grotii Introductionem.*

Van der Keessel may be regarded as the last of the great Dutch exponents of the Roman-Dutch law. His influence upon the development of the Roman-Dutch law in South Africa has been very great, partly because he is the last commentator on Grotius and partly on account of his reputation in Holland at the time South Africa was annexed to the British Crown. His only printed work on the Roman-Dutch law is the collection of notes on Grotius known as the *Theses Selectae*, but his *magnum opus* was the *Dictata ad Jus Hodiernum*. This, in accordance with Van der Keessel's will, has never been printed. It consists of the text of the lectures he used to deliver at Leyden. The manuscript is deposited in the university library at Leyden, and owing to the generosity of Mr. C. H. van Zyl a typed copy is now in the library of the Supreme Court at Capetown.

It was as a lecturer rather than as a publicist that Van der Keessel earned his fame. Van der Keessel was a great admirer of the civil law, and did not approve of the school of lawyers that grew up during the latter half of the eighteenth century. This school tried to persuade the people of the Netherlands that the Roman law was a foreign law, whose influence had been greatly exaggerated. Van der Keessel's strong sense did not allow political sentiment to obscure truth. Though steeped in the knowledge of Roman law, he did not strive to exalt the Roman law above the system of law which then prevailed in Holland, nor, on the other hand, did he refer to German customs those rules of law which were most obviously taken from the *Corpus Juris*. He studied the Roman law, the German customs and the statutory law, and gave to each its proper place in the system of Roman-Dutch law. Hence the *Theses Selectae* reflect the law as it prevailed in his day, and is by no means a mere academical commentary on the work of Grotius. Owing to Van der Keessel's popularity as a jurist during the first quarter of the nineteenth century his opinions were readily adopted by the judges of the old Court of Justice at Capetown, and in this way he came to be regarded as an authority of the highest importance. At present the work of Van der Keessel is regarded as one of the standard commentaries to the *Introduction* of Grotius. The *Theses Selectae* have been translated into English by C. A. Lorens.

Johannes van der Linden (1756–1835).—Johannes van der Linden was born in 1756. He practised as an advocate at Amsterdam for many years, and when, after fifty years of practice, he was appointed a judge of first instance at Amsterdam, a great banquet was given by all the lawyers of Amsterdam in honour of his services to the profession. He was the author of a great many law-books, though in South Africa he is principally known by his text-book on the law of Holland known as the *Institutes of the Law of Holland.* This short sketch of the Roman-Dutch law as we know it to-day was published in 1806 with the title of *Regtsgeleerd Prakticaal en Koopmans Handboek ten dienste van Regters, praktizijns kooplieden en allen die een algemeen overzicht van Regtskennis verlangen.* From this it will be seen that the true title of the work is not the *Institutes of the Law of Holland,* but a *Practical Legal Manual for the use of judges, practitioners, merchants and all others who desire a general view of the Law.*

In his preface to this *Manual* he tells us that the bookseller Allart asked him to edit and amplify a small manual then in general use called *Burgerlijk Rechtsgeleerd Notarieel en Koopmans Handboek.* This little book was chiefly the work of Lybrecht. Van der Linden, however, found it impossible to edit this work, for, in his own words, "I had found the work executed in such a manner that, to speak candidly, nothing could be done with it" (Juta's trans. p. x). This request, however, led him to write a small work on the law of Holland, which would enable persons not versed in the study of law to grasp the principles of law adopted by the courts of Holland. It was therefore intended as a text-book for students, and for persons desirous of obtaining a general idea of the law and procedure of Holland.

The *Manual* was, however, more than a mere popular exposition of the law of Holland, for the author refers to most of the accepted authorities for the statements contained in the text. At the same time it cannot be denied that the work is very sketchy, and not to be compared with the *Introduction* of Grotius as a text-book for acquiring a knowledge of the Roman-Dutch law. As a text-book for the student who is already acquainted with the *Institutes* of Justinian, Van der Linden's *Manual* can certainly be recommended; but the student who thinks that he has acquired a fair knowledge of the Roman-Dutch law when he has mastered his Van der Linden is unhappily very greatly mistaken. Van der Linden never intended his *Manual* to be considered as more than a first book to the student or a legal *vade mecum* for the merchant. In his introduction he tells us how the Roman-Dutch law should be studied by a person desirous of obtaining a sound knowledge of that system. No one who reads that introduction can possibly imagine that

Van der Linden ever thought that his own little work was more than a mere preface to the study of the law of Holland. There are two English translations of Van der Linden's *Manual*—one published by Jabez Henry in 1828, and a more correct one published by Sir Henry Juta in 1897.

His next best-known work is the *Verhandeling over de Judicieele Praktyk of form van procedeeren voor de Hoven van Justitie in Holland gebruikelyk.* This is usually known as Van der Linden's *Judicial Practice.* It was a book of great importance during the earlier part of the nineteenth century, but at present the practice in the South African courts has been so modified by the various rules of court and by the influence of English procedure that the work is of comparatively little value to the practitioner.

In addition to the above Van der Linden edited Voet, and published a *Supplement* to the first eleven books of the *Commentaries.* This *Supplement* was intended to elucidate the text of Voet and to bring his work up to date, but Napoleon's conquest of Holland and the adoption of the *Code Napoléon* made such a work unnecessary, and Van der Linden discontinued the *Supplement.* He also translated several of Pothier's works, *e.g.* the treatises on *Obligations,* on *Legacies,* on *Partnership* and on *Bills of Exchange,* and added valuable notes on the law of Holland. In 1798 he edited the two last volumes of the *Placaat Boek* and published a *Life of Catherine II, Empress of Russia.* His last work on the Roman-Dutch law was a collection of *Important Decisions of the Courts of Holland.* This was published in 1809. After the *Code Napoléon* took the place of the indigenous law of Holland

Van der Linden devoted the rest of his life to elucidate the *Code* and the new legal practice introduced by the French.

He died at Amsterdam in 1835 at the age of seventy-nine, and is, therefore, the last great Dutch lawyer who practised both the old Roman-Dutch law and the law of the *Code Napoléon*.

CHAPTER XXXIII.

ADMINISTRATION OF JUSTICE IN SOUTH AFRICA.

THE East India Company, as we have seen, was founded by a charter granted by the States-General in 1602. By sec. 35 of this charter provision was made for the establishment of courts of justice. In consequence of this a court was established at the Cape called the Raad van Justitie. Its judgments and sentences were pronounced in the name of the States-General and the Prince of Orange, and not in the name of the East India Company. The following was the formula used by the courts of justice in pronouncing judgment: *Zoo is 't dat den Edel achtbaren Rade van Justitie doende regt in de naam en van wegen de Hoog Moogende Heeren Staten Generaal der vrije vereenigde Nederlanden mitsgaders zyn Hoogheijt den Heere Prince van Orange als derzelver Erv-stadhouder*, &c. (Thus it is that the Council of Justice doing right in the name and on behalf of their High Mightinesses the States-General of the free and united Netherlands and of his Highness the Prince of Orange as their hereditary stadhouder, &c.).

The number of members of the Raad van Justitie varied. I have not been able to ascertain the exact number of its members prior to 1783. At that date the full number was thirteen, though at the capitulation of 1795 only eleven sat, owing to the close family relationship of two of its members. In 1797, during the British occupation, the number of members was reduced from thirteen to seven, but after the annexation of 1806 the court was composed of a president, a secretary and eight members. Some of its members sat as judicial commissioners to deal with petty cases. The full court had plenary jurisdiction in all criminal and civil matters. Its seat was at Capetown. It was the court of appeal for all the inferior and district courts in criminal as well as civil matters. From the Raad van Justitie an appeal lay to the Supreme Court at Batavia.

I learn from Mr. Leibrandt, the keeper of the Archives in the Cape Colony, that in 1682 a court of first instance for petty cases was created in Capetown and the Cape district, whilst courts of landdrost and heemraden were established at Stellenbosch and Drakenstein. That a court for the hearing of petty cases existed at Capetown towards the latter half of the eighteenth century admits of no doubt. It was called the Collegie van Commissarissen van Kleine Civiele Zaken, and was composed of members of the Raad van Justitie (Administration of Justice Ordinance, 17th July, 1797).

I can find no confirmation of the view that schepenen existed in South Africa, though they did apparently exist in India and Batavia. I am also informed by Mr. Leibrandt that the procedure of the early inferior courts at the Cape was regulated by Instructions issued to Johannes Mulder, landdrost of Stellenbosch and Drakenstein. These Instructions were no doubt based on the rules of procedure laid down by the Ordinances of 1570 and 1580 for the inferior courts of Holland.

The common law of the province of Holland was accepted as the common law of the settlement of the Cape of Good

Hope. All ordinances, therefore, of the States-General and of the States of Holland which were not of purely local application were recognised as law at the Cape of Good Hope. Of the ordinances passed either by the States-General or by the States of Holland, those which were enacted for the Dutch Republic and its dependencies or for the province of Holland undoubtedly applied to the Cape as well. Whether any placaat after 1652, which is not *ex facie* of universal operation or which was not specially proclaimed as law at the Cape of Good Hope, can be regarded as part of the law of the Cape Colony has not been definitely decided as far as I am aware.

In *Herbert* v. *Anderson* (2 Menz. 166 [174]) the Court decided that certain placaats, including two of 1677, were merely fiscal or revenue ordinances of Holland, and inasmuch as they had never become or been made law in the Cape Colony, they did not form part of the law of that colony. In *Maynard* v. *Usher* (2 Menz. 170 [178]) the Court held that a placaat of 1774 (9th May) did not apply to the colony, apparently because it was a fiscal ordinance; but Sir Henry de Villiers rightly remarked in *Green* v. *Griffiths* (4 S.C. 349): "In the case of *Herbert* v. *Anderson* this Court held that a parole lease for a year followed by possession is paramount to a subsequent written lease. The Court also held that the placaats to which I have just referred, being fiscal, have never been incorporated into the law of this colony. . . . Such portions of the placaats, if any, as had been incorporated in the general law of Holland and are applicable to the circumstances of this country, need not be excluded because the parts relating to the revenue are inapplicable." In other words, the mere fact that a portion of a placaat is fiscal is not enough to exclude its operation with regard to other matters contained in the placaat. In *London Discount Bank* v. *Dawes* (1 Menz. 386) the court referred to a placaat of the 5th February, 1665, as a valid authority.

Besides the Dutch placaats there were ordinances issued by the Government of Batavia. These applied not only to the East Indies, but to all dependencies connected with the East India Company. It was usual to insert in these ordinances a saving clause: "In so far as the conditions of the respective dependencies will permit." In time placaats were also issued at the Cape by the Governor-General subject to a veto from Batavia or Holland, so that towards the end of the eighteenth century the confusion at the Cape was very considerable. The Cape therefore received its statute law partly from the placaats of the States-General and the States of Holland, partly from the East India Company's directorate in Holland, partly from the Governor-General in Batavia, and partly from the Governor and Council at the Cape.

To what extent the Batavian ordinances applied it is difficult to say. From an article by Mr. Roos in the *Cape Law Journal* (vol. 14, p. 6) it would appear that no copy of the general statutes of Batavia of 1642 existed at the Cape in 1708. Before that date, therefore, these statutes could not have been very strongly relied upon. Mr. Roos says: "In 1715 the Cape Council of Justice presented a request to the Governor, De Chavonnes, pointing out that up to that time there had been no instruction to guide the said Council in the administration of justice, and asking that the Statutes of

India might be taken as a basis for laws with and in addition to the Roman law and modern laws, and without derogating from the plakaten and ordinances issued here at various times." Upon which the Governor in Council resolved "that in future in judicial and petty causes the Statutes of India should be observed in so far as they do not conflict with the plakaten, ordinances and respective Council resolutions given and resolved upon by the Government from time to time."

This Code of Batavian laws (also called the Statutes of India) was constantly amended and amplified, until it assumed a permanent form in 1766. It was then called the New Statutes of Batavia. Mr. Roos cannot tell us whether this New Code has ever been formally adopted at the Cape, and from inquiries made by me I should very much doubt its acceptance by the Government. It certainly was not sanctioned by the East India Company's directorate.

So great was the confusion at the Cape that De Mist was sent out as a Commissioner to inquire into the state of affairs. He made severe remarks upon the administration of justice, and said, amongst other things (again I quote Mr. Roos): "A Council of Justice without instructions, except as to the number, rank and emoluments of the members, a Fiscaal independent of the Council, of which he should have been the most subordinate minister, the sentences of the Council lying in appeal to India, while the Fiscaal alone was responsible to the Netherlands directly; no statute book for the colony, no instructions for landdrost and heemraden; behold the sorry state into which justice and its administration had fallen into at the Cape in 1795."

In consequence of this report an attempt was made to reform

the administration. The Government began by defining the authority of the landdrosts and heemraden. Hence we find that on the 23rd of October, 1805, General Janssens and the Council of Polity passed an ordinance for the administration of the country districts. This was in consequence of the report of the Commissary-General, De Mist. The ordinance dealt partly with the civil and partly with the judicial administration of the country districts. Five magistracies or *drosdyen* were established at Stellenbosch, Swellendam, Graaff-Reinet, Uitenhage and Tulbagh. Each drosdy was administered by a landdrost assisted by a secretary and as many burghers or heemraden, as they were called, as the Governor might appoint. This board, consisting of landdrost and heemraden, exercised both civil and judicial functions. Under the landdrost and heemraden stood the field-cornet. The landdrosts in their respective districts had the direction of all prosecutions for crimes committed in their districts, and were required to send the criminals to Capetown for trial.

In civil matters the jurisdiction of landdrost and heemraden extended to all disputes respecting lands, boundaries of the same, servitudes and impounding of cattle; but disputes regarding *leeningsplaatsen* (loan places) were reserved to the Governor and Council. The landdrost could entertain "any real and personal suits for money or money's worth without including therein interest and costs not amounting to the sum of three hundred Rds.," and all suits regarding the district auctioneers. Before proceeding to give judgment landdrosts were required to use every endeavour to bring parties to amicable terms.

The proceedings before a landdrost and heemraden had to

be conducted by the parties in person, unless the landdrost thought fit to allow an agent to appear. In any case the proceedings were to be conducted verbally, and not in writing. The defendant to a suit was allowed two defaults, subject to a fine of 3 Rds. for the first and 6 Rds. for the second default; on being summoned the third time and not attending the defaulter was declared contumacious, the case was heard and, if a sufficient case was made out, judgment given against him. The judgments of landdrost and heemraden were executed by the *Desolate Boedels Kamer* at Capetown, either by their own officers or by deputies. The landdrost presided over the court of landdrost and heemraden, and pronounced the judgment of the court. From this judgment an appeal lay to the Court of Justice at Capetown. The landdrosts also acted as Commissioners of the Court of Justice, as marriage officers and as coroners.

The whole of the civil administration of the district was entrusted to the board of landdrost and heemraden. They caused roads to be made, supervised prisons and all other public buildings, saw that proper weights and measures were used, that the food sold to the people was sound and not adulterated, and that the taxes were duly collected and paid. Special instructions defining the scope of their duties were issued to the secretary of the court, to the *onder-schout* (a chief police officer) and to the messengers.

The procedure of the Court of Justice at Capetown was regulated both by local instructions or rules of court, and by the rules of procedure which prevailed in the courts of Holland. The Instructions were, however, inadequate, and De Mist complained of their inadequacy, though his report is couched in such terms that one might conclude that there were no Instructions. Reference, however, is made to Instructies van de Raad van Justitie in several proclamations, so that it would be wrong to infer that there were no rules of court at all.

The procedure adopted by the Court of Justice was that laid down by the Civil and Criminal Procedure Ordinances of 1570 and 1580. The various books on procedure which I have referred to in an earlier chapter were used as authorities at the Cape. Of these the *Papegaai*, Merula, Van Leeuwen's *Manier van Procedeeren,* and Wassenaar and Van der Linden's *Judicieele Praktijk* were the most important.

Until 1813 all the proceedings of the court were not conducted with open doors. It is true the pleadings were public, but the court heard the witnesses in private, of course in the presence of the practitioners who appeared for the parties. By a proclamation of Sir John Cradock all proceedings before the court were ordered to be held with open doors, and the accused was to be confronted with the witnesses.

Such, then, was the state of affairs at the beginning of the nineteenth century. On the 10th of January, 1806, the Cape capitulated to Sir David Baird and Commodore Popham, and from that date to 1814 the British forces held the settlement as conquerors. In 1814 the Dutch possessions in South Africa were formally ceded to Great Britain by a convention between the King of England and the Sovereign Prince of the Netherlands. It was the practice of the British Government not to alter the laws and institutions of conquered territories except in so far as laws were inconsistent with British occupation. Hence the annexation of the Cape made no difference to the common law of South Africa.

The British Government recognised the judicial institutions then existing, and left the people to be governed by the system of law to which they had grown accustomed. In the first few years of the occupation no drastic alterations were made. It is true the services of the judges of the Raad van Justitie were dispensed with, but a new court was instantly constituted consisting of Willem van Ryneveld as president, Mathiessen, Struberg, Fleck, Truter, Diemel and Hiddingh as members, and Gerard Belaerts van Blokland as secretary.

In May, 1807, the Governor constituted himself a court of appeal for civil cases, with an appeal from his decision to the Privy Council. In the following year the Governor and two assessors became the final court of appeal in criminal cases.

Gradually, however, statutory alterations were made in the law and practice of the colony. In 1811 circuit courts were first established. The proclamation which established these courts recited that prior to this the cognisance and punishment of all crimes and the adjudication of all civil suits in which considerable property was at stake took place at Capetown. The language of this proclamation strikes us at the present day as very peculiar. Here is an example: "Now as the removal of such inconveniences and obstructions and the application of a Process by which justice may be more speedily administered must be productive of the most beneficial result, not only as inspiring the Good with an increased confidence in the superintending care of the Government, but by intimidating the Wicked and thus preventing the frequency of crimes," &c.

In 1813 the perpetual quitrent was fixed upon a proper

basis. In 1819 a new mode of proceeding in criminal cases was introduced. In this procedure some of the provisions of English criminal practice were introduced, but the old Dutch *Crimineele Procedure* still formed the basis of the new practice. I shall deal with this more fully in the next chapter.

In 1826 an ordinance was promulgated creating justices of the peace. From the date of the annexation the Dutch and English languages had been used in judicial proceedings, but after the 1st of January, 1827, all judicial acts and proceedings were required to be conducted in the English language. During this year the first Charter of Justice was promulgated establishing a Supreme Court. This was amended and repealed by the New Charter of 1832. In 1828 the duties of the sheriff were more explicitly defined, and the procedure in criminal cases considerably altered from the old Dutch practice so as to bring it more in accord with English procedure. During the same year the office of Registrar of Deeds was created. In the following year the legal age of majority was reduced from twenty-five years to twenty-one.

In 1830 the law of evidence was altered in such a way that the practice of the courts of Westminster rather than that of the Dutch courts was followed. The Ordinance (72 of 1830) attempted to codify the law of evidence for the colony, and based its provisions upon the principles which prevailed in English courts. This same year saw the criminal procedure considerably amplified. In 1831 the jury system was fully introduced, and an ordinance passed relative to the qualification and method of appointing Grand and Petit Jurors.

On the 2nd May, 1832, letters patent were issued to take effect from 1st March, 1834, known as the New Charter of

Justice. By this statute the judicial institutions which had existed since the annexation were completely swept away, and new courts appointed upon an entirely new plan. With the Charter of Justice of 1827 the Raad van Justitie passed away, and was replaced by a Supreme Court of three judges appointed by the Crown for life. The landdrosts and heemraden also disappeared, and their functions were taken over by resident magistrates and civil commissioners. The laws with regard to resident magistrates were consolidated in 1856 by Act 20 of that year.

In 1857 a Commission was appointed to inquire into the state of the law. The Commission consisted of the Chief Justice Sir Sydney Bell, judges Cloete and Watermeyer, Mr. Porter the Attorney-General, and Mr. Rawson the Colonial Secretary. It issued its report on the 10th November, 1858. To this was attached a list, framed by the Commissioners, of all the placaats, proclamations, advertisements, &c., which had had the effect of law in the Cape Colony. The Commission found that most of these were either repealed or obsolete. The list is to be found in the old editions of the Cape statutes. The Commission also found that the Roman-Dutch law, which consists of the civil or Roman law as modified by the laws passed by the legislature of Holland and by the customs of that country, forms the great bulk of the law of the colony, and that a large body of statute law scattered throughout the British imperial Statute Book had the force of law within the colony. Besides these there existed ordinances and proclamations of the colonial legislature and certain orders in council. The Commission recommended that all the laws still of force in the colony should be published in one collection. The result of this was the publication in 1862 of the statute law of the Cape of Good Hope, comprising the placaats, proclamations and ordinances enacted before the establishment of the colonial Parliament, and still wholly or in part in force. This volume has been the basis upon which all the subsequent editions of the Statute Book of the Cape Colony have been formed.

We see, therefore, that after 1834 the Supreme Court of the Cape of Good Hope assumed its present form. There was a considerable difference between the procedure of the old Raad van Justitie and that of the Supreme Court. As stated above, the Dutch courts recognised two classes of legal practitioners—the attorney and the advocate. As these practitioners were also known to the English practice, there was no difference in this respect after the establishment of the new court. The procedure before the Raad van Justitie was much more elaborate than that before the Supreme Court. It was the practice in the Dutch courts for the advocate not only to address the court, but to hand to the court a summary of his argument. This practice was followed even after the cession of the Cape, and was probably kept up until the formation of the first Supreme Court in 1827.

In 1864 an Eastern Districts' Court was established. In 1879 the Act of 1864 was repealed, and in addition to the Supreme Court of the Cape of Good Hope two other courts of superior jurisdiction were created—the Eastern Districts' Court, as at present constituted, and the High Court of Griqualand West—each with a judge-president and two puisne judges. The judges of these courts were also judges of the Supreme Court. A court of appeal was established consisting of the three judges of the Supreme Court and the two judges-president, but this court had a short life. At present the Supreme Court at Capetown is the court of appeal for the whole Cape Colony and for Southern Rhodesia. From the Supreme Court an appeal lies to the Privy Council. It is unnecessary to consider in detail the various modifications introduced from time to time into the judicial system. The above is a brief sketch of the gradual alteration which the administration of justice has undergone in the Cape Colony from the time of its settlement until it assumed its present form.

Natal.—The Roman-Dutch law was established in Natal by Ordinance 12 of 1845, which enacted that "the system, code or body of law commonly called the Roman-Dutch law, as the same has been and is accepted by the tribunals of the Colony of the Cape of Good Hope, shall be and the same is hereby established as the law for the time being of the district of Natal." In 1896 a law was passed (Act 39) consolidating the laws with reference to the Supreme Court, and the provision of Ordinance 12, above quoted, was incorporated in the new law. Besides the Roman-Dutch law there is a code of laws known as the Native Code, which applies to disputes between natives of a nature other than commercial. It was enacted as law by Ordinance 3 of 1849. In a later chapter I shall show how profoundly English law has modified the Roman-Dutch law in this colony.

The Transvaal.—The earlier laws of the Transvaal referred to the *Hollandsche Wet* (Dutch law) as the common law of that State. In 1859 this was explained to mean the Roman-Dutch law. It was then further enacted that the *Koopman's Handboek* of Van der Linden should be the law-book of the State. In other words, the Roman-Dutch law as contained in Van der Linden's manual should be the common law, except in so far as it was modified by the grondwet, by other ordinances or by resolutions of the Volksraad. If Van der Linden did not deal with a question the judges were referred to Van Leeuwen's *Roman-Dutch Law* or Grotius' *Introduction* (V.R.B. 5th May, 1859, appendix 1). In 1864 it was further explained that the Roman-Dutch law was the basis of the law of the State, but that it had to be interpreted according to South African usages (Notice, 12th April, 1864). In 1902, after the annexation, it was provided in the Administration of Justice Ordinance (sec. 17) that the Roman-Dutch law, except in so far as it is modified by legislative enactments, shall be the law of the Transvaal colony. This means presumably the Roman-Dutch law as it existed at the Cape at the time of the annexation of 1806.

The inferior courts of the Transvaal Republic were modelled upon the old Cape courts of landdrost and landdrost and heemraden. The number of heemraden varied from four to six until 1873, when it was definitely fixed at six. In 1877 the court of landdrost and heemraden was abolished. During the first English occupation the landdrost became a resident magistrate, though the term landdrost was again adopted after the retrocession in 1881, and continued in use until the annexation of 1900.

The superior court, according to the Grondwet of 1858, consisted of three landdrosts and twelve jurymen (or *Gezworenen*). This court was finally abolished in 1881. In 1877 a law was passed amending the grondwet and constituting a High Court of three judges and circuit courts. In terms of this law judges were appointed and the High Court of the Republic established. This court sat during the first English occupation, and its constitution was confirmed first by the Triumvirate and later by Law 3 of 1883. The High Court of the Transvaal thus constituted was modelled upon the Supreme Court of the Cape Colony.

After the disappearance of the heemraden the landdrost performed the functions of a magistrate, with a jurisdiction somewhat greater than the resident magistrate of the Cape Colony.

After the annexation of 1900 two superior courts were created—the Supreme Court at Pretoria, consisting at present of seven judges, and the High Court of the Witwatersrand, which is a single judge court presided over by one of the judges of the Supreme Court.

Instead of landdrosts, resident magistrates have been appointed similar to those of the Cape Colony. In addition to magistrates there are inspectors of Chinese, who have special jurisdiction over Chinese labourers.

Orange River Colony.—Prior to the annexation the Orange Free State, like the Transvaal and the Cape Colony, adopted the Roman-Dutch law. In the amended constitution of 1898 we find the following: "That the Roman-Dutch law is accepted as the fundamental law of this State in so far as it was found in force in the Cape Colony at the time of the appointment of the English judges, in the place of the previously existing Council of Justice, and not to include any new laws and institutions, local and general, which may have been introduced into Holland and which are not based on or are in conflict with the old Roman-Dutch law as expounded in the text-books of Voet, Van Leeuwen, Grotius, *De Papegaai*, Merula, Lybrecht, Van der Linden, Van der Keessel and the authorities cited by them" (ch. 1, sec. 1). After the annexation no alteration was made in this respect.

In the old days the Orange Free State, like the Transvaal, had courts of landdrost and heemraden; but after the establishment of the High Court the superior courts were like those of the Cape Colony—a Supreme or High Court and circuit courts. The landdrosts were similar to the resident magistrates of the Cape. Since the annexation the High Court of the Republic gave place to the present High Court under Ordinance 4 of 1902, and the landdrost courts became courts of resident magistrates.

Southern Rhodesia.—Here, too, the Roman-Dutch law is the common law, and a great number of the Rhodesian statutes are almost identical with those of the Cape Colony. The Supreme Court of Rhodesia is the highest court of the colony, and from this court there is an appeal to the Supreme Court of the Cape Colony at Capetown. The inferior courts are presided over by resident magistrates similar to those of the Cape Colony.

It will therefore be seen that from the Zambesi to Cape Point the Roman-Dutch law as it prevailed in the province of Holland prior to the foundation of the Cape Settlement in 1652 is the common law of South Africa. The procedure of the superior courts of each colony is regulated by a set of rules published for that particular court, but these rules are all so similar to the rules of the Supreme Court of the

Cape of Good Hope that the difference in judicial procedure of the various courts is very slight. The practice of the courts of Natal differs more from that of the Cape Colony than that of any other of the South African courts. Where the rules of court do not apply the practice of the old courts of Holland is generally adopted, though English precedent is often followed.

The Roman-Dutch law has, however, been profoundly modified in the various colonies since its first introduction into the Cape. To give a detailed account of this modification would be a work of considerable labour, and would occupy too great a space. In a later chapter I shall, however, point out briefly how English legal ideas have modified the principles of the Roman-Dutch law.

CHAPTER XXXIV.

CRIMINAL PROCEDURE FROM THE SIXTEENTH CENTURY TO THE PRESENT DAY.

In dealing with the administration of the Courts of Justice I endeavoured to show that during the early German period, during the Frankish rule and even after the institution of the counts, the assembly of the *mallum* was the Supreme Court in criminal matters. In addition to this court there were assize courts and inferior district and town courts. The latter took cognisance of lesser offences, whilst the assize and Supreme Courts dealt with all crimes for which the death penalty or other severe punishment could be exacted. The idea that the sovereign was the fountain of law, and that crimes were punished in his name, originated with the Frankish monarchs, and grew stronger as the power of the sovereign or count increased. The criminal procedure during the earlier period, when ordeals were still in vogue, has been sufficiently explained.

Gradually the procedure of the courts came to be moulded upon the procedure of the Roman law as modified by the Canon law, so that by the fifteenth century a considerable advance had been made in the method of bringing criminals to justice. The law of evidence had been brought into some system by the Canon law, and the harshness of the old criminal practice had been considerably modified. In 1507 the *Constitutio criminalis Carolina* had been enacted in Germany, and it soon formed the model for the criminal procedure of the Netherlands. Towards the end of the sixteenth century the criminal procedure of Holland was laid down by a statute passed for better regulating the method of criminal proceedings. Although the statute was promulgated during the early years of the struggle with Philip of Spain (1570), it was not revoked after the union of the provinces, and consequently formed the basis of the criminal procedure of the seventeenth and eighteenth centuries.

The lower courts, as we have seen, consisted as a general rule of baljuw and mannen in the country districts, and of schout and schepenen in the towns. From these an appeal lay with the Court of Holland. The statute of 1570 regulated the procedure in the lower courts. The same procedure was followed in the Supreme Court of Holland except in so far as it was modified by the rules of that court (*Instructiën van den Hove*). The first part of this Ordinance gives us a good insight into the abuses which existed in former centuries. It shows how the personal influence and feudal rights of the lords of manors had prevented delinquents from being brought to justice. The right of pardon and the right of remission of punishment were claimed and exercised not only by feudal lords, but by a whole series of State functionaries. The first salutary provision of the Ordinance of 1570 was the abolition of all these rights and privileges and the establishment of the principle that the stadhouder was the only official besides the king who could grant pardon and remission of penalty.

No person could be arrested without the order of a judge or magistrate unless caught in *flagrante delicto*. It was therefore necessary to lay a criminal information before the magistrate or judge, who heard evidence and determined whether leave to arrest should or should not be granted. No private prosecution was allowed, and all criminals were pursued by a public prosecutor before the judge of the domicile of the accused. A prisoner could only be tried before the judge of the place where a crime was committed if caught there *flagrante delicto*. With us the preliminary examination is held after the affidavit has been lodged that a crime was committed, and after the accused is arrested. By the old Dutch practice the complainant laid the information before the judge, called his witnesses in support of the charge, and the judge then determined whether leave to arrest should be granted. Unless the crime was of a serious nature no arrest was granted. In smaller delicts a personal citation was deemed sufficient. If the accused failed to appear upon the personal citation the trial could proceed without him. Our modern practice of a trial in open court and of insisting upon the presence of the criminal is derived from English procedure.

Besides this practice of citing the accused there also existed a method of inquisition. Van der Linden says (bk. 3, pt. 2, ch. 1, sec. 11): "An indirect method of procuring the attendance of the party accused is sometimes practised, namely, in case of one against whom there is a certain degree of suspicion, but not strong enough to ground a decree thereon, to send for him or to request his attendance in order to question him regarding the matter, and when anything is obtained from his own answers then to apprehend him; but this method is not to be commended, and ought to be banished from all tribunals." Our modern practice, of course, does not tolerate this course. Another arbitrary method of arrest was the one known as *political arrest.* In that case, for the purposes of public safety, magistrates were entitled to arrest citizens against whom there was suspicion, but no proof (Van der Linden, *loc. cit.* sec. 11).

A curious procedure was the demand on the part of a suspected person to have himself declared free of crime. He took out a *writ of purgation,* and called upon the Attorney-General of the court and all others interested to show cause why he should not be declared innocent of the crime mentioned in the writ. He appeared on the day named in the writ, and could be subjected to a severe cross-examination. If the applicant did not obtain his *purge* he usually found himself the subject of a criminal prosecution. There is no room for such a proceeding in our present procedure. The trial itself was conducted like any other trial, and the Crown made use of all informations, interrogatories, &c., in its possession. The prisoner was not only a competent witness, but could be interrogated.

When we altered the Dutch procedure we abolished not only the interrogatories, but also the right of a prisoner to give evidence. In time, however, we went back to the old Dutch practice, for in 1886 the Cape legislature passed an Act making the accused and his wife competent, but not compellable, witnesses in the case in which he is being tried. The other South African colonies have since then followed suit. On the Continent of Europe the accused can be interrogated, but our law, following English practice, which has always had a tender regard for the feelings of accused persons, refuses to admit the interrogation of prisoners. In the hands of a competent and well-trained magistrate interrogatories are extremely useful in the detection and punishment of crime, but in the hands of inferior magistrates and insufficiently trained prosecutors it would no doubt lead to tyranny and injustice.

It is a curious fact that by the general law of Holland a criminal could not as of right demand that he should be defended by an attorney or advocate: special leave had to be obtained from the judge. Thus art. 14 of the Ordinance of 1570 provides that a criminal cannot employ an advocate to speak for him unless the judge thinks it necessary. In some towns, however, the burghers had the privilege of insisting upon their defence being conducted by an advocate (*Rechts. Obs.* vol. 2, obs. 72).

Such were the general features of the criminal procedure that prevailed in Holland during the eighteenth century. In what respects it was modified at the Cape before the end of the eighteenth century I have not been able to ascertain, though some modifications were introduced by an Ordinance of the 7th July, 1760, on the mode of proceeding in criminal cases. We know, however, from General Janssen's Ordinance for the administration of country districts and his instructions to landdrosts and heemraden, that the Criminal Procedure Ordinance of 1570 constituted the criminal practice of the Cape (art. 54). There was only one judicial body at the Cape which dealt with the trial of serious crimes, and that was the Raad van Justitie at Capetown. The landdrost and heemraden were only entitled to deal with trifling offences, for which the ordinary penalty was a pecuniary fine.

The prosecution of all crimes committed in Capetown was

entrusted to the Fiscaal or Procureur-Generaal, as, subsequent to De Mist's commission, he was sometimes called. For crimes committed outside of the Cape district the landdrost of the district in which the crime was committed was *ex officio* the prosecutor, though he was entitled to employ an advocate in Capetown to conduct the prosecution before the Court of Justice on his behalf (Instructions to Heemraden, arts. 54 and 58).

When a crime was committed in a country district, it was the duty of the landdrost to acquaint the Attorney-General and the President of the Court of Justice with the fact. His next step was to hold an inquest and to conduct a preparatory examination, then already called by that name (*praeparatoire informatie*). This examination had to be conducted in the presence of the heemraden, and if a witness was to be summoned from another district the consent of the Court of Justice at Capetown had to be obtained. If the landdrost thought that there was a *primâ facie* case he was to "exhibit the said examinations to the Court of Justice together with a detailed *species facti* and a summary description of the crime," praying at the same time for a decree of the Court for apprehension or for citation of the suspected person (art. 60).

Without such a decree of the Court the landdrost had no right to summon, much less to arrest, unless there was a real danger that the delinquent would escape justice. If the landdrost arrested without sufficient ground for believing that there was *periculum in morâ*, then he could be mulcted in costs and subjected to "such further correction as the Court might judge necessary" (arts. 61 and 62).

If, however, the case was trifling, punishable by fine only, the landdrost could proceed without a special decree. If the papers were returned from Capetown with a decree to arrest, then he was to see to the transport of the prisoners to Capetown and to transmit to his advocate all the evidence collected by him, the *corpus delicti* and such particulars as might be required for the prosecution (art. 65).

If the decree merely directed him to summon, he was not allowed to arrest or interfere with the liberty of the accused. He had to see that the summons was served in good time to allow the accused to attend at the Court in Capetown. If he failed in this, he was liable to the costs in person. Persons caught in *flagrante delicto*, vagabonds and deserters could be summarily arrested by the landdrost and sent to Capetown for trial. There are two curious articles about the compounding of offences, and so alien to our modern practice that I give them here in full:—

> Art. 71.—The Landdrost shall not be allowed on his own authority to compound any offence whatsoever except in minor cases on which the law has affixed a penalty of some small fine not exceeding 50 Rds., the distribution of which, if not particularly prescribed by law, shall be directed according to article 13 of these Instructions.
>
> Art. 72.—In graver cases the Landdrost can compound only with the consent of the Court of Justice and in the presence of a commission of the Court, after the Court, on a petition of the offending party and the report thereon by the Landdrost, shall have declared the case to admit of such adjustment.

When the case was sent up to the Court of Justice at Capetown it was tried before the president and members of the Raad van Justitie. This was a court of judge and jury rolled into one. The president was always a qualified lawyer, but though many of the members were lawyers, it was not obligatory for them to possess legal qualifications. They were, however, all gentlemen of standing and education and owners of considerable property. The pleadings in court were conducted partly orally and partly in writing. It was the custom for the prosecuting as well as the defending counsel to hand in a resumé of his argument, and then to elaborate it orally. The evidence of the witnesses was not as a rule taken in open court. When the hearing of the case was over the members of the Court retired, and the view of the majority formed the judgment of the Court. When the judges had come to a conclusion the president delivered the judgment and pronounced the sentence. The punishments were very much the same as prevail at present. Torture was not allowed, and the confiscation of property even in case of treason had been abolished in Holland in 1779.

After the occupation of the Cape the criminal procedure then in vogue was continued without any alteration for some years. In 1808 a court of appeal for criminal cases was constituted. It consisted of the Governor and such assessors as he might from time to time appoint.

In 1811 the first great innovation in the trial of criminals was made by the establishment of a circuit court. This court consisted of two or more members of the Court of Justice, who were required to proceed through the districts of Swellendam, George, Uitenhage, Graaff-Reinet and Tulbagh for the purpose of hearing both civil and criminal cases. If, however, after investigation it appeared that the penalty for the crime was death, the case was reserved for the full Court at Capetown. The first members were appointed by the

Governor, but after that they were elected by the majority of the Court. In each district the landdrost acted as prosecutor. The practice of electing the judges soon led to abuse and inconvenience, and in 1813 a proclamation was issued by which the judges were required to go on circuit by turns. By proclamation of the 25th September, 1813, all criminal cases before the Court of Justice were required to be conducted with open doors, and the same regulation was to apply to all inferior courts.

As we saw above, the proceedings had been previously conducted partly with open doors and partly in private; after 1813 they were all conducted in public. I have also stated that part of the pleadings of the advocate were in writing, and if he thought fit he could elaborate his argument orally before the Court. This, however, was not always done, and therefore a criminal case might be heard by the Court without a public address by counsel. This was contrary to the English practice, and therefore the Proclamation of 1813 (art. 6) required that the proceedings should be conducted orally. The counsel for the prosecution and defence still, however, continued to put in a written plea, which in all probability was read in open court.

I have been favoured by Mr. C. H. van Zyl of Capetown with a copy of a trial conducted in 1822, in which the written pleadings of counsel signed by them were put in. As this case gives a clearer notion of how a criminal trial was conducted in those days than a mere description, a translation of the proceedings is given in an Appendix.

It was found that the *manier van procedeeren* as laid down in the Ordinance of 1570 was no longer suitable, and that extensive amendments were necessary in order to bring the procedure in accord with the practice prevailing in England; so the Court of Justice was requested to draw up a set of regulations. On the 2nd September, 1819 (Proclamations, p. 709), a new mode of procedure in criminal cases was established. The preamble said that for the purposes of uniformity and distinctness a new mode of proceeding in criminal cases was necessary, "containing the spirit of the existing laws, proclamations and ordinances under such modifications as may tend to combine the benevolent principles of the present Government with the mode of proceeding in the prosecution for crimes and misdemeanours heretofore in use in this colony in as far as the nature of the case will permit."

Three courts were recognised—the Raad van Justitie or full Court, the court of two commissioners from the Court of Justice, and the court of landdrost and heemraden. Crimes which were not subject to a more severe punishment than public scourging, transportation, banishment or confinement for a limited period were brought before the landdrost and heemraden of the district in which the crimes were committed. The court of commissioners tried all cases where the crime was committed in Capetown and where the punishment was more severe than is mentioned above. Cases in which the death penalty could be inflicted were tried by the full Court.

The secretary of the landdrost's court became the prosecutor for crimes committed in his district, but in all serious cases from the country districts referred to the Supreme Court at Capetown the landdrost still continued to prosecute through an advocate, known as the landdrost's official agent. The prosecutions before the court of commissioners and before the full Court of cases from Capetown and the Cape district were conducted by the Fiscaal or Attorney-General. The landdrost was still unable to arrest without first having obtained a decree. The Fiscaal's duties were, however, somewhat extended, and not only was a general supervision of prosecutions granted to him, but if he discovered any informality he could report the same to the Court of Justice or the Governor for rectification.

The indictment was drawn by the Public Prosecutor, and it contained not only the nature of the crime, but a statement of the circumstances which preceded, attended or followed the commission of the crime. The trial was conducted with open doors and in the presence of the accused. The accused could, however, be questioned on every circumstance relating to the accusation (art. 44), and if he refused to answer he could be committed for contempt of court. The old practice was so far modified that the trial proceeded nevertheless, and the refusal to answer was considered as a denial of guilt. The imprisonment for contempt meant nothing more than imprisonment as long as the trial lasted. In other words, no bail was recognised in such a case.

The accused could make his defence either verbally or in writing (art. 48). A curious proceeding was the provisional liberation of an accused upon giving security in case the evidence against him was not sufficient (art. 55). This decree lasted for twelve months, and if no proceedings were taken within that time the accused was regarded as acquitted (art. 56).

The Court was bound at any time from the commencement of the proceedings up to the execution of the sentence to hear any evidence tending to exculpate the accused (art. 59). The new rules allowed the accused to employ an advocate as of right. The proceedings in case the accused absconded or concealed himself were very different from our own. The accused who absented himself on the day of trial was summoned by edict to appear on a fixed day; if he failed to appear the court bell was rung and the accused summoned. After the third summons the case was proceeded with. A fourth summons was then issued, and if he still failed to appear a decree of *prise de corps* was pronounced against the accused, which made him subject to instant arrest. If arrested he was still allowed to defend himself, but the evidence taken in his absence held good, and the Crown was not required to call these witnesses *de novo.* The trial then went on in the usual way. Where the penalty was a fine the case could be compounded, as was customary in Janssen's time.

Minor criminal offences were tried in Capetown before one commissioner of the Court of Justice, and in the country districts by the landdrost and heemraden. The mode of procedure was almost identical with that which had prevailed since Janssen's Instructions. The sentences of the commissioners, or of a single commissioner or of the landdrost and heemraden could be brought in review before the full Court in two ways — either by rehearing (*reauditie*) or by appeal. The former was a more summary proceeding than the latter. In *reauditie* the person convicted deposited 25 Rds., which were forfeited if the decision of the full Court went against him (art. 130).

Appeals could not be noted after confession, and no appeal was entertained from the full Court unless the death sentence had been pronounced. From the other courts appeals only lay where the sentence involved public punishment or a fine of more than 1000 Rds. Appeals from landdrost and heemraden could be brought either before the circuit court or before the full Court.

The following year the procedure with regard to the arrest of criminals was somewhat modified. We have seen that by the procedure of 1570 and by that of 1819 no arrest could take place without a decree of the Raad van Justitie. By a proclamation of the 15th September, 1820, a new court consisting of a single heemraad was established, and power was given to the heemraad to arrest without a previous decree. From this court an appeal lay with the court of landdrost and heemraden. In 1825 petty police cases were taken from the Fiscaal and entrusted to the chief police officer.

In 1826 the court of the commissioner was separated from the Court of Justice, and a separate magistrate appointed. In 1827 a charter of justice was issued establishing the Supreme Court, and resident magistrates instead of landdrosts and heemraden. By Ordinance 40 of 1828 the criminal procedure of the various courts was again altered, and established upon the basis which still prevails. It is not necessary to deal with this Ordinance fully, as it differs only in detail from the criminal practice which prevails to-day. By this Ordinance the criminal procedure of the colony was brought still more into line with that which prevailed in England, and the old Dutch procedure, where it materially differed from the English practice, was swept away. During the same year a police court and a court of resident magistrate for Capetown and the Cape district were established.

In 1830 the basis of the present law of evidence was introduced, and the qualification of persons liable to serve on Grand and Petit Juries fixed. Since then changes have been made in the criminal procedure, some of considerable moment, such as allowing accused persons to give evidence; but on the whole the main principles of the criminal procedure as laid down by Ordinance 40 of 1828 have been adhered to. As the later alterations are mere matters of detail, well known to all students of colonial law, no useful purpose will be served in tracing the history of criminal procedure from 1828 to the present day.

CHAPTER XXXV.

THE INFLUENCE OF ENGLISH LAW ON THE DEVELOPMENT OF THE ROMAN-DUTCH LAW IN SOUTH AFRICA.

ENGLISH law has exerted a very strong influence upon the law of South Africa, and that influence is steadily growing greater in almost every department of law. In some respects the introduction of English law into South Africa has been slow and insidious; in other respects it has been rapid and overwhelming. The influence exerted by English text-books and by the decisions of the English courts has tended gradually to modify the principles of the Roman-Dutch law and to bend them so as to assume the form of similar English principles. On the other hand, English statutory law has frequently been taken over by the South African legislatures, and with the statute have been incorporated those principles of English law which accompany its interpretation.

Thus the introduction of the English jury system necessitated the adoption of the English rules of evidence. If, therefore, we analyse the different ways in which English law has been infused into the Roman-Dutch system of law as it prevailed in the Cape Colony prior to the annexation, I think we shall find that there are three principal channels:—

(1) The English legal text-books and the decisions of the common law and equity courts.

(2) The decisions of the Privy Council.

(3) The statute law

Besides these main channels there are numerous other ways in which both the law and practice in South Africa have been affected, but these are far too subtle to follow with any degree of accuracy. Thus, for instance, the large commercial relations between the colonies and the mother-country have caused English forms of contract to be adopted which contain terms that are unknown to the Roman-Dutch law, and the frequent use of these terms has sometimes led both the courts and practitioners to incorporate into contracts English legal ideas of which the Roman-Dutch law was ignorant. For our purposes, however, I think this kind of influence may well be classed under the first head.

(1) Text-books and Decisions.—The English barrister who attends a South African court must often wonder what we really mean when we say that the Roman-Dutch law is the common law of South Africa. He hears a dispute about a contract, or perhaps an action for damages in a running down case. He hears the pleadings read, and to him the claim in convention and claim in reconvention, the declaration, plea and rejoinder are familiar terms. The very form in which these are couched is the same as he was accustomed to in England. The rules of evidence are the same he learnt at his Inn or College, and when the argument is reached he hears quotations from such familiar books as Addison or Leake on *Contracts*, Addison or Pollock on *Torts*, and he finds that both Bench and Bar refer to the same law reports with which he was familiar in England. The arguments are closed, and the decision is given upon

English authorities, and sometimes not a single Dutch authority is even casually touched upon.

I open the twentieth volume of the reports of the Supreme Court of the Cape Colony, the first that comes to hand, and I find the case of *Murray* v. *Findlay & Co.* (p. 144). It is a question of partnership. Several English and not a single Roman-Dutch authority are referred to. On page 154 is the case of *Fairbairn* v. *Pepper*. It is a case of principal and agent. Again English authorities are quoted and no reference is made to Dutch books. Next I shall take an appeal from Rhodesia (p. 238). The question was whether a tenant was liable for rent where the leased property had been burnt down during the currency of the lease. Upon this point one would hardly have expected any English authorities, because our law of lease differs so materially from English law; yet I find no less than a dozen English authorities referred to. So one might take up any volume of South African law reports, and find either English authorities alone or else English and Roman-Dutch authorities quoted side by side.

This was the case even in the South African Republic and the Orange Free State before they became British territory. Wherever the English law is at all similar to the Roman-Dutch law we find the English cases referred to more frequently than the Dutch writers. The reason for this is not far to seek. The barristers who practise before the South African courts have most of them received their legal education at some English university, or have been called to the Bar at the Inns of Court. Those who have studied law in South Africa have had to pass examinations in which English law forms no small factor.

Moreover, Roman-Dutch law ceased to be practised in Holland after the end of the eighteenth century, and therefore there can be no reference to modern cases except such as have occurred in South Africa. Here the field has been very small in comparison with that of England and America, and therefore the practitioners naturally search for principles and precedents in those text-books and reports with which they have become familiar. These are generally English law-books, though American text-writers and reports are also referred to. The latter have principally found their way into South African courts through the excellent works of Judge Story.

Again, many of the earlier judges at the Cape were men advanced in years when they came to South Africa, and their legal training had been confined entirely to English and Scotch law. It is therefore no wonder that English ideas have gradually modified the principles of the Roman-Dutch law.

It would scarcely be profitable to deal with this matter in detail, though reference to a few cases may not be out of place. It has been a matter of considerable discussion whether the Roman-Dutch law required consideration to support a contract. In the Supreme Court of the Cape Colony Sir Henry de Villiers held that it was necessary; in the Transvaal Supreme Court Sir James Rose-Innes held that it was not. Now there can be very little doubt that the decision of *Alexander* v. *Perry* was very much influenced by the fact that in England consideration was required to support a contract. Sir Henry de Villiers decided that our law required consideration to found a claim on a contract for service; Judge Denyssen was not prepared to adopt that view, but

Judge Fitzpatrick clearly based his decision on the English law. It is also noteworthy that the only authorities quoted from the Bar in support of the view that consideration was necessary to support a contract were English text-books and English decisions. It is true that Sir Henry de Villiers based his decision on the Roman-Dutch law; but his view found no favour with Judge Denyssen, and but for the aid of Judge Fitzpatrick the view of the Chief Justice might not have been accepted. The doctrine of consideration was well known to the English law, but even if known to the Dutch law it was not universally recognised and was extremely doubtful. In the Cape Colony English influence decided the point in favour of the principle adopted by English law.

Again, in *Seaville* v. *Colley* (9 S.C. 39) one of the issues was whether the *Lex Anastasiana*, by which the cessionary of a debt could within a year be made to disclose what he paid for it and compelled to accept that amount from the debtor, applied to the case in question. There is very little doubt that the *Lex Anastasiana* was considered law by the Dutch jurists of the latter half of the eighteenth century (Van der Keessel, 663, 664) in so far that the debtor had the right, within a year, of paying the cessionary what the latter had given for the debt. There was, however, in Holland even in the seventeenth century a tendency to do away with the *Lex Anastasiana*. It interfered with commerce, and was unknown to the English law. Sir Henry de Villiers, who has always shown a desire so to interpret the Roman-Dutch law as to bring it into line with modern ideas and modern practice, came to the conclusion that the *Lex Anastasiana* was inconsistent with South African usages, and that it should be regarded as an abrogated law. He says: "The conclusion at which I have arrived as to the obligatory nature of the body of laws in force in this colony at the date of the British occupation in 1806 may be briefly stated. The presumption is that every one of these laws, if not repealed by the local legislature, is still in force. This presumption will not, however, prevail in regard to any rule of law which is inconsistent with South African usages. . . . Any Dutch law which is inconsistent with such well-established custom, and has not, although relating to matters of frequent occurrence, been distinctly recognised and acted upon by the Supreme Court, may fairly be held to have been abrogated by disuse" (p. 44).

Now South African usages are often built up on the commercial practice prevalent in England, and in this way the English commercial law is gradually improving the Roman-Dutch law by adapting it to modern customs. In many branches of law this tendency is very obvious, such as partnership and agency. In other matters the influence is more subtle, but at the same time very real.

(2) The judgments of the Judicial Committee of the Privy Council have had a very great influence upon the decisions of the South African courts. I do not allude to those cases which have gone to the Privy Council from South African courts, and where their decision is that of an ultimate court of appeal, but to decisions of the Privy Council on commercial questions raised in other colonies where the Roman-Dutch law does not prevail.

Judges as a rule do not like their decisions upset on appeal, and where they find a decision of the Privy Council on a question raised in Australia, they will apply it to a similar set of facts brought before a South African court, unless the distinction between Roman-Dutch and English law is very flagrant. If the two systems can, with not too much subtlety, be brought to harmonise, the voice of the Privy Council will prevail. Even to *obiter dicta* of the Privy Council great weight is attached. This is only natural, for the Roman-Dutch law is not a system with which the Judicial Committee has grown up, and it must often be difficult for the judges who have laid down a principle as applying to an Australian case to recognise the finer distinctions between the law of contract as it prevails in England and the principles adopted by the Roman-Dutch law. Hence South African judges conclude that what the Privy Council has applied to an Australian case they will in all probability apply to a South African dispute, and therefore they attach more importance to a dictum of the Privy Council than to the decisions of other courts.

Again, as the Judicial Committee is more conversant with English than with Roman-Dutch law, even in those cases which come to them from South African courts, they are apt to find a greater similarity between Roman-Dutch law and English law than South African lawyers can discover, and, having found the similarity, the decisions of English courts are applied to the solution of the problem. In this way, therefore, a great deal of English law has been incorporated into the law of South Africa. The decision of the Privy Council is then extended to other cases, and the English principles upon which the Privy Council relied are regarded as identical with those of the Roman-Dutch law, and reference is afterwards made rather to the decisions of the English courts to which the Privy Council has gone for its law than to the principles of the civil law as they prevailed in Holland.

Both these influences have operated in all the South African courts. I have given a few instances from the courts of the Cape Colony. If reference is made to the Natal Law Reports it will be found that the influence of English legal ideas has been greater in Natal than in any other South African colony. Of the earlier judges and advocates the majority were educated in England, and only acquired a knowledge of Roman-Dutch law late in life. An exception must be made in favour of Chief Justice Sir Henry Connor, who always strove to uphold the principles of the civil law. Besides these there are other reasons, upon which it is unnecessary to dwell here, which induced the Natal courts to lean more upon English than upon the Roman-Dutch law.

The practice of referring to English decisions was not confined to the English colonies of South Africa. During the period that the Transvaal and Orange Free State were free Republics, and whilst the official language of their superior courts was Dutch, English authorities were cited from the Bar and received by the Bench with approval. The decisions of the Supreme Court of the Cape of Good Hope were almost as authoritative in the Transvaal and Orange Free State as they were in the Cape Colony; and as these decisions are tinged with English ideas, so naturally the decisions of the Republican courts based upon them were also affected by English jurisprudence. The process is still going on, and now that the most important part of South Africa is

British it is likely to be greater than it was before the annexation of the two Republics.

(3) I now come to the statute law. Here the influence of English legal ideas is overwhelming. Many branches of law have been wholly taken out of the Roman-Dutch system, and English law substituted in their stead. This process naturally began in the Cape Colony, but through the great moral influence exerted by that colony in South Africa it was extended to the Republics and other colonies. Besides the cases where English law was entirely substituted for Roman-Dutch law, there are other cases in which the substitution has been partial only. Then there are cases where the principles of the Roman-Dutch law were retained, but slight modifications introduced based upon English practice.

First, then, there are certain Imperial statutes which apply to South Africa as well as to the other colonies. These, of course, are based exclusively upon English law. Next we come to a series of statutes where the Roman-Dutch law and practice are completely swept away, and a new law and practice based upon English law is substituted. Though a great part of the criminal law of South Africa is based upon the Roman-Dutch law, the criminal procedure is far more English than it is Dutch. The criminal practice in South Africa may be described as English, with here and there a remnant of the old Dutch procedure.

The introduction of the jury system and the method of examining and cross-examining witnesses led to the adoption of the English law of evidence with slight modifications. Thus the Evidence Act of 1830 provided certain rules for the admission of evidence in courts of law differing very largely from the old Dutch practice. Moreover, where cases arose for which the new law makes no provision the judges are required to go for their law not to the common law of the Cape Colony, but to the law of England as administered in English courts. Act 17 of 1859 introduced similar provisions into Natal.

A great deal of the Cape Evidence Act was embodied in the statute laws of the two Republics, but apart from statute law the High Courts of the Transvaal and Orange Free State always referred to English authorities in matters of evidence. This was partly due to the fact that the Cape decisions on questions of evidence were based upon English law, and partly because English law is so immeasurably superior to Roman-Dutch law on this point, besides being so much more accessible.

The introduction of the jury system in criminal cases, which was taken over by all the colonies and states of South Africa, rendered this change imperative. After the annexation of the Transvaal and Orange River Colony, ordinances regarding evidence were passed assimilating their statute law in this respect to that of the Cape. These statutes in no way altered the procedure which had existed in the Republics, though they established the practice on a firm basis.

In 1855 a Merchant Shipping Act was passed in the Cape Colony, the provisions of which were based upon English maritime law. Into this was incorporated a number of sections of the Imperial Merchant Shipping Act of 1854. In consequence of the report of a commission appointed to inquire into the reform of the law of the Cape Colony, an Act was passed in 1879 by the Cape Parliament, called the

General Law Amendment Act. The preamble says that the existing general law of the colony is in several instances unsuited to the advancing trade and the altered circumstances of the country, and that it is advisable to bring the colonial law more in accord with modern principles of legislation. For these reasons the legislature enacted that in all maritime cases English law should take the place of the Roman-Dutch law. The same rule was to apply to marine, life and fire insurance, stoppage *in transitu* and bills of lading. With regard to these subjects local Acts take precedence to the English practice, but where the local Ordinances are silent resort is to be had to the decisions of the English courts explanatory of the law as it then existed. Later English statutes, unless specially adopted by the colonial legislature, are not binding. *Laesio enormis* and the right of remission of rent (*remissio mercedis*) on account of injury to leasehold land arising from tempest, inundation or other unavoidable misfortune were also abolished.

Prior to the passing of Acts 26 of 1873 and 23 of 1874 the right of free testation did not exist in the Cape Colony. Every child had a claim upon the estate of its parents unless it had been so undutiful as to merit disinheritance. The Roman-Dutch law also made provision for the children of a former marriage in case either parent desired to marry again. These principles were repugnant to English law, and were swept away by the above-mentioned Acts, which enacted that the *Lex hâc edictali*, the Falcidian and Trebellian fourths as well as the legitimate portion should be abolished. Natal followed suit in 1885, but the Republics retained the old law. After the annexation of 1900 the new colonies adopted the same law as the Cape, so that the restrictions on parents which exist in countries where the civil law prevails no longer exist in South Africa.

By the Roman-Dutch law certain persons had prior rights over the property of others. These rights are called tacit mortgage or tacit hypothecation, though legal mortgage or legal hypothec is a preferable term. Thus the Government had a prior claim over auctioneers and postmasters for moneys due to it; minors over the estates of their protutors; and persons who repaired ships or houses were granted a preferent right over mortgagees. These and other similar preferent rights were abolished by Act of Parliament; so that our law was brought into line with English law in this respect also.

The Roman-Dutch law of insolvency, like the old English bankruptcy law, was very crude. The English bankruptcy law was greatly improved during the first half of the nineteenth century. During the latter half the amendments were more in the details than in principle. In 1843 the Cape Colony introduced an Insolvency Ordinance upon which the insolvency law of the whole of South Africa was afterwards modelled. This Ordinance was founded partly upon Dutch practice and partly upon earlier English statutes, and in this way a great deal of English bankruptcy law was introduced. Although the main principles of the insolvency law of South Africa are founded upon English ideas, yet the Roman-Dutch law applies to many of the details, such as preference, the vesting of ownership, &c.

In fixing the age of majority at twenty-one and in several of the ceremonies of marriage Roman-Dutch law has given way to English law. The same is the case in the execution of the so-called underhand wills.

Natal has taken over all or almost all the modifications introduced into the Cape, and has outstripped the Cape Colony in the desire to anglicise our law. This colony allows post-nuptial contracts, and has introduced many of the objectionable elements of the Statute of Frauds. Here also the Attorney-General, like the king's proctor, may interfere in divorce suits for a period of three months after the order is granted, and divorces for malicious desertion are not considered final until the lapse of ten months.

The new colonies have largely followed the lead of the Cape legislature in the introduction of English mercantile law and the right of free testation. The *Lex hâc edictali* and many of the tacit hypothecs have been abolished in these colonies since the annexation.

There is another class of statute law in which English law has been introduced, though not at the expense of the Roman-Dutch law. I allude to such institutions as were unknown to the eighteenth century. To this class of case belong the limited liability laws, the winding up of companies, the telegraph laws, laws relating to benefit societies, and generally to such matters as were not dealt with by the Roman-Dutch writers. In suits arising under the statutes on these subjects our courts naturally go to English cases to assist them in the interpretation of laws founded upon English precedents. The instances mentioned above are not by any means exhaustive, but they serve as typical examples to show

how in the statute law of the South African colonies English ideas have modified the Roman-Dutch law.

Has this wholesale incorporation of English law improved our South African law? On the whole the answer must be in the affirmative, though in many cases the introduction has been done in an unscientific manner. Lazy and ignorant draughtsmen have copied whole sections from English statutes without first inquiring how these conflicted with the principles of our law. Terms have been used which have a meaning in English law, but which are either meaningless in our law or have quite a different signification. It is always extremely difficult to incorporate isolated sections from the statute law of one country into the statute law of another, especially where a different common law prevails. Often the new law does not harmonise with the old. Thus we find the word "consideration" in many English statutes. In England it has a definite and well-ascertained meaning; in the Cape Colony it has a similar meaning in many cases, but in other cases it will not bear the meaning given to it by English courts. The executor and administrator of English law are not the same as the executor and administrator of the Roman-Dutch law. The English easement often corresponds with our servitude, but the English law of easements does not correspond with our law of servitudes. Hereditament has a technical meaning in English law derived from feudal customs; to our law it is wholly unknown. The words "deed" and "indenture" convey to English lawyers what they do not convey to South African practitioners. We talk of conveyancers in this country, though our law of conveyancing is entirely different from that of English law. We find phrases used such as "that a person shall not convert a thing to his own use" and "guilty of embezzlement or larceny," though the bulk of the English law of conversion is wholly foreign to our jurisprudence, and the English definitions of larceny and embezzlement do not apply to our law of theft. Similar instances may be multiplied. Now by incorporating in our ordinances sections from English statutes including these terms great confusion may arise.

Then certain branches of English law have been taken over as they applied in England at a certain date, and the South African courts have been required to go to the decisions of the English courts for their law in these branches. Nothing can be more slipshod and unscientific. Men trained in the study of the Roman-Dutch law, whose knowledge of English law is often very imperfect, are required to be familiar not only with the decisions of English courts, but with all the shades of English law upon which the decisions are based. The introduction of the English law of evidence, English maritime and English insurance law cannot be found fault with; but the manner of introduction is not a subject upon which we can congratulate ourselves.

The proper course to adopt is not to take over a whole department of English law *en globe,* and to say that all English decisions up to a certain date shall apply, but to determine what principles of the English law are to be incorporated into our law, to formulate these principles so that they harmonise with the principles of our law, and then to give them legislative sanction; in other words, to have a clear idea of what you are taking over from the

English law, and to know that there is little or no likelihood of a conflict between what you take over and what you already have. This has been done in the case of the Bills of Exchange Act, and there is no reason why it cannot be done in other cases as well. What the English law is in any special branch can be ascertained, and where there are divergent views one or other of these can be adopted. The law so ascertained can be enacted by the local legislature either in the form of a Code or in such other form as may be convenient.

In this way modern English ideas may be incorporated into our system of law in a correct and scientific manner instead of in the haphazard way in which it has been done in the past. Judges will then not be required to interpret English law sometimes by the canons of Roman-Dutch interpretation, and at other times by such rules as have been from time to time adopted by judges of the courts at Westminster or the High Court of Judicature.

If the scientific method were adopted, then, instead of having a heterogeneous mass of legal systems, as we have in South Africa to-day, we would have a homogeneous system based indeed upon principles both of the civil and of the common law, but so adjusted as to form one harmonious whole.

PART II.

LAW OF PERSONS, THINGS AND OBLIGATIONS.

CHAPTER I.

CONDITIONS OF PERSONS.

HAVING completed a survey of the judicial institutions and the general law of the Netherlands, as well as a brief account of the various jurists who systematised and expounded the Roman-Dutch law, I shall now turn to particular rules of law and endeavour to explain how the law which we apply to-day in our courts is connected with the customs of the past.

In the foregoing part of this work I have taken a general view of the development of our law: in this part I shall take particular branches of the law and strive to show how the rules and maxims which our judges follow are derived from the practice that prevailed in ancient days. In some cases we shall be able to find the origin of our present rules in the crude laws of the ancient Germans; in other cases the Franks, Saxons or Frisians will be responsible for the law. Space will not allow me to do more than trace briefly a few of our more important rules. I shall take the *Introduction* of Grotius as my guide, and shall consider such subdivisions of the law as are likely to interest the modern student, tracing the history of particular rules of law from its fountain-head to the present day.

First, then, I shall deal with the Law of Persons. Grotius divides persons into men and women, and these again into natives and foreigners, nobles and commoners, clergy and laity. The two last divisions are manifestly cross-divisions.

Justinian's familiar division of persons into freeborn and slaves is not touched upon, though we know that slavery existed with both the Germans and the Gauls (Hein. *Jus. Germ.* bk. 1, tit. 1; Tacit. *Germ.* c. 24, 25). The reason why Grotius omits slaves from his division of persons is because in his time it was a well-established principle of the law of Holland that if a slave set foot upon Dutch soil he became a free man whether his master desired it or not (Groenewegen, *De Leg. Abrog. ad Inst.* 1, 8).

Let us consider how this change was brought about, and whether it applied to South Africa.

In dealing with the laws and customs of the early Germans we saw that the people were divided into nobles, freemen and slaves. The latter were not domestic servants, as with the Romans, but tillers of the soil, compelled to supply their masters with a certain fixed quantity of grain, cattle or cloth. They were often liberated by their masters, but such freed men (*liberti*) were very little superior to slaves (Tacit. *Germ.* c. 25). The principle of slavery was adopted by the Franks, and prevailed in Holland long after the introduction of the feudal system.

The Franks admitted, as a general rule, that persons were either free or not free. The equality of all freemen which may have existed with the Germans whilst they were wandering from place to place had certainly ceased to exist after they settled down into separate nations. Social distinctions existed amongst the Franks, and they divided the freeborn into different classes; those who were on a footing of familiarity with the king formed the first rank of the freeborn. It has been disputed whether the Franks recognised a caste of hereditary nobles. The *Lex Salica* apparently did not recognise such a caste, though the leaders of the army and those persons who were in the immediate service of the king (*in truste*) were regarded as more privileged than the rank and file of freeborn citizens. The freemen (*in truste dominica*), afterwards called *antrustiones*, were persons raised as it were to the peerage. Gradually those who belonged to the *entourage* of the king came to be regarded as hereditary nobles. Those who were not free were either slaves or persons who held a position between the freeborn and the slaves. The latter were called *liti* or *lites* in Latin, and *laten* or *hoorigen* in Dutch. Hence during the period that the Netherlands formed part of the Frankish Empire the king stood at the head of the nation. In theory his office was elective, in practice it was hereditary. If the son of a king was as capable a man as his father he succeeded to the throne; if he was inferior to his nobles they might at a critical period elect one of their own number to the kingship. The next in rank were the nobles (*nobiles, adel*), and then came the mass of freeborn (*ingenui, vrijen, vrijling, vryhals, vrymannen*). Between the freeborn and the slaves proper came the *liti* or *hoorigen*, and in the lowest rank were found the slaves (*servi, slaven*).

The freeborn who belonged to the household of the king possessed as a rule a larger holding of land than the others, and consequently had a larger number of liti and slaves dependent upon them. In this way there gradually grew up a difference between the wealthier agrarian owners and the great bulk of the ingenui (*minoflides*). In the relation, therefore, of king to nobles, of nobles to other ingenui, of ingenui to liti and of liti to slaves we find one of the germs of feudalism (Noordewier, pp. 65–70; Raepsaet, vol. 4, c. 11; Fockema Andreae, *Bijdragen*, vol. 3; Schröder, pp. 214 *et seq.*; Arntzenius, *De Cond. Hom.* vol. 1).

The Freeborn (Ingenui).—The freeborn (*ingenui, ingenulis ordo*) were persons who had been born free, and who had never ceased to be such. They formed the important part of the people. Whether an actual distinction was made between the freeborn Frank and the freeborn Roman it is difficult to say, though one would infer such to have been the case from the fact that the *wergeld* for killing a Frank was greater than that attached to a Roman.

The principal advantages of the freeborn were (Raepsaet, vol. 4, p. 138):—

(1) He had a free right to dispose of his property.

(2) He was exempted from menial service.

(3) He had a capacity for civil and military service.

(4) He was exempted from all forms of corporal punishment.

(5) His cattle could not be seized for debt.

Slaves (Servi).—During the Frankish rule the number of slaves was very great, and their condition deplorable. They were of two kinds—those employed in agricultural work, who were attached to the soil (*adscripti glebae*), and those who were in the personal service of their masters. It is difficult to find out who composed the bulk of the slave class. In all probability the majority were persons captured in war, though an individual could become a slave through debt, through marriage with a slave, through being abandoned as a child and in many other ways.

The owner of a slave had almost absolute power over him. Though the master did not have a complete *jus vitae necisque* over his slave, he could legally kill him for a mere trifle. For a theft for which a freeman could be mulcted in a fine of 45 soldi a slave could be killed (*Lex Sal.* tit. 42, arts. 1, 4, 7, 8 and 9). The master could punish his slave with such corporal punishment as he thought fit (*Lex Sal.* tit. 37, art. 4). This harsh lot of the slave was considerably ameliorated by the Church, and cruel masters were often punished with excommunication.

The law, however, gave to the slave no *persona in judicio.* In the eyes of the law he was regarded as a mere chattel. If a slave injured a freeborn citizen his master was responsible in the same way as he was liable for the acts of his animals. Originally the slave could not contract a legal marriage, but through the influence of the Church a capitulare of 869 A.D. recognised the legality of slave marriages contracted with the consent of their masters. The goods of the slave belonged to his master, and if the children of a slave succeeded to the goods of their father it was solely due to the permission of the master (*Lex Sal.* tit. 28, art. 2).

These are the main features of slavery during the Frankish monarchy. Raepsaet thinks that the slaves who fell under the category of domestic slaves were of Roman, whilst the slaves who lived on the land were of German, origin. The condition of the latter was probably in many respects better than that of the former (Raepsaet, vol. 4, pp. 142 *et seq.*). In these two classes of slaves there were, however, many grades with different privileges.

The Enfranchised (Liberti).—If a person had voluntarily

passed into slavery for debt, the payment of the debt rendered him once more a free man. The usual mode, however, by which a person passed from slavery to the condition of a freeman was by enfranchisement. The Church constantly strove to ameliorate the condition of slaves, and so far gained its point that in several cases slaves who joined the Church could become freemen against the will of their masters. As a general rule, however, a slave could not be liberated except with the consent of his master. There were two methods of enfranchisement — a German and a Roman method. The former was a symbolic act by which the master threw a coin at the feet of the king (*per denarium ante regem*) as representing the value of the slave (*Lex Sal.* tit. 28). The principal Roman modes of enfranchisement in vogue with the Franks were the *manumissio in ecclesiâ* and the *manumissio per chartam et epistolam.*

The privileges of the manumitted slave were in many respects similar to those of the ingenuus, though in two respects there was a great difference. (1) The libertus required some protector, usually his former master or a church, and (2) his master could exact from him certain services, called *obsequia libertatis.* These services were usually of a very light nature, and never menial. He might be required to burn a candle once a year at the tomb of his master or to provide him with some trivial household matter. Sometimes, however, the enfranchised slave had to render services to his master of an onerous nature, and then the enfranchisement could hardly be regarded as complete. The liberti, therefore, upon whom onerous services were imposed occupied a position between ingenui and servi. These were the people known as liti, lites or laten.

Lites.—When a slave was manumitted, but fell under the class known as liti, he might be required to pay a yearly tribute. This tribute was known as *ledimonium*, and he himself as a litus. Fockema Andreae, speaking of this class, says: "Between the freeborn and the slaves there appeared in the Frankish period some who were clearly half free (*liten*). They were probably persons, originally attached to the soil, who belonged with the farm upon which they lived to their master, but who were so closely related to the farm that they could not be separated from it at the wish of either party, and with reference to whose services certain rules had grown up which could not be modified by the master without the consent of the litus."

The litus possessed most of the privileges of a freeborn citizen, except that he was compelled to occupy the farm upon which he lived and to pay a fixed tribute; he had, moreover, no right to take part in public assemblies. The position of the litus in the Frankish period no doubt formed an element in the conception of the relation between the lord and vassal of the feudal period.

Gradually the bond between dominus and litus (*heer* and *hoorigen*) began to slacken. First of all the Church insisted that the litus who took orders should be regarded as free, and then the towns claimed the right to regard those liti who lived within their walls for a certain period as having gained their freedom by right of prescription. The litus who lived in a town came to be regarded as a hoorigen of the town (*nostri proprii homines qui vulgariter dicuntur eigenluyde*), and could therefore not be claimed by his heer or master. During the fourteenth century, as a general rule, residence for a year in a town conferred freedom on a slave or a litus. Often to prevent the litus from leaving his estate, the master was himself compelled to grant that freedom which his litus would seek in the town. In this way the slave and the litus gradually disappeared, until here and there only traces remained.

Van Leeuwen tells us that even as late as 1532 the Court of Holland recognised the division of persons into nobles, commoners and serfs (*Cens. For.* pt. 1, 1, 2, 6). Grotius tells us that traces of this system of slavery existed in his time, "for some persons are even at the present day subject to certain personal services—to purchase permission to marry with some present—to live upon the land or to purchase freedom from this obligation, and at their death to leave their most valuable chattel to their lord." According to Fockema Andreae these traces did not disappear until 1795, when all men were declared free and equal and the state of *hoorigheid* was completely swept away. The law that a slave when he touched the soil of Holland was free did not apply to fugitive slaves from the Dutch colonies (Van der Keessel, 46).

Though the slavery of the Roman law did not exist in Holland after the tenth century, the same rule was not applicable to the over-sea possessions of the Republic. In the East Indies, the Cape Colony and the West Indies slavery existed even after all traces had disappeared in Holland. The slavery of the Dutch colonies was regulated by the Roman law, but in a very modified form. The master had the right to compel his slaves to work for him, but only for a certain number of hours a day. He could not compel his slaves to work on Sundays or holidays. Masters who treated their slaves cruelly were punished, and though they might chastise their slaves moderately they could not beat them severely. This had to be done at the request of the master by a public official.

The attitude of the Dutch Government at the Cape towards slavery can be gathered from General Janssen's Instructions to landdrosts. Article 68 is as follows:—

> As long as the use of slaves in the Colony shall not be abandoned the landdrost shall consider it amongst his most sacred duties to watch over these most unfortunate beings. The Government can never tolerate that the title of property in human beings should ever have a tendency towards maltreating them, and therefore it most decidedly expects that all constituted authorities and civil servants will by their own example accustom their fellow-civil servants will by their own example accustom their fellow-inhabitants to consider and to treat their slaves as their fellow-creatures and not to suffer that any cruelty be ever practised towards them. The respective landdrosts are enjoined in the strongest manner to attend to whatever can promote the civilisation of these people, and by having moral principles instilled into the slaves to render them useful members of society.

The master had to lodge a complaint with the landdrost, the latter investigated the case and punished the slave. The maximum imprisonment was six months. If, on the other hand, the slave complained against his owner the landdrost could send the owner for trial to Capetown before the Raad van Justitie (arts. 69 and 70).

In the West Indies if a person was the master of a family he could not sell the individuals of the family separately *ne fiat divortium.* If he did the sale was void

(Arntzenius, *De Cond. Hom.* vol. 1, p. 114). The States-General as well as the States of Holland passed a number of ordinances which strove to make the relation of master to slave as humane as possible. (*Vide G.P.B.* ii, pp. 1245, 1256; iii, p. 1426; Octroi van W. I. Co., 31st December, 1761; Placaat, 23rd May, 1776; *Ned. Jaar Boek,* 1764; Zurck, *Codex Bat.* vol. 2, p. 1030.)

In 1833 the English Parliament passed a general Emancipation Ordinance, and it was decreed that after the 1st of December, 1834, slavery should cease in the Cape of Good Hope. Since then slavery as an institution has been unknown to the British colonies and independent states of South Africa.

Nobles and Commoners.—This distinction never formed part of the law of the Cape Colony, though in Holland it had a political significance. During the twelfth and following centuries the nobles of Holland were distinguished from the commoners by the fact that they belonged to some class or order of knights (*ridderorden, ridderschap*). They bore the distinctive title of nobiles or welgeborenen, welgeboren, mannen or schildboortigen. To the ridderschap belonged those who were born of noble parents as well as those who had obtained patents of nobility from the count. In time a person who had obtained the degree of doctor in a learned profession was regarded as equivalent to a noble, and acquired many of the privileges of nobles. As long as the system of *wergeld* existed the penalty for injuring a nobleman was nearly double that paid for a commoner. The oath of a nobleman was accepted before that of a commoner, and he could only be brought before a court by a special form of summons (Fockema Andreae, *Oud Ned. Burg. Recht*, vol. 1, pp. 21 *et seq.*).

In the time of Grotius, besides the fact that the nobles had certain social and political privileges, the only distinction between them and commoners was that they were exclusively entitled to the chase of hares and rabbits (Grotius, 1, 14, 7).

Laity and Clergy. — Before the establishment of the Dutch Republic the clergy in the Netherlands, as in other parts of western Europe, enjoyed certain historical privileges. Their principal privilege was that of a special forum. In the Frankish Empire the bishops and other high ecclesiastics had a large jurisdiction over the minor clergy. In Utrecht the clergy were almost entirely exempted from the jurisdiction of temporal courts. During the early part of the fourteenth century the ordinances of the bishopric of Cologne were taken over by Utrecht, and amongst other matters it was provided that a person who cited a cleric before a temporal court laid himself open to excommunication. On the other hand, an ecclesiastic could cite a defendant either before a temporal or an ecclesiastical court.

These large privileges of the clergy, which were almost universally respected during the middle ages, began to be cut down in all the non-spiritual provinces, even before the Reformation. After the reformed religion had been accepted by Holland, and after the overthrow of Spanish rule, all special privileges of the clergy disappeared, and they were placed on the same footing as the ordinary citizen (Fockema Andreae, *Oud Ned. Burg. Recht*, pp. 106 *et seq.*; Grotius, 1, 15, 1).

In the Cape Colony the clergy had no special political or civil status. By an ordinance of 1852 a sum of £16,000 was set aside every year for the payment of certain clergymen. This was abolished by Act 5 of 1875, known as the Voluntary Act. Since then the clergy possess neither political nor pecuniary privileges.

CHAPTER II.

MINORS AND MAJORS.

Minors.—In dealing with the Law of Persons an important topic is the law regarding minors. Here, as elsewhere, the Roman-Dutch law has developed a system entirely at variance with that of the Roman law. The power of the father over his children is the outcome of German customs, and has nothing whatever to do with the *patria potestas* of the Romans. The *patria potestas* was never in the slightest degree recognised by the law of Holland, neither in remote nor in recent times (Grotius, 1, 6, 3). Grotius tells us that the extensive and peculiar *patria potestas* of fathers over their children did not obtain in Holland, and that consequently children who had attained years of discretion were free to do and act as they pleased, and could dispose of their property by will to whomsoever they thought fit.

The Roman-Dutch law recognises a minor as a person who has not reached a sufficiently advanced age to be able to look after his own affairs, and therefore places him under the legal control of his parents or guardians; but, unlike the Roman son, directly he reaches the age of majority or gets married he becomes his own master. That marriage makes a child of either sex a major is a doctrine unknown to the Roman law, though prevalent with nearly all the branches of the German nation (Sande, *Decis.* 2, 7, 5). The age of majority varied at different times.

It has been frequently remarked by writers who have compared the characteristics of the Germans with those of the Romans, that the German youth of both sexes developed physically at a much later age than the Roman. *Sera juvenum Venus ideoque inexhausta pubertas* (Tacit. *M. G.* c. 20). The German youths were at the age of twenty often under direct parental control. At that age they were still called *jungen* or *buben*, and were flogged by their parents for disobedience. This differed very materially from the treatment of the Roman youth, who at the age of sixteen was clad in the *toga virilis* (Hein. *de Jur. Germ.* sec. 334). The Roman youth ceased to be under tutorship at the age of fourteen, whilst girls were liberated at the age of twelve. These ages were commonly accepted by the Romans as the age of puberty. Amongst the ancient Germans there was no fixed age at which a young man became his own master. His emancipation depended entirely upon his physical and mental development. The boy became a man as soon as he could wield a spear, or as soon as he was strong enough to use a sword (*swertleite*). The German youth who was strong enough to meet the enemies of his tribe on the field of battle was *ipso facto* emancipated (Schröder, p. 36).

According to Tacitus the German youth was publicly recognised as a major in the assembly of the tribe. He was declared capable of bearing arms and looking after his own affairs (*Haec apud illos toga, hic primus juventae honos*). Before that public acknowledgment of his capacity to bear arms he was regarded as part of his father's family; after it he became a major and a member of the State (*Ante hoc domus pars videntur non reipublicae*) (Tacit. *Germ.* 13).

In time a distinction came to be made between becoming capable of bearing arms and becoming capable of performing legal acts. In this way an age of majority for performing certain acts came to be fixed, whilst the age for bearing arms was left open to be determined by the actual physical capacity of the youth. The Anglo-Saxons, Salic Franks and Lombards allowed boys of ten years to give evidence. The Ripuarian laws fixed the age for marrying and doing other legal acts at fifteen. With the Visigoths the age of majority was twenty years (Fockema Andreae, *Bijdr.* vol. 1, p. 4).

Up to the sixteenth century the age of majority varied very much in the different provinces of the Netherlands. Thus the *Lex Frisionum* fixed the age of majority at twelve years, whilst many of the stadboeken of the fifteenth century provided that a youth should be *mondich* at fourteen and a girl at thirteen years. During the sixteenth century the Roman law had gained such authority in Friesland that the general rule of that system was established, and minority ended at twenty-five years with males and twenty with females. In Groningen the stadboeken of the fifteenth century made a youth *sui juris* at eighteen and a girl at fifteen years. In Utrecht, on the contrary, before the fifteenth century the young man became a major at eighteen, whilst girls remained minors until their twentieth year.

In Holland and West Friesland the tutelage during the fourteenth century lasted until the twelfth year, but gradually it was extended to the fourteenth and fifteenth years. In the Keurboek of Leyden majority was fixed in 1406 at seventeen years, in 1545 at twenty-one years, and in 1566 at twenty-five years for males and twenty for females. In

Zeeland during the thirteenth century majority was reached by boys at the fifteenth and by girls at the twelfth year. Gradually, however, the Roman law began to be more universally followed, so that during the sixteenth century the age of twenty-five for males and twenty for females was uniformly accepted as the age of majority (Fockema Andreae, *Bijdr.* vol. 1, pp. 5–19).

Grotius tells us that in Holland in early times a young man came of age at fifteen, and a young woman at twelve. Subsequently the time was extended to eighteen, and ultimately to twenty-five; whilst the distinction between the first minority under tutors (*aetas pupillaris sub tutoribus*) and the second minority under curators (*aetas pupillaris sub curatoribus*) was never accepted in any part of the Netherlands (Grotius, *Intro.* 1, 7, 3).

By the Roman-Dutch law a person was either under tutelage or completely his own master. Until he reached his twenty-fifth year he was a minor, and under the control of his parent or guardian. In the language of the Dutch writers he was called an *onbejaarde wees,* and the guardian to whose power he was subjected was his *voogd.* Neither arrogation, adoption nor captivity put an end to the rights of this guardian.

The age of twenty-five for males and twenty for females was accepted in South Africa as the age of majority, and remained such until 1829, when an ordinance was passed by which the law of the Cape Colony was assimilated to that of England. The English age of majority is probably derived from the Norman customs. The words of the *Lex Normanica* are as follows: *Minorem aetatem habere, qui nondum spatium*

20 *annorum compleverint et adolescentes in tutela usque ad vicessimum annum completum tenendos esse: unum ultra annum iisdem concedi ex usu Normanniae* (Hein, *Jus. Germ.* sec. 338). The law of the Cape has therefore in all probability had its origin in a Norman custom.

Although the age of twenty-five was the age of majority in Holland, yet for some purposes an earlier age was fixed. Thus, following the Roman law, a youth of fourteen or a girl of twelve years can make a will, and if they obtain the consent of their parents they may marry. The effect of marriage in our law is to make both the youth and the girl *sui juris.* In this respect the Roman-Dutch law followed German custom, and not the Roman law. I shall deal more fully with this when I come to speak of marriage. This was always the case in the Netherlands, following the Frankish custom, with regard to males, but not with respect to females. It is true the married girl was freed from parental control, but directly she married she fell under the tutelage of her husband, and was to that extent regarded as a minor in the eye of the law. Where, however, she exercised some special trade or calling she could, with her husband's consent, bind both his and her estate by her contracts. With this I shall deal more fully later.

The age of twenty-one as the age of majority for both males and females was adopted by all the South African states and colonies, so that at present there is one uniform age of majority throughout South Africa.

Venia Aetatis.—When majority is removed to so late a period in life as twenty-five years, there are many difficulties in the way of an inflexible rule that all acts shall be done with the sanction of a guardian. This was recognised in the Netherlands, and young men were allowed to become majors at an earlier age under certain special circumstances. In this the Netherlands adopted a rule of the Roman law, by which the Emperor upon request of the minor could grant him *venia aetatis* (*D.* 4, 4, 3 pr.; *C.* 2, tit. 44).

It would appear that in Holland the *venia aetatis* could only be obtained from the States of Holland or the sovereign power of the province. In Friesland, however, and in the other provinces, the court, as representing the sovereign power, was the proper body to grant *veniam aetatis* (Munnik's *Hed. Rechts.* p. 72). There have been several conflicting decisions in South Africa, but as we follow the law of Holland, the correct view seems to be laid down in the decision of Sir Henry de Villiers in the case of *Cachet* (8 C.T.R. 9), where he refused to grant *veniam aetatis* on the ground that he did not think that the court had the power. Moreover, now that majority is attained at twenty-one instead of at twenty-five, the necessity for granting *veniam aetatis* is not so apparent.

Guardianship.—As we have seen, the *patria potestas* of the Roman law never formed part of the law of Holland. The father is, however, the natural guardian of his children, looks after their interests during their minority, and can bring actions on their behalf. If the father dies the mother always retains that control over her children to which she is entitled by natural law (Grotius, 1, 7, 8). The father may, however, appoint guardians to his children by will, and in that case the appointed guardians will administer the property of the minor and assist him in legal proceedings; but in matters of education, marriage and the personal welfare of the children the mother has not only a voice, but a large control. The grandfather has, however, no legal right to interfere in the affairs of his grandchildren.

In these respects, then, the Roman-Dutch law differs greatly from the Roman law, for by the latter the grandfather, if alive, by virtue of the *patria potestas* was superior to the child's own father. If the father had appointed no testamentary tutor, then some of the German nations allowed the mother to act as guardian, whilst others, again, appointed the nearest relative (Hein. *Elem. Jus. Germ.* 1, 15, sec. 351). The Capitularia of Charlemagne and the law of the Lombards provided that if the father was dead the nearest male relative should be the legal tutor and defender of the minor. It was also a custom of the Franks, where there was no fit and proper relative, to allow a magistrate to appoint a tutor to the minor (Hein. *loc. cit.* sec. 355). The principle that the princeps was the upper guardian of all minors was common to a great section of the German people. It was known as *Die obervormundschaft* or *Suprema tutela*, and mention is made of it in the Capitularia, the *Lex Normanica*, and in several other collections of German laws (Hein. *loc. cit.* sec. 370).

In feudal times the feudal lord received the profits from the lands of the minor. Now, we find all these customs taken over by the law of Holland. In 1346 the Empress Margaret granted a handvest to the inhabitants of North Holland, by which she proclaimed that the legal guardians to a minor should be the nearest relatives on the side of the paternal and maternal grandfathers and grandmothers (*Regts. Obser.* vol. 4, obs. 9). The *obervormundschaft* was very strongly developed in Holland, and prior to the fourteenth century in South Holland the count appointed guardians to minors even in cases where guardians had been appointed by will. This was a source of grievance during the fourteenth century, and in 1412 we find Count William granting a privilege to Rotterdam "that the burghers and inhabitants of Rotterdam may appoint guardians to their own children" (Mieris, *Groot Chart Boek*, vol. 4, p. 211). It is by virtue of this *obervormundschaft* of the princeps or count that the Court of Holland, as his representative, assumed to itself the right as upper guardian of all minors to appoint tutors dative within its jurisdiction.

In addition to the Court of Holland the Orphan Chambers and the town or provincial courts also possessed the power of appointing guardians. In the Cape Colony the Orphan Chamber was replaced by the Master of the Supreme Court (Ordinance 105), but that court still remained the upper guardian of all minors, and it therefore exercised in South Africa the same *obervormundschaft* that was exercised by the German chiefs and the Hollander counts.

With regard, therefore, to the appointment of guardians, the Roman law was never followed in Holland, and the Dutch gave to the mother the same power of appointing guardians to her minor children as the father possessed; and even where the father had appointed guardians the mother could appoint co-guardians with equal power (Grotius, 1, 7, 9). When, however, we come to the duties of guardians, then we find that the Roman-Dutch law drew very largely on the Roman law for its principles, though even here there was a good deal that had been taken from early customs.

With regard to the appointment of curators to persons labouring under mental defects, the Court of Holland decided in 1579 that the power of appointing curators lay with the Court, and not with the nearest relatives (Neostad. *Cur. Hol. Decis.* 60).

Tutelage of Women.—In the early German period the only persons capable of exercising legal rights were those who could defend themselves. Hence the women, like the children, were regarded as *pars domus.* The head of the family represented the *domus,* and therefore also the women. It was he, and not the tribe, that protected the women of his family. As, however, the tribe extended and became the state, and nomadic life gave place to more settled and civilised communities, women gradually came to be regarded as also capable of possessing rights. The growth of this view was gradual, and as legal institutions are extremely slow in changing, the idea that women cannot exercise the same rights as men has prevailed even to our own times.

It is interesting to trace back to a remote antiquity the present incapacities of women. According to the ancient German customs all women were under some form of tutelage. The married woman was under the tutelage of her husband. The widow was under the tutelage of her nearest male relative if she were childless; but if she had children then both she and her children fell under the tutelage of their ascendant (Hein. *Jus. Germ,* 1, 15, sec. 358). The spinster, whatever her age, was under the tutelage of some male relative (Hein. *loc. cit.* sec. 357). By the *Jus Frisionum,* if a woman were raped, not she but her tutor or her father claimed the penalty (*patri sive tutori puellae*) (*Lex Fris.* ix, 8, 11).

The *Lex Saxonica* gives elaborate rules for the tutelage of women (c. 42), and similar provisions exist in the *Sachsenspiel*. A like practice was followed by the Franks, though after their contact with the Gallo-Romans they seem to have relaxed the stringency of their earlier customs. The Church's justification of the tutelage of women is so extraordinary that I give it here: *Adam per Evam deceptus est non Eva per Adam. Quem vocavit ad culpam mulier, justum est ut eum gubernatorem assumat ne iterum feminea facilitate labatur* (*Decret.* ii, 9, 32, c. 17). This is equivalent to saying that because Eve was clever enough to deceive Adam, man ought to manage woman's affairs in the future. In the Netherlands the tutelage of women can be traced in many of the provinces.

In Friesland the old law placed all women under tutelage, and in the stadboeken of some of the towns we find as late as the fifteenth century that women could not dispose of their immovable property or appear in court without assistance of a guardian. It made no difference whether they were wives, widows or spinsters. In Overijssel and Gelderland the same incapacity on the part of women is found in many of the stadboeken. Towards the seventeenth century the general incapacity of women to transact their own business had disappeared in Gelderland, though widows reverted to the state of minority if, when their husbands died, they were still under age. This also applied to widowers when their wives died.

In Holland there are several stadboeken which tell us that during the fourteenth century women were under tutelage. Thus in the Stadboek of Haarlem (1309) we find the following: *Een wijf zonder horen rechten voecht en mach noch panden geven noch panden keren verder dan si waren mach na inhout der handvesten en na den keur.*

The Keurboeken of Leyden and Amsterdam also show that the women (*vrouwen* and *joncvrouwen*) of those cities were incapable of depriving themselves of their goods without the consent of their guardian (*momboir* or *rechte voecht*). It would appear that women of full age had the right to choose their fixed guardian or *straat voogd,* as he came to be called, and in the town of Hoorn this right existed as late as 1528. Zeeland was apparently one of the first provinces to grant to women who were majors the same privileges that were enjoyed by men (Fockema Andreae, *Bijdr.* vol. 1, pp. 40–62).

In the time of Grotius all traces of this guardianship had disappeared, for he tells us that "formerly all women were minors in this country; so much so that fatherless spinsters and widows of full age could not appear in court nor alienate property except through guardians, whence we have the custom of employing a guardian called a *straat voogd* in such cases. This law, however, has fallen into disuse through lapse of time, so that whatever is now done by unmarried women of full age, though without the intervention of their guardians, cannot be otherwise than valid" (Grotius, *Intro.* 1, 4, 7).

The fact that married women cannot appear in court without the assistance of their husbands is a relic of this ancient custom. It is quite contrary to the principle of the Roman law, which allowed the wife to sue in her own name without the consent or assistance of her husband (Voet, 5, 1, 14, &c.).

Brouwer and Voet tell us that the law of Holland during the seventeenth century regarded both widowers and widows as majors, even though at the dissolution of the marriage they had not yet attained the age of majority (Voet, 1, 7, 14, 15). This view of the law of Holland has been adopted by all the South African colonies.

CHAPTER III.

MARRIAGE AND DIVORCE.

THE next subject that presents itself is the Law of Marriage. I have to a certain extent touched upon this branch of the law when I made a comparison between Grotius and Gudelinus. Every student of law is aware of the fact that a great deal of the Dutch law of marriage has its origin in the Roman law, but how that law has gradually been adapted and modified into the marriage law of to-day is not so widely known. The definition of the *Digest* (23, 2, 1) is as follows: "Marriage is the union of a man and a woman and lifelong fellowship, sharing rights divine and human." This definition is modified by Grotius into "Marriage is the union of man and woman with the object of living together, and which confers the lawful use of each other's bodies" (bk. 1, c. 5, 1). The later Roman-Dutch lawyers modify the latter part of the definition of Grotius, and thus we find Arntzenius defining marriage as the union of man and woman, entered into for the purpose of begetting children and for mutual assistance through life (*De Cond. Hom.* vol. 2, pt. 2, tit. 3, 1), and this definition is practically adopted by Van der Linden (1, 3, 1).

The requisites of the Roman law for a valid marriage in the time of Justinian were (1) consent; (2) a certain age; (3) capacity to contract; (4) no legal impediments. In Roman times the marriage was a simple contract; in practice, however, there were always some ceremonies as well as the mere consent of parties. In later times the ceremonies which formed an essential part of the *Jus Antiquum* had disappeared as a necessary part of the contract.

Betrothal (*sponsalia, trouwbeloften*).—The Germans, however, attached great importance to the marriage ceremony, and this no doubt followed from their rigorous customs with regard to the union. Tacitus in his *Germania* (c. 22) tells us that it was a custom of the Germans to have a public betrothal, which depended upon the consent not only of the bride and bridegroom, but also of their nearest relatives. The parties bestowed mutual gifts upon one another. This custom apparently prevailed amongst all the Teutonic tribes (Arntzenius, *De Cond. Hom.*). In addition to the gift of arms and oxen, coins were also exchanged between the parents to serve as evidence of the betrothal. These and other facts have led antiquarians to believe that the early German marriage, like the marriages amongst so many of the ancient nations, was in its origin nothing more or less than a contract of sale. The gifts of cattle, which so often formed an essential part of the ceremony, really represented the price for which the bride was sold by her parents.

Homer calls marriageable girls αλφεσὶβοιαι (from αλφάνειν, to yield, and βοῦς, an ox), *i.e.* girls who bring to their parents oxen when they marry. The Romans called their ancient form of marriage *co-emptio.* In German-speaking countries *Ein weib zu kaufen: een wyf koopen,* to buy a wife, was a common expression in the middle ages, and even to-day in Friesland the country people speak of a bride or a betrothed girl as *verkocht* or sold. Christianity, however, strove to blot out the idea of a sale as much as possible, and to put marriage on a much higher plane; but the rudiments of the primitive ideas of marriage prevalent amongst the Teutons have survived even to our own times (Noordewier, p. 177).

During the early German period it seems clear that the consent of the bride was not required. She was in the power of her father or other male relative (*in mundio*), and could be transferred into the power of a suitor without her having any voice in the matter. The marriage promise, therefore, was a contract not between bride and bridegroom, but between the suitor and the father or the male relative who was the *mundoaldus* (guardian) of the bride. In form it was a contract of sale. It was usually made in the presence of the relatives of the bride (*in kreise, ringe*). Thus in the *Niebelungen Lied* the betrothal takes place in the ring of the blood relations. The bride was the subject of the sale, and therefore her consent was not required. The bridegroom paid over the price or portion of the price (*wittum, meta, muntschatz*), and the contract was completed. The only formality besides the payment of the price was the handing over of a spear by the father to the suitor as symbolic of the change of *munt* or guardianship (Schröder, p. 70). We see traces of this in some of the old formulae, *e.g.* where the father says to the suitor: *Andrea per hunc ensem et wantonem istum* (glove) *sponsa Christinam filiam.*

In the early Germanic period the distinction between the sponsalia and the actual marriage was not great. Hence we find that often immediately after the sponsalia the bridegroom led the bride home (*heimführung*), and *concubitus* completed the marriage.

In the Frankish period the distinction between the betrothal and the actual marriage was more marked. The betrothal (*fabula firmata sponsalia*) consisted in the promise on the part of the father or guardian to hand over the bride at some future time, and on the part of the bridegroom to pay the *meta*. The marriage itself (*nuptiae, traditio, dies traditionis nuptiarum*) took place at some later date (Schröder, p. 300).

About this time, also, the consent of the bride came to be considered necessary, and after the introduction of Christianity we may assume that in most cases it was insisted on by the Church. The betrothal with the Franks was a public act. It took place in the presence of the inhabitants of the mark or commune. The Dutch word *gemaal*, meaning husband, is derived from the practice prevalent among the Salic Franks of betrothing a widow in the *mahal, mallum*, or assembly of the tribe. In course of time the term came to signify any husband. The betrothal usually took place in the presence of the relatives (*in den ring*) with ceremonious questions for man and maid. The ceremony was concluded by the bridegroom kissing the bride before the assembled people (Noordewier, p. 180).

The appearance of a sale was maintained by the Franks in the *sponsalia per solidum et denarium*. The formula of Bigonius reads thus: *Ego in nomine Dei dulcissimae conjugi, dum ego te per solidum et denarium secundum legem salicam visus sum despondare* (Van der Spiegel, p. 121). Later on the outward symbol of the betrothal was an exchange of rings between bride and bridegroom. This exchange of rings became almost universal, and received the approval of the Church. It was probably derived from some Roman practice

(c. 5, tit. 1). By the Visigoths such a promise was looked upon as extremely sacred: *Ut nullatenus promissio violetur si annulus arrarum nomine datus fuerit vel acceptus* (*Lex Vis.* bk. 3, tit. 1, sec. 3).

The consequences of the betrothal were (1) that the father or guardian had to deliver the bride against payment of the price; (2) that the bride had to be true to the bridegroom, so that adultery on her part annulled the contract. From this it followed that the Germans did not, like the Romans, allow a solemn betrothal to be lightly set aside at the desire of one of the parties (Hein. *Jus. Germ.* bk. 1, tit. 8, secs. 179, 184), and the refractory party could be compelled to complete his contract. This German custom prevailed in Holland, and became one of the important ancient customs of the country. In 1656 it obtained statutory recognition in the *Echtregelment* of that year, and the courts were empowered to compel the marriage to take place whatever might be the difference between the wealth or dignity of the parties (*Hol. Cons.* 4, c. 368). In the seventeenth century, therefore, two courses were open to the rejected party—either to sue for damages or for specific performance of the marriage.

In South Africa the action for specific performance of marriage has been abolished, and the only redress left to the injured party is to sue for damages for breach of promise to marry. Here, then, we have abandoned the Teutonic custom in favour of the rule of the Roman law, which corresponds with the law of England.

The second consequence has also been adopted by the law of Holland, and *stuprum* on the part of the bride always enabled the bridegroom without fear of any penalty to refuse to complete the contract of marriage. There are several decisions to this effect in the South African courts (*Horak* v. *Horak*, 3 Searle, 389).

The Ceremony.—As we saw above, the marriage ceremony in early German days was practically the same as the betrothal. The concubitus which followed upon the *heimführung* really constituted the marriage. The *Sachsenspiegel* says that the marriage is complete as soon as *die decke mann und frau beschlägt*, or as soon as the *bett beschutten is* (Noordewier, p. 183). This remained the law in several of the provinces of the Netherlands. Huber tells us this was the law of Friesland, and it gave rise to the maxim, *Femme gagne son douaire à mettre son pied au lit* (Huber, *Hed. Recht.* 1, 5, 9).

After the introduction of Christianity the old forms were still preserved, but the priest came to occupy the place of the father or *mundoaldus*, and he it was who gave the bride to the bridegroom. Instead of the betrothal before the inhabitants of the village the priest published the banns, and the usual course was for the priest, after the publication, on the wedding-day to give the sacerdotal blessing and to place the hand of the bride in that of the bridegroom.

With regard to the marriage ceremony, the gifts of arms and oxen of which Tacitus speaks were continued well into the middle ages. Olaus Magnus speaks of this custom as still prevalent in northern Europe during the fifteenth century (*Hist. Gent. Sept.* bk. 13, c. 4). Gradually, however, this custom disappeared throughout western Europe, and in its place the Christian marriage rites (or *copula sacerdotalis*) were adopted. The Christian marriage was required by the Visigoths, the Lombards and the Franks, but the old German practice was not abolished altogether, and consequently for a long time both the Christian and Germanic rites were used side by side (Hein. *Jus. Germ.* 1, sec. 201). The early Church recognised the validity of a marriage even though the parties had not been married by a priest. All that the Church required was a contract that the man took the woman with an intention to make her his wife, together with a physical union following upon such promise. If the marriage was not consummated, either party was free to make a similar contract with some other party, and if consummation followed upon the latter contract, this and not the former promise constituted the marriage.

After the Decretals of Gratian the Canon law drew a distinction between a promise to marry *now* and a promise to marry *at some future time.* The promise to marry now, called *sponsalia de praesenti* or *sponsalia per verba de praesenti,* established a bond between the parties which was regarded equivalent to a marriage. As a general rule *sponsalia de praesenti* could not be set aside, and the party who had carnal connection with another was guilty of adultery. There were, however, exceptions, for the woman might take the veil, and then the bond was severed, or else the Pope might grant dispensation.

The promise to marry in the future, *sponsalia per verba de futuro* or *sponsalia de futuro,* created no bond unless there was also *copula carnalis.* In that case it became a marriage. The canonist therefore looked to the intention of the parties, and did not require a church ceremony to make the marriage valid. It is, however, true that the Church urged that there should be a public notification of the betrothal, and that the priest should pronounce a benediction over the spouses; but this was an exhortation of the Church, not a necessary ceremony of the Canon law.

The unsatisfactory state of a promise which might be *de praesenti* or *de futuro* as it suited circumstances was felt by the Council of Trent (1563), and this body, in order to have satisfactory evidence of the *sponsalia de praesenti*, provided that the parties must express their willingness to become man and wife before the parish priest and two witnesses (Esmein, *Droit Canonique*, vol. 1, pp. 95–137). Nothing, however, was said about the necessity of a marriage ceremony in the church. The provisions of the Council of Trent were never accepted by the Dutch Republic (Fockema Andreae, vol. 1, p. 72).

From the Stadboek of Groningen (1425) it is clear that there was no necessity for both bride and bridegroom to go to the church before the concubitus took place. After concubitus the bride alone was required to go, though the bridegroom could, if he wished, accompany her. *Als de brudegom de bruet beslapen hevet, so sal he des morgens tho kerke gaan mijt synen vrienden en de syne misse horen gelyk der bruet of he wil* (art. 215). That the law required the bride to go to the church the morning after the wedding with or without the bridegroom appears in a number of other stadboeken. It is clear, therefore, that the benediction of the church was often given after the real wedding. In time, however, this practice died out and the benediction was given only before the actual concubitus (Fockema Andreae, vol. 1, pp. 73–79).

In Holland as late as the fifteenth century a marriage could be validly contracted by a public declaration of an intention to marry, and by concubitus following upon such declaration. In 1434 Philip of Burgundy said: *Veele luyden in Holland, Zeeland en Friesland hijlicken ende malkanderen eer dat zy haer geboden hebben in der heylicher kercken* (Fockema Andreae, p. 123; *G.P.B.* 3, 392).

Later on we find that absolution was paid for marriages contracted without the *copula sacerdotalis.* In 1525 it was decreed in Amsterdam that "every citizen or inhabitant who marries in any way whatever without three proclamations or banns from the pulpit should forfeit 18 guldens." The marriage, therefore, was a civil act, and all that the Church could do was to fine the person who married without its aid (Fockema Andreae, p. 124). There are several judicial acts in which persons swear that they were secretly married *getruwet hadde tot sinen wive tusschen hem ende haar.* These were, however, the exception, for by far the most of the marriages in Holland during the fifteenth century were before witnesses and in the church.

In many parts of Holland the marriage was not complete until there had been concubitus, but the general trend of custom in that province was to regard the marriage as complete after the conclusion of the ceremony, even where there had been no concubitus. We have seen that most German tribes regarded concubitus essential to the completion of the marriage ceremony; but other tribes, again, attached so great an importance to the espousals contracted with all the attendant ceremonies that the woman engaged to be married was almost looked upon as a matron, and when once the marriage ceremony was completed she was held to be no longer a virgin. *Tanto enim honore pudicitia apud barbaros colitur ut femina de cujus nuptiis actum est, etiamsi corpore sit integra, pro corrupta habeatur.* It would seem as if this idea lay at the root of the rule of the Hollanders that the completion of the marriage ceremony and not the consummation of the marriage was to be looked to in order to determine when the marriage was legally effected (Grotius, *Intro.* 1, 5, 17).

In 1576 the baljuw and mannen of Rynland took a definite step towards invalidating secret marriages. It was enacted that persons secretly married since 1572 should have fourteen days allowed to them within which to make a declaration and register the fact that they lived together as husband and wife. This declaration was to be proclaimed either in the church or in the Court of Rynland. After the third proclamation the marriage was indissoluble. After 1576 leave could be obtained from the court to proclaim banns, and then the marriage might be celebrated either before the civil or church officials: all other marriages were void. In 1580 the States of Holland passed the Political Ordinance, and fixed the marriage ceremony which, with a few modifications, we follow in South Africa. By this Ordinance the marriage could take place either before a magistrate or before a church official. Each town drew up its own formula to be read to the bride and bridegroom, and questions were put to which they were required to make suitable answers.

We have seen that with regard to the marriage ceremony the *copula sacerdotalis* superseded the Roman as well as the

German customs of marriage. Before the Politique Ordonnantie of 1580 became law there was no uniform practice in Holland as to what were the ceremonial requisites of a valid marriage. The marriage ceremony usually adopted was that prescribed by the Catholic Church in the Canon law, but to the church ceremony were added various traditional practices in vogue in the different provinces and cities. It was therefore in order to have a uniform method of celebration that the Politique Ordonnantie laid down definitely the essential details of the ceremony. Whatever the religion to which the parties belonged, there were certain requisites that had to be adhered to: (1) The parties had to appear before the magistrate or church official to request that their banns might be published; (2) the banns were to be published on three successive Sundays or market days in the church or other recognised place at the residences of the spouses; (3) the church ceremony or the ceremony before the magistrate. It made no difference to what religion the parties belonged, and though the Jews apparently adopted their own regulations, after 1656 they were bound to conform to the requirements of the Politique Ordonnantie. This was the law of Cape Colony until the Order in Council of 1838. In the essential requisites, however, the Order of 1838 did not differ from those of the Politique Ordonnantie. All the other colonies in South Africa have similar marriage ordinances differing only in detail, so that we may say, broadly speaking, that the marriage ceremony in South Africa is identical with that instituted by the Politique Ordonnantie in 1580.

An important feature of the German marriage ceremony

was the bridal feast. I have shown in the chapter on the Stadboek of Groningen that the authorities of that town made provisions against too sumptuous feasts, and it would appear that throughout western Europe the bridal feasts were great gatherings usually ending in general intoxication. Though we do not indulge in all these mediæval excesses, the Germanic spirit still exists in many of our weddings. Even the wedding presents, so very prevalent nowadays, have their origin in an inveterate German custom. The *braut taffel* or *hochzeit geschenke* was a feature of the richest as well as of the poorest Teutonic marriage (Hein. *loc. cit.* 219).

Requisites and Hindrances.—Age.—According to our present law any person, male or female, over the age of twenty-one may contract a valid marriage. Under the age of fourteen for males and twelve for females there can be no valid marriage. Over these ages a valid marriage may be contracted if the consent of parents be obtained. Our law of marriage has gone through many vicissitudes before it reached this simple form.

The early Germans had no fixed age below which a marriage could not be contracted. They considered the physical conditions of the parties, and as long as the bridegroom had reached the age of puberty and the bride was *viripotens* the marriage could be celebrated. As a rule, however, the man was not regarded as fit to be a husband unless he had reached his twentieth year. Caesar tells us that it was considered scandalous for a youth to have any intercourse with women before he reached that age (*B.G.* 6, 22): *Intra annum vicesimum feminae notitiam habuisse, in turpissimis habent rebus.* The Franks recognised no age limit below which marriage was not allowed, but when we consider the age at which their kings married, then eighteen seems to have been the average age (Hein. *Jus. Germ.* bk. 1, sec. 203).

By the Roman law a youth under fourteen and a maid under twelve could not marry. The Canon law took over the provisions of the Roman law in this respect as a guiding though not as a rigid rule. We may therefore say that from the days of the counts to the present day a marriage of a youth under fourteen or a maid under twelve was not encouraged. In some cases no doubt the Church, for special reasons, permitted marriages of younger persons, though as a general rule it insisted on the parties having the apparent capacity of procreating children. In the time of Grotius the rule of the Roman law was rigidly adhered to, so that young men under fourteen and young girls under twelve could not contract a valid marriage (Grotius, *Intro.* 1, 5, 3).

Consent of Parents or Guardians. — We saw that by the early German customs the girl was no party to the contract. At that time, therefore, her marriage could only take place where her father or guardian had given his consent. The youth could not marry as long as he was *pars domus*, but as soon as he was publicly recognised as capable of defending himself and supporting a family he could purchase his wife. This custom was preserved by the Franks, for we find in the *Lex Salica*, tit. 70: *Si quis puellam alienam ad conjugium quaesiverit praesentibus suis et puellae parentibus.* Here *parentes* does not mean the father and mother only, but the nearest relatives as well, for this is the sense in which the word was used during the middle ages

(Faber, *Thesaurus, sub voce Parens; cf.* French *parent* = relative).

In Zeeland, where so many of the customs of the Salic Franks were preserved, we see from the Politique Ordonnantie of 1580 that orphan minors were required to have the consent not only of their guardians, but of their nearest relatives, and that even majors must either have the consent of their parents and relatives or explain why this consent has not been obtained.

It was only after the introduction of Christianity, and after the Church had attained considerable influence, that the consent of the bride was insisted upon. The Church recognised the validity of a marriage of minors where no parental consent had been obtained. *Sufficiat secundum leges solus eorum consensus de quorum conjunctionibus agitur* (*Decret.* Grat. c. 27, 9, 2, c. 2).

So rooted, however, was the idea that a girl could not marry unless her father or guardian gave her away, that we find the laws of many of the Netherlands provinces requiring the consent of parents. Without the consent the marriage was not as a rule void, but the bridegroom could obtain no pecuniary advantage from the marriage. We see this in Friesland and in Holland. In an old keur of Delft a penalty was imposed upon persons who married *een knechtekijn beneden sinen* 15 *jaren ende een maechdekijn beneden sinen* 14 *jaren.* What applied, therefore, at first only to the girl came in time to apply to both young man and girl. Before the Union of the Provinces, however, the influence of the Church was too great to render the marriage of minors without parental consent void (Fockema Andreae, vol. 1, p. 145).

By the civil law the marriage was void, but the reason of that law did not apply to Holland, for the prohibition arose from the law regarding *patria potestas,* and this peculiar power of the Roman ancestor did not form part of the law of Holland. Public opinion was therefore the only influence which restrained clandestine marriages. In the sixteenth century, however, public opinion seems to have lost its restraining influence, and we find Charles V in 1540 attempting to check clandestine marriages by imposing severe penalties upon the parties. Notwithstanding that the parties could be punished, and that they forfeited the benefits arising from community, the number of clandestine marriages increased. In 1580, however, the States of Holland boldly broke away from the Canon law and pronounced all marriages of minors void unless the consent of parents had been obtained, even though the marriage had been duly celebrated by an officer of the Church. The law was therefore brought into accord with that public opinion which had prevailed in the Netherlands from the earliest German period.

Though the legal age has been reduced to twenty-one years, the requirement of the Political Ordinance that the parents must give their consent to the marriages of children under the age of majority has been retained (Order in Council, 7th September, 1838, sec. 10), and a marriage of minors without the consent of parents is as void with us as it was in Holland.

After the passing of the Political Ordinance of 1580 the consent of parents, as we have seen, was indispensable to the marriage of a minor. The power of the father in that respect was regarded as unlimited, and no court could interfere with his discretion. This seems to have been the view which prevailed in Holland during the former half of the seventeenth century. During the latter half of that century the finality of the father's decision came to be questioned, and Voet held the opinion that the court could interfere where the father's decision was false, frivolous or foolish (Voet, 23, 2, 22). The Supreme Court of Holland and Zeeland adopted Voet's view, and decided in 1707 that the court could pass the father's decision by and grant an order to marry (Munniks, vol. 2, p. 85). Schorer and Van der Keessel express a similar view. In the Cape Colony the Chief Justice, like the Lord Chancellor in England, was selected in 1838 as the judicial officer before whom such matters had to be brought. Where, however, no special legislation exists, the court is the proper authority to try the validity of the father's objections. There is a decision in the Transvaal to that effect (December, 1906).

Prohibited Degrees of Consanguinity and Affinity.—To what extent consanguinity was a bar to marriage during the German period we do not know. There was, however, no prohibition against the marriage of persons connected by affinity. The introduction of Christianity effected a great change, and the prohibitions of the civil law came in the course of time to be followed by the Franks. The Salic law prohibited marriage between the children of brothers and sisters or between a man and the widow of a deceased brother or uncle. In the time of Charlemagne marriages within the sixth degree of consanguinity were forbidden.

Our rules with regard to the prohibited degrees of consanguinity and affinity are derived partly from the Roman and partly from the Canon law, and the readiness with which the Franks and the Frisians accepted these rules seems to point to the fact that Teutonic custom had also set its face against the marriage of persons nearly related in blood. Just as the royal houses were often allowed to contract polygamous marriages (Hein. *Jus. Germ.* bk. 1, sec. 206), so dispensation was often granted to them to marry within the forbidden degrees.

By the Roman law children by adoption were considered in the same light as children by birth, and the same prohibition to marry that applied to the former also applied to the latter. As, however, the *patria potestas* was not recognised in Holland, adoption never created a bar to marriage, and the adopted person was regarded in the light of a stranger (Ortwijn, *ad Inst.* 1, 10, 2). The Roman law provided within what degrees of consanguinity or affinity marriages were prohibited. With the Germans the prohibition was not quite so extensive, and varied with the different nations. The Canon law, however, considerably differed from the Civil law with regard to the prohibited degrees. In calculating the degrees of relationship the Canon and Civil law differed. For example, by the Canon law I am removed two degrees from my first cousin; by the Civil law I am considered to be four degrees removed (*Cens. For.* 1, 5, 9, and 1, 5, 12). By the Roman law persons in the fourth degree could marry according to the Roman computation, but by the Canon law persons within the fourth degree by ecclesiastical computation could not marry. Hence by the Roman law first cousins could marry, but not so by the Canon law, for by that law even second cousins were prohibited from contracting a marriage.

It will therefore be easily understood that after the Reformation, when the hold of the Canon law upon the people was so considerably relaxed, marriages took place which were valid by the Civil law, but invalid by the Canon law. This led to great disputes in cases of succession *ab intestato*, as to whether the claimant was legitimate or not. In order to obviate all these disputes and to introduce uniformity into the law of marriage, the degrees within which in Holland marriages were prohibited were regulated by the Politique Ordonnantie of 1580. The preamble to the chapter on Marriage states that the law is passed in order to obviate the irregularities which are daily committed and the lawsuits which constantly arise with regard to succession.

In 1664 (*G.P.B.* vol. 2, p. 3170) an Ordinance was passed explaining the Politique Ordonnantie of 1580, by which it was enacted that a person could not marry his wife's brother's or sister's child. In 1736 (*G.P.B.* vol. 6, p. 541) a further explanatory Act was passed prohibiting marriage with a deceased wife's step-mother. In 1789 (*Ned. Jaarboeken*, 1789, p. 1131) it was further enacted that a man could not marry the daughter of the brother or sister, full or half-blood, of his deceased wife, nor her step-mother; and that a woman could not marry the son of a brother or sister, full or half-blood, of her husband, nor her husband's step-father. In these matters, however, the States often granted dispensation; for instance, in 1644 a man was allowed to marry the half-sister of his deceased wife's mother (*G.P.B.* vol. 7, p. 808).

The Placaat of 1580, and in all probability the other placaats above cited, establish the law of South Africa with regard to the degrees of consanguinity or affinity within which marriage is prohibited, except in so far that marriage with a deceased wife's sister has been allowed in the Cape Colony and in the Orange River Colony, but not in the Transvaal. The latter country, however, went back to the Canon law in so far that it prohibited the marriage of first cousins whose parents were related as full brothers or sisters. This was, however, repealed in 1903 (Ordinance 40); so that the Transvaal law is now uniform with that of the rest of South Africa as regards the marriage of cousins.

Religious Differences.—The laws which forbade Christians from marrying Jews or Roman Catholics from marrying heretics had their origin in the decrees of the Church. But though a Jew could not marry a Christian, he could always contract a valid marriage in Holland with a Jewess. Before 1656 the Jews apparently disregarded the provisions of the Politique Ordonnantie, and contracted marriages in accordance with the Mosaic law and their own rites and ceremonies. In 1656, however, a placaat was passed requiring the Jews to adhere to the same regulations as to publication of banns and the consent of parents as Christians were required to regard, and also to be subject to the same prohibitions as the other citizens of Holland (*G.P.B.* vol. 3, p. 504). In the same way marriages between members of different Christian sects were valid, provided the requirements of the Politique Ordonnantie of 1580 were adhered to.

In the time of Grotius, even though religious feeling ran very high, there were no penalties against the marriage of Protestant and Catholic. Gradually, however, the Protestants adopted views as intolerant as those of the Roman Catholics of the sixteenth century. If military men married Catholics they lost their commissions (*G.P.B.* 1737, vol. 5, p. 682). Not satisfied with imposing penalties upon the marriages of Protestant and Catholic officers in the army, the States in 1755 (*G.P.B.* vol. 6, p. 536) decreed that no Protestant official, whether civil or military, who married a Catholic could retain his office, and furthermore that no minor of the Protestant faith could marry a Catholic even with consent of parents. In 1795, however, under the influence of the French Revolution all these restrictions were swept away, and Protestant and Catholic were left free to marry each other without any pains or penalties. In this respect, therefore, there was complete equality in South Africa when the Cape was ceded to the English Crown.

Adulterer and Adulteress.—Another restriction which did not exist in the days of Grotius, and which does not exist in England, was introduced into the law of Holland—that adulterer and adulteress could not marry one another. Groenewegen tells us (*C.* 9, 9, 27) that in his time the adulterer could in all cases marry the adulteress. The Roman law apparently did not tolerate such marriages, though the Canon law adopted a different rule (Voet, 23, 2, 27). In the Amsterdam third volume of the *Consultations* we find that seven lawyers all agree in the view that a man may marry the woman with whom he has committed adultery after the death of his wife, provided that he made no promise of marriage and that he did not plot against the life of his spouse (*Cons.* vol. 3 (Amst.), 52, 53, 54). This appears to have been the rule of the Canon law. The States of Holland, however, in 1674 (*G.P.B.* vol 3, p. 507) passed a special Ordinance prohibiting all persons who lived in adultery from marrying one another at any time, and decreed that such marriages should be null and void, and that the parties could be arbitrarily punished. This law has never been repealed, and forms part of the common law of South Africa.

Annus Luctus.—We have seen that all women, widows included, were during the early German period under the *mundium* of some male relative. Hence when a widow wished to remarry she had to get the consent of her guardian, and for this consent something was usually paid. In time the *mundium* over a widow became merely formal, and was in consequence transferred from the relative to the magistrate or other judicial functionary of her place of residence. Hence a curious custom arose in many parts of Germany requiring a widow who married to present a purse with silver coins to the magistrate.

I am not aware of any such custom in the Netherlands. There was, however, an old custom in the Netherlands which required a widow to wait at least a year before she contracted a new marriage. During the sixteenth and seventeenth centuries statutory enactments to that effect were passed in several of the provinces. No such ordinance, however, was passed by the province of Holland. In that province the matter was regulated by the local laws of the towns. Thus in Amsterdam a widow over the age of fifty could marry at any time she chose after her husband's death. Under the age of fifty she had to wait for a year. In Enckhuisen the period was six months if the widow was not pregnant (*Rechts. Obs.* vol. 3, obs. 7). The object, of course, was to prevent the so-called *confusio sanguinis.* Grotius says a widow may not marry within the period of probable pregnancy by her deceased husband (Grotius, *Intro.* 1, 5, 3).

According to the present law of the Cape Colony there is no *annus luctus.* The Marriage Law of the South African Republic (3 of 1871) provided that a widower might not marry within three months after the death of his spouse, and that a widow, unless she got dispensation from the Government, could not marry within three hundred days of the death of her previous spouse; but this has been repealed by Proclamation 34 of 1901.

Effect of Marriage upon the Persons of the Spouses. —We have seen above that part of the marriage ceremony of the early Germans was the handing over of the bride by her father or guardian to the bridegroom, and that this was accompanied with the delivery of a spear to the bridegroom as symbolic of the transfer of guardianship. This transfer of the guardianship of the wife upon marriage has persisted throughout the history of the Roman-Dutch law, and is to-day an important effect of our law of marriage. In the older Roman law the Roman wife passed into the guardianship of her husband (*in manum mariti*) in much the same way as the German wife passed into the *munt* of her spouse. In the later Roman law, however, all traces of *manus* disappeared, and the one spouse, as far as legal relations were concerned, was entirely independent of the other.

Although there has been a tendency in our law, through

the antenuptial contract, to bring the relationship of husband to wife in accordance with that of the later Roman law, in our common law we have not yet reached that stage. The effect of the old German custom has not yet worn off, and with us the wife is still regarded as a minor and her husband as her guardian. This power of the husband over his wife extends not only to her person, but even to her property. It makes no difference whether in point of years the husband is a major or a minor, in either case he is the guardian of his wife. A youth of sixteen may marry a widow of forty, and after the union the widow will in the eye of the law be a minor without the power of appearing in court or of alienating her property. This power of the husband over his wife is known as the marital power (*potestas maritalis, maritale macht*).

The marital power is intimately connected with the law of community of property, and its history is closely interwoven with the latter. The rule of the German law was, *Virum uxorem suam habere in potestate,* and we find it thus stated in the laws of the Visigoths, Burgundians, Alemanni, Lombards and Saxons. Heineccius thus defines the marital power of the German husband: "The marital power and guardianship of the husband is the right of the husband to rule over and to defend the person of his wife, and to administer her goods in such a way as to dispose of them at his own will, or at any rate to prevent his wife from dealing with them except with his knowledge and consent (*Jus. Germ.* bk. 1, sec. 285).

The marital power and guardianship of the husband always formed part of the law of the Netherlands, and is expressed in a number of laws and keuren. In the Costumen of Friesland (sixteenth century) it was thus expressed: *Dat die mannen hier te lande huer dragen als voechden van huer wyven goeden ende dat sonder enige distinctie of te dieselve goederen zijn dotalia of te parafernalia.* That is to say, the husband is the guardian of his wife's property whether such be dotal or paraphernalia.

In a keur of Zutphen of 1376 it was provided that a child of less than sixteen could not alienate property or choose a guardian without consent of the schepenen, unless such child had contracted a marriage. In the province of Holland there are several handvesten which show that in the fourteenth century marriage made the husband a major and the wife a minor. In the Groot-Privilegie of 1476 the Lady Mary promises that she will choose by the advice of the States a husband and guardian (*eenen vooght ende man*) (*Rechts. Obs.* vol. 2, obs. 3). Grotius says that by a legally contracted marriage the wife becomes a minor, and her husband becomes her guardian or *kerk voogd,* as it was sometimes called (Grotius, *Intro.* 1, 5, 19).

By virtue of the marital power the husband acquired the full and free administration of the goods his wife brought into the marriage. The origin of this right is clearly German, and not Roman. At the same time it is interesting to see how the Roman law constantly strove to supersede the German law with respect to this power. By the *Lex Romana* of Theodosius the husband could not alienate the property of the wife without her consent. It was sought to introduce this practice into Zeeland during the reign of Floris V, but it soon fell into disuse. In Gelderland the rule of the *Lex*

Romana seems to have taken root (Schomaker, vol. 3, pp. 141, 144), but in Holland it was never recognised.

Effect of Marriage on the Property o the Spouses.— According to the *Jus Antiquum Romanorum*, when the wife passed *in manum viri*, she fell into the position of a daughter of the house, and consequently had no property of her own. Everything she brought into the marriage belonged to the paterfamilias. In Justinian's time, however, each spouse retained the free disposition over the property which he or she had previous to the marriage, and no community of goods existed between them. By the common law of Holland, which is also our law, as soon as the marriage is celebrated the goods which belonged to the husband and the wife prior to the marriage form one mass, and each spouse or his or her heirs takes one-half of this mass upon the dissolution of the marriage. The spouses are said to be married in community of goods (*communio bonorum*), but the administration of the entire mass lies in the hands of the husband. This community can, however, be varied by antenuptial contract.

Our law, therefore, differs materially from the *Jus Antiquum* and the Roman law of Justinian. Its origin is to be sought in the customs of the Germans, and not in the Roman law. That community of goods existed with the early Germans in the form in which we know it is most unlikely. Neither Tacitus nor Caesar mentions such a community of goods. Caesar, it is true, tells us (*Bel. Gal.* bk. 6, c. 18), that amongst the Gauls the husband added from his own resources as much as the wife brought him, and this formed a fund which was held in common, and upon the death of either spouse the whole fund and its profits went to the survivor. Tacitus (*Germ.* c. 18) merely informs us that it was customary for bride and bridegroom to give presents to one another. The *Lex Ripuaria* (c. 87, sec. 1) tells us that after the death of the husband the wife gets a certain sum of money *et tertiam de omne re quod simul conlaboraverint.* In the *Capitularia* we find the following (*Cap. Carol. Mag.* lib. 4, sec. 9): *Volumus ut uxores defunctorum post obitum maritorum tertiam partem collaborationis quam simul in beneficio conlaboraverunt capiant.* So in the division of the goods of Dagobert the queen took a third part of the things acquired *stante matrimonio* (Hein. *Jus. Germ.* bk. 1, sec. 271).

The Saxons gave the wife a half of what was acquired during the marriage. Thus we find in the *Lex Saxonica,* tit. 8: *De eo quod vir et mulier simul conquisiverint mulier mediam portionem accipiat* (Hein. *loc. cit.* 272). Heineccius (sec. 273) tells us that he can find no trace of community in the laws of the Alemanni, Bavarians, Angles, Frisians or Lombards. The idea that the wife was entitled to some portion seems, therefore, common to both the Franks and the Saxons, but the equal division between husband and wife seems to have its origin in the Saxon law. It was the law of Westphalia and Thuringia, and in the Stadbuch of Bremen we find the following: *So woor twee tesamende kahmen an echtschap wat se hebben dat is ohrer beyder na stadts recht.* According to the local law of Bremen, the property brought by each spouse into the marriage was owned by them in common (Hein. *loc. cit.* 276–78; Arntzenius, *De Cond. Hom.* bk. 2, tit. 4, secs. 1 *et seq.*).

In the Dutch *Saksenspiegel* of Johan von Buch we find the following (sec. 44): *Een man en zijn echte wijf en hebben gheen ghesceiden goet zoo lange als si beide leven* (husband and wife have no separate property so long as they live). Where the Saxons got their community from we do not know, but it is safe to assume that some form of joint property was recognised by several German tribes. It certainly was not part of the Roman law, and was not borrowed from that source. Nor is it likely that it existed amongst the Saxons in exactly the same form as it existed in the law of Holland during the seventeenth century. The introduction of Christianity and the principle that husband and wife are one in spirit gave a new *ratio existendi* to the German custom, and it was accepted as a legal principle that the spouses should share fortune and misfortune together both as to person and property.

At what period the law of community as it exists at present was introduced into the Netherlands it is difficult to say. Fockema Andreae quotes an old Frisian source of the eleventh century, which says that a woman may choose to whom she will give her body and with whom she shall share her goods. There is, however, abundant proof that during the thirteenth and fourteenth centuries the *communio quaestuum* was recognised in Friesland (Fock. And. vol. 2, p. 55). The Frisian law made some distinction between movable and immovable property; the latter always fell into the community if bought *stante matrimonio*.

In Groningen the community of goods was recognised before the fourteenth century as soon as a child was born, but not before. Towards the end of the fourteenth century

(1374) community of goods became the general rule as soon as the marriage was consummated: *Alsoe vro als he se (zyne vrouw) beslapen heuet* (Stadboek, 1425, art. 24). Arntzenius thinks that community was introduced into Holland during the rule of the counts (*De Cond. Hom.* bk. 2, tit. 4, sec. 4). It certainly existed in Zeeland during the reign of Floris the Guardian: *Als si twee mit huwelijk syn vergadert ende de eene stervet die andere die te leve blivet sal hebben half die arve ende half die have dat ander deel sullen hebben die kinderen* (Van Mieris, *G.C.B.* 1, 313, art. 56).

In a handvest given to the Land van Arkel, 1382, we find: *Man en wijf wettelyk vergadert sijnde is haer goet gemeijn.* It is therefore clear that in Holland and Zeeland community of goods existed long before the sixteenth century. We saw that in Friesland and in Groningen the community took place only after the consummation of the marriage. This seems to have been the general German rule, and probably followed from the fact that a marriage was not regarded as complete until the wife had entered the nuptial couch. In Holland and Zeeland, however, the community followed upon the completion of the marriage ceremony. Thus Grotius says: "Marriage is considered as completed as soon as it has been celebrated in the church or before the authorities, so that all rights arising out of marriage vest and take effect at once, although no sexual intercourse follows (Grotius, *Intro.* 1, 5, 17).

The earliest ideas of community of goods naturally only concerned itself with a division of the corporeal goods of husband and wife. In time, however, it came to be applied to incorporeal rights as well. As the property of husband

and wife were *stante matrimonio* held in common, and as the husband had the full control of the whole mass, there can be no doubt that as soon as this community was recognised the debts incurred during the marriage were also common. Indeed it was early called a community of profit and loss (*eene gemeenschaap van baete en laste*).

A more difficult question is, When was the one spouse made responsible for the debts of the other spouse, contracted before marriage? The earliest reference I can find to this principle is the Keuren of Schoonhoven, 1557 (*Rechts. Obs.* vol. 3, obs. 37): *De schulden de man en wijf te samen of te en in 't bijzonder gemaekt hebben voor de vergadering des huwelijks zal men met recht den hun beyden mogen verhalen.* That this was the general law of Holland towards the end of the sixteenth century admits of no doubt. The older authorities speak of community of debts, but they always refer to debts contracted *stante matrimonio*.

Antenuptial Contracts.—It would be futile to seek for antenuptial contracts in the early German marriages. The form of marriage was a sale in the presence of the blood relations (*intersunt parentes et propinqui et munera probant*), and the price was paid over in exchange for the bride. Later on, however, the transaction became less mercenary, and instead of the purchase-price being paid over to the father or guardian there was either a pledge given or a trifle was handed over as symbolic of the price. Still later, when the consent of the bride became essential, a promise was made by the bridegroom at the marriage ceremony to endow his bride with certain property. It was when this stage was reached that a pre-marriage contract was no longer out of place.

This period could hardly have arrived before the introduction of Christianity.

Again, the very idea of an antenuptial contract conflicts with the idea of community of goods. It must, therefore, have been introduced at a stage when people realised that it was possible to contract a marriage in such a way that the general rule of community could be excluded either partially or wholly. It is more likely that the partial exclusion of certain property (*e.g.* a farm or cattle) preceded the general exclusion of community. Originally no written contract was thought of. The exclusion of certain property from the community was declared to a number of witnesses at the celebration of the marriage. This practice we find in several of the old keuren (*e.g.* Gornichem, 1382). Later on antenuptial contracts were declared before schepenen, and in some towns besides the declaration before schepenen the contract had to be registered within a certain time. Thus in the Willekeuren of Naarden we find that the contract had to be registered within six weeks: *Item desgelijke die in Hijlicks voorwaerden goet loofde of voorwaerde maekte dat soud men mede bebrieven binnen ses weecken of die tuygen souden van geenen waerden weezen* (*Rechts. Obs.* vol. 2, obs. 35).

In the older keuren of the town of Delft the antenuptial contracts had to be declared before the schepenen; the later keuren required not only the declaration before schepenen, but registration as well. Originally, therefore, the declaration was only by way of proof, though later it became part of the solemnity of the contract. This registration was, however, not insisted upon by the general law of Holland during the sixteenth and earlier part of the seventeenth centuries.

Grotius in his *Introduction* says that the antenuptial agreement may be either verbal or in writing; the writing, however, was only required as evidence, and witnesses were therefore competent to prove the agreement (Grotius, bk. 2, c. 12, 4). At Utrecht, on the other hand, the only proof of an antenuptial contract admitted by the courts was the document itself (Voet, 23, 4, 3).

The idea of requiring an antenuptial contract to be in writing is undoubtedly to be sought in the *Instrumenta dotalia* of the Roman law. The regular method amongst the Romans for constituting the *dos* and the *donatio propter nuptias* was by a written instrument executed prior to the marriage. This practice was followed by the Gallo-Romans, and was borrowed from them by the Franks. The Canon law also recognised the advantage of having the promises made by the spouses put into writing and confirmed by an oath. The canonist lawyers considered that it was this oath attached to the antenuptial contract which gave to it a solemn and binding character. Besides the *juramentum* the Canon law also required the antenuptial contract to be witnessed. These *juramenta dotalia* of the Canon law began to take the form of the antenuptial contract as we now know it during the rule of the counts (Arntzenius, *De Cond. Hom.* pt. 2, tit. 1, 2 and 3, and tit. 5, 1; Rosbach, *Comp. Jur. Civ. et Con.* bk. 1, c. 8).

In 1624 a placaat was passed which required the terms of the antenuptial contract, so far as regards immovables, to be registered *coram lege loci.* This placaat, however, soon fell into disuse, and in 1658 the States of Holland admitted that the placaat was a dead letter. De Haas tells us in a note to the *Censura Forensis* (1, 12, 9) that since 1677 writing was essential for the validity of antenuptial contracts. Whether that is correct or not, it would appear that it was the constant practice to register antenuptial contracts in the public registers (Van der Linden, 1, 3, 4; *Rechts. Obs.* vol 1, obs. 42; Kersteman, *Woordenboek*, p. 195).

In the Cape Colony a Proclamation of 1793 required antenuptial contracts to be registered. This was re-enacted in 1805 by a proclamation which required that "all antenuptial contracts must be publicly notified in the Debt Registry at the Government secretary's office" (*Steytler* v. *Dekkers*, 2 Roscoe, 103).

In 1875 an Act was passed in the Cape Colony amending the law relating to antenuptial contracts. Art. 2 provides that no antenuptial contract shall be valid or effectual as against any creditor unless the same shall be registered in the Deeds Registry of the colony. Art. 9 provides that no antenuptial contract executed in the colony shall be capable of being registered unless notarially executed, though such contracts, if executed abroad, need not be notarial. Hence in the Cape Colony an antenuptial contract must be a notarial contract, and must be registered to be of any effect against third parties. As between the spouses themselves the non-registration is not fatal to the validity of the deed, and the courts have often allowed such contracts to be registered after the marriage (*Twentyman* v. *Hewitt*, 1 Menz. 156; *Steele's* case, 10 S.C. 206; *In re Houghton*, 15 S.C. 8). The law which obtains in the Cape Colony regarding the execution of antenuptial contracts is practically at present the law of South Africa.

The object of the antenuptial contract was to regulate the disposal of the property brought into the marriage, and to state in how far the law of community should apply to the particular marriage. In this respect it therefore resembled the Roman law contracts regarding the *dos* and the *donatio propter nuptias*. Hence it is not surprising to find that in the interpretation of antenuptial contracts the courts were chiefly guided by the principles of the Roman law as found in the various titles dealing with dotal property and dotal pacts.

The great bulk of our present law regarding antenuptial contracts is therefore judge-made law. Besides modifying the law of community, the antenuptial contract can also modify indirectly the relation of the spouses by stipulating that the marital power shall be excluded with regard to all or part of the wife's property. In this way the ancient *munt* of the husband can be materially modified.

Dos, Douarie and Morgengave.—Though I have said above that the principles of the *pacta dotalia* of the Roman law are consulted in order to solve disputes arising out of antenuptial contracts, I do not wish to be understood to imply that the Roman dotal law forms part of our law. The *dos* was not an institution of the early German nations.

There was a radical difference between the Roman and the German customs in regard to marriage. The Roman bride always brought some goods or money to her husband for the purposes of the joint household, called the *dos*. The rules with regard to this *dos* formed a very important section of the Roman law, and they occupy a considerable space in the *Corpus Juris*. Now, with the Germans it was not the wife who endowed the husband, but the husband who made the marriage gift to the wife. Tacitus tells us in the *Germania* (c. 18) that the wife brought no *dos* to her husband, but she received one from him. In the laws of the Franks and of the Frisians the *dos* does not appear. The *Lex Ripuaria* makes provision for the dowry which the husband gives to the wife, but not *vice versâ*, and even provides for a *dos legitima* from the husband upon his death (Hein. *Jus. Germ.* 237). The same will be found in the *Lex Saxonica*, the *Lex Lombardica*, and in the laws of the Burgundians and Bavarians (Hein. *loc. cit.* 238–40). Some German laws, however, speak of the Roman *dos*, *e.g.* the laws of the Visigoths.

It would be an error to imagine that the wife never brought anything into the marriage, for all the world over women have found more favour in men's eyes when richly endowed. With the Romans however, the custom was so general and so ingrained that a marriage without a *dos* was almost inconceivable; whilst with the Germans it was an exception for the husband to receive anything from his wife, because the general custom decreed that the husband should provide for his wife and family. This gift bore various names, such as *maritagium, dotalitium, donatio propter nuptias, vidualitium* and *doarium.* Of these the last became the most general, and gave rise to the Dutch word *douarie.* In early times *douarie* was the name given to the settlement made by the husband on the wife, to be paid out to her upon death. Gradually, however, the word obtained an extended meaning, and Bynkershoek defines it as a gift which the first-dying spouse bequeaths to the surviving spouse, and which becomes due on the day of the death of the first dying (Bynk. *Q. J. Priv.* bk. 2, c. 7). At present, therefore, *douarie* includes *dos*.

There is another gift that the German husband gave his wife which, though distinct from the *douarie*, is often confused with it. This is the *morgengaba, donum matutinum, morgengave*, or morning gift. After the spouses had passed together the first night it was a German custom for the husband to give his wife some gift as evidence that the marriage had been consummated and, as some allege, *propter virginitatem*. It differs from both the *dos* and the *douarie* in that it became the absolute property of the wife, completely out of the husband's control.

According, therefore, to the German laws of the middle ages, we had various marriage gifts, some deriving their origin from the German customs of our forefathers, whilst others were taken over from the Roman law. (1) The *dos* or *braut schatte* was a gift from the bride or her relatives to the husband; of this he enjoyed the usufruct, at his death it reverted to his widow, and upon her death it went to the children. (2) The *douarie* (*doarium*) was a gift from the husband to the wife. He administered the property during his lifetime, but upon his death the widow had the usufruct until her death or until she married again. (3) The *morgengave* (*donum matutinum*) was an out-and-out gift made to the wife on the morning after the marriage. It became the absolute property of the wife (*als ihre freie eigenthum*), and she could dispose of it as she pleased; the income derived from it was her exclusive property.

Protection of Creditors.—I shall now pass over to consider the history of the legislation of the old Hollanders and of our modern parliaments to protect the creditors of unscrupulous persons who settle their property on their wives by antenuptial contracts. The stringent provisions of the States of Holland have been very much relaxed by our modern legislators, whether wisely or not time will show.

The practice of the German husband to endow the wife was, as we have seen, continued in Holland, and the Roman custom of *dos* was also introduced. In both cases where the goods belonged to the spouses an antenuptial contract was necessary, for if no such contract existed the goods of the spouses were commingled in the *communio bonorum* Where the *dos* is given by the parents of the bride the extent of the gift will depend upon the conditions of the donation.

As trade and commerce began to extend unscrupulous merchants gave their wives such large *douarien* and marriage gifts that creditors were often grossly defrauded. In order to meet this Charles V provided in the Perpetual Edict of 1540 that the wives could not participate in these gifts unless the creditors were paid in full or unless the marriage gift came from some source other than the husband (*G.P.B.* vol. 1, p. 316). This provision of the Perpetual Edict was recognised as still binding on the colonial courts in the case of *S. A. Bank* v. *Chiappini* (Buch. 1869, p. 143); but as modern views with regard to the claims of creditors, when they conflict with those of the wife, are not so favourable to the creditors as those of the old Hollanders, the Cape legislature in 1875 repealed the 6th article of the Placaat of 1540 and enacted in its stead: (1) That no antenuptial contract shall be valid unless registered. (2) That if sequestration takes place within two years the creditors shall be preferred to the spouse upon whom a settlement has been made. (3) That if the sequestration takes place five years after registration the settlement is unimpeachable. (4) If the sequestration takes place within five years after registration then it can still be impeached, provided the creditors can prove that the alienation was made *in fraudem creditorum* and when the alienor's liabilities exceeded his assets. The Act also protects settlements by way of life policy.

In the Transvaal the spirit of this Act has also been approved of, though in detail there is some difference. Sec. 39 of Law 13 of 1895 provides that the benefits conferred by antenuptial contract are secured to the spouse in whose favour they have been made, provided that the donor was not insolvent when the gift was made, and that two years had elapsed between the settlement and the insolvency. Though the frauds on creditors by means of antenuptial contracts have not decreased, we have so modified the salutary law of Charles V that unscrupulous speculators must restrain themselves in the Cape Colony for five years and in the Transvaal for two years; after that they may launch forth in the wildest speculation and, provided they have married with a wise settlement, they need never fear that their comfort will be interfered with. When will the pendulum swing back again?

Boedelhouderschap.—In some of the provinces of the Netherlands when either of the spouses died the survivor remained in possession of the whole estate until the eldest child became a major. This custom was not confined to the

Netherlands, for we find it in some parts of Germany (Hein. *Jus. Germ.* bk. 1, sec. 293). In 1256 we find in the Keuren of Zeeland that the mother remained in possession of the estate with her children until the eldest reached the age of majority. *Mater tenebit pueros suos cum omni haereditate et rebus mobilibus donec senior habuerit annos discretionis* (*Rechts. Obs.* vol. 3, obs. 39). During the fifteenth century this was still the practice, but in the following century the law was apparently altered, and an obligation imposed upon the survivor to make an inventory within a certain time and to allot the shares to the children (Fock. And. vol. 2, p. 159).

Grotius tells us that *boedelhouderschap* was also the practice in Holland in early times, even when there was no will; but at the period when he wrote (1631) this practice had discontinued. The question is discussed by several jurists, and there can be no doubt that during the seventeenth century there was no community of goods between the survivor and the heirs of the deceased, who are considered as strangers to one another (Voet, 24, 3, 28). Within what time the inventory had to be made and the deed of partition filed depended on the rules of the orphan chambers of the towns where the deceased died. In Batavia the *boedelhouderschap* seems to have existed in 1731 (*Rechts. Obs.* vol. 3, obs. 40).

In the Cape Colony and the other South African colonies there is no *boedelhouderschap*. The estate is divided between the survivor and the heirs of the deceased, and a mortgage is passed by the survivor by which the children are guaranteed their share. This mortgage is called *kinderbewys*.

Second Marriages.—According to Tacitus some German tribes set their faces against the marriage of widows: *Tantum virgines nubebant et cum spe votoque uxoris semel transigebatur* (*Germ.* c. 19). There is, however, no trace of any such prohibition in the later bodies of German laws. Where, after the death of the first husband, the property was divided between the widow and her children by the deceased no great difficulty arose as regards a second marriage; but where the estate was kept intact and *boedelhouderschap* prevailed it was extremely awkward to have two sets of children laying claim to the property. Hence the practice became almost universal to compel the widow who sought to remarry to execute a *kinderbewys,* and so secure the property to the issue of the first marriage.

In order effectively to protect the children of the first marriage the *Lex hâc edictali* of the Roman law was introduced into Holland as part of its common law. By this *lex* the survivor could not stipulate in favour of the second spouse either by will or donation or antenuptial contract more than the smallest portion due to a child. At what period this *lex* was fully incorporated I do not know, but it certainly was in full vigour during the latter half of the sixteenth century.

The *Lex hâc edictali* formed part of the law of the Cape Colony until 1873, when by Act 26 of that year it was repealed. In the Orange Free State and Transvaal it was recognised as law to a much later date, and was only repealed in the former colony in 1891 and in the latter in 1902.

Divorce.—According to the customs of the early Germans

divorce could be arranged between the parties, or the husband could, without assigning any reason, put aside his wife. Physical incapacity or criminal conduct was always a good reason. What the formalities were of an early German divorce we do not know, though in later times the handing up of the keys by the wife appears to have been a formal act (Noordewier, p. 188). Tacitus tells us that the German husband expelled his adulterous wife from his house after cutting off her hair. She was apparently also whipped through the streets of the village (*Germ.* c. 19).

When we compare the Roman law we find that by the *Jus Antiquum* there was no practical restriction to the right of either spouse to divorce the other. Divorce proper, or *Divortium*, took place when both the spouses agreed to terminate their contractual relationship, and if the act was unilateral it was called *Repudium*. In the time of Justinian marriage could be dissolved by informal private divorce without the concurrence of the judge or the priest. From the time of Constantine, however, attempts were made to place difficulties in the way of divorces. In all cases not based upon adultery or other misconduct penalties were imposed upon the party who procured the divorce.

Bonifacius in a letter, dated *circa* A.D. 745, tells us that according to the old Saxon law if a wife committed adultery the husband had the right to kill both his wife and her seducer (Hein. 1, sec. 321). The Franks freely admitted divorce on account of adultery, and during the rule of the Frankish emperors both the secular and ecclesiastical laws permitted the husband to divorce his wife on account of her adultery (sec. 323). By the laws of the Franks the one spouse could legally divorce the other if the latter fled or maliciously deserted the former. By one of the capitularia of Pipin (A.D. 752) special provision was made that a husband who migrated from his home *ex justâ causâ*, and whose wife refused to follow him, could lawfully divorce her and marry another woman (sec. 326).

Although the Church gradually came to set its face against divorce on any ground, without papal dispensation, up to the twelfth century it had not yet made its power felt in that direction (sec. 330). After the twelfth century, however, the authority of the Church grew greater in matrimonial matters, and the early German custom of divorce gave way to the decrees of the Popes and to the Canon law. The Canon law, as we have seen, did not acknowledge the right of one spouse to divorce the other except under papal dispensation. The most that the Church allowed was a *separatio a mensâ et thoro.* The Canon law, however, recognised a decree of nullity of marriage on account of an incapacity either on the part of the husband or of the wife. The complaint was made to the bishop by either spouse; he inquired into the matter, and decided according to the circumstances. The oath of the husband, however, was always to prevail over the oath of the wife. The whole matter is fully discussed in the title *De frigidis et maleficiatis et impotentia coeundi* (*Decret.* Greg. bk. 4, tit. 15).

The Canon law as to divorce was accepted throughout the greater part of the Netherlands, but in Holland and Zeeland the customs of the Franks appear to have prevailed over the law of the Church. In these two provinces, therefore, divorce on account of adultery was always permitted by decree of the judge. Divorce on account of malicious desertion presents greater difficulty. We have seen that by the laws of the Franks divorce was granted on account of malicious desertion. How far this custom of the Franks prevailed in Holland during the middle ages it is difficult to say. I have not been able to find out whether divorce by reason of malicious desertion has always been the custom of Holland and Zeeland, or whether it was only introduced in the seventeenth century. The earliest reference to divorce on account of malicious desertion that I have been able to find is a Consultation dated 1623 (vol. 4, cons. 151). Three lawyers sign the Consultation and express the view that *maliciosa et diuturna desertio conjugis* is sufficient ground for a divorce. As this was given some eight years before Grotius published his *Introduction*, it seems strange that he makes no mention of malicious desertion as a ground for divorce. All that Grotius tells us is that "in accordance with the teachings of Christ no dissolution of marriage is allowed in this country except by the death of either of the spouses or on the ground of adultery" (1, 5, 18). Groenewegen, however, in a note to this section says, "Besides this, if one of the spouses wilfully and entirely deserts the other divorce may be applied for and granted, as was decided by the Court of Amsterdam in 1650." Brouwer quotes several other decisions to the same effect, and amongst others a decision of the Court of Holland, dated the 26th February, 1658 (*De Jure con.* 2, 18, 12).

As I have not been able to lay my hands upon the full text of these decisions, I cannot say upon what grounds they are based. In the Regelment van de Staten Generaal, 18th March, 1656, art. 91 (2 *G.P.B.* p. 2429), the States-General declared that a marriage could be dissolved on account of malicious desertion. Professor Scheltinga, in his notes to Grotius, tells us though this Ordinance was passed by the States-General it merely embodied the laws and customs of each province, and that therefore we may safely affirm that it was a pre-existing custom in Holland. The same rule was adopted by the States of Zeeland and of Friesland. De Haas in his *Consultations* (p. 352) discusses the question whether malicious desertion is a ground for divorce, but he bases his whole argument upon biblical references and the authority of the Church ordinances of Geneva.

It is therefore difficult to determine whether the right to divorce a wife on the grounds of malicious desertion is derived from the laws and customs of the Franks, or whether it was introduced into Holland after the Reformation and in accordance with the views of the Calvinists. On the one hand we have no definite authority prior to the Consultation of 1623 that such was the law of Holland, whilst on the other hand it seems inconceivable that the Court of Amsterdam would have decided a purely legal question upon the authority of the New Testament and the Church ordinances of Geneva. Moreover, if Scheltinga's account of the *Echtregelment* is correct, then there must have existed, at least in Holland and Zeeland, some prior custom allowing such divorces.

It appears to me that the probable solution of the difficulty is that there existed in olden times a custom in Holland similar to that of the Franks by which a decree of divorce was granted in cases of malicious desertion, but that this had fallen into desuetude at the time when the Canon law regulated all matrimonial causes. When, however, Holland became a Protestant province, the old custom was revived and justified upon the biblical texts referred to by Beza in his *De Divortiis*, and upon the ordinances of the Church of Geneva. At any rate, since 1650 divorce on account of malicious desertion has been a rule of the Roman-Dutch law, and has been constantly acted upon both in Holland and in South Africa.

The Canon law, as we have seen, recognised a decree of nullity of marriage on account of impotence, and our law followed the practice of the Canon law in this respect.

Legitimation.—The Roman-Dutch law, like the Roman law, admitted the *legitimatio post nuptias*, but in doing so the old Dutch law required certain formalities that were quite unknown to the Roman law, and that had their origin in the customs of the Franks (Van der Spiegel, p. 120). If the parents wished to legitimise their bastard children at their marriage, then it was a part of the ceremony for the mother to make her bastard children creep out from under her dress *ut amittant maculam geniturae*.

We see, therefore, that in the marriage law of Holland the relation between husband and wife, father and child, guardian and ward, the woman's position in the family, and in fact the general family law of Holland, were all based upon ancient indigenous customs, and not upon the Roman law; and if, therefore, we wish to go to the origin of the family law of Holland, and to trace its development, we must go to the customs of our German forefathers as we find them in Tacitus, in the *Lex Salica*, the *Jus Frisicum*, and the other collections of German laws. At the same time we must not forget that the *Lex Romana* had a great influence both on the form and on the substance of the family law of Holland as we know it to-day.

CHAPTER IV.

LAW OF THINGS.

WHEN we pass from the family law to the Law of Things we find that the influence of the Roman law becomes much greater, yet even here we constantly see how tenacious the old Hollanders were of their ancient customs. By the Roman law all rivers and harbours were *res communes,* and any one could fish in them at pleasure; but this principle was never adopted in Holland. In the days of the counts the right of fishing belonged exclusively to them, and they were entitled to make sub-grants of this right. The manner in which this right of the counts was modified in later times is a good example of the way the law of Holland was built up by various State bodies.

We have in the *Groot Placaat Boek* (vol. 1, pp. 1276 *et seq.*) a series of statutory enactments regulating the right of fishing in rivers and arms of the sea. In 1609 the States of Holland made certain provisions by which fishing with the rod was allowed, but fishing in shallow boats along the shores of the harbours and inland seas was prohibited. In 1641 the same States allowed the netting of fish in certain cases, but made very strict regulations with regard to waste and the killing of small fish. In 1621 Prince Maurice issued a proclamation prohibiting the netting of fish in Holland and West Friesland; whilst in 1613 and in 1643 the Court of Holland prohibited going on private property under the pretence of fishing with the rod. In 1649 the States-General took the matter up, and positively forbade the netting of fish in the Maas except by the lessees of fishing rights. We see, therefore, that in this one matter of fishing we have laws made by the States-General, the States of Holland, the stadhouder Prince Maurice, and by the courts. In 1795, under the influence of the Rights of Man and natural law, the right of fishing was thrown open to all, subject to certain regulations, and the law of Holland was made the same as the Roman law of Justinian.

The division of things by Justinian into *Res sacrae et religiosae et sanctae* is well known, as also the fact that these things could not be the subjects of ownership. This was the law of Holland prior to the Reformation, but after the establishment of the United Netherlands the views of men began to change, and Grotius tells us: "On mature reflection, however, it will be seen that all these things belong to man, but for different purposes; nay, more, nothing is so entirely dedicated to God that it may not occasionally be converted to other uses" (Grotius, 2, 1, 15). He therefore abandons the division of Justinian, and divides things into *Res communes, Res publicae* or *Universitatis, Res singulorum* and *Res nullius.*

The division of things into *Res mobiles* and *Res immobiles* is very important in the Roman-Dutch law. The Romans divided *Res* into *Res corporales* and *Res incorporales. Res corporales* were again divided into *Res mobiles* and *Res immobiles.* This division was based upon the fact that some things could be physically displaced without injury and others could not. Thus a definite piece of land or a house was regarded as immovable, whilst a horse or the gathered fruit from a farm was considered movable. The Roman jurists extended the meaning of the word *res* to rights and duties, and called these incorporeal things. The Roman law therefore recognised immovable and movable things, and in contradistinction to these incorporeal things, such as *jura*, *nomina* and *actiones*.

The usual division of things adopted by the early Germans was into movables and immovables. They recognised land as immovable (*vaste, liggende, onroerende goederen*) and cattle as movables (*tilbare, roerende goederen*), and into these two categories all things had to fall. When they came to deal with incorporeal things they placed them, quite illogically, in one or other of these divisions. Thus Matthaeus tells us in his *De Auctionibus* (1, 3, 13) that in the various customs and keuren of the different towns things are divided into movables and immovables, and no mention is made of the division into corporeal and incorporeal things, and that therefore debts and rents have to be classed either as movables or immovables. Voet says much the same (bk. 1, tit. 8, 18 *et seq.*). The commentators distinguish between immovables and incorporeal rights which are regarded as immovables by calling the former *immobilia* and the latter *res quae in loco immobilium habentur*. So also a similar distinction is made between *mobilia* and *res quae in loco mobilium habentur*.

It was determined at the Hague in 1572 that by the custom of that place amongst movables are included "annuities, debenture bonds of the province or towns, obligations and debts, credits, money, gold and silver, clothes, jewellery . . . horses and other living animals." To say whether a particular incorporeal right is a movable or an immovable is by no means easy. It is difficult to extract any general principle from the authorities, and this is probably due to the fact that the customs of one province or town were different from those of its neighbours.

It is sometimes said that rights affecting immovables are to be regarded as immovable, whilst those regarding movables are themselves movable. In many cases this rule works fairly well, but there are so many exceptions that it is a very unsafe guide. Thus the Court of Holland decided in 1549 that *losrenten* (*i.e. losbare rentebrieven op de comptoiren van de Provincien ofte Steden* or treasury bills) are movable.

In *Eaton* v. *Registrar of Deeds* (7 S.C. 249) the Supreme Court of the Cape Colony held that a mortgage debt is a movable asset. Now a mortgage bond undoubtedly affects immovable property, but because its principal aim is to establish a *jus in personam* it is regarded by some as a movable (Voet, 1, 8, 27). On the other hand, Groenewegen (*ad Dig.* 13, 7, 18) says: *Nomina debitorum pro quibus immobilia hypothecata sunt immobilibus annumerari solent.* The Transvaal courts have had occasion to decide whether leases for ninety-nine years should be pledged like land or like movables. The opinion expressed by Chief Justice Kotzé in *Collins, N.O.*, v. *Hugo, N.O.* (10 C.L.J. 344 and Hertzog's Rep. 176) was that leases *in longum tempus* are to be regarded as falling under the category of *res quae in loco immobilium habentur*, and this has been followed by the present Supreme Court. The above is sufficient to show how peculiar and unsatisfactory our law is upon this point.

Justinian, in dealing with the division of the Law of Things, discusses how ownership is acquired in wild beasts, in treasure-trove, and in those cases where the property of one person becomes mixed up with that of another. In most cases the Roman-Dutch law follows the Roman law, but here and there we find an important distinction. For instance, Justinian tells us that if a person knowingly builds upon the ground of another he is held voluntarily to have abandoned the materials to the owner of the soil. We learn from Zypaeus and Groenewegen that this was not the custom in Holland, for the builder under these circumstances was entitled to the value of his materials and to the necessary expenses incurred by him (Zypaeus, *Not. Jur. Belg.* p. 111; Groen. *De Leg. Abrog. ad Inst.* 2, 1, 30).

In *De Beers Consolidated Mines* v. *The London and South African Exploration Co.* (10 S.C. 368) Sir Henry de Villiers says in a judgment of extreme importance: "I am inclined to agree with those writers who regard a *malâ fide* possession as being in the nature of a spoliation, and who hold that the land should first be restored before any question of compensation can arise. As to the nature of that compensation, the high authority of Groenewegen and Voet as to the state of the law in their time cannot be gainsaid; but a different conception of the law does appear to have gained ground in the time of Van der Keessel, who places the *malâ fide* possessor on the same footing as a lessee who has made improvements without the consent of the lessor (Van der Keessel, *Thes.* 214)." On page 372 the learned Chief Justice states our law with regard to the *malâ fide* possessor to be as follows: "A *malâ fide* possessor who has affixed materials to the land and, before demand has been made by the owner, has disannexed and removed them, is not deemed to have parted with his ownership in the materials. After demand he no longer has the right to retain the land or remove the materials from the land, nor is he entitled to compensation, except for such expenditure as he may have necessarily incurred for the protection or preservation of the land. If, however, the rightful owner has stood by and allowed the erection to proceed without notice of his own claim, he will not be allowed to avail himself of his own fraud, and the possessor, though he may not have believed himself to be the owner, will have the same rights to retention and compensation as the *bonâ fide* possessor."

CHAPTER V.

POSSESSION AND OWNERSHIP.

Possession.—In a later chapter we shall see that the German nations attached a great importance to the publicity of the transfer of ownership. It is therefore not extraordinary that they should have regarded possession, one of the most important outward signs of ownership, with favour. At the same time, they were not acquainted with the Roman law right of protecting ownership as a substantive right.

In ancient times self-help was resorted to where possession had been disturbed. Gradually, however, as the State came to be recognised as the defender of rights, the importance of protecting the possessor came to be appreciated. Several of the German Codes followed the principles of the Roman law with regard to possession. Professor Fockema Andreae quotes a *lex* of the Visigoths to the effect that a person who violently deprived the possessor of a thing before appealing to a judge lost his cause, and he compares this with a *lex* of Justinian's *Code* (*Lex Visigoth.* viii, 1, c. 2, before 586 A.D. and c. 8, 4, 7; Fock. And. *Oud Ned. Burg. Recht.* vol. 1, p. 201).

In a law of the Bavarians we find the following: *Si quis homo pratum vel agrum vel exartum alterius contra legem malo ordine invaserit et dicit suum esse propter praesumptionem cum sex solidis componat et exeat* (*Lex Baiur.* xvi, c. 1, sec. 1). In one of the Frisian *kesten* of the eleventh century we find a similar provision. These provisions, however, were established not so much for the benefit of the possessor as such, but in favour of the owner and possessor.

The Canon law in the middle ages took over from the Roman law the principle that the possessor should be protected as such, and gave to the possessor the *exceptio spolii*. Thus a bishop who is deprived of his property, and brought into a court of law, need not answer the plaintiff until his property has been restored to him. After the recognition of the *exceptio spolii* the idea of an *actio spolii* was developed, by virtue of which the possessor could appear as a plaintiff and claim restitution of the property which was in his possession, but which was taken away from him by force. From the Canon law it passed into the Common law of the temporal courts. The Germanic term for possession was *weer* and the person who deprived another of the possession of a thing was guilty of *craft* or *cracht* (*vis*), as it was called at Middelburg.

In Utrecht we find the maxim *Spoliatus ante omnia restituendus sit* accepted as law in 1367. In the Instructiën van 't Hof van Holland of 1462 we find that possessory remedies were admitted "in accordance with the customs of the Supreme Court" (Fock. And. *Oud Ned. Burg. Recht.* vol. 1, pp. 200 *et seq.*). By this time the principles of the Roman law as regards possession were accepted by the Dutch courts, and so our law of possession came to be moulded upon the rules of the *Corpus Juris.*

The effects of possession are with us very much the same as they were with the Romans. In the manner, however, in which the possessor asserts and vindicates his rights there-has been a gradual development from the less to the more simple. The Roman-Dutch jurists recognised three remedies against disturbed possession—the *mandament van maintenue*, the *mandament van complainte* and the *mandament van spolie.*

In the case of the *mandament van maintenue* the applicant asked the Court to intervene, and to decree that he might retain the possession wherein he was disturbed or threatened to be disturbed. The *mandament van complainte* was for the purpose of recovering possession; whilst the *mandament van spolie* was granted where the ejectment was accompanied by force or violence. The procedure in all three cases was very formal and cumbersome, and has long ago been superseded in South Africa by a far simpler practice. We nowadays effect the same object by the ordinary interdicts, by an action, or by a writ of spoliation; the latter, though the same in name as the old Dutch *mandament*, is far simpler in its nature.

Ownership.—We saw in a former chapter that the early Germans were migratory in their habits. Caesar tells us that their principal occupations were hunting and fighting: *Vita omnis in venationibus atque in studiis rei militaris consistit;* also *agriculturae non student.* . . . *Neque quisquam agri modum certum aut fines habet proprios sed magistratus ac principes in annos singulos gentibus cognationibusque hominum, qui una coierunt, quantum et quo loco visum est agri attribuunt atque anno post alio transire cogunt* (Caesar, *De Bel. Gal.* vi, 21, 22, 29; *cf.* iv, 1).

The general meaning of Caesar is that the Germans were a migratory people, whose settlements were only temporary, and who therefore did not recognise the right of the individual *in perpetuo* to a definite plot of ground. The land was parcelled out to family groups, and was owned in common by the members of the family. As circumstances compelled the Germans to give up their migratory habits, so they gradually developed, besides their lust for fighting, a pastoral and agricultural life. Even in the days of Tacitus we find the individual occupying a house surrounded with a few acres, whilst the pasturage and lands fit for agriculture were held in common (Tacit. *Germ.* c. 16; c. 26). Every year plots were parcelled out to the various families—*arva per annos mutant.* A fixed abode, therefore, takes the place of constant migration.

During the Frankish occupation of the Netherlands individual ownership was recognised, though ownership in common by no means disappeared. In many of the villages common ownership of forest lands and pasturage existed in the Netherlands even after the eighteenth century. This was called *Markegemeenschap* or *Gemeenschap van leide, weide en bosch.* The idea was introduced into South Africa by the early settlers, and our commonages or *dorpsgronden*, so often found around South African villages, have their origin in this ancient conception of common ownership.

In the Frankish period the largest land-owner was the king, and next to him came the Church. Large tracts of the royal domain were granted to various nobles, with either a full or a limited right of alienation. Besides these there were numerous small plots which were recognised as the property of the individual freeman. Hand in hand with the development of the idea of individual ownership went the development of the means of passing ownership from one person to another. In other words, the idea of individual ownership gave birth to the ideas of tradition, division and devolution (Fock. And. *Oud Ned. Burg. Recht.* pp. 175–88).

The Romans had reached an accurate conception of individual ownership many centuries before the Germans invaded Europe. Their views of ownership were spread with their conquests through western Europe, and when the Franks drove out the Roman legions they found that the Gallo-Romans were in possession of a law of ownership far in advance of their own. The Church, through the Canon law, helped to spread the Roman law of *dominium,* so that even before the revival of the study of Roman law its doctrines as regards ownership were pretty widely accepted throughout western Europe.

After the establishment of feudal law the *dominium utile* was contrasted with the *dominium civile,* and through the *Jus Feudorum* the Roman conceptions of *dominium* and *emphyteusis* became stereotyped. The jurists of the fourteenth and fifteenth centuries took the *Corpus Juris* of Justinian as their basis, and regarded the theory of *dominium* of that system as the last word on the law of ownership. Here and there old customs were clung to by the people with great tenacity, and where they were too strong to disappear they were absorbed in the Roman system. Thus, as we shall see in a later chapter, the transfer of land *coram judice loci rei sitae* prevailed over the Roman principle, and registration came to be regarded as equivalent to tradition. Grotius therefore follows the Roman law when he says that ownership is that attribute of a thing whereby a person, though not actually in possession of it, may acquire the same by legal process, and that it consists in the right to recover lost possession (Grotius, *Intro.* 2, 3, 1 and 4; *D.* 6, 1, 23).

In its broad features, therefore, our law of ownership differs very little from that of the *Corpus Juris.* Whether the theory of the Roman law is a correct one or whether we should accept the views of modern jurists is a subject beyond the scope of this work. I shall confine my attention to the development of the law of ownership and the modifications that have been introduced at various times. How change of ownership has been effected at various times will be considered in a subsequent chapter.

In the present chapter I shall point out how we have come to vary some of the well-known Roman rules as to the acquisition of property. Thus it is a principle both of the Roman and the Roman-Dutch law that wild animals or animals *ferae naturae* are incapable of being the subject of the *dominium* of an individual except during the period that they are actually under his control. This principle has been considerably varied by the legislatures of the different South African colonies. Bees, for instance, are wild and are not considered by the Roman-Dutch law as private property until they have settled in the hive, and they continue such private property until they have flown away so far that there is no hope of their returning. Before they have become such private property and after they have ceased to be such, they and their combs become the property of the first occupant (Grotius, *Intro.* bk. 2, c. 4, 15). This principle has been modified in the Cape Colony by Act 9 of 1869, sec. 1, which provides that every bees' nest with all the bees, honey and wax is deemed to be the property of the occupier of the land.

Act 24 of 1875 of the Cape Colony placed the owner of ostriches in a better position than did the common law. The common law regarded ostriches as animals *ferae naturae*, but as the domestication of these birds increased, and as they came to be regarded as valuable assets on account of the high market value of their feathers, the legislature of the Cape Colony provided that when ostriches are domesticated they can be followed up by the owner even though they have escaped and strayed on to the land of another. By Act 12 of 1885 they have been included under the term cattle in provisions regarding the theft of cattle.

In general, however, with regard to the capture of game and fish the principles and rules of the Roman-Dutch law still apply (*Langley* v. *Muller*, 3 Menz. 588). In one respect, however, in various parts of South Africa a considerable change has been made in the law of ownership. I allude to the legislation with regard to the mining for precious metals, stones and other minerals. The Dutch jurists accepted the principle of the Roman law that the owner of land is the owner not only of the superficies, but of all that is found below the surface. Hence by the law of Holland the minerals under the ground belong to the owner of the land. Where there was no reservation in the title this was the law throughout South Africa until the mineral wealth came to be explored. The fear that the benefit resulting to the whole community from the development of the mineral resources might be curtailed if the owner had the exclusive right to the minerals led the legislatures of the Transvaal and Rhodesia to modify the principle *Cujus est solum ejus est usque ad coelum et ad inferos.*

It may be interesting to trace briefly the history of this legislation. In 1867 diamonds were discovered in Griqualand West, and legislation was soon after proceeded with to meet the new conditions. The various ordinances passed by the Griqualand West Government were eventually repealed, and a general Act for the mining of precious stones and minerals passed in 1883 (19 of 1883). By this Act the right to mine precious minerals and stones lies with the Crown where the mine is situated on Crown lands or where there is a reservation on the title in favour of the Crown. The private owner remains the owner of any precious minerals or stones found on his property. In the case of Crown lands various elaborate provisions were made for the pegging of the superficies by diggers and for extracting the minerals from the soil. In the Cape Colony, however, the legislature did not go so far as to divest the owner of his *dominium* in the precious minerals or to suspend his rights of ownership over the superficies of his property.

When gold, however, came to be discovered in the Transvaal the principle of the diamond mining Act of the Cape Colony, which applied to Crown lands, was adopted and extended to private land as well. The first interference in the Transvaal with private ownership in minerals was in 1870, when the person who found diamonds was required to pay a certain percentage of their value to the State. In

1871 the Volksraad declared that the right to mine precious minerals belonged to the State. In 1883 they went further, and enacted that the *dominium* in all precious metals and stones belonged to the State. This was modified in 1885 by giving the State the exclusive right to mine for and dispose of all precious stones and metals. This principle has been adopted by all the subsequent gold and diamond laws.

The owner's common law *dominium* in the minerals under the soil has been reduced to a very shadowy right. If in theory the *dominium* in the minerals still belongs to him, in practice he is completely debarred from enjoying his rights of ownership. The farm itself can in certain cases be thrown open to the public, and when proclaimed as a gold-field the owner's rights over the farm are to a large extent suspended. It still remains his property, but as long as the field is proclaimed he can only enjoy such parts as are not occupied by the public as claims or stands. If, however, the farm is deproclaimed, so that it is no longer subject to the gold or diamond law, then the owner resumes his suspended *dominium*.

In the Transvaal one step has led to another, and laws for the precious metals have induced legislation for the base metals as well, so that the old maxim that the owner of the soil is the owner of all that is found in it has been considerably shaken of late years. This maxim, of course, only referred to such things as nature had placed in the soil. If man placed them there, and they were afterwards unearthed, they were regarded as treasure-trove. *Thesaurus est vetus quaedam depositio pecuniae* (not necessarily coins, but anything valuable) *cujus non extat memoria ut jam dominium non habeat* (*D.* 41, 1, 31, 1). In this case we still follow the ordinary rule of the Roman law: the man who finds the treasure on his own land takes all, whilst the accidental finder of it on the land of another takes half, the other half going to the owner.

CHAPTER VI.

THE ALIENATION OF PROPERTY—IMMOVABLES.

I NOW propose to deal with the development of our law with regard to the alienation of property. I shall first confine my attention to immovable property. As soon as the individual ownership of property came to be recognised, it follows that provision for its alienation had to be made. We therefore find that the conception of individual ownership precedes the forms and ceremonies which are deemed necessary for its alienation. The object of elaborate formalities in the transfer of ground was to make all persons interested in the matter acquainted with the fact that the new occupant of the ground has established himself upon it as rightful owner.

It is, therefore, not astonishing to find that the development of the law of alienation of property ran on similar lines both at Rome and in western Europe. To a great extent the same causes no doubt produced the same results, and it is difficult to say in how far the system of alienation of property which prevailed with the Gallo-Romans influenced the German nations when they came to establish their laws upon this subject.

With regard to the Roman law as to the alienation of land we must consider two periods. The first is that period when the distinction between *res mancipi* and *res nec mancipi* was rigorously observed, and the second when all the differences between *res mancipi* and *res nec mancipi* were swept away. According to the *Jus Antiquum* things were divided into *res mancipi* and *res nec mancipi*. To the former class belonged all land, houses, rural servitudes, slaves, and beasts of burden and of draught. To the latter belonged all such things as did not fall in the category of *res mancipi*.

Now it was a characteristic of the *res mancipi* that they could not be alienated except by that formal mode of transfer which the Romans called *mancipatio*. It was not enough for the owner of a *res mancipi* to have the intention to divest himself of the ownership of the thing and to hand it over to another. In the eye of the law the consent to part with the ownership and the physical tradition of the thing were not enough to transfer the *dominium* in the *res mancipi* to the person to whom it had been handed over. A judicial and sacramental act was absolutely necessary. Without the presence of the *libripens*, the five Roman citizens, the thing to be alienated or the clod representing the land, the scales and brass, there could be no legal alienation of the property. By the solemn and formal *mancipatio* alone could *dominium ex jure Quiritium* be transferred from one Roman citizen to another.

If, however, the thing to be alienated was a *res nec mancipi*, the mere physical handing over with an intention to invest the transferee with the ownership or *dominium* in the thing was all that the *Jus Civile* required in order to make the alienation complete and legal. As the *Jus Civile Antiquum* came to be modified in the course of time, the formality and solemnity in the alienation of *res mancipi* were dispensed with, and mere *traditio* took the place of *mancipatio.* Justinian by a rescript formally abolished all distinction between the alienation of *res mancipi* and *res nec mancipi* (*C.* bk. 7, tit. 25).

At the time of Justinian, therefore, the law demanded no greater formality or solemnity in the transfer of a piece of land than in the delivery of a movable. In order to effect a legal alienation there must be an intention to transfer and an act manifesting that intention. In other words, there must be consent and tradition. Movable property could be passed from hand to hand, and therefore delivery of the thing from one person to another with the intention to transfer was all that was necessary to make the transferee the owner. Land, however, by its nature was incapable of physical delivery or *traditio*; and therefore the Romans required the transferor to point out the land to the transferee, and the occupation of the land by the transferee was considered equivalent to the delivery of a movable. No witnesses were required and no solemnity formed part of the alienation.

If now we turn to the German nations we shall find that the development of their laws regarding the alienation of property is very similar to that of the Romans. In some respects, however, there is a difference—the Germans clung to a solemn transfer far longer than did the Romans. The informal *traditio* of the later Roman law did not commend itself to the people of western Europe. The Germans preferred to adopt a more solemn form of delivery in the case of an alienation of land. They did not take over the *mancipatio* of the old Roman law, but they adopted a form of alienation in which we find some of the characteristics of the old *mancipatio*. We have seen that the *mancipatio* required five witnesses, and I shall point out presently that many of the German Codes also required the presence of witnesses (*salamannen*) in order to make the transfer legal and effective. The whole object of the *mancipatio* was to give publicity to the act of alienation, and the object of the Germans in requiring certain formalities and solemnities was also directed towards that end.

But the similarity does not end here. Just as the old Romans made use of the scales and weights as symbols, so the Germans used either a straw (*halm, calamus, stipula* or *festuca*—Noordewier, p. 238; Matthaeus, *Paroem.* 5, 2) or a clod of earth or other symbol. In different provinces different ceremonies prevailed in which the straw played an important part. One of the best known was the custom called *halmworp*. The seller repeated the conditions of sale in the presence of several witnesses, and threw the straw or twig towards the purchaser. There was a modification of this custom in which a master of ceremonies, corresponding to the *libripens* of the *mancipatio*, took charge of the straw, and when the transaction was concluded handed the straw to the purchaser. Besides the *halmworp* there were other ceremonies in connection with the purchase and sale of land, such as the *traditio curvatis digitis*, though the former seems to have been the most widely adopted.

After the introduction of writing the terms and conditions of sale were written upon parchment, and each party kept a copy of the deed. This was the practice of the Ripuarian Franks as well as of the later Saxons (Hein. 394, 396). It was probably derived from the Gallo-Romans, for we know that the *traditio per cartam* was prevalent in the Roman provinces. For a long time the *traditio per cartam* formed part of the traditional modes of transfer, such as the *traditio curvatis digitis* and the *halmworp.* The usual procedure after the introduction of the deed into the old ceremony was as follows: The terms upon which the alienation took place were set out on a parchment deed, and the clod of earth, straw or other symbol was placed upon the document. The master of ceremonies then lifted up the parchment with the symbol, held it on high and publicly announced the sale. This was called *cartae levatio.* Later on, towards the eighth century, the person who conducted the ceremony and lifted the parchment was the local judge. About this time also the practice grew up for the judge to affix his seal to the parchment (Noordewier, p. 239; Matthaeus, *Paroem.* 5). In time the parchment came to be registered with the local judge, and in this way in all probability began our registration of sales of land.

If we turn to the old German Codes we find that the Visigoths refused to recognise a sale of land unless some deed of sale was drawn up and the ground pointed out to several witnesses. The Salic law seems to have recognised some form of tradition before public officers, though this is not quite clear (Hein. *Elem. Jur. Germ.* 2, tit. 3, sec. 73).

When we turn to the laws and customs of the Netherlands we find that they adopted a practice very similar to that which prevailed in the German Codes of western Europe. As early as A.D. 1217 we find that a *traditio coram judice* was prevalent in the province of Zeeland. In the Keuren of Middelburg (1217) the following occurs: *Nullus oppidanus poterit dominium terrae dare nisi ante scabinos de Middelburch, nullus extra commanentium poterit terram dare oppidano nisi ante scabinos de extra* (No citizen can transfer *dominium* in land except before the schepenen of Middelburg, and no person living outside the town can give transfer to a citizen except before the country schepenen).

In the Keuren of West Cappel we find in A.D. 1223 the following provision: *Certa terrae emptio vel alienatio non nisi per scabinos fieri poterit.* A similar provision is found in a handvest of Count William (dated 1246), given to the town of Delft. In fact, all through the thirteenth and fourteenth centuries we find similar provisions throughout all the towns of the Netherlands, so that we may fairly infer that the custom of transferring land before some judicial officer was almost universal (*Rechts. Obs.* vol. 3, obs. 32, p. 96). Although it is difficult to find out at what date this custom was first introduced, there can be but little doubt that even before the thirteenth century a practice had been established in the Netherlands similar to that which prevailed in the adjoining German and Frankish States.

Matthaeus (*Paroem.* 5) was of opinion that the reason for this alienation *coram judice* was in order to pass the succession to land, inasmuch as the early Hollanders did not know of testamentary succession; but Noordewier points out that no solemnities were required to pass property upon the death of one member of a family to another. The editor of Matthaeus points out that the reason given by Matthaeus is incorrect, and suggests that the true reason is in order to secure publicity for the act of alienation, so that innocent third parties may not be prejudiced.

If we consider some of the additional solemnities required by the handvesten and keuren, there can be no doubt that the object of the *traditio coram judice* was to have some public record of the fact of alienation, in order to protect the innocent purchaser as well as those who had claims to the land. In a handvest to the town of Hoorne and to the district of Altena we find that a sale of land had to be notified on three Sundays in the church of Workom. In Utrecht three times a year the church bell sounded to collect the citizens to hear a public announcement of all the alienations which had taken place since the last proclamation. Similar proclamations took place at Amersfoort and other towns. We may therefore fairly infer that the system of judicial transfer was introduced (1) to secure publicity; (2) to prevent the same thing being alienated to different alienees; and (3) to allow claimants to assert their rights of *naasting*, servitude, &c.

In many towns (*e.g.* Rotterdam) it was not enough that the sale took place before the schepenen, but in order to get an indisputable title the purchaser must also have possessed the land without complaint for a year and a day. If both these conditions were fulfilled he would be protected against all claimants except minors and absentees. In order, therefore, during the time of the counts, to obtain good title to land the purchaser must have acquired the property *bonâ fide*, before schepenen, and must have been in possession for a year and a day (Grotius, 2, 7, 8). Minors and absentees, however, could still defeat the purchaser's title. Such was the customary law of Holland until 1529 (*G.P.B.* vol. 1, c. 373).

It would appear from the Placaat of the 10th May of that year, promulgated by the Emperor Charles, that the practice had grown up of declaring the sale not only to the schepenen of the place where the land was situated, but to the schepenen of a court where the property was not situated For instance, land situated outside a town was frequently transferred before the schepenen of the town, whereas the transfer should have been made before the schepenen of the district or village. In order to stop this the Placaat of 1529 provided that no subject or resident of Holland and West Friesland could sell, burden or hypothecate any land, houses, erven, tithes or other immovable property, except before the judge of the place, and at the place where the property was situated: any sale made contrary to these provisions was regarded as null and void. This proclamation did not refer to feudal property, but only to allodial, for the former kind of property was by custom transferred before the feudal lord and his court. The proclamation required the fact to be stated in a solemn document that the sale was made before the judge of the place (*coram lege loci*).

It is not clear whether at this time it was the universal practice to keep registers at the courts where the transfers took place, or whether the seal of the schepenen upon the document recording the transfer was sufficient. However, on the 22nd December, 1598 (*G.P.B.* vol. 1, c. 1956) a Placaat was issued by which 2½ per cent. had to be paid upon the purchase-price of all immovable property. By the 12th and 17th sections of this Placaat the secretaries of towns and villages are required to keep registers of all such transactions. This Placaat is therefore the probable origin of our Deeds Registry Office. The duty of seeing to the payment of the various imposts lay upon the secretary or Registrar, and this was our custom in South Africa until the Civil Commissioner was substituted for the Registrar of Deeds in this respect. The system of registration applied to all transfers, hypothecations and encumbrances of immovable property or of property *quae in loco immobilium habentur.*

In 1624 a Placaat was issued which provided against the establishment of secret burdens upon property by way of *fidei-commissum.* This Placaat enacted that no secret burden on property would be of any avail against an innocent purchaser unless the document by which the burden was created was duly registered before the court of the place where the property was situated. After the passing of these Placaats no servitude could be of any value unless registered.

We see, therefore, that as regards the tradition of immovable property from the very earliest times the Roman law did not apply. The customary law of Holland required some declaration before the schepenen, but the exact requirements depended largely on the special regulations of the place where the property was situated. In some places a declaration before any schepenen was regarded as sufficient. Charles V compelled parties to go before the schepenen of the *situs* of the property, and made all transfers void which did not comply with the requirements of his placaat. In 1598 it was not enough to go before the schepenen, but the document of sale had to be registered by the secretary upon transfer duty being paid; and later on no secret burdens were acknowledged, but every burden to be of any value had to be registered *coram lege loci.* By these means was inaugurated a complete system of land registration, and legal principles were established entirely at variance with the rules that governed the *traditio* of the Roman law.

The far-reaching consequences of these principles, entirely new to the civil law, may be seen by referring to the well-known case of *Harris* v. *Buissinné's Trustee* (3 Menz. 256). This registration system was introduced into the Cape Colony in 1714, and the Commissioners of Justice took the place of the schepenen. The Governor of the settlement granted the title to a piece of land; a copy of this title was given to the grantee and another copy lodged with the Commissioners; any transfer of, dealing with or burden imposed upon the property was noted on the copy lodged with the Commissioners; and unless the transfer, alienation or burden was noted in the register no legal consequences followed.

Such remained the practice until 1829, when the Registrar of Deeds was created, and he took upon his shoulders the functions of the Commissioners of Justice or of the secretary of the schepenen. To him, therefore, was entrusted the registration of all deeds relating to land as well as such other deeds as required registration. An indorsement upon the Register of Land became notice to all the world as to the person in whom the *dominium* lay, and as to the burdens to which the owner of the land was subject. All the various colonies of South Africa have adopted this system of land registration, and consequently land can be transferred in South Africa with very little more trouble than movables, and the purchaser knows exactly the value and extent of his title.

To sum up, therefore, the history of our law regarding the alienation of immovable property, we find:—

(1) The *Jus Antiquum* required a formal and solemn transfer of land, called *mancipatio*.

(2) The later Roman law abolished *mancipatio*, and land was transferred with no greater solemnity than movables.

(3) The early Germans required some solemnity in the transfer of land.

(4) In the fifth and sixth centuries, the transfer of land in western Europe was more like the Roman transfer of a *res mancipi* than of a *res nec mancipi*, and was carried out in the presence of witnesses.

(5) In the seventh and eighth centuries the local judge took part in the alienation, and affixed his seal to the deed of transfer.

(6) This practice was probably prevalent in Holland before the thirteenth century, for during that century we find it well recognised.

(7) During the thirteenth and fourteenth centuries the alienation of land took place *coram judice*.

(8) The Placaat of 1529 only recognised transfers, hypothecations and burdens before the schepenen of the place where the land was situated.

(9) The Placaat of 1598 established registers.

(10) In the Cape Colony, under the Dutch, the registration took place before the Judicial Commissioners.

(11) After the cession of the colony to the British this practice continued until 1829, when the Registrar of Deeds took the place of the Judicial Commissioners.

We see, therefore, that the Registrar of Deeds is the direct representative of the Judicial Commissioners, who in their turn represent the schepenen, and that these took the place of the old German judge who handed the straw to the purchaser. Is it perhaps too fanciful to go one step further back, and to connect this *halmwerper*, or straw-caster, and the *libripens* of the old *mancipatio* with some similar Aryan functionary, and to say that our Registrar of Deeds is the lineal descendant of that ancient person?

CHAPTER VII.

TRANSFER OF MOVABLES.

WE saw in the last chapter that although the early Germans owned most of their land in common, the individual ownership of immovable property was not unknown to them. With regard to movable property, however, they had attained a fairly advanced idea of individual ownership. The freeman's arms, his booty and what he had acquired in the chase were recognised as his exclusive property, and the community respected his ownership. By what procedure a German could recover his property in the earliest period we do not know. The recovery of stolen and lost property is dealt with by the Salic as well as by the Ripuarian law (*Lex Sal.* c. 37, 47; *Lex Rip.* 33, sec. 1; 47, sec. 1). If an animal was stolen the owner could recover it without the aid of legal process, provided he followed its track and found it within three days. If, however, the possessor openly bought it or obtained it by exchange, the claimant must give security that he will bring his suit against the person from whom the possessor obtained it (the *auctor*). If the claimant was unable to follow the track, or if he found it after three days, he could not recover his animal except by a formal suit. If the possessor could show that he bought the animal openly or that it formed part of his father's estate, his defence was a complete answer to the claim (Fock. And. *Oud Ned. Burg. Recht.* vol. 1, pp. 388 *et seq.*). This right of vindication was not confined to stolen goods, but applied to lost property and goods lent.

We see, therefore, from the laws of the early Franks that if the possessor could show that the stolen article had been openly bought by him from a person who was the apparent owner his title was preferred to that of the true owner. This rule prevailed in many parts of the Netherlands, and had its origin in the fact that it was inconvenient that the true owner of property which bore no special mark should be able to claim his property from one who had openly and innocently purchased it from an apparent owner. This rule was expressed by the maxim *Mobilia non habent sequelam* (*Meubelen hebben geen gevolg* or "Movables cannot be followed up").

In many places, however, the true owner was protected to a certain extent by laws which required a formal tradition not only of immovables, but of movables as well. This tradition was called *saljan* (Anglo-Saxon, *sellan*) or later *mei sale geven*. In order that the tradition might pass ownership it had to take place in the presence of witnesses (Noordewier, p. 237). In some provinces the tradition, in order to protect the alienee, required more than the mere presence of witnesses. In an old ordinance of Utrecht we find the practice set out in the following terms: "If a person delivers movable property to another in the presence of schepenen, then the person to whom the delivery has been made must take up the goods before the next day, and not leave them with the owner or hand them back to him; if the transferee omits to do this he cannot claim the goods if they come into the hands of a third person." Here the schepenen had already replaced the witnesses of the Teutonic customs, and the tradition of movables was to a certain extent assimilated to that of immovables.

The Saxon law had also adopted the maxim *Mobilia non habent sequelam*, and it provided that if the owner of a movable lent or hired out the thing to a third person, and this person sold it openly to another, the true owner lost his right of vindicating his property. The innocent purchaser acquired a better title to the property than the person who allowed it to go out of his possession (Matthaeus, *Paroem.* 7, 7).

This rule of the Saxon law was adopted by many of the cities of the Netherlands. In Holland, however, the maxim *Mobilia non habent sequelam* was not adopted to its full extent. The influence of the Roman law caused the Hollanders to adopt the rule that the owner of stolen property could follow up his property and claim possession of it.

According to the Roman law a valid transfer of movables was constituted when the rightful owner or his agent delivered the goods to the transferee with the intention of passing ownership. The mere agreement to transfer a thing did not enable the person in whose favour the agreement was made to exercise the rights of owner (*Traditionibus et usucapionibus non nudis pactis dominia rerum transferuntur*).

It was a rule of the Roman law that the *dominus* of a movable could vindicate his property in the hands of a third party. Being owner, he could bring an action *in rem* against any person in whose hands he found his property (*D.* 6, 1, 23). This is often expressed by saying that the owner has the right to follow up his property in the hands of third persons. It is therefore diametrically opposed to the maxim *Mobilia non habent sequelam.* There is very little doubt that those provinces, like Holland, which allowed the owner to follow up his property, were influenced rather by the Roman law than by Teutonic custom.

Again, it is a well-recognised principle of the Roman law that if a thing is sold for cash, and the purchase-price is not paid, the seller can claim his property in the hands of a person who has innocently bought it from the first purchaser (*Inst.* 2, 1, 41). Many cities of the Netherlands did not recognise this rule, but allowed the innocent purchaser to retain the property even though the purchase-price in the first sale had not been paid.

The city of Antwerp was one of the principal cities that rejected the Roman law rule and adopted with all its consequences the maxim *Mobilia non habent sequelam.* The reason why Antwerp adopted the latter rule was because it was a great trading centre, and because it found the right of following up property a great hindrance to trade (Matthaeus, *loc. cit.*). The Hollanders followed the Roman law, and Grotius tells us (bk. 2, c. 5, sec. 11) "that movable property may be delivered under hand or privately; nay, if any one sells or gives me any property of his which is already in my possession, it is regarded as delivered." In Holland there was no necessity to deliver the goods before witnesses or schepenen; any actual delivery transferred the ownership, and the former owner had no right to deal with the property. Unless, however, there has been a valid delivery the mere possessor, whether he had acquired the property by a just title or not, could pass no greater right to a third party, however innocent such third party might be.

With regard to sales also the Hollanders adopted the rule of the Roman law: "With regard to delivery consequent upon the sale of movable property, it is to be observed that it does not pass the ownership unless the purchaser has paid the purchase-price or given security for the same, or has got credit from the seller for the amount" (Grotius, 2, 5, 14). Though the Hollanders and Zeelanders followed this general rule they were not unaffected by the ancient customs of the Netherlands and the customs of the great trading cities of the neighbouring provinces. They admitted the maxim of the Roman law, *Nemo in alium transferre potest plus quam ipse haberet*, and they applied this to the vindication of movables in whatever way such movables may have got into the hands of a third party; but upon this rule the Zeelanders engrafted exceptions foreign to the Roman law, but prevalent in the laws and customs of their neighbours.

In Zeeland one of the principal exceptions to the right of following up property is to be found in the case where goods are sold in market overt (*vrije markt*). According to Grotius the Hollanders also adopted in this case the maxim *Meubelen hebben geen gevolg*, and did not allow the true owner to claim back from a *boná fide* purchaser at a *vrije markt* goods which had been there exposed. If the owner wished to get back again his goods so sold, he had to pay to the purchaser whatever the latter had paid at the market for such goods. Even if the goods had been stolen from the owner and sold at the *vrije markt*, the owner had first to tender the price before he could reclaim them (Grotius, 2, 3, 6). It is, however, open to very great doubt whether Grotius is correct in making this exception part of the law of Holland.

There can be no doubt that it did actually form part of the law of Zeeland, but it is not so clear that it formed part of the law of Holland. Professor Scheltinga in his commentary on the passage cited from Grotius has the following: "At the same time, although (this exception) is admitted in Zeeland and in many other places, it is not an exception universally adopted, and for that reason one has to be very careful, whenever this point is raised, to consult the local customs of the places where the case occurs, and if these are in favour of the exception they must be followed, but if there is no local custom the general rule of law must be followed, . . . viz., that the owner is entitled to claim his property from a third person without tendering any money for it, even though the latter should have purchased it *bonâ fide*."

This question has cropped up in South Africa, and different opinions have been expressed by the Chief Justice of the Cape Colony and the Chief Justice of the South African Republic. The Transvaal court in *Retief* v. *Hamerslach* (1 C.L.J. 346) held that it was a rule of the Roman-Dutch law that goods sold in market overt could not be reclaimed except after tendering the price paid for them, and that our public markets corresponded to the Dutch *vrije markt*. The Eastern Districts' Court in *Van der Merwe* v. *Webb* (3 E.D.C. 97) adopted a different view, and in *Woodhead, Plant & Co.*

v. *Gunn* (11 S.C. 4) Sir Henry de Villiers, C.J., expressed his approval of the latter decision. Sir Henry de Villiers does not say that the exception does not form part of the Roman-Dutch law, but he says, "The custom was so general that *it was regarded by some authorities* as being part of the law of the land." If, however, we go to the *fontes* of this exception, the greater probability seems to be that the custom was not actually incorporated in the general law of Holland as it had been in that of Zeeland. In the latter case, however, Sir Henry de Villiers (differing from Chief Justice Kotzé) says that markets never existed, and do not exist, in South Africa similar to the *vrije markten* of the Netherlands. Other exceptions similar to the one above mentioned are to be found in the case of goods exposed for sale by public pawnbrokers and old clothes men.

We see, therefore, if we trace the history of the law regarding sales in market overt, that in several of the German Codes the Roman law rules, *Nemo potest in alium transferre plus quam ipse haberet,* and *Id quod nostrum est sine facto nostro ad alium transferri non potest,* were modified into the principle *Mobilia non habent sequelam.* Some of the cities of the Netherlands adopted this principle in its entirety; others, again, followed the Roman law, but protected the innocent purchaser in certain specified cases—such as sales in market overt; whilst in other places there was no derogation from the general Roman rule that an owner could claim his property wheresoever it might be found. What would, therefore, at first appear to be an arbitrary exception, we find by historical investigation to be the remnant of an almost universal German principle, that an innocent third party who *bonâ fide* acquires property has a stronger claim to that property than the rightful owner.

When we turn to the law regarding negotiable instruments we find that the *Lex Mercatoria* adopted the principle of the German Codes which followed the maxim *Mobilia non habent sequelam*, and rejected the rule of the Roman law. Whatever the law of Holland may have been with regard to a horse which was stolen and sold in market overt, there is no doubt that the *bonâ fide* holder of a negotiable instrument got an indefeasible title by delivery (*Woodhead, Plant & Co.* v. *Gunn*, 11 S.C. 4). It has been a matter of some dispute whether negotiable instruments were known to the Roman law; but whether they were or not there is no authority in the Roman law which supports the view that the owner of a bill of exchange could not follow it up in the hands of a third party, and that bills formed an exception to the general rule. The better view seems to be that bills of exchange were unknown to the Roman law, and that they were first introduced long after the Roman rule had disappeared. One fact, however, is clear, that with regard to their transfer and ownership the maxim *Id quod nostrum est sine facto nostro ad alium transferri non potest* was abandoned, and the rule adopted *Mobilia non habent sequelam.*

CHAPTER VIII.

TRANSFER OF PROPERTY POST MORTEM.

I SHALL now leave the law regarding the transfer of property *inter vivos* and pass over to the succession of property *post mortem.* I have no intention of writing a disquisition on the law of succession, but I shall endeavour to trace the history of our law and to point out how it has developed into what it now is.

I must preface my remarks on the historical development of testamentary and intestate succession by stating at once that the bulk of our law upon these subjects is taken almost bodily from the Roman law. If any one has any doubt about the enormous influence which the Roman and Canon laws have exerted upon the Dutch law, I should refer him to these important branches of our law.

It is true that Germanic customs have survived and altered in detail the Roman law, but these modifications are quite insignificant as compared with the mass of Roman law principles which govern our law of testamentary and intestate succession. Our law with regard to the interpretation of wills, the whole of our law of legacy and the bulk of our law of intestate succession are to be found in the *Digest, Code* and *Novels* of Justinian. The law of executors is due to the Canon law. At the same time many of the details in the execution of wills, a part of our law with regard to the distribution of the property of deceased persons and many of our rules of intestate succession vary considerably from the *Jus Civile.*

In South Africa English influence has also modified the old Roman law in many respects, and by increasing the power of the executor has deprived the Roman law heir of his important position. The English idea of a full and free power of bequeathing one's movable property has entirely swept away the Falcidian and the Trebellian Fourth, and has so modified the law regarding second marriages as to do away with the provisions of the *Lex hâc edictali.*

Testamentary Succession. — There can be but little doubt that the succession *ab intestato* is an older institution than testamentary disposition. The goods of the deceased were at first seized by his nearest relatives and divided amongst themselves. As society became more organised custom determined what persons were entitled to the goods of the dead man. The will of the deceased must, however, in many cases have determined how the property should be divided, though in Europe it was not until a comparatively late date that the will of the owner came to be regarded as an effective legal method of disposing of property. As we are chiefly concerned with the customs of the Germans and the law of the Romans in tracing the development of this branch of our subject, we can follow with a fair amount of accuracy the change from intestate to testamentary succession.

Tacitus tells us in his *Germania* (c. 20) that the Germans were not acquainted with the custom of making wills. According to him the goods of the father were divided amongst his children, and if there were no children, then amongst his brothers. If there were no brothers the succession went first to his paternal and then to his maternal uncles. (*Heredes tamen successores suicuique liberi: et nullum testamentum. Si liberi non sunt proximus gradus in possessione fratres, patrui, avunculi.*) Amongst the Romans, on the other hand, the will was quite an old institution. It has been pointed out by Maine (*Ancient Law,* p. 190) and others that the Roman will was really a means by which the devolution of the family was regulated. It was a mode of declaring who was to be the head of the family upon the decease of the person in whom was vested the *patria potestas.* Inasmuch, however, as the whole tribe was interested in the succession, we find that the oldest form of Roman will was made before the whole tribe (*testamentum calatis comitiis*). Later on the will was made by a solemn and fictitious sale of the inheritance (*testamentum per aes et libram*).

During the Empire the idea that the will designated the person into whose hands the *patria postestas* was to pass had been completely lost, and the forms and ceremonies were in consequence considerably relaxed. Codicils were recognised as valid, even though devoid of the formalities required by a will, and by them legacies and *fidei-commissa* might be imposed on the heir. Already in the time of Cicero the will signed by the testator and seven witnesses was recognised by the praetor as a document capable of transferring the inheritance.

It is not my intention to go deeply into the history of the Roman will. I only wish to recall to the mind of the reader the fact that when the Romans overran western Europe they introduced amongst the Gauls and Germans the form of testament which was then in general use. Although, as we have seen, it was not the custom of the German tribes of western Europe to make wills before the advent of the Roman legions, yet we must not suppose that the will of the father as to how his property was to be divided was entirely ignored by his sons, for even in very primitive people we find the wish of the father respected. But there was no law that enforced the will of the deceased.

After the Roman conquest, and after Roman ideas had spread throughout western Europe, the Roman testament became part of the law of the conquered tribes, and was adopted almost universally wherever the Roman rule prevailed. When the Franks overthrew the Roman power they did not cast aside the Roman law, but adopted the greater part of its provisions. The Roman testament was one of the customs they took over from the Romans, and there is a number of wills extant in the time of Dagobert (seventh century) executed according to the provisions of the Roman law (Hein. *De Historia Juris,* 11, 19; Matthaeus, *De Nobil.* c. 27).

In the Netherlands, however, free testation was not recognised universally. Schelling, in his *Histori van het Notarisschap,* p. 406, tells us that in some parts of the Netherlands wills were not recognised at all, whilst in others the testator could only legally dispose of his movables by testament. In Gelderland and at Roermond only such immovable property could be disposed of as the testator had acquired by his own industry, whilst all inherited land went to the person to whom it would have gone if the deceased had died intestate. In these places, however, movable property could be disposed of by will. This was the law at Roermond even as late as the eighteenth century.

In how far the Batavians took over the Roman will, or in what way, we cannot tell, for there are no wills extant which were made in the Low Countries earlier than the sixth century. There are copies of some wills in existence made by ecclesiastics (*geestelyken*) during that century, *e.g.* the wills of Remigius, who spread the Christian faith in Belgium, and of Willibrod, Archbishop of Utrecht. Their wills were made in Latin, and more or less according to the Roman form; but whether they made their wills according to the law of the Netherlands or according to the customs of the neighbouring provinces, whence they came, is an open question.

There is no doubt that the strict requirements of the Roman law were not adhered to in western Gaul. Nor is this to be wondered at when we consider that the Roman soldier could make a valid will without the solemnities of the civil law, and that these soldier wills must have been very prevalent in the conquered provinces, where the military element was so predominant. Some of the wills were only signed by the testator; others, again, were signed by the priest who executed the will. It is clear that many of the formalities of the Roman law were considered unnecessary, and the Canon law did a great deal towards simplifying the old Roman will (Ritterhuisius, *Differentiae*, bk. 4, c. 1).

By the Canon law a will could be executed by a parishioner before his priest and two witnesses. It was the aim of the ecclesiastical lawyers to follow the *Jus gentium* as much as possible, and to do away with such solemnities as did not affect the Church; hence it admitted women as witnesses to a will. *Praeterea jus canonicum etiam feminas testes in testamento admittit quas repudiat jus civile. Rationem reddunt doctores hanc, quia jus canonicum in testamentis spectet jus gentium quo jure nulla debet esse differentia inter masculum et feminam* (*ibid.*).

Owing to the great power and influence of the bishops in the Netherlands, there can be but little doubt that the provisions of the Canon law with regard to solemnities in the execution of wills were very largely adopted throughout the Netherlands. It is in the priest and the two parishioners that we are to seek the origin of our will before the notary and two witnesses, and not, as I shall show later on, because a notary is supposed to be equivalent to three witnesses (*Hol. Cons.* vol. 4, c. 245; Coren, *Obs. Decis.* 31). During the ninth century we have the will of Count Ansfrid, which was written by a priest named Walther and signed by two witnesses who were named, and by two others who were not named in the will. Sometimes the will was only signed by the priest and not by the testator, as is the case with the will of Theodoric of Sassem (1270 A.D.) (Schelling, pp. 451, 452).

It appears, therefore, that it was customary for the testator to dictate the will to a priest and to get some persons to sign as witnesses. The number of witnesses varied, and there existed apparently no fixed rule as to the exact number required. The rule of the Canon law requiring the priest and two witnesses was not a rigid one until it was incorporated in the *Corpus Juris Canonici* of Gregory IX, though the Church had already intimated in the twelfth century that

HH 2

a will should be passed before a priest and two witnesses (*Decretales* of Alexander III).

In Holland during the rule of the counts a testator sometimes wrote out his will, and added a request to the count to affix his written approbation. The count put his seal to the will, and it was then recognised as legal even though unwitnessed. In Utrecht and Middelburg the seal of the bishops took the place of that of the count. All that the secular and ecclesiastical courts required during the twelfth and thirteenth centuries was that the will should be executed in such a public way as to leave but little doubt about its authenticity. This method of proof for so important a document came to be regarded during the fourteenth century as insufficient, and therefore during this century we find the practice growing up of requiring a will to be passed before the secretary or the schout and two schepenen (Schelling, p. 459). In 1372 we find in a handvest of Jan Blois, given to Texel, that "no person can deprive his heirs of their inheritance unless he does this before a baljuw and two mannen or before a schout and four schepenen."

This custom of making a will before some public officers as representing the count became more and more widely spread, and seems to have been the most general way of making a will during the earlier part of the fifteenth century. Towards the middle of the fifteenth century, however, the notary and two witnesses appear as persons before whom a will could be executed (Schelling, p. 462). The notary was an old institution, well known in the time of Justinian to both the eastern and the western Empire. In France and in the Netherlands he was very often a priest, and was attached either to the imperial court or to the court of a bishop. It is more than likely, therefore, that the priests who drew up wills before the fifteenth century were notaries as well, and thus acquainted with the legal requisites of a will. The custom of allowing wills to be executed before a priest and two witnesses appears to have survived in the country (*ten platte lande*) even as late as the beginning of the seventeenth century (Coren, *Obs.* 31).

Van Leeuwen is of opinion that wills were not executed before a notary and two witnesses until the middle of the fifteenth century, and we know that in Leyden in 1449 the seals of two schepenen were still required. The exact date, however, at which the practice of allowing a will to be executed before a notary and two witnesses was introduced into the Netherlands is a matter of doubt. Some writers think that the general practice of making wills before notaries grew out of the Placaat of Charles V of May, 1524, by which the office and number of notaries was regulated. We know, however, this much, that the practice of making wills before notaries was general in Holland during the latter half of the sixteenth century, and rapidly spread throughout the whole of the Netherlands. In 1583 we find in the Keuren of Leyden: "No legacy or last will, whether by way of testament or codicil, will be valid unless made before the Court, or before two or more schepenen, or before an approved and admitted notary and at least two witnesses" (Schelling, p. 463).

It would therefore appear that the Roman rule requiring seven witnesses to a will was never a prevalent custom in the Netherlands, although a will so executed was not regarded as invalid. The Canon law had at an early date introduced the priest and two parishioners, and these were later on superseded first by the schout and two schepenen, and then by the notary and two witnesses. After the sixteenth century the favourite way of executing a will was before a notary and two witnesses, though the will before the schout and schepenen never completely died out; for even in the time of Van der Keessel (*Thes.* 294) such a will was the only one by which children could be validly disinherited.

We find it stated by some writers (*e.g.* Van Leeuwen, *Roomsch. Holl. Recht.* 3, 2, 7) that the notary and two witnesses had their origin in the five witnesses required by the constitutions of Leo the Sophist, the notary being equivalent to three witnesses. This is clearly a very fanciful suggestion. It was never the custom of western Europe to require five witnesses, whilst a notary's signature in the case of wills was never held to be equivalent to three witnesses. The constitutions of Leo were never accepted as law in the western Empire. They are included in many editions of the *Corpus Juris*, but Cujacius says of them: *Novellarum constitutionum Leonis Sophi . . . tantum abest ut aliqua sit apud nos auctoritas ut nec aetate ejus unquam obtinuerit*" (Cujac. *Obs.* 17, vol. 3, p. 467). The provision, therefore, of Leo that five witnesses instead of seven would suffice in order to make a valid will was never recognised as law. Moreover, the Roman law nowhere states, as far as I can find, that the signature of a notary is equivalent to that of three witnesses. Van Leeuwen relies on *Novel* 73, c. 7, sec. 1, but that passage certainly does not justify the conclusion he draws from it. Nowhere in the middle ages do we find that five witnesses were taken as the requisite number in the execution of wills.

I have asked myself the question why the canonists have hit upon a priest and *two* witnesses, and the Hollanders upon a baljuw and *two* mannen or a schout and *two* schepenen, and later on upon a notary and *two* witnesses. I would venture the following explanation, though I must confess I have not seen it suggested by any Dutch writer. The Roman law required at least two witnesses to attest a fact (*C.* 4, 20, 9; *D.* 22, 5, 12). Documents to prove a debt, such as receipts, required three witnesses, and the same rule applied to loans and deposits (*C.* 4, 2, 17; *Novel* 73, c. 2). As these documents formed the bulk of every-day transactions, the number three came to be looked upon as the accepted number of witnesses to documents in general. From these documents the rule was extended to wills, and as the priest was the person who usually drew up the will in the middle ages, he was naturally one of the persons to sign it. Moreover, as an ecclesiastic his testimony was of great value in the courts, especially when wills were referred to the ecclesiastical courts. When later on the notary took the place of the priest, he also signed as one of the three witnesses which most documents required. The testimony of the notary always carried weight, but when it stood alone it was of no more value than that of any other single witness. *Tabellionis solius fides non sufficit*, says Cujacius (*ad Nov.* 73, vol. 2, p. 975). It therefore became customary for the notary, like the priest, to draw up the will and to sign it with two other persons, so as to make up the three witnesses which occurred upon most documents.

We have seen that the ordinary will of the Roman law required seven witnesses, and that this will was retained by the law of Holland. The privileged or holograph will of the *Code* of Justinian (*C.* 6, 23, 21, 1) was also taken over by the Dutch law. In the Cape Colony, however, another form of will taken from the English law was introduced side by side with the testament of the old Roman-Dutch law. This form was found to be so convenient that it has become universal in South Africa, and is usually known as the "underhand will." Ordinance 15 of 1845 provides that a will signed at the foot or end thereof by the testator and two witnesses shall be regarded as a valid will; though, if the document is composed of two or more leaves, each leaf must bear the signatures of the testator and the witnesses. Such a form of will was wholly unknown to the Roman-Dutch law, and is one of those numerous examples in South Africa where English law and English practice have been introduced in order to modernise and simplify that Roman practice which had been adopted by custom, by legislation or by judicial decision as part of the law of Holland.

By the Roman law the heir could not be a witness; but the legatee was admitted, because he did not represent the testator, and could merely claim his legacy from the heir. Women and children under fourteen years were also rejected by the civil law. The Roman-Dutch law followed the civil law in this matter, but modified it to this extent, that no one whose testimony was suspected on account of interest could witness a will (Lybrecht, vol. 1, pp. 252–57). Legatees, relatives of the testator within the fifth degree, the son or father of the heir, the father or son of the notary, were excluded by the Roman-Dutch law from being witnesses. Some authorities also exclude executors and guardians appointed under the will. All this was simplified in the Cape Colony by Act 22 of 1876, and since then every person above the age of fourteen years, who is competent to give evidence in any court of law, is competent and qualified to attest the execution of a will; but if the person who witnesses a will is benefited by that will, then he forfeits any interest or appointment conferred upon him by the will, as well as any interest conferred upon his wife, or, in the case of a woman, upon her husband.

It will therefore be noticed that the Roman law adopted the principle that a person who could not make a will could not witness one, and that certain specified persons could not attest a will, not because they were interested in the will, but for other reasons. The Roman-Dutch law took over the disqualifications of the civil law and added to them certain other persons, because their testimony as interested persons might be liable to suspicion. If the will was signed by these persons the document was void *in toto*, for "documents which are not executed according to the formalities required by the common or statute law are void, even though the omission is of a trifling nature" (Wassenaar, *Prak. Not.* c. 18, n. 12). The principle adopted by the colonial statute is diametrically opposite. The document remains valid, but the person who testifies to the document loses all his interest therein. This carries out to the fullest extent the rule of the civil law, *Nullus idoneus testis in rē suā intelligitur* (*D.* 22, 5, 10).

It is a well-known principle of the Roman law that the institution of the heir was an absolute necessity to the validity of the will. The institution of the heir was the *caput et fundamentum totius testamenti.* This rule was never adopted in the Netherlands, and in the laws of many places it was specially laid down that the institution of the heir was not necessary to the validity of a will. From this it followed that a person could die partly testate and partly intestate. In this way another inroad was made upon the Roman law, for by that system if two or more persons were instituted heirs for a certain or uncertain part, and one did not succeed to the inheritance, then the other took the whole estate as the representative of the deceased. But inasmuch as by Dutch custom a person could die both testate and intestate, the heir who has been instituted to a definite portion of the estate succeeded to that portion and to no more; and if the succession of a co-heir who had also been instituted to a definite portion failed, then his share went to the next of kin. By the Roman law a person could not be instituted heir *ex certo tempore vel ad certum tempus,* but by the customs of the Netherlands there was nothing to prevent such an institution. Nor did the Hollanders take over the rule that the testator must disinherit those children who are in his power *nominatim;* for, as we have seen, the peculiar power of the Roman father was never recognised by the Germans. A father could, therefore, pass over his child in silence, and yet the will remained valid (Van der Keessel, 306). The child in such a case was left to claim his legitimate portion by the *querela inofficiosi testamenti.* For the same reasons the Roman-Dutch law rejected the pupillary and exemplary substitutions.

We see, therefore, that a great deal of the subtlety of the

Roman law relating to wills was done away with in Holland. This arose from the fact that the idea of bequeathing one's property was unknown to the German people, and therefore when they did adopt the practice of making wills they took over such portions only as were essential. The Roman law itself showed them how this could be done in a way far simpler than the law that applied to the ordinary population of the Empire, for the law regarding wills had been, even before Justinian's time, considerably modified with regard to soldiers. The Germans of western Europe were brought in contact far more with Roman soldiers than with Roman civilians, and so they became better acquainted with the simpler form of Roman will.

Reservatory and Codicillary Clauses.—There are two clauses that we constantly find in our wills, which have their origin not in the Roman law, but in the customs of the Netherlands. I refer to the reservatory and codicillary clauses. We do not find any mention made of the reservatory clause in the Roman law, and we do not know precisely at what time the clause became universal in the Netherlands. It was not introduced by any special enactment, but its use gradually spread until it came to be regarded by custom as a necessary part of a will. Van der Schelling (*Geschied. der Notarisschap,* p. 239) tells us that he has not found any will earlier than 1349 which contains the reservatory clause. In that year a will was made at Utrecht with the clause substantially in the form we know it to-day. The words used are: *Salvo tamen mihi jure revocandi, mutandi et disponendi aliter de praemissis quamdiu vitam duxero in humanis.* It seems difficult to assign any reason for the introduction of this clause; for the testator, according to the civil law and according to all the German Codes, always had the right to alter his last will either by a new will or to a certain extent by codicil.

In the fourteenth century it does not appear to have been the practice to reserve to the testator the right to alter or add to the will either upon the document itself or upon a separate sheet over his signature. In the next century, however, the reservatory clause was considerably amplified, and in a will of 1433 we find a testator instructing his executors not only to carry out his wishes as expressed in his will, but also those expressed upon any document signed by him, or sealed by him, or executed under his instructions by a notary or some other trustworthy person, and that any such document should be regarded as having the same force and effect as if it formed part of the will.

The codicillary clause, or salutary clause, as it is often called, was introduced into Holland some time prior to the fourteenth century, for during that century it was freely used all over the Netherlands. In the will of 1349, mentioned above, the words of the codicillary clause are, "This is my last will and testament, . . . and if it be not valid as a testament, I desire that it will at least have effect as any other kind of testamentary disposition." Both these clauses were of extreme importance when the distinction between wills and codicils was rigidly attended to. If the testator forgot to put in a reservatory clause he could not alter his will by an informal testamentary instrument. In 1896 the Supreme Court of the Cape Colony decided that unless a testamentary instrument purports to be executed under the reservatory clause, it will not be valid unless duly witnessed (*Van der Wall* v. *Van der Wall's Executors*, 13 S.C. 316). Now, however, that all the technical distinctions between wills and codicils have disappeared, for an heir can be appointed as well by codicil as by will, it seems difficult to understand why these clauses should retain the effect which they had in olden times; one would have thought that *cessante ratione cessat lex.*

CHAPTER IX.

EXECUTORS.

Grotius does not treat of the duties of executors, but as we have been dealing with testaments it will be advisable to consider at this stage the history and development of the law with regard to executors. Testamentary executors do not occur anywhere in the *Corpus Juris*. The idea, however, of requesting some person to see to the due execution of the will of the testator seems to have prevailed in the time of Justinian. The Emperor Julian in one of his decrees (*C.* 1, 3, 46) states that if a dying person makes a disposition *ad pias causas,* and requests the bishop to see that his wishes are carried out, then the bishop should act in accordance with these instructions. Here we have the idea of executorship in a crude form. The passage refers to a charitable gift, and the person empowered to see it carried out is an ecclesiastic, and so far as we know the appointment of executors was confined to cases of this kind. There may have been executors in other cases, but we do not know of their employment. The early German Codes, as far as I can discover, make no mention of executors.

In the middle ages it became the custom for the clergy, when disposing of their goods by will, to appoint some trusted friend to supervise the execution of their wills (Glück, vol. 34, p. 5). This was done in order to prevent the bishop from seizing the goods of the deceased for such purposes as he might deem fit. The Council of Cologne in 1266 recognised the custom, and decreed that every cleric had the right of appointing an executor to supervise the execution of his will and the disposition of his property. Any person other than the executor who interfered in the matter rendered himself liable to excommunication. When there was a charitable gift in the will the request was generally addressed to the bishop. In the course of time the bishops came to regard it as their right to carry out the wishes of the testator whenever the will contained a gift *ad pias causas*, and in this way the bishop of the diocese gradually came to assume the functions of an executor *perpetuus* (Ritterhuisius, *ad Nov.* p. 97, sec. 78).

From gifts *ad pias causas* the practice gradually spread to other cases, and as a rule the executor remained an ecclesiastic. The Canon law came in time to deal with the subject, and laid down certain rules which executors were required to follow. They were obliged (1) to make an inventory; (2) to sell the goods by public auction; (3) to pay the testator's debts; (4) to hand over to the Church the legacies due to it *pro salute animae;* and (5) to hand the balance over to the heir. This procedure was adopted mainly with a view to secure bequests made to the Church without the outside interference of laymen. The advantage was soon perceived of requesting some trusted person to see that the heir did not fail in his duty of distributing the estate in accordance with the testator's wishes.

During the fourteenth century we find in Holland numerous Latin wills in which executors are appointed (Schelling, pp. 493 *et seq.*). Sometimes he is called executor, sometimes *testamentarius*, and at other times *manufidelis*. In one extant will the testator appoints his executors in these terms: *Suos executores, manufideles, fideicommissarios et dispositores videlicet honestos viros.* In another the executors are described as *executores manufideles et procuratores in rem suam.*

During the sixteenth century the custom of appointing executors was already fairly general, and we find wills both in Latin and Dutch in which the appointed executors are requested not only to supervise, but also actively to take part in the distribution of the testator's assets. Gudelinus, writing probably about the end of the sixteenth century, tells us that it was a custom in the Netherlands to appoint executors, and where no executor was appointed the bishop *ex officio* acted as executor in all matters relating to charitable gifts (*De Jur. Nov.* bk. 2, c. 9, *in fin*). Whether, however, the bishop had the right to act in other matters as an executor *ex lege* was a matter of dispute.

The ecclesiastics claimed the right to act as *legitimi executores* in all cases, and they based their right upon the fact that the execution of the last will of a deceased person was in itself a *pia causa*, and that it was therefore their peculiar Christian duty to see that the will was properly carried out. They contended that the execution of a will belonged to that class of case where the Canon law should be preferred to the Civil law. It was also manifest that they did not always act from motives entirely disinterested. Though this view seems to have met with some approval in the southern provinces of the Netherlands, it certainly found no favour in Holland. After the establishment of the Republic this view was not even seriously urged so far as I am aware.

Executors were therefore introduced by no special law, but in the course of time came to be recognised by custom. It was usual for the testator to request some person during his lifetime to act as his executor, and because the executor was a creature of later custom and not of the civil law, he was free to accept or reject the burden. In this respect he differed from the tutor, who was bound to accept the tutorship unless he could plead some valid excuse recognised by the law. There was no law which could compel an executor to act as such if he did not choose to.

In the early wills (fourteenth and fifteenth centuries) the appointment of executors is generally found at the head of the will, and the executors often appear and declare that they will undertake the duty imposed upon them. Sometimes the executor seals the will with his own seal. An executor was therefore an agent appointed by the testator during his lifetime for the sole purpose of seeing that his wishes were duly attended to after his death. The Church stepped in and framed provisions as to how the agent was to carry out his mandate, and these rules were gradually adopted by the civil courts. Before the fifteenth century executors were not given the powers of assumption and surrogation: these arose at a later date.

During the sixteenth century the custom of appointing executors was fairly general, and during the seventeenth century their duties were so clearly established by custom that they came to be incorporated into the common law of the country, and were as clear and well defined as those of the heir (Wassenaar, *N.P.* c. 18, secs. 168 *et seq.*).

From what has been said it is manifest that the law of Holland dealt almost exclusively with the duties of the testamentary executor. At the same time there is some probability that the executor dative was to a certain, though very slight, degree also known to the law of Holland. Voet tells us that executors were sometimes appointed by the court *sed potius bona hereditaria per executores aut tutores testamento datos, vel a magistratu dandos, administranda sunt donec certum fuit posthumos nullos nascituros esse,* unless indeed the phrase *vel a magistratu dandos* only refers to the word *tutores.* I have searched all the authorities known to me, and nowhere can I find a specific case where an executor dative had been appointed. The ecclesiastical law undoubtedly did recognise the executor *legitimus,* and it is quite possible that in Holland the bishop may have appointed some person in his stead to administer the gifts *ad pias causas.* Such a person would have been an "executor dative." In England we know the ordinary did appoint executors dative to administer intestate estates.

In the powers of the executor *legitimus* of the ecclesiastical courts we have no doubt the germ of the appointment of an executor dative, but as he was not recognised in the province of Holland he could only have supplied the idea of appointing some one other than the heir to administer intestate estates. The name *executor dativus* is no doubt derived from the Canon law, where it is used to distinguish the person who administers an intestate estate from the executor *testamentarius* and the executor *legitimus* or a *lege constitutus.*

The executor dative, as we know him in South Africa, was

created by Ordinance 104 of 1833, and it would appear as if the executor dative of that Ordinance owes his origin more to English than to Roman-Dutch law. The practice, however, of appointing officials to act as the executors of persons who died without wills was not unknown at the Cape at the time of the English occupation, and was no doubt derived from a similar practice in Holland. Every town in Holland had its Orphan Chamber, and amongst the duties of the Orphan Chamber was the administration of intestate estates of which the heirs were minors. At the Cape the Orphan Chamber was established, according to Tennant, in 1691 for the administration of testate and intestate estates in which there were minor heirs or heirs resident abroad. The duties of the orphan masters were constantly revised and amplified.

In 1803 were drawn up (though first printed in 1804) a number of instructions (of which I have a manuscript copy) for the administration of insolvent as well as of intestate estates. It would appear from these instructions that the Orphan Chamber and the *Desolate Boedelkamer* were the only bodies who administered intestate estates, and that the estate was never handed over to a kinsman or friend of the deceased in order to be wound up by him. The winding up and administration of an intestate estate was apparently confined to the heir and to officials appointed for that purpose. Art. 3 of these instructions says: "The orphan masters shall as a general rule take charge of and administer the estates of all persons who die in this settlement or its dependencies and whose heirs, either *ex testamento* or *ab intestato*, are minors or absentees, unless the Orphan Chamber has been specially excluded." If the estate was found to be insolvent by the orphan masters they handed the matter over to another official body called the *Desolate Boedelkamer.* This latter institution had charge of all insolvent estates, all estates to which there were no heirs *ex testamento* or *ab intestato*, and, lastly, of all estates over which a curator had been appointed (*Instructie voor Desolate Boedels*, ch. 1, art. 1). Whenever the heirs, either *ex testamento* or *ab intestato*, refused to adiate either *simpliciter* or under benefit of inventory or refused to make use of their *jus deliberationis*, then the creditors could apply to have the estate placed in charge of the *Desolate Boedelkamer* (ch. 2. art. 10).

It would therefore appear that all estates *ex testamento* were liquidated by the testamentary executors, or, if there were none, by the heirs and then administered by the latter. If, however, the heirs were minors or absentees the Orphan Chamber, unless specially excluded, took charge of and administered the estate. Should it happen, however, that the heirs repudiated the inheritance the *Desolate Boedelkamer* administered the estate for the benefit of the creditors. If the inheritance devolved *ab intestato* the legal heirs, if majors, took charge of the estate, but if minors the estate was placed under the administration of the Orphan Chamber. If the estate was insolvent it was handed over to the *Desolate Boedelkamer.* Such was the practice until 1833, when the whole administration was altered into the system now in vogue throughout the greater part of South Africa. I shall revert later on to the change which was then introduced, but in order to appreciate the alteration I shall first deal with the duties of executors.

The duties of the testamentary executor began with the

death of the testator and ended when the estate of the deceased was liquidated and settled. In the early days he was a *nudus mandatarius*, whose only duty was to see that the heir carried out the wishes of the testator *ut haeres defuncti voluntatem impleat et perficiat*. He did not so entirely take the place of the heir that he acquired any real right by virtue of which he could demand to be placed in possession of the goods of the deceased (Schrassert, vol. 3, c. 102, sec. 6). If, however, he was entrusted with the administration as well, his powers were somewhat greater. In this case he was called *erffuijter*, and then *per omnia repraesentat personam defuncti ad tempus statuto praefixum*. Gradually, however, his powers and duties were enlarged, and in the eighteenth century they may be roughly said to have been: (1) In the presence of a secretary and schepenen or of a notary and witnesses to put his seal to all the rooms and coffers of the deceased; (2) to see to the burial of the deceased; (3) to make an inventory of the assets of the deceased; (4) to pay all debts due by, and to receive all debts due to, the estate; (5) to liquidate the estate by sale of all such property as was not specially disposed of by will; (6) to pay out to the legatees and creditors what was due to them; and (7) to hand over the balance to the heir (Kersteman, vol. 1, p. 128, *sub voce Executeur*).

The executor therefore gradually usurped the functions of the Roman law heir. In practice the executor appointed a notary or other qualified person to make the inventory, to draw up any deed of partition that might be necessary, and to frame a general account of the administration of the estate. The executor was also entitled to incur such expenses as were necessary to liquidate the estate. Inasmuch as the executor was regarded as the trusted friend of the deceased, the law did not require him to pass a bond of suretyship for the due administration of the estate; but if he abused his trust, or acted *dolo malo,* he laid himself open to a criminal prosecution known as *raroof.* If the testator appointed two or more executors *conjunctim,* then the law presumed that he relied upon their joint judgment as long as it was possible for them to act together, and therefore they had to perform their acts of administration in conjunction; but if one of them died the survivor was entrusted with the sole management of the estate.

It was often very inconvenient for an executor to liquidate an estate which consisted of assets scattered over the various provinces. Where the testator appreciated this difficulty during his lifetime he specially provided in his will that the executor might assume some definite person to act with him. In time a general power was given to the executor to employ any person or persons he might think necessary. In this way arose the powers of assumption and surrogation with which executors were usually clothed. In the early wills these powers were never given to executors and were unknown to the law of Holland.

This was the law with regard to testamentary executors which prevailed at the Cape during the first quarter of the nineteenth century. There may have been some special modifications introduced by the various instructions to the orphan masters, but materially the law prevailed as above stated.

In 1833, by Ordinance 104, a great change was made in the relation between the heir and the executor, and also in the administration of intestate estates. As we have seen above, the old Roman-Dutch law placed the administration of the estates of deceased persons in the hands of the heir. After the practice of appointing executors had grown into a recognised custom the most important duties connected with the administration of estates passed from the heir into the hands of the executor. Towards the end of the eighteenth century there was a growing tendency on the part of the testamentary executor to usurp the functions of the heir. This usurpation was completed in the Cape Colony by fusing the rights and duties of the Dutch executor with those of the English executor of personal estate. According to the English practice the personal property of the deceased vests in his executor upon his death, but the executor does not become the administrator of the estate until he is armed with letters of administration. These letters of administration were granted before 1857 by the ecclesiastical courts, and are now granted by the Probate Division of the High Court of Justice.

The English practice differed, therefore, considerably from the Roman-Dutch practice with regard to the administration of estates *ex testamento*. In dealing with estates *ab intestato* a statute of Edward III (31 Edw. III, c. 11) provided that where a person died intestate the ordinaries should depute the next of kin or the nearest friends of the deceased to administer his personal estate. The administrator derived his right from the ecclesiastical court, and that right only vested upon receipt of letters of administration. Until the letters were granted the intestate estate vested in the judge ordinary, and now vests in the President of the Probate Division. In the administration of intestate estates the difference between the Roman-Dutch and English law was most marked, and the English procedure was infinitely simpler and better. Ordinance 104 aimed at a fusion of the Dutch and English practice, and succeeded in establishing a simple and satisfactory system of administration.

Just as the ordinary of the ecclesiastical court was entrusted with the duty of looking after the estates of deceased persons, so Ordinance 104 conferred upon the Master of the Supreme Court similar duties. If there was an executor testamentary, then the Master, by granting him the letters of administration taken from the English practice, recognised him as the true representative of the deceased; and if there was no will the Master took certain prescribed steps in order to enable the nearest friends of the deceased to appoint a representative called an executor dative. After letters of administration have been granted either to the executor testamentary or dative, the whole estate of the deceased vests in the executor. The heir, whether *ex testamento* or *ab intestato*, therefore ceased to hold the important position he held under the old Roman-Dutch law, and became very nearly akin to a legatee. The administration of the estate is no longer entrusted to his care, but devolves entirely upon the appointed executor, and the heir is consequently no longer responsible for the debts of the deceased whether he adiates or not (*Oosthuysen* v. *Oosthuysen*, Buch. 1868, p. 63).

If the heir under the old Roman-Dutch law adiated and did not claim the benefit of inventory, he was liable for all the debts of the deceased. In 1890 the Supreme Court of the Cape Colony was called upon to decide whether Ordinance 104 had or had not modified this rule of the common law. The court decided that the law had been altered and that the heir was no longer liable. Sir Henry de Villiers in the course of the judgment said: "I am quite satisfied that whether the heir be sued by the creditor or by the executor, he stands in no worse position than an ordinary legatee who has received his legacy from the executor. Such a legatee may be liable to the *condictio indebiti* at the suit of the executor who overpaid him, or to a direct action for a refund at the suit of a creditor, but beyond what he has received his liability does not extend" (*Fischer* v. *Liquidators of Union Bank*, 8 S.C. 54). Ordinance 104 gave some new rights to executors, and placed upon them some new duties, but on the whole executors retained the rights and duties which they had under the common law. The English practice which was taken over related in England entirely to the personal estate of the deceased; but as by the Roman-Dutch law no distinction was drawn between the administration of real and personal estate, the Ordinance adopted the same procedure whether the estate consisted entirely of land or of movable property or both. The result of the change has been somewhat curious. As we have seen above, the origin of the executorship was a desire to provide some person to see that the heir duly administered and properly distributed the assets of the deceased; whereas now the heir, who is the residuary legatee, has in his own interests to see that the executor does not fail in his duties as a due and proper distributor of the assets entrusted to his care.

Formerly the executor looked after the heir, now the heir looks after the executor.

The words executor and administrator are so constantly used together that we are apt to forget that they differed originally very considerably with respect to their rights and duties. Moreover, the term administrator as used in English law-books is not the same person as our administrator. By the term "executor" the Roman-Dutch lawyers meant the person appointed by the testator in order to liquidate the estate, to pay the debts, call in all moneys due to the estate, sell the goods, pay the legatees, and hand over the balance either to the heir or to some other person mentioned in the will. The administrator was the person to whom the executor was required to hand over the assets of the deceased, and whose duty it was to deal with such assets according to the directions of the testator. In most cases the executor and administrator would be the same person, but sometimes they were different. Suppose, for instance, the testator had left a large part of his estate under a *fidei-commissum*, in that case the executor would liquidate the estate and hand over the property subject to the trust to the administrator, who would collect the rents or other revenues and pay them out to the appointed heirs (Lybrecht, vol. 1, c. 30, sec. 4). In the Canon law the administrator of an intestate estate was the person appointed by the ordinary or executor *a lege constitutus*, and was called the *executor dativus*. These terms were taken over by the English law, and an administrator was an executor appointed by the ordinary to represent the intestate estate of a deceased person. Sir Henry de Villiers stated the distinction very clearly in *Hiddingh* v. *Denyssen et al.* (3 S.C. 441), in the following terms: "Some confusion was caused through the introduction of English legal phraseology into the arguments. The English 'administrator' corresponds to our 'executor dative,' our 'administrator corresponds to some extent to the English 'trustee,' and the English 'executor' corresponds to our 'executor testamentary.'"

CHAPTER X.

LAW OF INTESTATE SUCCESSION.

HAVING touched upon the principal points in the law of testamentary succession, I shall now consider the origin and development of the law of succession *ab intestato*. There is no portion of the Roman-Dutch law which is more confusing to the student than the law of intestate succession which prevailed in Holland and the neighbouring provinces. Van der Vorm in his *Versterfrecht* deals with more than thirty different forms of intestate succession. The differences, it is true, are often insignificant, though in many cases they are considerable.

If we ask ourselves how these differences arose, a little investigation will show that the cause is to be sought in the fact that the provinces of the Netherlands were occupied by Franks, Frisians and Saxons, and that each of these nations left behind some portion of its law of intestacy. Not only did the Netherlands start with at least three systems of intestacy, but no section of the people rigidly adhered to any one system, for each district, nay, almost every town, introduced variations in the law. There was no general law of succession like the 118th *Novel* of Justinian, though at the same time there were certain fundamental principles adopted by the Germans, and these were not unlike the rules of the Roman law. After the almost universal reception of the Roman law some order was introduced into the law of succession, though particular customs survived in different provinces.

Hence we find towards the end of the sixteenth century the legislatures of the various provinces were anxious to introduce the principles of the 118th *Novel* into the various systems of succession, but the people were unwilling to accept the Roman law in its entirety. The result of this was a compromise, such as the Intestate Succession Law of 1580. I shall now proceed to trace as briefly as possible how we in South Africa came to adopt the law of intestate succession which prevails in all the colonies.

In very ancient times the Germans had no legal conception of individual ownership of land. The ground belonged not to the individual, but to a group of persons. This idea of joint ownership of land has not yet died out even in Europe, for common ownership of land prevails to-day in many parts of Russia. The only occupations of the ancient Germans were fighting and agriculture.

It was comparatively late in the history of the Germans that they lost their habit of migrating from one part of Europe to another. A people with such nomadic habits could hardly have acquired an idea of individual ownership. When the tribe had settled for a time in a particular locality the land fit for ploughing was parcelled out to the various families, and the head of each family administered the portion assigned to his household. When, therefore, the head of the family died the other members naturally continued to occupy the land which had been parcelled out to them. In this way the children of the deceased house-father came to be recognised as his intestate successors. At first in all probability the daughters were not recognised as having any right, and the sons took all the property.

If the father died without leaving any children, his wife was not considered capable of looking after the property. She herself was regarded as a minor, *in mundio*, and therefore unfit to deal with her husband's land. Hence the nearest male relatives of her deceased husband became the heirs to the property (Schröder, pp. 62, 276, 326, 717, 748; Brissaud, pp. 1520 *et seq.*). If the father of the deceased was alive, he no doubt succeeded to the land and took charge of the widow. If he were dead his sons, the brothers of the deceased, had the prior claim.

There were apparently at a very early date two principles of succession recognised. According to the one, women were excluded from the succession, whilst according to the other their rights were recognised. Where the exclusion of women prevailed the mother transmitted no rights to her son, and the relatives of the mother had consequently no claim upon her goods. Where, however, the woman had a right to succeed to the property, two sources were recognised, and the property was divided into the part which came from the father's side and that which came from the mother's family. Hence, according to the customs of some of the German nations the property which came from the paternal relatives went back to them, whilst the maternal relatives took what had come from the mother's side. This was embodied in the maxim *Paterna paternis materna maternis* (Brissaud, p. 1522).

The importance of these customs will be more fully appreciated when we come to deal with the Aasdoms and

Schependoms succession of the Roman-Dutch law. We see, therefore, that the ancient German customs provided that the goods of the deceased should go first to his descendants, then to his ascendants, and lastly to the collateral relatives in the family. Although this was the general principle the details of the law of succession varied considerably. In the succession of children some Codes admitted the sons and daughters to equal shares, whilst others preferred the sons to the daughters (Hein. *Elem. Jur. Germ.* bk. 2, tit. 9, sec. 216).

The Salic Franks excluded the daughters from any share in the immovable property (*ibid.* sec. 219). The Ripuarian Franks excluded the daughters from that part of the father's estate which he had inherited from his ancestors. In dealing with the succession of ascendants, the Salic and Ripuarian Franks called the father and mother to the succession of their children with equal rights, whilst the later Saxons preferred the father to the mother. When we come to the succession of the collaterals we find the greatest diversity in the various German Codes (*ibid.* secs. 234 and 240). There was no uniform law as to succession *per stirpes* or representation. The Franks and Saxons admitted the principle in many cases, but in some parts of the Netherlands, *e.g.* in Utrecht, it was not introduced until the sixteenth century.

Many of the peculiarities of the old German Codes are reproduced in the Netherlands. In the province of Holland and West Friesland there were two distinct systems of succession, generally known as the Aasdoms and Schependoms Recht. And as it is from these two systems that we in South Africa have derived our law of intestacy, it is necessary to know the principles of these modes of succession and the later legislation which modified them into our present law.

Grotius (bk. 2, c. 28) deals very fully with the origin of these systems and the districts in which they prevailed. He tells us that originally the province of Holland and West Friesland was divided into two provinces. The northern province was more inclined to adopt the Frisian laws and customs, whilst the southern province preferred those of Zeeland. The northern parts therefore followed in their law of intestate succession the *Jus Frisicum*, whilst the southern parts adopted the law of the Salian Franks. The two systems came in course of time to be known as the North Holland or Aasdoms Law, and the South Holland, Zeeland, or Schependoms Law. As the terms "Aasdom" and "Schependom" are frequently used, it will be as well to get an accurate idea of what they mean.

The term "Schependoms Recht" means the *recht* or law prevailing in those parts where the schepenen pronounce the verdict or *doem*. The "Aasdoms Recht" means the *recht* or law prevailing in those parts where the *asing* pronounce their *doems* or judgments. In Friesland law was administered by a kind of jury system; the judge was the schout, and the jury that gave the verdict was called the *geburen*. Now the *asing* was the person who was chosen as foreman by the *geburen*, and as he pronounced the verdict or *doem* of the jury the law administered in Friesland was said to be the *asing-doems recht* or Aasdoms Recht.

It would be quite out of our province to discuss in detail

these two systems, and it will be sufficient to point out their radical differences. The rule of the Schependoms recht was *Het goed moet gaan aan de zyde daar het van gekomen is* (Van der Vorm, p. 29)—the property must go to that side whence it came. Representation *ad infinitum* was also a cardinal principle (Grotius, 2, 28, 6). Since, however, it would have been difficult to ascertain with certainty from whom the property came, the rule of the Roman law was followed—*Ad ea potius debet aptari jus quae et frequenter et facile quam quae perraro eveniunt*, and therefore it was taken as a *presumptio juris et de jure* that the property should never go to the surviving side because no property of the survivor had to be distributed. If, therefore, a child dies without descendants, and there is one surviving parent, then that parent does not succeed, but the inheritance will go to the next of kin of the deceased parent, *i.e.* in the first instance to the brothers and sisters of the deceased. If both parents are dead the property goes to the four quarters, *i.e.* to the relations of the four grandparents.

The cardinal principle of the Aasdoms law was *Het naaste bloed erft het goed* (Van der Vorm, p. 29)—the nearest blood relation succeeds to the property; but the *jus representationis* was not admitted. This maxim, however, is far from correct, for a grandchild was preferred to a father. It must therefore be so qualified that the descendants are preferred to ascendants or collaterals. Inasmuch as these two systems started with such different principles, when we come to the details of distribution the diversity becomes very great.

In 1580 the States of Holland attempted to bring some uniformity into the laws of intestate succession, and a law was promulgated which contained to a great extent the provisions of the Schependoms recht, but also took over some of the provisions of the Aasdoms recht (art. 19, *G.P.B.* vol. 1, p. 335). This law, on the whole, met with the approval of South Holland, but the northern portion, and especially West Friesland, could not be persuaded to adopt it, more especially as by their Grondwet they could not be compelled to admit any change in their ancient laws (Scheltinga, *ad Grot.* 2, 28, 2).

One of the greatest innovations introduced by the Ordinance of 1580 into the Frisian law of North Holland was the *jus representationis.* The principle of representation had always been familiar to the Franks, and is distinctly laid down by one of the capitularia of Childebert (Hein. bk. 2, sec. 228). It was also admitted as part of the later Saxon law (*ibid.* sec. 233). It apparently never formed part of the Frisian law, and was certainly not the law of Gelderland. The law of Zeeland and South Holland, which adopted the Frankish customs, recognised representation in the Schependoms recht, but the law of North Holland rejected it from the Aasdoms recht. This principle had in all probability been taken over by the Franks from the *Lex Romana,* where it was a recognised rule. The Ordinance of 1580 provided that representation should take place *ad infinitum;* but this did not please the inhabitants of the northern parts, and therefore an attempt was made by means of an Interpretation Act in 1594 to remove the difficulties, but this was of no avail (13th May, 1594, *G.P.B.*).

To give another example of the radical difference between the Ordinance of 1580 and the pre-existing law: If there were one surviving parent and brothers and sisters of the deceased, then the old Aasdoms law gave the whole of the deceased's estate to the surviving parent, as the nearest in blood, whilst the old Schependoms recht divided all the assets between the brothers and sisters, to the exclusion of the surviving parent. The Ordinance of 1580 (art. 21) gave to the surviving parent the whole estate in accordance with the Aasdoms law. This greatly displeased the inhabitants of South Holland, who were willing to compromise, but were not willing to accept the law of the North Hollanders in its entirety, and therefore on the 18th December, 1599 (*G.P.B.* vol. 1, p. 343) a new Placaat was issued, which met with the approval of both North and South Holland, and by this Placaat the law of intestacy was henceforth regulated.

The preamble to this Placaat states that inasmuch as the burgomasters of Harlem, Leyden, Amsterdam and other towns on the east side of the Rhine have often complained that the rules of succession laid down by the Politique Ordonnantie of 1580 differed too much from the Aasdoms recht, to which the people of North Holland and West Friesland were deeply attached, and inasmuch as it is impossible to frame a law of succession that will satisfy both North and South Holland, therefore the States of Holland and West Friesland decree that a new law be framed applicable to the districts and towns of North Holland and West Friesland named in the Ordinance.

The consequence of this Placaat was that there was one system of intestate succession in South Holland and some other specially named towns regulated by the Political Ordinance of 1580, and another system for North Holland and West Friesland regulated by the Placaat of 1599. As an example of the compromise effected by the Placaat of 1599, I shall mention the case before alluded to, where there is a surviving parent and brothers and sisters of the deceased. The Schependoms law as contained in the Ordinance of 1580 was rejected, and so also the old Aasdom's law, and a course midway between the two was adopted by which the surviving parent took half and the brothers and sisters the other half of the intestate estate. The effect of these Placaats was to do away entirely with the old Aasdoms and the old Schependoms recht, and therefore the law introduced by these new statutes was known respectively as the *New Schependoms Recht* and the *New Aasdoms Recht.*

This was the state of the law in Holland; but outside of Holland in her colonies grave doubts arose as to what law should be applied in the case of persons resident in or journeying to or from the East and West Indies. The case of the West Indies was first dealt with, and in 1629 the States-General passed a resolution that the law of succession as contained in the Political Ordinance of 1580, together with the customs of South Holland and Zeeland, as being the best known, should be henceforth followed in the possessions of the West India Company.

In 1634 (*G.P.B.* vol. 2, p. 1322) the question of intestate succession was raised before the States-General with reference to a person who died in India, and it was then decided that a person in the service of the East India Company was considered to remain a citizen of the place where he had lived in Holland before he went to India, and his estate was to be distributed in accordance with the laws of his original domicile. This apparently gave rise to great difficulties and confusion, and therefore in 1661 the States-General of the United Netherlands devoted their attention to the East India Company, and an Ordinance or Charter was passed (*G.P.B.* vol. 2, p. 2634) of which the following is an abridgment:—

The States-General proclaim that whereas it has been represented to them that it is advisable to pass an Ordinance establishing a fixed law upon the matter of the intestate succession of such persons as die either when resident in the East Indies or when on their way thither or on the return journey, and whereas the Political Ordinance of 1580 has already been adopted for the West Indies, where it has become an established law, therefore they decree and determine that henceforth the intestate succession of all persons dying in the *East Indies* or on the journey should be regulated by the provisions of the Political Ordinance of 1580 and the amendment of the 13th May, 1594, with this further proviso: "That if only one of the parents of the deceased be alive, whether mother or father, then the surviving parent together with the brothers and sisters of the deceased, whether of the whole or the half-blood, together with their children and grandchildren by representation, shall be called to the succession of the deceased in this proportion, the surviving parent whether mother or father shall take one-half and the brothers and sisters and their children and grandchildren shall take the other half. It must, however, be well understood that in such a case the half brothers and sisters, their children and grandchildren, must be the descendants of the deceased parent. If, however, the deceased has left no brothers and sisters, but brothers' and sisters' children or grandchildren, then these children and grandchildren succeed *per representationem* together with the surviving father or mother to one-half of the deceased's estate. If there are no brothers, sisters, or brothers' or sisters' children or grandchildren living, then the surviving father or mother succeeds to all the goods of the deceased in preference to any collateral; but if there should be any immovable property, land or houses in the estate of the deceased, then the law of the province or place where the immovable property is situated shall be followed with regard thereto."

In this Placaat the States-General make special mention of all lands, towns and people in the East Indies, but do not in any way refer to the Cape Colony or other dependencies of the East India Company. In Berbice and the island of St. Eustatius the same law was applied that obtained in the East Indies, but, strange to say, in Surinam and in Curaçao the Aasdoms law was adopted as contained in the Placaat of 1599.

The Ordinance of 1661 does not mention the Cape settlement, which was then very recent, and no doubt persons who died there in the early days were considered in the same light as those who died on the voyage. Later on, however, the settlement became considerable, and then no doubt some definite system of succession must have been adopted. Tennant in his *Notary's Manual* (7th ed. p. 168) tells us that the administration of intestate estates at the Cape of Good Hope was vested in the Orphan Chamber. In 1714 the Orphan Chamber had a difficulty with regard to succession, and asked the Governor to furnish it with instructions for the distribution of the estates of intestate orphans. Tennant does not tell us why the Orphan Chamber had the difficulty, nor does he say that the difficulty arose out of the interpretation of the Ordinance of 1661. The Governor in Council did not clear up the special difficulty submitted, but passed a resolution directing the Orphan Chamber in future to follow the Placaat of 1580 and the Interpretation Ordinance of 1594.

According to Tennant no mention was then made of the Ordinance of 1661 applying to the East Indies, nor does he tell us when and how it was declared to apply to the Cape as well as to India. It does seem strange that if the Ordinance applied to the Cape Colony as well as to the Indies that the Orphan Chamber should have had the difficulties it had. Moreover, if there was no doubt as to the applicability of the Ordinance of 1661, why did not the Governor refer to it, but direct the Chamber to follow the Ordinances of 1580 and 1594? The more so because the Ordinance of 1661 not only refers to the former Ordinances, but introduces something new. It is true Tennant tells us (p. 166) that the Charter of 1661 and the Ordinances to which it refers establish the order of succession *ab intestato* at the Cape, but he quotes no authority for this proposition. In *Raubenheimer* v. *Executors of Breda* Sir Henry de Villiers makes the same statement, but the only authority for the proposition which was quoted by the Bar or by the Bench was the *Notary's Manual.*

It may of course be correct that the Ordinance of 1661 did apply to the Cape, but the words do not justify that view, for the Ordinance says that it shall apply "to all lands, towns and people in India," and to persons dying on the outward or home journey. Nor does the fact that the Governor in Council in 1714 made no mention of the Ordinance of 1661 tend to show that it was regarded as obtaining at the Cape. There may be some other authority for the statement that the Ordinance of 1661 established the Cape law of succession. I regret, however, that I cannot give it here.

In 1838 the case of *Spies* v. *Spies* (2 Menz. 476) came before the Supreme Court, and counsel in that case made the following admission: "That by the Placaat of 10th January, 1661, the law of North Holland, including the Political Ordinance of the 1st April, 1580, and the interpreting Ordinance of 13th May, 1594, was made the law of this Colony."

It was assumed after that date that the law of North Holland, that is to say, the Aasdoms recht, was the law of intestacy in the Cape Colony. In 1880, however, the question was again raised in *Raubenheimer* v. *Executors of Breda* (Foord, 111), and then the Supreme Court decided that the law of the Cape Colony as to intestate succession was regulated by the Ordinance or Charter granted by the States-General to the East India Company on the 10th January, 1661. The law of the Cape Colony is therefore based upon the Political Ordinance of 1580 (which is not the law of North Holland), upon the Interpretation Ordinance of 1594, and upon the Charter of 1661. In all these cases it has been assumed that the law of the 10th January, 1661, applied to the Cape as well as to the East Indies.

We have seen that in *Spies* v. *Spies* the Court decided that the intestate law of the Cape Colony was the law of North Holland, *i.e.* the Aasdoms recht. In *Raubenheimer* v. *Executors of Breda* the Court overruled *Spies* v. *Spies*, and decided that the intestate succession on the whole is regulated by the Politique Ordonnantie of 1580. Now this Ordinance is founded upon the law of South Holland, that is to say, upon the Schependoms recht. Article 19 of the Ordinance of 1580 provides that with regard to the inheritance and rights of succession the States abolish and annul the civil law, the customs and usages in the said territories of Holland and Friesland hitherto in existence with regard to the rights *ab intestato* where there has been no will or testament with respect to allodial and immovable property, and they decree that in future the provisions of the Ordinance shall be followed.

Grotius (2, 28, 27) in commenting upon this article says: "If any cases should occur which are not clearly provided for they will have to be decided not according to the Roman law, for that has by the above-mentioned Ordinance been abolished, but according to the general principles which we have laid down, and, moreover, according to Schependoms law wherever the same used to obtain." Later writers (Scheltinga, *ad Grot.* 2, 28, 2; Van der Vorm, p. 49) have expressed grave doubts as to the correctness of this interpretation of Grotius, and some maintain that the Roman law has only been repealed in so far as it is in conflict with the provisions of the Ordinance of 1580. Voet, however, seems to approve of the view expressed by Grotius (Voet, 38, 17, 26).

We see, therefore, that the law of intestate succession of the Cape has its origin in the old Frankish law of succession, but that this old law was considerably modified by the principles of the Frisian laws as contained in the Aasdoms recht; whilst the *Lex Romana*, as part of the ancient customs of both Frisians and Franks, modified the German law of inheritance to a considerable extent. The law of intestate succession is therefore an excellent example to show us how necessary it is to understand the history of the Roman-Dutch law in order to appreciate the links of that historical chain which binds us so indissolubly to the remote past of that race from which both Dutch and English are sprung.

CHAPTER XI.

SUCCESSION OF FISCUS.

THE early Germans in all probability knew nothing about inheritances reverting to the chief upon the failure of near relatives. The succession of the Fiscus was taken over from the Roman law, and was well recognised in West Friesland in 1289. It would appear that the Fiscus could claim if there were no relatives nearer than the fourth degree. Grotius was of opinion that by the Roman law the Fiscus took the inheritance if there were no relatives nearer than the tenth degree, and therefore he regards this as the Roman-Dutch law (2, 30, 1). Voet and Van der Keessel show that Grotius made a mistake, and that though his proposition might have been true for the older Roman law, it was not true as regards the law at a later period. They therefore reject Grotius' limitation to the tenth degree. Van der Keessel, moreover, tells us that the Supreme Court in 1622 decided that there existed no limit to the right of succession (*Thes.* 364).

The Roman law by the edict *unde vir et uxor* allowed one spouse to succeed to the goods of the other where the deceased had left no relatives, but Grotius tells us that such rights of succession *ab intestato* were never recognised in Holland. It has been pointed out by several writers that this statement is too general, and that the exclusion of the spouse was not the practice where the Aasdoms law prevailed. The Schependoms law did, however, exclude the spouse, and if by the Politique Ordonnantie, art. 19, the Roman law is entirely excluded, then it would appear that in South Africa also the Treasury, and not the surviving spouse, would be entitled to the *bona vacantia.*

Another ground of forfeiture to the Crown was the failure on the part of relatives to claim their inheritance within a year and a day. This seems to have been a custom pretty widespread in Holland, though it was never admitted in Utrecht. In the latter place the Crown could only step in after the lapse of the third of a century.

By the Cape Ordinance 105 of 1833, sec. 36, all inheritances not claimed within forty years are forfeited to the Crown. Our present law in the Cape Colony is therefore far more liberal than the law of Holland.

CHAPTER XII.

SUCCESSION "AB INTESTATO" AS REGARDS ILLEGITIMATE PERSONS.

THE law with regard to the succession of illegitimate persons in the time of Grotius was as follows: An illegitimate person was just as much his mother's heir as her legitimate offspring. When an illegitimate child died and left no descendants his mother, if alive, took nothing, but if she were dead the estate was divided into two parts, the one half going to the Crown and the other half to her nearest relatives; if, however, the child was born *ex prohibito concubitu*, the whole inheritance went to the Crown (Grotius, 2, 31, 4).

The origin of this law is to be sought partly in the Roman law and partly in that modification of the *Lex Romana* which had been adopted by the Germans. The German law undoubtedly excluded illegitimate children from succeeding to their father (Hein. *Elem. Jur. Germ.* bk. 1, p. 156). Unlike the Roman law, the Germans made no difference between *naturales liberi* and *spurii*. This rule was universally followed in Holland, so that nowhere in Holland did the illegitimate child succeed to the goods of his father. With regard, however, to the intestate estate of the mother, the law of Holland in very early times adopted the maxim *Een wyf maakt geen bastaard* (Matthaeus, *Paroem.* 1, 4, 8), and therefore the illegitimate children succeeded to the estate of their mother even though she had legitimate offspring. The illegitimate succeeded in the same way as the legitimate.

When, however, we come to consider the succession of the mother to the goods of her illegitimate child, we shall find that different rules prevailed at different times. In the early days of the counts the mother did not succeed at all to the property of her illegitimate child, for the whole estate went to the count. Gradually, however, various handvesten allowed the mother to succeed to some portion, and usually one-half went to the mother, whilst the count took the other half. Later on several towns obtained the privilege of allowing the mother to succeed to the whole of her illegitimate child's estate. Grotius, however, did not recognise this change in the law, for he held that in no case could the mother or her relatives succeed to the whole.

Later writers have pointed out that though this may have been the Schependoms law, it never was the Aasdoms law, for there the rule prevailed, *Het naaste bloed erft het goed.* If the mother be not dead, then according to Schependoms law the property must go whence it comes, and as it cannot come from a living person the mother and her relatives are excluded. Now inasmuch as the law did not recognise the father, the goods were *bona vacantia,* and so reverted to the Crown. If, however, the mother was dead, then her relatives would be entitled to one-half, and the other half would go to the Crown as taking the place of the father.

Blondeel, in his *Verhandelingen over Van der Vorm's Versterfrecht* (p. 237), discusses the whole question and adopts the view of Van der Vorm that the mother should succeed if she is alive, and that the mother's relatives, and not the Fiscus, should take the whole property if she herself had predeceased her illegitimate child. The whole discussion shows how much more humane men had grown since the time of Grotius. In one respect, however, the law remained as harsh, cruel and barbarous as it was in the seventeenth century. Unfortunate children born *ex prohibito concubitu* or *ex damnato coitu,* as the canonists say, were wholly cut off from the inheritance of their parents, and if such children died without having disposed of their property the Crown, and not the parents, was entitled to the succession. Some writers go so far as to class among these unfortunates the offspring of a married man and an unmarried woman. The origin of this harsh law, which visits the sins of the parents upon the children, is to be found in the *Code* of Justinian (*C.* 5, 5, 6).

The Emperors Arcadius and Honorius deprived the offspring of an incestuous union of all right to succeed to their mother; Justinian went further and deprived them even of aliment. The law of Holland took over the Roman law with all its cruelty, and cut off the child born in incest from the succession to its mother's estate. It is difficult to see any reason for this law, and its inhumanity seems revolting to modern ideas. I can understand a provision whereby the parents are deprived of enjoying the estate of the child, but why the child born of incest should not succeed to its mother's estate like any other illegitimate child I fail to appreciate.

CHAPTER XIII.

SERVITUDES AND EMPHYTEUSIS.

Servitudes.—Our law regarding servitudes is based almost entirely on the Roman law. The influence of German customs on this branch of our law is extremely small. During the middle ages the Germans introduced servitudes which were hardly known to the Roman law, as, for instance, where my slave had to work so many days for my neighbour; where I had to put my sheep in my neighbour's fold so that he might acquire the manure; where I was obliged to grind my corn at my neighbour's mill or buy my beer from his brewery. Many of the German servitudes consisted not only in *patiendo*, but also in *faciendo:* this was the case with the rights instanced above, called *jura bannaria.* These rights are called servitudes by the writers on German customs (*e.g.* Strijkius and the author of the *Speculum*), though they do not conform to the Roman law definition of a servitude (Hein. *Jus. Germ.* ii, secs. 37 and 38). They are created by grant, and cannot be acquired by prescription.

Some of these *jura bannaria* existed in the Province of Holland. They resembled servitudes in so far that the obligation went over from the owner of a property to his alienee. Thus if I, as the owner of Blackacre, were compelled to grind my corn at the mill on Whiteacre, by the sale of the property I got rid of the obligation as far as I myself was concerned, but the new owner was compelled to grind his corn at the mill on Whiteacre. The right, therefore, consisted in *faciendo*, whereas the Roman servitude, with perhaps a few doubtful exceptions, consisted in *patiendo*.

With regard to the constitution of servitudes, Grotius simply tells us that they are created by grant and subsequent sufferance (Grotius, *Intro.* 2, 36, 2). He draws no distinction between the Roman law and the Roman-Dutch law upon this point. Groenewegen, however, in his note on Grotius as well as in his *De Legibus Abrogatis* (*Inst.* 2, 3, *ult.*) points out that the constitution of servitudes in Holland differed from that adopted by the Roman law. Servitudes were placed by the Hollanders under the same category as alienations of immovable property, and as the latter could not be effected so as to prejudice third parties except before the judge of the place where the immovable was situated (*coram lege loci*), it followed that a servitude affecting land could not be created so as to bind third parties unless registered before the judge of the place where the land was situated.

As far as I know, there are no special placaats which provide for the registration of servitudes, nor are there any special provisions in the Placaats of 1529 or 1598 relating to servitudes. The practice of requiring servitudes to be registered is apparently due to an extension of the spirit of the placaats by analogy.

The *Code* (4, 15, 7) provides that where a testator or where the law prohibits the alienation of a property a servitude could not be imposed upon that property. It was therefore argued that where the law prescribed a certain procedure in the case of an alienation of land no servitude could be imposed upon that land except in the same way as an alienation was effected. This was apparently the view taken by the Court of Holland when it decided in 1627 that the grant of a servitude executed underhand or before a notary and witnesses could not prejudice the grantor's creditors (Groen. *ad Grot. Intro.* 2, 36, 1).

The principle that servitudes must be registered against the title of the *praedium serviens* in order to bind the innocent purchaser of the *praedium serviens* has been adopted by the courts of the Cape Colony (*Parkin* v. *Titterton*, 2 Menz. 296; *Judd* v. *Fourie*, 2 E.D.C. 41). In the Transvaal provision was made by Law 3 of 1886 for the registration of servitudes then still unregistered, and future servitudes were declared not to bind third persons unless registered. *Inter partes* a servitude would appear to be binding even though not registered; nay, the courts of the Cape Colony have gone so far as to hold that if a person purchases land with the knowledge of an unregistered servitude the person in whose favour the servitude is created can compel the purchaser to allow its registration (*Richards* v. *Nash*, 1 S.C. 312). The decision in this case is based on *Le Neve* v. *Le Neve*, the leading English case on the doctrine of notice. It has been doubted whether this doctrine is applicable to a person who buys land with notice of a servitude verbally created *inter partes*, but not registered *coram lege loci* (*vide* judgment of Shippard, J., in *Judd* v. *Fourie*, 2 E.D.C. pp. 65 *et seq.*).

It is unnecessary to consider the particular servitudes mentioned in the text-books, as they are all based upon the well-known servitudes of the Roman law. I shall conclude this chapter with a few remarks on some passages of Grotius and a short sketch of the history of emphyteusis, which is classed by Grotius under servitudes. Grotius says (bk. 2, c, 34, sec. 21) that by the common law one may build or plant trees on his own land, but no one may allow his trees to overhang the ground of his neighbour, and the latter may cause the overhanging branches to be cut off or else may gather the fruit on these branches. The authors of the *Rechtsgeleerde Observatiën* point out that this is not wholly founded upon the Roman law, but owes its origin to certain keuren and customs so prevalent in Holland that Grotius calls it the common law. By the Costumen van Rhynland the owner of the ground over which the branches hang may cut them down. Other keuren require the owner to cut them down at the request of his neighbour. In some towns, again, the owner of overhanging trees gets half the fruit and his neighbour the other half. The usual custom, however, was as stated by Grotius (*Rechts. Obs.* vol. 3, obs. 54).

Emphyteusis.—The contract of emphyteusis (or *erfpacht-recht,* as it is called by Dutch writers) has its origin in the Roman law. It was originally the form of contract by which municipalities leased their lands (*D.* 6, 3, 1; Gai, *Inst.* 3, 145); but it was afterwards adopted by other corporations. Its chief feature in early times was the long period of the lease, often extending to a hundred years. Later on the emphyteusis came to be regarded as a lease of land *in perpetuo,* subject to the payment of an annual rent. Grotius defines *erfpachtrecht* as the hereditary usufruct of another's immovable property, subject to a yearly canon or quitrent (Grotius, *Intro.* bk. 2, c. 40, 2).

Grotius tells us that according to the Roman law an *emphyteuta* or quitrent holder could not alienate his right without the consent of the owner, though the property could be bequeathed to his family, but that by the Roman-Dutch law this was not the rule. Our law allowed alienation, reserving to the owner a *jus retractus* (2, 40, 7). In most respects it was considered as immovable property. The erfpacht holder had the *utile dominium* in the property and the right of vindication. He had to keep the property in good condition, and even to improve it. Failure to pay rent for three years enabled the owner to resume possession.

The nearest approach to emphyteusis in South Africa were the *leenings plaatsen* created by the old East India Company. Plots of ground were originally granted merely for the temporary use of squatters. In time these squatters' rights were converted into *leenings plaatsen*, subject to the annual payment of a certain sum, called a *recognitie*. In other words, they were converted from a mere concession into an emphyteutic lease. The issue of actual titles was apparently delayed until 1743. In 1813 these emphyteutic leases were converted into the perpetual quitrent tenure which we know to-day. This tenure is not emphyteusis, but is a special kind of tenure created by Sir John Cradock's proclamation of the 6th August, 1813, although the term perpetual quitrent might lead one to assume that the tenure is the same as emphyteusis (Maasdorp, *Institutes of Cape Law*, vol. 2, c. 35).

The rules, however, which applied to the old Dutch *erfpachten* do not apply to the perpetual quitrent tenure of the Cape Colony. It is a tenure *sui generis* dependent on the title-deed and on Sir John Cradock's Act, though in its general complexion it resembles emphyteusis (*Stellenbosch Divisional Council* v. *Myburgh*, 5 S.C. 8; *Colonial Government* v. *Stephan Bros.*, 17 S.C. 393). As far as I am aware emphyteusis or erfpacht proper has ceased to exist in South Africa.

CHAPTER XIV.

OBLIGATIONS.

In the preceding chapters I have attempted to show that the Roman-Dutch law is the outcome of German customs and Roman jurisprudence. It is but natural that German customs should have been most persistent in that branch of law usually called Family law, and that in those divisions of law where abstract ideas play an important part the highly developed Roman jurisprudence should prevail. When, therefore, we turn from Family law to the law of Obligations we necessarily find that its fundamental principles have their roots in the Roman law.

In the time of Grotius the Dutch people understood the principles of the law of Obligations almost as well as we do, and the law they relied upon to solve their difficulties was the law of the *Corpus Juris.* This, however, had not always been the case, for there was a time when the Roman law of Obligations was not understood in the Netherlands. German law had independently developed some principles of the law of Contract, and after the revival of learning the Roman law came to be used as a solvent, so that though the bulk of our law of Contract was derived from the *Corpus Juris* there was still a good deal of the Germanic element to be found in it. When, therefore, we step aside from the main road of fundamental principles, and proceed to investigate the by-paths of the law of Contract, we find that German custom has left its mark in that division of our law as well as in Family law. The deviations from the Roman law are not so great and so noticeable in the law of Obligations as they are in Family law or in the law of Things; yet they do exist, and we can readily discover some of the traces of German custom.

In dealing with the law of Obligations we have to distinguish between a promise to do an act and a promise which gives rise to a legal obligation. Promises men have no doubt made to each other in all ages, but the promise which gives rise to a legal obligation *juris vinculum quo necessitate adstringimur alicujus solvendae rei* is only found when the idea of State control has been well developed. Besides the promise to pay a gambling debt, we do not know of any promises that the early German community regarded as specially binding.

Tacitus certainly believed that the Germans attached a great importance to a promise. He tells us (*Germ.* c. 24) that they played dice when sober as a serious business, and even staked their liberty upon the throw. If a player lost he voluntarily went into servitude, and patiently allowed himself to be bound and sold. Tacitus thought this a bad practice, yet he adds that the Germans themselves considered it an honourable thing to keep their promises (*est ea in re pervicacia—ipsi fidem vocant*). In the case of wagers, therefore, the Germans recognised that a promise seriously made should be scrupulously kept. But Tacitus tells us that the Germans regarded it base to violate other promises as well, and that they thought that no people in the world were superior to them either in war or in keeping promises (*nullos mortalium armis aut fide ante se esse.—Tacit. Annals XIII*, c. 54).

At a later period we find the same idea of the sanctity of a promise in the maxims of the people, *e.g. ein mann, ein mann, ein wort, ein wort. Zuzagen macht schuld* (Hein. *Jus. Germ.* bk. 2, tit. 12, sec. 337). Heineccius quotes a proverb of the Saxon law to show their respect for a promise: *Wer etwas borget oder gelobet der soll es gelten und was er thut das soll er stett halten* (He who becomes surety or who makes a promise must carry it out, and if he undertakes to do a thing he must act up to his undertaking). The Salic law had a chapter *de eo qui fide facta alteri debitum reddere noluit.*

The Dutch writers of the sixteenth and seventeenth centuries who collected the old German laws and commented upon them constantly refer to the sanctity of the old German promise. Zypaeus, Gudelinus, Grotius, Groenewegen, Vinnius and Matthaeus all express the opinion that the ancient Germans attached great importance to their promises. The promise was usually strengthened by the grasp of the hand (*manu firmatio*). This in all probability was connected with some old religious rite. In the *Lex Baiuvariorum* (tit. 16) there is a provision that if several witnesses swear to a fact they must give each other in turn the right hand. A promise was probably regarded as something sacred to the gods, and this may explain why the Church attached such importance to the *fides manu data.* We see, therefore, that the early Germans had a great regard for a promise, and that after they became Christianised the promise with hand-shake was regarded as a solemn obligation.

This promise was, however, different in character from the contract or *obligatio juris*. It created no *vinculum* by which the promissor could be compelled by the community to carry out his undertaking. There was no agreement which could be enforced by the judge. It was only after the power of the State became well established that the specific performance of a promise could be demanded. In other words, the power of judicial execution preceded the idea of a binding contract. Most recent German writers maintain that the early Germans were wholly unacquainted with the consensual contract, and that they only knew the so-called "real contract," where there is no promise to do something in the future, but where the whole transaction is carried out at once (Schröder, p. 283, Heusler, *Inst.* 2, 225).

Exchange is probably the earliest type of the real contract. If an ox is to be exchanged for three sheep, they are all brought to one place, and the owner of the ox then hands his beast over to the other party, who in turn delivers the sheep. Here the whole transaction is completed at once. The next step is probably where one person undertakes to deliver to another some article or animal at a future time in exchange for something handed over at the present time. In such a case many investigators think that the transaction was carried out by the debtor handing over to his creditor something of greater value than the thing to be delivered *in futuro*. The debtor could release the article of greater value by delivering to his creditor the promised thing. The object given as security for the due performance of the contract was known as *vadium* (*wedde*), and the whole transaction may be called the vadium contract. If the debtor performed his contract the vadium was returned, but if he failed to carry out the agreement within a specified time the vadium became the property of him to whom it was delivered. If the value of the vadium was greater than that of the promised article, then a considerable pressure was brought to bear upon the debtor to perform his contract. In this way the vadium came to be, as it were, a *vinculum juris* (Fock. And. *Oud-Ned. Burg. Recht.* vol. 2, p. 2).

When once the State intervened and took steps to carry out a solemn promise, the vadium came to be regarded as traditional rather than as necessary, and so it took the form of the *festuca* or rod. The symbol sometimes represented the power of the owner over a thing (*e.g.* the *festuca*), whilst at other times it represented the thing itself (*e.g.* a clod). Later the vadium dwindled into some trifling token like a small coin, and became similar to the *arrha* of the Roman law (Schröder, pp. 63, 289, 721; Brissaud, p. 1377). During the middle ages, before the Roman law of Justinian was well understood, a legal obligation was usually rendered binding by the *fides manu data*. The result of a breach of such an agreement was that the defaulter was declared a dishonourable perjurer. Thus Jan van Arkel, for not carrying out an agreement, was declared *witteloes, trouweloes, eerloes ende meyneedich* (Van Mieris, *G.C.B.* 3, 451). The next step was, apparently in order to give a greater solemnity to a contract, to require the agreement to be stated before a judicial officer. The *fides manu data* of the Church became the *ghewedde hant* of the court of schout and schepenen. The following formula was used at Nijmwegen: *Nos scabini testamur quod Jacobus noster concivis dedit wedde ad manus Conradi,* &c.

Later the *wedde* disappears, and the formula is: *Nos scabini testamur quod constitutus coram nobis talis promisit ad manus talis*, &c. (Fock. And. *Oud-Ned. Burg. Recht.* vol. 2, p. 7).

When the study of the Roman law had made such progress that its principles were well understood by the lawyers of the larger towns, and its rules were adopted by the higher courts, the Germanic forms and symbols gradually disappeared, and the law of Contract in the Netherlands became almost identical with that of the *Corpus Juris*. The tendency to deal with contracts on the basis of the Roman law is visible in the fourteenth century, whilst the fifteenth century saw a great advance in that direction. During the sixteenth and following centuries Dutch contracts were almost entirely interpreted according to the rules of the Roman law, and their binding effect was tested exclusively by the principles of that system.

We find, therefore, that when Zypaeus, Gudelinus and Grotius have to expound the law of Obligations they refer not to German customs, but to the law of Justinian. At the same time there is no doubt that the influence of German custom had not entirely disappeared. Thus it was a maxim of the Roman law that no action could be brought on an informal contract—*Ex nudo pacto non oritur actio.* This was not the principle of the Roman-Dutch law. The Hollanders adopted the view of their ancestors, that a serious promise was binding and that legal effect should be given to it. If we accept the view that the early Germans attached some sanctity to a serious promise, or even if we admit that the lawyers of the fifteenth and sixteenth centuries were of opinion that the customs of their ancestors regarded the promise or *fides manu data* as legally binding, then we can understand how the Roman-Dutch law of the seventeenth century came to adopt the maxim *Ex nudo pacto oritur actio.*

That the Dutch writers of the sixteenth and seventeenth centuries thought that the Germans attached the utmost importance to a promise admits of no doubt whatever. The authors above quoted repeatedly say so. This view was adopted in Germany as well as in Holland. Heineccius says: "The Romans considered that there was a great distinction between pacts and contracts. The former they divided into *nuda* and *non nuda*, and these last again into *legitima, praetoria* and *adjecta.* The Germans, however, were clearly ignorant of this distinction, and they attributed no less force to agreements deliberately made than did the Romans to their contracts entered into with due solemnity" (Hein. *Jus. Germ.* bk. 2, tit. 12, sec. 330).

He also points out that the Romans at any rate were of opinion that the Germans regarded good faith as a part of their religion, and that a man who broke his word was considered infamous. Such persons were known as *schelmen, ehren und treu vergessene leute.* He shows that the same principle appears in many of the German Codes, and then sums up the matter in the following terms: "Pacts, therefore, gave with the Germans not only an exception, but also a right of action, unless the promissor was either a person who could not bind himself or unless it appeared *ex ipso negotio* that the promise was merely part of a jest" (*ibid.* sec. 340).

This was the view taken by most of the eminent Dutch jurists of the seventeenth century. Thus Grotius tells us that in his time this principle of the German law, that a deliberate and serious promise must be performed, was part of the law of Holland. His words are: "But as the Germans from times of old esteemed no virtue higher than good faith, these subtleties were not adopted by them, but it was the rule and practice that all promises based upon any reasonable ground (*redelyke oorzaak*), in whatever terms expressed, and whether the parties were together at the same place or not, gave a right both of action and of exception" (*Inst.* 3, 1, 52).

It is difficult to see how the *redelyke oorzaak* of Grotius and the *causa* or *causa legitima* of those writers who used the Latin language can mean a *quid pro quo*, or consideration in the sense used by English lawyers. Those writers, like Grotius, who refer to the good faith of the Germans as the stable basis of their contracts, cannot possibly mean by *redelyke oorzaak* or *causa* a *quid pro quo*, for if they did it seems inexplicable why they should have wrapped up the matter in such obscurity. Grotius says in effect we do not require the formalities of the Roman law in order to establish a contract, for we attach the same importance as did the Germans to good faith; all we require is that there shall be some good ground for concluding that the parties really intended to bind themselves legally. What, then, is this good ground for a belief that the parties intended to bind themselves, other than the fact that a promise was made, and that seriously and with the deliberate intent that it should be carried out? If we give this simple and ordinary meaning to *redelyke oorzaak* or *causa* we can understand why Grotius refers to the German custom of abiding by a promise; but if we give to these words a meaning similar to the English consideration, the reference to the good faith of the Germans seems beside the mark and wholly misleading.

By *nudum pactum* the Romans meant an agreement which was concluded without the necessary solemnities which the civil law required for a valid contract. Consequently the maxim *Ex nudo pacto non oritur actio* meant that an agreement which was not made with due solemnity could not give rise to a claim in a court of law. The later commentators gave to *nudum pactum* a somewhat wider meaning, and with them these words conveyed the idea of a contract based upon the agreement of parties and upon that alone (Voet's *Beginselen*, 3, 14, 13). Hence when Groenewegen and others use the phrase *Ex nudo pacto oritur actio* they mean that where there is a valid agreement between two parties there is a contract upon which an action can be brought. At any rate from the thirteenth century onwards the maxim *Ex nudo pacto oritur actio* meant that all serious and deliberate agreements could be sued upon even though they were entered into without any formality. Hence the Germans could not have required any consideration in the English law sense of the term, for if they did they would have required some formality besides the mere proof of the contract.

Heineccius, who reviewed the greater portion of the ancient German Codes, nowhere suggests that they required more than a bare agreement seriously entered into. He nowhere suggests that the Germans required a *quid pro quo* in order to support a contract. It is therefore most unlikely that Grotius, who appeals to the respect of the Germans for good faith, would have meant by *redelyke oorzaak* anything more than that there was some serious agreement which gave rise to the contract. Zypaeus, a contemporary of Grotius, expressed the same view that no formality was required to make a contract binding. He is an authority for the law of the southern States of the Republic, and he bases his opinion upon the Canon law and *quod magis fidei datae in rebus licitis habenda sit ratio* (*De Contrahenda Stipulatione*, bk. 8). Gudelinus, another contemporary of Grotius, expresses the same view, and also bases his opinion on the fact that the early Germans esteemed good faith before all things (l. 3, c. 5, *porro*).

Vinnius (*ad Inst.* 3, 16, 1, n. 4) says that an informal agreement, provided it was made seriously and deliberately, gives a right of action, and he attributes this change either to the Canon law or to the fact that the ancients regarded any breach of promise as an immoral act. *Sive hoc ex jure Pontificio, ejusve juris interpretatione invaluit sive ex eo quod posterioribus saeculis grave visum fuit etiam in nudis pactis fidem fallere.* Groenewegen (*ad Cod.* 2, 3, 10) was also of opinion that an informal agreement would support a valid action, *moribus nostris ex nudo pacto non solum exceptionem sed et actionem competere constat.*

Paul Voet (*ad Inst.* 3, 14, 5), the great commentator's *pater piae memoriae*, is also of opinion that the law of Holland adopted the maxim *Ex nudo pacto oritur actio.* He points out that in Friesland, where the Roman law was more rigidly followed, the maxim of the civil law, *Ex nudo pacto non oritur actio*, was the practice. He attributes the practice of Holland to the customs of their forefathers, and not to the influence of the Canonists. The fact that he points out the difference between the law of Holland and of Friesland shows clearly that in his time it was regarded as a matter of considerable importance that no formality was required in Holland in order to make a contract binding, whilst in Friesland a mere agreement did not bring with it a right of action.

Jan Voet discusses the question in his *Beginselen des Rechts* (bk. 3, c. 14, secs. 13 and 14), and tells us that a nude pact is one which depends on agreement alone, and that such a nude pact has the same effect as a formal contract provided it is made seriously and deliberately. His words as given in the Dutch translation of the *Elementa Juris* are as follows: *Een bloot verdrag is het welk in de bloote en enkele paelen van een overeenkomst bestaet. . . . Het blijkt al eertyds door 't gebruik aangenomen te zijn dat ook uit een bloot en enkel verdrag actie gegeven worde zoo dat een verdrag nu de kracht van eene toezegging heeft: laeten wy ons alleen erineren dat ernstig en overdachte en nutte beloften van de onbedachtzaeme roekelooze en onnutte (wanneer iemant niet besluitenderwyze zoo ze 't noemen noch ernstelyk maer of verhaelens gewyze of uit boertery en wat anders doende iets voortbrengt) moeten worden onderscheiden; dat uit die alleen niet uit deze eene verbinbenis en actie geboren wordt. En 't zelve houdt ook het Pauselyke recht uit drukkelyk genoeg in. En wy zien insgelijks de meeste andere hedensdaegs weder tot de een vondigheid van 't recht der volkeren gebracht te zijn.* This little work of Voet was one of the principal student's text-books in the eighteenth century, and is quoted very freely by Lybrecht.

It would appear, therefore, that, at any rate during the seventeenth century, such authorities as Grotius, Gudelinus, Zypaeus, Groenewegen and the two Voets were of opinion that the law of Holland did not recognise the Roman doctrine that some formality was required to establish a contract, but followed the practice of the Germans and of the Canonists, and only required (1) consent; (2) a voluntary and deliberate agreement; (3) persons capable of contracting; and (4) an agreement physically possible and not contrary to the moral sense of the community.

Though some authorities think that the origin of the maxim *Ex nudó pacto oritur actio* is to be sought in the Canon law, it seems to be more probable that the Canonists found the custom prevalent amongst the German nations of western Europe, and incorporated it into the Canon law as part of the *jus gentium* of the middle ages. Whether, however, the later Roman-Dutch law required more than a deliberate agreement is a question which still forms part of the *jus controversum* of South Africa. If we regard the question from a purely historical standpoint it would appear that, at any rate in the first half of the seventeenth century, there was an almost unanimous opinion that no formality (and therefore no consideration as required by English law) was necessary to enable a person to sue upon a contract.

Van Leeuwen, who wrote in the second half of the seventeenth century, in his *Censura Forensis* (4, 2, 2) seems to be of a different opinion, but he appears to stand alone as an upholder of the view that *Ex nudo pacto non oritur actio.* Voet (2, 14, 9), referring to this passage of Van Leeuwen, says, *Lapsus ergo est Simon van Leeuwen asserens id in praxi quoque receptum esse quod ex nudo pacto actio non detur.* Dekker, Van Leeuwen's annotator and no mean lawyer, also takes pains to show that Van Leeuwen is wrong. It is also worth noting that in his *Roman-Dutch Law*, a later work than the *Censura Forensis* and more exclusively devoted to Roman-Dutch law, there is no such statement as is contained in the *Censura Forensis.*

If, then, we accept the view of Grotius and Voet as a fair exposition of the law of Holland as it prevailed in the seventeenth century, it becomes somewhat difficult to see when and in what way the law and practice of that time was altered. From a purely historical point of view it would therefore appear to be more probable that the Roman-Dutch lawyers disregarded the formalities of the Roman law, and adopted the simpler rule that if a man made a serious and a deliberate promise he should abide by it, even though there was no consideration for the promise at the time when it was made. When we view the matter from an ethical standpoint, it seems to require a great deal of special pleading to enable the ordinary man to see why a promise without a consideration should be less binding than where the *quid pro quo* is a peppercorn or a mere fanciful consideration.

In the Cape Colony the Supreme Court in a series of decisions has held that a contract, however serious, which was not based upon consideration, could not be sued upon; whilst the present Supreme Court of the Transvaal as well as the late High Court and the Court of Ceylon have expressed the opinion that consideration is not necessary to uphold a serious promise, and that therefore the maxim *Ex nudo pacto non oritur actio* is not a maxim of the Roman-Dutch law. (Cape courts: *Louisa* v. *Van den Berg,* 1 Menz. 472; *Jacobson* v. *Norton,* 2 Menz. 221; *Alexander* v. *Perry,* Buch. 1874, p. 59; *Malan and Van der Merwe* v. *Secretan, Boon & Co.,* Foord, 94; *Colonial Secretary* v. *Davidson,* Buch. 1876, p. 131; *Tembu* v. *Webster,* 21 S.A.L.J. 202. Transvaal: *Rood* v. *Wallach,* [1904] T.S. 187. Ceylon: *Lipton* v. *Buchanan,* 22 S.A.L.J. 169.)

When I say that the Germans did not adopt the formalism of the Romans, I do not wish to be understood to mean that their contracts were entirely void of forms and ceremonies. It would be incorrect to suppose that the contracts of the Germans were not also in many cases attended with certain external forms. The difference, however, between the formalism of the Romans and of the Germans was that the former attached as great an importance to the circumstances attending the promise as to the promise itself, whilst the latter looked to the promise as the essential part, and regarded the symbolical acts which attended the promise as mere evidence of the seriousness of the contracting parties. In certain cases, however, as in the sale and transfer of land, and in the contract of vadium, the Germans exacted as great a formalism in their contracts as the Romans, but on the whole the formalism of the Germans was not so strict as that of the Romans.

From the twelfth century onwards the German nations strove to get rid of all unnecessary ceremonies in making contracts, and regarded the consensus of the parties as the essential element of every agreement. This disregard for form was no doubt greatly encouraged by the ecclesiastics, for the authors of the Canon law strove to do away as much as possible with forms, and to give full authority to the deliberate and serious promises of the contracting parties.

The man who broke his promise was regarded as a scoundrel, and he might freely be stigmatised as a *schelm* either by word or picture. *Schelm durch schimpfen oder schandgemälde öffentlich zu brandmarken* (Grimm, *R.A.* 612).

Hence when we come to consider the various codes and law-books which were in vogue in western Europe, we find that they no longer adopted the divisions and distinctions of the Roman law. No doubt in many cases the terminology of the Roman law was retained, but the exact meaning of terms was no longer the same as in the days of Justinian. Heineccius, in dealing with this part of the subject, says that we may disregard the divisions of the Roman law into *contractus nominati et innominati, reales et verbales, bonae fidei et stricti juris.* In their place he proposes a division into *conventiones principales* and *conventiones beneficae.*

By *conventio benefica* the jurists of the middle ages meant a contract by which I agree that something should be given to me or done for me by another without any remuneration being due by me to the other party. This class will include such contracts as *donatio, commodatum, mutuum, precarium* and *mandatum.*

By *conventio principalis* they meant bilateral contracts, in which the obligations were mutual, such as sale, lease, partnership, or contracts of the nature of the *do ut des, facio ut facias* contracts (Hein. *Jus. Germ.* bk. 2, tit. 13, secs. 352 and 579).

Although we find the words *stipulatio, stipulo,* frequently used in the German Codes and by Roman-Dutch writers, we must remember that the technical meaning which the Roman jurists attached to the word *stipulatio* was never given to it by the jurists of western Europe, and certainly not by those of Holland. The word *stipulatio* came to mean any agreement between parties in whatsoever way it might have been brought about (Groen. *ad Inst.* 3, tit. 19).

According to the ancient Roman law a stipulation was invalid unless the parties employed the solemn words which the law required in order to make the promise binding. The promise must be made in reply to a question, and the words used must be Latin words, such as *spondes? spondeo; promittis? promitto; fide dabis? dabo.* A question in Greek answered by a Latin word created no binding contract. The object of the question and answer was to prevent any confusion, and to assure that both parties clearly understood one another. Gradually the rigour of the ancient law was broken down, so that in the time of Severus if a document stated that a promise had been made, the law presumed that it was made by a formal stipulation (Roby, *Roman Law,* vol. 2, p. 13).

The idea, however, that the two parties were present and that a question was put and answered prevailed even in the reign of Justinian (*Inst.* 3, 15, 1). Hence it was accepted that the answer should follow close upon the question, and a day's interval would prevent any obligation arising. Thus we see in the *Digest* (45, 2, 12 pr.) that if there are two persons who desire to contract, and one promises to-day, whilst the other promises to-morrow, they do not constitute two co-debtors, for the second is not bound (*ac ne obligatum quidem intelligi eum qui postera die responderat*). As the one party asked the question, and the other had to give the reply within a reasonable time, not longer than a day, it followed that a person could not as a rule exact a promise on behalf of an absentee. To this, however, the Roman jurists made this exception, that a person could stipulate on behalf of one in whose power he was. This is also expressed by saying that a contract can only be enforced by one who has an interest in it and is a party to it. Any stipulation, therefore, framed in the interests of an outsider was invalid. Directly, however, the jurists of the middle ages came to disregard the strict formality of the *stipulatio,* and did away with the necessity of question and answer *inter praesentes,* they extended the scope of the verbal obligation far beyond the limits of the Roman law.

The abolition of the technical *stipulatio* had far-reaching consequences. As the parties were no longer required to be present or to put questions and receive the answers in their own interests, a verbal contract could be made by an agent, and a promise could be enforced though made on behalf of a third party. By the Roman law if a person promised to do an act it meant that he himself was to do it, and he could not be held bound if he promised that the act should be done by another unless a penalty for non-performance was added, or unless the question and answer were both so framed that it was clear that if the third party did not perform the act the promissor was obliged to do it. But nowadays such a promise implies, even though no penalty be stipulated for, or no mention be made that the promissor will do the act, that the promissor will see that the third party does the act or else he will do it himself or pay damages (Grotius, 3, 3, 3; Voet, 45, 1, 5).

The Canon law rejected the rigid principle of the Roman

law *nemo alteri stipulari potest,* and adopted the rule that if a person promised that a third person would do an act he was tacitly understood to have promised that he would see that the act was performed (Ritterhuisius, *Different. Juris, Civil et Canon,* bk. 3, ch. 6). Grotius in discussing this question says: "No one can make a promise which shall be binding on another. Consequently, if any one promises that a third person shall do or give something, he is with us understood to mean that he promises to cause such a thing to happen" (Grotius, 3, 3, 3); and Voet adds that even if the promissor dies his heir can be compelled to see that the promise made by the deceased is carried out (45, 1, 5). In such a case, therefore, if the third person does not do the act which has been promised, the one contracting party can sue the other either to see that the act is done or else to pay damages for the non-performance of the act.

From what has been said above it is clear that by the Roman law a stipulation made by one party for the benefit of a third party could not have been sued upon by the third party, for he was not considered to have a pecuniary interest in the stipulation; *Ea in obligatione consistere quae pecunia lui praestarique possunt* (*D.* 17, 1, 54). The Romans got over this difficulty by attaching a penalty to non-performance. Thus the Roman stipulator would not be bound if he promised affirmatively to the question *Dabisne Titio servum illum?* where Titius was a third party. Hence the stipulator added, *Si non dederis centum nummos mihi dabis?* Here there was a pecuniary interest to the stipulator in the performance of the contract, and he could sue for the penalty though Titius himself could exact neither the performance nor the penalty.

This technical difficulty was done away with, and we find that the Roman-Dutch jurists in the time of Grotius no longer recognised the principle of the Roman law above enunciated. Grotius allows the third party to sue in several cases where he could not sue by the civil law. Thus he says (3, 3, 38): "But a simple stipulation in favour of, or acceptance for, a third party (except for one who can, as stated above, acquire a personal claim through another), is null and void unless made for the service of God, or for the poor, or unless the acceptor has himself an interest in the same or unless a penalty is thereby imposed upon the promissor, in case of non-performance; but, besides these exceptions, as equity is more regarded with us than legal subtleties, a third person may accept the promise and thus acquire a right, unless the promissor revokes the promise before such acceptance by such third person." Grotius therefore requires the acceptance of the third party in order to bind the promissor.

Groenewegen, however, uses more general terms, and according to his view a stipulation on behalf of a third party is quite valid, and gives the third party a right of action. *Hinc moribus hodiernis ex nudo pacto datur actio et stipulando alteri obligatio acquiritur* (*ad Inst.* 3, 20, 19, 5). Voet adopts the same view. His words are: *Quin et moribus hodiernis obtinuit, unumquemque alteri aeque ac sibi posse stipulari adeo ut et domino ex stipulatione procuratoris agere liceat etiamsi actio ei a procuratore cessa non sit.*

Van Scheltinga, in commenting on the passage of Grotius above cited, adopts the views of Groenewegen and Voet, though Van der Keessel (*Thes.* 510) differs from both Voet and Groenewegen, and thinks that a third party will not acquire a right to sue merely because between two outsiders a stipulation has been made in his favour. But even Van der Keessel is prepared to admit that if the third party has accepted the benefit of what was stipulated in his favour he can sue, so also if he is a public notary. Why the notary is put in a more favourable position is not stated. Van der Linden seems to prefer the view of Van der Keessel (bk. 1, c. 14, sec. 3).

Dekker, the commentator of Van Leeuwen, discussed the question, and seems to agree with the view of Groenewegen (*R. D. L.* bk. 4, c. 2, 5 (*n*) *h*). Dekker takes the view of Heineccius (*De Jure Germ.* bk. 2, secs. 346 and 347), that the Germans had in this respect modified the Roman law, so that the true statement of the law should be in the words of Huber (*Hed. Recht.* 3, 21, 40): "The custom is that whenever I have stipulated something for another of which he afterwards approves, a claim may be made by him for it." I am not aware that this controverted point has been argued and settled in any South African court.

I have frequently had to refer to the fact that the Roman-Dutch law did not recognise the *patria potestas* of the Roman law. This is of importance in the law of Obligations, for by the civil law a *stipulatio* between a father and a son *in potestate ejus* could not be enforced; but by our law such a contract will be perfectly valid, and the son, provided he is of age or emancipated, can sue upon such a contract.

I shall now pass over to the consideration of the modifications which were introduced into the Roman-Dutch law in some of the different well-known branches of the law of Contract. It is unnecessary to deal at length with such contracts as *depositum, commodatum, mutuum* or agency, for the rules of the Roman law which apply to these contracts have been taken over almost in their entirety by the Roman-Dutch law, provided, of course, they do not conflict with the fundamental principles of the latter. The small discrepancies here and there need hardly be touched upon in so brief a sketch as this.

CHAPTER XV.

SURETYSHIP.

By far the greatest portion of our law of suretyship is derived from the Roman law. There are, however, several peculiarities in the law of Holland which owe their origin to the customs of the Germans. It will therefore not be deemed out of place if I give here a short history of the law of suretyship as it has been developed in Holland and the neighbouring States.

Contracts of suretyship were well known to the Germans. They were, like the Roman *fidejussiones*, contracts between a creditor and some person who promised to pay a debt in case the principal debtor could not pay. The sureties were sometimes called *vadii* and sometimes *gesiles* by the writers of the middle ages. The contract called *vadium* was one which was attended with considerable solemnity, and does not always appear to have had the same meaning. Thus a freeman could make a contract to pay, and further agree that, if he did not pay, his creditor could exact services from him in payment of what was due *se loco vadii in alterius potestatem committere* (Noordewier, p. 133). The usual solemnity was the cutting off of the hair of the person who surrendered himself to his creditor, and placing his head under the arm of the latter (*ibid.* p. 37). In this case the freeman pledged his person. He might also pledge his immovable property by way of vadium. An accused person might also agree to appear before the court by a contract of vadium, and then his failure to appear would justify his imprisonment.

The contract by which a freeman pledged his person was also called *geisel, gijsel* or *ghijsel. Gijsel* was thus a form of pledge, and if the person who entered into this kind of suretyship could not perform the terms he could be locked up until the contract was performed. It is from this word *gijzel* that the Dutch words *gyzelaar,* a hostage, and *gijzeling,* are derived; the latter came to mean civil imprisonment. These two forms of contract were both considered of so solemn a nature that the surety was regarded in the same light as if he were a principal debtor. Such a surety could not claim the *beneficium ordinis.*

In 1327 the Bishop of Utrecht promised the Count of Holland a certain sum of money, and agreed *inter alia* that if upon the appointed day he did not pay the money then he and his sureties would come to the city of Leyden to an inn, and they would there remain until the money was paid. A feast, therefore, which cost a great deal of money and which might lead to the calamity of the host being locked up for debt, was called a *gijzel maal, i.e.* an expensive feast (Noordewier, pp. 270 *et seq.*). Some of the German nations (*e.g.* the Franks) gave the creditor the option of suing either the debtor or the surety, but if he pursued the debtor he had no further claim upon the surety (Hein. *Jus. Germ.* bk. 2, sec. 448).

Most of the German nations did not give the surety the right of claiming that the debtor should first be excussed; his only valid plea was that the debtor had paid the principal debt (Hein. sec. 449). Some tribes, however, followed the *Lex Romana*, and allowed the surety to plead the *beneficium ordinis*. Throughout the Netherlands the *Lex Romana* has been accepted as the common law, and sureties can always claim the *beneficium excussionis* unless they have renounced the benefit. It was, however, doubtful whether a person who had bound himself as surety and co-principal debtor could not demand that the principal debtor should be first excussed. The question was raised in a contested case at Middelburg in 1610, and the court decided that the co-principal debtor stood upon the same footing as a principal debtor, and could not claim the *beneficium excussionis* (*Holl. Cons.* vol. 6, p. 323).

It has been a matter of dispute among Roman-Dutch writers whether a surety can bind himself for more than the principal debt. By the Roman law (*Inst.* 3, 20, 5) a surety could not bind himself for more than the principal debt. Ulpian tells us that in such a case the surety was not bound at all, and that therefore he could not be sued, even for a sum equal to that of the principal debt, *quod si fuerint in duriorem causam adhibiti, placuit eos omnino non obligari* (*D.* 46, 1, 8, 7). This gave rise to great controversy during the middle ages, some holding with Ulpian, and others adopting a more liberal view. Grotius adopted the Roman law, for he tells us (3, 3, 23), "Sureties may not bind themselves to more than their principal whether as to subject-matter, time, place or other particular, but may to less and also conditionally, or from or up to a certain time, in which last case when the time arrives the surety ceases to be bound, although the principal still remains liable." This view may be summed up in the maxim of the commentators, *Fidejussor intensive obligari potest extensive non potest.*

Groenewegen not only rejected this view of the law, but even went so far as to hold that the surety who stipulated for a greater sum was liable not only for the amount for which the principal was indebted, but even for the excess to which he, the surety, had agreed. "It is more in accordance," he says, "with equity and modern practice to hold with those who say that a surety who binds himself for an amount greater than the principal debt is liable at least to the extent of the principal debt. And, moreover, I hold that a surety who knowingly and with deliberate intent binds himself to perform something greater than the obligation of the principal debtor (*qui se in duriorem causam obligavit*) should be bound as a principal debtor, by virtue of his stipulation or promise, for the amount for which he has become surety" (*ad Dig.* 46, 1, 8, 7). This is indeed carrying out the German idea of the sacredness of a promise to its extreme logical consequence.

Schorer is also of opinion that the subtlety of the Roman law, which Grotius approves of, has no place in the Roman-Dutch law, and follows in this respect the views of Van Leeuwen and Voet (*Cens. For.* 4, 17, 8; Voet, 41, 1, 4). Van der Keessel adopts both the principles of Groenewegen, though in a modified form (*Thes.* 499): "A surety who has engaged himself for a larger sum is by our law bound, without distinction, for the principal; and even for such larger sum, *if the principal debtor has subsequently become indebted therein.*"

Suretyship of Women.—As long as women were subjected to the *mundium* of some male relative they could hardly have bound themselves as sureties. When, however, women were enabled to transact business in their own name there was nothing in the Teutonic customs to forbid them from becoming sureties. The *Lex Romana*, however, recognised the *beneficium Senatus Consulti Velleiani;* hence we find that in some portions of the Netherlands the benefit of the *Senatus Consultum* was admitted, whilst in others it was rejected (*e.g.* Harderwyk).

In Holland from very early times women could not be sureties unless they renounced the benefits of the *Senatus Consultum*, and, if married, of the *Authentica si qua mulier* as well. When Grotius wrote his *Introduction* this was well settled and established law. The whole matter was regulated by the provisions of the Roman law. The same law prevails in the various South African colonies, where the *Senatus Consultum Velleianum* and the *Authentica si qua mulier* have the same force as they had in the Roman Empire.

CHAPTER XVI.

PLEDGE AND MORTGAGE.

MODERN investigators of ancient law have come to the conclusion that the German pledge was originally akin to a form of payment. We have seen that in the vadium contract the debtor gave his creditor some article of greater value than the thing promised. The debtor therefore gave to his creditor as provisional payment something different from the object that had been promised. If the promised article was forthcoming the object handed over provisionally could be redeemed. In this sense it was a pledge. But unlike our pledge, it was not an accessory agreement; it was more of the nature of an altërnative payment. If the debtor chose he could fulfil his agreement by allowing the object to remain in the hands of the creditor. The creditor was regarded so far as owner of the pledged article that if he sold it to a third party the debtor could not reclaim it.

The phrase *betalen met panden* occurs as late as the fourteenth century. The very expression to redeem a pledge (*redimere*) shows that the debtor was regarded as if he bought it back from the creditor. If a condition was added that the agreement should be performed within a certain period, and the debtor allowed the time to elapse without redeeming his pledge, then the creditor *remained* the owner of the thing given in pledge (Schröder, pp. 273, 288, 711, 724;

Brissaud, p. 1484; Fock. And. *Oud-Ned. Burg. Recht.* vol. 2, pp. 97 *et seq.*).

Delivery was an essential element in the constitution of a pledge. We find the necessity of delivery mentioned in several old local ordinances. Thus in the Stadboek of Groningen the debtor is required to place the object in the hands of the creditor or in his control—*in die hant ofte in die were doen* (*Stad. Gron. Pro excolendo,* vii, 13).

Gradually, however, the contract of pledge came to be regarded as an accessory obligation, and after the Roman law was resorted to its principles of *pignus* and *hypothecatio* were completely taken over. Hence the law of Holland in the time of Grotius with respect to pledge was very much the same as the Roman law, though in some instances the Roman-Dutch departed from the law of Justinian and adopted a practice founded on German custom. The Roman law required no special formality to create a valid pledge of movable property or a hypothecation of land. In the Netherlands, however, in early times a distinction was drawn between the pledge of movables and the mortgage of immovable property. Although some towns required a pledge of movable property for a debt of above a certain sum to be executed before schepenen in order to allow the creditor to become owner of the pledged article if the debtor failed to repay the loan, yet the general practice was to allow a pledge of movables to be constituted without special formality. Delivery was essential, and the pledge of movables lasted only so long as the pledgee had possession of the pledge.

As regards the formalities necessary to constitute a valid pledge of immovable property, the German customs differed considerably from the Roman practice. Immovable property was originally pledged in very much the same way as movable property. The creditor became the *dominus* of the property, with a promise to transfer it back again to the debtor if the loan were repaid. The creditor had the full usufruct of the land until the debt was paid. In a deed of 1219, referred to by Professor Fockema Andreae, we find the following words: *Curtem in Oye sub tali conditione eidem ecclesiae assignari quod uxori meae aut liberis meis eandem curtem cum L marcis redimere licebit et interim usque ad ultimam solutionem ecclesia in possessione et fructuum perceptione pacifice residebit* (*Oud-Ned. Burg. Recht.* vol. 2, p. 106). If the loan were not repaid within the specified time the mortgagee remained the owner.

Gradually the practice was introduced of leaving the mortgagor in possession of his property. This was the general practice during the fourteenth century. This practice necessitated not only a deed of hypothecation, but a certain amount of publicity so that the mortgagee could rest assured that the property was not already mortgaged. In some districts, as in Selwerden, the mortgage took place with the formality called *stock legging*, or the passing of the rod from mortgagor to mortgagee in the presence of witnesses. According to many of the German Codes the property pledged, as I have said, passed out of the *dominium* of the mortgagor into that of the mortgagee. A pledge was therefore treated as a *venditio cum pacto de retrovendendo* (Hein. *Elem. Jur. Germ.* bk. 2, sec. 443).

Now a transfer of immovable property, as we saw in a former chapter, was generally executed by solemn deed before the magistrate of the locality in which the land was situated (*coram lege loci*). Hence the practice of executing a mortgage before the local judge was assimilated to that of sale, and when the mortgagor was allowed to remain in possession the registration of the deed gave the necessary publicity to the transaction. The placaats of the sixteenth century firmly established the practice by requiring the payment of $2\frac{1}{2}$ per cent. upon the execution of every mortgage. In this way it came to be recognised law that the hypothecation of land which was not executed *coram lege loci*, and upon which the proper dues were not paid, only held good *inter partes*, but was of no effect against a *bonâ fide* purchaser for value.

I remarked above that many German Codes treated the mortgagee as the person in whom the *dominium* was vested. Heineccius sums up the matter as follows: *Itaque vere dici potest* (1) *inter venditionem cum pacto de retrovendendo et pignus vix quidquam apud Germanos fuisse discriminis adeoque?* (2) *ea quae de pignore et pacto antichreseos jure Romano prodita sunt moribus Germanorum vix quadrare.* This general principle of the German law was modified in the thirteenth century in such a way that the pledgee was not entitled to treat the pledged property as his own, but was required to sell it by judicial sale.

Whatever rule the ancient law of Holland may have adopted, the later Roman-Dutch law seems to have followed the practice which had grown up in Germany. The Hollanders followed the Frisians, who adhered more strictly to the Roman law in not divesting the owner of his *dominium* in the thing mortgaged. The consequence of this was that the law of Holland was always favourable to the mortgagor, and its policy was to allow the debtor to recover the property pledged up to the time that it was actually sold in execution by judicial decree. So far did the law of Holland carry its protection of the debtor that it did not recognise *parate executie,* or a stipulation by which the debtor agreed to allow the creditor to sell the property pledged if the debt were not paid. In this respect the Hollanders did not follow the Roman law and the law of Friesland (Sande, 3, 12, 20), for both these systems allowed the pledgee to sell the pledge if he had contracted to do so, upon non-payment of the principal debt.

That the prohibition of *parate executie* was the law in the time of Grotius admits of little doubt (Grotius, 2, 48, 41; Neostad. *Decis.* 89; Kotzé's Van Leeuwen, vol. 2, p. 407, notes), though the question whether a pact of this kind was void by the later law of Holland still belongs to the *jus controversum.* The late Transvaal High Court decided in favour of the rule laid down by Grotius (*Gundelfinger* v. *De Villiers*), and held that a pledgee could not sell the pledge without the authority of the court. It is difficult to say whether the Dutch jurists followed some ancient custom, or whether they adopted the rule because they attached so much importance to the principle that the mortgagor retained the *dominium* of the thing pledged.

This practice was not peculiar to the Dutch, for we find that in the thirteenth century the Germans adopted the same principle of compelling the pledgee to go to the court before foreclosing. In a Constitution of 1235 we find *Nullus aliquem sine auctoritate judicis provinciae pignorare presumat quod qui fecerit tanquam praedo punitur* and *Quod creditor suum debitorem per poenam pignoris non prius requisito judicio non offendat: quod si aliquis praeter praenotatam formam pignus alstulerit, praeda potius quam pignoratio reputatur.*

At the same time we find in many old pledge-contracts the so-called *pfändungs clausel*, whereby the pledgor agrees that the pledgee can take the pledge *non requisito judicio.* Heusler, in his *Institutionem* (vol. 2, p. 208), thinks that the existence of this clause can be explained if we assume that in such pledge-contracts the pledgor and pledgee lived under different jurisdictions, for he does not think that where both lived under the same jurisdiction a contract so contrary to the statutory provisions would have been recognised as valid. Moreover, we find in many German *landfrieden* that special legislation was introduced permitting the use of the *pfändungs clausel.*

If there were not a general prohibition against *parate executie*, it is difficult to see why these special provisions should have been introduced. If this prohibition against *parate executie* became so general in Germany it may explain why the Hollanders departed from the old custom of regarding the pledge as a sort of *pactum de retrovendendo*, and why they adopted the custom of regarding *parate executie* as illegal.

CHAPTER XVII.

SALE.

THE law of sale in Holland is founded in its main features upon the Roman law. Here and there, however, we find that the Roman-Dutch law has not adhered rigidly to the rules of the *Corpus Juris.* Where differences do exist, as in the case of sale of immovable property, *naasting* and the specific performance of a contract of sale, we may assert with considerable confidence that these differences owe their origin to the influence of German customs, so strong as to withstand the influence of the Roman law.

In a former chapter, when dealing with the alienation of immovable property, we saw that the law of Holland only recognised one mode of transfer of land, viz., *traditio coram lege loci*, and that this mode of alienation was probably derived from the bodies of German law which prevailed in western Europe. We saw that the alienation took place before the schout and schepenen or before the schepenen alone, and that there is evidence that this practice existed in the thirteenth century. In dealing with the history of the law of sale in the present chapter, I have thought that it might interest students to know something more of the early history of this very important branch of law.

The old law of Holland, like the old law of most European countries, recognised a great deal of symbolism. This symbolism was carried to great lengths in all the very important contracts of daily occurrence. It is therefore not surprising to find that in the Contract of Sale we are met with a large number of symbolical acts. First, then, with regard to the sale of land. The Franks, Frisians, Saxons and other German tribes had a great variety of ceremonies and solemnities in carrying out a sale of land. Some of these have so completely disappeared that they would only interest the law student who has antiquarian tastes, whilst others have left behind them traces in the language of the people and the practice of the courts. It is to this latter kind that I shall confine my attention.

One of the most prevalent methods of selling land in vogue in the Netherlands during the middle ages was that of *stock legging*, as it was technically called. This consisted in its simplest form of seller and purchaser holding a rod and reciting to some witnesses (generally three) the conditions of the sale of the land. In the Landrecht of Selwerden (4, 4) the following passage occurs: "No ownership can pass in goods sold by the mere conclusion of an agreement to sell; there must be a clear delivery." In the sale of movables the goods must pass from hand to hand, whilst in the case of immovables there must be a sale with the rod (*in roerlycke goederen geschieden moet van handt tot handt ende in onroerlycke met stocklegginge*). The symbol of the rod is a very old and a very prevalent one. Antiquarians trace it to the sceptre, which appears to have been a universal sign of kingly power. This rod was unquestionably used by the judge as one of his insignia of office. He always used a rod when pronouncing his doom or judgment (*so neemt hy (de regter) eene roede in de handt en leit die op't aerde ende vraagt vonnes).*

Now this sale with the rod was conducted in some places with greater solemnity than the mere presence of the parties and three witnesses. In Vossmaer, for instance, the sale was concluded in the presence of the judge and of several witnesses, and the rod was also a part of the ceremony. The procedure adopted in that locality was as follows: The parties proceeded together with the judge (schout) and several witnesses to the land which was to be sold or to be let for a long period. The boundaries of the parcel sold were then pointed out, and the judge took his rod or staff in the centre, whilst the parties to the sale held the ends. The judge then declared in a loud voice the conditions of the sale or long lease. Here then we have the interposition of the judge in its simplest form—the earliest *traditio coram lege loci.*

Later on we find the sale conducted in a still more solemn form. The purchaser could in certain cases demand that the seller should cause the sale to be published by banns on three successive Sundays. On the appointed day the parties assembled on the ground together with the judge (schout), three schepenen and a land-surveyor. The rod (which now appears to have become a land-surveyor's measuring rod) was also used. After several ceremonies the judge took the rod in his hand, declared the conditions, and then handed the rod to the surveyor and ordered him then and there to measure the ground. A sale conducted in this fashion gave the purchaser an indefeasible title. Later on the ceremonial was simplified and a mere declaration by the seller in the presence of the schout and schepenen (which was in all probability written down by an official) came to be considered as sufficient (Noordewier, pp. 259 *et seq.*).

There were several other methods of symbolical tradition, but two deserve special mention. They were both used in connection with the sale of movable property. The one was to touch the article with the tips of the fingers (*aanstooten met de finger toppen*); this signified that the conditions were settled and the sale agreed upon. It is from this symbolical tradition that we get in Dutch the interjection *Top!* meaning "agreed." This expression *Top!* when two parties have come to an agreement or understanding, is very frequently heard amongst the Dutch-speaking people of South Africa, and very few who use it know its derivation.

The other symbolical method of delivery was to place the right foot upon the thing sold. This symbol afterwards came to have a specialised meaning, and to sell a thing *voetstoots* meant to sell the thing without any undertaking as to warranty.

In the early days, therefore, all sales were accompanied by certain ceremonies and solemnities, but gradually the only ceremony in the sale of movables, after the parties had come to an agreement, was the delivery. The sale of immovable property, however, was always accompanied with a considerable ceremonial, and the presence of witnesses was one of the most important requisites. These witnesses were no doubt the precursors of the schout and schepenen. In the thirteenth century the sale before schout and schepenen, or before schepenen only, was the regular practice, though in some parts of the Netherlands a written document was essential to the validity of the sale (*Recht. Obs.* vol. 2, p. 172).

The Placaat of 1529, requiring all sales to be *coram lege loci*, introduced nothing new, but merely regulated and systematised the ancient customs of the country, and when the Transvaal legislature required all sales of land to be in writing they reintroduced a practice which was once in vogue in certain parts of the Netherlands.

The next point with regard to the sale of land which I wish to touch upon is the *periculum rei venditae.* In the Roman law the rule of the *periculum rei venditae* was quite general, and applied equally to movables and to immovables. Upon the completion of the contract all risk attaching to the thing sold fell upon the purchaser whether there had been delivery or not. The Roman-Dutch law adopted this rule in its entirety with regard to movables, but with regard to immovables the doctrine was not accepted unconditionally.

We have seen that the Placaat of Charles V did not recognise as valid the transfer of immovable property unless it took place *coram lege loci* and unless the proper transfer duty was paid. Neostadius (*Sup. Cur. Decis.* 70) tells us that if land is sold to two persons, then in a competition between them the person who gets transfer *coram lege loci* will be in a better position than the one to whom it was first sold, but who failed to get the proper transfer. If, however, the land were sold to two persons, neither of whom gets transfer, the rule *qui prior in tempore potior in jure* applies. The person, therefore, who has made a contract with regard to the purchase of a piece of land has certain rights as against the owner even though there has been no actual transfer. Hence Groenewegen tells us (*ad Grot.* 3, 14, 34, and *Inst.* 3, 24, 3) that the *periculum rei venditae* applies also to the sale of immovable property which has been sold, but of which no transfer has been given. If, however, there is a condition in the contract of sale that the purchaser is not immediately to get possession of the thing sold, but is to wait a certain time for it, then the *periculum rei venditae* will not lie with the purchaser from the date of the sale, but will only begin to run against him from the day on which delivery was to be made. Even if delivery had been made to him previous to the time stipulated, the risk will still lie with the seller until the stipulated date of delivery has arrived.

Neostadius, however (*Cur. Hol. Decis.* 32), seems to have taken a different view. The following is a free rendering of the decision referred to: "It is a well-known legal principle that when a contract of sale is arrived at the *periculum rei venditae* lies with the purchaser even though the subject-matter of the sale has not yet been delivered, and therefore even if the thing sold is destroyed or spoilt the purchaser will have to pay for it. The Placaat of 1529, however, provides that no one shall sell land, &c., except before the judge of the place where such lands are situated, and further that all sales, &c., otherwise made shall be considered valueless and void. Now it has occurred that Titius has sold to Seius certain land and houses of which Seius has had the usufruct, but the land had not been transferred to Seius *coram lege loci.* According to the civil law the tradition to Seius was complete, but no tradition has taken place before the magistrate. Now the houses were burnt down and the land was inundated, and the question has arisen—Who has to bear the loss? According to the civil law the risk lay with Seius, the purchaser, but according to the Placaat the sale is void, and it is a rule of law that what the law forbids is to be considered null and void. The opinions of the judges differed and no judgment was given upon the matter."

Voet discusses the question (18, 6, 6) and says: "Since, therefore, the only change introduced by modern practice relates to the mode of delivery, that is, to the transfer of the *dominium* of immovable property, and the transfer of the risk does not depend on the transfer of ownership, there is no reason why a change in the form of the one should involve a change in the other." Although in his *Introduction* Grotius does not mention the rider added by Groenewegen, he states it as a rule of law in his *De Jure Belli ac Pacis* (2, 12, 15, 2), and Voet approves of this view in the passage cited above.

With regard to movables, therefore, our law as to the risk is the same as the Roman law, but in regard to immovables our law differs from the Roman law where a period has been fixed when transfer is to be given, for then during the interim period the risk will lie with the vendor.

The spread of the Protestant religion in Holland had a very far-reaching effect upon the relation of the individual to the Church and to Church property. Justinian protected the immovable property belonging to the Church from alienation generally, and where such alienation was permitted it was hedged in with most difficult and onerous conditions. The Canon law also placed grave restrictions upon the sale of Church property. By the Roman law, if a person bought Church property from the State, he obtained a valid title; but the Canon law did not recognise such a sale even when made by the Fiscus. All distinctions, however, were swept away after the Reformation, and Church property was placed on the same plane as any other, and the same formalities were required for the sale of ecclesiastical as for private property.

There was a curious custom prevalent in a great many towns of Holland, though never actually forming part of its common law, known as the *jus retractus* or *naasting*. Grotius defines *naasting* as the right of a person over immovable property, as also against the purchaser and seller thereof, to step into the place of the purchaser whenever the property is sold. The origin of this custom has been the subject of considerable dispute. Bynkershoek thought that its origin was to be sought in the feudal customs, but Van der Spiegel (p. 133) says: "If I mistake not the origin of this custom is to be found in the ancient customs of the Germans which were brought over by the Franks."

A favourite form of *naasting* was that by which the blood relations of the seller had the right to claim the property from the purchaser for the same price the latter paid for it (*jus retractus familiae*). Van der Spiegel tells us that with the Germans the family ties were so closely knit that in any dealing with land the relatives had to be consulted. The principle pervaded the whole of the German law. We see it in the marriage law and in the law of inheritance. The immovable property was always regarded as family property, which could not be alienated without the consent of the nearest relatives. In return for this privilege they had to take part in the family feud. (*Suscipere tam immicitias seu patris seu propinqui quam amicitias necesse est.*—Tacit. *Germ.* 21.) This vendetta formed for a long time part of the customary law of Holland, and we constantly find it cropping up in the *Lex Salica* and the old keuren of the Netherlands, where it was known as the *Maagzoen.*

Inasmuch as this *jus retractus* did not form part of the common law of Holland, it was not taken over into the law of the Cape Colony. The idea, however, was not entirely lost, for there are still many old properties at the Cape burdened with the condition that they may not be sold out of the family, and this condition is nothing more nor less than the ancient *naasting* in a different form.

CHAPTER XVIII.

LAESIO ENORMIS.

ANOTHER custom connected with sale which formed a part of the common law of Holland, but which no longer obtains in the Cape Colony, is the doctrine of *laesio enormis.*

This had its origin not in the customs of the Germans, but in the *Lex Romana.* If the seller or purchaser was prejudiced to the extent of more than half the real value the sale could be rescinded. Such a law is hostile to commerce, and it shows once more how tenacious the Hollanders were of their ancient customs, that, even after they became a commercial nation, trading with the greater portion of the known world, they still retained a law so fatal to free commercial intercourse. They no doubt felt the burden it was to their trade, for they tried by all manner of means to whittle away the injurious effect of the *laesio enormis.* This fragment of old-world law is still of full force and effect in the Transvaal.

This doctrine affords an excellent example of the phenomenon, so frequent in the history of the Roman-Dutch law, where a principle taken over from the Roman law is so modified and extended by custom, and by the interpretation of jurist and judge, that the very reason of the principle is lost amidst the vast mass of subsequent accretion. A reaction then sets in, and the original principle together with all the subtleties that have grown up around it are swept away to make room for new ideas.

It was a general principle of the old Roman law that a

vendor and purchaser were at arms' length, and that each could seek for himself the greatest possible advantage. Ulpian (*D.* 4, 4, 16, 4) tells us that it was a dictum of Pomponius that buyer and seller could get the better of one another. *Idem Pomponius ait in pretio emptionis et venditionis naturaliter licere contrahentibus se circumvenire.* Later on it was found that persons in needy circumstances were often compelled to sell their land for prices far beneath the market value, and to meet such cases an equitable doctrine of the praetor was invoked by which in *bonae fidei* transactions parties could be put on an equal footing *quia in bonae fidei judiciis, quod inaequaliter factum esse constiterit in melius reformabitur.* If, therefore, in a contract of sale the one party got an extraordinary advantage over the other, this equitable doctrine of the praetor seems to have been relied upon by the party who had been placed in the worse position.

At any rate the Emperors Diocletian and Maximilian thought that provision ought to be made in case a vendor sold his land at too low a price, and came to his assistance with a rescript which is embodied in the *Code* (4, 44, 2). The words of this rescript are, "If you or your father have sold land (*fundus*) for a price less than its value, it is just that if you offer to the purchasers the price they paid they should, upon order of a judge, restore to you the property; or otherwise, if the buyer prefers it, you should receive the amount that will make up the proper price. You will be considered to have sold for a price less than the value if the price paid to you is half of the true value."

The *Code* therefore provided that the vendor of land could set aside a sale if the purchaser had paid less than half the true value of the estate. The reason of the *lex* usually given is that owners of property were often compelled to sell owing to the fact that they were reduced to great straits by circumstances over which they had no control, and unscrupulous purchasers took advantage of their dire distress. We see, therefore, that the Roman law only contemplated the special case where the vendor sold land for less than half the value.

The glossators thought that it would be unjust to give the benefit of this *lex* to the vendor alone and to deny it to the purchaser, and they therefore interpreted the *lex* to apply as well to the purchaser as to the seller. Donellus puts the case very clearly: *Beneficium autem quod hic venditori tribuitur aperte beneficium est causae non personae. Tribuitur enim laesioni, id est venditori non quia est venditor sed quia venditor laesus est* (*ad*, 4, 44, 2, par. 48). This view was adopted by the great jurists of the sixteenth century, and came thus to be incorporated into the Roman-Dutch law. Hence Voet (18, 5, 5) lays it down that there is no difference between the purchaser and the vendor as regards *laesio enormis*, and quotes the Amsterdam volume of the Consultations (*Amst.* vol. 3, cons. 14), where an opinion is found to that effect dated 1596. This was the first deviation from the original provision of the Roman law.

Again, the *Code* only speaks of sales of land (*fundus*). In this respect also the *lex* was extended by the jurists, and Voet tells us that in Holland, at any rate, the practice prevailed of allowing the remedy to be extended first to house property and then to the more valuable kinds of movables. This view of Voet was approved of by Sir Henry de Villiers in *Levisohn* v. *Williams* (Buch. 1875, p. 108).

Exceptions, however, soon came to be engrafted upon the general principle, and certain transactions were excluded from the operation of the doctrine. If the subject of the sale were of so uncertain a value that no estimate could be made of what would be a fair price, then the doctrine of *laesio enormis* did not apply. Hence were excluded the sale of an inheritance, an *emptio spei* like the cast of a net, and later on the same was decided with regard to the sale of minerals and turf (Sande, 3, 4, 16). The doctrine was interpreted not to apply to the sale of an annuity or of crops to be raised on a certain piece of land, nor generally to all cases where the value is unascertainable (Huber, *Hed. Recht.* 3, 6, 6). Sales by judicial decree or by public auction, as well as all transactions arising out of compromise, were also excluded. On the other hand, the doctrine was extended first to all *bonae fidei* contracts which resemble sale, and later on in Holland even *stricti juris* contracts were included (Voet, 18, 5, 14).

We see, therefore, that the original principle of law was that buyer and seller could circumvent one another in any way short of fraud. An equitable rule was then adopted that there must be some ratio between the true value and the price. Later on the ratio was fixed with regard to land at half the true value. The doctrine was then extended to movables, and the purchaser was placed on the same footing as the vendor. Not only in true sales, but also in transactions similar to sales, the right of rescission was admitted on account of *laesio enormis*. Meanwhile the impossibility of applying the doctrine to all cases of sale became manifest, and numerous exceptions were grafted upon the rule, and eventually wherever the element of chance prevailed, the injustice of allowing the sale to stand when the transaction turned out favourable, and to be upset when a loss ensued, came to be universally recognised. As commerce increased the great difficulty of upholding the doctrine became manifest.

In France the *lex* of the *Code* was adopted in its restricted form, and the right of rescission was restricted to the sale of land. For a short period it was specially abolished, but later on it was re-enacted in its restricted form (*Code*, arts. 1674 *et seq.*). In some States where the civil law prevails the principle was adopted in a restricted form, whilst in others it was altogether abandoned.

This doctrine of the civil law never formed part of the common law of England. The tendency of modern ideas is therefore clearly towards a curtailment of the doctrine, if not towards its total abrogation. It is therefore not astonishing that the Cape legislature in 1879 passed an Act by which the whole doctrine of *laesio enormis* was entirely swept away, and in that respect the law of the Cape Colony has been assimilated to the law of England.

CHAPTER XIX.

SPECIFIC PERFORMANCE.

WITH regard to the specific performance of contracts generally, and more especially with regard to the specific performance of a contract of sale, there has always been a dispute between the various jurists as to whether specific performance formed part of the law of Holland. As the history of this subject is of great interest, I shall deal with it somewhat fully. The controversy is one which dates back to a very remote period. It was very acute in the time of the *Quatuor Doctores* (twelfth century), though it is hardly necessary to consider the views of all the ancient jurists who took part in this controversy. Donellus was of opinion that no one could be compelled to do an act, and that he could always get rid of an *obligatio faciendi* by paying *id quod interest* (Donel. *ad*, l. 72; *De Verb. Obl.* n. 32, vol. 11, p. 1218). Cujacius, on the other hand, held the view that the civil law allowed the one party to a contract to compel the other to do an act.

There were, therefore, two schools, both relying on the *Corpus Juris* for their different views. Zoesius (45, 1, 52) adhered to the opinion of Cujacius, whilst Grotius adopted the view of Donellus. Grotius (3, 3, 41) says: "But although by natural law a person who has promised to do something is bound to do it if it is in his power, he may, nevertheless, by municipal law release himself by paying the other contracting party or acceptor the value of his interest in the same or the penalty, if any has been agreed upon, in default of payment." Groenewegen in his note to this passage says that in his time this was not the law, and that a person could not release himself by paying damages, but could be compelled by civil imprisonment to the strict fulfilment of what he had promised. In support of this view he quotes the *Instructiën van den Hoogen Raad* and the decisions of the Court of Mechlin, but he adds at the same time "that some jurists, not without reason, declare this to be in accordance with the Roman law." The *Instructie* (275) referred to is to the effect that judgments or orders containing a *condemnatio ad factum* are to be executed by civil imprisonment (*gijzeling*), and the refractory person is to be imprisoned until he carries out the sentence.

In the *De Legibus Abrogatis* (*ad Dig.* 42, 1, 13, 1) Groenewegen says: "*Hodie in omnibus faciendi obligationibus praecise ad factum cogi potest neque solvendo interesse liberatur promissor qui faciendi facultatem habet. Ita judicatum refert Christinaeus* (vol. 1, dec. 323, n. 8)." Groenewegen therefore had no doubt whatever that not only in contracts *ad dandum*, but also in contracts *ad faciendum*, specific performance could be enforced. In referring to Christinaeus we find that he is of the same opinion, and he also tells us that this view was actually followed by the Court of Brabant.

Van Leeuwen (Kotzé, vol. 2, p. 118) in treating of the contracts *do ut des*, &c. (bk. 4, c. 14, s. 3) says "that by the Canon law, which in this respect we follow, a simple promise made premeditatedly begets a complete obligation, so at the present day in these innominate contracts and all other transactions all change of intention and withdrawal are excluded, except where it has been otherwise expressly stipulated. But he who has on his side completed the transaction has the right of compelling his adversary to perform his part thereof, and need not be satisfied with *id quod interest* if the doing consisted in something which it was in the power of the adversary to perform, but may compel him by means of imprisonment to perform that which he has promised." He relies on the same authorities for this view of Groenwegen.

Ulrich Huber, in his *Praelectiones ad*, bk. 3, tit. 16 (vol. 1, p. 296) (*De Verborum Obligationibus*) expresses an opinion in favour of specific performance being admissible in contracts *ad faciendum* as well as in contracts *ad dandum*. Van der Keessel (*Thes.* 512) holds that by the proper interpretation of the civil law a person who has promised to do an act can be compelled to perform his promise. He refers to a decision of the Supreme Court of Holland, reported in Neostadius. But later on we shall see that this decision only refers to cases of sale.

Professor Scheltinga, in his annotations on Grotius (*ad*, 3, 3, 41), says: "With regard to the doctrine of Grotius, as expressed in this paragraph, we must remark that it is certain that if a person promises to do a thing *or* to pay a penalty if he fails, he can fulfil his obligation by paying the penalty; but with regard to the question whether a person who has promised to do a thing can fulfil his obligation by paying the *id quod interest*, there is some doubt. We, however, are of opinion that if the promissor can do the act promised, then, according to the civil law, he cannot escape his promise by paying the *id quod interest*, but he is bound to perform the act promised. This was also the view of Groenewegen, and it appears from his remarks that this was the law of Holland, so that a promissor *facti* can in Holland be compelled by civil imprisonment *ad factum praestandum*."

From the passages of Van der Keessel and Scheltinga referred to, it would appear that this was the view of eminent professors of law towards the end of the eighteenth century. Voet, on the other hand, adopts the view of Donellus, that *nemo cogi potest ad factum praestandum*. His words are (45, 1, 8): *In iis, quae faciendi obligationem continent, generaliter placuit, neminem ad factum obligatum, praecise ad implementum facti cogi posse sed liberari praestando id quod interest.* He discusses the civil law, and comes to the conclusion that this is the proper view to be gathered from the texts. Voet's view is adopted by Dekker in his notes on Van Leeuwen (2 Kotzé, p. 33).

We see, therefore, that the view that specific performance can be enforced has been defended by reference to texts in the civil law, whilst those who attack specific performance rely on the same law for their opinions. Heineccius is of opinion that the Germans adopted the view that a person could be compelled to do an act which he had promised, and that he could not free himself from his obligation by tendering the *id quod interest* (*Elem. Jur. Germ.* bk. 2, sec. 346).

Thus far I have dealt with the general question as to whether a person can be compelled *ad factum praestandum*. I shall now proceed to consider the question whether in the case of sale a vendor can be compelled to deliver the actual thing sold. Of course if it be conceded that *in omnibus obligationibus promissor ad factum praestandum cogi potest*, then it follows that he can be compelled to perform specifically the contract of sale. At the same time the general rule may not be true, but the contract of sale may give a special right of specific performance.

This question is discussed by Mr. Justice Kotzé in his second volume of Van Leeuwen, p. 141. In addition to some of the authors quoted above he refers to Huber's *Hedendaegse Rechtsgeleerdheyt.* There is a misprint in the reference; it should be 3, 2, 9 and 10. Huber says, "As soon as the parties have come to an agreement they cannot recede from the sale; the seller must deliver the article sold and the purchaser must pay the price, nor can the seller escape delivery and free himself by tendering the *id quod interest,* even if he offered double the price."

Van Leeuwen says the same (Kotzé, vol. 2, p. 140), and he bases this view upon a decision of the Supreme Court quoted by Neostadius (*Decis.* 50). As this case was decided in the sixteenth century, and is quoted with approval by many authorities, I will give it here. The headnote reads as follows: "A person who has the power of delivering a thing sold will not be liberated by paying the damages of the *id quod interest* for non-delivery. A certain vendor was condemned to deliver to a purchaser a certain piece of land; he declared that he could not deliver the land inasmuch as he had already delivered it to another, but he offered the damages which the purchaser had suffered by his failure to deliver. When, however, it was found that in truth he had not yet delivered the land to the second purchaser, the court ordered that the vendor should be civilly imprisoned until he had given delivery of the land. The reason was because a person who had it in his power to deliver an article sold could not escape his liability to deliver by tendering damages. If the vendor remained obstinate and would not deliver, notwithstanding the civil imprisonment, then the land must be taken from him by a judge or he must be compelled to make delivery. If the vendor refuses, the purchaser may put a value on what it is worth to him to have delivery, and take a pledge for the amount. The vendor, however, will remain in prison until the purchaser is recouped out of the sale of the pledges and the full amount is paid."

It would appear, therefore, that the purchaser could either enforce specific performance or claim the value, and that in order to enforce specific performance the purchaser could call in the aid of the court.

With regard to the contract of sale, Grotius adopts the view of Neostadius and says (3, 15, 6): "If delivery is delayed by the seller, the purchaser has the option of either claiming delivery together with all profits and compensation for loss or merely compensation to the extent of his interest in the delivery, which frequently is more advantageous to him, for instance, when the property is destroyed or damaged." To this Groenewegen adds a note, "To this delivery the seller may be compelled by *gijzeling* or civil imprisonment, nor can the seller escape it by offering to pay the damage caused by the non-delivery."

Voet, however, in his *Commentary* (19, 1, 14) discusses the question fully, and comes to the conclusion that specific performance should not be decreed in a case of sale. If we look closely into the language of Voet it is manifest that he does not say that the law of Holland does not allow specific performance, but he argues that it is not advisable to admit specific performance of a sale. Towards the end of par. 14 he says: *Nostros vero mores quod attinet scriptum quidem a pluribus invenio venditorem habentem rei tradendae facultatem compelli posse ut tradat nec liberari praestando id quod interest.* He then quotes Neostadius, Van Leeuwen and Grotius. If the judges have the power of taking away the ownership from one person and giving it to another, then he thinks specific performance can be enforced; but if they do not possess that power, then the better course would be to adopt the rule of the Roman law and to allow the vendor to compensate with *id quod interest.* In his *Compendium*, however, Voet expresses clearly the view that in case of sale specific performance can be claimed (*ad*, 19, 1, 8). *Potest autem jure hodierno venditor habens rei tradendae facultatem cogi ut rem praecise tradat nec liberatur praestando id quod interest.* It would therefore appear that Voet did not always hold the view that specific performance should not be decreed in cases of sale.

The impression which the passage (19, 1, 14) leaves upon my mind is that Voet thought that the true view with regard to the civil law is the view of Donellus, that *nemo praecise cogi potest ad faciendum,* and that therefore a vendor should not be compelled to make delivery ; that it is inadvisable to give a judge the power of specifically enforcing contracts by *gijzeling,* and that therefore we should return to what Voet considers the true view of the Roman law. I do not understand Voet to say authoritatively that it was not the law and custom of Holland to compel a vendor to make delivery.

In the Cape Colony the case of *Malan* v. *Schalkwyk and*

Odendaal (1 Searle, 225) has been cited as an authority in favour of the power of the court to decree specific performance of a contract of sale. The case is, however, badly reported, and the matter was never actually raised in argument. The court no doubt said that the plaintiff was entitled to the property in dispute on paying certain sums to the defendant Schalkwyk, but there is nothing in the report which justifies one in concluding that specific performance was decreed. It is true the summons prayed that the defendant might be compelled to deliver up possession of the land, but in the way the judgment is reported it may be construed to be a mere declaration of rights.

In *Norden* v. *Rennie* (1879, Buch. p. 155) the plaintiff brought an action for specific performance of a contract of sale of landed property sold by defendant to the plaintiff. Sir Henry de Villiers, C.J., said: "It is clear that the plaintiff is entitled to have specific performance of the contract, *but the judgment of the court must be in the alternative.* The declaration simply asks for specific performance, and does not pray for damages, but under the prayer for general relief the court will be able to award damages as an alternative." There is nothing in this report to show that the question was argued at the Bar.

In *Kettles* v. *Bennett* (8 E.D.C. 89) Barry, J.P., expressed an opinion in favour of the court's power to decree specific performance of a contract of sale: "Where a vendor sells property, some of which he cannot deliver, he cannot be heard to say, 'Because I cannot deliver some you cannot make me deliver the rest.' The rule of law is, where a purchaser buys property and the vendor cannot deliver part, the vendor may at the request of the purchaser be ordered to deliver what he can deliver. But the court will not make such order unless the plaintiff insists upon it, and unless it could see its way clearly to apportion the purchase amount which will have to be paid if only part is delivered."

In *Van der Westhuysen* v. *Velenski* (15 S.C. 237) the court decreed specific performance of an undertaking to sign a formal contract, but gave an alternative judgment for damages, so that this case is no authority that specific performance of a contract of sale without an alternative of damages can be decreed. Sir Henry de Villiers, C.J., said: "The court must declare that the contract embodied in the memorandum was a valid and binding one, and must grant an order compelling the defendant to duly execute the formal contract. . . . It is usual, however, to fix an amount as damages in case of refusal to comply with the order of court. The court in such cases has never gone minutely into the question of damages sustained, but has taken a round sum *for the purpose of enforcing its judgment.*"

In a note to ch. 4, bk. 18, sec. 1, of his translation of Van Leeuwen's *Commentary,* Mr. Justice Kotzé expresses a decided opinion in favour of the contention that the Roman-Dutch law gave the purchaser the right of demanding the delivery of the article sold, and that he was not obliged to be satisfied with the *id quod interest* (Kotzé's trans. vol. 2, p. 141). He seems, however, to have gone somewhat too far when he asserts that it is the settled practice of South Africa, for *Norden* v. *Rennie* hardly seems to justify this view. The High Court of the South African Republic unhesitatingly adopted the doctrine of specific performance of a contract of sale in the unreported case of *Cohen* v. *Shires* (1882) and in the reported case of *Thompson* v. *Pullinger* (1 Off. Rep. (Eng.), 298).

The Natal Supreme Court in *Trollip* v. *Tromp and Van Zweel* (1 N.L.R. 130, 166) granted specific performance in an action on a contract for sale of land, and ordered the judgment to be carried out by the Master, inasmuch as the plaintiff could not get the necessary authority from the registered owner, one of the defendants in the action.

The Supreme Court of the Transvaal has adopted the principle of specific performance in a contract of sale, and has carried out this principle to its logical consequence. It has said to the vendor: "What you have sold you must deliver, and you must deliver in accordance with your promise, and if you fail to deliver in terms of the contract the court will not only compel you to deliver, but will compel you to make good any loss which the purchaser has suffered on account of your failure to deliver in accordance with your contract." In the case of *Silverton Estates Co.* v. *Bellevue Syndicate* ([1904] T.S. 462) Sir James Rose Innes said: "The court will lay down the rule that where a seller has made default in delivery of the thing sold and is *in mora*, the purchaser, in addition to demanding specific performance, may, where he has sustained damages which the law recognises and allows, claim those damages in the same action" (at p. 470).

In the Transvaal, therefore, no alternative claim for damages is required, for the courts will decree specific performance of a contract of sale and damages as well, if such have been caused by default in delivery.

CHAPTER XX.

LETTING AND HIRING.

In dealing with the development of the Roman-Dutch law of Letting and Hiring, the first thing that strikes us is the peculiar doctrine embodied in the maxim *Huur gaat voor koop*. Grotius tells us that it was a custom of Holland that a purchaser must continue a lease granted by his vendor. Groenewegen points out that this custom was diametrically opposed to the Roman civil law (*C.* 4, 65, 9), which provided that the purchaser of a property was not bound to leave the lessee upon the property until the expiration of his lease, unless the sale was concluded subject to that condition. I have not been able to find out whether this practice was derived from some ancient German custom or whether it grew up in the Netherlands. Heineccius mentions no such German custom, and, as far as I know, none of the old Roman-Dutch lawyers discuss its origin. We find the principle enunciated in several of the local Codes in the Netherlands (*Regts. Obser.* vol. 3, obs. 79). In the Customs of Rhynland we find, "It is a common custom and law that not only the heirs of the deceased, but also the purchaser, must acknowledge the lease entered into by his predecessor in title, viz., the vendor, according to the maxim *Huur gaat voor koop*."

Similar provisions are found in the Keuren of Leyden, Amsterdam, Middelburg, Zierikzee, Flushing, Antwerp and Mechlin. In Friesland, however, a modified form of the

Roman rule prevailed. It would therefore appear that the custom grew up in Holland not from any general principle, but because it had been specially adopted by several of the most important cities of the Netherlands. Nor did this principle apply to all leases, for when the lease was one *in longum tempus* the purchaser could eject the lessee unless the agreement was made in writing and registered before the judge of the place where the property was situated. This at any rate was the view of the Court of Holland, for Groenewegen (*ad Grot.* 3, 19, 9) tells us that it was well understood that land could not be leased for more than ten years unless a written lease was executed *coram lege loci*, and that this view was based upon a decision of the Court of Holland given in 1609 (*Sup. Cur. Decis.* 30). Neostadius quotes a decision of the Supreme Court of Holland and West Friesland, in which it was definitely laid down that according to the law of Holland land could not be sold otherwise than subject to the rule that Lease goes before Sale, and, as far as I know, this is the first judicial declaration of such a general custom.

With regard to the necessity for registering leases for more than ten years in order to bind a purchaser, there has been some dispute, though there can be little doubt that according to the view of the older lawyers registration was necessary. Groenewegen, in addition to the passage cited above, tells us in his *De Legibus* (*ad Cod.* 4, 65, 9): *Ceterum si ad longum tempus privatim fundus locatus sit aliud dicendum existimo. . . . In locatione enim longi temporis eadem solemnitas intervenire debet quae in alienatione cujus naturam induit atque sortitur ex communi atque inveterata doctorum sententia.* The decision referred to by Groenewegen is given in the appendix to the Amsterdam third volume of the Consultations, and as it is an important decision I give a translation of the text. "Some one having leased a house or land for as long as the lessee pleased, and the lessee having enjoyed it for a period of more than ten years, a dispute arose whether the lessor could eject the lessee; the court decided that the lessor could eject because leases do not run for more than ten years unless passed *coram lege loci,* when they affect the land."

In *Green* v. *Griffiths* (4 S.C. 346) the question was raised by Sir Henry de Villiers, but not decided. He says: "It is another question whether a lease for a long period, such as ten years or more, whether parole or in writing, will avail against a particular successor of the lessor unless in some form or another registered or indorsed upon the title-deeds of the land in the Deeds Register of the colony. The case of *Maynard* v. *Usher* (2 Menz. 170) is generally cited in support of the proposition that a lease, however long, is binding upon a purchaser of land from the lessor; but this proposition is too widely stated, for the purchaser in that case had full notice of the long lease of ninety-nine years, which was in fact annexed to and registered with his deed of transfer. The court decided that the Placaat of the 9th May, 1744, was not in force in this colony, but even before 1744 it was the better opinion that a lease was not binding upon the particular successor unless it was made *coram judice rei sitae,* or unless if made by a private contract it was for a shorter period than ten years (Groen. *C.* 4 65, 9)." The learned Chief Justice then points out that the Placaat of 1744 extended the period to twenty-five years, and required leases for that period or longer to be registered in the same way as the alienation of immovable property.

Voet has been cited as an authority for the contrary view. It seems to me, however, that Voet (19, 2, 1) says this: "A lease confers a *jus ad personam* and not a *jus in rem,* and the length of time for which a lease runs cannot alter its nature from an obligation *ad personam* to an obligation *in rem.* Theoretically, therefore, a lease for more than ten years should not require greater formalities than a lease for a less period. If, however, leases for long terms need not be registered, then sellers who have granted such long leases may defraud purchasers. It would therefore be well to make leases for a period longer than ten years binding between the parties themselves and their heirs, but not binding on creditors or singular successors. This view has been taken by the Court of Holland and by Matthaeus, and if taken with the above limitations I have no objection against such a custom."

Now if we turn from his *Commentary* to his *Compendium* we find the following: "By the law of Holland and Utrecht the purchaser of land or houses must recognise the leases made by the seller *if they do not exceed ten years,* even though such leases are not disclosed." It seems to me, therefore, that Voet never intended to go so far as to say that leases over ten years were by the customs of Holland not binding upon particular successors. He seems rather to have accepted the law as laid down by Groenewegen, Neostadius and Matthaeus, subject to the limitation that a lease over ten years was binding on the contracting parties and their heirs.

I have tried to discover why the Placaat of 1744 extended the time to twenty-five years, but I have not yet been successful. It is, however, possible that this Placaat did not alter the law, but only fixed a definite period for which a duty of 2½ per cent. had to be paid. In other words, the old law requiring a lease over ten years to be registered in order to bind the particular successor still remained in force, but upon such leases under twenty-five years no duty had to be paid. If, however, the lease was for a period of twenty-five years or more it had not only to be registered, but a duty of 2½ per cent. had to be paid as well. If the ten-year period of the old law was extended to twenty-five years, it does seem strange that no mention is made in the law itself of the alteration.

In the Transvaal the question has been set at rest by sub-sec. 1 of sec. 29 of Proclamation 8 of 1902, which provides that leases of over ten years, to be binding upon particular successors for a period longer than ten years, must be registered.

Another important difference between the Roman law and the Roman-Dutch law is the law relating to the subletting of rural tenements. The rule of the Roman law was *Nemo prohibetur rem quam conduxit fruendam, alii locare, si nihil aliud convenit* (*C.* 4, 65, 6). Here, then, there was no restriction whatever upon the right to sublet either the whole or part of the property leased. This principle did not commend itself to several of the big towns of Holland (Grot. 3, 21, 10). In Amsterdam, Gouda, Utrecht, Middelburg and 's Hertogenbosch the subletting of houses was forbidden unless with the consent of the owners. The general law of Holland, however, allowed the subletting of urban tenements, and this view has been adopted by the Cape courts (*Swarts* v. *Landmark*, 2 S.C. 5). With respect to farm lands (*praedia rustica*), the law of Holland, as interpreted by the courts of Holland and by the Supreme Court of the Cape Colony, did not allow a sub-lease without the express consent of the owner (*De Vries* v. *Alexander*, Foord, 43). The Transvaal court in *Eckhart* v. *Nolte* (3 C.L.J. 43) held a contrary view, and decided that *praedia rustica* could be sublet.

There is no doubt whatever that the great authorities on the Roman-Dutch law were of opinion that *praedia rustica* could not be sublet without the special consent of the lessor. On the other hand, they all rely on the Placaats of 1515 and 1580,* and, as Mr. Justice Kotzé has rightly pointed out, these Placaats do not speak of lease (*huur*), but of *na huur*, *i.e.* after lease. What the Placaats sought to avoid was that a lessee should refuse to give up his lease because of some alleged custom which gave him the right to retain it. The Placaats do not speak of subletting; they are only directed against holding over (*na huur*). The arguments for and against the view that *praedia rustica* can be sublet are fully set out in the controversial articles of Chief Justice Maasdorp and Mr. Justice Kotzé in the CAPE LAW JOURNAL for the years 1886 and 1887. No amount of argument can, however, get away from the fact that Voet, Neostadius and other

* The Placaat of 1658, mentioned by Van der Keessel in *Thes.* 674, merely repeats the *ipsissima verba* of the Placaats of 1515 and 1580.

great authorities of the Roman-Dutch law were of opinion that *praedia rustica* could not be sublet unless the lessor gave his consent to such sub-lease.

Considering that the Placaats of 1515 and 1580 do not mention subletting, I have asked myself why, with the Placaats before them and with the fact that *na huur* and not *huur* is mentioned, did they persist in the view that *praedia rustica* could not be sublet. Mr. Justice Kotzé thinks *aliquando dormitat bonus Homerus,* but this view does not seem adequate. It has struck me that there may be some other explanation. Although the Placaats do not expressly prohibit the subletting of *praedia rustica,* they may have had that effect indirectly. Now if we look at the wording of the Placaats, we find they say that no lessees and occupiers of land which they have taken on lease may enjoy the land longer than a period of four years except by the leave and consent of the owner, and *that they must have proper written deeds of lease thereof.* In other words, the Placaats prohibit the lessees from holding over on a pretext that they have some *jus retractus,* unless they can produce a written lease. In order to defeat the claim of a landlord to quit, the person who claims a lease over the land must produce a written lease from the landlord. If, therefore, the lessee sublets to a third party, such third party would never be in the position to produce a written lease from the landlord. Now I would suggest that it was this failure to produce a written lease from the landlord, when such was demanded, which made the sub-leases of *praedia rustica* impossible in law, unless the sub-lessee was protected by a written instrument of the landlord. It was not enough for the sub-tenant to say to the owner, "I have no lease from you, but you have a written lease with A B, and I hold from him." The occupier had to prove his title by the production of a written lease, and if he were a sub-tenant he would fail to show his title unless fortified with the written consent of the owner. I have been led to this view by the words of Vinnius (*Inst.* 3, tit. 25, pr. 3). He says, *Apud nos locatio agrorum non procedit sine interventu instrumenti aut publici aut privati nec absque instrumento locationis ullo colono jus est agro conducto frui. Extat de ea re Constitutio Principis Caroli edita,* 1515 *Confirmata, art.* 30, *Polit. Ord.*

The effect of requiring a written lease from the person who claims the enjoyment of the property would be to prevent sub-leases without the owner's written consent. The Placaats according to this view were directed, as correctly stated by Mr. Justice Kotzé, against *na huur* or holding over, but incidentally they came to be regarded as preventing subletting without the written consent of the owner. This view reconciles to some extent the law as stated by Voet and others with the sense and meaning of the Placaats. To this it may be objected that the production of the written lease to prove that there was a *na huur* could only be demanded after the expiration of the lease. But how could the original lease be proved in a case of conflict of evidence except by reference to the written document? In most cases the document would be all the court could rely on, and so in actual practice a written lease from the lessor came to be the only defence which the occupier of *praedia rustica* could set up against the owner.

The sub-lessee would not be heard to set up a sub-lease unless he had the owner's written consent, and so subletting came to be regarded, first, as exceedingly difficult of proof, and afterwards as illegal unless fortified with the written consent of the owner. I merely put this forward as a suggestion of the probable explanation why the text-writers state so categorically that the subletting of *praedia rustica* without the owner's consent is contrary to law, and why they rely for their proposition upon the Placaats.

By the Roman law a lease both of lands and houses could be completed by mere consent, and no writing was necessary to ensure its validity. This was also apparently the law of Holland until the sixteenth century. During that century several placaats were issued by which a lease of lands was declared null and void unless made by a public instrument or by a private writing signed by the owner. Grotius (3, 19, 3) therefore states the law in his day to be that a lease of lands cannot be contracted in Holland without a *schepenkennis* or deed signed by the owner: a lease contracted otherwise is null and void. He makes no mention of the law with regard to *praedia urbana,* though inferentially we may conclude that he did not think that writing was necessary to constitute a lease of houses.

Groenewegen (*De Leg. Abrog.* c. 4, 65, 24) distinctly states that with regard to *praedia urbana* the civil law still prevailed, and that it was customary in Holland to let houses without written leases. *Caeterum in praediorum urbanorum locatione in Hollandia tamen jus civile adeoque et haec lex incorrecta remansit communi et recepta pragmaticorum sententia.* He points out, however, that a difference of opinion existed upon this point, and refers to a Consultation (1 *Holl. Cons.* 262) where the jurist Willemsz held that a written lease was required for houses as well as lands. Groenewegen, however, asserts the custom and relies on the maxim *Optima enim est legum interpretes consuetudo.*

Van Leeuwen (*R.D.L.* bk. 4, c. 21, 3) says that it was the general opinion in his day that no writing was necessary for the lease of a house. Voet (19, 2, 2) refers to this controversy, and holds it to be the better opinion that by the customary law of Holland writing was necessary for leases of houses as well as of lands. He adds, "However, all doubt was subsequently removed by the promulgation of the Placaat of the 3rd April, 1677 (*G.P.B.* vol. 3, p. 1037), which provides that no leases of lands or houses or any immovable property should be made without writing and a sealed instrument."

Van der Keessel (*Thes.* 670–72) boldly states that both houses and lands may be let without any writing, and he infers this with regard to houses from the very law Voet relies upon. With regard to lands, he quotes a decision of the Court of Holland that if a person is the lessee of land on a parole lease he may prove the existence of this lease on oath. He forgets, however, to mention that this case was decided in 1532, and therefore prior to the Placaat of 1580, and that in the same volume of the *Sententiën van den Hove* there is an earlier decision in which a diametrically opposite view is expressed.

It is manifest, therefore, that the law upon this subject was by no means clear even in the eighteenth century. The question cropped up at the Cape in 1839, when the court was called upon to decide whether a written lease was necessary for urban tenements (*Herbert* v. *Anderson*, 2 Menz. 174). The court held "that the four Placaats of 1452, 1515, 1580, and 1677 were merely fiscal or revenue Ordinances of Holland, and had never become or been made law in this colony. That although writing may be necessary to the validity of leases in the cases mentioned in Van Leeuwen's *Roman-Dutch Law*, it is not by the law of this colony required in leases of urban tenements even when the term is a year, at least when followed with possession." The decision is not very lucid, and it is difficult to accept the statement that all the Placaats mentioned are entirely revenue Ordinances, yet this decision established the law in the Cape Colony that writing was not necessary for leases of urban tenements followed with possession.

It is an open question whether a parole lease not followed by possession is valid, though no doubt it would not be difficult to show that the custom of South Africa admits as valid parole leases of urban tenements. In *Green* v. *Griffiths* (4 S.C. 346) Sir Henry de Villiers felt the weakness of the decision of *Herbert* v. *Anderson*. He did not in that case decide the law upon this point, but held that an assignment of a lease need not be in writing.

The Roman-Dutch law with regard to the necessity of writing for leases of *praedia rustica* was apparently in Van der Keessel's time *jus controversum*. In *Friedlander* v. *Croxford & Rhodes* (5 Searle, 395) no decision was given upon this point, though the court decided that a tenant of a *praedium rusticum* cannot sublet without the written consent of the landlord; the same view was afterwards adopted in *De Vries*

v. *Alexander* (Foord, 43). In *Swarts* v. *Landmark* (2 S.C. 5) and in *Nieuwoudt* v. *Slavin* (13 S.C. 58) the Supreme Court of the Cape Colony decided that the test whether a tenement is rural or urban is not the place where the property is situated, but the use to which it is devoted. *Praedium rusticum* is therefore not property situated in the country, but land used for farming purposes.

CHAPTER XXI.

PRESCRIPTION.

ACCORDING to the Roman law Prescription was one of the modes of acquiring ownership. The long-continued possession of a thing was regarded as presumptive evidence that the person in possession was the owner. In French the prescription by which we acquire ownership is called *préscription acquisitive,* whilst the prescription which operates as a bar to a claim is called *préscription extinctive.* The Roman-Dutch lawyers have not made use of any verbal distinction to denote the different kinds of prescription, and therefore there is some confusion between the prescription by which ownership is acquired and the prescription which is equivalent to the English "limitation."

As there are few Roman-Dutch text-books in which the gradual development of our law of prescription has been set out, it may be useful to sketch the history of that branch of law. The origin of our prescription by which ownership is acquired is to be found in the *usucapion* of the Roman law. In the Twelve Tables we find that the term for *usucapio* was *usus auctoritas* (*usus et auctoritas*). The *usus* here refers to the possession, whilst the *auctoritas* refers to the legal protection, the guarantee accorded by the people. The rules with regard to usucapion were highly technical in the very olden Roman times. It is enough to remind the reader that only a Roman citizen could acquire property by usucapion, that the property which could be acquired by usucapion had to be a *res in commercio,* and that land could be acquired by continuous possession for two years, whilst for other things a year sufficed; and, lastly, that the original mode of acquisition was a *justa causa* or *justus titulus. Peregrini,* therefore, could not acquire property on Roman soil by *usucapio.*

In the provinces, however, a similar mode of acquiring property gradually grew up. If a person had been in possession of property for a long time, the praetor allowed the possessor to defend his right to that possession by an exception called the *praescriptio longi temporis.* The *longum tempus* of one province was not always the same as that of another. The period of ten years *inter praesentes* and twenty years *inter absentes* seems to have been the one most generally recognised. This possession gave a *securitas possessionis,* but no *dominium.* The requisites for the *praescriptio longi temporis* were continuous possession and a *justum initium possessionis.* This prescription at first only applied to provincial land, and not to things movable. In the time of Severus (146–211), however, it was extended to movables.

In theory there was no doubt a difference between the acquisition of ownership by usucapion and the *securitas possessionis* which the possessor acquired by the *praescriptio longi temporis,* but in practice the distinction was not very great. The *praescriptio longi temporis* which prevailed in the provinces came gradually to be regarded as more equitable than the *usucapio* of the *Jus Antiquum.* Constitutions of the emperors had apparently fixed the periods of ten years *inter praesentes* and twenty years *inter absentes.* This was the state of the law when the Emperor Theodosius II introduced a prescription of thirty years, usually called by the glossators the *praescriptio longissimi temporis.* By means of this prescription the possessor of a thing, whether movable or immovable, could resist any claim by the mere fact that he had been in possession for thirty years irrespective of whether he had a *justus titulus* or good faith (Cuq. *Institutions Juridiques*, vol. 2, pp. 247 *et seq.*).

In the time of Justinian, therefore, there existed the old Roman law of *usucapio* for the *Solum Italicum*, the *praescriptio longi temporis* for land in the provinces, and the *praescriptio longissimi temporis* of Theodosius. Justinian introduced a complete reform and simplified the whole law as to prescription. In the *Institutes* (2, 6, pr.) he tells us: "We have accordingly published a constitution providing that movables shall be acquired by use extending for three years, and immovables by the possession of long time, *i.e.* ten years for persons present and twenty for persons absent." This mode of acquisition, however, required a *justa causa*.

The *praescriptio longissimi temporis* of Theodosius is not met with either in the *Institutes* or in the *Digest*, but it occurs in the *Code* (bk. 7, tit. 39) under the title *De Praescriptione XXX, vel XL annorum.* By this form of prescription all manner of rights could be acquired, whether they referred to movables or immovables, or even if they were only mere rights of action. From this mode of prescription were excluded things *extra commercium*, the *fundus dotalis*, *peculium adventitium* and a few other rights of minor importance. No *justus titulus* was required, and if there had been good faith this prescription was a mode of acquiring ownership, whilst it served as an exception where the subject was originally acquired without good faith. The prescription of forty years referred to hypothecary actions, things belonging to the Emperor or the Church.

Such then, briefly stated, was the law of prescription in the time of Justinian. In a former chapter we saw that before the revival of the study of Roman law western Europe was indebted for its law more to the *Code* of Theodosius than to the legislation of Justinian. We find, therefore, that long before the reign of Justinian the German nations had already adopted the *praescriptio longissimi temporis* of Theodosius II. Very few of the German Codes took over the *usucapio* of the early Roman law, and the almost universal period of prescription for movables as well as immovables was the period of thirty years (Hein. *Elem. Jur. Germ.* bk 2, c. 4). No distinction as a rule was made between prescription *inter praesentes* and *inter absentes*, nor between acquisition *bonae fidei* and *malae fidei*. All that the Germans regarded was the lapse of thirty years. If thirty years' continuous possession could be proved, then the person who could prove such possession was the absolute owner of the property, no matter how it had been acquired (Hein. *loc. cit.* sec. 120).

The above statement of the German law is true for the greater bulk of German laws; but it is not true with respect to every body of German law, for we undoubtedly find some nations who admitted a short as well as a long period of prescription. The Saxons are said to have recognised a prescription of a year and a day, but Heineccius tells us that he has not been able to find such a prescription in any of the sources of Saxon law (Hein. *loc. cit.* sec. 108).

In several bodies of German law we find some extra period added to the almost universally adopted thirty years. Thus the Saxons in the case of immovable property added a year and a day, making the period of prescription thirty-one years and a day. In the Netherlands the usual period of prescription was thirty years; but in Holland, though thirty years applied to movables, a third of a century was required for the prescription of immovables (Groen. *De Leg. Abrog. ad Cod.* 7, 39). In Zeeland twenty years sufficed *inter praesentes*, whilst *inter absentes* thirty years were required.

When, however, we come to consider the various towns of the Netherlands we are astonished at the different rules that prevailed with regard to the period of prescription. In many places if the sale of immovable property took place before schepenen, and if the sale was registered, a year and a day sufficed to give the purchaser complete title against an adverse claimant. This form of prescription seems to have been abandoned some time in the seventeenth century (Van der Keessel, *Thes.* 208).

At what precise time the Hollanders varied the general German rule that a prescription of thirty years was sufficient to give a good title I have not been able to discover. It is, however, certain that in 1476 A.D. the prescription of a third of a century was already the customary period of prescription as regards immovables, for we find in the *Groot Privilegie* of the Lady Mary of Burgundy that the third of a century was the period of prescription—*Voor leenen ende erfelijke goederen.* Noordewier, however, mentions that in

1383 a document of title was given for prescription of thirty years: *Caerte van het stille der goederen van het besitten van dartich jaren.* It is therefore not unreasonable to suppose that the prescription of thirty years existed in Holland, as it did in most German countries, but that sometime in the fifteenth century it was increased to the third of a century as regards immovables.

In 1530 the Feudal Court of Holland decided that the possession of land for the period of a third of a century gave good title as well to feudal as to allodial land (Neos. *Observ. Feud.* 1). About this time the rule of law as to a third of a century was embodied in a number of Dutch maxims, such as, "*Praescriptie van een derden deel van hondert jaren gaet voor alle segel en brief;*" "*Alle gerechtigheden werden verkregen bij het verloop van het derden deel van hondert jaren*" (Matthaeus, *Paroem.* 9).

A question which has given rise to a considerable amount of discussion is whether the prescription of a third of a century applied only to immovables, or whether it extended to movables as well. Some maintain that the thirty-three and a third years' prescription never applied to movables, and that the prescription of the latter was always governed by the thirty years of the Theodosian *Code.* Others, again, maintain that the usucapion of three years and ten years of the Roman law, as well as the thirty years' prescription for movables, formed part of the law of Holland. It may safely be asserted that until the new impulse was given to the study of Roman law, and the legislation of Justinian became generally studied, the prescription of three and ten years was not recognised as part of the customs of the

Netherlands. Whether it was introduced after the revival of learning is a moot point.

Some authorities argue that the prescription of a third of a century only applied to the acquisition of immovables, and that therefore in this respect only the Roman law was modified by the customs of Holland (Van der Keessel, *Thes.* 207). The better opinion, however, seems to be that the usucapion of the Roman law never formed part of the law of Holland and was never recognised by the courts of that province. Groenewegen (*ad Inst.* 2, 6) says: *Usucapiones et longi temporis praescriptiones nostris et aliorum moribus in desuetudinem abierunt.* Zypaeus in his *Notitia juris Belgici* had already expressed the same view (*De Praes.* pr.). Voet in his *Compendium juris* (41, 3, 12) says: *Usucapio trienii decennii vel vicenii non ita recepta est ut de jure Romano; sed magis in plerisque negotiis obtinuit praescriptio triginta annorum vel tertiae partis annorum centum.*

This brings us to the further question whether the thirty years' prescription of the Theodosian *Code* existed side by side with the prescription of a third of a century. Groenewegen (*ad Cod.* 7, tit. 39) was of opinion that the prescription of thirty years applied to movables, and that of a third of a century to immovables. Van Leeuwen (Kotzé, vol. 1, p. 201) was of the same opinion, and Bynkershoek (*Q.J.P.* 2, 15) tells us that the Supreme Court of Holland had definitely settled this disputed point and decreed that movables could be acquired by a prescription of thirty years. Van der Keessel unhesitatingly accepts this as the correct view (*Thes.* 206). We may therefore safely accept it as the law of

Holland in the eighteenth century that immovable property could be acquired by possession for a third of a century, whilst the acquisition of movables required the lapse of thirty years.

In the Cape Colony the period of prescription in the case of immovable property was altered in 1865 by an insignificant paragraph squeezed into the many sections of the Land Beacons Act (Act 7 of 1865, sec. 106). This section provides that "the period of prescription in regard to immovable property in this colony and servitudes upon or connected therewith shall from and after the 1st of January, 1867, be thirty years instead of the third of a century." The law of the Theodosian *Code* was therefore restored, and the period of prescription was made the same for both movable and immovable property. The legislature of the Cape Colony in 1865 reverted to the old law of the German Codes, which provided a uniform period of thirty years for the prescription of both movables and immovables. In the Transvaal the period of prescription is still that of the old Roman-Dutch law.

The next point of difference between the Roman law and the Roman-Dutch law as regards prescription is the nature of the original possession. We have seen that for usucapion both *justus titulus* and *bona fides* were essential. With regard to the *praescriptio longissimi temporis,* a distinction was made between the person who obtained possession *bonâ fide* and one who was a *malâ fide* possessor. The former acquired the *dominium,* whilst the latter could only repel a claimant. The Germans ignored all difference between *bonâ fide* and *malâ fide* possession. This was no doubt the law of Holland in very early times.

QQ

After the introduction of the Canon law, however, the ecclesiastics sought to introduce into the law of prescription the element of conscience. The canonists required not only that there should have been *bona fides* when the possession was acquired, but that it should exist all through the period of prescription. If ever the possessor became aware of the fact that the property was really that of another, then the prescription was interrupted in such a way that the possessor could never become the lawful owner (Ritterhusius, *Diff Jur. Can. et. Civ.* bk. 4, c. 13). Some authorities held that the rules of the Canon law in this respect were taken over by the law of Holland, whilst others were of opinion that the Canon law did not prevail (Grot. 2, 7, 5). Although Grotius does not expressly state that *bona fides* was not necessary, he does so by implication (Grot. 2, 7, 6 and 8). Matthaeus discusses the question fully (*Paroem.* 9, nn. 2 and 3), and expresses the opinion that the law of Holland did not adopt the rule of the Canon law in this respect. Van der Keessel (*Thes.* 207) says: "In these prescriptions of a third of a century and of thirty years, neither *bona fides* nor a just title is required," and this statement of the law appears to be the correct view. Grotius (3, 46, 4) tells us, however, that it is a well-recognised fact that from these periods of thirty years or the third of a century must be deducted the claimant's minority or the period of his absence from the country.

The *lex* of the *Code* upon which, according to Groenewegen, this statement of the law is based, reads as follows: *Non sexus fragilitate, non absentia, non militia contra hanc legem defendenda sed pupillari aetate duntaxat (quamvis sub tutoris defensione consistat) huic eximenda sanctioni. Nam cum ad eos annos pervenerint qui ad solicitudinem pertinent curatoris necessario similiter ut aliis annorum triginta intervalla servanda sunt* (*C.* 7, 39, 3). The *Code*, therefore, did not consider that the period of absence should be taken into consideration, nor did it extend any consideration to the minor after he was freed from tutorship. Groenewegen, however, in commenting upon this *lex* of the *Code*, says, *Absens tamen adversus praescriptionem restituitur*, and he quotes a decision of the Supreme Court of Mechlin in support of this view (Christ. vol. 4, decis. 84, n. 4).

With regard to minors, also, the Roman-Dutch law differed from the Roman law, for by the latter the rule was *Praescriptio non currit contra impuberem sed currit contra puberem*, whilst the rule of the Roman-Dutch law is *Praescriptio non currit contra puberem aut impuberem usque ad minorennitatem* (Voet, 4, 4, 29). The other exceptions fall under the rule *Praescriptio non currit contra non valentem agere*, *e.g.* against a married woman with regard to the alienation by the husband *stante matrimonio* of property which he could not legally alienate (Voet, 44, 3, 11). Grotius states the rule with regard to minors and absentees in the following words: "Against the effect of lapse of time minors and other wards might pray for relief within four years after the termination of their guardianship. Other persons could only do so for lawful reasons, such as unavoidable absence, especially in the service of the State, imprisonment, want of a tribunal or ignorance resting on reasonable grounds."

Having considered the *préscription acquisitive*, I shall now pass over to the *préscription extinctive*, or limitation of actions. By this latter form of prescription no property is acquired, but the person against whom a claim is made, the *causa debendi* of which arose some time before, can repel the claim on the ground that the time has elapsed within which such claim should have been preferred. The first question to determine is whether according to our law the debt is discharged or whether the lapse of time merely gives the defendant the right to except. Is the debt extinguished *ipso jure* or is the remedy barred?

By the Roman law lapse of time gave rise to an exception, but did not extinguish the claim *ipso jure.* The judge had no right to take cognisance of the fact that the claim was instituted after the period of prescription had lapsed. He could only decide this point if the defendant raised the plea of prescription by way of exception. I am aware that this is a controversial point, but it appears to me that the balance of authority is in favour of the conclusion as stated above. It must be remembered that this applies only to extinctive and not to acquisitive prescription. By the latter form of prescription the former proprietor completely lost his right to the ownership of the thing, and therefore also his right of action. This controversy is fully treated by Savigny in his *System* (vol. 5, secs. 248–51).

Grotius (3, 46, 2) is of opinion that the rule of the Roman law did not apply in Holland, and that not only was the remedy barred, but the debt was wholly extinguished. His words are: "It is indeed true that under the Roman law obligations are not extinguished by lapse of time, but that it merely gives a ground of exception; but if we observe closely the practice obtaining amongst us in olden times it will be found that, in the same way as ownership is with us acquired by prescription, so also obligations are extinguished *ipso jure* by lapse of time, and, as is clearly proved by some laws, are regarded as discharged, so as to give no right of action; whence it follows that the judge when the lapse of time is proved ought to declare the plaintiff as not admissible."

The laws to which Grotius refers are the Placaat of 1540, sec. 16, and several old handvesten and keuren (*Recht. Obs.* vol. 2, obs. 97). The words of sec. 16 of the Perpetual Edict which refer to this matter are: *Maer nae de expiratie van den voorsz: tydt sulcke schulden sullen geacht worden behoorlijck gequeten ende van de selve zal men geen actie hebben* (*G.P.B.* vol. 1, p. 319). [" But after the expiration of the aforesaid period such debts shall be regarded as having been duly paid, and no action can be brought for the same."] If the debts are to be regarded as paid the obligation must be considered as extinguished, and therefore not only is the remedy barred, but the right must be held to have completely ceased to exist even as a *naturalis obligatio.* Voet (44, 3, 10) is of the same opinion, though Van der Keessel doubts the accuracy of this view (*Thes.* 874).

Van Scheltinga, on the other hand, almost as recent a writer as Van der Keessel, holds that as soon as the judge is satisfied that the plaintiff's claim is prescribed he must give judgment against the plaintiff, even though prescription had not been pleaded. For this proposition he relies on Voet (5, 1, 49). The Natal Supreme Court in *In re Webster* (12 N.L.R. 129) held that it is incorrect to say that a claim is effaced by prescription (in the sense of limitation of action);

it is only the remedy for recovery of the debt that is affected. An executor may therefore rightly admit a claim part of which is barred by prescription.

The time within which an action was prescribed varied according to the nature of the action. Hypothecary actions were only prescribed after a lapse of forty years (*Schonberg's Executors* v. *Executors of De Vos*, 1 S.C. 325), but all other actions affecting immovables were extinguished after the expiration of a third of a century, whilst actions affecting movables were prescribed after thirty years. This was the general rule of law with regard to prescription, but there were many exceptions introduced by the statute law of Holland. Grotius states the law of the Placaat of 1540 thus: "The fees of advocates, attorneys and surgeons, salaries of clerks, the wages of servants, the price of merchandise sold by retail and of medicines sold in the shop, and accounts for which security must be given, must be claimed within two years after the rendering of the service, the delivery of the merchandise, or the giving of the security, unless a written acknowledgment is given for it, in which case such claim must be prosecuted within ten years against the original debtor, but against his heirs, in the case of his death, within two years after the creditor has notice of the death."

Groenewegen, in his notes to the *Code* (7, 34, 5), tells us that the Placaat of Charles V of 1540, sec. 16, with regard to prescription had fallen into desuetude, though Coren (*Cons.* 92, n. 20) is of a different opinion. The latter tells us that a mere demand is not enough to justify the view that "the claim has been prosecuted"; there must be an actual joinder of issue or *litis contestatio.* Van der Keessel seems to adopt the view of Coren (*Thes.* 876).

This question came before the High Court of the Transvaal in *Van Diggelen* v. *Wepener* (1 Off. Rep. 38) and *Little* v. *Rothman* (2 Off. Rep. 215), when it was held that the Placaat of 1540 as to prescription formed part of the law of the Transvaal. In the Orange Free State, in *Rabie* v. *Neebe*, the Court adopted a similar view. In the Cape Colony the Supreme Court in 1858 (*Drew* v. *Wolfe's Executors*, Buch. 1868, p. 119) held that the Placaat formed part of the law of the colony, at least with regard to medical men. This decision led to the passing of Act 6 of 1861, which amended the common law in respect of certain suits and actions. This Act repealed all laws and usages repugnant to or inconsistent with the provisions of the Act, and then provided that no suit or action on such documents as will give rise to provisional sentence can be brought after the expiration of eight years from the time when the cause of action accrued. Sec. 5 of the Act then provided that in certain specified cases, *e.g.* fees of advocates and attorneys, butchers', bakers,' and tailors' bills, &c., the period of prescription should be three years. Minors and persons under legal disability are protected for a period of eight years. If, however, they happen to die their representatives have three years within which to institute the action. If there has been an acknowledgment of the debt then the rules of *English law* and not the rule of the *Roman-Dutch law* shall apply. If the debtor is absent from the colony he cannot avail himself of the plea of prescription during the time of his absence. If there are joint debtors and the one is an absentee, then the absentee debtor cannot avail himself of the plea for the time of his absence, though the debtor who remained in the colony is free to raise the exception of prescription.

The wording of this Act is based upon the English law of limitation of actions, and it may be that the scope of the Roman-Dutch law has been very much modified by the Act. The practice of grafting fragments of English law upon the Roman-Dutch law, not infrequently met with in the Acts of the Cape Colony, cannot be said to be a sound practice, for it is bound in many cases to lead to great confusion. It would be far better to incorporate so much of the English law as is taken over in the statute itself, and not to require the colonial courts to extract from a multitude of cases, frequently conflicting, the rule of the English law. It is often difficult for English judges of great learning and of great experience in their own law to say definitely what the English law is upon any particular subject, and therefore colonial judges, whose knowledge of English law must, in the nature of things, be far from accurate, can hardly be expected to judge a case according to the "rules and principles as it would be judged of and determined in any of his Majesty's Courts of Record at Westminster."

There are, however, cases of prescription in the Roman-Dutch law which are not dealt with in the Cape Act of 1861. Actions for libel and slander are prescribed after the period of a year and a day if not proceeded with within a year and six weeks (*C.* 9, t. 35, l. 5). In cases of fraud the action is prescribed after two years (*C.* 2, 21, l. ult.). Restitution or relief in cases of contract after four years (*C.* 2, 53, l. ult.); actions for divorce and defloration after five years; actions for breach of promise of marriage after two years. In criminal matters the period of prescription is twenty years after the crime became known to the officials, except in cases of murder, arson and theft. These and other cases are apparently not dealt with in Act 6 of 1861.

From the above we see that in the Transvaal and Orange River Colony the period of prescription is the same as that of the old Roman-Dutch law, which, again, is largely based upon the Roman law; whilst in the Cape Colony the law of prescription is based partly upon the old Roman-Dutch law, partly upon the provisions of the statute law, and partly upon the law of limitation of actions as followed by the Courts of Record at Westminster.

CHAPTER XXII.

PARTNERSHIP.

OUR law of partnership is based upon the Roman law of *societas.* The *societas* of the Romans was not quite the same as our partnership. The word *societas* was sometimes used to designate various voluntary associations for religious, literary or other purposes, *e.g. societas actuariorum.* The *societas vectigalium* differed considerably from the ordinary commercial partnership, and was governed by rules not always applicable to the latter.

The idea of several persons associating themselves for the purpose not only of trade, but of mutual benefit, was considerably extended during the middle ages. It was then that community of goods in case of marriage grew up, and that the foundations were laid of the numerous guilds, associations and societies. These associations were not confined to the people of the towns, for in the country the *lites* and other agriculturists also established partnerships. These partnerships were not trading ventures, but rather benefit societies established for the advantage of all their members.

Besides these benefit societies there existed partnerships in which one party contributed the capital and the other the labour. These partnerships were no doubt well known to the Romans, though the principal period during which they flourished was immediately after the Crusades. A special class of these partnerships was known throughout Italy and France as *socida.* This was probably a corruption of its

Italian name—*soccita accommandita di bestiame.* In France it was called *commande de bestiaux,* and is in all probability the origin of the French term *société en commandite* (Du Cange, *sub voce Socida*).

Originally it was an agreement between the owner of a herd of cattle and a farmer, by which the latter undertook to look after the cattle and find pasturage for them. The increase and the profits were divided between them. At first it was not a trade partnership, but an arrangement between agriculturists. In time, however, the idea was applied to merchandise, and partnerships were established between the capitalist who furnished the goods and the trader who sold them at the various markets and fairs throughout Europe. These trade partnerships, like the *commande de bestiaux,* spread from Italy to France, where they flourished as *sociétés en commandite.* From France it was brought into Holland, where it was known by its French name (Troplong, *Contrat de Société,* Preface).

Van der Linden defines the partnership *en commandite* as follows: "The company or partnership termed *en commandite, i.e.* when a merchant agrees with some person to carry on a trade or business in partnership, but to be conducted in the name of this merchant alone, and the other merely brings in a certain sum of money as the capital under the condition that he shall draw a certain proportion of the profits" (Van der Linden, bk. 4, c. 3, sec. 12).

Besides the partnership *en commandite* and the *société anonyme* (*naamloze vernootschap*) there is nothing in the history of the law of partnership which calls for special attention.

As the French and Roman-Dutch law of partnership are both founded on the Roman law, it will not be surprising to learn that the decisions of the French courts and the works of French lawyers have considerably influenced our law of partnership. Pothier's treatise on Partnership was regarded towards the end of the eighteenth century as an authority of great weight. It was translated into Dutch by Van der Linden, and is constantly cited by him in his *Institutes.* In the South African courts also Pothier has been regarded as an important authority, though the influence of English law in this branch has been markedly great. English cases on partnership usually have great weight with our courts, because in their main principles the English and the Roman-Dutch law are very similar. It is unnecessary to deal with this matter in detail, as the student will find the comparison between our law and that of England fully set out in Mr Morice's work—*English and Roman-Dutch Law.*

CHAPTER XXIII.

LAWS LIMITING LIABILITY.

It is not my intention to write a complete history of the laws which in the course of time brought about our modern limited liability company. I merely wish to point out briefly that the idea of limiting the liability of members of a trading venture is not nearly so recent as some imagine. The idea dates back to the Romans, though the machinery for facilitating the establishment of limited companies is recent.

There is very little doubt that the Romans fully appreciated the advantages to be gained from the association of numerous individuals to carry out large enterprises. Livy tells us (bk. 23, c. 48, 49) that when the two Scipios were operating in Spain against Hasdrubal in order to prevent his junction with Hannibal they were sadly in want of money and provisions. They appealed to Rome. The Romans themselves were far from prosperous. Sicily and Sardinia, the granaries of the Republic could hardly feed their own garrisons. The Praetor Fulvius called together an assembly of the people and explained to them how absolutely necessary it was to find provisions for the army in Spain. He fixed a day on which he would make contracts for the provisioning of the army. When the day arrived three partnerships, each of nineteen persons, came forward to enter into the contracts. They made two requests: one was that they should be exempted from service whilst engaged in this public business, and the other that the Republic should bear all losses which might arise either from the attacks of the enemy or from storms (*ubi ea dies venit, ad conducendum tres societates aderant hominum undeviginti quorum duo postulata fuere,* &c.).

These companies carried out their contracts so well that the army in Spain was provisioned quite as effectually as when the treasury was full. Here then we have a number of persons coming together and contributing each so much money that it sufficed to provide for an army. As the work was carried on so satisfactorily, we must presume that an excellent organisation existed, and this seems to show further that these large associations of men for trade purposes could not have been isolated instances.

The banking houses (*socii argentarii, argentariae societates*) were also in all probability partnerships consisting of numerous persons each contributing towards the capital. But of all the Roman partnerships those which most closely approached our modern limited liability companies were the *societates vectigales* or *societates vectigalium.* The Romans farmed out their tolls and customs (*portoria*), the pasture lands belonging to the State, their mines and other similar sources of revenue. The persons who obtained these concessions were called *publicani.* These concessions for Italy as well as for the distant provinces were granted at Rome, and the *equites* were as a rule the favoured persons who obtained the concessions. It was quite impossible for a single knight to carry out these complicated concessions, hence he was obliged to call in the aid of others. It therefore became the practice to form partnerships for the purpose of exploiting the concession, much in the same way as concessions in the Transvaal before the war were granted to individuals and promptly ceded by them to limited liability companies.

These partnerships are so constantly referred to by Cicero that it is unnecessary to do more than call to mind their wealth and importance. Sometimes the whole concession was exploited by the partners themselves, and each one had a definite share assigned to him (*D.* 39, 4, 9, 4). Usually, however, the partnership or company appointed one or more managers (*magistri*) to conduct its business (Cicero, *in Verrem*, 3, 71). These managers lived in Rome, whilst the sub-managers (*promagistri*) lived in the province where the business was being transacted. Besides these there were hosts of officials of various grades, some freemen, others slaves (Cic. *in Ver.* 2, 77). Some kept books, others attended to the correspondence, whilst the letters were carried to the head offices in Rome by a large number of messengers (Cic. *in Ver.* 3, 47; *Epist. ad Atticum,* bk. 5, epist. 15, 18, 21). It was impossible to run so huge a concern in the same way as an ordinary partnership. Hence special rules were adopted which regulated the *societates vectigalium*, but which did not apply to ordinary partnerships.

The partnership was not dissolved by the death of one of the members (*D.* 17, 2, 59), and if the heir of the deceased was registered in the books of the partnership (*adscriptus*) he became thereby a partner (*adscitus*). In this respect they resemble our modern companies. This, however, is not the only resemblance. Like our companies, the *societates vectigalium* were regarded as corporations, and could sue and be sued in the name of their *magistri* or syndics (Roby, *Rom. Priv. Law*, vol. 2, p. 133). *Neque societas neque collegium neque hujus-*

modi corpus passim omnibus habere conceditur nam et legibus . . . ea res coërcetur paucis admodum in causis concessa sunt hujusmodi corpora ut ecce vectigalium publicorum sociis permissum est corpus habere (*D.* 3, 4, 1, pr. 1). In the social and political life they exercised the same influence that the wealthy companies exercise in South Africa. From the above it will appear that the Romans had in addition to the notion of an ordinary commercial partnership also a well-developed idea of what we know as limited liability companies.

The idea of associations for the purpose of gain was not lost in the middle ages. In France it took the form of several families combining together to till the soil and to rear cattle. As the associates lived together and had their meals together they were called companions (from *cumpanio*=*cum,* with, and *panis,* bread; hence *compagnie,* our company: the derivation from *compaganus* is now regarded as incorrect). In Italy during the fourteenth century nobles like the Bardi, the Corsini and the Peruzi established large trading companies, whose operations were not confined to the country south of the Alps. During the seventeenth century the *Compagnie en Actions,* or company with a capital divided into a number of shares which could freely pass from hand to hand, became a well-recognised institution.

The English East India Company was founded in 1600. In 1602 the Amsterdam merchants founded the Dutch East India Company, and in 1607 the States-General granted a charter to the Dutch merchants who traded in the West Indies. These companies were large trading partnerships in which the liability was limited to the calls on the shares held by the partners, and as they obtained State recognition they were regarded as corporations like the *societates vectigalium*. Similar companies existed in France during the sixteenth century, though it was not until the seventeenth century that Louis XIII granted royal charters to several companies. During the eighteenth century the great Bank of Law was established on the lines of the Bank of England, and this was imitated by the Dutch, who founded not only banks, but companies of all kinds that indulged in the wildest speculations (Troplong, *Contrat de Société*, Preface).

All the great trading companies, however, of the eighteenth and early part of the nineteenth century were incorporated by special charter, and as this was a cumbersome process limited liability companies were by no means plentiful either in England or on the Continent. The great activity in trade after the Napoleonic wars led to the establishment of numerous trading partnerships to exploit mines and other industries. When the railways had been perfected speculation in this and other concerns became exceedingly active, and men strove to reap profits from a combination of capital without incurring risks beyond the capital invested in the concern. In this way was gradually evolved not the idea of a partnership with limited liability, but a less cumbersome machinery than a royal charter for accomplishing the purpose. In England the outcome of this idea was the Joint-Stock Companies Act of 1844, and the Limited Liability Act of 1855. The facility with which joint-stock companies with limited liability could be created gave a great impetus to trade and commerce, and the passion for speculation and for the combination of capital spread from England to the Cape.

The Cape Colony in 1861 took its company law from the English Joint-Stock Companies Act of 1844, and the Limited Liability Act of 1855. The Transvaal took its Law (5 of 1874) from the Cape Act of 1861. In the case of the *Contributories of the Rosemount Syndicate* ([1905] T.H., at p. 181) Judge Bristowe has traced the history of our company law from the English statutes, and I can do no better than quote his words: "At the date of the Act of 1844 there were in existence institutions called joint-stock companies, which were simply large partnerships constituted by a deed called a deed of settlement, which all the original members of the company and all persons to whom shares were subsequently issued had to execute. The management of the concern was usually entrusted by the deed to a body of directors, and shareholders were empowered to transfer their shares without the consent of other members. It was well settled that the individual shareholders in such a company were, like ordinary partners, liable for the debts of the concern 'to their last shilling and their last acre,' and that they could not by any arrangement between themselves or by any provision in the deed of settlement rid themselves of this liability. The Act of 1844 compelled all these companies to be registered and incorporated, and preserved the direct rights of creditors against the individual shareholders (which otherwise would have been lost by incorporation) by enabling any creditor who failed to obtain satisfaction for a judgment debt out of the corporate assets to levy, by leave of the court, against the private estate of any present or (subject to certain limitations) past shareholders. At the same time it provided for public registration of the deed of settlement and of all changes in the list of shareholders. The Act of 1855 enabled companies formed under the Act of 1844 to obtain limited liability, and provided that in that case the right of an unsatisfied creditor to levy against a shareholder should be limited to the amount remaining unpaid on his shares. Joint-stock companies under these Acts were therefore simply partnerships constituted by deed, which by statutory provision were required to be publicly registered, were endowed with an individuality of their own, and were accorded the enormous privilege of limited liability. They became subject to a variety of statutory obligations, chiefly conceived with the view of securing publicity, but the rights and obligations of the members *inter se* were primarily dependent upon and regulated by the deed by which each of them was required to expressly bind himself." Neither the Cape Act of 1861 nor the Transvaal Act of 1874 expressly makes a registered company a *universitas* or corporation. It seems, however, to do so by implication.

In the Cape Colony the formation and liquidation of companies are now regulated by the Companies Act (25 of 1892); in Natal by Law 19 of 1866; in the Transvaal by Law 5 of 1874, Law 1 of 1894, V.R.R. of 1893 and the Liquidation Law (1 of 1894); in the Orange River Colony by Law 2 of 1892; and in Rhodesia by the Companies Ordinance of 1895.

The company law in most of the South African colonies is very imperfect, inasmuch as they followed the old English Acts, and not the newer Act of 1862 and its numerous amendments. The Companies Acts of the Cape Colony of 1892 and of Rhodesia of 1895 have endeavoured to place companies in those colonies on much the same footing as they are in England.

The establishment of limited liability companies necessitated laws for the winding up of such companies in cases of failure; for though by the common law corporations ceased to exist if they no longer had the requisite number of members, the mere death of the company was not the only matter to consider. If a trading company can no longer pay its debts or carry out its objects it must be wound up and its assets equitably distributed. The South African colonies and states followed the English legislation upon this subject, though in many respects their liquidation laws require considerable amendment.

CHAPTER XXIV.

PROCEDURE IN INSOLVENCY.

OUR present procedure in bankruptcy or insolvency, for there is no distinction now between the two, owes its origin partly to the Roman-Dutch and partly to the English law. Both these systems have taken the main principles of their insolvency law from the Roman law.

The earliest source of our law of insolvency is the Twelve Tables (Tab. iii, 1). The judgment debtor was given thirty days' grace to see if he could find some one to come to his assistance. If not the debtor was arrested, taken into court, and the judge gave the creditor the right to imprison him. If after a time the money was still unpaid the debtor could be sold across the Tiber, and according to Bynkershoek the price was divided amongst the creditors (*Obs. Jur. Rom.* 1, 1). The literal interpretation of cutting the debtor's body into pieces and dividing these amongst the creditors is nowadays rejected by the best authorities. Some doubt whether the debtor was sold as a slave. He may have been held as a pledge compellable to redeem the debt by the services of himself and family. Besides the attachment of the person the Roman law allowed an attachment of the debtor's property. The praetor granted a *missio in possessionem* to the creditor, who took charge of the debtor's property on behalf of himself and other creditors. In Labeo's time several creditors could be put in possession, and if they could not agree as to the management the praetor intervened and appointed one of them as the manager (*D.* 42, 5, 8, 4).

The dispossession of the debtor was publicly advertised (*proscriptio bonorum*), so that all the creditors might make their claims on the estate. If the debtor after a certain lapse of time could come to no arrangement with his creditors he was declared infamous, and could never again appear in court without giving security (Gai, iv, 102).

The next step was to appoint a manager (*magister*, or, as we should call him, a trustee) and to proceed to the *venditio bonorum* or sale of the bankrupt's estate. The highest bidder bought the estate (*massa*) as a whole, and became the *universalis* successor of the debtor. This procedure was adopted not only where the debtor was *judicatus*, and could not pay, but also where he fled to escape his creditors. The proceeds of the sale were divided amongst the creditors in the following order: first the mortgage creditors were paid in full, next the privileged creditors, *e.g.* the wife, who had a claim for her *dos*, the persons who paid the funeral expenses, and, lastly, the *chirographarii* and other creditors (Cuq. *Institutions juridiques des Romains*, vol. 2, pp. 766 *et seq.*).

Here we have the main elements of our modern law of bankruptcy. From time to time alterations were introduced, but the principles remained the same. In Justinian's time a debtor could either voluntarily surrender his goods to his creditors, or he could be compelled to do so by order of court. *Cessio bonorum* liberated the debtor from imprisonment for debt. The debtor was bound to make an inventory and to swear that he had withheld nothing (*Nov.* 135, 1). He was left his wearing apparel and probably the implements of his trade: also any monthly or yearly allowance—*misericordiae causâ relictum* (*D.* 42, 3, 6). He could not be troubled after this, but directly he acquired property his creditors could again require him to pay any balance due (*D.* 42, 3, 7). Sometimes a respite (called a *moratorium*) was granted to debtors: this allowed them a certain time within which to pay their debts (*C.* 1, 19, 2 and 4).

The *cessio bonorum* was apparently introduced into Holland during the fifteenth or sixteenth century, and with it the *moratorium* or *respijt*. The history of the cessio bonorum is given in the *Rechtsgeleerde Observatiën* (vol. 2, obs. 100), and I can do no better than give here an abstract of that *Observatie.* According to the old Dutch law, as we find it in the handvesten given by the counts from time to time to the towns, if a debtor was unable to pay his creditor the former was handed over to the latter until such time as the debt was paid. In support of this the authors quote some dozen handvesten between 1245 and 1412. In the Handvest of Dort of 1252 we find the following: *Si debitor non habuerit unde solvere valeat ejus personam creditori presentare debemus.* In a Handvest of Alkmaar of 1254 we read the following: "If a person owes money to another and cannot pay, then upon a judgment against him the judge shall order his detention for two weeks by the messenger, who will be required to feed him. After the expiration of the two weeks the judge must give the debtor into the hands of the creditor, who is responsible for his maintenance and safety; the creditor shall, moreover, have the right to detain the debtor until the debt is paid or until the latter is released."

In a former chapter we have seen that according to German custom a freeman could be sold into slavery for debt, and that during the feudal régime the debtor could be compelled to work for the creditor. There are still vestiges of this practice in our present law, viz., the arrest of the person and civil imprisonment. Until the introduction of the cessio bonorum (*boedelafstand*) the law of Holland apparently only knew of attachment of the person of the debtor in satisfaction of the debt. The exact date of the introduction of the cessio bonorum is not accurately known.

The cessio bonorum is not mentioned in the *Instructiën van den Hove van Holland* (Rules of Court) of 1462, though reference is made to it in the *Instructie* of 1531. Between these dates we find the cessio bonorum mentioned in various towns. It was the law at Leyden in 1501, at Rotterdam in 1519, and at Briel in 1521. It would therefore appear that the cessio bonorum was gradually introduced into Holland towards the beginning of the sixteenth century.

To obtain the cessio bonorum was a difficult and costly procedure. The insolvent was required to address to the Court of Holland a petition stating the causes of his insolvency. This had to be accompanied with an inventory of his goods. The Court referred this petition to the burgomaster and governing body of the place of the insolvent's domicile. The Court upon receipt of this report granted a writ, or, as we should say, a rule *nisi* calling upon all persons interested to show cause before the judge of the petitioner's domicile why the writ of cessio bonorum (*brieven van cessie*) provisionally issued to the insolvent should not be confirmed. The effect of granting the rule was to free the petitioner from future arrest, whilst the effect of its confirmation was to stay all execution against his goods, and to place his property in charge of a curator (Van der Linden, *Jud. Prak.* vol. 2, c. 31).

The writ of cession did not discharge the insolvent from his debts. If he acquired property after the confirmation of the writ his creditors could claim the property. The only benefit it conferred upon the insolvent was to free him from personal arrest and the worry of being sued.

From what has been said above, it appears that the benefit of cession was virtually a voluntary surrender by an insolvent of all his estate for the benefit of his creditors. In dealing with the petition of the insolvent the Court only granted the brieven van cessie if it were satisfied that the insolvency was due to misfortune. If at the hearing before the local judge the petitioner's actions were shown to have been fraudulent, or if he had not made an honest declaration as to his assets, the petition was not only refused, but the applicant could then and there by order of the judge be imprisoned. The costs incurred in making the application were preferent, and ranked even before the claims of mortgage creditors.

As we have seen above, with the Romans insolvency brought infamy in its train. In France the insolvent who had obtained the benefit of cession was obliged to wear a green cap, whilst during the sixteenth century at Rotterdam and Leyden persons who had obtained brieven van cessie were required to stand before the steps of the town-hall in their underclothing for an hour a day during three successive days.

The insolvent was allowed to retain his clothes, his tools

and such other trifles as might enable him to earn a living. In the brieven van cessie was inserted a clause to the effect that "if hereafter the petitioner should by good fortune obtain any goods he shall be obliged to pay his creditors in full" (Van Alphen, *Pap.* pt. 1, p. 224).

By the Roman law the debtor could make a valid composition with all his creditors, but if some of his creditors objected to the arrangement the composition fell through. In one case, however, the majority of creditors could bind the minority to accept the composition. When an heir refused to adiate unless his creditors were agreeable to accept less than was due, the approval of the majority bound the minority (*D.* 2, 14, 7, 17–19).

By a Placaat of 1544 the rule of the Roman law was approved of. Later, however, a practice was adopted in various towns that a majority of the creditors could bind the minority if three-fourths of the creditors, who were entitled to two-thirds of the debt, consented to the agreement (Van der Keessel, *Thes.* 829). There gradually grew up a tendency to allow an insolvent to be discharged from all liability provided he could obtain the consent of one-half of his creditors to whom half of the debts were due.

During the seventeenth century the insolvent estates of deceased persons were administered by commissioners under the supervision of the schout and schepenen (Merula, vol. 2, p. 23). As chambers for the administration of derelict estates were gradually established in the various towns the insolvency commissioners were chosen from the members of these bodies. Besides the insolvent estates of deceased persons these chambers came to be charged in many towns with the administration of the estates of persons who had obtained cessio bonorum; so that instead of appointing private persons to administer the estate of the insolvent, it became a custom during the eighteenth century to place all insolvent estates under the administration of boards called *Desolate Boedelkamers.*

Hitherto I have only dealt with the insolvent who had become such through misfortune, and who at his own request desired to surrender his estate, There was, however, another class of person, called a *bankroetier* or *bankbreeker* (bankrupt), whose estate was also sometimes administered by the *Desolate Boedelkamer.* The person who contracted debts and fled the country to escape payment or the consequences of his fraudulent acts was regarded in the same light as a thief. For him the law knew no mercy. There were a number of placaten promulgated for the purpose of punishing bankrupts and all persons who connived at their flight. The estates of such persons were originally handed over to a curator appointed by the Court, but later they were placed in the hands of the commissioners of the *Desolate Boedelkamers.*

The insolvent could not make any contract or appear in court as plaintiff or defendant so long as his estate was being administered by the Insolvency Chamber, and so long as he had not obtained his rehabilitation. The bankrupt could never be rehabilitated, and therefore he could never make a valid contract or have a *personam legitimam standi in judicio* (Kersteman, *sub voce Insolventie*).

In 1777 an insolvent Ordinance was granted to the city of Amsterdam (*Ned. Jaarboeken,* p. 291). This is important to us, as it was the source of the insolvency practice of the

Cape of Good Hope at the time of the annexation. The main principles of this Ordinance were introduced into the various colonial ordinances, and still form the basis of our bankruptcy practice. The provisions of this Amsterdam Ordinance were briefly as follows: Whenever any one within the city or its jurisdiction was so situated that he was obliged to stop payment, and notice thereof was given to the commissioners of the *Desolate Boedelkamer*, either by himself or any of his creditors with a request that they should take charge of his goods, two members of the board were appointed to administer the estate. The commissioners first tried to make an arrangement with the creditors, but if the latter refused or if the insolvent was deemed unworthy of a composition, then these commissioners proceeded to make a rough inventory of the estate and to examine the insolvent. The next step was to call a meeting of creditors and to elect provisional sequestrators. The sequestrators then made a complete inventory and took charge of the estate. The insolvent was given a month to compound with his creditors. If he succeeded the estate was released from sequestration, but if not then the commissioners adjudged the debtor insolvent, and the sequestrators became curators (trustees). Claims were filed against the estate, and the assets were liquidated by the curators. The curators could, when they deemed it necessary, summon the insolvent before the commissioners and examine him. For non-attendance and for fraud he could be punished. The estate after being liquidated was divided amongst the creditors, the preferent claims being first paid. If the insolvent had acted honestly he was allowed a certain percentage out of the assets, and a certificate was granted to him. Upon receipt of this certificate the insolvent could obtain from the commissioners a discharge from all debts due previous to his insolvency. The certificate had to be signed by six-eighths of his creditors, and to contain a declaration by the curators and the creditors that nothing fraudulent was discovered in his actions.

In 1803 De Mist established a Chamber at the Cape in whose charge were placed insolvent estates, unadministered estates (*desolate boedels*) and estates under curatorship. The commissioners were also entrusted with the execution of sentences. To this Chamber De Mist issued certain instructions which, as regards insolvent estates, were almost identical with the instructions of the Amsterdam Chamber. In two important respects they differed from the latter: creditors could only apply for the sequestration of an estate if there remained unpaid more than one sentence lodged with the Chamber for execution, and, secondly, the creditors had no share in the administration of the estate. This was conducted officially by the Chamber. This Chamber was abolished in 1818, and in its place an official sequestrator was appointed with the powers originally entrusted to the Chamber.

In 1819 instructions were issued to the sequestrator and other functionaries of his department, and an Ordinance was promulgated for the judicial administration of estates. To the department of the sequestrator were entrusted all estates that were insolvent, unadministered or placed under curatorship as well as the execution of all civil sentences except those entrusted specially to the boards of landdrost and heemraden. The procedure in matters of insolvency was very little altered from that established by De Mist's instructions (Proclamation, 2nd September, 1819).

In 1829 an Ordinance (No. 64) was passed for the regulation of bankrupt and insolvent estates. This formed the basis of our present law of bankruptcy. In its form and in many of its principles it was based upon English procedure; at the same time it did not entirely do away with the Dutch principles, as a comparison between our Ordinance and the Amsterdam law will show. The groundwork of the new Ordinance was, however, English, and into it was woven a great deal of the Dutch practice. This Ordinance recognised the principles that a person could surrender his estate voluntarily, and that creditors could obtain an order for sequestration if certain acts of insolvency had been committed. The order for sequestration as soon as it was made had the effect in law of divesting the insolvent of his estate and of vesting the same in the Master. The Master then called a meeting of creditors, and they elected a trustee. The rest of the administration was carried out by the trustee under the supervision of the creditors. The Master took the place of the official sequestrator, and took over many of the functions of the Amsterdam commissioners. In many respects the Ordinance of 1829 was more like the Amsterdam law than like the practice introduced by De Mist.

The Ordinance of 1829 was superseded by that of 1843, which has established the bankruptcy procedure for the whole of South Africa. Here and there alterations have been made, but the main principles and most of the details of procedure are the same in all the South African colonies. Since 1843 several amendments have been made, the most important of which is the Cape Colony Act of 1884, many of the provisions of which have been taken over by the rest of South Africa. During the existence of the Republics their insolvency procedure was almost identical with that established by the Cape Ordinance of 1843.

If we compare the Dutch law of insolvency with that of the law of England as it prevailed in 1829, we shall see that there was a remarkable similarity, and in many matters where the law of England differed from the law of Holland the colonial Ordinance of 1843 followed the latter. Judge Burton in his *Observations on the Insolvent Law of the Cape of Good Hope*, published in 1829, mentions a number of differences, and in nearly every case our law is nearer to the Dutch law than to the English law of that time. It would not be profitable to mention all these differences, so I shall only select a few: (1) The law of England applied to traders only, the law of Holland to all persons. (2) The law of Holland allowed voluntary surrender to all unfortunate persons whether under arrest or not; the English law only permitted a debtor under arrest to surrender. (3) By the law of England there were two tribunals and two systems, one for the bankrupt and one for the insolvent; by Dutch law there was only one tribunal and one mode of procedure. It will be noted in each of these cases we have followed the Dutch practice. Incidental questions, such as the preference of mortgage creditors, the vesting of property, &c., are determined by the law of Holland. To sum up:—

(1) The Roman law recognised imprisonment for debt, and handed over the debtor to his creditor. It divided the goods of the debtor amongst his

creditors with the assistance of the praetor, who granted the *immissio in possessionem, cessio bonorum, proscriptio* and *venditio bonorum.*

(2) The German law allowed the creditor to enslave the debtor, and the later law of the Franks made the debtor work for his creditor.

(3) The law of Holland recognised the attachment of the person, and towards the beginning of the sixteenth century admitted the *cessio bonorum.*

(4) During the seventeenth century the insolvent estates of deceased persons and the estates of absentees were administered by commissioners under the supervision of the schout and schepenen. During this century the practice grew up in certain towns of administering the insolvent estates of those who had obtained *brieven van cessie* in the same way.

(5) Except as regards the administration of the insolvent estates of deceased persons, of *desolate boedels* and the *cessio bonorum,* there was no general law of insolvency during the seventeenth century. The bankrupt was dealt with as a criminal.

(6) During the eighteenth century various local ordinances were framed for the administration of insolvent estates, which were then placed in the hands of the *Desolate Boedelkamers.* The principle of rehabilitation began to receive recognition during this century.

(7) The most perfect law of insolvency was that of Amsterdam of 1777. It recognised compulsory sequestration, the administration of the insolvent

estate by a trustee under the direction of creditors, and rehabilitation.

(8) De Mist in 1803 introduced most of the principles of the Amsterdam Ordinance, and handed over insolvent estates to commissioners of the *Desolate Boedelkamer.*

(9) In 1818 the official sequestrator took the place of the commissioners.

(10) In 1829 the Insolvent Ordinance wove English and Dutch practice together, and established the principles of our present practice.

(11) The Ordinance of 1843 superseded that of 1829 and fixed our modern South African law of insolvency.

CHAPTER XXV.

HISTORY OF OUR LAW OF ARREST TO FOUND JURISDICTION.

THE courts of Holland recognised two kinds of arrest. The one kind was said to arise *ex necessitate* and the other *ex utilitate.* The latter was conceded in order to found jurisdiction, the former to conserve the thing or debt. The former class of arrests was granted both against the citizen and the non-resident stranger, as, for instance, when the defendant was *suspectus de fugâ.* Movable goods could also be arrested when a fear existed that they would be removed. The arrest *ex necessitate* was regarded as consonant with the principles of the Roman law (Voet, 2, 5, 18), whilst the arrest to found jurisdiction was considered to be hostile to its principles, and therefore odious. The arrest *ex necessitate* is recognised by the Roman law in many cases, as, for instance, when a *res litigiosa* was ordered to be deposited with a sequester or in a temple pending the decision to whom it should be awarded (*Dig.* 2, 8, 7). The arrest *ex utilitate* appears, however, to be peculiar to the laws of western Europe after the fall of the Empire.

Our law of arrest to found jurisdiction differs very considerably from the practice which prevailed in the Roman Empire, where the plaintiff was required to sue the defendant in the court of the latter's domicile. The reason for the Roman rule arose from the fact that the Romans, Italians and other provincials were all *cives Romani.* Modern investigators into the history of the Roman law have come to the conclusion that the true foreigner (*advena*) could not claim the assistance of the Roman courts unless he lived under the protection of a Roman citizen. In Rome the *peregrinus* of the *Corpus Juris* was not a true foreigner: he was a subject of Rome, a free inhabitant of Roman territory who was neither a citizen nor a Latin (Gérard, *Droit Romain,* p. 109, and authorities there cited). He could in many cases have recourse to the ordinary courts, though in special matters he had his own tribunals.

The arrest to found jurisdiction was unknown to the Roman law; it is therefore a matter of great interest to endeavour to ascertain how it came to be introduced into our law, and what its exact scope was. As it is foreign to the Roman law, it must have had its origin in some German or other custom, which was so inveterate that it survived the introduction of the Roman law and practice into Holland. It will therefore be necessary at the outset to inquire into the condition of foreigners in western Europe from the earliest German times to the sixteenth century in order to ascertain how strangers were treated by the local courts.

In the earliest German period all persons who did not belong to a particular tribe were regarded as foreigners. They could claim no protection from the tribe, and were considered to be devoid of all rights. The foreign guest (*hospes*) was under the protection either of the princeps or of some particular person, and if he was attacked or injured his host defended him or claimed reparation. When the tribe became the nation the foreigner was no longer a person who did not belong to the same tribe, but a person who owed allegiance to some other king. During the period of the Frankish Empire all who owed allegiance to the Emperor were citizens of the Empire, irrespective of whether they were Franks, Saxons or Gallo-Romans. All others were regarded as *peregrini*, and were entirely devoid of any rights *à l'époque barbare les seuls sujets francs pouvaient se prévaloir de leur loi nationale et non les étrangers, car le viel usage germanique les met hors la loi* (Brissaud, *Histoire du Droit Franc*, vol. 1, p. 55).

When, however, the Frankish Empire fell to pieces, and the various principalities, countships and dukedoms were carved out of the imperial domain, each dukedom, &c., was practically an independent State, and the inhabitant of one province came to regard the inhabitant of another as a foreigner. This practice applied to the Netherlands as well as to the other divisions of the Empire. The word foreigner (*buitenlander* or *uitlander*) was applied either to a person who did not belong to the Netherlands at all (like a Frenchman), or else to the inhabitant of another province. Thus a Frisian was regarded as an *uitlander* in Holland, as opposed to an *inboorling* or native Hollander. A distinction, however, was drawn between the *uitlander* who lived permanently in the province and the person who merely passed through or took up a temporary residence there. The former was called an *inwonende vreemdeling* (*incola*), whilst the latter was termed an *uitwonende vreemdeling* (*extraneus* or *peregrinus*) (Fock. And. *Oud-Ned. Burg. Recht.* vol. 1, pp. 77 *et seq.*).

The domiciled foreigner (*incola*) possessed as a rule the same private rights as the citizen. His status was determined by the law of his origin, but he could approach the law courts in exactly the same way as any citizen. The *peregrinus,* however, who fell under the category of *uitwonende vreemdeling,* laboured under several disadvantages; of these the principal were that he and his property could be arrested and brought before the court to determine whether he owed an *incola* money or not, and that if he wished to appear as a plaintiff his adversary could demand security for the costs likely to be incurred. The lawyers of the sixteenth century usually expressed these disadvantages by saying that the *peregrinus* had to give security for costs and was subject to an *arrestum fundandae jurisdictionis causa* and a *cautio de judicio sistendo et de judicato solvendo.* On the other hand, the *peregrinus* had the advantage that any matter in which he was a party was speedily dealt with. He was said to have *kort recht.* In Overijssel, for instance, the lawsuits between *incolae* were always adjourned at midday, whereas foreigners were entitled *die sonne te baten nemen,* or to demand a hearing in the afternoon (Fock. And. *ibid.* p. 86). In case of arrest the foreigner could demand a prompt decision upon the matter upon which he was detained (Voet, 5, 1, 56, and Van der Keessel, *Thes.* 175).

The practice of arresting a *peregrinus* and of bringing him before the local judge in order to determine whether he owes an *incola* a debt is diametrically opposed to the rule which prevailed in the Roman Empire. The practice of the civil law is usually expressed by the rule *actor sequitur forum rei,* and this rule was adopted everywhere in western Europe with regard to *incolae;* but with regard to *peregrini* a different rule was followed in many parts of Germany, in some parts of France and in most of the provinces of the Netherlands (Sande, 1, 3, 17; Gail, 1, 12; Voet, 2, 4, 22). In Holland and in several other Dutch provinces the *incola* was allowed to arrest the *peregrinus* or his property and to bring him before the local judge, in order to compel him to give security for his appearance in court, and to pay whatever the amount of the judgment might be.

What is the origin of this practice? Peckius, who is one of the earliest Dutch writers on the subject of arrests, does not trace the history of the arrest of a foreigner. He merely states that the reason this practice was introduced was to avoid the costs which citizens would have to incur if they had to pursue the foreigner to the court of his domicile (Peckius, *De Jur. Sist.* 2, 6). Merula (bk. 4, tit. 2, c. 25) thinks that the arrest was a kind of compulsion to which the foreigner was subjected so that he could be driven to pay his creditor rather than endure the worry of an arrest. *Daar door de persoon wòrd bekommert ten einde hy door verdriet van 't Arrest eindelyk gedrongen zy te Compareren voor den Juge.* He calls it *kommer-recht,* and says that by such arrest the jurisdiction of the court was established *word bevestigt de jurisdictie van den Hove.*

Bort, who wrote in the following century, adopts the reason of Merula. "Arrests have been introduced by us in order that the arrested person, affected by the worry of his arrest, may appear before the local judge and pay the debt or give security that he will appear before the court and pay the amount of the judgment, so that lawsuits may be cut short and the costs or expenses avoided which are necessarily incurred when a foreign debtor domiciled in another country has to be sued there." He also tells us that it was introduced in favour of Dutch commerce, inasmuch as merchants would not lightly enter into transactions with foreigners unless they were assured that the person and property of the foreigner could be arrested for the debt. He also points out that commerce is the life of the Netherlands, and that the prosperity of the inhabitants depends entirely on its trade (*Arresten*, 1, 12 *et seq.*).

These reasons, however, do not appear to be the only ones. From what has been said above it is clear that the foreigner was not regarded in the same light as the *incola* in many countries of western Europe. He suffered several disabilities besides being subject to arrest. I need only mention the fact that, during the eleventh century, if a foreigner died in the Netherlands his property was seized by the count. Fockema Andreae quotes a handvest of Alblas of 1332 to the same effect: *So wat goed dat besterft van overlantsche luyden dat salmen deelen ons die twee deelen en den ambachts heer het derde deel.* This right of *keurmede* existed as late as the seventeenth century (Fock. And. *loc. cit.*). In some provinces the testimony of a foreigner was not admissible against an *incola*.

From all these facts we can easily infer that between the tenth and the sixteenth centuries the lot of the foreigner in the Netherlands was not a happy one. In those times foreigners were not treated with the same tenderness that we extend to them nowadays. If a foreigner came in conflict with a citizen the interests of the latter were first studied. If he owed a debt to a citizen the judge saw that he paid his debt before he left the country. Jurists gradually sought to introduce the more humane laws of the *Corpus Juris*; but the people clung to their ancient rights and customs, and amongst these a respect for the interests of the foreigner can hardly be said to have existed. Gradually, no doubt, the position of the foreigner was ameliorated, but in the matter of arrest the Dutch courts adhered to their old customs, and they detained the foreigner *ut arrestatus taedio arrestationis affectus coram judice loci arresti compareat, pacta conventa servet, et debitum exsolvat* (Bort). The origin of the practice of arresting a foreigner in order to make him pay his debts is therefore to be sought in the fact that the early Germans, the Franks and the people of the Netherlands, before the fourteenth century at any rate, regarded the foreigner to a certain extent as outside of the protection of the law.

As commerce increased, and as foreigners came to be regarded in a more favourable light, many of their disabilities disappeared. They could vindicate their rights before the local courts, but if they owed citizens money they could be compelled to remain in the country until they either paid their debts or gave security that they would appear before the judge and pay the amount of the judgment. A rude kind of justice, however, attempted to give them some compensation for the disabilities imposed on them. The foreigner could demand that the judge should then and there determine whether the *incola* had a *primâ facie* case against him. If this was decided against him he was heard as speedily as possible, so that he might not be detained in a foreign land longer than was absolutely necessary.

The next question to inquire into is, Why is the arrest

said to found jurisdiction? On the threshold of this inquiry we are met with a difficulty—Was the arrest made for the purpose of establishing a jurisdiction which was supposed not to exist, or was it made with the object of strengthening a jurisdiction which already existed?

Mr. Justice Buchanan in his translation of Voet, bk. 2, tit. 4, 5, 22, has rendered the words *jurisdictionis firmandae gratiâ* by the words "for the purpose of strengthening his jurisdiction." Sir Henry de Villiers accepted this view in *Einwald* v. *German West African Co.* and in *Ex parte Kahn.*

Is this correct? Did the Roman-Dutch jurists really consider that the jurisdiction of the judge was strengthened by the arrest, or did they think that the arrest founded a jurisdiction which they considered did not exist without it? In order to determine this, we must first consider whether Voet really meant to convey by the words *firmandae jurisdictionis gratiâ* that the jurisdiction of the judge was *strengthened.* There can be no doubt that the usual expression used by the Dutch jurists is "to found jurisdiction." Those who write in Latin use the term *jurisdictionis fundandae causâ,* and those who write in Dutch use the phrase *arrest fundeert jurisdictie.* Voet is apparently the only Dutch jurist who makes use of the words *jurisdictionis firmandae gratiâ.*

It seems difficult to see how a jurisdiction which already existed over a foreigner could be increased or strengthened by an arrest. If the judge has the jurisdiction to compel the foreigner either to pay the debt due to an *incola* or to give security *judicatum solvi,* he has all the power that he can wish for. Why should he want to strengthen so abstract a right as jurisdiction? If the translation of *jurisdictionis firmandae gratiâ* is really "for the purpose of strengthening his jurisdiction," then no doubt Voet at any rate held that view, though in this respect he would stand alone. If we examine title 4 of book 2 of Voet's *Commentary* we shall find that he uses three expressions in order to convey the meaning that there is a relation between arrest and jurisdiction. Thus in secs. 22, 25 and 42 the words *firmandae jurisdictionis gratiâ* occur, whilst in secs. 18, 26, 31 and 33 the words *fundandae jurisdictionis gratiâ* are used. In secs. 42 and 49 of the same title we find the words *stabiliendae jurisdictionis gratiâ*. Now *stabiliendae jurisdictionis gratiâ* is synonymous with *fundandae jurisdictionis gratiâ*, for the words *fundare* and *stabilire* both mean "to establish." We have, therefore, three sections in which the words *firmandae gratiâ* are used, and at least six where *fundandae gratiâ* or its equivalent are made use of. It is true that the word *firmare* both in classical and low Latin will bear the meaning of "to strengthen," but this is not its only meaning. It also means "to assert, to declare." Thus in Tacitus we have the expression *Paratis omnium animis reversuros firmaverunt* (*Hist.* 2, 9), where the word undoubtedly means "to assert." In the classical jurists we find the same meaning (Heumann, *Lexicon*).

I would therefore suggest that by the words *firmandae jurisdictionis gratiâ* Voet meant at the most "for the purpose of asserting his jurisdiction." If then we examine sec. 18 we find that Voet means that, if the judge intervenes merely for the purpose of asserting his jurisdiction, he acts not so much *ex necessitate* as *ex utilitate*, because it is cheaper for a creditor to sue foreigners before the local judge than to sue them in their own courts. I am not, however, sure that Voet meant more by *firmare* than he did by *fundare*. He seems to use the phrases above quoted quite indiscriminately. The word *firmare*, unless used in its classical sense, will easily bear the meaning of "making firm or establishing." It certainly was used in an extraordinary way by mediæval writers. Thus we find such expressions as *firmare psalmos* for singing psalms; *firmare in palam altari S. M.; firmare in directum (jurer que sa cause est juste); firmare* in the sense of *sera occludere*, French *fermer* (Magne D'Arnis).

Why should Voet have given so very peculiar a meaning to the phrase in the three sections mentioned, and not in the others? Add to this, that almost every other writer during the sixteenth and seventeenth centuries uses the phrases *arrest fundeert jurisdictie* and *arrestum jurisdictionis fundandae causâ*, then, I think, it will be conceded that the probabilities are strongly in favour of Voet having used the words *firmandae gratiâ* as synonymous with *fundandae gratiâ*. If, however, he did not use the words as synonymous, he stands alone in asserting that the arrest was made to strengthen and not to found jurisdiction, and as he quotes no authority for this statement we cannot accept it as historically correct.

If then the arrest was made *fundandae gratiâ, i.e.* in order to establish jurisdiction, where is the idea derived from? Merula tells us that the arrest was made *ten einde hy door verdriet van 't Arrest eindelyk gedrongen zy te Compareren voor den Juge* ("so that, by reason of his miserable plight caused by the arrest, he is at length driven to appear before the judge"). The foreigner, therefore, who was arrested, was not brought before the magistrate, but was simply detained until he agreed to appear before the judge. The arrest was not in practice carried out by order of the judge, but by the messenger, and the judge had nothing to do with the matter until the foreigner chose to appear before him *soodanige arresten als geschieden om het regts gebied van den regter te fundeeren werden allen door den Bode gedaan sonder daar over eenige Schepenen te bemoeyen* (Van Leeuwen, *Manier van Procedeeren,* p. 94). The *incola* addressed a request to the messenger to detain the foreigner and to summon him to appear before the schepenen to hear such claim as the *incola* will make on the afore-mentioned day (Van Leeuwen, *Prakt. Not.* bk. 4, c. 5). It was only upon his appearance in court that the judge acquired a jurisdiction over him.

The jurists after the reception of the Roman law in Holland had no doubt an aversion to interfere with the Roman rule of *actor sequitur forum rei.* The arrest of a foreigner was "odious," and therefore not to be encouraged. Yet the customs of the country permitted the arrest. The local judge, therefore, would not cite the foreigner to appear before him in the ordinary way, but if he were brought into court by way of arrest, then the judge asserted his jurisdiction *ex moribus.* The foreigner was probably considered by a fiction to have submitted himself to the jurisdiction. The actual presence of the foreigner was required before a jurisdiction was established, which the judge could not claim to exercise by virtue of the civil law. In this way, then, an arrest founded a jurisdiction which did not exist *ex jure scripto.*

From the person of the foreigner the arrest was extended

to his goods, so that, in order to release them, he might be induced to appear before the local judge. Originally, no doubt, the goods that were arrested were such as a traveller usually possessed; thus in certain parts of France an arrest of the horse or other belongings of a traveller was specially provided for (Rebuffus, *Tract. de Oblig.* art. 2, n. 70). The debts, no doubt, were originally such as a stranger would incur in a foreign country, as money due at an inn or small purchases made at the local shops. As trade increased, however, the debts would become more and more complicated, and as a popular idea existed that these arrests were introduced on behalf of Dutch merchants trading with foreigners, many cases must have arisen where the *locus contractus* and the *locus solutionis* were outside of Holland. It is, therefore, interesting to inquire whether the jurisdiction of the local judge over the foreigner was limited to the case of contracts entered into or torts committed in the country of the arrest. Different opinions have been expressed on this subject by the Supreme Courts of the Cape Colony and of the Transvaal—*Ex parte Paul Kahn* (17 C.T.R. 840) and *Lecomte* v. *W. and B. Syndicate of Madagascar* ([1905] T.S. 696).

It is not my desire to express any opinion as to the law of the Cape Colony or of the Transvaal, but merely to inquire into the practice of the old courts of Holland. If we examine the authorities we find that they all lay down the general proposition that an *incola* may arrest a foreigner or his property in order to found jurisdiction. The value of the property was not considered: *Tegenwoordig wordt Arrest om Jurisdictie te funderen, verleent op eene zake, hoe gering dezelve ook zoude mogen wezen* (Merula, vol. 1, p. 238, in notes). The inquiry of the judge was therefore not limited to the property under arrest, but to the whole claim of the local creditor.

Now if we consult Peckius, Bort, Voet or any of the writers who deal with arrests, we find that they all devote a chapter to the inquiry as to when a foreigner cannot be arrested. Thus no arrest can be made where the claim of a local creditor is founded upon an immovable situated abroad (Voet, 2, 5, 25). If, however, the plaintiff demands the restoration of a movable, then the foreigner can be arrested to found jurisdiction even if the movable happens to be out of the jurisdiction of the local judge and in the foreigner's own country (Voet, *ibid.* 25). Not one of these authorities mentions the fact that a foreigner cannot be arrested if the debt was contracted elsewhere than in the country where the arrest is made. All the authorities are agreed that the claim must be founded on a contract, quasi-contract, delict or quasi-delict; but not a single one restricts the jurisdiction of the local judge to claims arising out of contracts entered into or to be performed in the country.

Sir Henry de Villiers, in *Ex parte Kahn*, has relied on Groenewegen (3, 18, 4) as an authority for the view that the local judge's jurisdiction was limited to contracts entered into in the *locus arresti.* I do not understand Groenewegen to hold that view. He refers to the French practice, and says that in those countries a person is not cited before the court of the *locus contractus* or *delicti,* unless he is found there. He then goes on to say that this has no doubt given rise to our custom of arrest, and he quotes Peckius (c. 2, n. 5) as his authority. Now Peckius points out that the Dutch practice differs materially from the Roman rule, and says that "a burgher of Louvain can arrest a rich and influential burgher of Mechlin, who can easily be sued in his native city, which is not far off; there is no necessity for it, no fear of flight: all that we look to is the advantage and convenience that I can cite him before the court of my domicile, contrary to the Roman law, which requires the creditor to sue the debtor at the domicile of the latter." Sande uses similar language (*Decis,* 1, 3, 17). What Groenewegen therefore means is that, because the Roman rule was found to be inconvenient to *incolae,* the Dutch introduced in opposition to it the law of arrest to found jurisdiction. If, therefore, anything is to be inferred from Groenewegen it is that, in case of arrest, the practice of the Romans and French does not prevail in Holland. Voet seems to have understood Groenewegen in the same way (Voet, 2, tit. 5, 22).

If this is not the meaning of Groenewegen, then he would stand quite alone in suggesting that the right to attach property *ad fundandam jurisdictionem* only arises at the place where the defendant has committed a tort or made or broken a contract. Every writer points out how peculiar and unusual this practice of the Dutch courts was, and how it was based on the theory that by worrying the foreigner by arrest you indirectly compel him to allow the local judge to try the dispute between the *incola* and himself. Why should the *incola* go to another country if the foreigner owed him a debt *ex contractu alibi facto,* when the whole doctrine of arrest is based on the ground that the *incola* must be protected against the foreigner? It was to save the *incola* the expense of a costly lawsuit in a foreign country that the Court allowed him to obtain judgment and to levy execution in his own province.

It is also noteworthy that when in 1667 an inquiry was directed into the existence of this right of arrest to found jurisdiction, the question put to the advocates and attorneys whose opinion was sought made no mention of any exception. The question was as follows: "Does there exist in the province of Holland a practice founded upon an ancient right or custom, observed and acted upon, whereby a burgher or permanent resident (*ingezeten, incola*) of one town, who has a claim against the burgher or resident of another town, or of the country, or against a foreigner resident in another kingdom or province, may cause the non-resident person or foreigner or his goods to be arrested both to found jurisdiction and to obtain security for the payment of the debt?" (Bort). To this an affirmative answer was given. Surely, if the claims referred only to those which arose out of contracts entered into in the town or province, this important exception would have been mentioned and the question qualified to that extent.

The extensive privilege claimed by the Hollanders has existed in a modified form in France, and the present Code allows the seizure of the property of a *debiteur forain* who has no fixed domicile in France. In Holland art. 764 of the Procedure Code gives a Dutch creditor, who gets leave of a judge, the right to arrest the goods of a person who has no fixed domicile in Holland. Boneval Faure points out that this is a survival of the old *saisie foraine*, but that the present rule makes no distinction between *peregrinus* and *incola;* all that it requires is that there should be no fixed domicile in Holland on the part of the debtor.

Whether the rule of the Dutch courts, by which the goods of a foreigner can be attached to found jurisdiction, is a wise and salutary rule or one tinged with selfishness and barbarity, does not affect an historical investigation into the origin of the rule or the practice of the Dutch courts. Like so many of the old customs of Holland, it was introduced into South Africa, and has been repeatedly acted upon by the South African courts. As I have pointed out above, a difference of opinion exists between the courts of the Cape Colony and of the Transvaal as to the scope of the rule. I think all the South African courts are agreed that a resident can arrest a foreigner if the debt upon which the claim is founded arose out of a contract entered into and to be performed in the colony where the arrest is made, or if the claim arises out of a delict committed there; but a difference of opinion exists whether the right should extend to claims which arise out of contracts entered into and to be performed elsewhere.

In *Dunell and Stainbridge* v. *Van der Plank,* or the *Louisa* case (3 Menz. 113), the Supreme Court of the Cape Colony, after the case had been fully argued, granted an arrest to found jurisdiction where the applicant was an *incola,* the respondent a *peregrinus,* and where the contract was made and had to be performed in England, and therefore out of the jurisdiction of the colonial court. It has been alleged that in *Wilhelm* v *Francis* (Buch. 1876, p. 216) the court departed from the position taken up in the *Louisa* case. This hardly seems correct. In *Wilhelm's* case both the parties to the suit were out of the jurisdiction of the court, the cause of action arose out of the jurisdiction, and there was no allegation that the contract was to be fulfilled within the colony. This, therefore, is a case of one *peregrinus* attempting to arrest the goods of another *peregrinus*, and differs thus materially from the case of the *Louisa*.

In *Einwald* v. *German West African Co.* (5 S.C. 87) the court also refused to allow a foreigner to arrest the goods of another foreigner, where the contract was to be performed elsewhere. Quite recently the Supreme Court of the Cape Colony has refused to allow a domiciled citizen to attach the goods of a foreigner on a claim arising out of a contract entered into and to be performed in German South-West Africa (*Ex parte Kahn*). In the late South African Republic Chief Justice Kotzé adopted the rule that an *incola* can arrest a foreigner upon a claim for a debt arising out of a contract which may have been entered into elsewhere and which may have to be performed elsewhere (*Cloete* v. *Benjamin*, 1 S.A.R. 180; *De Villiers* v. *Benjamin*, 1 S.A.R. 224; *Middelvlei Black Reef Syndicate* v. *Tucker*, 4 Off. Rep. 17; *McBride & Thompson* v. *Vause*, 6 S.A.R. 3). The decisions of the late High Court were followed by the present Supreme Court in *Lecomte* v. *W. and B. Syndicate of Madagascar* ([1905] T.S. 696). Though there is a great deal to be said in favour of the old Dutch practice as followed in the Transvaal, the rule adopted by the Cape courts is no doubt more in accordance with the modern practice of commercial nations.

The next point to consider is whether a *peregrinus* had the right to arrest another *peregrinus* in order to found jurisdiction. I am not aware of any Dutch writer who deals specifically with this question, though it seems unlikely that such a right could have been accorded, without qualification, to the non-resident stranger. There can be no doubt that a foreigner, who had settled more or less permanently in a town so as to have come to be regarded as an *ingezeten*, had that right; but it is by no means certain that an *advena*, who happened to be temporarily in a town of Holland, could arrest another *advena* there, both being *buytengezetenen*. As we have seen above, in ancient times the foreigner (*advena*) was considered to be *hors la loi*. In time, however, privileges were accorded to him, and he certainly had the right in the Netherlands during the fifteenth and sixteenth centuries to sue in the local courts on contract or for a tort. Besides the advantage of *kort recht*, he had no special privilege. The right to arrest the person and goods of a foreigner was regarded as the special privilege of the inhabitants of the towns of Holland. It was the burgher or resident of the town, and not the *advena*, who was allowed to make an exception to the rule *actor sequitur forum rei*.

The Hollanders were very jealous of the right that every burgher should be cited before his daily judge, and the only exceptions were the arrest of strangers to found jurisdiction, and the arrest *ex necessitate* under special circumstances. Thus by the Great Privilege of the Lady Mary it was provided that no citizen should cite another citizen elsewhere than before the court of their town, and the *Instructiën* of the Court of Holland provided "that no subject of this country shall sue another in the first instance except before his daily or ordinary judge" (Van Leeuwen's *Commentaries*, Kotzé's tr.

vol. 2, p. 399). The right to arrest a foreigner was, therefore, a special privilege contrary to the Roman law, contrary to the Great Privilege and contrary to the usual practice of the courts. Maevius (*De Arr.* c. 7, n. 49) says that the right of arrest is in all cases a *privilegium civibus concessum non facile extraneis esse concedendum et eo casu caute a judice procedendum.*

It was a subject of considerable discussion whether a burgher, who lived in the suburbs of a large city (*voorstede*), had the right to arrest a foreigner. As against such a right was advanced the argument that the right was a special privilege, and that the inhabitant of a *voorstede* was not an *ingezeten.* The right was conceded, but apparently not readily (Peckius). It is therefore difficult to conceive that to a foreigner would have been granted what was regarded as the special privilege of the burgher. Moreover, it was not the practice of the local courts to encourage lawsuits to be brought before them. It was the practice, where two *peregrini* belonging to one province appeared before a judge, to refer them to their own court (Voet, 2, 5, 45). Bort (*Arrest,* 3, 14), however, says: *Cum arresti vis ea fit ut omnimodo parere ei oporteat et justitia rem saisiat;* therefore, if a person, who is a foreigner and unknown, requests the messenger to make an arrest, the latter must demand security for damage which the arrested person may suffer. Bort, however, relies for this view on a passage of Argentré on the customs of Brittany. It certainly appears extraordinary that Argentré should be called in to say what the practice of Holland was. Again, it is not clear that Bort is referring to an arrest to found jurisdiction. It is more likely that he is referring to one of the arrests *ex necessitate*, *e.g.* to impound the *res litigiosa* pending the lawsuit.

On the whole, therefore, it seems more reasonable to hold that a *peregrinus*, who was not a resident in a town, could not arrest an *advena* to found jurisdiction, inasmuch as this right of arrest was a special privilege accorded to burghers and residents. If an *advena* could in every case arrest another *advena*, the authorities would have made some definite statement to that effect, or would have said that every person could arrest every other person, not being an *incola*, in order to found jurisdiction.

The form of the interrogatories quoted by Bort (*loc. cit.*) seems to show that the idea of a non-resident stranger arresting another non-resident stranger to found jurisdiction never presented itself to the practitioners of his time. That two non-resident strangers, who were not the inhabitants of one province, might have been allowed to arrest one another not *ex utilitate*, but *ex necessitate*, is quite possible, as, for instance, where the place of arrest was the *locus solutionis* of a contract made between them. Thus, if a foreigner agreed to deliver to another foreigner a movable in Holland, and if both happened to be in that province, the creditor might arrest the matter in dispute; for by making Holland the *locus solutionis* the debtor may be considered to have intended to submit himself to the jurisdiction of its courts. In such a case the court had jurisdiction *ex ratione solutionis*. It is, however, inconceivable that one foreigner could have been allowed to arrest another in Holland to found jurisdiction, in order to try a cause where the contract was to be performed outside the province.

As commerce extended, and as the intercourse of the various towns increased, the privilege of arrest was sought to be curtailed. Treaties were made between several provinces by which the right to arrest one another's subjects was considerably diminished. Most of the laws and treaties, however, seem to refer rather to the arrest *ex necessitate* than to the arrest to found jurisdiction. In *Hornblow* v. *Fotheringham* (1 Menz. 364) Judge Menzies expressed a strong doubt whether a *peregrinus* could arrest another *peregrinus* to found jurisdiction. In *Einwald* v. *German West African Co.* the Supreme Court of the Cape Colony refused to allow a *peregrinus* to arrest another *peregrinus* where the contract had to be performed outside the limits of the Cape Colony. However, from what has been said by Sir Henry de Villiers in *Ex parte Kahn,* the ground for this decision was not so much because a *peregrinus* was suing a *peregrinus,* but because the *locus solutionis* was outside the Cape Colony.

The view expressed above that in Holland a *peregrinus* could not arrest another *peregrinus* in order to found jurisdiction was approved of by Chief Justice Kotzé in *Cloete* v. *Benjamin* (1 S.A.R. 180), and followed by the present Transvaal Supreme Court in *Springle* v. *Mercantile Association of Swaziland, Ltd.* ([1904] T.S. 163). This question, therefore, also appears to form part of the *jus controversum* of South Africa.

CHAPTER XXVI.

DELICTS AND CRIMES.

Development of Delicts and Crimes. — According to the theory of the Roman law obligations flow either from contracts or from delicts or from a multitude of other causes (*Obligationes aut ex contractu nascuntur aut ex maleficio aut proprio quodam jure ex variis causarum figuris.—D.* 44, 7, 1). These numerous other causes are divided into quasi-contracts and quasi-delicts according to whether the fact which gives rise to the obligation resembles a contract or a delict. Certain acts give rise to a legal relationship (called *obligatio*) between two parties, by virtue of which the one can demand something from the other (*Obligatio est vinculum juris quo necessitate adstringimur alicujus solvendae rei secundum nostrae civitatis jura.—Inst.* 3, 13 pr.).

If there has been an agreement between two or more persons, and if by virtue of such an agreement the *jus civile* allowed an action to be brought, then an obligation *ex contractu* arose. If, on the other hand, by a voluntary premeditated act, illicit according to the Roman law, one person injured another, then the latter was bound to make reparation to the former: an obligation was then said to arise *ex delicto.* It made no difference whether this illicit act was directed against the person, property or reputation of another. Leaving aside the question whether it is scientifically correct to say that contracts and delicts are species of the genus obligation, it is sufficient for our purposes that this was the theory of the Roman law, and that it was accepted by the Roman-Dutch jurists during the sixteenth and seventeenth centuries as the basis upon which they built up their system of jurisprudence.

In the development of law, however, the idea of compensation for a delict precedes the idea of demanding the fulfilment of a promise or of exacting a money payment on account of a breach of contract. In other words, payment for a delict is older than payment of damages for breach of contract. If, therefore, we go back to the German customs we find that the early Germans had a fairly advanced conception of the law of delicts, though their notions of contract were crude. To attack a person's body or his goods or his good name is to do him and his family an injury for which compensation can be claimed.

The early Germans had so far advanced in their appreciation of law that the attack on the person, goods and honour was regarded as an attack on the freedom of a member of the tribe (Schröder, p. 73). At first, no doubt, the compensation was paid in cattle, corn or other goods (Tacit. *Germ.* c. 21), though later, when money freely circulated among them, a delict could be compensated in money. A penalty in kind existed in the Netherlands as late as the fifteenth century. In Saxony quarrelling wives were obliged to bring to the court a bag of corn tied with a silk thread. Later on each delict had a particular money value attached to it.

The Germans had, however, not advanced so far as to appreciate that it was the duty of the collective tribe or nation to prevent the individual from seeking his own redress and to procure satisfaction for him in the name of the community. At first the injured person and his relatives took the matter into their own hands and exacted their own vengeance. When, however, the redress sought came to be of a pecuniary nature, the tribe stepped in and determined the value of each assault and of each insult. If the value was paid the community forbade the exaction of any further vengeance. We find that when a scale of charges had been formulated for delicts the tribe or nation demanded its share of the damages. It is doubtful on what principle this share was exacted. Some think that the share demanded by the community was to cover the expenses necessarily attached to some organisation to compel the payment of the damages; others that it was demanded as a reward for the assistance lent in its recovery; whilst others, again, are inclined to see in the tribe's share a compensation for allowing the injured party to pursue the tortfeasor. This was the period of the blood-feud and wergeld.

It must not be imagined for one moment that payment for delicts was the only mode of punishment. As far as we know there was no period when a settled community did not visit its vengeance on criminals whose conduct was so grave as to endanger the peace of the community. So also, where the injury to the individual was extremely serious he could take his personal vengeance on the wrong-doer. In the history of law amongst the Germans we find that though punishment for serious crimes was not unknown, the exaction of a money penalty loomed large, and the punishment of the wrong-doer by the community was still in the background.

Gradually, however, the idea of penalty grows weaker and that of punishment grows stronger. Wrongful acts which were regarded as purely private wrongs lose that character and come to be dealt with as public offences. Penalties claimable by the injured party often disappear entirely and are replaced by punishments (Noordewier, pp. 272 and 273; Schröder, pp. 73 *et seq.* and 755 *et seq.*).

When, therefore, we investigate the law of delicts as it obtained amongst the German nations after they had begun to occupy definite territories, we are struck by the fact that there are few general principles regarding the exaction of penalties, but a mass of rules dealing with injuries in detail. The price to be paid depends on the nature of the injury. Hence it becomes absolutely necessary to define each particular injury, to give it a definite name and to affix to it a definite price. The difference in the depth or length of a wound, the place where the wound is inflicted, the weapon with which the blow was dealt are carefully considered, and to the result is given a definite name with a definite price attached to it. It would be wearisome and unprofitable to go into minute detail; a few examples will therefore serve to make the above statements clear (Noordewier, pp. 274 *et seq.*).

Thus *moord brand* was originally the putting fire to a house with intent to kill the inmates as they tried to escape. Later it came to mean arson. To murder and secretly to dispose of the body was *mord rit* or *mord tot.* It differs from *manslag* in its secrecy. In the assizes of Jerusalem we read: "*Homecide* est quant home est tué en apert devant la gent et meslée; *meurtre* est fait en repos." The penalty differed greatly, and if the murder was a very base act the death penalty was exacted from the culprit. *Maiming* was another serious crime. Some wounds were said to support a complaint, others not (*klaag bare wonden*). If the wound were the depth of the nail it was *klaag baar*. A blow followed by blood was *dolg* or *ser*, a simple blow *slahs*. If a bone was broken and the blood flowed on to the ground it was called *bloedrisen*. The length and breadth of the wound, whether the wound was visible or not, the number of bones broken, not only altered its name, but altered its value as well. To throw a man into the water (*walpuldepene*), to pull his beard (*berdfang*), to stop him on his way (*wegwending*), were some of the many injuries to the person for which a high wergeld was demanded.

The night thief was a far greater criminal than the day thief. The secret thief had to pay a larger measure of compensation than the thief who stole openly. To steal cattle and corn was a much more serious act than the theft of other movables. Both in manslaughter and in theft the *corpus delicti* must be produced much in the same condition as it was found. Hence the thief was brought before the judge *with the stolen property tied on his back.* Even as late as 1245 A.D. we find a similar provision in a keur of Haarlem: *Dat hi hem des scoonen dages den rechter mach leveren met den dinge dat hi gestolen heeft op sijn rugge gebonden.*

To insult a freeman by using towards him opprobrious words was a delict for which satisfaction could be exacted. The amount of the penalty depended on the period and on the words used. To call a man a traitor or a defrauder cost *fyf punt;* to call him a thief, *een punt;* whilst calling a man a liar was very inexpensive (Noordewier, pp. 275 *et seq*).

The next step in the law of delicts and crimes was to do away with the injured person's right to claim vengeance, and to allow the State to pursue the wrong-doer and exact the penalty. The growth of this conception was extremely slow. Blood-feud and outlawry were prevalent in the thirteenth century, and though the former was disappearing the latter was still vigorous. The system of composition slowly gave way to the system of punishment by an officer of the State. As this system grew stronger the practice of declaring a man an outlaw grew weaker.

I have said above that there never was a period at which the tribe did not punish at all. Even the early Germans, we learn from Tacitus (*Germ.* c. 12), accused persons before the mallum, and the tribe caused them to be punished: *Licet apud concilium accusare quoque et discrimen capitis intendere.* But what I desire to point out is that the general practice before the thirteenth century was the system of outlawry and composition, and the system of State punishment the exception. After that period the system of punishment gradually replaces the system of composition, until in the sixteenth century the idea of our present system of criminal law is fully established. Delicts are gradually distinguished from crimes. Penalty for the former is recovered by the injured party, whilst punishment for the latter is exacted not by the individual, but by the State.

The State's gradual usurpation of the right of the individual to claim blood vengeance was brought about by a series of causes, among which the influence of the Church must be regarded as important. The Canon law contains a number of provisions with regard to crimes which, taken together, form a kind of penal code. This penal code began about the seventh and was quite considerable during the eleventh century. It was not only for the humble, for it reached equally well the great feudal lords. Through the terrors of eternal torture in an after life the Church was able to punish the great. It did so by striking at their pride or by compelling them to suffer corporal punishment by means of the penance. It showed men that the mere payment of money was not a sufficient restraint. The right of asylum no doubt did harm, but it had its good side also. The Church threw her shield over the victim pursued by the blood vengeance of the injured man's family. She helped, therefore, to put down private feud and private vengeance, and to substitute corporal punishment for money satisfaction. In this way the Church lent its aid to the State to suppress lawlessness and crime and to punish the criminal instead of allowing the injured man and his friends to do so (Poullet, *Origines*, vol. 1, p. 109).

After the idea that the State should pursue the criminal became once fixed the distinction between crime and delict became more and more clearly appreciated. In Grotius' time it was fully understood. He tells us (bk. 3, c. 32, sec. 7) that "a twofold obligation may arise out of one and the same delict—the one liability to punishment, the other the obligation to remove the inequality" (*i.e.* to give compensation); "further, the right to inflict punishment belongs to the sovereign, but the right to claim removal of an inequality (damages) to whoever is wronged thereby."

When the system of blood-feud and composition prevailed the relatives of the injured man sought vengeance and reparation not only from the perpetrator of the wrong, but from his relatives as well. Hence arose the terrible and cruel family feuds. In time, however, the wrong-doer alone was punished, and his heirs were only held liable to make reparation out of the funds which came into their hands through the wrong-doer, and then only when the action had already been commenced against the deceased wrong-doer (Grot. 3, 32, 10).

The law as to damages for a delict is thus stated by Grotius (3, 32, 12): "Every one is liable for damages who has injured another through crime, even though he has not done the deed himself, but has by act or omission in some way or other caused the deed or its consequences in so far as any one is injured thereby."

Delicts.—I have given above a brief account of the historical development of delict and crime in western Europe. I shall now consider how the law regarding delicts developed in the Netherlands and in South Africa. During the period that the Netherlands formed part of the Frankish Empire the penalties of the Salic law and of the capitularia applied to the Low Countries as well as to the other parts of the Empire. No definite line was drawn between the tort and the crime: the two merged insensibly into one another. In the same way the English common law in its earlier days failed to draw an accurate distinction. "In the mediæval period the procedure whereby redress was obtained for many of the injuries now classified as torts bore plain traces of a criminal or quasi-criminal character, the defendant against whom judgment passed being liable not only to compensate the plaintiff, but to pay a fine to the king (Pollock, *Torts*, 4th ed. p. 3).

After the breaking up of the Frankish Empire the old customs still prevailed, so that during the rule of the counts blood-feud, outlawry and composition were still the main features of the law of delicts as well as of the criminal law. The amount of the penalties was gradually varied by charters and handvesten in the different provinces and towns. The stadboeken during the thirteenth, fourteenth and even the fifteenth centuries are our principal authorities as regards the law of torts. To what extent the principles of the Roman law of delicts were applied in the Netherlands during these centuries it is difficult to say, though the probability is that the influence of the Roman law in this department was so insignificant that it may be disregarded. No doubt towards the end of the fifteenth century it may have begun to influence the law of delicts, but it is not until the latter half of the sixteenth century that we can say with any certainty that the rules of the Roman law as regards delicts were generally adopted.

In a former chapter, when dealing with the Stadboek of Groningen of 1425, I pointed out that the third, fourth and fifth books dealt chiefly with the penalties attached to particular delicts. In the other stadboeken we find similar provisions. Thus in Jan Mathyssen's Law-book of the town of Briel (p. 167, ed. of Fruin and Pols) he tells us that according to the ancient customs if a person strikes another with his fist the penalty is twelve groats; if the blow is dealt with the open hand on the ears (a box on the ears) the penalty is thirty schellings. If a wound is given with a forbidden weapon, then according to the handvesten the penalty is three pounds. If the tortfeasor is not a citizen the penalty is increased fourfold. In the *Utrechtsche Keurboeken* we find similar provisions, though from Muller's *Middeleeuwsche Rechtsbronnen der Stad Utrecht* it would appear that the notion of a criminal law was considerably higher in Utrecht than in Groningen.

The gradual introduction of the Roman law drove out the idea of a fixed penalty attached to each delict, and the courts of justice came to disregard the penalties imposed by the stadboeken and to determine the amount of damages in accordance with the circumstances surrounding each case. In the sixteenth century the Roman-Dutch jurists began to consider the delict as an illegal act directed against a person, his property or his reputation, or as an omission to do something which the law requires a person to do, whereby another is injured, and on account of the act or omission the injured person is entitled to claim damages; whilst a crime came to be regarded as an act or omission which is punishable according to the municipal law. In the eighteenth century this distinction was clearly understood (Moorman, *Misdaden*, p. 3), though in expounding the law of crimes and delicts the Dutch jurists so mixed them up that the student experiences considerable difficulty in keeping delicts separate from crimes.

Grotius deals with obligations arising out of delicts, then proceeds to discuss crimes against life and crimes to the person. This is followed by chapters on injury (*hoon*), slander and crimes against property, and after treating of these he proceeds to discuss the quasi-delicts *si quid dejectum effusumve sit, si quid positum suspensumve sit* and others. The arrangement here is manifestly not suggested by a desire to distinguish accurately between torts and crimes.

Van Leeuwen, again, treats of obligations arising from crime, defines crime and states who cannot commit a crime. He next proceeds to consider the various classes of crime, and whilst dealing with these he proceeds to discuss the compensation due to those who are injured through the killing of another person, and the damages recoverable by the person wounded, maimed or injured. He then passes on to discuss civil and criminal libel, seduction and the damages arising therefrom. A separate chapter is, however, devoted to the obligations which arise either through the act of those in our power or service or to the damage caused to others by our property (quasi-delicts). Van der Linden's method of treating torts and crimes is little better.

It was, however, the influence of the great English jurists like Bentham and Austin which led English writers to draw accurate distinctions between crimes and torts, and through them we in South Africa have learnt to keep the law of delicts and quasi-delicts distinct from the law of crimes. No doubt the great difference now existing in the civil and criminal procedure of our courts has helped to emphasise the distinction. Our law of torts is therefore not to be found in some separate chapter in our great law-books, but is mixed up with the chapters on the criminal law, or in the commentators on the *Digest* is found under the titles of *De Injuriis*, bk. 47, tit. 10; *De Lege Aquilia* (*D.* 9, tit. 2); *De Obligationibus quae ex delicto nascuntur* (*Inst.* bk. 4, tit. 1); *De Pauperie* (*D.* 9, tit. 1); *De Damno Infecto* (*D.* 39, tit. 2); *De Dolo Malo* (*D.* 4, tit. 3); *Quod Metus Causâ* (*D*, 4, tit. 2), and others.

In elaborating the law of delicts the Roman-Dutch jurists of the sixteenth and seventeenth centuries went to the *Corpus Juris* for their principles. The *Lex Aquilia* and the commentaries on this law became one of the most important sources of the Roman-Dutch law of delicts. The title *De Injuriis* also afforded them a number of important principles. Voet's *Commentary* on this title is one of the best treatises we possess on certain sections of the law of torts. It has been translated into English by Professor Melius de Villiers, late Chief Justice of the Orange River Colony, and the notes and excursus added by the professor has made this translation an excellent exposition of our law of torts.

In South Africa our common law as regards delicts is still the Roman-Dutch law of the eighteenth century, and is therefore founded upon the Roman law. The Canon law has added some principles such as the *amende honorable* (or the *actio ad palinodiam*), whilst several of the ancient laws and customs of the people were respected by the Roman-Dutch jurists. English law has, however, considerably modified our law of torts, especially by its successful distinction between torts and crimes.

Criminal Law.—We have seen that the early German law, like the *Jus Antiquum* of the Romans, had no well-defined line between criminal law and private wrong. Theft and robbery were regarded not as public, but as private wrongs. Even the killing of a man could be compensated by the payment of cattle or money. Gradually, however, the

State stepped in and claimed the right not only to exact compensation from the wrong-doer, but also to punish him. We can point to no specific period when this first took place. As we have seen, even the early Germans in certain cases punished the dangerous criminal. It was an ancient maxim, *Morth mot ma mit morthe kela* (Murder must be cooled with murder), though at first the retribution was sought not by the State, but by the family of the murdered man. In very early times the traitor, the deserter and the cowardly soldier were punished by the chief and the members of the tribe (Tacit. *Germ.* c. 12). We can also well imagine that any wrong to the chief or to the army was avenged by the punishment of the wrong-doer.

During the Frankish Empire the State extended its right of punishing wrong-doers, as we see from many of the capitularia. The assembly of freemen in the mallum exercised criminal jurisdiction and punished the offender. At first the mallum only punished where a complaint had been laid (*daar geen klager was, was ook geen regter*). Later on certain officials were allowed to lodge complaints if the family of the injured man did not appear (*Zo geen bloedts beware klagt zal de amptman een klager stellen en een Hegemaal laten hegen.—Verhandelingen, Pro excolendo,* vol. 1, p. 406).

In Gelderland the friends of a murdered man might appeal to the feudal lord to pursue the criminal. Thus we find in the Landrecht van Veluwen: *De vrienden des dooden zal den Heer aanroepen om den misdadiger na te schryven.* The right of the feudal lord in council to punish offenders was gradually extended to the various town and district courts.

In Utrecht the schepenen assumed jurisdiction as early as 1315, though their right was not formally acknowledged until the reign of the Emperor Charles (Muller, pp. 79 and 127). The various stadboeken show that the town courts had acquired the right to punish criminals during the fourteenth and fifteenth centuries.

The criminal law during the middle ages was contained in no special code. Whether an act was a crime or not was very largely in the discretion of the count and his council. The ancient customs and the various charters had, however, fixed certain punishments for particular acts, and in this way the punishment very often determined whether the act was a crime or merely a private wrong. Thus hanging was decreed for traitors and deserters, decapitation for certain forms of theft, burning for witches, whipping with rods for those who broke the peace and wounded or injured citizens, and so on (Noordewier, pp. 305 *et seq.*).

Prior to the sixteenth century there was no definite criminal code, and ancient customs, town ordinances and the opinion of the judicial council determined whether an act was punishable as a crime or not. During the sixteenth century the Roman criminal law was appealed to, especially in the form that was practised in Germany. The principles of the Roman criminal law were adopted by the German Emperors and modified by them to suit the requirements of the day. The Canon law was also a fruitful source of penal law. In 1532 appeared the *Constitutio Criminalis Carolina*, at that time the best European criminal code. From these German sources the Dutch criminalists borrowed very largely in order to systematise their criminal law. They incorporated with the principles of the Roman law a great deal of the old customs of the Germans and Franks, and where their own law was insufficient they referred to the *Constitutio Carolina.* Hence when Antonius Matthaeus wrote a treatise on the criminal law he made it assume the form of a commentary on some of the titles of the 47th and 48th books of the *Digest.* These books deal with the general principles of the *Crimina extraordinaria* and *Crimina publica,* and with special crimes such as *furtum, stellionatus, concussio,* &c.

With the above explanation it will be easy to understand why Van der Linden in his *Institutes* quotes as authorities of great weight in criminal matters such works as Leyser's *Meditationes,* Boehmer's *Constitutions of Charles V,* Carpzovius' *Practica rerum Criminalium,* and Von Quisdorp's *Grundsätze des Deutschen Peinlichen Rechts,* all of which were written by German authors for use in German courts. The reason is because both the German and Dutch criminalists started with the Roman law as their basis, and inasmuch as the Germans had worked out their system of criminal jurisprudence before the Dutch, the latter followed in the wake of the former, making such alterations as their different circumstances required. Of pure Dutch works besides Matthaeus' *De Criminibus* and the various chapters on criminal law in the text-books of Grotius, Van Leeuwen and Voet, the *Verhandelingen over de Misdaden* of Moorman and Van Hasselt is perhaps the best known.

The criminal law of the Cape Colony is set out in Mr. Clarkson Tredgold's *Handbook of Colonial Criminal Law.* The criminal law of Holland was followed by the Dutch courts of South Africa with such modifications as altered conditions required. When the British annexed the Cape Colony no alteration was made in the criminal law, though numerous statutes were introduced by which this branch of law was assimilated to the criminal law of England. The criminal law of the Cape Colony has therefore as its basis the Roman-Dutch law of crimes, though this has been largely modified by Imperial statute law applicable to the colonies, and by special colonial statutes. Where crimes are defined by statute the definition of the Roman-Dutch law falls away, but where the statute law is silent we have recourse to the Roman-Dutch law. The same applies to the other South African colonies.

In many respects the principles of the Roman-Dutch penal law agree with those of the English criminal law, and where such is the case English authorities and precedents are followed as being more recent and better adapted to modern society. Where, however, our principles differ from those of English law, the latter are not adopted by our courts. The Roman-Dutch law, for instance, recognises no distinction between felonies and misdemeanours, nor between principals in the first and second degree. In the scope and definition of the crimes there is also here and there a difference, though on the whole there is a remarkable similarity. Thus we do not know embezzlement as a crime distinct from theft, and with us many of the technicalities of larceny do not exist. For the difference between our law and the law of England I refer the reader to Mr. Morice's excellent work—*English and Roman-Dutch Law.*

APPENDIX.

R. v. GEBHARDT.

[A copy of the record of the above case was kindly given to me by Mr. C. H. van Zyl. The original is in Dutch, and for the translation which follows I am indebted to Mr. Advocate H. Reitz of Pretoria.]

THE PROSECUTION IN ITS ENTIRETY OF WM. GEBHARDT FOR THE MURDER OF THE SLAVE JORIS VAN MOSAMBIEK.

Proceedings before the Honourable the Chief Justice Dr. J. A. Truter, Knight; and with him the Honourable the Councillors of Justice for the Settlement of the Cape of Good Hope and places under its jurisdiction, in the matter of the Magistrate of Stellenbosch and Drakenstein, Mr. D. J. van Ryneveld, prosecutor in criminal matters, versus William Gebhardt, the accused, for grievous ill-treatment of the slave Joris van Mosambiek, which resulted in his death, held on Saturday the 21st of September, 1822, at 9 A.M. in the ordinary Council Chamber, the secretary of the Council being substituted in the absence of Mr. Matthiessen (on account of indisposition) and of Messrs. Bentink and Buissinne (they being busy elsewhere).

The doors of the Chamber being opened, and Dr. J. J. Lind in his capacity as official agent of the magistrate above mentioned and the above-mentioned accused having appeared before the Court, the Court said prayers. After which the agent hands in :—

(1) The indictment together with the preliminary examination.

(2) A list of the witnesses for the defence and for the prosecution.

(3) The report of the inquest held on the slave Joris, together with the doctor's *post mortem* certificate.

1. INDICTMENT.

Whereas from the preliminary examination held by the Magistrate of the District of Stellenbosch, prosecutor (having obtained an order of arrest from the Council) against you William Gebhardt, it has appeared to him that on Tuesday the 10th of the month of September towards evening you went to the vineyard of the small farm which forms part of the farm Simons Valey, situate on the Great Drakenstein, being the property of your father, Johan Willem Ludwich Gebhardt, where you found certain slaves of J. W. L. Gebhardt busy digging in the vineyard, that David Heyder (overseer in the service of the aforesaid J. W. L. Gebhardt) informed you on your arrival that he had that day chastised one of the slaves named Joris van Mosambiek because of his laziness in digging in the vineyard; that you thereupon went to the aforesaid Joris van Mosambiek, who was still busy digging with the other slaves, and urged him to dig faster (which the said Joris on account of the weakness of his constitution and because he was unaccustomed to this kind of work could not accomplish to your satisfaction), thereupon because of this you had him thrown upon the ground, and while four slaves held him down you with your own hand thrice successively chastised him in a most brutal manner on his naked body with quince sticks, and not yet content herewith you commanded certain of the slaves to take the said Joris to the wine cellar in order to have him chastised afresh in that place, but the said Joris, being no longer able to walk on account of the former chastisements, had to be supported by the arms by two of the slaves, and having traversed half the distance to the said cellar sank down and complained that he could go no further, whereupon the slave November took him upon his shoulder and carried him up to the gate of the homestead, his head being supported by one of the slaves, and put him down there; that you, seeing his infirmness and the weak state wherein the said Joris was, nevertheless ordered him to be dragged into the said wine cellar, which was done upon your orders by two of the slaves, and after the said Joris had been dragged into the cellar on his stomach, you there and then by candle-light had him thrown upon the ground, and whilst held down by four slaves you caused him to be cruelly chastised on his naked body by the slave November with many strokes of an ox hide about four feet in length and about one inch thick; that you not being able to quench your malignity against this slave gave orders to have quince sticks cut, the said slave meanwhile remaining prostrate upon the ground, and when the quince sticks were brought the said slave Joris was once more chastised therewith by the said November by your orders on his naked body in a most brutal manner. During this chastisement you urged November with threats of punishment to give the slave Joris many strokes, and by your orders salt and vinegar were brought and these you caused to be rubbed in copiously on the bleeding and smarting parts of the body of that slave, and then you caused him to be beaten over and over again with the aforesaid quince sticks on the parts thus rubbed in, so that the said slave remained prostrate and unconscious on the ground. After this you caused vinegar to be poured into his mouth, and finally he was carried away in an unconscious state by one of the slaves and put to bed, which terrible and brutal ill-treatment resulted in the death of the said slave Joris van Mosambiek at about 8 o'clock on the following morning.

And in case the investigation of this matter shall show that all this is in accordance with truth, then will you, William Gebhardt, be found guilty of brutal ill-treatment of the slave Joris van Mosambiek, resulting in the death of the said slave, which crime the maintenance of the authority and dignity of his Majesty's Government and of an unpolluted system of justice demands shall be punished according to law.

Fiscal Office, 18th *Sept.*, 1822.

(Sgd.) J. J. Lind,
Assistant Fiscal Officer.

3. Report of the Inquest.

On this the 12th day of September, 1822, at 4 o'clock in the afternoon, the undersigned Committee of Heemraden, Christoffel Jacobus Briers and Willem Wium, duly assisted by the first sworn clerk of the secretary's office of this town, Johan Godfried Gabriel Lindenberg (the secretary himself being otherwise occupied), and by the district surgeon, Robert Shand, at the request and in the presence of the magistrate of this district, Mr. Daniel Johannes van Ryneveld, officer of justice, on the declaration of the slave Bastiaan van de Kaap, the slave of the Rev. J. W. L. Gebhardt, made before the honourable magistrate this morning at 11 o'clock . . . "that his fellow-slave Joris, after having received a correction on the day before yesterday at the hands of the overseer David Heyder, and thereafter being chastised over and over again by the orders of the son of the said Gebhardt, by name William Gebhardt, expired yesterday" . . . betook themselves to the farm Simons Valey, situate on the Great Drakenstein in this district, belonging to the said Rev. Gebhardt, and there held an inquest on the body of a man identified by the said Rev. Gebhardt, who was present at the inquest, as that of one of his slaves, by name Joris (alias George), hailing from Mosambiek, and being about forty-five years old, and after the body had been denuded they came to the conclusion that—

(*a*) On the back of the body from the neck down to the lowest edge of the buttocks there were to be seen the marks of a chastisement, being weals, some of which laid bare the lower skin.

(*b*) That the skin of the left knee was off.

(*c*) The head having been opened by the said surgeon, and having been minutely examined, nothing whatever was there found which could have been the cause of the death of the said Joris.

(*d*) The body being opened, after a minute examination still nothing was found which could have caused a sudden death (according to the statement of the said surgeon) except a slight redness on one of the small intestines, which, however, the said surgeon positively stated could not have contributed to his death and was of very little importance, as also that the stomach was filled with a quantity of water mixed with slime, which according to the statement above mentioned emitted a sour smell.

(*e*) Thereupon the hind parts having been opened and carefully examined it was found that the whole back was badly bruised from the neck right down to the lowest edge of both buttocks, more especially along the loins and the kidneys on both sides, and that the back was covered with thick coagulated and also with liquid blood, bearing traces of a terrible beating; and the said surgeon stated with regard to this that no other cause was to be found in the body which could have resulted in death except the beating which had been administered.

Finally, the thong was shown to the commissioners with which the slave Joris had been beaten in the cellar. It was made of ox-riems twisted together, and being about an inch in thickness and about four feet in length; the one end of this was smeared with blood.

And hereof the above statement was drawn up.

Thus done at the above-mentioned place on the day of the year above stated.

(in my presence)
(Sgd.) J. G. G. Lindenberg, Sworn Clerk.

as commissioners,
(Sgd.) C. J. Briers,
W. Wium.

Certificate of the Doctor with Regard to the Post Mortem Examination.

I certify hereby that on this day, together with a committee, I went to the farm of the Rev. Gebhardt in order to examine the body of the slave Joris, and I found as follows:—

Internal examination.—Having opened the head and examined the brains and membranes, I found with the exception of a small quantity of water in the stomach no signs of disease or derangement.

On examining the thorax or chest I found it to be in a healthy condition, and nothing whatever characteristic of any disease was noticeable. The viscera or intestines of the abdomen or stomach were equally healthy, with this one exception that there was a slight redness about three inches in length on one of the convolutions of one of the small intestines, the ileum, but this could not have had any fatal consequences. The stomach was perfectly sound, slightly swollen and contained a quantity of liquid, clear and colourless, mixed with slime and having a sour smell.

External examination.—On examining the external parts of the body a totally different scene presented itself: the loins showed a large mass of extravasated blood, congealed liquid and bruised sinewy substances; the loins and sinews of the back were bruised to such an extent that their fibres in several places could not be traced. This outpour of blood and liquid, the clearest consequence of a severe bruising, extended from the hips up to the square sinews of the neck, while on either side as far down as the external oblique sinews of the stomach there were broad blotches of coagulated blood under the different bands. The whole fleshy and hollow substance of the loins indeed appeared to be a misformed heap of coagulated blood, liquid, and sinewy substance.

After the most minute and careful examination of the internal parts of the body, I found no signs of disease or disorder which could have caused death, and hence the inevitable conclusion is that the slave in question owes his death to the destruction of the tissues about the loins and adjoining parts, causing such a weakening of the constitution, exhaustion of strength and agony as gradually tended to lessen the working or pulsation of the heart to such an extent that death resulted therefrom.

(Sgd.) ROBERT SHAND, M.D.,
District Surgeon.

Finally, the agent handed in the interrogatories, upon which the accused had to be heard.

The secretary then publicly read aloud the above-mentioned indictment, after which the accused was informed by the Honourable Chief Justice that the questions which had been handed in *in judicio* with regard to the matters mentioned in the said indictment would be put to him, together with such questions as the judge himself might deem necessary. These interrogatories were then handed to the accused and answered as set forth hereunder.

EXAMINATION OF THE ACCUSED.

1. Your name? Age? Birth-place? Residence and Occupation? Johan William Louis Gebhardt—21 years of age—born in London—residing with my father on the farm Simons Valey—manager of the farm.

2. Do you not admit that you are guilty of having brutally ill-treated the slave Joris belonging to your father, in the manner set forth in the indictment which has just been read to you? No.

The accused having pleaded not guilty, thereupon in accordance with art. 49 of the Criminal Ordinance the witnesses were called, both those whose evidence is included in the preliminary examination and those called later on by the accused. First of all the witnesses for the prosecution were heard, being called in one after the other, and they made the following statements in the presence of the accused.

*　　*　　*　　*　　*　　*

Address by the Counsel for the prosecution in the matter of the assistant fiscal officer, Dr. J. J. Lind, representing the Magistrate of Stellenbosch and Drakenstein, D. J. van Ryneveld, judicial officer, versus Gebhardt, the accused in the above-mentioned criminal matter.

Honourable Sir and Gentlemen,—The crime which is now being investigated by this Court is one which has been perpetrated so often recently that the welfare of this colony demands that it should be severely punished in order to serve as a warning that one cannot ruthlessly and with impunity take the life of a slave and fellow-being. The condition of these people is already pitiable enough. Is it then to be rendered still worse by ill-treatment and brutality on the part of those placed over them, so that they are really treated as if on a par with brute animals? No, Honourable Judges, the gentle and humane laws of the colony, the kindly feelings with regard to their lot on the part of his Majesty's Government, will not permit these beings, who are our fellow-creatures and fellow-men, to be ill-treated without reason; nay, not only ill-treated, but most cruelly done to death. Who would not speak feelingly on seeing before him one of our citizens who had caused to be beaten to death in a most cruel manner a defenceless and helpless being entrusted to his care, who had even stained his own hands—hands which he should have used in the defence of this being—with the blood of this poor creature? It is not necessary to call the attention of your Lordship and the Honourable Gentlemen who are the judges in this matter to the enormity of this crime: I am convinced that you have each and all been deeply touched; a holy duty has called you hither to watch not only over the well-being of Christians and free men, but over the well-being also of the slaves specially entrusted to your care; you watch over their fate as fathers and mitigate their truly hard lot.

The offence, or rather the brutal crime, became known to the Magistrate of the district of Stellenbosch, whose representative I am, and the circumstances have now been brought before your Lordship and Honourable Gentlemen for trial.

The slave Bastiaan, belonging to Johan Willem Ludwich Gebhardt, the father of the accused, informed the magistrate on the 12th of September last that his fellow-slave Joris van Mosambiek, after first of all having received a beating from the manager, David Heyder, on the 10th of September, had been chastised so severely by the accused that he died from it. The magistrate immediately on receiving this complaint summoned two heemraden as a committee in order to obtain further particulars from the said slave Bastiaan. When this was done the magistrate on the same day ordered the two heemraden and the district surgeon, Robert Shand, to hold an inspection *in loco*, and an inquest with the magistrate as presiding officer was held at the farm of the said Johan Willem Ludwich Gebhardt on the death of the slave Joris and the condition of his body. This took place on that very day at about 4 o'clock P.M., and the commission having completed their investigations they reported as follows. [The report of the inquest is read.] After the return of the commission appointed to hold the inquest the magistrate proceeded on the following morning with the examination of the witnesses, and after all the witnesses who were present when the crime was perpetrated had been heard the further preliminary investigations were made and sent hither, and upon them an order of arrest against the accused was asked for from your Lordship and the Honourable Gentlemen. This order was granted on the 16th of September last, and at the same time the case was set down for trial to-day. From the evidence given by the witnesses it clearly appears that the circumstances were as follows: Towards evening on the 10th of September last the accused proceeded to the vineyard of his father, Johan Willem Ludwich Gebhardt, where certain slaves were busy digging. He there met a certain David Heyder, who was in the service of his father, and who was placed over the slaves as superintendent. The latter informed the accused on his arrival that he had that morning beaten the slave Joris, alias George van Mosambiek, because he was lazy and stubborn while digging in the vineyard. The accused, who did not seem to be satisfied with this chastisement, at once went to the said slave, who was then busy digging in the vineyard, and urged him to work faster, although as has appeared from the statements of the witnesses the deceased was weak and not fitted for this kind of work. When the accused saw that this slave did not work as fast as the other slaves he attributed it to sulkiness, and without inquiring into the real cause he ordered him to be thrown upon the ground, to be held down by four slaves, and to be chastised three times in a brutal manner on his bare buttocks with quince sticks, which were renewed during the beating. After this beating, which had already weakened the said slave Joris very much, the accused was not yet satisfied, but ordered Joris to be taken to the cellar and to be beaten there once more, whereas the said slave had not given the slightest cause either for this or for the former beating; on the contrary, his condition after the chastisement was such that the poor creature could neither walk nor speak. Nothing, however, satisfied the brutality of the accused; the slave Joris, supported by two of his fellow-slaves, was led to the cellar, there to be beaten once more, but having come half-way he was no longer able to stand, and intimated this to one of his fellow-slaves who had held and supported him, and one of them, the slave November, convinced of his weakness, took him on his shoulders and carried him to the gate of the homestead; arrived here he put him down. The accused hereupon came up, looked on with indifference and continued in his cruel resolve to have Joris beaten once more in the cellar. This want of feeling and this gruesome indifference at once proclaim the brutal character of the accused; he saw before him a creature in this pitiable condition, who at that moment could not have been guilty of disobedience or of any crime not even the very least. The accused cannot say that this slave was pretending to be ill or weak. It appears but too clearly from the evidence of the slaves November and Geduld that Joris was quite unable to walk, and for that reason had to be led. So weak was he that November had to take him on his shoulders while Geduld supported his head; the severe chastisement which had already been administered to the slave in the vineyard by the accused himself produced a state of collapse, and the accused must have been convinced of this. But this did not move the accused from his cruel resolve; no, he thought only of devising means for punishing and ill-treating him still more cruelly. He ordered him to be dragged into the cellar, and when this cruel order was carried out he was dragged along on his stomach into the cellar and there the further diabolical cruelty was effected. The accused ordered him to be thrown down and commanded the slave November to chastise him brutally on his naked back with an ox-hide thong which has been produced for inspection to your Lordship and to you Gentlemen of the Court. The severity of this chastisement appears sufficiently from the evidence of the slave November, who admits having administered it, whilst the other slaves who were present corroborate his statement. The very instrument itself is proof of how terrible this chastisement must have been. But the accused had not yet completed his inhuman cruelty. No! he wished to have the unfortunate slave done to death; he ordered fresh quince sticks to be brought, and once more had him beaten on his bare back. And even then he did not think that he had tortured him sufficiently, for he sent for salt and vinegar and caused almost a bucketful of the latter mixed with salt to be rubbed into the lacerated parts, and after that he had Joris beaten again—a cruelty which even the most barbarous person could not contemplate without aversion, a brutality which casts dishonour upon humanity and causes man to sink down to the level of a beast. This chastisement carried on in the cellar by candle-light lasted for about two hours. To spend almost two hours in torturing to death a fellow-being is the work of a person dead to all feelings of duty, of a person who treads under foot the laws of nature. The ill-used, tortured and unconscious slave was conveyed to a bed by one of his fellow-slaves and left to his fate.

The consequence of this terrible chastisement and torture undergone by the slave Joris was that on the next morning at about 8 o'clock death released and set free the unhappy Joris van Mosambiek from his unfortunate and pitiable condition. This picture is a true account of the way in which the crime was committed, and it has been vouched for by several witnesses, who agree to the facts. These witnesses are slaves partly, it is true, under the control of the accused. Should we for that reason reject their evidence? If so, how, Honourable Gentlemen and your Lordship, could this crime ever be proved? These witnesses alone were present when the crime was perpetrated, and are therefore the only witnesses whom the judges have to assist them in deciding this case. The accused himself has called several of these slaves as witnesses. If it were that the facts stated had been declared to by only one or two of them, then one might perhaps doubt the veracity of their evidence and hold that they were influenced by their hatred of the accused; but no, there is a crowd of witnesses who saw the deed committed, and the circumstances have been minutely and consistently related by all of them, so that with regard to this [there can be no possible doubt] in the minds of the judges. This crime appears, moreover, conclusively from the *post mortem* examination, which states and proves that the slave Joris died from the consequences of ill-treatment. This ill-treatment was committed partly by the accused with his own hands and partly at his behest, and he must therefore be held guilty of the crime with which he is charged. It would be unnecessary to delay the judges with an explanation of the theory of evidence in criminal cases; it all depends upon the judge as to how much belief he shall attach to the witnesses and other evidence produced in a criminal case, and with him rests in this case the decision. The crime with which the accused is charged in the indictment rests on the statements of witnesses and other evidence which is of such a nature that there can be no possible doubt in the minds of the judges. The law of the land has fixed capital punishment as the punishment for this crime, and on account of what has been said alone we now make the following claim and declaration. Wherefore and for other reasons which, if necessary, can be brought forward, the Officer of Justice as plaintiff claims that the accused be condemned by a sentence of your Lordship and Honourable Gentlemen to be taken to the place in which it is customary here to carry out criminal sentences, and there having been handed over to the executioner to be hanged with a rope round his neck until death follows, and that the accused be condemned to pay the costs and expenses of this trial—or for alternative relief.

(Sgd.) J. J. LIND.
Assistant Fiscal Officer.

Defence in the matter of William Gebhardt versus the Magistrate of Stellenbosch and Drakenstein, D. J. van Ryneveld, Officer of Justice.

Your Lordship and Gentlemen,—*Audi et alteram partem* is a maxim which has been so carefully instilled into every judge, and which this Honourable Court has followed so religiously that it is almost unnecessary to repeat it before the trial of a case of such importance as the present one, which, though painted black, has nevertheless a brighter side as well. I say this not in order to excuse the accused from all blame, but in order to free him in the minds of the judges from the suspicion that he, for whom from the very beginning all presumptions should plead both as regards the crime and as regards the punishment, is on a par with those wilful evildoers who, regardless of all laws, take a delight in and get a living by murder, robbery and plunder. Without being led away by our feelings or without trying to work upon the feelings of the judges, without being disturbed by the awe-inspiring claim of the Officer of Justice, we must calmly inquire whether in the case before us the accused is guilty of any *homocidium dolosum*, in which case alone the claim of the prosecutor can be granted, and then the judges will be convinced, as I am, that the accused, however wrongly he may have acted, can nevertheless not be found guilty of that crime.

In considering this point the judges will notice first of all that the *judicium medicum* itself is not free from conclusions which very often the mere idea itself of a case of gross ill-treatment brings with it (*i.e.* that the doctor found symptoms which he knows would follow such ill-treatment). Nor should the judges lose sight of the fact that all the circumstances of this case rest on the unsworn testimony of slaves who were all under the control of the accused, and are certainly not well disposed to him. Let us, gentlemen, for a moment allow all these circumstances to appear as black against the accused as the prosecutor wishes them to appear, even then they would not make him a murderer; nay, even if all this were so, your Lordships will find many facts which militate against the conclusion that he is guilty of such a serious crime. How much the more, then, will this be the case after your Lordships have given your attention to such circumstances as plead for the accused. For argument's sake, let us admit that the unfortunate death of the slave Joris, alias George, was caused solely by the chastisement which he had received; let us now consider whether this act can be classified among the *homicidia dolosa*. It has been proved that the slave Joris, otherwise a strong, sturdy workman, was very lazy and loth to work on the 10th of this month during the absence of the accused, that being exhorted by the superintendent, D. Heyder, to work harder, he had made fun of him, and after receiving a single slap he had continued in his laziness and had even shouted at the superintendent, and clapping his hands had derided him. The latter felt that it was necessary to report this to the accused, who was the manager of his father's farm, on his arrival in the evening to inspect the progress of the work. The maintenance of discipline among a set of such slaves demanded, therefore, that he should be punished for this, and this punishment took place first of all in the field in a manner and with an instrument by no means uncommon, and consequently neither because of the circumstances accompanying the beating nor on account of the severity thereof can the accused be considered as guilty of any unlawful act. And when this slave thereupon pretended not to be able to walk the accused could ascribe it to nothing else than those clever tricks which this slave had played off on the accused so often before, and for this reason he had him punished in a manner which surely does not merit that terrible accusation and claim which the prosecutor has made against him. All this will appear to the judges by means of the following points in the defence, which counsel for the accused herewith takes the liberty of bringing forward. While considering this matter the judges will surely be mindful of the precept contained in "Lex 14 ff ad Leg. Corn. de Sicariis": *in malificiis voluntatem non exitum spectari debere*, which precept Cicero in his *Oratio pro Milone* reminded the judge of in the following words: *Non exitus rerum, sed hominum consilia vindicantur.* Mindful of this lesson, the judges will now investigate with me whether while committing this deed the accused was imbued with such a *consilium* or *propositum occidendi*, or whether from all the circumstances such an *animus occidendi* does appear. If it does not, then as a matter of course the prosecutor must fail in establishing his claim. We know that a slight but very important distinction should be drawn with regard to *homicidia*, for *homicidia* committed with *culpa lata* are not on a par with *homicidia dolosa*, and cannot be punished with death. *Vide* Voet, *Comment. ad ff. ad Leg. Corneliam de Secariis*, sec. 9.

(*a*) This being so, the judge will notice first of all that the accused at the beginning was doing what was lawful, for on account of the laziness and stubbornness of the slave Joris or George he had a lawful reason for punishing him, and therefore he is not guilty on account of the chastisement itself, but only because of excess of chastisement.

Every excess makes him guilty of *culpa lata*, but in no way of *dolus* or malice aforethought. Hence, too, even in English law excess in chastisement is not looked upon as murder nor punished as such (Blackstone, bk. 4, chap. 14, p. 200: "But if the person, so provoked, had unfortunately killed another, by beating him in such a manner as showed only an intent to chastise and not to kill him, the law so far considers the provocation of contumelious behaviour as to adjudge it only manslaughter and not murder.") So, too, in our law, where persons had attacked others with murderous weapons and injured them so severely that death resulted, yet as it appeared that they only intended to injure and not to kill they were not punished with death. Vide *Crim. Advyzen*, No. 68.

(*b*) Secondly, it is worthy of mention that the accused did not make use of a murderous or dangerous weapon, but only of such an one as is usually made use of for chastisement, and from which fatal results have never before followed. A horsewhip or thin quince sticks are not classified among malicious instruments. *Vide* Carpzovius, chap. 3, secs. 8 and 11.

(*c*) Thirdly, the number of strokes was not such as to cause death; all the witnesses declare unanimously that the beating in the vineyard was not severe, and that the beating administered in the cellar by Bastiaan, and mentioned as the severest, was only 139 strokes, a number which can surely not be looked upon as fatal, when as we know in the military or marine service 700 to 800 strokes with the rod and with other far more dangerous instruments are often administered without fatal consequences to a white person, whose skin is far more tender than that of a black.

(*d*) Fourthly, it appears that the accused only desired to correct, and in no way had any *animus occidendi* from the fact that he positively forbade November, who administered the chastisement, to strike on the loins, where a stroke might be dangerous. This the slave Geduld voluntarily stated, and his evidence deserves credit herein.

(*e*) Fifthly, we have it in evidence that after the chastisement he specially ordered the slave Jan to care for the slave Joris and to administer such medicines and apply such remedies as best heal such injuries, therefore no *animus occidendi* can lie therein. When in addition to all these circumstances, which acquit the accused from any murderous intent, we add the fact that the accused is a young man under whose care his father had placed his farm and slaves, and who could have no other object than the interest of his father, and who was responsible for the welfare of these slaves who had been entrusted to his care as well as to that of his father, then every suspicion that he bore any malice or had any thought of compassing the death of this slave must surely fall to the ground. Counsel for the accused cannot but draw attention to the fact that the prosecutor, carried away by his feelings, has painted the whole affair in the very blackest colours, and, besides, merely to gratify his own feelings he has accused the prisoner of brutal ill-treatment which never actually took place. The prisoner has been accused of having beaten the slave after he had already been chastised twice on that same day by the inspector Heyder. This is true, but the prosecutor forgets to add that it appears from the preliminary investigation and has been proved that he knew nothing about these previous chastisements (*vide* statement of D. Heyder). He has been accused of having chastised the slave in the cellar for two hours; but here, too, it must not be forgotten that it has been proved that the slave Joris received at most 139 strokes in that place (*vide* statement of Bastiaan), which number the other witnesses place at 100, so that this can in no way be considered to have been excessive. And we must not forget that of those two hours fully an hour was spent in having quince sticks cut (*vide* statement of Mei).

We should not forget that November himself, who administered the beating, declares that he only hit at intervals, and continually at the command of the accused gave the slave Joris the opportunity of escaping further punishment by asking for pardon.

Lastly, the prisoner has also been accused of having culminated his cruelty by having the parts which were sore and had been rubbed in beaten again. But this is absolutely untrue. The salt and vinegar was applied in order to prevent ulceration, in order to preserve the skin and in no way to cause suffering; this has always been the custom everywhere. After the slave Joris had been beaten on his buttocks, and they had been rubbed in, the accused ordered him to be beaten only on the shoulders and not to touch his loins (*vide* statement of November). How can the prosecutor then twist the truth, or at all events the evidence of the witnesses, thus against the accused? Has not this very evidence proved that even during the punishment there were pauses, and when we add to these the time necessary in order to fetch the salt and to tap the vinegar, &c., then the time of the actual chastisement just corresponds to the number of strokes mentioned by the witnesses. This number has been pretty accurately fixed, and thus we should fix the degree of punishment in accordance therewith, and by no means according to any presumption or duration of time. The accused has been depicted as a monster who caused the parts of the unfortunate Joris which had been rubbed in to be once again beaten, all of which November and Geduld, as we said above, absolutely deny.

Where, then, is there any presumption to the contrary? We should also add that the slave Joris was a huge Mosambique, as appears from the statements of Geduld and November, in whom consequently there could have been no such weakness as is pretended to have been the result of the chastisement in the vineyard unless the beatings administered by the superintendent Heyder had been excessive; but for this the accused is not to blame. At all events it has been proved that the accused could not and did not wish to do anything else than correct and punish the slave Joris, therefore he cannot have had any *animus occidendi*, which alone can render him liable to capital punishment, and as the unfortunate Joris succumbed to the combined chastisements of the inspector Heyder and of the accused and of November, hence the accused cannot alone be held responsible for the consequences of all three chastisements, but the responsibility rests on all three equally according to the "Lex Ult ff. ad Leg. Corn. de Sicariis": *Si in rixa percussus homo perierit ictus unius cujusque in hoc collectorum contemplari debet. Vide* Carpzovius, chap. 24, secs. 16, 17, 19, 20 and 21.

Accordingly the counsel for the accused asks that the claim of the prosecutor be refused, and that your Lordships may grant such lesser unishment as to you shall seem right and according to law.

(Sgd.) H. Cloete, Lz.
Advocate.

Judgment and Sentence.

The Court having heard the claim of the prosecutor, as also the defence, and having taken notice of everything which in a case like this it should take notice of, and administering justice in the name and on behalf of his Britannic Majesty, and considering that notwithstanding the defect that the depositions of all the witnesses for the prosecution except one were not made under oath, yet from all the circumstances which appeared and which had nothing to do with the said defect in the depositions, it has legally been made sufficiently clear to the judges that the accused is the deliberate perpetrator of the ill-treatment inflicted on the slave Joris which resulted in his death, declares the accused to be guilty of the crime of murder, and consequently sentences the accused to be taken to the place in which it is customary here to execute criminal sentences, and being handed over to the executioner there to be punished by being hanged to the gallows with a rope round his neck until death shall follow, and to pay the costs and expenses of the trial.

Thus done and decided in the Council of Justice at the Cape of Good Hope. *Die et anno ut supra* and delivered on the same day.

(Sgd.) J. A. Truter.
W. Hiddingh.
J. H. Neethling.
F. R. Bresler.
J. C. Fleck.
P. J. Truter.
D. F. Berrange.

In my presence,
D. F. Berrange,
Secretary.

INDEX.

INDEX.

Printed by the AFRICAN BOOK COMPANY, LTD.,
Grahamstown, Cape Colony.

www.ingramcontent.com/pod-product-compliance
Lightning Source LLC
LaVergne TN
LVHW062242200926
848484LV00006B/1591

* 9 7 8 1 5 8 4 7 7 6 5 7 4 *